THE LETTERS
OF
HUGH MACDIARMID

BOOKS BY ALAN BOLD

Poetry

SOCIETY INEBRIOUS
THE VOYAGE
TO FIND THE NEW
A PERPETUAL MOTION MACHINE
PENGUIN MODERN POETS 15 (with Morgan and Brathwaite)
THE STATE OF THE NATION
THE AULD SYMIE
HE WILL BE GREATLY MISSED
A CENTURY OF PEOPLE
A PINT OF BITTER
SCOTLAND, YES
THIS FINE DAY
IN THIS CORNER: SELECTED POEMS 1963–83
A CELTIC QUINTET (with Bellany)

Stories

HAMMER AND THISTLE (with Morrison)
THE EDGE OF THE WOOD

Criticism

THOM GUNN & TED HUGHES
GEORGE MACKAY BROWN
THE BALLAD
(ed) SMOLLETT: AUTHOR OF THE FIRST DISTINCTION
(ed) THE SEXUAL DIMENSION IN LITERATURE
THE SENSUAL SCOT
MODERN SCOTTISH LITERATURE
MACDIARMID: THE TERRIBLE CRYSTAL
(ed) SCOTT: THE LONG-FORGOTTEN MELODY
(ed) BYRON: WRATH AND RHYME

Anthologies

THE PENGUIN BOOK OF SOCIALIST VERSE
THE MARTIAL MUSE: SEVEN CENTURIES OF WAR POETRY
THE CAMBRIDGE BOOK OF ENGLISH VERSE 1939–75
MAKING LOVE: THE PICADOR BOOK OF EROTIC VERSE
THE BAWDY BEAUTIFUL: THE SPHERE BOOK OF IMPROPER VERSE
MOUNTS OF VENUS: THE PICADOR BOOK OF EROTIC PROSE
DRINK TO ME ONLY: THE PROSE (AND CONS) OF DRINKING
A SCOTTISH POETRY BOOK
THE POETRY OF MOTION
THE THISTLE RISES: A MACDIARMID MISCELLANY

THE LETTERS
OF
HUGH MACDIARMID

Edited
with an Introduction
by

Alan Bold

Hamish Hamilton London

The Publisher acknowledges subsidy from the
Scottish Arts Council towards the publication of this volume.

314018

First published in Great Britain 1984
by Hamish Hamilton Ltd
Garden House 57-59 Long Acre London WC2E 9JZ

Copyright © 1984 by Alan Bold and Valda Grieve

British Library Cataloguing in Publication Data

MacDiarmid, Hugh, *1892–1978*
   The letters of Hugh MacDiarmid.
   1. MacDiarmid, Hugh, *1892–1978* – Biography
   2. Poets, Scottish – 20th century – Biography
   I. Title   II. Bold, Alan
   821'.912   PR6013.R735/
ISBN 0-241-11220-6

Printed in Great Britain by
Redwood Burn Limited, Trowbridge, Wiltshire

Contents

List of plates

Introduction

On the evidence assembled here Hugh MacDiarmid was not only a great poet and indefatigable propagandist but a prodigious and remarkable man of letters. Despite the size of this book it represents a careful selection of the letters MacDiarmid wrote in his long life (1892-1978). Clearly some letters have been lost through natural causes and unavoidable accidents but there are thousands extant in institutions and private collections. Some of the available letters have been omitted from this book: a very few on deeply personal grounds, one or two on legal advice, and a large proportion because they were merely of a routine nature concerned with the details of various assignations. What remains represents, I believe, the authentic core of MacDiarmid's correspondence; he is revealed as one of the great letter-writers of the twentieth century.

Writing to Helen Cruickshank on 7 October 1930, MacDiarmid said, 'I'd as soon write a letter that isn't a purely and unavoidably business one as have a tooth drawn or join a Rotary Club or the Kirk nowadays ... I just can't write letters.' On 6 February 1924, however, he had confessed to Neil Gunn, 'This is my 40th letter tonight and I am ink-sick.' Allowing for the hyperbole typically present in both statements it is nevertheless apparent that Mac-Diarmid was a prolific and self-conscious correspondent. He took letter writing seriously as he acknowledged when he told George Ogilvie, on 8 January 1928, 'my biggest work has been correspondence. You would scarcely credit the amount of it – the affiliations I have made all over the world – the continuous effort to knit it all up into a definite and determined movement.' In later years he considered his career in a retrospective way and claimed that letter-writing had become his principal literary activity. He told Duncan Glen on 19 September 1962:

> my output in the early to middle 'twenties was incredible – how the devil I did it I can't now imagine; I only wish I had the same energy now – and yet you know, perhaps I have; only instead of pouring out articles, it goes now into correspondence – my range of letter-writing nowadays is really phenomenal.

All through his life, then, MacDiarmid kept up a vast correspondence with a purpose. 'I'm all for GIANTISM in the arts', he once

vii

exclaimed.[1] As well as being, in his later years, an epic poet he was an almighty epistolary performer.

The letters range in time from 1911, when MacDiarmid was finding his feet in local journalism; to 1978, when he was a world figure who had largely remade Scotland in his own energetic image. MacDiarmid served in two World Wars and fought countless cultural and political battles. In the letters he constantly announces campaign plans. For example, writing to George Ogilvie from Salonika in a long letter of 20 August 1916, he says, 'I shall come back [to Scotland] and start a new Neo-Catholic movement. I shall enter heart and body and soul into a new Scots Nationalist propaganda.' On 22 June 1933, having settled into his island exile on Whalsay, he tells Neil Gunn:

> My coming up here is no retirement from the fight [since] if I am not already literally an impossible person I intend to become one ... I will pursue a course calculated to the last degree to give me opportunities for 'making things difficult' to say the least of it. No considerations of personal prestige or any favours that may be bestowed upon me will induce me to hold my hand a moment longer than I think the most effective moment for striking; I will 'hit below the belt' in the matter either of 'personalities' or leading people on to the ice by not disclosing what I intend to do or say until what I judge to be the psychological moment or unscrupulously saying one thing to one person and the opposite to another etc. In short – whatever other people or parties may do in Scotland – my own course at all events is perfectly clear and insusceptible of the slightest deviation and if health and harness hold I will have an amusing time during the next few years. The shots in my locker are far from spent and it will become increasingly difficult to bottle me up in any way.

Born Christopher Murray Grieve in the little Border burgh of Langholm on 11 August 1892, MacDiarmid (to use the pseudonym he adopted in 1922) was aware from an early age of his unusual position as a Scottish poet. Partly because of his religious background – which brought him into Langholm South United Free Church and under the influence of the literary minister, the Rev T. S. Cairncross – MacDiarmid saw himself as a man destined to be a saviour. His intellectual elitism is arguably an extension of the Calvinist doctrine of the elect and his poetry consistently preaches the gospel of salvation through sacrifice. In *A Drunk Man Looks at the*

[1] Hugh MacDiarmid, *The Company I've Kept* (London 1966, p. 56).

Thistle (1926) he anticipated the coming of a 'greater Christ, a greater Burns' (86) and wrote, towards the end of the poem,

> *A Scottish poet maun assume*
> *The burden o' his people's doom,*
> *And dee to brak' their livin' tomb.*
>
> *Mony ha'e tried, but a' ha'e failed.*
> *Their sacrifice has nocht availed.*
> *Upon the thistle they're impaled.* (165)[2]

For his part MacDiarmid was not willing to contemplate failure. Like the eponymous Drunk Man he wanted to transcend the spirit-sodden sentimentality associated with Scottishness and replace it with an illuminating spirituality. The Scotsman was no longer to be impaled on the thistle but to rise to resurrection and renaissance and stand absolutely independently as an individual in an autonomous nation. MacDiarmid felt his own self-sacrifice and prophetic poetry would provide Scotland with a new pride, a fresh philosophical ideal of independence and a radical ideology. The powerful and deliberately blasphemous notion he exploited in *A Drunk Man* was to project himself as a Scottish symbol of a Second Coming:

> Millions o' wimmen bring forth in pain
> Millions o' bairns that are no' worth ha'en'.
>
> Wull ever a wumman be big again
> Wi's muckle's a Christ? Yech, there's nae sayin'. (103)

Poetically too MacDiarmid adopted a biblical precedent. 'In the beginning was the Word' says St John (1:1) and MacDiarmid endorsed that opinion in one of his few statements on his technical approach to the making of verse. For him 'the act of poetry [is] the reverse of what it is usually thought to be; not an idea gradually shaping itself in words, but deriving entirely from words – and it was in fact [precisely] in this way that I wrote all the best of my Scots poems.'[3] A similar hypersensitivity to words is apparent in the finest letters written by MacDiarmid. Readers of his published books, from *Annals of the Five Senses* (Montrose 1923) onwards, have 'been frequently astonished' (197) by the quotation-encrusted texture of the prose. MacDiarmid wished to create a forceful intellectual presence in his books and believed he could command attention most readily by making an assertion then citing, often at great length,

[2] All poetic quotations are followed by parentheses whose numbers correspond to pages in MacDiarmid's *Complete Poems 1920–1976* (London 1978) edited by Michael Grieve and W. R. Aitken.

[3] Hugh MacDiarmid, *Lucky Poet* (London 1943, p. xxiii).

authorities he felt were in its favour. So when he assesses literature or politics he piles on the illustrative quotations relentlessly to create an anthological atmosphere. When writing letters he is generally addressing admirers and colleagues and therefore takes for granted an appreciation of his interests. The prose is still assertive but infinitely more personal. MacDiarmid the letter writer does not need the protective plating he requires in his books – and in some of the letters to the press.

'I never saw afore a thistle quite/Sae intimately' (92) says MacDiarmid in *A Drunk Man Looks at the Thistle*. The same sort of scrutiny can now be applied to the man who wrote the letters in this book. As a public figure MacDiarmid was not expansive about the everyday details of his life. *Lucky Poet* (London 1943) was, by design, 'A Self-Study in Literature and Political Ideas' (as the subtitle has it) rather than a confessional composition. In the autobiographical sequel MacDiarmid was still 'not disposed to be any more forthcoming ... with regard to intimate personal matters.'[4] Naturally the letters provide many of the facts of life he preferred to eschew in the books. He was well aware that autobiographical avenues would open up when his correspondence was published and considered the subject with an admirable objectivity. When I first suggested an edition of his letters he replied, on 26 January 1977,

> Re my letters, I know that something along the lines you suggest is inevitable, but it will be a hell of a job for whoever does it ... I have never kept copies of any of my letters. I know a few friends who almost certainly have kept my letters but I am sure most of my correspondents haven't and consequently the whole collection will be lacking in that essential counterpart.

In fact most of his correspondents did keep MacDiarmid letters and from an early stage. George Ogilvie, his teacher at Broughton, understood the enormity of what MacDiarmid was attempting and realised the importance of the letters sent to him regularly from 1911. Other Scots such as William Soutar and Pittendrigh Macgillivray also kept their MacDiarmid letters; as did international literary celebrities such as T. S. Eliot and Ezra Pound. That they did so was both a tribute to the status of the poet and a tribute to the quality of his correspondence.

Grieve the man and MacDiarmid the poet are equally visible, if not indivisible, in the letters. His experiences in Greece and Glasgow, in the First and Second World Wars respectively, are colourfully conveyed. Then there is his astonishingly active life in

[4] *The Company I've Kept*, p. 16.

Montrose (as local politician, founder of the Scottish Literary Renaissance, accomplished editor, journalist, family man and author of *Sangschaw, Penny Wheep, A Drunk Man Looks at the Thistle*); his disastrous move to London leading to the collapse of his first marriage; his period of island exile in Whalsay when he suffered a severe breakdown; his later years as Scotland's most acclaimed writer. Though the passing of time brought recognition it did not, for long enough, bring financial security and MacDiarmid never settled in the easy chair occupied by the Grand Old Men of other countries. He continued to embody the fighting spirit he felt so necessary for Scotland. As he said to R. E. Muirhead in a letter of 5 November 1928:

> My task is to be unpopular – a fighter – an enemy of accepted things; not in any captious fashion but out of profound conviction, and while I may often mistake the promptings of my heart and be merely factitious, I have reason to know that the best of my work at all events is proving a powerful influence because it springs from the deeps of the destined.

With Muirhead and others he developed a political programme for Scottish independence. He was expelled from both the Scottish National and Communist parties but maintained his own singular point of view as a demonstrative individual whose creative powers and evolutionary ideals put him above any rigid party-political discipline. He injected into his political philosophy a good deal of Social Credit and could even combine his innate radicalism with reactionary lapses. A letter of 11 April 1929 to Compton Mackenzie enthuses over 'a species of Scottish Fascism' while another, of 7 January 1930 to Oliver St John Gogarty, has the poet admitting to being 'a crusted old Tory'. It should, of course, always be remembered that MacDiarmid delighted in controversy and that his intelligence and marvellous sense of humour prevailed upon him to be polemical and provocative most of the time.

From a literary point of view the letters show MacDiarmid in the process of making crucial creative decisions. There have been, for example, persistent rumours that F. G. Scott, the composer to whom *A Drunk Man Looks at the Thistle* is dedicated, was responsible not only for the final ordering of the poem but for supplying the last two lines. In letters to Ogilvie and Macgillivray, for instance, MacDiarmid suggests how he shaped the poem; at Macgillivray's request he even supplies a coda to his masterpiece. The switch from Synthetic Scots to a highly charged English idiom is justified in letters to Soutar and others. Moreover, many letters relate to MacDiarmid's plans for two uncompleted projects, *Clann Albann* and *Mature Art*. MacDiarmid always operated on a grand scale since his ambition was to produce a great epic poem for Scotland, something as endurable as Dante's *Divine Comedy* or Milton's *Paradise Lost*. In his own opinion *A Drunk Man Looks at the Thistle* was not extended enough and so he went further, in length if not in breadth, in *To Circumjack Cencrastus* (Edinburgh 1930). That poem was completed in distressing personal circumstances and was not well received. MacDiarmid thus turned his talents to a new project.

Clann Albann was to be a huge autobiographical poem that was also to serve as the Scottish *Faust* for the poet told Compton Mackenzie, in a letter of 7 September 1931,

> Am making great headway myself with the Scottish *Faust* – two long separate poems from it are being used by Lascelles Abercrombie in a miscellany of hithero unpublished poems Victor Gollancz are putting out shortly. It's certainly the best stuff I've done yet.

The two poems included in Abercrombie's anthology of *New English Poems* (1931) are 'Charisma and My Relatives' (301-2) and 'First Hymn to Lenin' (297-9) which are collected in *First Hymn to Lenin and Other Poems* (London 1931). That volume, as well as *Second Hymn to Lenin* (Thakeham 1932) and *Scots Unbound and Other Poems* (Stirling 1932) were promoted as separable parts of the first volume of *Clann Albann*. The Scottish *Faust* was to comprise a Prologue plus five volumes: *The Muckle Toon, Fier Comme un Ecossasis, Dimidium Animae Meae, The Uncanny Scot, With a Lifting of the Head*. In the *Scots Observer* of 12 August 1933 MacDiarmid explained the project:

> The poem is an autobiographical one and a study in the evolution of my mentality and development as a poet, and, in particular, my knowledge of and attitude towards Scotland. The first book deals with *The Muckle Toon* (i.e. Langholm, in Dumfriesshire) my birthplace, and my boyhood days; and this involves poems about my parents, about the hills, woods, and streams of that district, about my first contacts with Love and Death, about the Church influence which bulked so largely in my life then, about Border history, and about the actual – and symbolic – significance of the frontier. The second book, *Fier Comme un Ecossasis*, is concerned with my widening knowledge of Scotland and its history and literature and the emergence of the Scottish nationalist ideas with which I have since been so actively concerned ... The third book, *Dimidium Animae Meae* , concerns my marriage (a marriage – since my wife was a Highlander – symbolising the Union of Scotland, the bridging of the gulf between Highland and Lowland, and, inci-

dentally, treating Gaeldom as the feminine principle), and where the second book is predominantly political and objective, this one is mainly psychological ... The fourth book, *The Uncanny Scot*, deals with my furthest conceptions of the Scottish genius; and the fifth and final book, *With a Lifting of the Head* (from Plotinus), represents [essentially] the abandonment by the spirit of the poet of all that has preceded this stage and his ascent into a different order of consciousness altogether ... Whether I am able to carry out this scheme with any completeness remains to be seen ...

When he moved to Whalsay in 1933 MacDiarmid abandoned *Clann Albann* but this colossal concept lurks in the background of many letters written during the early 1930s.

Settling in Whalsay, in the Shetlands, MacDiarmid was confronted by a new set of circumstances and responded to them with great poetic fervour. Again, the biblical background intrudes as he was surrounded by stones and able to regard the individual stone as a symbol of the obstacle to the resurrection of Christ — or even a 'greater Christ, a greater Burns'. 'On a Raised Beach', one of the most majestic poems written by MacDiarmid in the 1930s, establishes this symbolism with imaginative brilliance as the poet contemplates his human condition in a metaphysical manner;

> — I lift a stone; it is the meaning of life I clasp
> Which is death, for that is the meaning of death;
> How else does any man yet participate
>   In the life of a stone,
> How else can any man yet become
> Sufficiently at one with creation, sufficiently alone,
> Till as the stone that covers him he lies dumb
> And the stone at the mouth of his grave is not overthrown?
> — Each of the stones on this raised beach,
>   Every stone in the world,
> Covers infinite death, beyond the reach
> Of the dead it hides; and cannot be hurled
> Aside yet to let any of them come forth, as love
>   Once made a stone move ...
> It is not more difficult in death than here
> — Though slow as the stones and powers develop
> To rise from the grave — to get a life worth having,
> And in death — unlike life — we lose nothing that is truly
>   ours. (432-3)

Knowing himself in possession of such poetic power MacDiarmid was ready to begin another project that would enable other obstacles to be pushed back so that individuals could rise to resurrection.

One of the most potent influences on MacDiarmid was the work of James Joyce; it was, after all, in 1922 – the year of *Ulysses* – that Christopher Grieve adopted the pseudonym 'Hugh MacDiarmid'. The Synthetic Scots MacDiarmid derived, in the 1920s, from the etymological dictionary and his own flow or oral rhythms seemed to him experimentally sound. Quite specifically he claimed, when expounding 'A Theory of Scots Letters' in *The Scottish Chapbook* of February 1923, that there was a strong cultural connexion 'between Jamieson's Etymological Dictionary of the Scottish Language and James Joyce's *Ulysses* '. I have argued elsewhere[5] that *A Drunk Man Looks at the Thistle* is partly an attempt to emulate Joyce's *Ulysses* and have stressed the structural similarity between Leopold Bloom's diurnal odyssey through Dublin and the Drunk Man's nocturnal odyssey over a Scottish hillside. Both men win home to a particular Penelope which for Joyce is an affirmative earth-mother and for MacDiarmid the feminine principle of Scotland. MacDiarmid's new epic was to be quintessentially Celtic like the best of Joyce. As he was not a fluent Gaelic speaker MacDiarmid cast the Celtic theme, of eternal longing for spiritual ascent, in a multilingual idiom owing much to Joyce's linguistic precedent in Work in Progress (or *Finnegans Wake* as it became on publication in 1939) and much to Pound's allusive practice in the Cantos. *Mature Art*, as MacDiarmid's Celtic epic was to be called, was described in an advertisement prepared by the poet for the abortive Obelisk Press edition planned for 1939:

> [*Mature Art*] is an enormous poem of over 20,000 lines, dealing with the interrelated themes of the evolution of world literature and world consciousness, the problems of linguistics, the place and potentialities of the Gaelic genius, from its origin in Georgia to its modern expressions in Scotland, Ireland, Wales, Cornwall, Galicia and the Pays Basque, the synthesis of East and West, and the future of civilisation.
>
> It is a very learned poem involving a stupendous range of reference, especially to Gaelic, Russian, Italian and Indian literatures, German literature and philosophy, and modern physics and the physiology of the brain, and while mainly in English, utilises elements of over a score of languages, Oriental and Occidental.

In connexion with this multilingual mode it is interesting to recall that Sergeant Grieve wrote to George Ogilvie from Salonika on 2 September 1916:

> East and west meet and mingle here in an indescribable fashion. Soldiers of half-a-dozen different nations fraternize in canteens

---

[5] Alan Bold, *MacDiarmid: The Terrible Crystal* (London, 1983).

and cafés. Naturally and necessarily one picks up an incredible polyglottery.

Indeed MacDiarmid's insistence to Ogilvie that he had, as early as World War One, mapped out his literary future is substantiated in some of the letters.

As letters to T. S. Eliot in particular show, MacDiarmid believed *Mature Art* to be his monumental contribution to the art of the twentieth century. However the collapse of the plans to publish the poem in 1939, the financial problems of publishing a work of that size, the return to mainland Scotland for the Second World War, and the increasing demands on the poet's time in later years meant that *Mature Art* was never published in its entirety. *In Memoriam James Joyce* (Glasgow 1955) and *The Kind of Poetry I Want* (Edinburgh 1961) were the only two volumes of *Mature Art* that appeared in MacDiarmid's lifetime – a letter of 3 January 1941 to Albert Mackie shows that *The Battle Continues* (Edinburgh 1957) was not part of *Mature Art* . The other volumes, such as *Impavidi Progrediamur*, were never given the authority of print as entities and at the end of his life MacDiarmid declared that 'large-scale projects, such as *Clann Albann* . . . and the complete *Cornish Heroic Song for Valda Trevlyn* [an alternative title he later preferred to *Mature Art*], were either abandoned or subsumed in other works' (vi). Precisely because so much of MacDiarmid's poetic work was completed by 1940 the majority of the letters come from the period between the two World Wars.

Surveying MacDiarmid's achievement as a totality is an exhilarating experience: there is the mystical verse and prose of *Annals of the Five Senses* (Montrose 1923), the coalescence of delicately metaphysical and harshly physical images in the Synthetic Scots poems of the 1920s, the angry political utterances of the hymns to Lenin, the discovery of universal connotations in his native Langholm in the *Clann Albann* poems, the stunning range of reference in the *Mature Art* project. The contention, made by MacDiarmid in 1972, that there is a 'basic unity',[6] running through all his activities, is supported by the persistent pursuit of fundamental aims in the letters he composed during his most creative years, that is from the outbreak of World War One to the advent of World War Two. Eliot said, in 'East Coker'

> So here I am, in the middle way, having had twenty years –
> Twenty years largely wasted, the years of *l'entre deux guerres* –
> Trying to learn to use words, and every attempt
> Is a wholly new start, and a different kind of failure . . .

---

[6] *Lucky Poet*, Author's Note to the reprint of 1972, p. xi.

In that same inter-war span MacDiarmid had the creative time of his life 'Trying to learn to use words'. He felt that 'most of the important words were killed in the First World War' (1156) and avoided vague abstractions by rescuing words from Scots dictionaries and scientific texts and putting them into poetic practice. In this endeavour he had conspicuous success for the defeatist tone that Eliot brought to such a fine art is absent from MacDiarmid. His utterances, whether in Synthetic Scots or idiosyncratic English, are positively defiant and ultimately certain of diverse victories. Politically the triumph is conceived in terms of an independent state of Scotland and the poet is confident enough to offer himself as a personification of the area he wishes to explore: 'I am Scotland itself to-day ... Scotland will shine like the sun in my song' (1277).

A complete Scotland, though, needed more than 'to-day'; it needed an eternally valid synthesis that would accept both the masculine aggression of MacDiarmid and the eternal feminine principle of creativity. Increasingly the 'Lost world of Gaeldom' (415) became the feminine principle the poet could penetrate as a prelude to rebirth. MacDiarmid's political statements were often formulated on the basis of such literary symbolism. Hence the difficulties political parties had in accommodating him.

Though endlessly involved in organisational meetings and the affairs of movements such as the Committee of 100, MacDiarmid was never an orthodox practitioner of politics. Poetry was always his priority. He believed that language was the instrument that could change the world. His political demand for independence was an application of his poetic faith in individuality. Books and letters to the press, containing his propagandist and programmatic prose, generalised about the urgent need for social and political improvements. His poems sought the universal in the particular and their characteristic method is to draw attention to an earthly image then reach out for a cosmic conclusion. Working on the assumption that Everyman (or at least Everyscot) could become a spiritual Superman (and at times MacDiarmid linked his Christian symbolism to a Nietzschean existentialism) he offered himself as an example: the postman's son from the Borders surmounting all obstacles to become the voice of Scotland speaking to the rest of the world. This may seem arrogant yet as MacDiarmid was fond of saying, 'I may be vain but then I've something to be vain about.' He could view himself dispassionately as a representative of the timeless values he perceived in Scotland and was, above all, never afraid to be himself and to insist to his readers that they should accept his precedent as a guiding principle:

xvi

And let the lesson be – to be yersel's,
Ye needna fash gin it's to be ocht else.
To be yersel's – and to mak' that worth bein'.
Nae harder job to mortals has been gi'en. (107)

At times MacDiarmid could be himself by giving vent to his anger about injustice in violent vituperation. His own revision of the biblical precepts he had absorbed in his youth included an absolute refusal to turn the other cheek. When he was attacked or insulted he hit back ferociously. This militant mentality is obvious in many of the letters, particularly the letters to newspapers and some of those addressed to the British Broadcasting Corporation. MacDiarmid was always on guard, eager to defend his position and carry the fight forward. If an ideal is at issue then he is in his element as a poetic warrior. He was also willing to pursue his enemies with a tenacity that made him the terror of the more timid sections of the Scottish literati. Not for MacDiarmid the stab in the back or the insidious spreading of malicious gossip. He preferred open confrontation and enjoyed conflict which doubtless he saw as a further example of the dialectical impulse. When MacDiarmid was on the offensive he named names and did not spare the feelings of those who got in the way of the action. He was glad to be a Borderer by birth and a battler by temperament.

The most bitter comments contained in MacDiarmid's letters are probably those directed towards Edwin Muir. The two poets had been friendly in the 1920s when MacDiarmid, as editorial adviser for Routledge's Voice of Scotland series in the 1930s, was content that Muir should contribute the title on Sir Walter Scott. The result, *Scott and Scotland* (1936), seemed to MacDiarmid an appalling act of treachery. Muir had been one of the greatest supporters of Mac-Diarmid's Scots poetry. Reviewing *Sangschaw*, in *The Saturday Review of Literature* on 31 October 1925, he said that MacDiarmid's use of Synthetic Scots 'may turn out to be a fact of great importance for Scottish letters ... For if a Scottish literary language is possible then a Scottish literature is possible too.' In *Scott and Scotland* , however, Muir dismissed MacDiarmid's Scots poetry as ingenious but irrelevant and argued that

a Scottish writer who wishes to achieve some approximation to completeness has no choice except to absorb the English tradition, and [when] he thoroughly does so his work belongs not merely to Scottish literature but to English literature as well. On the other hand, if he wishes to add to an indigenous Scottish literature, and roots himself deliberately in Scotland, he will find ... neither an organic community to round off his conceptions, nor a major literary tradition to support him, nor even a faith among the people themselves that a Scottish literature is possible or desirable ... Scotland can only create a national literature by writing in English. [7]

MacDiarmid attacked Muir in the Introduction to *The Golden Treasury of Scottish Poetry* (London 1940) and in *Lucky Poet* and was even more explicit in letters written at the time of the dispute and for some time after it. He felt that Muir had been turned into a time-server by his wife Willa, and expressed a cordial dislike of the couple. Lest readers find MacDiarmid's abuse difficult to reconcile with Muir's saintly reputation it is interesting to note that Wyndham Lewis, in *The Apes of God* (1930), had a view of the Muirs very similar to that of MacDiarmid. Muir appears, in Lewis's satire, as Keith of Ravelstone:

He is as you see, a very earnest, rather melancholy freckled little being – whose dossier is that [eventually] he fell in with that massive, elderly scottish lady next to him – that is his wife. She opened her jaws and swallowed him comfortably. There he was once more inside a woman, as it were – tucked up in her old tummy. In no way embarrassed with this slight additional burden ... she started off upon the *grand tour*. And there in the remoter capitals of Europe the happy pair remained for some time, in erotic-material trance no doubt – the speckled foetus acquiring the german alphabet, learning to list italian greek and portuguese. [8]

It is also meaningful to mention that George Orwell once 'crossed the street rather than pass the Muirs'.[9] Apparently MacDiarmid was not alone in his assessment of the Muirs. As an exponent of the fabulous dimension to everyday life Muir was an attractive figure; as a man he rubbed several contemporaries the wrong way.

As well as being mentally pugnacious MacDiarmid was physically robust; indeed he gave the appearance, at times, of being indestructible. During the First World War he survived cerebral malaria and returned to Scotland to write the great poems of the 1920s. When he moved to London in 1929, as London editor of *Vox* , he fell from the top deck of an open-deck bus and sustained severe concussion; after a few weeks he was fit again though he told George Ogilvie, on 6 January 1930, that he was obliged to 'avoid all mental stress and excitement, alcoholic stimulants, spicy foods, etc.' In 1935

[7] Edwin Muir, *Scott and Scotland* (London 1936, pp. 14–15 and p. 178).
[8] Wyndham Lewis, *The Apes of God* (London 1930, Penguin edtn p. 315).
[9] Bernard Crick, *George Orwell : A Life* (London 1980, Penguin edtn p. 263).

the poet had a serious breakdown in Whalsay and had to be hospitalised, in Perth, for seven weeks but returned to Shetland to work on *Mature Art*. During the Second World War he became a fitter in an engineering company in Glasgow where he 'suffered serious injuries when a stock of copper-cuttings fell on me and cut both my legs very severely'.[10] MacDiarmid was not a man to complain about difficulties and he managed to make light of these trials and tribulations. Surprisingly enough the one omnipresent medical obsession in the letters is a fascination with flu whose symptoms, of course, are almost identical with those of the hangover. It can, quite reasonably, be conjectured that his frequent bouts of flu were, in some cases anyway, simulated by the after-effects of alcohol. He was, as the letters confirm, a connoisseur of whisky. It must also be said, though, that MacDiarmid had more reason than most to be apprehensive about influenza, for at the end of World War One he was posted to the Sections Lahore Indian General Hospital stationed at the Château Mirabeau at Estaque near Marseilles. There he witnessed, at first hand, the devastating consequences of the great influenza epidemic of 1918.

It was only towards the end of MacDiarmid's life that his health was seriously undermined. The collapses he describes – in letters of 9 August 1973 to David and Pippa Wright, 23 April 1974 to Morven Cameron, 3 June 1974 to David Craig – were a result of erratic syncope, often occasioned by the arterial wear-and-tear of old age. What finally killed the poet was an inoperable carcinoma of the large bowel though the precise nature of the illness was not, initially, disclosed to him. Instead he was persuaded that he had a rectal ulcer and accepted treatment first by cauterisation under anaesthesia then by radiotherapy. When he realised he was suffering from an incurable disease he adjusted to the facts with a wonderful display of courage. Those letters that discuss the imminence of his death have the same philosophical attitude shown by J.B.S. Haldane's poem 'Cancer's a Funny Thing' (published in the *New Statesman* on 21 February 1964):

> I wish I had the voice of Homer
> To sing of rectal carcinoma,
> Which kills a lot more chaps, in fact,
> Than were bumped off when Troy was sacked.

MacDiarmid had a similarly matter-of-factual way of discussing his illness. He wrote to W.R. Aitken, on 18 June 1978 – less than three months before he died in an Edinburgh hospital on 13 September 1978 – of his predicament:

[10] *The Company I've Kept*, p. 187.

I've been a week out of hospital now and as I think I told you had two major operations there – one of which confirmed the fact that the basic cause of my troubles is a cancer of the rectum. It is temporarily quiescent. Cancers do that – go into latencies. The doctors had told Valda and Mike I'd probably 6 months to live, but I'm a tough old guy and may live far longer. I'm not anxious to and feel I've done my best work and am unlikely to be able now to add to that, so there's no point living on.

The supposition that the purpose of his life was entirely artistic is typical of the poet who wrote

> To hell wi' happiness!
> I sing the terrifying discipline
> O' the free mind that gars a man
> Mak' his joys kill his joys ... (281)

Yet MacDairmid was a man who created much happiness, who was genuinely loved by those who knew him well. Indeed Norman MacCaig, one of his closest friends, observed in a poem called 'After His Death'

> We sat with astonishment
> enjoying the shade
> of the vicious words he had planted.

Though MacDiarmid was materialist and mystic, nationalist and communist, intellectually elitist and socially egalitarian, I have never subscribed to the notion that he was a dangerously divided personality who was by turns Dr Grieve and Mr MacDiarmid. He was, instead, a poet determined to heal 'a broken unity of the human spirit' (753). Given his Christian-cum-Nietzschean belief in the ability of the individual to surmount all obstacles and achieve a transfiguration it is arguable that MacDiarmid was the name Grieve put on his evolutionary aims. Surveying the prevailing condition of inhumanity he wanted to oppose injustice so MacDiarmid was Grieve ready to do battle. It should be remembered that most of the letters in this book — apart, that is, from those intended for immediate public consumption in the correspondence columns of newspapers — are signed by Grieve not MacDiarmid. For that reason they are capable of exhibiting a more accessibly human image of the artist.

Those who know MacDiarmid only as a name on a series of books might have expected the man to be, judged on the basis of his public anger, a ferociously argumentative person who never relaxed his grip on Scotland. In fact he was a perfectly gentle man in private. In an article I contributed to *The Scotsman* shortly after his death I tried to account for his internal dialectic by examining two aspects of the phenomenon who was both Hugh MacDiarmid (public personality) and Chris Grieve (private person). Those who had the privilege of knowing him were confronted by demonstrations of this personal dialectic and had to supply their own synthesis to understand the subtlety of his character. A session with the man, in a pub in Edinburgh or at his cottage near Biggar, provided several surprises. One moment he would be Chris, contentedly going over day-to-day matters: he would ask after family and friends, politely enquire after a mutual acquaintance, relish the opportunity of topping a fine story with an even finer flash of wit. He would chuckle at some amusing or absurd incident, his eyes would twinkle, and the sheer warmth of his personality would flood out. At such times the world seemed worthwhile and it was possible to judge the emotional limits he put on his Scotocentric universe. Then, if a matter of principle was touched on, he would literally rise to the occasion. His face would harden into features of sheer determination and he would command all the eloquence of a man of destiny addressing a multitude, appealing to humanity itself. That was Hugh MacDiarmid, the artistic embodiment of the principles Chris Grieve embraced, and when that serious mood took him there was an acute awareness in those present of being face to face with the indomitable spirit of Scotland. His ability to switch from a cosy chat to a shatteringly incisive discourse never ceased to astonish but then he was an amazing man.

His realisation that he had within himself the power to, at the very least, rouse Scotland from the soporific state that had characterised the country since the catastrophe of Culloden made MacDiarmid a tireless literary worker whose time was spent either expounding his aims or expressing them poetically. His letters were not a peripheral part of his output but an indispensable contribution to his lifelong campaign to rouse Scotland from her slumber and give the nation a major poet to be proud of. With an enormous amount of energy at his disposal he sent out thousands of letters and gave them the function of a one-to-one exposition of his poetic and political determination to ensure that 'The thistle rises and forever will!' (152). Perhaps more than any other major writer MacDiarmid addressed his letters to the ideals that sustained the creative gifts he had in such abundance. The recipients invariably understood that and treated his correspondence with the care normally reserved for historic documents.

The principle of selection I applied to these letters was relatively straightforward as I took as my editorial criterion a high degree of literary and autobiographical significance. MacDiarmid was not an obsessive rewriter and though his poems were based on theoretical

xxi

premisses the substance of them came to him in an inspirational manner. The letters, too, were composed in a direct way and were written to elucidate his mood of the moment. There are hardly any holographic hesitations or scorings-out in search of synonyms; the elaborately formal epistolary style came to him naturally as the result of a childhood spent devouring as many books as he could lay his hands on. Because the letters carry their meaning with great clarity there is a drastic distinction between the relevant and the routine. When the poet comments on an important subject such as the making of actual poems these letters ask to be included in a truly representative edition. Moreover, letters full of illuminating remarks tend to have been produced on the spur of a MacDiarmidian moment. For example it would be impossible to ignore the import of the following sentiments in a letter of 4 March 1953 to Kenneth Buthlay:

> I have always felt that the resumption and redevelopment of Scots as a literary medium was only a stage in that return to our Gaelic background which alone would enable us to conceive and achieve major work . . . As you know I have been silent and comparatively unproductive for a good few years now, but I have not been idle and I have been pursuing the purpose of which these statements give you only the faintest adumbration unceasingly all the time, and I have now a tremendous programme of poetry in hand which I hope will carry the whole complex process into the sunlight of achieved poetry ere long.

Other letters, too, chose themselves; MacDiarmid's guided missives to Routledge in the 1930s arguing the case for his book *Red Scotland* (now, alas, lost though an extract from it appears in his letter in *New Scotland* of 26 October 1935); his letter (of 25 November 1948 to Douglas Young) responding to criticisms of his inadequate edition of Soutar's *Collected Poems*; the emotionally emphatic letter of 1 August 1972 to Alex McCrindle on hearing that Honor (Arundel) McCrindle had cancer; and the letters written to Mary MacDonald shortly before his own death from cancer. When a letter had claimed its right for inclusion then it was decided to give it *in toto*; the very few excisions – marked by the convention [. . .] – were determined by discretion with regard to the living and not by any wish to delete less intense passages.

Those letters I omitted were, with a few exceptions, of a perfunctory nature. I also decided to avoid easily available letters already in print such as the one to the *Shetland News* printed in *Lucky Poet* (p. 87) or those given in their proper place in the 1977 reprint of *Contemporary Scottish Studies*. As MacDiarmid, who never learned to type, wrote everything in manuscript (except for those brief periods when he had access to a typist) it was possible to transcribe the vast majority of the letters from the handwritten originals (or photocopies of the originals). The letters to the press were a problem since few newspapers retain originals after they have been printed thereby making it impossible to compare a manuscript letter with the text given in columns of public correspondence. MacDiarmid once demonstrated, in an article in *The National Weekly* of 28 June 1952, that his letters to newspapers were sometimes ruthlessly cut and complained of 'the ethics of putting in only a fraction of a letter and leaving out all the real guts of it'. However this was less likely to happen in his later years when his letters were welcomed as excellent and controversial copy by editors eager to prolong a public debate by admitting MacDiarmid's polemical presence to a contentious issue. In clarifying the letters, personal and printed, I have – where appropriate – adopted a system of autonomous annotation so the reader can rely on the footnotes without having to go back and forward to the index of what is a large book.

From the erudite flair of the early letters to the valedictory flourish of the late ones. MacDiarmid operates as a man possessed by a large vision. Everything that happened to him was related to this vision which amounted to a poetic view of the world as a life-enhancing sphere turning gracefully in a space full of spiritual significance. He was convinced that 'The astronomical universe is *not* all there is' (822) and crystal-clear in his visionary intensity;

> I know that in the final artistic
> – The highest human – vision
> There is neither good nor evil,
> Better nor worse,
> But only the harmony
> Of that which is,
> The pure phenomenon
> Abiding in the eternal radiance. (835)

This 'eternal radiance' lights up the letters in this book which is the cumulative credo of a man whose artistic integrity made him both an apostle of individuality and a poet whose love of the Olympian heights did not detach him from the earth he inhabited with such distinction.

ALAN BOLD

Acknowledgements

In editing these letters I owe a debt of gratitude to various individuals and institutions who readily supplied me with copies of MacDiarmid's correspondence and patiently answered questions. Stanley Simpson of the Department of Manuscripts, National Library of Scotland, gave me invaluable advice and erudite assistance throughout the project and clarified the context of various letters. J.T.D. Hall, Keeper of Special Collections, Edinburgh University Library, was also most attentive in providing manuscript material and information. Mrs Valda Grieve and Michael Grieve, executors of the Hugh MacDiarmid Estate, graciously permitted me to edit the letters and were unfailingly helpful at every stage of the preparation of the book. J.K. Annand kindly gave me the benefit of his extensive research into MacDiarmid's early life and relationship with George Ogilvie. Those superlative MacDiarmid scholars, W.R. Aitken and Duncan Glen, were (as ever) immensely encouraging and expansive on bibliographical and textual matters. The Scottish Arts Council generously awarded me a research grant to complete the project, and I had the benefit of advice from Walter Cairns, the SAC's Literature Director. My wife, Alice, sustained me (as usual) through all the work and I am most fortunate in having as publishers Hamish Hamilton: Christopher Sinclair-Stevenson, Managing Director, championed the project from its earliest stages; Julian Evans and Jane Everard supervised the text with skill and sensitivity. I would also like to cite, with appreciation, the following individuals who helped in diverse ways: John Bett; Grace Brown; George Bruce; Norman Buchan; John Calder; John Carswell; Linda Christie; Alex Clark; G. E. Davie; Valerie Eliot; G.D. Fergusson; David Fletcher; Dairmid Gunn; Colin Hamilton; Hamish Henderson; Gwyniver Jones; P.J. Keating; Frida Knight; Maurice Lindsay; Robin Lorimer; Eileen Lyons; Rhea Martin; Sorley Maclean; Elizabeth Malcolm; Bernard Meehan; Eileen O'Casey; John O'Riordan; Hannah Royle; Trevor Royle; Alexander Scott; Brian Smith; Ronald Stevenson; Meta Viles; Jean White; Gordon Wright. To Kate Chapman I owe the excellent Index.

I am most grateful to The Trustees of the National Library of Scotland and all the institutions, identified in the List of Abbreviations on p. xxv, for the provision of texts of letters; and all the individuals who possess the letters still in private collections.

List of Abbreviations

In identifying the source of letters in specific collections the following abbreviations have been used:

AEDC = Annandale and Eskdale District Council
BBC = British Broadcasting Corporation
BRB = Beinecke Rare Book and Manuscript Library, Yale University (Collection of American Literature)
ECB = Ellen Clarke Bertrand Library, Bucknell University
EUL = Edinburgh University Library
HRC = Humanities Research Center, The University of Texas at Austin
LLI = Lilly Library, Indiana University
McM = McMaster University Library, Hamilton, Ontario
NLS = National Library of Scotland
PMO = Prime Minister's Office
SUNYB = State University of New York at Buffalo (The Poetry/ Rare Books Collection)
ULL = University of London Library (Sterling Library)
UR = University of Reading
UV = University of Victoria

In quoting from books by and about MacDiarmid the following abbreviations have been used:
Company = *The Company I've Kept* (London 1966)
Contemporary = *Contemporary Scottish Studies* (Edinburgh 1976)
Festschrift = *Hugh MacDiarmid : A Festschrift* (Edinburgh 1962), edited by Kulgin Duval and Sydney Goodsir Smith
LP = *Lucky Poet* (London 1972)

Note on the Text

The vast majority of MacDiarmid's letters are in manuscript; though he trained as a journalist he never typed. Only when he worked on *Vox* (1929) and with the Unicorn Press (1931) was he able to utilise the services of a secretary; then, again, when he prepared *Mature Art* in Whalsay in the 1930s he was given secretarial assistance by Henry Grant Taylor. Unless a letter is marked TS (for typescript) it has been transcribed from a manuscript (or photocopy of a manuscript).

All the letters included in this book are complete with the exception of the excisions indicated by [. . .]. Four dots represent the poet's own punctuation, three dots denote omissions in quoted material.

In the text, quotations from MacDiarmid's poetry are identified by numbers in parentheses which refer to appropriate pages in *Complete Poems 1920–76*, edited by Michael Grieve and W. R. Aitken, and published by Martin Brian & O'Keeffe of London in 1978.

All the sources of the letters in specific collections are given in abbreviations explained on p. xxv. Letters in private collections are either in the possession of the recipient or the family of the recipient.

The letters are given as MacDiarmid wrote them though a few syntactical slips have been silently corrected.

The letters have been arranged by correspondent in clusters whose chronology is established by the first letter in each main group. The chronological arrangement is also observed in the two general groups: open letters to the press and isolated letters to individuals (who are identified as correspondents in the Index). Those interested in a particular chronological period should consult the 'home and career' section of the Grieve entry in the Index.

Chronology

(In the Chronology the following abbreviations are used for books by MacDiarmid: LP for Lucky Poet *(1943),* SE *for* Selected Essays *(1969),* Company *for* The Company I've Kept *(1966),* Annals *for* Annals of the Five Senses *(1923),* Uncanny *for* The Uncanny Scot *(1968).)*

My life has been an adventure, or series of adventures, in the exploration of the mystery of Scotland's self-suppression.

LP, 381

1892 *11 August: born at Arkinholm Terrace, Langholm.* I am of the opinion that 'my native place' – the muckle toon of Langholm, in Dumfriesshire – is the bonniest place I know, by virtue, not of the little burgh in itelf . . . but of wonderful variety and quality of the scenery in which it is set. (SE, 53)

1894 It was some fourteen months later that I was caught in the act of trying to commit my first murder – attempting, in short, to smash in the head of my newly-born brother [Andrew] with a poker, and, when I was disarmed, continuing to insist that, despite that horrible red-faced object, I 'was still Mummy's boy, too.' (LP, 218–19)

1899 *Enrolled in primary department, Langholm Academy. Moved to house in Library Buildings.* It was that library, however, that was the great determining factor. My father was a rural postman, his beat running up the Ewes Road to Fiddleton Toll, and we lived in the post office buildings. The library, the nucleus of which had been left by Thomas Telford, the famous engineer, was upstairs. I had constant access to it, and used to fill a big washing-basket with books and bring it downstairs as often as I wanted to . . . There were upwards of twelve thousand books in the library (though it was strangely deficient in Scottish books), and a fair number of new books, chiefly novels, was constantly bought. Before I left home (when I was fourteen) I could go up into that library in the dark and find any book I wanted ... I certainly read almost every one of them ... (LP, 8–9)

1904 *Transferred to secondary department, Langholm Academy.* But even as a boy ... I drew an assurance that I felt and understood the spirit of Scotland and the Scottish country folk in no common measure, and that that made it at any rate possible that I would in due course become a great national poet of Scotland. (LP, 3)

1905 *Taught in Langholm South United Free Church Sunday School.* My parents were very devout believers and very Churchy people ... (LP, 40) Another poet – Thomas Scott Cairncross, who was, when I was a boy, minister of the church my parents attended, introduced me to the work of many poets ... but ... subsequently ceased to be friendly with me ... (LP, 222) *Taught English by William Burt and Francis George Scott* who were teachers at Langholm Academy when I was a boy ... and, in my opinion, [rank] among the strictly limited number of the best brains in Scotland ... (LP, 228–9)

1908 *Admitted as pupil teacher to Broughton Higher Grade School and Junior Student Centre, Edinburgh.* [George Ogilvie] my English master at the Junior Student Centre in Edinburgh was a man in ten thousand, who meant a very great deal to me ... (LP, 228–9) *Joined the Edinburgh Central Branch of the Independent Labour Party of Great Britain and the Edinburgh University branch of the Fabian Society.*

1909 *Edited* **The Broughton Magazine**.

1911 *Death of father, James Grieve.* A lean, hardy, weather-beaten man, he died at forty-seven after a few days' illness of pneumonia. He had never been ill in his life before. (LP, 18) *Left Scotland to work in South Wales on the* **Monmouthshire Labour News**. My father died suddenly before I was finished at the Junior Student Centre. I took immediate advantage of the fact to abandon my plans for becoming a teacher. That is one thing which I have never, for one moment, regretted ... If I had gone on and qualified and become a teacher, my sojourn in the profession would have been of short duration in any event, and I would have been dismissed as Thomas Davidson and John Maclean and my friend, A. S. Neill, were dismissed. (LP, 228–9)

1912 *Returned to Langholm.* The old Radicalism was still strong all over the Borders, though already a great deal of it had been dissipated away into the channels of religious sectarianism and such moralitarian crusades as the Temperance Movement, the Anti-Gambling agitation, and so forth ... But what I personally owed to the Langholm of that time was an out-and-out Radicalism and Republicanism, combined with an extreme anti-English feeling. (LP, 225) *Moved to Clydebank to work on the **Clydebank and Renfrew Press**. Rejoined Independent Labour Party. Moved to Cupar, met Peggy Skinner.*

1913 *Moved to Forfar to work on **The Forfar Review**.*

1915 *Enlisted.* I served in the Royal Army Medical Corps in the First World War, rising to the rank of Quartermaster-Sergeant. From 1916 to 1918 I was in Salonika with the 42nd General Hospital, which, located on the outskirts of the city towards Kalamaria, was established in the marble-floored premises of L'Orphenilat Grec. I was invalided home with malaria in 1918, but, after a period in a malaria concentration centre near Rhyl, was pronounced A1 again and fit for another spell of service overseas. After a brief stay near Dieppe, I was posted to the Sections Lahore Indian General Hospital stationed at the Château Mirabeau at Estaque near Marseilles. This hospital had been established to deal with Indian and other Asiatic soldiers who had been broken down psychologically on the Western Front. We had always several hundred insane there and the death-rate was very high, culminating in the great Influenza Epidemic in 1918 when our patients had little or no power of resistance and died in great numbers. The officers of the hospital were all Indians, mostly Edinburgh-trained, and there were only, in addition to myself, four white NCOs. I returned to Britain and was demobilised in 1920. (Company, 184)

1918 *Married Peggy Skinner.* [1] came back with an *idée fixe* – never again must men be made to suffer as in these years of war. (Annals, 89)

1919 *Found job with* **The Montrose Review** *and moved to Montrose.*

1920 *Moved to Kildermorie, E. Ross and Cromarty. Edited* **Northern Numbers.** Looking back, and recollecting my own conviction even as a mere boy that I was going to be a famous poet, it is surprising that I wrote little or nothing until after I was demobilized in 1919. (LP, 65)

1921 *Returned to Montrose to work for* **The Montrose Review.** *Edited* **Northern Numbers: Second Series.**

1922 *Edited* **Northern Numbers: Third Series.** *Founded and edited* **The Scottish Chapbook.** I became editor-reporter of *The Montrose Review*, and held that position until 1929. I threw myself whole-heartedly into the life of that community and became a Town Councillor, Parish Councillor, member of the School Management Committee and Justice of the Peace for the county. (Company, 184) *Began to use pseudonym Hugh MacDiarmid.* It was an immediate realization of [the] ultimate reach of the implications of my experiment which made me adopt, when I began writing Scots poetry, the Gaelic pseudonym of Hugh MacDiarmid (Hugh has a traditional association and essential rightness in conjunction with MacDiarmid) ... (LP, 6)

1923 *Edited* **The Scottish Chapbook**, *edited* **The Scottish Nation**, *published* **Annals of the Five Senses**, *contributed to* **The New Age**. When Orage gave up *The New Age* [in 1922] and went to America to promulgate the doctrines of Ouspensky and Gurdjieff I took over the literary editorship of *The New Age* and was a prolific contributor to it over my own name and various pseudonyms for several years – until, in fact, Orage returned to England. (Company, 271)

1924 *Peggy gave birth to Christine. Edited* **The Northern Review**.

1925 **Sangschaw.**.

1926 **Penny Wheep**. I was in the thick of the General Strike too. I was the only Socialist Town Councillor in Montrose and a Justice of the Peace for the county, and we had the whole area sewn up. One of my most poignant memories is of how, when the news of the great betrayal came through, I was in the act of addressing a packed meeting mainly of railwaymen. When I told them the terrible news most of them burst into tears – and I am not ashamed to say I did too. (Company, 158) **A Drunk Man Looks at the Thistle. Contemporary Scottish Studies.**

1927 *Founded the Scottish Centre of PEN.* **Albyn. The Lucky Bag. The Present Position of Scottish Music.**

1928 *Founder member of the National Party of Scotland.*

1929 *Peggy gave birth to Walter. Moved to London to edit* **Vox.** In 1929 I left Montrose and went to London to become London editor of *Vox*, a radio critical journal which had been promoted by Compton (afterwards Sir Compton) Mackenzie ... Alas, *Vox* was under-capitalised and premature – radio was not sufficiently far developed to yield an adequate readership concerned with critical assessments of home and foreign programme material of all kinds; and very shortly the venture collapsed. (Company, 186) [In December 1929] I had fallen from the top of a London double-decker motor-bus going at speed, and landed on my head on the pavement, sustaining severe concussion. I did not fracture, but it was a miracle I did not break my neck. (LP, 38)

1930 *Separated from Peggy.* **To Circumjack Cencrastus.** I realized, with terrible distress, that, against my will, the ties between my wife and two children, Christine and Walter, were about to be broken no less completely than I had allowed the ties between myself and my relatives in Langholm and elsewhere to break. (LP, 19) *Moved to Liverpool to work as public relations officer.* After ... one most unfortunate interlude in London, and a subsequent year in Liverpool (equally unfortunate, but for other and far more painful reasons, and owing perhaps to a considerable extent to my own blame), I have been desperately anxious not to leave Scotland again ... (LP, 41)

1931 *Divorced from Peggy. Met Valda Trevlyn in London.* My domestic affairs were in a bad way and I was divorced in 1931. Shortly afterwards I married again. I had, however, no money or income … (Company, 186) **First Hymn to Lenin and Other Poems**.

1932 *Moved to Thakeham in Surrey. Valda gave birth to Michael.* My friends included, too, such extraordinary characters as Count Geoffrey Potocki de Montalk, editor of the *Right Review* (who went … about London wearing a long red cloak – as did his brother, Count Cedric – and whose cottage at Thakeham in Sussex I 'took on' while he was in gaol for publishing obscene literature) … (LP, 48) **Second Hymn to Lenin. Scots Unbound and Other Poems**.

1933 *Moved to the Shetland island of Whalsay.* I came to Whalsay, this little north Isle of the Shetland group, in 1933. I was absolutely down-and-out at the time – with no money behind me at all, broken down in health, unable to secure remunerative employment of any kind, and wholly con- centrated on projects in poetry and other literary fields which could bring me no monetary return whatever … I could not have lived anywhere else … without recourse to the poorhouse. We were not only penniless when we arrived in Whalsay – I was in exceedingly bad state, psychologically and physically. *Expelled from the National Party of Scotland.* (LP, 41, 45)

1934 *Joined the Communist Party of Great Britain.* My coming to Communist membership was not the resolution of a conflict, but the completion, as it were, of a career … From the beginning I took as my motto – and I have adhered to it all through my literary work – Thomas Hardy's declaration: 'Literature is the written expression of revolt against accepted things.' (LP, 232) **Stony Limits and Other Poems**. *Death of mother, Elizabeth.* My mother … and I were always great friends and had a profound understanding of the ultimate worth of each other's beliefs … (LP, 224)

1935 *Suffered nervous breakdown.* I have been Scotland's Public Enemy No. 1 for over a decade now, and I have certain accounts to settle while (a recent very grave illness prompts the phrase) there is yet time. (LP, 34) **Second Hymn to Lenin and Other Poems**.

1938   *Edited* **The Voice of Scotland**. *Expelled from the Communist Party for Nationalist deviation.*

1941   *Conscripted for National Service.*

1942   *Left Shetland.* In February [1942] I had to abandon my Shetland retreat, and since then I have been doing hard manual labour in big Clydeside engineering shops. Going from one extreme to the other like this is, of course, in keeping with my (and Gurdjieff's) philosophy of life, and, happily, at fifty, my constitution has been able to stand the long hours, foul conditions, and totally unaccustomed, heavy and filthy work perfectly well ... my Leontiev-like detestation of all the bourgeoisie, and, especially, teachers, ministers, lawyers, bankers, and journalists, and my preference for the barbarous and illiterate lower classes of workers, has been completely confirmed by my Clydeside experiences. (LP, xxxiii) *Rejoined the Scottish National Party. Member of SNP National Council.*

1943   *Transferred to the Merchant Service.* I had made a good recovery from a serious general break-down I had had in 1935, but the very rough conditions at Mechans [engineering firm] and the fact that I suffered serious injuries when a stack of copper-cuttings fell on me and cut both my legs very severely led me to seek a transfer to the Merchant Service. This was granted and I became first a deck hand – and then first engineer – on a Norwegian vessel, MFV *Gurli*, chartered by the British Admiralty and engaged in servicing vessels of the British and American Navies in the waters of the Clyde Estuary. (Company, 187) **Lucky Poet**.

1945   *Registered as unemployed in Glasgow. Revived* **The Voice of Scotland**.

1948   *Left the Scottish National Party.*

1950   *Visited Russia with members of the Scottish-USSR Friendship Society. Moved to Dungavel House, Strathaven.* At a meeting of the Saltire Society the Earl of Selkirk praised my work for Scotland and the quality of my lyrics, and a little later at his instance his brother, the Duke of Hamilton, offered me a commodious house adjacent to his Lanarkshire mansion of Dungavel, near Strathaven. Standing in a fine wood, it is an ideal dwelling, but unfortunately we had barely moved in and got ourselves settled when the National Coal Board bought over the whole estate, to establish a School for Miners in the mansion and in the adjoining lodges like ours houses for the school staff. So we had to get out . . . *Received a Civil List Pension.* I received a letter from the Prime Minister's office asking if I would accept a Civil List pension. This was a Godsend and put me on my feet at last. (Company, 188, 189)

1951 *Moved into Brownsbank Cottage, near Biggar, Lanarkshire.* It was in a derelict condition, not having been occupied for several years, but it had the supreme advantage of being rent-free, and my wife speedily made it not only habitable but comfortable. We had no 'mod cons', and were getting too old to put up with really primitive conditions. In a year or two, however, some of the Edinburgh University students, members of the Young Communist League, and other friends came to the rescue and did all the necessary digging, draining, etc., and we soon found ourselves equipped with a kitchenette, bathroom, hot and cold water, flush lavatory, and electric light and other gadgets. The long spell of hardship and near destitution was over and after about twenty years' tough struggle we were very comfortably ensconced in a house of our own with every likelihood that it would prove a permanency. (Company, 188–9)

1955 **In Memoriam James Joyce**. *Again revived* **The Voice of Scotland**.

1956 *Rejoined the Communist Party.* I rejoined at the time of what I would call the suppression of the threatened counter-revolution in Hungary. Those who came out then, I think, did so for reasons I would call purely sentimental. They had probably never been convinced Communists and the party was well shot of most of them. (Uncanny, 170)

1957 *Visited China with the British-Chinese Friendship Society. Awarded Honorary LL.D. by Edinburgh University.*

1959 *Visited Czechoslovakia, Rumania, Bulgaria and Hungary as part of the Burns bi-centenary celebration.*

1961 **The Kind of Poetry I Want**.

1962 **Collected Poems**. It was in 1962, however, that the real break-through came. The occasion of my seventieth birthday was celebrated all over the world. There were scores of articles about my poetry in newspapers and periodicals in every so-called civilised country. I had hundreds of greetings telegrams and letters from many countries – so many that for several days round about 11th August ... Biggar Post Office had to run what was virtually a shuttle-service several times a day to deliver the masses of mail. (Company, 189)

1963 *Presented with the William Foyle Poetry Prize for 1962.*

1964 *Visited Canada. Communist candidate for Kinross and West Perthshire in General Election.* It was essential to oppose the Prime Minister [Sir Alec Douglas-Home], as a Communist and as a Scotsman. (Company, 203)

1966 **The Company I've Kept**.

1967 *Visited the USA.*

1971 *Visited Italy.*

1973 *Visited Ireland.*

1976 *Visited Canada.*

1978 *Awarded Honorary Litt. D. by Dublin University. 9 September: died in hospital in Edinburgh. 13 September: buried in Langholm Cemetery.* **Complete Poems**.

To George Ogilvie

At three important formative stages of his life – as a boy in Langholm, as an adolescent in Edinburgh and as a prophet in Montrose – MacDiarmid turned to older men for advice and encouragement. These men were, respectively, the Rev. Thomas Scott Cairncross, the poet and novelist who ministered at the Langholm South United Free Church from 1901 to 1907; George Ogilvie, MacDiarmid's English teacher at Broughton Junior Student Centre; and F. G. Scott who taught MacDiarmid at Langholm Academy then dramatically re-entered the poet's life in the period when *A Drunk Man Looks at the Thistle* was taking shape. Until J. K. Annand edited and introduced MacDiarmid's *Early Lyrics* (Preston 1968), the Ogilvie connexion was unsuspected since it was assumed that F. G. Scott, to whom *A Drunk Man* is dedicated, had been the teacher who most influenced the poet. As Annand observes, there are only isolated references to Ogilvie before MacDiarmid's appreciation in *Early Lyrics*: 'A Moment in Eternity' (3–8) is dedicated to Ogilvie; in *Lucky Poet* (LP, p. 288) MacDiarmid refers to, but does not name, 'my English master at the Junior Student Centre in Edinburgh [who] was a man in ten thousand'; and in *The Company I've Kept* (Company, p. 271) MacDiarmid records the fact that 'I was put in touch with *The New Age* and its editor A. R. Orage when I was still at school by a very remarkable school-master, George Ogilvie.'

Ogilvie, an engineer's son, was born in Glasgow in 1871; when his mother died the family moved to Kilmarnock and George left Kilmarnock Academy at the age of fifteen to serve his time as an engineering draughtsman. He won an entrance bursary to Glasgow University where he intended, initially, to train for the ministry then, when the evangelical impulse passed, turned (albeit with religious fervour) to literature and graduated in 1899 with a First Class Honours degree in English. After teaching in Glasgow and Fife he was, in 1904, appointed Principal Teacher of English at the new Pupil Teacher Centre at Broughton in Edinburgh and taught there for twenty-four years (during which time the Centre became Broughton Higher Grade School and Junior Student Centre and, subsequently, Broughton Secondary School). Although Ogilvie

1

hoped for eventual promotion to the headmastership of Broughton he never achieved this ambition and became, in 1928, headmaster of Couper Street Primary School, Leith, Edinburgh. Forced to retire through ill-health in February 1934 he died a month later (on 31 March 1934).

Evidently, Ogilvie was an inspired teacher. C. M. Grieve was not alone in finding that Ogilvie's Broughton was an institution devoted to the promotion of creative writing. In Ogilvie's period at Broughton he developed the twice-yearly school magazine into an attractive literary periodical. Grieve edited *The Broughton Magazine* 1909–10; other editors were Roderick Watson Kerr and John Gould (joint editors 1910–11); Albert Mackie (1922–3); and J. K. Annand (1925–6). Ogilvie also taught Edward Albert, author of *Kirk o' Field* (1924) and Mary Baird Aitken, author of *Soon Bright Day* (1944).

C. M. Grieve arrived at Broughton on 2 September 1908 and Ogilvie, in an article in the Christmas 1920 issue of *The Broughton Magazine*, recalled the impact this sixteen-year-old Borderer made on him:

> I remember vividly Grieve's arrival amongst us. I see the little, slimly built figure in hodden grey, the small, sharp-featured face with its piercing eyes, the striking head with its broad brow and great mass of flaxen curly hair. He hailed from Langholm, and had a Border accent you could have cut with a knife. I am afraid some of the city students smiled at first at the newcomer, but he very speedily won their respect. He certainly very quickly established himself in mine. His first essay (an unseen done in class) is still to my mind the finest bit of work I have got in Broughton. The subject was 'A Country Road', and Grieve hedged it with the wayside beauty and paved it with the golden romance of the Borders. You may be sure that I made it my chief business from that day onwards to keep my eye on Grieve. He did not belie the promise of his start . . . He wrote poetry and prose with equal facility; indeed, his facility was positively uncanny, and the amazing thing was that everything he did was superlatively good. That is, everything he did in the line of literature. He was not, it must be admitted, a model student . . . As a matter of fact he became the despair of most of his teachers.

Grieve spent two years at Broughton then left, in 1910, to freelance in Langholm. Ogilvie helped him find work as a journalist with the Edinburgh *Evening Dispatch* but, as the following letters reveal, he lost this job in unfortunate circumstances and returned to Langholm.

When Grieve left Broughton he requested, from Ogilvie, two

Valedictory Poems for the summer 1910 issue of the magazine, then responded to them. Grieve's first poem, a sonnet, hinted at his deep admiration for Ogilvie:

> Pilot, farewell! By labyrinthine ways
> Down to the deep'ning of uncharted seas
> Thou hast me led. On flashing seas like these
> Did dreaming young Columbus big-eyed gaze.

It was not the end of the relationship, however, for Grieve made sure he remained in touch with Ogilvie: wherever he was he wrote to his old teacher and when he was in Edinburgh he came to see him if he could. Ogilvie suggested the notion of *Northern Numbers*, an annual anthology to do for Scottish verse what Edward Marsh's *Georgian Poetry* (1912–22) was doing for English verse. He also encouraged Grieve in his plans for *The Scottish Chapbook* and applauded the early MacDiarmid lyrics. MacDiarmid acknowledged his debt to Ogilvie in his contribution to *Early Lyrics* (pp. 21–3):

> It may seem absurd to call Ogilvie a revolutionary. He was far too gentle, too humble, too self-effacing to fill the stereotype of that role – yet perhaps it is the quiet revolutionaries who are most revolutionary. Ogilvie was a Socialist, was already a reader of A. R. Orage's *New Age*, with which he put me in touch, and this led to my subsequent friendship with Orage and with Major C. H. Douglas and all the other early promulgators of the Social Credit Movement, notably such later friends of mine as T. S. Eliot, Ezra Pound, and Sir Herbert Read, and resulted finally in my serving as literary editor of that journal for several years. This is only one instance of the way in which Ogilvie affected people, opening up perspectives for them, indicating what he felt was the right direction in which they should develop . . . He was perfectly certain that I would effect a change in Scottish poetry and probably in Scottish life. He hailed my early Scots lyrics with enthusiasm, and as to politics he rejoiced that I was on the side of the working class. I saw him last in the early thirties, ravaged by illness, and reduced to a shadow of his former self. He was not the sort of man to 'get on' in the teaching, or perhaps any, profession and I felt he had been hardly done by and that the established system was such that preferment was always given to his spiritual inferiors. He was incapable of competing on that level. While so many Scots ignore the cultural riches of their people, and even pride themselves on such ignorance, Ogilvie regarded it as an abnormality in a citizen of any land to despise the culture of his people. His influence was potent at the root of the effort to create a better attitude in

Scotland, and in the long run I am certain the effort will succeed, and his part in it win the recognition it deserves.

NLS

c/o J. W. Storey,
55 Harcourt Street,
Ebbw Vale. Mon.
S. Wales.

Today, (Friday, I think, or
Saturday).
[October 1911]

Dear Mr Ogilvy [sic]:-

It's one in the morning and I've just transcribed my last sheaf of notes.

I don't know why I feel that I must write to you now or never. I have tried to do it a dozen times.

I will never return to Edinburgh – to stay at all events. Probably I'll never see you again, but I feel that you understand better than anybody else I know – that you will be glad to know that it is all right, that I have at last emerged from chaos – from the hurricane of mental and moral anarchy which has tossed me hither and thither these last twelve months.

I am in a good position, earning good money, working fifteen or sixteen hours a day.[1]

And I look back to you as I look back to my dead father, to my mother and one or two others.

Enclose[d] you will find a cutting – which perhaps may interest Mr Ross[2] more than you. I should be glad if you would return it, as it is the only copy I possess.

Yours sincerely,
Christopher Grieve

P.S. Please let us keep up a correspondence.

[1] In October 1911 Grieve moved to Ebbw Vale to work as a reporter on the *Monmouthshire Labour News*, a paper published by the South Wales Miners' Federation.
[2] Peter Ross, Head of Mathematics at Broughton.

4

55 Harcourt Street,
Ebbw Vale,
Mon. S. Wales.

24/10/11

Dear Mr Ogilvie:-

Forging ahead aye! I have already been instrumental in forming four new branches of the ILP down here. In Tredegar a policeman took my name and address on the grounds that it was illegal to speak off the top of a soap-box.

I asked him if a match box was within the meaning of the act and he put something else down in his note-book: what I do not know.

However, as a branch of 25 members was the outcome, I can afford to be generous.

Did you see my account of the recent pogroms in Bargoed, Tredegar, Rhymney, Ebbw Vale & Cwm?[1] They gave me my first taste of war corresponding: and I narrowly escaped being bludgeoned more than once. I heard the Riot Act read thrice in one night (in different towns, of course) and saw seventeen baton charges. My attack on the police, for their conduct during these riots, sent up the sales of the paper considerably. I did not get to bed for four consecutive nights and was the only reporter present at the meeting of the rioters – the riots were almost as admirably directed as the present Chinese revolution – held at Nantybuch at midnight and my editor thought fit to warn me that in all probability I would be arrested for aiding and abetting.

I have since investigated the matter very thoroughly: and the Urban District Councils are agog at the outcome, which reveals an almost incredibly inhuman system of rack-renting and blood-sucking on the part of the Jews in the district.

Several police cases are already filed: I will post you cuttings of my revelations shortly.

I am also busy every minute I can spare in doing up the Broughton business[2] – in anonymous terms, of course – after the

[1] For details of the Tredegar anti-Jewish riots see *The Welsh History Review* (December 1982). In a letter, of 7 December 1982 to the present editor, the Rt Hon Michael Foot suggested that 'The "recent pogroms" may have referred to some of the so-called Rebecca riots or some of the riots directed against the Irish.'

[2] In a letter, of November 1982 to the present editor, J. K. Annand clarified the Broughton business as follows: 'There had been a break-in at Broughton, books and other items stolen. Two students arrested – one pleaded guilty & put on probation. Case against other dropped – books belonged to Ogilvie in his case.

style of these 'Tales for Men only' that have been appearing in the *New Age*[3] to which my efforts will also be directed as soon as I complete and polish – say in a fortnight or three weeks.

When you write that Mr Ross did not seem to understand my article, do you mean that he could not understand such an article coming from me: or do you mean it literally, because, if so, I might post him a little scientific dictionary in memory of old times.

I will send you cuttings of all original stuff from my pen-nib and ink bottle.

I have piles of stuff in chaos: and if I had not such an impossible district to cover, could sort some of it out and dress it up. But my district includes several large mining towns – with all sorts of sectional strikes, inquests, colliery accidents and Federation meetings.

It's like living on the top of a volcano down here. You never know what's going to happen next. I have had three triple murders this last fortnight and have two strikes in hand now. Tomorrow there is County Court in Tredegar – over 400 cases filed, nearly all connected with mining compensation etc.

I am kept pretty well informed of Broughton affairs – (Do not press the point. Open confession may be good for the soul: but there are other things to consider.) but would like to have a syllabus of this winter's lit: and copies of the Magazine.

The astrological article was – I think I did not mention it before – only one of a forthcoming series. I have several important new and absolutely original propositions to enunciate: and have quite a long and interesting correspondence with Camille Flammarion and Prof. A. W. Bickerton (of Yale Observatory)[4]. More of that anon.

I wish I could find time to formulate them soon: also I want to publish a little booklet on Theology.

I wish some device could be patented whereby my flying thoughts could be photographed: that might give me a chance to express my present mental stage with some adequacy.

As to physique, I am constantly crossing mountains (by unutterably rocky tracks) and the wind and rain and constant outdoor work is doing good. My hair is as outré as ever.

Both had to leave school. Grieve saved by Ogilvie's attitude, and refusal of fellow-students to give evidence against him & the other student. Grieve allowed to resign on 27/1/1911 on ground that he had mistaken his vocation.'
[3] 'A Tale for Men Only' by R. H. Congreve was serialised, in five parts, in *The New Age* from 10 August to 7 September 1911.
[4] Camille Flammarion (1842–1925) was founder of the Societé Astronomique de France and a well known popularizer of astronomy. A. W. Bickerton (1842–1929) was Professor of Chemistry at Christchurch University, New Zealand.

Hoping to hear from you soon.

                            Yours etc.
                            C. M. Grieve.

P.S. There must be a hiatus somewhere in my humanitarianism. A
society for the prevention of cruelty to friends should be formed and I
should be sentenced to death for inflicting such an atrociously long
and aimless letter in such execrable calligraphy, on an unfortunate
friend.
    Do tell me about your Canadian trip and give my kindest respects
to Mrs Ogilvie.
C.M.G.

NLS   Somewhere in Macedonia.[1]
                                                20th Aug. 1916

Dear Mr Ogilvie:-

    The Sergeant-Caterer of the Officers' Mess (that's my new post in
our little military world here) has to go 'on deck' at dinner – dinner
commencing at 7.30 p.m. and running to some five courses – freshly
shaven, boots and buttons mirror-bright, properly dressed with belt
and all. He does nothing, of course, save supervision. A spot of
tarnish on a knife or fork – lack-lustre of a wine glass – uneven
flaming of one of the hanging lamps – slackness on the part of the
waiters – slow, slovenly, or uneven dishing-up on the part of the
cooks – what an eye one develops for detail on such a job! Between
the Mess-Marquee, and the Mess cook-house, is a strip of open
hillside over which waiters run backwards and forwards in the
moony Macedonian night. Brightly the beans fall on platefuls of
white vegetable soup, patum peperium entrées, portions of cottage
pie enlivened with rice-stuffed peppers, liberal helpings of rice and
raisons, coffee pots and later when the Mess has come to the walnuts
and almonds and the wine-steward is busy supplying Vin Blanc, Vin
Russe, or Vin Muscat de Samos (my favourite wine, recalling with

---

[1] Grieve joined the army in July 1915 and went to Salonika in August 1916 as a
sergeant with the R.A.M.C.

every sip the wonderful tribute of a poem of Mr Sturge Moore's[2] and unreservedly endorsing every adjective therein), the Sergeant-Caterer and his staff dine too. (What an awful war, to be sure!)

Then down the hill a bit to the Sergeants' Mess Marquee to see if there are any letters – to play a hand at solo-whist at a penny a corner, or, out of purest spite perhaps, or because the courses of the dinner ran too like true love or simply from nostalgia talk like a Bernard Shaw preface, irritatingly over their heads, with bewildering rapidity and not very obvious consequence, and yet with sufficient point and wit to make them endure me. And then up the hill again to my store tent here where amid stacks of Nestle's Milk, tinned Jams and Cakes, sacks of potatoes, bags of flour and oatmeal, tins of tapioca and rice and café-au-lait and cocoanut and cornflour, bottles of wine and whisky and A1 relish I have my bed and my desk and an excellent lamp and a book or two – Gardiner's *Prophets, Priests and Kings*, Birrell's *Selected Essays*, R.L.'s *Familiar Studies of Men and Books*,[3] assorted copies of the *Nation*, *Spectator*, and *New Witness*.

And I read an hour or two. Perhaps do a little scribbling. Another paragraph or two or merely a note of a line of thought, for my *Scots Church Essays*, or *Scots Arts Essays*, thus (extracted from my notebook at random)

8/ The Calibre of Modern Scottish Priests (Contrast with America where, vide Monsignor Benson,[4] 'catholicism is the only living religion'.)

9/ Neo-Catholicism's debt to Sir Walter Scott. (This completed – based on Newman's and Borrow's acknowledgements.)

10/ The Indisseverable Association. (i.e. of Catholicism in Scotland – like Bells of Ys.[5] Placenames, social functions, sacraments, etc. etc. This also completed.)

[2] T. Sturge Moore's poem 'Sent from Egypt with a Fair Robe of Tissue to a Sicilian Vine-Dresser. 276BC' is included in *The Poems of T. Sturge Moore* (1932). In the opening lines of 'Cornish Heroic Song for Valda Trevlyn' (704-12) MacDiarmid refers to 'the Coan wine my friend Sturge Moore has sung/In one of the first longish poems my boyhood knew'.

[3] The books referred to are Alfred George Gardiner's *Prophets, Priests and Kings* (1908), Augustine Birrell's *Selected Essays* (1909), Robert Louis Stevenson's *Familiar Studies of Men and Books* (1882).

[4] Very Rev. Monsignor Robert Hugh Benson (1871 – 1914) was appointed Private Chamberlain to His Holiness Pius X in 1911.

[5] In the Preface to his *The Bells of Is* (London 1894, p.v) F. B. Meyer writes: 'One of the most popular legends of Brittany is that relating to an imaginary town called Is (pronounced Iss), which is supposed to have been swallowed up by the sea at some unknown time ... According to [the fishermen], the tips of the spires of the churches may be seen in the hollow of the waves when the sea is rough; while during a calm the music of their bells ringing out the hymn appropriate to the day

The first series of these 'studies' runs to 50. So does the second, embracing

1/ The Religion of Wallace & Bruce (and all great figures of Scottish history – the religions which make the true atmosphere of Scottish tradition. Who shall put Peden beside Bonnie Prince Charlie, Jenny Geddes beside Queen Margaret? etc).

11/ On Scottish Religions & Moral Influences overseas.

17/ Files of Futility. (Scots Church papers – a distinctionless infinitude of number.)

18/ Scots Catholic Soldiery.

21/ Our Loss of Negative Capability.

40/ John Knox and Mrs 'General' Drummond: An Imaginary Interview. Completed. Not bad, I think, but deriving, of course, from R.L.S. on 'Knox's Relations with women'.[6] etc. etc.

Or is it Art?

I have my *The Scottish Vortex* (as per system exemplified in *Blast*), *Caricature in Scotland – and lost opportunities*, *A Copy of Burns I want* (suggestions to illustrators on a personal visualization of the national pictures evoked in the poems), *Scottish Colour – Thought* (a study of the aesthetic condition of Scottish nationality in the last three centuries) and *The Alienation of Our Artistic Ability* (the factors which prevent the formation of a 'national' school and drive our artists to other lands and to 'foreign portrayal'.

But tonight I have not added a note or thought of new topic. Tonight when dinner [was] over I went down to the Sergeants' Mess [where] your letter was lying for me. I opened it and a bottle of beer and sat down to read – and when I had finished the forgotten beer had gone hopelessly flat. And beer, not bad beer but not 'the good brown ale' by a long chalk, being sourer and thinner, is 80 leptae (eightpence) a kilo-bottle in this Paradise of War-Profiteers. But I did not grudge the eightpence nor did I have another bottle, but bought instead some sweets, remembering what Huxley says somewhere concerning the energising qualities of sugar, and knowing that I should require all my energy.

Your letter was not only in itself a joy: but because of myself an unspeakable relief. 'Twere hopeless to try to convey the state of mind it has occasioned to me – the mingling of memories, desires, regrets, hopes, aye and still fears. Fears – for I shall never read a letter of yours or think a thought of you without a sense of shame and a terrible unrest until I have something worth while [to] dedicate to

rises above the waters.' In his poem 'Homage to Dunbar' (1265-6) MacDiarmid refers to 'the bells o' Ys frae unplumbed deeps'.

6 The essay appears in Robert Louis Stevenson's *Familiar Studies of Men and Books* (1882).

you. But enough of that! You know and I know. And I have not done it yet.

And mention of that makes me think painfully of another debt I owe, to a dream unredeemed on this life but vital to me in the very fibre of my being, and unthinkable to go unpaid. You mention Nisbet.[7] What Nisbet was to me (although for long before his death we had not met nor corresponded) I cannot define – infinitely more than a brother, a very spiritual familiar – one of the many contrast-ing personalities in me was essentially Nisbet, thinking in me with his brain, working in me with his splendid sensuous vitality, reflec-ting upon the other personalities, part and parcel of the debating society which is my mental life. He must not go indedicate – I have the very poem (for poem it must be without saying). It trembles on my tongue – at times in semi-sleep I can read it in the volumes of my sub-conciousness as from a printed page – perfect, adequate. But I have not yet contrived to write it. Must I forever plan what I shall never execute? I am tortured worse than any Tantalus. (These personalities of mine stultify each other – I have meant what I have written – Nisbet was terribly my friend – but yet, close on the above, the Humourous Bit must interject, 'Those classical allusions again! You must stick to the times, you know. Leave Tantalus alone, and confess rather that you are a dead Barber's Cat, becalmed and suffering from a stricture of the urethra'.)

The sweets have justified Huxley. My mental machinery is running at top gear. It is only 9.30 p.m. My lamp I had filled an hour or so ago. Certain 'Salonika Nightingales' (the ubiquitous and raucous donkeys) are making the night hideous but I am used to them, and to the singing all evening long of irrepressible allied troops not far away. Otherwise there is no noise. Nor is there anybody about. I am unlikely to be disturbed again tonight. And you say that you would give much to know in some detail my psychological history since you last saw me: I wish I could comply. How often I have tried – modelling on Amiel's *Journal*, or in novel form, or in a set of essays, or somehow, anyhow. But I have not managed it so far. As you say of the war, so far I am too close to it all. If I could make peace between my contending spirits – cease to think new thoughts, dream new dreams, live so unceasingly and at such a rate (for I can think out novels and play in odd half-hours, visualize every detail, see

---

[7] John Bogue Nisbet, who died in the 1st Battle of Loos, was one of Grieve's fellow pupils at Broughton; it is interesting in connexion with the remarks in this letter that the first composition credited to 'Hugh M'Diarmid' was 'Nisbet, An Interlude in Post War Glasgow' which appeared in the first two issues of *The Scottish Chapbook* (August and September 1922). Nisbet was a 2nd Lieutenant in the Royal Scots.

them published and played, anticipate their criticisms in *The Times*, *The British Weekly*, and *The New Age* simultaneously, write prefaces to new editions, sum up carefully on the business side, grant interviews and talk at great length and with indescribable sense and spirit – and as promptly forget all about them; although they all stick in my conciousness and my thoughts are thus forever like a man moving through the ever-increasing and various confusion of an enormous higgledy-piggledy lumber room) – if, as I was saying before I put out that leafy branch, I could get a sufficient breathing space, then I think I could take stock and write myself forever out of the tangle. That done, I could obtain that variety which is the spice of life, by getting into another and quite different but no less complex tangle.

But I cannot get that breathing space. Nor can I hit on any super-shorthand to keep pace with my continuing mental 'spate' and make up back-time. The outlines are capable of being jotted down very barely perhaps.

1/ South Wales – working for Miners' Federation – delightfully immersed in labour movement, until perception into spiritual sides of question got beyond ILP stage – then found myself in an atmosphere suddenly transfused with hostility – youth and natural tactlessness accentuated difficulty – would I had been born jesuitical – as it was shipwrecked on hidden rocks of implacable liberalism and non-conformity suddenly in bright seas of labourist activity. Contrived to have published in sacro-sanct columns extremist articles galling to diplomatists like Tom Richards MP[8] and other Miners' Leaders on editorial committee. Was horrible unrepentant and truculent withal. Openly construed their statesmanship as a species of hypocrisy attributable to the partial development of too generous ideals in unsuitable natures. Re-organisation of paper afforded convenient opportunity of dispensing with my services.

2/ Back home again to Langholm. Living practically, as Bernard Shaw did, off my widowed mother. Reading inordinately (a fault persisted in to such an extent at too tender an age as to be largely responsible for my present predicament), and spasmodically writing enough to bring in an average of say £1 a week, of which I smoked and purchased papers to the extent of, say, 25%. Philandered extensively during this period. Intimate passages with three young ladies, all English, revived in me our racial antipathy to the English, which, recurring lately, has caused me to write quite a body (some thirty poems in all) of Anti-English verse, not dissimilar to certain products of Irish revival. More important is the way in which my

[8] Rt Hon Thomas Richards (1859–1931) sat as Labour MP for W. Monmouthshire from 1904 to 1918.

attention for the first time was turned to Scottish Nationalism and national problems – my continuing absorption in which is patent in the beginning of this document. Later fell seriously in love with a Scotch girl, a school teacher. Began to work hard, buoyed up with new dreams of honour, visions of a 'home of my own', etc. (You can easily complete the picture – ambition stirred, all better instincts at work, my whole being suffused with a new spirit.)

3/ As a consequence of this 'affaire', found work in Clydebank and Renfrew district.[9] A cushie job, but poorly paid. Lived a strenuous life there for some five months – little time for reading or original writing, all reporting. Did nothing discreditable during this period (albeit the ILP again reclaimed me, and poor Maxton and McLean and I were great friends and co-propagandists) except perhaps for a little interlude with a Dunoon girl, which clashed nastily with the other affaire owing to a rank inadvertence. But matters adjusted themselves nicely and my brother[10] securing for me an option on a job in Cupar, at a very much higher wage, this fitted in nicely with my unusually sustained dream of getting into a fairly well-to-do position and marrying and settling down.

4/ In Cupar as assistant-editor of the Innes papers – *The Fife Herald*, *St Andrew's Citizen*, and *Fife Coast Chronicle*. Unfortunately in the eyes of my well-wishing relatives Cupar happens to be a boozy little hole and my two-fellow pressmen, representatives respectively of the *Dundee Courier* and the *Dundee Advertiser*, were born boon-fellows both. I had heaps of work – holding the correspondencies for *The Glasgow Herald*, *Glasgow Evening Times*, *Scotsman*, *Edinburgh Evening Dispatch*, Press Assoc[iation] & Central News Agency in addition to reporting in extenso for my own three papers. I enjoyed Cupar immensely – worked harder than I should have believed it possible for me to do and simultaneously drank like a fish, acquiring in time the art, of which Dallas of *The Glasgow Herald* – (and perhaps the finest journalist in Scotland today) – is the best exponent, of accurately transcribing and telephonically transmitting while wildly intoxicated reports from the shorthand of brother-journalists, who collapsing under the strain of work and wine, had passed into hopeless conditions which left it up to the unbowled-over one of the party to see that their papers were not 'let down'.

Unfortunately or fortunately, I did not get on well with one of the bosses. We were mutually incompatible. A rupture beyond repair at last sent me to a new sphere in Forfar.

5/ Forfar is the booziest place in Earth. And again the men with

---

[9] Grieve worked on the *Clydebank and Renfrew Press*.
[10] Andrew Graham Grieve, the poet's brother.

whom I was associated were jolly good fellows. Our libations were limitless. So far did this go, in fact, (although my work never suffered – that is to say my work in the limited sense excluding what I am pleased to consider my life-work) that a sudden access of unaccountable good sense made me take a house, four miles in the country by Glamis Castle way, and invite my mother to keep house for me. The result was eminently satisfactory. I had an easy and well-paid-job: my mother had claims upon my time which kept me out of 'company' in my spare time, and I had peace to write. And write I had begun to do in very earnest: but by this time, just when my literary projects were at last emerging out of the tangle and bit by bit getting *actually and satisfactorily* – that is, fairly satisfactorily – written, it was becoming impossible for a young man physically fit to remain in 'civvies'. Besides, I was always susceptible to fits of wanderlust – and I had been a Territorial and loved camping out – and Nisbet's death finally settled matters. (N.B. No 'patriotism' no 'fight for civilisation'.)

6/ I joined the Army in July 1915. Within six months of joining I had risen from a recruit to be acting Quarter-Master-Sergeant of a company 1000 strong. I had acquired not only discipline, a certain mastery of and confidence in myself, and a command of men but a sense of responsibility, a certain business ability, and the habit of being trusted and trustworthy. Needless to say in a Sergeants' Mess sobriety is not strictly insisted upon. I drank as heavily as I possibly could without bad effect to my work and position – and it is wonderful how very heavily that is. In full rig-out with sling-sword belt, and polished crowns, and knee-breeches and tan boots, I was 'some nut' too, and English girls are notoriously 'free', especially since the war began – and I prosecuted feminist studies of the nature I have already mentioned to a great extent. But I got no black mark on my papers, and I never failed my C.O. or Sergeant-Major in the slightest respect.

7/ In July last I was sent to Aldershot; lost (by the curious custom) my acting rank of QMS; in a week or two came through in orders with the substantive (permanent) rank of Sergeant; and was detailed to proceed with this unit, which we did early in August.

So there you are. That's a bald outline. Of my progress through the pit of atheism to Roman Catholicism (adherent not member of the Church of Rome – I doubt my faiths and doubt my doubts of my faith too subtly to take the final step but at this house by the wayside am content meanwhile). I have said nothing but the course is familiar. And similar to it is that other from Labourism through anarchy to a form of Toryism. And not new either is the general lover whom multiplying loves but confirm in bachelordom. Nor of my

13

ceaseless reading, wide as the world of books, in every conceivable subject – or my own interests in activities ranging from gardening to bacteriology and from fox-hunting to scientific indexing – I have planned books and articles on a thousand and one topics (and written in rough draft a score or so – God only knows if they will ever come to more). My mental methods are only too well illustrated by the extracts from my notebook in the beginning of this letter. But I still hope to be allowed to fulfill a few of my intellectual engagements.

I shall come back and start a new Neo-Catholic movement. I shall enter heart and body and soul into a new Scots Nationalist propaganda. I shall – I may.

And now I must make an end. I have no time left for the nonce to animadvert on things Salonikan – to tell you of the life here where all the armies and navies of the world seem to have met – where Russian, Frenchman, Italian, Greek pro-ally revolutionary, Serb and Britisher meet and make friends in café and canteen and a curious polyglottery is the current medium of expression – of mosquitoes and rats and locusts and crickets – of heat-strokes at noon and frost-bite at night – of malaria (which I have had badly but have well recovered from, despite occasional agues) and enteric and dysentery – of 'swazi phantazeers' (or little merry-makings) in Sergeants' Mess – of Venizelos and Gshad Pashi and the wonders of Eastern sunsets, and the beauty of villages that clamber on hill-tops – and of a Greece that is not Helas, and yet has new and quite satisfactory Helens (in extenuation I must not forget to tell you that the young lady teacher of stage 2 broke off our engagement last New Year) – but these and other things will keep for again.

Probably I am more in touch even than you are with the Broughtonians contemporary with me.

A curious study in itself would be that of the relations between Miss Murray[11] and I. Months elapse during which we hear nothing of each other. Then suddenly from one or other of us comes a postcard or letter, with never a sense of interval and never a change in tone. We meet haphazardly at long intervals – here or there – Edinburgh or Aberdeenshire or London, and from her I derive my news, I know of Sutherland and Tommy Clow and Mr. Ross; and hear once in a while of Westwood and T. G. P. Walker and Templeton and Simpson.[12]

[11] Miss Helen Christine Murray taught at Hastings for thirty-seven years. She died in 1967.

[12] The names cited were all associated with Broughton: A. E. Sutherland, Tommy Clow, Peter Ross (a teacher), Jimmie Westwood, Tommy Walker, James Templeton.

From mother I had just heard before I got your letter of the honour awarded to Dr Drummond's[13] son, and in a sudden access of grateful recollection, have written to congratulate the good doctor.

I am sorry to hear of Mr Watson's recurring illness.

And wish inarticulately I could pop in to Broughton again and sit through a lesson with you: and canvass for contributions to the Magazine in the corridor afterwards: and help to revive the 'Lit': and infuse my tame successors with some new Macedonian madness.

But it is no new thing to wish one had one's life to live over again.

You do not mention any literary activity on your own part: nor tell me how time is dealing with yourself in the respect of health.

To end, may this long letter find you in the best of health and spirits, with many thanks,

Yours affectionately,
C. M. Grieve

NLS

Somewhere in the East.
2nd September 1916.

Dear Mr Ogilvie,

Why it should be vitally necessary for me to write to you I can no more indicate that I can indicate why, having unaccountably delayed in writing to you, I found it increasingly and finally absolutely impossible to write to you again. The loss has been mine, and an incalculable one. One of the chief considerations in the psychological tangle from which I have never freed myself is undoubtedly the fact that I have never done anything worthwhile. I have nursed my ambitions, dreamed my dreams – and grown older, that is all! Never a day has passed, however, but what I have thought

[13] Rev. Dr Drummond was Minister of Lothian Road Church. In a taped interview with J. K. Annand (National Library of Scotland, Acc. 7328) MacDiarmid says: '[Ogilvie] didn't approve of my drinking and other things. He was a great Christian, Ogilvie, he was an elder of Lothian Road Church under R. J. Drummond who was a great friend of mine too. I used to go to the Literary Society and Ogilvie was always there, you know, but I wasn't a Christian you see. I've always been a pagan.'

of you. Never a day but what I have said, 'Tomorrow I will write the Fine Thing – then I will write to him again.' But the tomorrow has never come. I have written and written and great are the piles of my MSS – but they have never taken the one shape I keep on hunting for. Someday yet perhaps – !

But in the meantime picture me lying here in the mouth of a tent on a Balkan hillside, looking out over the ancient city of Salonika and its crowded waterways, across the sun smitten gulf to high Olympus (not so very high, after all – only some 3000 feet).

And despite my booklessness, the total absence of such company as in pre-war days I would have found congenial – despite the ravages of mosquitoes which have paid me marked attentions since I came here (indeed marked me all over), the huge heat, and the fact that the ground beneath me is one mass of ant-hills – a very moving scene! – I am as healthy as ever I was, and happier than I had ever thought to be.

It is a big hospital, that down below there to which I am attached, on the Quartermaster's Staff – a cushie job! – and it will be to say enough concerning the life here, or rather the difficulty of living here, to say that business is brisk.

It is a wonderful place this ancient city with its huge new population of soldiers. So many Scotsmen are here that it has been suggested that it should be called, not Thessalonica, but Thistleonica. But that would not be just to our allies. East and west meet and mingle here in an indescribable fashion. Soldiers of half-a-dozen different nations fraternize in canteens and cafés. Naturally and necessarily one picks up an incredible polyglottery. Even the coins in one's pockets are representative of almost every nation in Europe.

One wearies here for letters in an unspeakable way. Perhaps you will understand and forgive and write me sometime – that is to say if you can make head or tail out of this extraordinary scribble. My address is 64020 Sergt. C. M. Grieve, R.A.M.C. 42nd General Hospital, British Salonika Force.

Now I must close. As least I have managed to write again. I earnestly hope that this letter will find you in good health and spirits, and that you will be interested a little to hear once more, after a long elapse of time, from your old pupil,

C. M. Grieve

THE BROUGHTON MAGAZINE[1]
Christmas 1917

Dear Mr Ogilvie,

Camped on a high and airy promontory jutting out into the blue Aegean, across which, a day's sail away, my usual station is on a very clear day dimly discernible on a further coast. I am at present enjoying a rest-cure and write in a holiday mood for the first time in close on fifteen months.

A recent recurrence of malignant malaria left me deplorably reduced in physique and stamina and, noting my debility, the authorities took compassion on me and sent me hither to this 'change of air camp' for a ten-days' spell, of which four or five days have still to run.

There are caller airs which would revive me more speedily and thoroughly, I know, but failing these yet awhile, (the wheels of the chariots of Mars stand badly in need of oiling), the change here is doing me a world of good – I feel a different fellow already and by the time my holiday is over I should be quite built up again for the winter. Now that the colder weather is setting in I need fear no further recurrence of the fever till next summer by which time I hope to have shaken the dust of Macedon off my Army Pattern boots finally and forever – but one never can tell.

In the meantime, however I have little to do but eat, sleep and bathe and remember old friends. The bathing is splendid, along a long sweep of beach (reached by a break-neck of goats' track down steep cliffs) in waters clear to a great depth and with a fine smooth, sandy bottom. On walking along the shore one may see some quaint native fisheries, with two rickety ladder erections sticking up out of the water like the skeletons of stupendous cranes. From seats on the top of these the fishermen can see their prey entering their nets some distance out. They then haul up the nets until they go out and secure their yield in a primitive old boat. Red mullet, for the most part, and an eel-like fish with silver belly and bright green back, and curious thin sword-like mouths, like a snipe's bill.

More curious still is a chance encounter with a lonely but well contented Scots highlander, line-fishing with an old cod-hook, baited with the entrails of mussels (with which the adjacent rocks are plentifully bestruck). He has a true highland knack of casting – power to his elbow! – and is doing great damage to a school of

---

[1] This letter was printed (*The Broughton Magazine*, Christmas 1917) with a headnote stating 'The following letter is from an F.P. and gives some delightful descriptions of life in a rest camp in the East.'

pink-and-silvery flounder-like fish. But as he says, no doubt he'd be 'nane the waur o' a wheen worms.'

But mostly I lie on the cliff-top – the climb back from the beach liking me not – lie in the sunshine on the almost bentless terrain, watching the crafts go up and down the shining waterways. All kinds and conditions of vessels are here. Modern men-of-war and motor-craft; old fashioned sailing-ships and native boats, Trireme and Submarine, galleon and collier, schooner and motor-yacht pass and repass in striking epitomes of naval history.

Behind, the ground rolls endlessly in almost desert stretches. Scarcely a tree is to be seen. But all that Masefield in his 'Gallipoli' says of Mudros and the Dardanelles, and the magic colours, which the powerful sunlight draws out of the rocky barrennesses there, is true also of my present location – and even Masefield's pen has not done full justice to the subtle wonders of these unsuspected colours that make it seem as if the wizardry of the slanting rays of the sun turned grey stone and brown clay into gold and silver and ruby and emerald.

And in such settings I lie and dream.

> Your old pupil,
> C. M. Grieve

NLS   Salonika
                                                                      4/12/17

Dear Mr Ogilvie:-

I have written you several letters at spaces in the great interval since I last heard from you and in the absence of any reply can only conclude that all of them have been turned into fish-food by the fortunes of War, the only alternative being a fear, which I will not give house room to, that something has happened to you. But once more in the hope that this time I may circumvent the conspiracy of circumstances – or, alternatively, lay that persistent little ghost of unformulated anxiety (perhaps after all it is your letters to me which have gone astray) – I must scribble a few lines to wish you in time the old wish of a merry Christmas and a happy New Year.

My malaria which ruined my summer is once more quiescent. It hibernates and is unlikely to give further trouble until the hot weather returns, but another of the endemic diseases of this unnatural country has been playing havoc this last fortnight or so with my debilitated constitution and I am only just pulling myself together and accomplishing what is really one of those feats of physiological acrobatics in which lies the real significance of the 'survival of the fittest'. A few more such successes – and I will be able to survive anything. In a Balkan Who's Who, I could safely put down my recreation as 'pathological equilibrism'.

Day succeeds day here in a monotony of existence in which an accident or an air-raid is a God-Sent diversion. The anatomical side of life is appallingly obstrusive. Conversation is practically monopolised by indecent discussions of 'how one feels today'. I share to the full 'Erewhon' Butler's revulsion from the tendencies of modern science.

Fortunately I am not without books and paper. Turgenev, Henry James, J. M. Synge, the Georgian poets, Galsworthy's *Fraternity*, Gilbert Murray's Greek translations, and a few others make me little worlds in my spare time that carnal considerations cannot violate – and for myself I have actually committed to paper in rough draft (which nothing will induce me to put into any more final shape as long as I am in khaki) two one-act plays, some seventy poems, and the first volume of a trilogy of autobiographic novels somewhat of a cross in nature between Gorki's *Childhood* and Wells' *Tono-Bungay* there. I shall arrive yet if I come scatheless out of the holocaust into civil life where there are personal rights again.

I hope time is being good to you and that I shall hear news of you again some happy day at no too great distance.

I wish you all good and desirable things and ascribe myself in affectionate respect.

Your Old Pupil.
C. M. Grieve.

Please remember me seasonably to Dr Drummond should you be seeing him.

Dear Mr Ogilvie:-

My state of mind at this writing can be best indicated by the following quotations from my current Suggestion Book. Vis. 'N.B. – See October 1917 *Little Review*, not allowed to be issued in America, on account of Wyndham Lewis's "Gentleman's Spring-Mate".[1] The case of Cantleman was taken into court in New York and brilliantly and humorously defended, but to no avail. The soldier Cantleman and the girl he met in the forest are still most damnably "wrapt in mystery".' Scots Bureau 27/7 (a reference number, which must go as merely adumbrating an extraordinary system I have evolved for not losing sight of workable material concerning Things Scottish – similar systems cover my other interests) – Rev. J. A. Ferguson, sportsman, dramatist, novelist and poet. *Campbell of Kilmohr*[2] – 'N.B. T. W. H. Crossland's *The English Sonnet*'. There are thousands of such entries now in these Suggestion books of mine, each indicating some time of creative endeavour, or journalistic intention. Will I ever be free to develop them? Looking over them I can only ejaculate Eureka, Zeugma, Catachresis, and all abominable things. I feel like a buried city.

The first thing I must do when I get into civilian clothes again is to go into a Committee of Ways & Means. Then, if the way is clear, I must first of all, however intriguing other speculations may be, dispose of my trilogy of novels. I could complete them in a year. My brother is now 1st Clerk in the 4th Inland Revenue Division, Edinburgh – I will live on him for that year, probably. After that I can work up the Suggestion Books – and my Catholic Adventures – and the one act play and poems, – The appalling thing is that there are additions every day to these Suggestion Books, new impulses for lyrics, new motifs – and I can finish nothing under present circumstances – and I have already mortgaged more than my allotted span

[1] 'Cantleman's Spring-Mate' is reprinted in *The Little Review Anthology* (New York 1953) edited by Margaret Anderson who explains (p. 143) that 'In the October 1917 number we published a story by Wyndham Lewis, which was promptly suppressed'. In Lewis's story Cantleman, about to leave for the Front, methodically seduces his 'Springmate' Stella: 'He felt that he was raiding the bowels of Nature: not fecundating the Aspasias of our flimsy flesh, or assuaging, or competing with the nightingale.'

[2] J. A. Ferguson's one-act play *Campbell of Kilmohr* (1915) was produced by the Scottish Repertory Theatre Company at the Royalty Theatre, Glasgow, on 23 March 1914. It is set after the Jacobite uprising of 1745 and was hailed as a landmark in Scottish drama; in his introduction to the printed text of the play G. Pratt Insh describes it as 'a new and significant type of Scottish drama.'

several times over. Verily as some one said 'Life is a predicament in which we find ourselves before death.'

I was glad to get your last letter. (I forget whether I have written you since receiving it or not.) I remember Roderick Kerr well[3] – He succeeded me as editor of the Mag. didn't he? – and went in for punning verse after Thomas Hood. I should like to see his *English Review* stuff. If you should be writing to him please congratulate him on my behalf of his 'arrival'. I shall hope someday to meet him, as you suggest the fates may allow, chez vous. Other Edinburgh news is scanty. Nisbet's sister has just been married. I am afraid that by the time I get back all the nice girls will be bespoken. Still we have our compensations here. One Maregena, a Spanish girl hailing from Barcelona, would interest you.[4] Only a Turgenev could write her up. Incidentally she writes herself. Curiously poignant little songs they are, somewhat like Heine's or Emily Dickinson's. I am collecting all she will permit to pass into my hands. One day I shall translate them perhaps. – There are others. Miss Murray is teaching down in Essex now. A friend of mine, a *New Age* writer and poet, lives there too in the same village – G. Reston Malloch.[5] And Miss Cecilia Murray is down in Bucks.

I am in excellent health just now and having a fairly lively time. We had a champion Burns' Night, the 'Immortal Memory' devolving upon me. I do a lot of talking and speechifying. Modern musical tendencies was the theme of a lovely discussion the other night: but when we got off generalities and down to names and motifs, I found that Rimsky Korsakov, Stravinsky and Debussy did not enter into the scheme of things for others, so I dropped out. The general ignorance of recent stringed-instrument experimentation is abysmal – and yet a fellow who can sing 'Annie Laurie' or has heard of Chopin & Handel contests my right to argue seeing I do not like music and am tone deaf. A mad world!

It is a terrible thought, shutting me in most horribly on myself, that of a list of say twelve people in whom I am for the moment pre-eminently interested, not one of them is known to any other

[3] Roderick Watson Kerr (1893–1960) was, with John Gould, editor of *The Broughton Magazine* 1910–11: he contributed the poem 'The Gaff' to the December 1917 issue of *The English Review*, 'June 1918' to the August 1918 issue, and (as Lieut. R. Watson Kerr) 'The Corpse' to the September 1918 issue. His book *War Daubs* appeared in 1919 and in 1922 he founded (with George Malcolm Thomson and John Gould) the Porpoise Press. From 1926 until his retirement he worked on the editorial staff of *The Liverpool Post*.

[4] See MacDiarmid's poem 'The Spanish Girl' (10–13).

[5] George Reston Malloch (1875–1953) became best known for his play *Soutarness Water* (1927). He was also a poet who published *Lyrics and Other Poems* (1913) and *Human Voices* (1930).

member of the mess – there are Paul Fort, the Sitwells, Rebecca West, Serge Asanoff, Remy de Goncourt (whose posthumous papers I am dying to read), Joyce Kilmer (an admirable appreciation of whose work I have just read in *The Month*), Theodore Maynard (quotations from whose *Drums of Defeat* – and in extenso his fine tribute to Padraic Pearse – I find in the latest Dublin *Leader*, the Sein Fein paper, to hand) – and so on.

Still one can always read. Under my pillow just now I have Chesterton's *Club of Queer Trades*, Alpha of the Plough's *Pebbles on the Shore*, E. V. Lucas's *A Little of Everything*, some *English Reviews* containing stories by Caradoc Evans, some copies of *Everyman* and of *The Month* and *The Tablet* and *The Sydney Bulletin* and *Life* and *La Revue Franco-Macedoniene*, and some *National News'* copies with instalments of Wells' *Soul of a Bishop*. – On the whole I cannot complain.

I have a letter from the Rev. T. S. Cairncross[6] – did I ever mention him to you? He has published several volumes of pleasant prose and two volumes of poetry. *The Margin of Rest* (Elkin Matthews), written largely under the influence of Heine on the one hand and Bliss Carman on the other, and *The Masters' Return* (Scott), a volume of rhymeless rhythms reminiscent of Henley. He could not be omitted from any adequate anthology of modern Scottish poetry. Several of his vernacular ballads are wonderfully good. But the great bulk of his stuff is still in MSS. He is just back from chaplaining in France and is likely to contribute something good to the literature of the War. I should like to send on some of his stuff to you – but must wait till I get home. I should like your opinion of him. He writes most delightful letters.

Excuse this paper and scribbling hand. I shall hope to hear from you again soon. It was fine of you to will my safe return. Any psychological force I can support the suggestion with, will be devoted to making you an effective master of Nietzschean methods.

Au revoir, then, with all good wishes.

Yours etc.
C. M. Grieve.

P.S. Please remember me to the Rev Dr Drummond.

---

[6] Thomas Scott Cairncross, who ran Langholm South United Free Church from 1901 to 1907, published several collections of poems, including *The Return of the Master* (1905) which influenced MacDiarmid in his use of images associated with Langholm.

Dear Mr Ogilvie:-

Yours of date a month ago today just to hand by mail which yielded me nothing else. The postal authorities have been dealing hardly with me lately. I have had no letters from home since 2/3/18. Imagine then the doubled joy with which I welcomed your letter.

I do not think I have ever felt better since the malaria microbe invaded my veins way back in September 1916 than I do at this writing. During the past fortnight or so I have been constantly in the open sharing all the strenuousness that is involved in the establishing of a new camp. I have experienced the sundry travails of a dreary porter, a navvy, a general contractor's ganger – and, if the weather has been progressively hot, well the good brown ale at intervals has been all the more refreshing. Our labours are nearly over. Soon we will resume the ordinary routine. But it has been good while it has lasted in hard work, long hours, willing comrades, a little period of hard playing and riotous fun, and then, the soundest of sleep.

Beneath my newly reissued solar topee my face is of a deep good-natured brown and there are no dark rings under eyes which are clearer and livelier perhaps than lately they were. Something deep in me has been stirred by the sensation of striving muscles and the sight of spaded clay that never responds to the disciplined system of more settled periods. Once but for my father (and that was after I had been to Broughton a year or so) I would have become a gardener . . . but that was so many centuries ago!

I wish I could lay my hands just now on Maurice Hewlett's *Epic of Hodge*.[1] I am just in the mood to appreciate it, as it is I shall be surprised if I do not find it to my hand any moment. I nearly always do. You comment on the strange way in which I seem to keep in touch. It is the operation of some law similar to that which makes birds of a feather flock together. Seek and you shall find – such urgent need as mine cannot be denied. Just now I have in my little Nestle's Milk Box library a recent number of *The Dublin Review*, Viola Meynell's *Lot Barrow*, Stella Callaghan's *Vision*, Turgenev's *Rudin* in Constance Garnett's translation, Austin Dobson's *Fielding*, a monograph on Landseer,[2] Archibald Marshall's *Richard Baldock* a presentation copy autographed by the author to his friend, Dion Clayton Calthorp, whom we also know, and a copy of the *English*

[1] Maurice Hewlett, *The Song of the Plow* (1916).
[2] Probably McDougall Scott, *Sir Edwin Landseer* (1903).

containing a very delightful review of the poems of George Reston Malloch[3] (erstwhile the GRM of the 'Ham & Meat' corner of the *Glasgow Herald*) who is one of my own correspondents too. It is strange, but it could not have been otherwise if it had been in the middle of the Sahara. At the worst I would have written (or more probably dreamt) my own library. – And it may further interest you to know that most of my reading comes from 'The Soldier's Recreation Friend, 29 Drumsheugh Gardens, Edinburgh'.

I am in one of my buoyant moods. When I wrote that last letter in which I despaired of ever producing anything I was in a 'Rudin' mood – but today! No, I will not be snowed under in my mental senses. What I do most desperately fear is that my physique will not carry me through, or that the free expression of myself will be inhibited by family and economic cares before I get a chance to establish myself in a monetary sense – which I must do before I can labour uninterruptedly and successfully at my work. – But today I am well in body and mind and all my diverse purposes are grouping themselves harmoniously into a delectable life's work with no confusion or failure anywhere. – If only the war would end soon and let me get begun in real earnest!

In a day or two per registered post I shall send on to you a series of poems, designed to fill a gap in the Soldier Poets' series published by Erskine MacDonald, which so far has mainly consisted of the work of men serving on the Western Front and at all events has not so far included anything from Salonika. I suggest calling the little collection *A Voice From Macedonia*.

They represent the work of three consecutive days, except one or two written earlier and at isolated times. Probably they might be the better of having more time spent on them but that would be rather against the idea of 'soldier-verse' – essentially a hasty and spontaneous thing. But I send them to you, rather than directly to Erskine MacDonald's, confident that I am not trespassing too far on your kindness in asking you to read them first and make any little alterations or corrections you deem good. Will you please then submit them to Erskine MacDonald for me. I can guarantee a circulation of at least 100 among my own immediate friends here – and advts in the *Balkan News* and the RAMC Corps Magazine would be profitable, while of course I have at least 50 personal friends at home who would have a copy.

Whatever happens to them I feel sure you will find some interest in these Active Service effusions and that in itself will amply redeem a few leisure hours they took to write. I heard that you utilised my

[3] George Reston Malloch, *Poems and Lyrics* (1916).

24

Karabouroun letter[4] for the BM and if any of these poems can be similarly used I shall be only too happy. It was, by the way, with remarkable indirectness through a Miss Mabel Leighton, now teaching at Ayton in Berwickshire, that I heard of my reappearance in the BM. She it seems knew me at Broughton. I do not remember her at all – but how nice to be remembered after all this time!

I have been definitely passed for invaliding home as a chronic malaria subject. The scheme was temporarily hung up but has just restarted. So expect a surprise call from me sometime during this summer.

I shall ask my mother in my next letter to post on to you two or three volumes of Cairncross's work I happen to have lying at home.

You refer to my letters showing a 'serene detachment from the War' – but please remember the strictness of the Censorship. However loyal I may be to certain ideals bound up in the Allied Cause I was never to say the least of it an Anglophile – and when I am free of his majesty's uniform again I shall have a very great deal indeed to say and to write that I have not nearly enough desire for premature and secret martyrdom to say or write until then.

In a postscript you ask me to give you my full denomination & address in this reply but your doubts seem to be groundless – you have correctly addressed me on this last envelope.

By the way if you hear anything about Miss Murray[5] – more particularly in regard to her health – please tell me. We write – but the intervals are always long and irregular. The last time I heard from her she was teaching down in Essex. I have not heard from her now for more than usually long – which generally means that she has had another breakdown. She scarcely ever alludes to such matters herself and after inexplicable silences resumes as casually as if she had never left off writing. I am not now in touch with anyone who is in the way of hearing anything about her, but at Broughton you may be. I am afraid my relations with the other sex are incredibly complicated and that between Nelly and I, if it could be written up, would be voted quite impossible, but it is nevertheless although so sketchy and haphazard vital in different ways to both of us – and part and parcel, as you say, of a group of associations I would not willingly let die.

Now I must cease. I shall post the poems on as soon as I can get them censored. Hoping to hear from you soon again – and ever with the kindest regards.

Yours,
C. M. Grieve

4 See above p. 17.   5 Helen Christine Murray.

Somewhere in France.
11/11/18

Dear Mr Ogilvie,

It is some time now since I wrote you: but you will understand that I have had a somewhat busy time of late. I called down to see you at Broughton when I was on final leave but you were off ill and I had not time to come to your house. Shortly afterwards I was transported hither[1] – to a great malaria concentration camp for a further course of treatment so called. Conditions are somewhat rough and we are kept pretty well at it. Still I am A1 – or rather B1. What leisure I do get I am devoting to giving courses of lectures on 'Political & Commercial Geography' and 'Civic & Town Planning' under the Army Educational Scheme. These monopolise three nights a week. I had little thought to return to teaching but the work is absorbing and I think greatly worth while.

News came today of the cessation of hostilities. It was taken very very quietly – incalculable relief, but no mafficking. Technically we are still invalids & may be sent home & demobilised all the sooner on that ground. Anyhow it is splendid knowing that the duration is over and that one is at last actually on the last lap.

My plans for after the war are all cut and dried – I am ready and eager for a time of systematic production. But I shall hope to talk all my plans over with you and I know that whatever I write you will give me the benefit of your advice and experience.

My present address is:- 64020 Sergt. C. M. Grieve, RAMC No 3 Group, Reception Camp, No 2 L of C area. B.E.F. France.

I hope your home has escaped the ravages of the 'flu epedemic and that you soon recovered from the indisposition you were suffering from when I was last in Edinburgh.

Please give my kindest regards to Mrs Ogilvie and the children. I hope this will find you all well in health and spirits.

With all good wishes.

Chris.

[1] 'After a brief stay near Dieppe, I was posted to the Sections Lahore Indian General Hospital stationed at the Château Mirabeau at Estaque near Marseilles.' (Company, p. 184)

Dear Mr Ogilvie:-

Your delightful letter to hand! It redeemed for me the unspeakable unprofitableness of a cold dull Sunday forenoon when I was vainly and with a stultifying sense of unworthiness endeavouring to mitigate my bleak untidy boredom by persuing the current issues of *La Vie Parisienne* and *Le Rire*. Forthwith as a sign of my gratitude I am going to scribble some sort of a return, for the inadequacy of which please blame my cramping comfortless circumstances. I am half-recumbent on damp and muddy tentboards, with blankets, slarried over with mud, wrapped round ice-cold feet, and unobliging vertebrae dove-tailing unevenly into the lumps & hollows of a stack of miscellaneous kit, while a woodfire in a biscuit-tin brazier flames & smokes unequally and disconcertingly in the mouth of the tent. Some setting!

I was greatly interested in what you say of the termination of hostilities and the future you forecast. I myself believe that we have lost this war – in everything but actuality! When I see scores of sheep go to a slaughter-house I do not feel constrained to admire their resignation. Nor do I believe that the majority of soldiers killed were sufficiently actuated by ideals or capable of entertaining ideas to justify such terms as 'supreme self-sacrifice, etc.' I have been oppressed by my perception of the wide-spread automatism – fortuity – of these great movements & holocausts. A painter covers a canvas with a number of rapid brush-marks – a critic comes along and writes it up at inordinate length, seeing in it all manner of technical and aesthetic qualities which the painter had probably not even the mentality to comprehend. So with 'patriotism' – 'a war of ideas' – 'democracy versus autocracy', etc. I more and more incline to the belief that human intelligence is a mere by-product of little account – that the purpose of destiny of the human race is something quite apart from it – that religion, civilisation and so forth are mere 'trimmings', irrelevant to the central issues. However I cannot justly present these opinions here nor have I the space or time to show what has led to my forming them. Only, more and more, with Matthew Arnold, do I believe in the necessity for 'keeping aloof from what is called the practical view of things.[1] To try and approach truth from one side after another, not to strive or cry, nor to persist in

---

[1] In quoting Arnold, Grieve runs together a phrase ('keeping aloof from practice') from the opening essay of *Essays in Criticism* (1865) with a passage (beginning 'To try and approach truth') from the Preface to *Essays in Criticism*.

pressing forward, on any one side, with violence and self-will – it is only thus, it seems to me, that mortals may hope to gain any vision of the mysterious Goddess, whom we shall never see except in outline but only thus even in outline'.

In saying in my last letter that all my plans for the future are cut and dry I should have qualified myself. What I meant was that my life-work is really done – that various books exist complete and unchangeable in my mind – what remains is only to do the actual writing. But alas in real affairs I must condescend to the practical view. It will be necessary for me to do my writing in what leisure and suitable atmosphere will be allowed to me by bread and butter employment – and my first duty will be to secure such employment as rapidly as possible in some suitable place. What an odious problem! I do not suppose for a moment that anything really suitable or adequately lucrative will turn up. Fortunately the fact that I am now married does not complicate these difficulties. But we will see in due course.

Did I tell you, by the way, that Colonel John Buchan expressed himself in very laudatory terms concerning my Salonika poems?

Where and how is Kerr? I have not yet contrived to see any of his stuff. Is he still active? I am greatly hoping to meet him in the not-too-distant future.

Please give my kindest regards to Mrs Ogilvie and the children. I hope they are all well and have successfully dodged the 'flu epidemic which has according to the papers been so bad in Edinburgh.

I hope you have completely recovered from your own indisposition.

You were, by the way, wrong in fearing that I had had a relapse of malaria. The phrase which led to the assumption was 'writ sarcastick'. I am afraid that, the Censorship being still unabated, I cannot make the matter clearer in the meantime. But I am really feeling marvellously fit although conditions here are in every way conducive to an opposite condition.

Hoping to hear from you again as soon as may be, and with all good wishes.

I remain,
C. M. Grieve.

P.S.
By the way I wonder (in connection with what you say of your relationship to the newer ideas) if you have read *A Schoolmaster's Diary* by S. P. B. Mais. Carelessly and impetuously written it is yet a

mine of good things. I have just been rereading it – also Professor Hugh Walker's *Outlines of Victorian Literature* – a glorious textbook.

NLS

Sections Lahore Indian General Hospital.
BEF France.
Marseilles 27/12/1918

Dear Mr Ogilvie:-

I am as happy – or more so – here than I was otherwise when I wrote you last from the wet muddy cold neighbourhood of Dieppe. There are about 30 whites of us attached to the above big native hospital. Four senior NCOs including myself occupy a delightful little flat in a fine old chateau set on a cliff on the outskirts of the city, overlooking the blue sea, surrounded by sub-tropical woodlands and old orchards and gardens where the red and yellow rosebuds still nod beside the walks and the oranges ripen slowly along the old walls in the strong sunshine. We have little neat bedrooms to ourselves complete with real beds furnished with sheets, mattresses, pillows and all the sumptuous rest of it. One could not be more cushily circumstanced on service. Perhaps I may be a trifle snobbish. But the status of a Sergeant here as Sub-Assistant-Surgeon mark you! instead of mere Wardmaster as in an all-British unit is infinitely satisfactory. Duties are nearly negligible. Routine is so relaxed that the oppression of the system is brought to the irreducible minimum. All discipline except self-discipline is practically non-existent. The old creeper-hung weather-coloured Chateau is a veritable martial Abbey of Thelema.

On the way down I spent a lively day in Paris and in an inadequate transatlantic fashion 'did' most of the 'lions' – but Marseilles for light, life, colour, music, gaiety and danger beats Paris hollow and I am revelling in its cosmopolitan excitements under the expert guidance of a young French lady[1] who speaks four languages and is capable of brains and beauty in each of them, and who is attached to the Norwegian Consulate here. In her company I kept the fête de Noël in quicksilver fashion. May no birds migrate to Gath! Suffice it to say that in the perfecting of my dexterity in the

---

[1] See the poem 'To a French Girl Friend' (1202) which first appeared in *The Broughton Magazine*, Summer 1919.

sweet Provencal patios and in penetrating the warm secrets of Southern life my volatile temperament is running with the swift delightful smoothness of a high-grade electrical contrivance: and once again I take as my temporary motto:- 'It is better to be an electric current for five years than a vegetable for fifty.' The dilly dally policy in demobilisation ceases to worry me.

Just before I came south your letter of Dec. 14th arrived. I read it in the Boulogne-Paris express – with enormous amusement and underlying impotent contempt at my own epistolary antics and no little dismay on fresh realization of all I really owe you. What leads me to write – above all to you – as I sometimes do I cannot imagine – no sooner is the unspeakable missive irretrievably despatched than I realise its unutterable crudity, my unfathomable failure in expression of the real content of my mind! However your gentle irony shows unfailing understanding and my own keen appreciation of the Anatole-France quality of your reply shows that I am not unutterably lost myself – to what? There's the rub.

I was certainly in a dreadful condition of mind when I wrote last. No fit of 'blues' approaching that in prolonged intensity has ever visited me before – nor have I often lost my deliberate pose of depersonalisation so completely. My state amounted to cerebral neuritis almost. However it is over. I regained myself by using my natural safety-valve and the result which I am busily licking into shape is a sheaf of studies similar in angle of approach to 'Cerebral'[2] but dealing with diverse psychological crises and reactions. But you shall read them at the earliest possible moment, as soon as I have purified and concentrated their excellent fury.

But that in my ineffably disconnected fashion I am not at all blind to certain boon qualities in your wonderful letters let me quote what my wife said of your last (I sent it to her – I hope you do not mind my doing so – because of its own real interest and because my experimental habit found a congenial speculative field in the possible interactions of her own thought and yours in regard to my own vagaries). She wrote – she is of course very young and instinct with a rectitude I have none of – 'Surely, Chris, you *cannot* fail when you have such a friend to trust in you & help you.' It is significant that even she should cast the sentences in interrogative form. Apart from that it shows that even to one, who knows me only slightly and you only by hearing me speaking of you, your perfect friendliness is evident. I may be unable to express myself normally and tactfully on such matters – but I want you to know that I do fully realize the spirit in which you write and hold our correspondence far from lightly.

[2] 'Cerebral' is the prose piece that opens Grieve's *Annals of the Five Senses* (1923).

30

Apart from that, however, I was enormously struck by your uncanny divination of the extraordinary possibility that I may 'disappear' again. I too recognise that it is possible – even under certain circumstances, highly probable. Yet I cannot explain. To do so (not explain – but disappear) will be black ingratitude to you and a matter of infinite impotent regret to myself. But in such matters I am not the captain of my fate. However, I promise to resist this inexplicable tendency to the full. If our relationship was a blood one or a business one or mainly one of ordinary friendship I am bound to confess that in all likelihood it would be impossible for me to organise myself as an active agent in the maintenance of any continuity or comprehensibility of intercourse actual or epistolary – but fortunately it is not so and I will endeavour, with an uneasy sense that you are having an uncommonly bad bargain of it, to evince a fidelity real enough if incurably erratic and to avoid the all-besetting tangents of unintellegibility as far as possible.

However, your anticipation of the possibility of my 'disappearance' shows a far-going understanding which I will happily be able to count on as an advocate against my unavoidable self-accusations of unaccountable business.

Please transmit to Kerr my congratulations on his MC & hopes for his speedy recovery. I shall look forward eagerly to seeing his book. No, Buchan[3] does not read for love now – he is one of Nelson's directors. Erskine MacDonald after as I told you provisionally accepting my stuff wrote that he found it impossible to put on the market for perhaps an indefinite interval so I withdrew the MSS – sent them to Buchan who seemed enthusiastic about some of them but was only able to promise after-the-war help: so I have done nothing further. My only disappointment lay in the fact that thus whatever happens they lose topicality. However. I'm not worrying.

I have now taken careful stock: and have decided to to seek any employment but to sink or fall as a free-lance pure & simple. I have accordingly filled up the necessary papers to secure priority of demob: I may be released in Feb. or March – but I am easy as to that and in the meantime I am, as I have said, writing (as well as living) a lot. Later on we'll see what we'll see.

Please write again whenever you can. I send my kindest regards to Mrs Ogilvie and the children, and to yourself, with all seasonable greetings and good wishes.

Yours sincerely,
C. M. Grieve.

[3] John Buchan (1875–1940), the novelist.

31

Dear Mr Ogilvie:-

It is now over a month since I got back to Marseilles and it is high time that I was reporting progress. (But that is not all. My slowness in writing this time has a new and graver aspect. Your last letter, which I received in St Andrews when on leave, established a new relation with new obligations. And this time, negligence has a worse complexion of vital inconsideration. Will I never overcome that mastering horror of rational sequence which has lost me already so many good friends, including the person I might have been if my life had ever been susceptible to ordinary order, and made me a sort of stepson of Hagar? – Thus belatedly it would be a further impertinence to essay an expression of gratitude for that letter. I wonder if when Peggy and I saw you in Edinburgh anything in the bearing of either of us told you without words that it had had its ineffaceable effect?)

I have had a busy month working with my accustomed jungles. I have ceased to marvel at the existence and enormity of them: but am industriously clearing paths. Evidence: (having made Peggy my agent and repository) these all new since I came back, and not drafted out or merely noted down further indefinitely-postponed treatment, but actually completed, worked out at high pressure and yet with all the care and thoroughness I can muster, dismissed from a mind eager to turn to other matters, and signed, sealed and sent home (Peggy can see to the business end of the matters – she has had a sound and well-varied journalistic experience despite her deceptive shyness and 'youngness') – 1/ a study of the technique and temper of Joseph Conrad's work; 2/ a Parisian sketch, designed for the back page of the *Manchester Guardian* 3/ several sketches for a book on *Marseilles, Moods & Memories* which I am doing in colloboration with one Leon Pavey who has 'appeared' frequently in the *Guardian, Punch, New Age, Passing Show* and other papers (the book consists of some 35 sketches – Pavey 20, 12 completed – myself 15, 3 completed and 1 which I am not sure will congenially fit in – but we'll see). 4/ eleven or twelve sets of verses: and 5/ a 20,000 word 'book' on *The Soviet State* comprising 1/ A Preface. 2/ A Selected Bibliography. 3/ An account of the present situation in Russia and the Allied attitude thereto. 4/ A discussion of the Old Regime and the causes of the Revolution. 5/ An account of the development of the Revolution through the Duma Provisional Govt. to the present Soviet Republic. 6/ A detailed description of the actual machinery of Bolshevik

Government. – I have told P. to try and place it with either P. S. King, Headly Bros, or Fifield. Whether she has already sent on *Salonika Poems* to Lane and I do not know. I expect she has. She has also in hand a huge unwieldy study called 'Triangular' somewhat after the manner of 'Cerebral' but not episodal. – If *Blast* were still being issued it might appear there. It is an essay in futurism.

The Soviet thing entailed a fearful amount of reading: but I have also found time to read in the original a big anthology of contemporary French Poets and am in communication now with Paul Valéry, André Gide, Albert Samhain and a few others endeavouring to secure permission to incorporate translations of certain poems and confessions of faith in an analysis which I propose to write of the motivation and method of modern French creative art. – In this I have been fortunate to secure the help of a really brilliant French Girl. I have re-read too with great delight George Moore's *Sister Theresa* and Alfred Olivant's *Owd Bob*, also Hilaire Belloc's *A Change in the Cabinet*. So I am far from idle – and I don't intend to be again. I am enormously satisfied to have been able to tick these things off my list as 'things done' and am turning to other projects – I believe I will get all my ideas worked out in time, after all, or at least, most of them. Whether they are worth anything or will secure publishers, Heaven only knows – I have shown Pavey much of my recent stuff, he being on the spot, and he enthuses, you and others have encouraged me before – anyhow the *cacoethes scribendi* gives me no rest! I am not going to mention what I am turning my attention to now – I will tell you when and as the things get done. I only wish that circumstances were more accommodating and that you were nearer so that I could benefit by your advice as I go along – but in the meantime the thing to do (as I know now that I shall not get out of the Army for nearly a year yet!) is to forge ahead and pile up completed stuff instead of listing intentions and dreams.

I am anxious to know how Kerr's book[1] is getting on and wearying to see some of his stuff. I hope that he has now satisfactorily recovered from his wounds and has been demobilised.

I find time, too, I must tell you, for other things beyond writing and reading. How wonderful I am!! I was away all last week-end on special leave playing Rugby, as a wing three-quarter (Can you see me in that role?) for the Marseilles Base Team against a crack team of French aviators (who won by 8 points to nil after a swift bitterly-contested game) at the wonderful little Riviera resort of St Raphael. I sustained gravelled knees, a split lip, and a priceless thirst which I satisfied – headache in lieu. The match was on the

[1] Roderick Watson Kerr, *War Daubs* (1919).

33

Sunday – on the Monday another player & I went on to Cannes where we had an unforgettable six hours' medley-treat of white sun, blue sea, blossoming almonds and mimosa, glittering cafés, music and merriment. Thence back by the night express, running through an incomparable countryside doubly magical under a sovereign moon to Marseilles!

I am afraid this letter is scrawled even more atrociously than usual – my pencil is too slow. The alarming account in the papers of the amount of illness prevalent at home makes me anxious that it may find you, and Mrs Ogilvie and the children, well. Exciting rumours of industrial happenings are trickling through – I wonder what's what really, and, if there is to be anything really *big* doing, cannot imagine how I will support existence away here out of it all, at all, at all.

But I have already put more than a sufficient strain on your patience and powers of decipheration. I will write again soon. In the meantime I am longing for one of your letters once more. Please write soon.

With all good wishes,

I remain,
Yours faithfully,
C. M. Grieve

64020 Sgt. C.M.G.
RAMC
Sections Lahore Indian General Hsp., Marseilles.

NLS   CARTE POSTALE

Villa de L'
Lourdes.
4/6/19

Dear Mr Ogilvie:-

You must excuse my slowness in writing you. I will write as soon as I get back to Marseilles – in a week's time. I have just returned from the Franco-Spanish frontier. This p.c. shows the great Semi-circle of rock and snow dividing the two lands. Yesterday over fields

34

of eternal snow I climbed right up the Brèche de Roland into Spain – about 3000 metres high – a wonderful experience. Tomorrow I am going on to Bayonne and Biarritz and thence into the Pays Basque and along the Silver Coast – Kindest regards to Mrs Ogilvie and the children. I hope this finds all well – Yours Grieve.

P.S. I expect to be home demobilised next month. Full details next letter.

NLS   S.L.I.G.H. Marseilles.
                                                        12/6/19

Dear Mr Ogilvie:-

Have just returned to find awaiting me your date of 29/5/; and am hastening (happily) to accede to the little request you make therein in the hope that I may not be too late. I am greatly interested in this idea of a Souvenir number[1] and shall hope to be able to secure a copy. Probably however I shall see you before it is out and I now find myself (rather unexpectedly) the next in this unit for demobilisation: which indeed may come through for me before the end of this week and at most cannot be delayed more than a fortnight or so.

I have unfortunately not got MSS here of *Salonika Poems* (or indeed of much else: as I have been sending stuff home for safekeeping or disposal otherwise practically as I wrote it) – nor can I rewrite more than one or two of them from memory. I enclose copy of one which you told me you liked. If you remember any one which you would prefer to this one, please drop a note to Peggy at 35 South Street, St Andrews: and she will send a copy on right away. (I told you I had left the stuff with her to 'place', etc. but other matters have so occupied me lately that I have not even asked her to report progress and curiously enough she has not herself mentioned the matter. – However, I'll be home soon now and get things properly in order).

I also enclose a set of verses I wrote on my Pyrennean holiday.[2] I wrote a great deal of various kinds but nothing else, I think, suitable

---

[1] The Summer 1919 issue of *The Broughton Magazine* which contained Grieve's story 'Casualties' and his poem 'To a French Girl Friend' (1202).
[2] 'To a French Girl Friend' is located 'Cirque de Gavarnie, Les Hautes-Pyrénées, June 1919'.

for your purpose. But I rather like this little thing myself and perhaps it will fill a corner.

As to the sketch, this has me frankly beat. Looking over the stuff I have, I have vainly and desperately ached 'which'? Thinking over the material in my brain I have demanded 'what?' and 'How?' till I have tottered on the verge of cerebral vertigo. (Please do not construe this as indicating that your request has caused me any trouble!) Only one thing I have written has done, I think, any justice to my war experience and opinions – particularly opinions – but as it runs to about 200,000 words and it is still in rough draft you will understand why I do not enclose it. But my month's demob. leave is to be dedicated to its finishing – I think you will like it and perhaps find in it some little reward for your long faith in me.

Anyhow I have at last (with a sense of utter inadequacy) fixed on the enclosed sketch.[3] I am sorry that I can do no better in the time at my disposal or under my present very unsettled circumstances.

You must please excuse too this quickly scribbled letter. If I have time here I shall write again in a day or so and tell you of my wonderful time on the Spanish Border – if not, I will instead tell you of it by word of mouth. I am looking forward enormously to seeing you again shortly.

Many thanks for your kind remarks re Peggy. She has been a bit run down but is now on holiday down Selkirk way.

My holiday did me a world of good. I don't remember ever feeling more fit.

Kindest regards to Mrs Ogilvie and the children: and to yourself.

> Faithfully,
> Grieve.

P.S. On second thoughts I'll send you another sketch tomorrow. Please use which you will.

NLS

65 Market Street,
St Andrews.
23/7/19

Dear Mr Ogilvie:-

I was unable to get to the concert after all, having had to come straight on here through news that my wife had taken suddenly ill –

[3] 'Casualties', reprinted in *The Thistle Rises* (1984).

chill and a sort of nervous breakdown – much better now. I hope I did not cause great inconvenience to Mrs Ogilvie and yourself by not turning up on the Saturday. Please accept my apologies. Peggy will look forward eagerly to the pleasure of meeting Mrs Ogilvie again – at Kingsbarns perhaps. To Kerr also I owe my apologies and, like myself, having lost his address.

Can you please manage to let him know that Foulis has jumped our way a treat over that selected verse idea[1] and that it is essential that I should have his selections (four or five if possible) at the earliest possible moment – and if you can get in touch with him, will you ask him to write me to above address so that I can send him on certain information he wants which he should have had ere this but for my misfortune with his address?

What a host of 'can you's'? – and there's one more. If Mr Stewart has succeeded in enlisting Donald MacKenzie's [2] cooperation, his selections also I should have as quickly as can be.

It struck me after our talk that perhaps Eddie Albert[3] has some stuff, too, and would like to come in? It is immaterial whether the stuff has appeared elsewhere before or not. If it has I will, if I have the writers' permission, secure the publisher's or editor's consent to inclusion.

So far as the matter stands the following are definitely 'in':-
T. S. Cairncross
R. W. Kerr
Joseph Lee
Myself
Also my hopes are to secure
Donald Mackenzie
John Ferguson
Edward Albert
and I am in correspondence with John Buchan and Will Ogilvie.

Please give my kindest regards to Mr Stewart: and accept for yourself, Mrs Ogilvie and the children the best wishes of Peggy and myself.

Yours sincerely,
C. M. Grieve

[1] *Northern Numbers* which T. N. Foulis published in November 1920. The book finally featured, in order of appearance, John Buchan, Violet Jacob, Neil Munro, Will Ogilvie, T. S. Cairncross, C. M. Grieve, Joseph Lee, John Ferguson, A. G. Grieve, Donald A. Mackenzie, Roderick Watson Kerr.
[2] Donald A. Mackenzie (1873–1936) was a journalist, folklorist and poet.
[3] Edward Albert, novelist and former pupil of Broughton, prepared with Ogilvie *A Practical Course in Secondary English* (1913). He was also the author of *Kirk o' Field* (1924), *Man's Chief End* (1928), *The Grey Wind* (1929), *Herrin' Jennie* (1931).

NLS   65 Market Street,
                                                     St Andrews.
                                                       7/8/19

Dear Mr Ogilvie:-

   Since I have not yet heard from you in answer to my letter asking
you to be good enough to link me up on to Kerr, and if possible to
rope in Albert, and to ask Mr Stewart[1] if he had succeeded in
securing Donald Mackenzie, I have regretted all the more that
instead of hurrying desperately to catch (by the skin of my teeth)
that train I did not wait for the next: and take my opportunity of
talking things over with you.
   I am anxious to know as soon as may be whether or not these three
are really coming in to this first volume of *Northern Numbers*. I shall be
greatly disappointed if they do not. If they are it is essential that I
should have their selections by the earliest possible post. I have
received all the others now and they are already in the hands of the
publishers. These are:- John Buchan, Will H. Ogilvie, John Ferguson (author of the Thyrea sonnets now in their sixth edition – Ye
Gods!) Thomas Scott Cairncross, and Joseph Lee, the author of
Ballads of Battle. Also mine.
   And by permission the first volume is to be dedicated to Neil
Munro.
   Please try to send me Kerr's address if you can.
   Apart from all that I have now clearly completed the devastating
task of writing out my novel – am on the very last lap – over 200,000
words.
   Also other things of which more anon.
   In our 'wee house' we have at present no fewer than three girl
friends staying – I feel as if I were imprisoned in Girton.
   You too will now be on holiday. I hope you are having a good time.
Please give my kindest regards to Mrs Ogilvie and Agnes and John.
And accept the same yourself. Peggy joins me in this.
   Hoping to hear from you soon and to see you soon.

                          I am,
                          As Ever,
                          C.M.G.

[1] Principal classics teacher at Broughton.

65 Market Street,
St Andrews.
10/8/19

Dear Mr Ogilvie:-

Glad to get your note of y'day's date. I expect that my trouble through the missing letter was really occasioned by my inveterate bad habit of sending letters to you to the J.S. Centre. I really must begin to keep an address book.

Yes. The first volume is to be entirely verse (with an intro., biographised short notes, and bibliographical notes where needed.) The subsequent numbers will also be all verse, except where one or two suitable one act plays may be procurable. Joseph Lee has promised to do something in that line, and I am hopeful of 'roping in' Eric Lyall. Even then, however, not so much one-act plays as dramatic poems will be used.

I should be extremely glad if you do manage to get Albert to let us have one or two of his poems – 5 is about the run, if his section is to be proportionate to the others.

By special permission the volume is to be dedicated to Neil Munro. (I do not know if I mentioned that before.)

I do not know what to do about Donald Mackenzie: as of course I have not Mr Stewart's address: and after the holidays will be too late.

I shall be extremely glad to see you some day this week.

Please give Mrs O. and the children my kindest regards.

Yours,
Grieve.

Kildermorie Forest Lodge,
Alness,
Ross-shire.
24th Oct. 1920

Dear Mr Ogilvie,

Will you not forgive me and write? Mr Stewart said that you would. But no letter has come.

You must have wondered how I was enjoying this.[1] It has been the most unqualifiedly successful experience I have yet made in a life of ups and downs. I intend to remain here as long as circumstances will permit.

But neither what was, nor is, still less what may be – must be the theme of this note. Mrs G. is holidaying and I am bird alone. So once again I have had to write poetry instead of living it.

A week ago it struck me that it would be an interesting exercise to write a volume of sonnets.[2] Forthwith I planned a book to consist of a dedicatory sonnet, 4 sequences of 12 each, and a valedictory sonnet – 50 in all. I have so far succeeded in writing (if they may be called sonnets) the 29 I enclose. I account it a creditable week's work. The quality is of course unequal. The form is not one in which I shall ever feel at home. I do not attempt to defend sestets which are impermissible with the octaves chosen – still less to defend the varied quatrains in one of the octaves. But . . . ?

Please tell me!

Hoping that this note may find you in fine fettle, and with kind inquiries as to the health and happiness of Mrs Ogilvie and Agnes and John.

I remain.
As Ever,
Grieve.

NLS   Kildermorie Forest Lodge,
                                                      Alness.
                                             2nd Nov. 1920

Dear Mr Ogilvie:-

I apologise for having trespassed so flagrantly upon your scanty leisure. It was characteristically thoughtless on my part not to have written first and asked whether you would care to see my sonnets

[1] Grieve accepted an offer to teach in a side school at Kildermorie, a deer forest and lodge ten miles north-west of Alness in E. Ross and Cromarty. His pupils were the two daughters of the head stalker.
[2] Eleven 'Sonnets of the Highland Hills' (1205–12) indicate the nature of this project.

and express an opinion on them. Much of the 'difficulty of my case' arises from the fact that au fond I am ill-bred. The frigid fairness of your reply perhaps punished me sufficiently. I shall not so presume again.

Your letter is, however, to a certain extent incomprehensible to me. For instance you say 'you don't seem to worry very much about yourself – it is a pity for your own sake, etc, that you don't keep a firmer hold upon yourself – I don't know what your peculiar temptation is but it has a good innings.' It would have been truer to say that I worry about nothing else – I have worried myself practically into insanity in the hopeless endeavour to realise the promise some people found in me. I have kept a strangle-hold upon everything but my imaging faculty. I live (as my wife can tell you) a life of constant discipline quite abnormally rigorous. The Spartans were libertines in comparison. I am mobilised to the last fraction of sentience to one end and one end only. My 'temptation' lies simply in the fact that when I recurrently reach a certain pitch everything outside me ceases to exist. At Montrose, despite this intense and monopolising inner life I nevertheless discharged my duties so well that I earned the esteem of all with whom I came into contact – so much so that when, to my employer's disgust, I left (which I did simply and solely because although I was flourishing financially and socially I was not getting sufficient leisure for original work, and consequently verging upon a breakdown) the almost blasphemously ironical incident happened of my receiving from the Town Council a vote of thanks for my eminent public services! My 'temptation' simply arises from the fact that it is impossible to serve God & Mammon – and I have a wife and myself to keep.

You say that you will treat me as I treat you. Except in my difficulty in maintaining a correspondence (which I have tried hard to explain) and my incorrigibly maladroit terminology when I do write (which you can discount), how have I treated you? I have turned to you in every need with utter confidence. I have loved you above all men and women. You have been constantly in my thoughts. I have sought in season and out of season to justify the faith you expressed in me. Can you not imagine the terror it has been to me to bear your predictions as to my literary abilities? I scarcely ever put pen to paper without first re-reading all your letters – just to make sure that they were really addressed to me – that it was of me you said all these impossible things! Do you think I want money or position or reputation? No. Do you think that it matters to my wife, for instance? I may dedicate my poems to her but do you think she reads them? And if she did do you think she would understand them, or me? No! I need not write. I can dream my books and enjoy them in my head. But I try to write incessantly and cannot help doing so because your commendation of my work is my only desire. If my work gives you no pleasure – if my work does not satisfy you that you saw true away back in these Broughton days – it is wasted, irrespective of anything else. I own no duty, in connection with any power of expression I may have, to anyone. God and man may be as they like. But for you I will do all that lies within my power. In the light of that, can you understand what it means to me, chaotic among my private tragedies and nourishing myself on this solitary flame, to have you write 'I have had no time to do more than glance at your sonnets'?

I wrote these sonnets under an urge of despair. If they are not good enough I shall try again and again. While your acute criticisms have been infinitely helpful to me in issues of detail, your reply did not tell me what I wanted to know. Did they *satisfy* you? Did they leave you with the same notion of my ability as before? and where do you place them? I wanted to know what relative position you thought they would if published procure for me among contemporary poets. I cannot determine for myself whether I am on the right lines or not.

For good or evil, beyond all turning back, I do regard myself, thanks to you, as dedicate and I will exhaust every endeavour as long as I live to win out on the highest level.

When I was a boy at school, my old Headmaster said to my ineffable disgust, 'If he is careful he will be another J. M. Barrie' – probably the cause of my scrupulous carelessness in many respects! – and if today you can say no more, I am spending myself in vain ambitions – and my 'peculiar temptation' is to keep on so spending myself.

I will go far beyond the stage of fragments – I have piles and piles of MSS – but not until in every case I am assured in advance of the precise place each volume will take in its particular field and its worthwhileness in view of my single goal.

And there is nobody who can so assure me, nobody whose opinion is of the least consequence to me, but yourself – and even your circumstances which I will not have altered debar me from consulting except on questions of literary merit.

Yours sincerely,
C. M. Grieve

Kildermorie Forest Lodge,
Alness.
13.11.20

Dear Mr Ogilvie

No! I do not believe in consistency. And I am not going to pretend that I attach any great importance to the merely reasonable. Oblivion and a life hereafter are complementary notions. Both attract me: and I am prepared for either. Their attraction predominates alternately.

> 'Grant it to come to me also to keep
> This small session in camp at end of day,
> To have this waking witness ere I sleep
> Of the world passed away;
> Whether dreams take me then, or heralds wait
> As singing children say;
> Or ushers of the stars, bewildering fate,
> Upon the walls of darkness: or not less
> To be desired than they
> Calmer forgetfulness!'

. . . . After all our powers of expression and perception are at best five dimensional: and the Universe. . . ?

Nor do I admit that I will anywhere find a wiser or safer guide, philosopher and friend than you are. I have my own opinion of my work – and my own general literary ideas – wherewith to offset the opinions you pass. I agree that your fondness for me may corrupt your judgement. I make the necessary allowances. But I value and want; and in fact need and will no matter how far I go continue to need your opinion first and foremost – It enables me to regard the showers of rejection slips with equanimity!

I am standing before the Citadel of the Dark Denizen all right: and I have my slughorn ready: and my lungs are splendidly sound – but unfortunately I am in the clutches of two Policemen – Indifference and Preconceived Ideas – who are determined to prevent me making what they call a breach of the peace. I shall break out of their hands all right – but in the meantime their clutch is too tight.

You must not imagine that I am devoting any material fraction of my time to building Spanish castles. My work is by no means all in the future. *Cerebral and Other Studies*[1] is in the hands of the publishers –

---

[1] This title was subsequently changed to *Annals of the Five Senses* (Montrose 1923), a phrase Grieve found in G. Gregory Smith's critical study of *Scottish Literature* (1919, p. 33).

and is the first of a series of 10 volumes of short stories all of which are either absolutely finished or in complete draft – over 100 stories in all, which will complete my work in this region of, shall I say, mystical psycho-analysis.

The Road to Spain, a volume descriptive of a holiday in Les Hautes Pyrénées – with sections of verse[2] – is also in the hands of the publishers.

In the Tents of Time is a series of post-war essays, psychological in interest and concerned principally with the reactions to war experience of the imaging and expressing faculties. Contributors – Joseph Lee, L. A. Pavey, Kerr and self. My own essay is completed (15,000 words) and is being typed. All MSS are promised me by the end of this month. Buchan is to write an analytical introduction. Foulis is publishing in the Spring.

I am also busy with a volume of *Contemporary Scottish Writers*[3] – R. B. Cunninghame Graham, Neil Munro, etc. etc. – for Leonard Parsons' 'Contemporary Series' and have promised the MSS not later than the first weeks of the year. Spring publication also.

Then articles of mine on Lee, Kerr, Cairncross, and Ferguson are appearing (starting this next week, I think) in *The National Outlook*.[4]

These are not intentions – but things actually done – written and accepted! And I think you will agree that they represent a fair amount of work especially when you take into consideration the fact that in addition to my other duties here I am local 'headmaster' under the Ross and Cromarty Education Authority and put in full school hours, and teach all the requisite subjects for Class V, Supplementary!

I would willingly share with you the fun connected with my appointment here. It is the most incredible mixture of phantasy and reality: and (permit me my oblique little satisfactions) overwhelmingly impossible to anyone less 'mixed' than myself. However, I must ask you to wait a little longer – I have drafted a book entitled *Oddman Out: Notes from a Highland Pantry*. Once I can get a start on it I will write it in no time. I am sure that you will enjoy it. I should like to know what you did in reply to Col. Cuthbert – who, by the way, is factor: my employer is C. W. Dyson-Perrins, the Worcester Sauce

[2] See the poem 'To a French Girl Friend' (1202).

[3] *Contemporary Scottish Studies* was published by Leonard Parsons in 1926; the essays originally appeared in *The Scottish Educational Journal*.

[4] Grieve's articles in *The National Outlook* appeared under the title 'Certain Newer Scottish Poets'. The first one, on T. S. Cairncross, was in Vol 2, No 12, December 1920; those on Roderick Watson Kerr, John Ferguson and Joseph Lee followed in the next three numbers (Vol 3, Nos 13-15).

multi-millionaire and one of the most delightful and original little good-hearted freaks in Christendom!

But after all, although I get a chance to write here which I could not get in Montrose, I am not apparently to be permitted to enjoy my wilderness as long as I had hoped. I had hoped to remain here for a couple of years anyway – and do not be surprised if I am in Edinburgh for good in a few weeks' time. I have applied for a job – but just for a time if I do get it. I do not care much either way. The *New Scotsman*,[5] is coming off! And I am just about 'snowed under' with preliminary correspondence and arrangements. It will be a very big thing. However as soon as matters are definitely fixed up and a date can be settled for launching out I will make an opportunity of seeing you and going as thoroughly into the matter with you as you have time for. What I feel I should really like and benefit by would be a thorough cross-examination into my theories of life, literature, politics and religion. I feel pretty sure of myself: but before taking on such a task I would like to 'mak' siccar'. In the meantime I am doing a power of reading – I have accumulated big reserves of practicable journalistic ideas – and I am in constant correspondence with several prominent Scottish politicians and writers who have promised to support the venture.

That is not all. Foulis has practically agreed to start a monthly (1/-) *Scottish Chapbook*[6] under my editorship – to set a national standard, to sort the grain from the chaff, to discover and encourage new Scottish poets, to move Towards a National Theatre, etc. etc. I just sent him my final proposals the other day and it is next to certain that he will decide to go forward immediately. Among the first contributors will be Lady Glenconner, General Sir Ian Hamilton, and Sir Ronald Ross.

I do not want you to imagine that I am in any danger of dissipating my energies by tackling too much. Not so! I feel equal to a bigger programme than that: and much of the energy called for to carry through these schemes is old stuff I have had bottled up for this emergency for several years. What I mean is that I am not attempting in any way to start making bricks without having seen to it that I have ample stores of straw available.

An egotistic epistle! Reading between the lines will reveal easily enough the sort of man I am. The reason why I am anxious to limit our expressed relationships to what seem safe grounds of literary interest merely is that, while I am afraid that you might find closer intimacy disappointing – nay, quickly insupportable, I am in certain

[5] This title was never used: Grieve launched *The Scottish Chapbook* in August 1922.
[6] Grieve himself published *The Scottish Chapbook* from his address in Montrose.

45

respects so definitely committed to courses of living (which I know you would not only not condone but could scarcely overlook – to your own sorrow, as I forsee, and increased anxiety, and finally perhaps, to a washing of your hands) that I am anxious to spare the few friends I do vehemently need to retain, the useless pain of endeavouring to help where I am unuttarably determined not to be helped. I hope that despite the length of the sentence I have contrived to make myself clear.

At the same time I am touched to my very heart's heart by your letter and profoundly grateful to whatever Gods there may be to have such a friend. I shall not disappear again: and I shall write you, storm or shine psychologically, as regular as clockwork, every week-end in future so that you may at least always know where I am and what I am doing.

You will know however that there is at least one chamber in the heart of every real man to which he can admit no other – to which under certain circumstances he dare scarcely venture himself – and it is in that secret chamber that the most terrible encounters of life which in any case never set much store by either material or spiritual happiness or peace must continue apparently without intermission to be fought. Which of course entails now and then such a participation of my external elements in the fray that I tumble before the incredulous eyes of one to whom I may be speaking into sudden and complete chaos – to all appearances!

Yours Ever.
C. M. Grieve.

P.S. And whatever you do please do not imagine that I pity or indulge myself in any way.

NLS

K[ildermorie] F[orest] L[odge],
[Alness]
15th Nov. '20

Dear Mr Ogilvie,

I have to thank you for your exceedingly helpful – really the word sh[oul]d be relieving – notes. The main reason for hurry is that my poetic output has run away with me lately – including sonnets, over 120 poems in less than five weeks! I want to get through with this phase as rapidly as possible – without sacrificing anything if possible – in order to disengage my mind, and apply it elsewhere.

I am afraid that 'The Following Day'[1] is even more of a mystery to me than to you. It came into my head just as it stands on paper. I was drying some dishes – stopped, wrote it down in a few seconds – and went on drying dishes, not however without feeling curiously shaken. I recognised quite impersonally the latent power of the thing – I tried to develop it afterwards: but soon found that it was impossible. The 'We' and 'I' in the Soldier's Song is easily put right – by making 'a song a soldier sung' instead of 'the soldiers sung' in first stanza. – Otherwise I shall just leave it. It is only a fragment of something infinitely bigger which will happen to me one of these days – and, have no fear, the big thing will be clear enough.

You must not think either that I am at the mercy of moods altogether. Things like this happen. How I know not. But as a rule I work with definite and perfectly controlled intention. And I detest obscurity just as much as you do. I will be the last man to mystify for mystification's sake. J. C. Squire's notes ran as follows:- 'I *do* think it "worthy of perusal" but not publishable (i.e. in *London Mercury*). It would be difficult to explain why. Had you sent 10 poems instead of 1 I would probably put my finger on things. It isn't only that the soldier's song doesn't ring quite true and isn't in a convincing metre* but there are things forced or not easy to understand. *But* there seem to me what I can only call *guts* in the poem and you should certainly stick to it and send us some more in the same vein. It is only a matter of finding yourself.'

Asterisk refers to side-note as follows (with which I am in utter disagreement) 'e.g. "But" as a single line might do in a slow-going ode but not in a reckless chorus'. My ear is faulty, I know – I am as you know tone-deaf in music and that does affect my work: - but I am convinced that it should be the other way about.

However, that's that.

I quite agree with your criticism of 'The Spanish Pro'.[2] I really wrote it round this quotation from Henri Barbusse:-[3]

> 'Peu a peu mes regards du jour
> S'habituent à votre tendresse. . . .
> Je comprends l'indistinct amour
> Et le mystère de caresse.

[1] 'The Following Day' (8-10) was first collected in *Annals of the Five Senses* (Montrose 1923).
[2] 'Spanish Girl' (10-13) was first collected in *Annals of the Five Senses*.
[3] The lines are taken from Henri Barbusse's poem 'Apothéose'.

Je vois votre coeur rayonnant
Dans la candeur crépusculaire.
A force de tranquillité
Vous brillez comme auprès d'un cierge
Dans le soir de réalité
Ou vous êtes un peu de Vierge.'

Since writing it too I have discovered this fine line of Victor Hugo's which I shall place above my 'Eden Regained'.

'Un instant d'amour r'ouvre l'Éden fermé.'[4]

I do not think that theologically you are in the best – shall I say – of modern company. Wells and many others have pictured the Lonely God – still continuing to discover Himself. If that conception is right – then it follows that there is quite room for little lapses and forgettings as well as developings of new attributes. I agree of course that the whole is greater than the part – and consequently have changed

'O wind of love, blow cold upon him them!'

to

'O force Creative fail within Him then!'[5]

Your view of 'The Windbags'[6] is just what I intended to convey.

I quite recognise that Death is a matter of comparative indifference to Humanity. This indifference I cannot share. One year with love will always remain to me more desirable than any celestial eternity. Whatever the Hereafter may be Death is to my mind a definite and irreparable loss, more or less serious – but serious always.

I know you are busy. It is selfish of me to keep on thus. But it does me good to unburden myself: and I know the breadth of your shoulders.

As Ever
C. M. Grieve.

P.S. No, no! I invite the public to share my hopes and fears. I do not pretend to omniscience: nor don the prophet's mantle. Final philosophic attitude should not be sought in a first book of poems. I must be permitted my ups and downs. I do not wish to be regarded as a

[4] 'Eden Regained' (1210) is one of Grieve's 'Sonnets of the Highland Hills'; as printed the line from Hugo reads 'Un seul instant d'amour r'ouvre l'Eden fermé.'
[5] The fourth line of 'Acme' (1210), the ninth of Grieve's 'Sonnets of the Highland Hills', is printed '(O Force Creative, fail within Him then!)'
[6] 'The Wind-bags' (1207) is the fourth of Grieve's 'Sonnets of the Highland Hills'.

'one-sided case'. The very fact that I have written them at all is proof of an underlying sense of the worthwhileness of everything – life and death, sorrow and joy, love and lust, hope and fear, Eternity & Oblivion. I do not claim to look at things from God's altitude – but from a human and therefore necessarily incomplete angle. The Ultimate Perspective may be all-inclusive – ours is not yet, nor likely to be. It is God's own point of view that He is neither young nor old – from the human point of view each day ages everything, and certain minutes superannuate Him.

2nd P.S. The 'F[ollowing] D[ay]' intrigues me more than anything I have yet written. Of course I may yet undergo the actual experience of which, this shadow, fell across my mind. Or, in the same way, a stanza I have not so far been given may yet come and throw all the others into perfect clarity.

By the way I am troubled about Mr Stewart.[7] Some weeks ago I wrote him a long letter criticising (on his invitation) certain translations and original poems of his. He has not written again: and I am very much afraid that he may have taken offence. I do not know what sort of man he is, you see. I expressed my view of his work with utter honesty and of course expected that he could sufficiently depersonalise himself to accept my views in the spirit in which I gave them. I shall be very sorry if I have lost his friendship in this way – especially as I emphasised the complete irreliability of my critical apparatus and was at considerable pains to let him know that although my opinions were as they were I attached little importance to them and hoped he would attach less.

NLS

Kildermorie Forest Lodge.
Saturday.
[November 1920]

Dear Mr Ogilvie,

A lean week! Nothing of interest to report. My wife returned (after 5 weeks absence) on Thursday: and we are busy entrenching ourselves, in all the ways that one needs must at a distance of 17 miles from the nearest village, against the rigours to come – rigours already most unmistakably adumbrated in a terrific and soul-

---

[7] Mr Stewart, Principal Classics teacher at Broughton.

freezing frost. Praise be it is luxuriously comfortable indoors – and I have barely five minutes walk to school.

'School', I should explain, is 2 pupils – girls – one Supplementary, one Standard V. The marriage of their former teacher and the practical impossibility of procuring another to sojourn in this fastness led to my being offered – and accepting – the appointment. I find it positively fascinating – which of course would not be the case under almost any other circumstances.

I apologise most unreservedly for setting up Wells as a scoring point. My odious journalistic instinct often betrays me into ill-considered retorts. Au fond I think I am fairly sound. I am, however, tremendously fond of arguing – often for arguing's sake – but I cannot argue really. Sometimes I think that I only think that I can think. It is difficult to know – and it doesn't matter.

I did apparently misunderstand certain of your criticisms. I thought that you were objecting to one sonnet embodying an eternal concept, and another prophesying oblivion. I sought to set up a defence for the duality of – shall I say – my desire in this matter: because, other differences aside, I do attach supreme importance to the fundamental thought or ethical content of all literary work. There would have been no argument if I had read your remarks as criticising a conflict or contrareity of view within the scope of a single sonnet – because there can be no two opinions on that. In the sonnet in question I think the line I substituted for

'O Wind of love blow cold upon Him then'

viz.

'O Force Creative fail within Him then'

disposed of the logician's objections and greatly strengthened the whole sonnet.

I am tremendously relieved to know that my tortuous spirit did Mr. Stewart the injustice of imagining the impossible reason for his delay in writing. I must endeavour to make up in some other way for this infirmity in my general disposition to Amity.

Excuse this scribble. Perhaps by next week I may have matter of creative moment to exercise my pencil upon. If you are busy, do not trouble to answer this note – wait till some communication of more consequence suggests a real need rather than my ordinary perpetual desire for a letter from you in reply.

With every good wish.

> Yours faithfully,
> C. M. Grieve.

Dear Mr Ogilvie:-

I shall certainly forego the keenest delight life can have in store for me if I do not achieve, in time, such a reputation as will enable you to put all that you have thought and dreamt of me into black and white.

C. M. Grieve: The Man and His Work by Geo. Ogilvie will certainly be a book worthy living the most difficult of lives for. . . . You obliterate my fears and all these disagreeable concomitants of a general uncertainty which spring from practical considerations of such matters as the perversity of publishers, the price of paper, etc. – so that I, too, share your desire that it were two years hence and my position secured.

Your all-too-generous article in the *B.M.*[1] has purged me, I think, of my last hesitancies and doubts. I have been reinfused with some of the exuberance I lost when I left Broughton. Almost I fancy that you have enabled me to recapture some at least of my old careless rapture. Certainly my pen is acquiring speed. MSS accumulate. Just as I owe the inception of the *N.N.*[2] idea to you, so now I am indebted to you for a fillip to the sales I am sure. These debts – can I ever succeed in putting something really substantial on the other side of such a balanceless account?

Why, I have so far even failed in such a matter as procuring a maid.[3] Another likely convert has just yielded a most disappointing blank. I could not have celebrated Christmas more happily than by succeeding in this quest. . . . I hope however that the third time will be lucky. In any case I shall not cease to do my utmost until either I succeed or you obtain otherwise the necessary girl.

Many thanks for *Scotsman* par! I wonder if you could look out any day this week for a letter from me in *Scotsman* correspondence.[4]

[1] In the Christmas 1920 number of *The Broughton Magazine* George Ogilvie wrote: '[Grieve] wrote poetry and prose with equal facility; indeed, his facility was positively uncanny, and the amazing thing was that everything he did was superlatively good. That is, everything he did in the line of literature.'

[2] Apparently Grieve developed the ideas of *Northern Numbers* in discussion with Ogilvie.

[3] Ogilvie had asked Grieve if he could find him a maidservant.

[4] *The Scotsman* of 20 December 1920 carried a paragraph on *Northern Numbers*: '[The poems included] may not all perhaps conform to average taste in selection . . . The explanation is to be found in the "foreword" in which the editor tells us that the contributors have been chosen for the most part among his personal friends.' Grieve's reply appeared in *The Scotsman* of 31 December 1920; he asked the

There may also be other letters before the end of the week. My methods in such matters are my own: and resemble those of the Heathen Chinese.

I shall certainly send on all reviews. Enclosed is quite a good one from the *Dispatch*.[5] The 'and Shadows' part of the title refers to subsequent paragraphs, unconnected with our book, but dealing with Murray's protest against unhealthy literature. The editor of *The Scottish Field* is having a special article on *N.N.*[6] It should be good. He's a good man – Brown, they call him.

He wrote re my article on Cairncross in December *National Outlook* – 'It is a piece of grand work which makes me envious.' The editor of *The Irish Times* also wrote in flattering terms of its merit as journalism. Other tributes re this article were surprisingly enthusiastic – and unanimous. And I wrote down to the level of the paper! Honestly I did. The thing astounds me. Did you see it? I haven't a copy – but I can get you one. My article on Kerr appears in the January issue. It is published on the 15th of each month – 3 Frederick St, Edinburgh.

Your final sentence stirs me as nothing else could. You say that you almost feel like writing yourself. I wish you would. Nothing has made me during these years lose whatever sureness of myself has occasionally been mine than my periodical reflection on the receipt of letters from you that I was confirmed in my unfaith in the utility of literary endeavour by your contentment with the fallow-lying of gifts so immeasurably greater than mine.

You may be sure of me. I am infinitely more sure of you. And I know that whatever I may do will be a small achievement in comparison with what (for excellent reasons into which I shall never probe) you have deemed it best to leave undone.

I shall write you again as soon as I know definitely when I shall be in Edinburgh and when and where the dinner is to be.

Accept my assurance (as one who inter alia has written on 'Scientific Management' and 'Publicity and Propaganda Methods' in the *Advertisers' Weekly*) that I am alive to the fact that I have secured in you at any rate an incomparable press-agent: and have quite fallen in love again with the boy I used to be, as you picture the Then Me.

reviewer to 'name any other contemporary Scottish writers whose work approaches the standard taken'.
5 In *The Evening Dispatch*, 15 December 1920, 'Man O' Moray' devoted part of his 'Among the Books' feature to a favourable review of *Northern Numbers*.
6 *Scottish Field* did not carry a 'special article'.

With best wishes to yourself and to Mrs Ogilvie and the children –
in which Mrs G. joins me.

> Yours,
> Grieve.

NLS   K[ildermorie] F[orest] L[odge].
                                                                    26/1/21

Dear Mr Ogilvie:-

I enclose herewith a few cuttings. I have others somewhere but
can't lay my hands upon them at the moment – particularly a
column one in *Glasgow Evening News* and my column-long reply
thereto.[1] But these may interest and amuse you in the meantime.
There are quite a number still to come in: also certain special articles
based on *N.N.* I'll send these on as they come to hand. Who the
'W.J.'[2] of the Glasgow *Bulletin* is I do not know? I shall be glad if you
can return them in a few days' time, as they are travelling round.

No luck yet in my search for a girl.[3] I would not have believed so
simple a commission could have proved so impossible to discharge.
Fortunately – or rather unfortunately – your own experience will
enable you to understand the reasons for 'this thusness' better than I
do. I am told that a letter to the official in charge of the *Inverness*
Labour Exchange would secure applications all right: unemployment is rife there: and perhaps a good girl might be secured in that
way, although it is not so satisfactory as knowing a girl would be.

I am busy now making arrangements for the second series of *N.N.*.
I will let you know who the contributors will be – and in what
proportions – as soon as I get matters fixed up.

I am also making headway with a volume of vers libre – all on
Scottish subjects, such as Edinburgh, the Black Watch Barracks, the

[1] *The Evening News* (Glasgow) 23 December 1920, criticised Grieve's Foreword to
Northern Numbers for promoting the notion of a Group: 'I find it difficult to believe
that there is any such Group at all.' Grieve's reply was published on 6 January
1921 and stated: 'The contributors to *Northern Numbers* were a group only in the
sense that they agreed to associate themselves with the same book. Beyond that,
and beyond nationality and contemporaneity, they had obviously nothing in
common.'
[2] Probably William Jeffrey (1896–1946), Scottish poet and journalist.
[3] This refers to Ogilvie's request that Grieve should help him find a maidservant.

Cowcaddens, Verhaeren in Glasgow, etc. I believe I will be able to place this all right. Some of it is humorous, as enclosed example – least I think it humorous! A mixture of parody and passion!

I had hoped to be in Edinburgh ere this but flu' broke out here. Mrs G. had quite a bad time. I escaped rather easily. But that, and the fact that it prevented my getting on with my 'timetable' as I should otherwise have done, rendered a jaunt South out of the question. To my great disappointment I have no option but to adjourn my prospect of a break 'sine die'.

I am wading through quotations for *The New Scotsman*. I am afraid that it is commercially out of the question to float such a paper in the immediate future – would cost over £20,000 per annum. But we'll see. – – – I'll write soon again. I hope all well.

> Yours Ever.
> Grieve.

NLS   Kildermorie
                                                                  8/2/21

Dear Mr Ogilvie,

I have always meant to dedicate to you something really good if – and as soon as – I could. This is not it.[1] I have put your name about it and am sending it to you simply because you are the subject of it and were in my mind to the exclusion of all else when I wrote it.

Please return it sometime in one of your letters. I haven't a copy: and am too lazy just now to make one. I have, as a matter of fact, had a bad turn – one of the worst since I came back. I took it in time. The diathesis of a severe relapse was there – but I managed, but dint of going to bed and staying there for a day or two, to prevent the development in it of the conditions of malaria and jaundice which threatened. I am however far from right: and must perforce ca' canny.

Progress is being made with the arrangements for the Second Series of *N.N.* Most of the contributors – if not all: I have not yet

---

[1] 'A Moment in Eternity' (3-8) is dedicated 'To George Ogilvie'; it is the first poem in *Annals of the Five Senses* (Montrose 1923) and was later incorporated (without the dedication) into *To Circumjack Cencrastus* (Edinburgh 1930).

54

heard from three of them – are appearing again: and all are out to make a Second Series which will technically and otherwise mark a great advance on No 1. Sir Ronald Ross is joining us.

I have lost Albert's[2] address again. Can you please give it to me? I am anxious to have him this time if he will come in. Have you seen any recent work of his?

I am anxious to know whether you are still without a girl. I can think of no avenue I have not explored, still open to me. And I am truly sorry. I would give a great deal to have been able to do you this small service.

I hope you, and Mrs Ogilvie & the children, keep well. All sorts of troubles seem to be going. Even up here we have had quite an abominable assortment.

I expect you are very busy.

Excuse this scrawl. All good wishes.

Yours as Ever,
Grieve.

NLS   Kildermorie
                                                        22.2.21

Dear Mr Ogilvie:-

Excuse a short scrawl! I am keeping better but not quite myself yet. It is becoming intensely cold here. Spring does not whisper in these latitudes – she roars like a fish-wife.

I was surprised and delighted to find that you thought so much of 'A Moment'. 'Blind' is a word that means something to me quite unlike its normal or proper meaning. – To me it is an antithesis of 'blazing', i.e. a steady light. Cf. Rupert Brooke's

'The unnameable sightless white
That lies behind the eyes'.[1]

However I have altered it. I agree particularly with your pencilled

[2] Edward Albert, the Scottish novelist.
[1] Grieve is misquoting, from memory, from Rupert Brooke's 'The Fish': 'Blue brilliant from dead starless skies,/And gold that lies behind the eyes,/The unknown unnameable sightless white/ That is the essential flame of night'.

55

suggestion of 'judgement' in lieu of 'criticism'. Judgement is *the* word.

A special review of *N.N.* is to appear in the *London Mercury*[2] shortly – so the editor (Mr J. C. Squire) tells me in a letter to hand today. Squire seems to expect me to do things yet. *N.N.* he says still keeps him to his view that I haven't quite found myself yet – but he repeats all he said as to my promise.

General Sir Ian Hamilton[3] is joining us in the next series of *N.N.*

I am worried about Kerr.[4] He sent me two pieces of deplorable stuff. I enclose these. Please return them. I should not perhaps send them without K's permission – but I want your help in dealing with him for his own good.

Kerr, however, also sent me the enclosed Ballad by a young Edinburgh fellow – an architect's clerk, called Wm. Ogilvie.[5]

I should be grateful for your opinion of its merits. I think it is extraordinarily good. I have however edited it here and there, – mainly by entirely omitting two very weak verses.

I am looking forward to receiving your suggestions as to 'A Moment'. By the way, did you get the letter containing the poem on 'Edinburgh' and the jeu-d'esprit, 'Playmates'.[6]

I hope this finds you recovered again: and Mrs Ogilvie and the children also well.

Best regards from Mrs. Grieve and myself.

> Yours ever.
> Grieve.

NLS   K[ildermorie] F[orest] L[odge.]
                                25/3/19 [? 1921]

Dear Mr Ogilvie:-

I was concerned to learn of your continued indisposition. The thought of you ill powerfully dismays me. Your holidays will have

[2] Nothing actually appeared in *The London Mercury*.

[3] Cf 'The well-known poets represented alongside *les jeunes* in [*Northern Numbers* such as General Sir Ian Hamilton] were speedily, and no doubt a trifle unceremoniously, "dropped", and the field was left to the rising school.' (LP, p. 179).

[4] Roderick Watson Kerr.

[5] MacDiarmid included Ogilvie's poem 'The Blades of Harden' in his *Golden Treasury of Scottish Poetry* (London 1941).

[6] 'Edinburgh' (1204) and 'Playmates' (1204–5) are early poems in English.

begun. Wherever you spend them I hope you will have a splendid recuperative time: and that the Spring will oust whatever sickness may be in your veins. But alas! There is so much strange trouble abroad – one is anxious. I, too, am feeling far from well. My last touch of malaria has left me singularly weak and jaundiced. I would give a great deal for a sensation of vim.

I am agog with all manner of ideas: but my cerebrations are too enfeebled to clutch the winged things soaring incessantly just out of reach. Rather than be idle, however – and, of course, I do not believe in merely doing my best under the circumstances, but prefer to wait until circumstances are more favourable for seizing all that is still troubling me with its apparent inseizability – I have occupied myself with the more mechanical work of trying to make good to some little extent my deficiencies in the departments of the epigram & the short poem.

I have not succeded in adding anything of moment to my little store of either: but I do not think what I have done is altogether wasted labour. I enclose a few examples[1] and will be glad to have your opinion. I was glad you liked the poem on Edinburgh: also the jeu-d'esprit 'Playmates' and thank you for your suggestions on both.

Mackenzie[2] is a nuisance. I have as a matter of fact gone a long way out of my usual to placate & propitiate him. He has given me more trouble – over nothing! – than all my other correspondents put together. His grouch originated from the fact that in the first volume of *N.N.* he was relegated to the back of the book – instead of figuring alongside the 'bigger men'! As a matter of fact I shirked my duty as editor: I did not arrange the order of contributors: and left it to Foulis. To save any similar dispute this time I am arranging contributors in alphabetical order. Mackenzie's all right – seems quite a decent sort of chap – but except in re his own poems. Egotism I understand & like: but egotism that is camouflaged as disinterested advice – the sunflower masquerading as the violet – I detest. As far as I am concerned I do not care if M's contributions are given first place – but if they were I should have all the other contributors rearing up. M. is not popular in any case: and he is to my mind in every way a smaller man than Ferguson, Lee, and one or two others.

But I am confident that if Mr Stewart or you were to read my letters to him (having read his to me) you will acquit me on any

---

[1] With this letter Grieve enclosed 'Ennui' (1113), 'A Fool' (8) – which was included in *Annals of the Five Senses* – 'She Whom I Love' (1113). 'Withered Wreaths' (14) – retitled 'A Last Song' in *Annals* – 'Tryst in the Forest' (1113), 'Truth' (1115), 'Two Gods' (1115), 'In Memory' (1114), 'To Margaret' (1114).
[2] The poet and folklorist Donald A. Mackenzie.

charge of want of tact: and see me in a peculiar light as a monument of superfluous patience.

Enough! As a matter of fact I do now understand so well the petty troubles and difficulties of literary work that I wholeheartedly sympathise with every foible, however preposterous, of every scribbler however small: – a sympathy that is, alas!, complicated and on certain cases nullified in exact proportion to the number of correspondents to whom I must simultaneously extend it.

With best wishes and renewed thanks.

Yours Ever.
C. M. Grieve.

NLS   19 Kincardine Street,
                                                        Montrose
                                                          [1921]

Dear Mr Ogilvie:-

I will write you fully in a few days – on Thursday perhaps. I shall be tremendously busy till then. This intermittent aboulia which renders me impotent to maintain regular relations with people has been extraordinarily well-developed this time. It has been physically impossible to write. However I objected strongly to passing out into the void again – and some time ago I shall ask my mother who is in Edinburgh to call upon you and explain why I wasn't writing. It is a horrible business and developed quite unexpectedly.

I have however, been writing a great deal all this time. The *Northern Numbers* volume is all right – but for typographical reasons publication has had to be postponed till early in the Spring. I have heaps of things to tell you and show you – mainly short stories. But I am making no effort to place them – all I feel interested in is to write them.

I was sorry to hear illness had spoiled your holiday: and hope you are completely rid of the trouble.

My own health is very shaky. The cold weather is playing me up in all sorts of unpleasant ways.

However, I'll write fully on Thursday.

Please forgive me.

C.M.G.

NLS

12 Whites Place
Montrose.
8th Sept. 1921

Dear Mr Ogilvie:-

I am sending you herewith a set of the proofs of my forthcoming book,[1] which I think you will like to see. There are many mistakes as you will see: but these I have all corrected already: and the book will be out very shortly now.

So will the Second Series of *N.N.*, – proofs of which I am now passing through.

I am sorry that neither of these volumes contains any poem of mine new to you: but I sent off on Tuesday last a set of seventy new ones – all, nearly, songs and little lyrics, written during two week-ends – to Andrew Melrose, publisher, who, I have reason to hope, will issue them under the title of *Shapes and Shadows* this season yet.

I had hoped to have seen you in Edinburgh ere this: but may do so soon. I hope you are keeping well – also Mrs Ogilvie and the children. Mrs Grieve joins me in sending our best regards to all.

As to other matters this kettle may have been exceptionally long in coming to the boil – a waited-on kettle has always a well in it however – but it is singing quite promisingly now.

With all love.
Chris.

P.S. Your name is wrongly spelt in dedication of 'A Moment' – but I corrected that all right. – I hope you do not mind it appearing: or my use in 'Four Years' Harvest' of a little bit of one of your letters to me.
P.S. In regard to *N.N.* I was greatly disappointed in Albert not coming up to the scratch, and joining us.

[1] *Annals of the Five Senses* (Montrose 1923).

12 White's Place,
Montrose.
26th Sept. 1921

Dear Mr Ogilvie:-

Many thanks for your letter characteristically over-generous as usual. Despite the clearest realisation of my actual desserts I would have been disappointed had it been otherwise. Variety is the spice of life – and your letters are variety to me in that sense coming as they generally do between batches of editorial rejections and regrets. I put my best into my work. Neither in subject, treatment or any other way do I write to suit this paper or that or any purpose to save my own reasonable satisfaction. So that I do not care whether you are a biased laudator or otherwise. If I please you that is almost enough for me – when I get more depressed than usual I even get defiantly proud of the fact that I am an author with a public of one, out-Landoring Landor so – in any event such a letter as yours counterbalances rightaway accumulating doubts and dejections of all kinds. Sometimes I re-read a whole batch of them until I purge myself of the presumption of disappointment and set to to write something spontaneously and unaccountably mine again utterly oblivious or contemptuous of the fact that it is 99 chances to 1 that it will be even more insusceptible of any editor's or publisher's acceptance.

I enclose a poem[1] just by way of example. Squire of the *London Mercury* wrote to me of it that he 'Liked it – but didn't see that they could publish it'. Concerning another little poem he said in the same letter that he would have taken it but they were so full up with accepted poems that a thing had to absolutely bowl them over before they could take it, in the meantime. He suggested that I should send this poem[2] (this second one of which I am speaking) to *The Outlook*. I have done so and await the result. – – – But obviously his couldn'tness in regard to this poem (which he did not advise me try elsewhere – not even in the *British Weekly*!) was based on considerations quite other than that overflowing drawer. He writes very exactly. 'Like' from him means a lot. Almost I can persuade myself that this poem did bowl him over, that he had a struggle with himself to refuse it, that his refusal is actually apologetic and shamefaced, and that he was actuated by sordid, horrible, and unmentionable reasons, philistine reasons, considerations of prudence and the

[1] 'Cattle Show' (462).
[2] 'The Universal Man' (1212–3).

fitness of things and les convenances. – But my poor little poem! In what way does it come under the operation of such considerations. I re-read it. If it is blasphemous then I do not know what blasphemy is. I – who upon occasion have tried to be deliberately blasphemous! If it is obscene, precisely where then? (It goes a long way beyond mere hermaphroditism of course.) – You see my point, of course. – What I want to know is what Deity was likely to be enraged or outraged by its publication – Mammon, Mrs. Grundy, or which of them?

Enough! – Seriously it is likely to mean a great deal to me in one way how then *Annals* go. If 2,000 copies sell all will be well. In other words I shall be able to get more work of the same sort published – and that's all I care about. I'm not limiting myself to its sort: but I have a lot of its sort I do want published: and I just want enough practical success to have as little difficulty as possible about that. – I have a feeling that if it doesn't go sufficiently well I shall be bound over to keep the peace and compelled to do so – gagged and bound. – I have no wish to let the Cursed Commercial System turn me into 'some mute inglorious Milton.'
– But it is necessary to remember that it may, and can, do so: and that if it decides to do so there is only one way in which the aspirant can avoid being reduced to impotence – and that's a way I refuse to take.

However, we'll see.

Yes! I am keeping rather splendid physically, or was, up to a week ago. In the interval I have almost boggled into jaundice again and am feeling still seismic and unsafe – but I think I'll be all right.

I am looking forward to seeing you soon. I think I may be in Edinburgh about 7th October – but will let you know.

I was sorry to hear of Mrs Ogilvie's uncle's death, and of her own consequent unrobustness. I hope she may soon recover the vitality of which that trial robbed her.

With kindest regards from Mrs G. & myself.

Yours Ever,
C.M.G.

NLS

12 White's Place,
Montrose.
14th Oct. 1921

Dear Mr Ogilvie:-

Your letter was a Godsend. It is weak of me but I do get
atrociously depressed at times: and the worst of it is that I do so not
without cause!

I shall be happy to advise Mr Watters[1] when the review copies are
issued. It was very good of you to think of this.

It occurs to me now that if you care to do so and feel that you can –
if you know Mr Watters sufficiently well – you might perhaps sound
him as to the possibility of there being any opening or any likelihood
of one in the near future on the *Scotsman* literary or Sub-Editorial
staffs.

I have done very well here: but I have to work far too hard. I get
practically no leisure. And the job is a cul-de-sac.[2] It leads to
nothing. My employer will testify to my unusual diligence, enterprise, competence, and reliability. He regards me as a perfect
paragon and (without immodesty) rightly so – I *am* a rara avis in
local journalism. Unfortunately any abilities I have are not called
into play – this job only takes brute endurance, solid slogging, and
routine experience.

Although I have meant for some time to seize the first Glasgow or
Edinburgh chance I could, I would not write to you but for another
reason. Montrose is not agreeing with Mrs G. I have to shift as soon
as I can, somewhere. Now Edinburgh does suit her – superlatively.
So I can scarcely hesitate to explore the possibilities that lie in your
acquaintanceship with Mr Watters. Such jobs are impossible to get
without influence. I do not wish a reportorial job – but am willing to
take anything on an editorial or literary staff. I have had a very
extensive experience now and can prove thorough competence.
Given a chance I shall certainly reward the giver by making
thoroughly good. I need say no more. If Mr Watters could secure me
an interview I could give all the necessary particulars etc.

Accept my best thanks for all you have done: and forgive my again
trying to make use of you. It is wretched of me.

---

[1] George (later Sir George) Watters was appointed Chief Assistant and Deputy
Editor of *The Scotsman* in 1919 and was, from 1924 to 1944, Editor of *The Scotsman*.
[2] In April 1921 Grieve returned to work on *The Montrose Review* at an increased
salary.

With kindest regards to Mrs Ogilvie, the children & yourself.

Yours ever,
Chris.

P.S. I had hoped to be in Edinburgh on the 7th inst. but was unexpectedly prevented. But I shall see you soon I think. I intend if possible to take a week's holiday before the end of this month.

NLS
12 White's Place,
Montrose.
9th Nov. 1921

Dear Mr Ogilvie:-

I am tremendously indebted to you and to Mr Stewart for what you have done and tried to do for me.

I wish it had occurred to me that the old *Dispatch* escapade[1] – as you call it – had any such jack-in-the-box capacity: or that, even so, its sudden reappearance would have had the effect it has had. I would certainly not have rendered your efforts liable to any such frustration. I did not count upon its having been forgotten: on the contrary – so defective is my conscience – I had for all practical purposes forgotten about it myself and did not even recall it when thinking about the possibilities of a job on the *Scotsman* – far less take it into account as a potential factor.

Escapade by the way is absolutely the right term to apply.

From what you say. . . . 'after hearing his (Watters') account, we could not press him' – I gather that Mr Watters must have given you a more serious impression.

It may be that it would arm me against not impossible contingencies in the future (this incident clearly shows that anything is possible) to know exactly what he did say. You will know best whether you can tell me that or not however.

I do not understand the lack of humour in the world: but I cannot

---

[1] In 1910 Grieve left Broughton and, after a few weeks freelancing in Langholm, secured – on the recommendation of Ogilvie – a job as a journalist with the *Edinburgh Evening Dispatch*. Apparently Grieve sold some review copies of books and this led to his dismissal.

imagine Mr Watters to be so entirely devoid of it as to rule me out on account of that escapade if he knows the true facts. I have every reason to believe that he is 'punishing' me for a 'crime' I never committed – although I can quite well believe that he has what he thinks are the best grounds for believing that I did.

It has been said that there is nothing more difficult than to forgive a person whom you have wronged. So I account for this attitude on the part of *The Scotsman*. For the Chief Reporter did a very cruel and, worse, a very stupid thing – and knew that I assessed his action at its correct value.

I write contemptuously, of course, ... I do not suffer fools of a different type to my own gladly . . . . but although I have no desire to 'Vindicate my character' as the horrible phrase goes I cannot permit these people to convert me into 'a young man with a terrible past before me' – and I should appreciate an opportunity of pointing out that what they are doing amounts to criminal libel.

I could as a matter of fact have cleared up the matter at the time by bringing an action against the proprietors of the *Dispatch* – but, as you may remember I was very ill with jaundice at the time: and too contemptuous of the possible consequences to bother.

I thank you for expressing your continued trust in me and can only reassure you that I did nothing that I am in the least degree ashamed of and nothing that I cannot defend.

Did you say in my note that I would be in Edinburgh on the Friday? If so I made a mistake in writing. It should have read Saturday at time stated. I was: and intended to have been in town all day – then caught last train here. Unfortunately, Mrs G. took ill: and I caught the next train for Methil (her home) and stayed there over the week-end. Mrs G. underwent a slight operation on Sunday – successfully: and is recovering nicely. I need not add that I was tremendously disappointed not to see you. I had been looking forward to a talk with you for weeks.

I will see what Buchan[2] can do. What Watters says about scope for men like me in the provinces no one knows better than I do. I have no delusions. Only I hoped that I might get something where the drudgery might be less unadulterated than here, the leisure slightly longer, in some centre where I would have a better library at my disposal than here, and, preferably in Edinburgh because Edinburgh suits Mrs G. & – for my own part – because you are there.

However, please do not worry! I shall be all right in the long run. Such an attitude towards an ancient and entirely trivial 'irregularity' as you discovered in Mr Watters confirms me in all my

[2] John Buchan.

64

best suspicions. It has quite bucked me up. Nothing is better calculated to renew in me the determination to make good in my own way than such dreadful examples of moral obscenity.

You will appreciate that I am writing flippantly, – but, on the contrary, passionately. 'For the moment' you say 'we looked foolish'. I can quite imagine your real feelings: and writhe in impotence at the thought. But – – – my time will come. And I think I will be able some day to write such an account of the *Dispatch* episode and this belated phase of it as will make 'the other side' look infinitely more foolish. I will judge my judge (d.v.) with a vengeance. I cannot understand why *N.N.* and *Annals* are not out.[3] I wired Foulis yesterday to find out but have received no reply yet. The delay is inexplicable and most unfortunate.

Again with all thanks to Mr Stewart & yourself: and kindest regards to Mrs Ogilvie & yourself.

Yours Ever.
CMG

NLS   Montrose 25th Sept. [? Nov] 1921

Dear Mr Ogilvie:-

I am sorry that it has been impossible for me to reply earlier, owing to troubles of various sorts which have more than monopolised my time and energy.

My letter was of course never intended to be taken literally. I merely meant to give you such a reply as you might show to Mr Watters. I quite understood that the whole business was inviolably private and, in 'asking' for it, know perfectly well that you could not and would not give any more than I could use any statement as to what Mr Watters actually did tell you.

My point is this – that the *Dispatch* made no charge against me at all: nor did I admit any offence. No reason was assigned for my dismissal – nor was any asked. I was too ill at the time both in body

---

[3] The publishers T. N. Foulis were in financial difficulties and eventually declared bankrupt. Grieve himself published the Third Series of *Northern Numbers* (Montrose 1922) and *Annals of the Five Senses* (Montrose 1923).

and in mind to show fight to circumstance or protect myself in any way from consequence.

I concluded from your letter (not the last one) that Mr Watters gave you the impression that, to say the least of it, my dismissal was justifiable. I suggest that after all these years it is surprising that he should remember with such particularity what was, however regarded, at worst a very minor misdemeanour: and question if he remembers correctly. I could not, I am afraid, disguise from the very first that I considered Donald[1] the chief reporter of the *Dispatch*, a very obnoxious kind of fool. I afflicted him in ways you can no doubt imagine with an intolerable sense of his inferiority, mentally at any rate – and he avenged himself when opportunity arose. I do not blame him for that. But I ought to have seen that he did not magnify the matter. I ought to have seen that he was rendered incapable of transmitting more than the exact facts – – – which probably he did not know himself.

What actually did happen was this. I did some book reviewing on the *Dispatch*. My wage left practically nothing over after paying my 'digs'. I was anxious to get on. I was trying to do free-lance articles in my spare time. I found it very difficult indeed to buy the necessary paper, envelopes and stamps to send them on their rounds. I got practically no return except in rejection slips. It was borne in upon me that the cause of this was that my articles were not typed. The cost of having them typed was a problem. I thought however that if I could surmount this difficulty it was only a question of time before I would 'arrive'. As books for review were handed to me I reviewed them – then sold them to second-hand shops – getting a few shillings for each which I used to get my stuff typed and sent out. I ordered the same books at a bookseller's and when they came gave them to the *Dispatch*. The effect was that I was getting the ready money I needed to carry on my literary efforts – while my account for books was mounting up. But I did not go too far. I knew that the acceptance of one or two articles would bring in sufficient to wipe out that account – perhaps to leave me even with a balance which would enable me to discontinue the unprofitable practice circumstances had compelled me to adopt – and I did not let my account mount beyond what could be so covered. I did get one or two articles accepted: but only for small sums: and one or two books I was accordingly able to pay cash for.

If I had had a little luck all would have been well – so I told myself, gambler-wise. I would have cleared my account at the booksellers.

---

[1] Isaac Donald, Chief Reporter of the *Dispatch*, had a reputation for treating the reporters under him as inferiors.

The *Dispatch* would not have suffered in the least – and would have had ordinary copies indeed of the books in question instead of copies stamped 'for review' – a slight gain!

But I was doing, or trying, too much & collapsed. I had a serious illness – jaundice.

The position then was that I owed a pound or two to the bookseller's – and that all the review copies I had had from the *Dispatch* had been replaced except one. The copy to replace that one had not been delivered when I took ill.

What transpired during my illness I do not know. But what I had been doing was discovered – somehow. At least I suppose so. Precisely what construction was put upon it I do not know – the worst, judging by the result – and Donald was incapable of anything else in any case. I returned to the office as soon as I was convalescent – ridiculously glad to get back to work – and was dismissed.

In the outcome the *Dispatch* did not lose a single copy and I paid the bookseller in full.

Was there theft or any other crime in what I did? I pleaded guilty only to unsuccess. Perhaps I should have 'bided a wee' – waited till my wages increased – or saved a penny or two a week to enable me to submit an article a year to one or perhaps two editors?

I hope that I have put matters clearly. It is the truth, *the whole truth*, and nothing but the truth. I did not, for instance, get the books from the bookseller on false pretences – pretending that I was ordering them on behalf of the *Dispatch* or anything like that.

The essence of my position was the belief that if I could only get one or two of my articles taken I could even up the difference between what I received from the review copies from the second-hand bookseller, and what I paid for the others to replace them.

Selling the review copies gave me working capital: getting the others on account gave me the necessary time.

I will only add that I am still convinced so absurdly sanguine is the temperament with which I am accursed that could I have at any time between then and now have made good as a free-lance writer if I had ever been in such a position that I had sufficient leisure and an appropriate environment to work in and sufficient spare cash to get my stuff typed and kept going the rounds.

But my mental & physical energy has also been so fully absorbed by drudgery – and my instincts so browbeaten & cowed by philistine surroundings – that I have had little time or heart to devote to original writing (apart from the other inherent difficulties): and I have never been able to afford to maintain a regular bombardment upon editorial entrenchments.

Apart from all else I knew then – and I know now – that I was *legally entitled to retain the Review books in question and to dispose of them as I thought fit.* I reviewed them and the law would be on my side if I claimed that ipso facto they were mine. So it is criminal libel if I am charged with having dishonestly sold review copies belonging to the *Dispatch*.

I do not accept your formula – simply because a formal application would only evoke a formal answer regretting that there was no vacancy – and we would be no forrader.

But I shall not do – or write – anything that can ever put any friend into any such position as my letter led Mr Stewart to imagine he or Mr Watters might occupy.

Disappointments continue without intermission. I have just been informed that the publication of *Annals* has been indefinitely postponed.

Excuse this scrawl and my delay. Believe me deeply appreciative of your unfailing sympathy & understanding.

Yours Ever,
C. M. Grieve.

P.S. Let me add, too, that I perfectly realise that the only victory is for me to make good as you put it, in the Big Way. . . . and let me reassure you in the most absolute sense of the words that no matter what trials and troubles of external or internal circumstances still await me, I shall – abundantly – despite the fact that art is always getting longer and life shorter.

NLS   12 White's Place,
                                                                  Montrose.
                                                                  29.XII.21

Dear Mr Ogilvie:-

Please excuse again my writing in pencil, and my delay in replying to your last two kind letters – a delay due to the fact that I have been more than usually 'busy', an excuse which is none the less sincere, despite the fact that I have been busy for the most part only in a cerebral sense. My most urgent affairs (to which haplessly I sacrifice all other considerations) continue to be almost entirely psychological. I am really very robust. – – – I was deeply concerned to hear that you yourself were off colour. I hope you have recovered. You will now be on holiday, glad, I know, of the respite, which I hope will be thoroughly profitable in health, as in other, respects.

*N.N.*2. is going splendidly. The reviews I have so far seen are very favourable but of course hopelessly uncritical – enough to make me follow Robert Buchanan's example and in sheer desperation review oneself. They are on the whole longer than last year's and more wholly commendatory. I will certainly send you my collection.

Despite the *Weekly Scotsman*'s[1] opinion that 'some of Mr. Grieve's sonnets are as difficult of access as the mountains which inspired them' and the *Edinburgh Evening News*'s[2] remark that 'they breathe the real tang of the heather', my own work has attracted this year far more attention from people whose opinion counts a little with me. Mrs Violet Jacob singles out my *'admirable* "Edinburgh"' and Agnes Falconer says 'nothing in the volume is more attractive to me than your own extraordinary little poem "Edinburgh" – an etching in a few lines in which the spiritual and the picturesque are powerfully blended. No one who reads this will easily forget it'. Miss Symon[3] says 'Your things are powerful – very' and intimates that in the strength of their appeal she has ordered a copy of *Annals* – which a literary friend of her own had told her was 'a remarkable work'. I wonder who the prophet was. Annals will be out early in the Spring. Delay was due to Mr Foulis' sudden collapse. He is now back to business. Probably it's all for the best. Review space will be more generously obtainable then.

I have been conducting a further stage of my guerrilla warfare with the Vernacular Circle of the London Burns Club in the columns of the *Aberdeen Free Press*.[4] J. M. Bulloch, editor of the *Graphic*, is my opposite number. The dispute arose out of a paper he gave on 'The delight of the diminutive in the Doric'. I replied with a few scornful phrases about 'Doric Infantilism'. He responded with a full column over the Henley-Stevenson business. I have replied again – to the effect that I believe that 'progress in sexual ethics is at length removing the "specific aboulia" so long responsible for the prevalence of the diminutive in Scotland' and that Burns like Christ (with whom he shares the distinction of having his birthday celebrated all

---

[1] *The Weekly Scotsman*, 17 December 1921.
[2] *The Edinburgh Evening News*, 13 December 1921, welcomed the Second Series of *Northern Numbers* (Edinburgh 1921) as 'a remarkable volume . . . Mention must also be made of the several "Songs of the Highlands" from the pen of Mr C. M. Grieve. These breathe the real tang of the heather.'
[3] Violet Jacob, Agnes Falconer and Mary Symon were minor Scottish poets.
[4] See pp. 749–56.

over the world) is a mere eponym giving his name to a cult entirely at variance with his own spirit – as a result of being subjected to a system of syncretism – the consequence being that Burnsism now is 'an unique abnormality of mob psychology, pickled in whisky', interesting only to students of literary pathology.

All this of course has its affect on *N.N.* If *N.N.* isn't a movement it will be. A group is going to emerge. The relations between Ferguson,[5] & others, & myself are greatly strengthened. Let drop out who will – or must. There will be enough left to go ahead. Short of unintelligibility I am more than ever determined to act on the 'Left Wing'. I shall shortly send you the draft of a long poem entitled 'Water of Life', the first two sections of which I have now completed – this is a preliminary credo: and I am also working hard at a sequence of poems on Edinburgh which I intend to make a complete and quite portly book of, entitled *Sic Itur ad Astra* (the city motto) – I have been moved to this by a perusal of Rosaline Masson's anthology *In Praise of Edinburgh*[6] – Edinburgh has never been praised either in prose or poetry – the poems given are horrible in the extreme. I do not flatter myself at all when I say that my own wee 'Edinburgh' is ten times better than anything in that burdensome tome.

Had a most encouraging & kindly letter from Stewart!

Mrs Grieve joins me in wishing Mrs Ogilvie & the children & yourself all happiness in the coming Year.

With love,
Chris

NLS   Note New Address:-   6 Links Avenue,
Montrose.
19th March 1922

Dear Mr Ogilvie:-

I have been intending to write you for weeks now – so strange and insupportable your long silence! I have wondered and worried. Of

---

[5] John Ferguson, poet and dramatist.
[6] (ed) Rosaline Masson, *In Praise of Edinburgh* (1912). It includes Rosaline Masson's own poem 'Edinburgh' which contains lines like 'Your beauty in the sunshine/No mortal can forget, – /But most I love the smell of you/When every stone is wet!'

course I know how incessantly too-busy you are: but, then, anything else might have happened also – illness – anything. Do drop me a note soon. All my own correspondence is in arrears – for a variety of reasons. Mr Stewart, in particular, deserved a letter long before this. I shall write him soon. Today I am just emerging from the turmoil of a flitting. Hitherto we have perforce been in a furnished house. A new house was allocated to us months ago: but took much longer to build than could be anticipated – as is always the case. However it is ready now: and we got our furniture in the day before yesterday and yesterday I had to be as energetic a spectator as I could possibly contrive while Mrs G. did the work of getting the place into order. So thoroughly did I fill my rôle, in fact, that I was very much more tired at the end of the day than she was: and today I am one of those pictures that tell stories – only my story is (although no one would think so to look at me) one of those kind which can only be properly articulated with one's tongue in one's cheek and the pupil of one eye at an angle of 30 degrees to the line of vision in the other.

The fact is that I have nothing but domesticities to relate. Since I wrote you last (but this too is deplorably domestic as well) I have become a member of Montrose Town Council and have thrown myself with more energy than I imagined I possessed into the Work of Local Government. I have also blossomed out as one of the leaders of the Scottish Free State Movement and have addressed a public meeting in Dundee, issued a public challenge to an Arbroath opponent, conducted an incredible variety of newspaper controversies, etc. etc.

Apart from that however I have been busy. I cannot tell you all about my different projects here. But I want to tell you about one. I have planned a book of 100 sonnets. I have over 40 of them written: – i.e. written in their final form, which I cannot improve. Others are in draft or I am now dissatisfied with them as yet than with the 40. All of them are obscure in at least one, and generally in more than one, respect. They deal with foreign subjects – Russian, French, Italian, Spanish, Bulgarian – for the most part: and are largely unintelligible to those who are not thoroughly familiar with the modern literatures of these countries. They are highly allusive – but I am supplying notes which will be interesting in themselves and thoroughly illuminating. I cannot apologise for obscurity of this kind. Some of them derive additional 'obscurity' from the fact that they seek to express in concentrated form as it were the essence of the para-doxical philosophies of Blake, Nietzsche etc. Again there are cases in which the fundamental metaphor cannot be understood without a knowledge of certain foreign ceremonies – i.e. in one sonnet the ceremony of Cursing and Expulsion from a Jewish synagogue is used as a basis. No one can understand this sonnet who doesn't know what a Sharof is, etc. – but to Jews it will be perfectly clear.

I have nowhere sought obscurity for obscurity's sake. To certain classes of readers – i.e. students of the literatures in question – these sonnets will all be perfectly clear. They all fit into one big scheme. What moved me in the first place to write them was Croce's statement as to the necessity of reckoning systematically with the enormous accumulation of moral doubts and psychological perceptions in the 19th Century – and the impossibility of thinking we can transcend them by merely being contemptuous and dismissing them as Mid-Victorian. That – and Clutton Brock's statement that art must be a desperate adventure – if not it ceases to be art and becomes merely a game of skill.

I think I have written my best sonnets so far in this sequence. I enclose a few upon which I beg you to give me your candid opinion. I have chosen the less recondite because I have not time yet to write out the explanatory notes which must accompany the others. But what do you think of these? I again emphasise that they were largely written for you – apart from other considerations the necessity of ultimately justifying your faith in me determines my efforts.

Excuse more in the meantime. Do please write soon and tell me how you are. *Annals* should be out very soon now. It has been a terrible wait. However all's well that ends well.

Mrs G. joins me in conveying every good wish.

> Ever Yours
> Chris.

NLS   16 Links Avenue.
                                                        [1922]

Dear Mr Ogilvie:-

No! I don't like your figure of the anchor. Rather let us say that you are an old friend – the oldest and best of friends – who has travelled far in and become familiar with the seas of thought in which I, who have hitherto been a coaster, am sometimes to navigate this new type of ship of mine (let me admit since you insist upon it that you know less than I do about this kind of ship – or the ultimate purpose of my voyage – although in the latter respect I must in turn insist that I am under sealed orders!). – Your query as to whether I was not overrating Amiel's importance, your criticism of the implied proposal to systemmatic poetry, etc., all these are so many hints as to cross-currents, 'snags' and the like. It is these things I so wish I could discuss with you – or with anyone in any way like you. I am exiled from my element here in this respect. . . . 'The artist has no right to complain if he is misunderstood by the large mass of his contemporaries. But he has the right to expect to be comprehended by a few. . . . Poe's isolation in America was of this unhappy and stultifying kind and its effects upon his poetry are plain. For the most remarkable thing about him as a poet is the contrast between his scanty production – and the natural facility, the unmistakable fecundity of his poetic genius. . . . Keats without his £2,000, Shelley without his private income, would they, we wonder, have written more, or more finely, than Poe? But they would at least have been sustained by a handful of understanding friends. It does not appear that Poe had one.'

Without flattering comparisons of my own case with Poe's – I have at least one: and I object to him calling himself an anchor – – – an anchor anxious to see the ship dispense with its services and be off!

Your letters mean a great deal to me – and, apart from all that, you are one of my very oldest friends and I was genuinely anxious to hear how you were keeping – apart from the delight your letters always give me – a delight I disassociate from the sensations produced by the fact that they refer to me and my work and your hopes & fears for me & my work, and find has a splendid independent existence, derived from the fact that these are the letters of a friend, and the letters of one of the very few friends one encounters nowadays who can write letters.

No more in the meantime. My sonnets continue to accumulate. My real reason for sonneteering instead of writing in other forms is that I want to write two or three sonnets which will live – which will rank with the great sonnets of British literature – and once I do write two or three sonnets which a competent critic assures me fill that bill I shall stop sonneteering. The sonnet form is not natural to me. But I won't be beaten by the 'demned little thing'. – Once I win I will proceed with all expedition to tackle other forms.

But I am not by any means confining myself to the sonnet as matters stand.

And this note is merely to thank you for your letter and to enclose the longer poem upon which I want just two or three words of opinion.

Mrs G. joins me in the kindest regards to Mrs Ogilvie, the children, and yourself.

Yours Ever,
C. M. G.

P.S. Will you please return the MS? I've no copy – and am too lazy to write one out.

NLS   16 Links Avenue,
                                                        Montrose.
                                                    April 5/1922

Dear Mr Ogilvie,

   The discovery that two recent letters of mine to different friends have not been received by them makes me anxious to know if you duly received my last letter containing MSS of a longish poem 'Water of Life'[1] – of which foolishly enough, I took no copy (owing to laziness).
   I particularly hope this MSS is safe in your hands. The poem is like the parson's egg – good only in parts – but I am anxious not to lose it.
   I know you must be very busy just now – Quarterlies, etc., I suppose – and perhaps that accounts for your not writing yet, even if you have safely received it.
   I am not trying to hustle any reply out of you – but I cannot shake off the feeling that in this particular case you have not received my letter and its enclosure.
   Please drop me a P.C. just to say whether the poem reached you or not.
   This worry serves me right. I musn't be so lazy in future and must take copies of my poems before entrusting them to the Postal Authorities.

[1] 'Water of Life', a poem in Scots, was collected in *First Hymn of Lenin and Other Poems* (London 1931). This reference is to an earlier poem using the same title (1213·5).

74

Kindest regards,

Yours Ever,
C. M. Grieve.

P.S. I posted the letter in question a week past Friday.

NLS   16 Links Avenue,
                                                                         Montrose.
                                                                         22.5.22

Dear Mr Ogilvie:-

Many thanks for your last letter. I am making various alterations
on 'Water of Life'. I think they will immensely improve it.

Foulis has now succeeded in transforming his firm into a Limited
Coy: and in a note yesterday promises me a definite decision within a
week as to whether they can or can't undertake *N.N.*3. this autumn.
If they can't then I'll either get another publisher or bring it out
myself. In any case I am determined to go on with it.

I enclose copy of a circular which I am sending out to such and
such as such. My letters on the matter to the Dailies last Monday
evoked a splendid response. As you will see the *G. Herald* went to
length of giving us a fine fillip in a leader.[1] So we're getting on.

But the difficulties of running such a periodical as I intend are
immense: and if it is not to appear a miserably attenuated shape, but
in substantial and worthy form, literally every Scottish poetry-lover
must be roped in.

Since I wrote you last I have written over 40,000 words of a new
novel – somewhat Henry Jamesy perhaps – but quite publishable I
think. I intend finishing it in time to permit of its being considered
for autumn publication.

Oh! and that reminds me, Foulis promises final arrangements
about *Annals* within the course of this week!!

Excuse this scrappy note: but I am of course nearly snowed under

---

[1] *The Glasgow Herald* of 15 May 1922 published Grieve's letter inviting readers to
subscribe to a new poetry monthly; the following day the *Herald* stated that 'Mr
Grieve's venture deserves support from every Scot who is interested in the poetry
of his native land.'

with correspondence in connection with this *Chapbook* business. But I wanted to drop you a note because I am sure that if there is anybody within reach you can persuade to subsidise creative literature in Scotland to the extent of some $2\frac{1}{2}^D$ per week in this way you'll want to have the chance of doing it. And I want to enrol as many subscribers as possible as soon as possible – for I want to curtail the circulation immediately I see my way to cover the costs. The arrangements I am making ensure that immediate bibliographical value will attend the first year's issues anyhow. But I am not to disclose these details – subscribers will find that, apart from literary value, they have made a good investment. – Enough! I am in great form. With kindest regards to Mrs Ogilvie, the children, and yourself, in which Mrs G. joins me.

Yours Ever,
C. M G.

NLS   16 Links Avenue.
                                                    20/9/22

Dear Mr Ogilvie

I should have written you long ere this: but have been, and remain, overwhelmed. Going off to Birmingham in the beginning of the month to tell the Burns Federation a few things did not help matters. I had a glorious and most useful time: but have not yet made up the arrears of correspondence which accumulated in my absence. I have various other lecture-dates cutting into my time shortly – then, in February, am speaking to the Vernacular Circle in London. I have determined to transform the Burns movement at home and abroad: and am conducting an extensive and very subtle press campaign to that end. My slogan is – 'the application of the spirit of Burns to practical affairs', 'first things first – would Burns have wasted time on bibliography, textual researches, genealogical investigations with Scotland in its present terrible social condition', 'the realisation of the full social & political programme implicit in Burns' works', etc. etc. – I have constructed so many phrases that I am like a merry-go-round myself – but I am open to wager that over 30 columns of 'Burns Movement Re-Orientation' stuff appears in the press within the next six months. I was the 'stormy petrel' at the Brum Conference but the September *Chapbook* will give you an indication of what I am driving at in this connection.

I am also busy with the Scottish Home Rule business – and expect to be very much busier this winter yet. The October Assocn. newsheet will eulogise 'my work for Scottish literature' next month: and in November will 'splash' a special article of mine on 'Scottish Home Rule and Revival of letters'.[1]

The *Chapbook* has gone splendidly. Sold out. Unable to supply scores of copies ordered. Roped in all sorts of desirable Scots from Stornoway to Hong Kong, Sunderland to New York.

Many thanks for your valuable letter on No 1. Glad you were interested in 'Nisbet'.[2] Haven't got a full sheaf of reviews but enclose a batch herewith. A mixed lot. But I know exactly how much to attach to each – who writes them, etc.

I was greatly delighted with *Broughton Mag*. Many thanks. I came out quite well. Splendid photo of Kerr. Had letter from Editor[3] (still unanswered, alas! but will answer soon) asking for article for next number. Barkis is willin! Will try to let him have it soon. Something quite short. Will you please tell him so?

Yes, Just heard from Mr Stewart, with 10/-: Many thanks for cheque for £2.10. What about postages? Would it not be better for me to send to the 5 direct rather than trouble you?

Please excuse this scrappiest of letters. Hope you, Mrs Ogilvie and the children had a good holiday and are fine & fit. I am in notorious form myself. Do wish I could see you and have a talk: but may do so at no distant date. Many many thanks!

Yours Ever,
Chris.

[1] *Scottish Home Rule* was the monthly organ of the Scottish Home Rule Association. In Vol 3, No 4, October 1922, the newsheet extended 'a most cordial welcome to the first number of *The Scottish Chapbook*, a courageous new venture published by Mr C. M. Grieve, who is the local secretary of the S.H.R.A. in Montrose... Mr Grieve is the right kind of Home Ruler, one of those who see in Home Rule only the political side of a movement that affects every phase of national life.' Vol 3, No 5, November 1922 featured, on the front page, Grieve's article 'Scottish Literature and Home Rule.'

[2] 'Nisbet', the first composition credited to 'Hugh M'Diarmid', appeared in two parts in the first two issues of *The Scottish Chapbook* in August and September 1922. It is reprinted in *The Thistle Rises* (1984).

[3] The editor of *The Broughton Magazine*, 1922-23, was Albert Mackie, see p. 409.

16 Links Avenue,
                                              Montrose,
                                              10/10/22

Dear Mr Ogilvie:-

   Excuse just the hastiest line in reply to your welcome note of 8th
inst. to hand today.

   I must have expressed myself most clumsily: for you have taken up
my last letter in a different sense altogether to what I intended. 10/-
is *Chapbook* cost per annum to original subscribers *post free*. It would
be slightly more expensive to send out your five copies individually: I
merely suggested it to save you trouble – I know you are busy
enough. Then I didn't know whether the five were living near or
whether you might have to repost the copies on to them, thus
involving you in expense. What I meant about the postage was that
if anything I owed you in respect of postage. You owed me nothing. I
accordingly return stamps herewith.

   I quite agree with you as to format of *Chapbook*. There are
difficulties about changing it: but I shall do so at the earliest possible
opportunity.

   I enclose cutting of article from *Glasgow Herald* you may not have
seen. Also others. Please return when you write again.

   Excuse this terrible scrawl. I am up to the first wrinkle on my
many-seamed brow – above the eyebrows – in work of all sorts.

                        Kindest regards.
                        Yours As Ever,
                        Chris.

16 Links Avenue,
                                              Montrose.
                                              15.1.23

Dear Mr Ogilvie:-

   Quite unexpectedly – bereavement calling Mrs G. in another
direction – I did not manage to get further south than Kirkcaldy at
Christmas & New Year. I was quite disappointed to lose the chance

of seeing you. But I shall certainly see you next month – either as I go to or return from London. And will have a good talk over things.

Your casual mention of Kerr's P.P.[1] – all you said was that you supposed I had heard of it – was the first I learned of it. But the weekend before last a mutual friend, Soutar, who writes for the *Chapbook* & *N.N.* spent a few days with me and told me precisely what it was. Then I was speaking in Dundee last Thursday (Scottish Free State) and met Lewis Spence who also spoke of it. I haven't seen the first issue, or any prospectus or newspaper reference. I am writing Kerr by this post, however, enclosing what I understand to be the subscription for twelve issues – in the hope that I am still in time. I am sorry to learn from you that they are in a struggling state, finding their enterprise a burden, and doubtful if they will win through. I have, as you may imagine, absolutely no wish to 'butt in' where I am not wanted – but if it is merely lack of sufficient subscribers I think I could put them all right. Of course it may not be that – 5/- may be too little – and an increase of subscribers might worsen instead of better their position. Under the circumstances I cannot see my way to make direct inquiries as to the nature of their difficulties. But I am of course eager to help if I may. Can you send me a paragraph about it for insertion in the *Chapbook*? – by return if possible, as I am issuing *Chapbook* a little earlier this month. I do not expect that that will help materially, however, though it will certainly make a few ask to become subscribers. If my own subscription is accepted and I get the first broadsheet, I will devote an article or two to the subject in certain papers and I can get helpful paragraphs inserted in certain quarters where they are likely to be influential. But direct appeal is the thing and I am in touch with plenty of people certain to subscribe. If this would help, can you procure copies of any prospectus or announcement sheet or anything? If so, I would send them out. – But, if you do this, please tell whoever you get them from merely that you want them for a friend who has a notion that he can rope in a good few subscribers. Don't mention my name to Kerr or anybody else as willing to help, or in any way interested in, the *Chapbook*.

The weekly is coming all right.[2] I am absolutely up to the neck in preliminary arrangements. The whole story is too involved – but I *do* see my way financially & otherwise: I am in touch with nearly all the right people! and pulling all sorts of Labour Party, Scottish Home

[1] Porpoise Press was the publishing firm founded, in Edinburgh in November 1922, by Roderick Watson Kerr, George Malcolm Thomson and John Gould. Kerr and Gould had succeeded Grieve as joint-editors of *The Broughton Magazine* in 1910-11.

[2] Grieve's weekly *The Scottish Nation* ran from May to September 1924.

79

Rule Assoctn, Scots National League, etc., strings. I am not yet quite sure when I will launch it – probably the beginning of March: but that will depend upon the final arrangements I make in London.

Annals has encountered another hitch. But don't worry. Either the people who have it in type just now must print it and let me publish it within the next week or two – or have it set up here de novo and publish it. My lawyers have the matter well in hand now. But it has been a ghastly business.

A lot of people have written to me more or less as you do – as to the desirability of expounding my theories clearly and straightforwardly in the Causerie. And I am to denote the next six causeries to that.

I was glad you were interested in 'Nisbet'. I will have my draft typed as soon as I can – in full – and let you have a read of it. Also progress is being made now with the typing of my novel: and if you are hard up for something to read during next summer holidays, let me know! I have just read over what you wrote about Kerr's P.P. and what I have just written. I hope I need not say that I bear Kerr no grudge of any kind at all and that I wish him anything he may try unbounded success. Only – while extremely eager to help him if I possibly can – I would prefer that he should not know that I was doing so. I do not wish to be associated by name in any case with his work – although I do not know what you mean at all when you say 'his ways are not exactly yours, and V.V.'.

Press reviews of *N.N.* 3. have been very good – heaps of very encouraging letters from people from whom encouragement is worth having – sales by no means satisfactory to date – but I'm not worrying.

Now I must knock off. I'm 'bunged up' with cold and nasal catarrh, and so any daily output is not quite what it should be. And I have vowed to at least treble it this year – in every direction. I intend to sling out MSS. of all sorts in 'every airt the wind can blaw' – by all sorts I mean political, & literary articles, short stories, etc. – work worth doing all the time, however, and not mere pot-boilers. I have not been pestering editors as I should have done, but I have been accumulating and I am ready at last to disgorge.

Excuse this scrappy note. I hope you have fully recovered and that this may find Mrs Ogilvie and the children in good condition. Please remember me to any friends.

Yours faithfully,
C. M Grieve.

P.S. Mackie (A.D.) is coming on! He has sent me some sonnets and some dialect stuff. He has unquestionably the root of the matter.

Sorry to hear that my good old friend Lily Bennett is in straits. I wish I could do something for her. I have most pleasant recollections of her black-and-red bespectacled vivacity. There's no telling what I may need once the weekly gets going however – and I'll keep her in mind all right.

No! I shall retain my present work *plus* the weekly. No reward that letters has to bestow would tempt me to sever my connection with the Town & Parish Council, and other Boards of which I am duly elected representative here. It's too funny for words – and my sense of humour must be provided for in the first place. Other things come after that.

Chris.

NLS

16 Links Avenue,
Montrose.
31/1/23

Dear Mr Ogilvie

I am going down to East Lothian on Saturday: but returning to Edinburgh on Monday forenoon. Soutar (who writes for the *Chapbook*) and another chap are to have tea with Mrs G. and I at Mackay's at 5 p.m. I don't know whether you can or would care to join us there: but in any case, I shall have a few hours to spare after that (going 10 p.m. train to London) so am keen to spend a bit of that time with you at any rate.

Of course you may be otherwise engaged that night. I know you are kept very busy with all sorts of things. Especially just now! I hope you have secured all the support that was necessary in re the headmasterships – although I could not imagine Broughton without you: and judging by the way Mackie writes some of the present studies there would be almost as much at a loss if you left them as I would have been if you had left during my first year.

Looking forward to seeing you: and hoping this finds all well at 14 St. Catherine's Place.

Yours,
C. M. Grieve.

81

16 Links Avenue,
Montrose.
[Feb 1925]

Dear Mr Ogilvie:-

For some time now I have been on the look-out for a suitable job of some kind – no easy matter, for my lack of academic qualifications, the fact that I have so far as journalism is concerned served only on little local papers on the one hand and specialised on the other in forms of literature which have little or no popular appeal, and then, my politics and my expertise generally in the gentle art of making enemies have all combined to make me an adept at falling between all sorts of stools. Still, I am anxious to 'better myself' – I think that is a phrase – indeed I owe it to my wife and daughter,[1] if not to myself, to lose no conceivable opportunity of doing so, and some time ago I thought that, with Buchan's help, I was about to do so. But Fleet St. is in a bad way, owing to amalgamations, etc. I wouldn't care but for the fact that I'm not getting any younger: indeed I am afraid that I getting older in some ways.

Now I've just seen an advt. which I think offers a job that would suit me. It reads:-

National Galleries of Scotland.

App[oin]tment of Keeper

Applications are invited for the post of keeper of the Galleries. The duty of the keeper is to assist the Director in the work of the National Gallery and National Portrait Gallery, and take control in his absence. Salary £350, rising by £15 per ann. to £450 plus Civil Service bonus, which at present is £145 on the minimum, etc.

I have applied: and am whipping up all the influence I possibly can. The advt. only appeared in Saturday's *Herald*, and I haven't had time yet to find out who the Trustees are. The appointment lies with them, and it occurs to me that you may know some of them or have means of getting at some of them through others. There is no forbidding of canvassing in the advt. so I am taking it for granted that it will be allowed and that it will go a long way. I shall be extremely glad if you can help me in any way.

Since I saw you last there has been little doing. I have been concentrating on foreign papers – *Les Nouvelles Littéraires*, etc. (although I have an article this week in the *Scottish Educational Journal*[2] of all places) – and maintaining my *New Age* stuff – and,

---

[1] Christine Grieve was born on 6 September 1924.
[2] 'Reviving the Scots Vernacular' by C. M. Grieve appeared in *The Scottish Educational Journal* of 6 February 1925.

apart from that confining myself to Braid Scots poetry (in which I think I am doing good work – at least Buchan and others are greatly taken with it) and ultra-modern experiments in English for which I cannot find a publisher and which I am not even trying to place with the limited number of periodicals which offer scope for work of that sort. As to the Scottish Renaissance useful articles have appeared on it, and my work in *The London Mercury*[3] and elsewhere.

I sincerely trust you are keeping much fitter than when I saw you last. Please give my kindest regards to Mrs Ogilvie, Agnes and John. We are all well here, despite a prevalence of illness of all kinds in the burgh.

What about trying Montrose this summer? Have you thought it over? Houses, etc., are booking up already.

I had a pleasant hour or two with Miss Manson[4] while in Glasgow lecturing to the English Assocn, and also met and am now corresponding with Miss Aitken,[5] another old Brotonian, who is doing WEA work on Scottish Literature in Greenock.

Every good wish.

Yours faithfully,
C. M. Grieve.

NLS

16 Links Avenue,
Montrose.
14th Feb. 1925

Dear Mr Ogilvie:-

It is extremely good of you to respond as quickly as ever to my latest appeal for your help. I acted at once on your suggestions and wrote to Dr Drummond. In the meantime John Buchan has written

[3] In Vol XI, No 61 of The London Mercury, November 1924, David Cleghorn Thomson praised Grieve's work as an editor – of *Northern Numbers, Scottish Nation,* and *Scottish Chapbook* – and added 'Mr Grieve has already done splendid work in affording publicity to the Doric poems . . . of Hugh MacDiarmid and others.'
[4] Miss Manson was a teacher at Broughton.
[5] Mary Baird Aitken was a contemporary of Grieve's at Broughton; she later taught at Broughton for twenty years. Her novel *Soon Bright Day* (1944) is about Thomas Muir of Huntershill.

strongly recommending me to Sir John Findlay (of *The Scotsman*, who is Chairman of the Trustees), Sir D. Y. Cameron & Sir J. M. Stirling Maxwell; and Professor Grierson has written too to the two-first named and also to Mr John Warrack.[1] My friend Dr Pittendrigh Macgillivray thinks I'm the last man in Scotland the Trustees are likely to favour – and that the only thing that could make my appointment a shade more impossible (to use an Irishism) would be any effort on his part to help me. But one never knows. If Dr Drummond and, perhaps, Mr Wm. Graham MP, supplement Buchan's and Grierson's recommendations I may have a sporting chance despite the fact that I have been (as I intend to remain – whatever the consequences, and they can hardly be worse than those I have already 'tholed') such a 'notorious rebel'.

I was deeply concerned to hear that you have been so unwell and that you are still in such deplorably poor fettle. I earnestly hope that you may recover strength soon.

We are all fine here and Baby is thriving beautifully.

Please give my kindest regards to Mrs Ogilvie, Agnes and John – all of whom I trust are well.

If I am at least lucky enough to secure an interview in connection with this job, I may have a chance of seeing you ere long.

Again with all thanks.

Yours Ever,
C. M. Grieve.

P.S. Kitchin meant kindly I know.[2] That didn't improve matters from my point of view. I didn't take his articles seriously at all – My motto being 'Speak weel o' my love, speak ill o' my love, but aye be speakin'.' I welcome any sort of publicity rather than a conspiracy of

---

[1] Dr Drummond, Minister of Lothian Road Church, Herbert Grierson of Edinburgh University, and John Buchan (who introduced MacDiarmid's *Sangschaw*) were sympathetic supporters of the poet. Sir John Findlay (1866–1930) was proprietor of *The Scotsman* and Chairman of the Board of Trustees for the National Galleries of Scotland. Sir David Young Cameron (1865–1945) was a painter and etcher; Sir J. M. Stirling Maxwell (1866–1956) inherited Pollok House which is now a museum run by Glasgow District Council; John Warrack was a patron of the arts who presented the National Gallery of Scotland with an Italian cassone in 1929.

[2] George Kitchin's article on 'The "Scottish Renaissance" Group' appeared in *The Scotsman* of 13 November 1924. MacDiarmid responded in the correspondence columns of *The Scotsman*, see p. 758, and *Forward*, No 51, Vol 18, 22 November 1924, carried C. M. Grieve's article 'Dr Kitchin, Moscow and the Scottish Renaissance'.

silence. But there was a great deal more in the matter than met the eye, and I am afraid I am impenitent in regard to the *Forward* article. I made it just as crude & vulgar as it was in the most calculating way. It may seem stupid – it certainly harms me a great deal more than it harms those I am attacking in the meantime, and it is precisely in the meantime in some ways that I can't stand much more harm than I've already let myself in for – but there are precedents and I think that in the long run I should count myself a more despicable failure than I am likely to be if I could recall any time I had neglected for any reason whatever to bang my head against a stone-wall. But I am free of the 'cursed conceit' of considering myself right: I am not making any virtue of what I recognise as the necessities of my being.

NLS   [prob. Nov 1925]

Dear Mr Ogilvie:-

I was more than delighted to hear from you. I have been often wondering how you were: but I never write letters if I can possibly help it – I hate pen and ink – and though I was through in Edinburgh on Friday night recently speaking at Patrick Geddes's[1] I got no chance of running up to see you. I do hope you'll keep on an even keel now.

I wish you could holiday in Montrose one summer soon. I'd give a great deal to have a few walks and talks with you. Please give my best remembrance to Mrs Ogilvie and the children (scarcely children now). Christine is a fine specimen of a lassie for fourteen months. She hasn't been well lately but I think it's only her being 'among her teeth'!

Sangschaw is only a beginning: Blackwood's have option on next two volumes. I have another half-ready. I expected *S.* to meet with a mixed reception, and it has. But the people to whose opinions I attach any importance are unanimous. Grierson had doubts as to the validity, practicality and desirability of what I proposed trying to do in my McDiarmid stuff: but after reading Sangschaw he writes as follows:-

'I have been reading it with unaffected and great pleasure. You

[1] Patrick Geddes (1854-1932) was an important intellectual influence on Mac-Diarmid. See note on p. 857.

85

have, I think, succeeded in writing Scottish poetry that is quite unaffected by the Burns (no disrespect to what is best in Burns)-Sentimental-Kailyaird tradition, and which is real poetry, imaginative and moving. One is glad to get in Scots such sincere, imaginative, musical poetry in so fine, and (for later Scotland) so surprising and fresh a strain. It makes me understand better your plea for a fresh reading of Scottish history. We have been too much "handin' doon" by the Knox-Covenanter-Shorter Catechism traditions and must recover our sense of a Scotland that was a great and prosperous country before John Knox was heard of, a country that was part of Europe in life and faith. . . . I do feel (which I do not often) that you have given me a fresh experience in poetry.'

Muir has written an article on *Sangschaw* for the *Saturday Review of Literature* (USA),[2] and Saurat has translated it for *Les Marges*. I am hopeful of arranging an American edition of *Annals* .

I enclose for your interest an article on myself which appeared in a Border paper the other week.

I am not anxious to put together my English verse – till I have some better stuff. Did you see a poem of mine some time ago in *Glasgow Herald* entitled 'A Herd of Does'?[3] If not, I'll send you a copy.

My *Contemporary Scottish Studies* appearing in *Scottish Educational Journal* are appearing – adjusted, with amplifications here and excision there, – next Autumn through Leonard Parsons.[4] I have material ready for another book on lines of *Annals*. I have just written a play which I expect to have produced in Glasgow ere long. And F. G. Scott, Professor McCanse (who is art-critic of *The Spectator*) and I are creating some Scottish Ballets, for which I am doing the libretti. I am writing for various papers – book-reviewing, etc. And I am to be speaking in Dundee next month, Falkirk (EIS) in December and Glasgow (English Assocn) in February.

I can't get out of Montrose though, do what I will, but I loathe my work here. I have tried in all directions. In other respects I am far from being out of the wood. I continue – and will continue – to make enemies. I will not allow myself to be judged by anything other than the quality of my work. People who demand that in addition to doing

[2] Edwin Muir's review of *Sangschaw* (Edinburgh 1925) appeared in *The Saturday Review of Literature*, 31 October 1925: '[*Sangschaw*]is written in Scots, and it has the best of justifications; it is perfectly original. Each of these poems is a single flash, vivid but brief. We wait for the further volume which will establish Mr M'Diarmid's title to our most serious attention.'

[3] 'A Herd of Does' (75–6) was published in *The Glasgow Herald* on 3 June 1925 prior to its inclusion in *Penny Wheep* (Edinburgh 1926).

[4] *Contemporary Scottish Studies* (London 1926) by C. M. Grieve.

work of a certain calibre a man must be respectable, sociable, God-fearing, compromising to meet them in one way or another, will not only find that I won't fit in, but that I will stall most violently. And my general opinions in most directions are impossible so far as contemporary Scotland is concerned. 'Determined things to destiny' must 'hold unbewailed their way.'

I agree as to the difficulties a pseudonym involves one in: but I am much more inclined to give every facility for the sort of malevolence I am encountering than otherwise. I think I'll get my own back with interest in the long run. At the same time – if only to please you – I'd shed the pseudonym now, if I could – but I can't for various reasons. There are the publishers of Scott's music, etc. to consider.

How's Albert? I've been looking for another novel from him. I thought a good deal of *Kirk o' Field*.[5]

With every good wish.

Yours ever.
C. M. Grieve.

Of course *Sangschaw* is like the curate's egg. There's about a third of it below par, which I'm sorry I included.

NLS

16 Links Avenue,
Montrose,
Scotland.
9th Dec. '25

Dear Mr Ogilvie:-

I have just discovered to my disgust that I forgot to reply to you re 'O Jesu Parvule'.[1] I need say that the *Broughton Magazine* is always welcome to anything of mine. I wrote to Scott re the music: and found that his publishers (Bayley & Ferguson) would be prepared to print you specially a copy of the leaflet with music and words to insert in the Magazine at between £2 and £3 for enough copies to cover your issue. But that would probably have been beyond the

---

[5] Edward Albert, *Kirk o' Field* (1924).
[1] 'O Jesu Parvule' (31) appeared in *The Broughton Magazine* of December 1925.

financial resources of the Mag. However, I'm afraid I'm too late now, owing to having been horribly rushed of late. I only hope you've taken my consent for granted and used the words. Excuse this hasty note. *Sangschaw* has been getting some rare reviews of late – *Glasgow Herald* (last Thursday), *Manchester Guardian* (yesterday) and *Saturday Review of Literature* (USA – 2 cols).

I do hope you are keeping more fit again. Kindest regards to Mrs Ogilvie and the children.

Yours ever.
C. M. Grieve.

NLS

Avondale,
St Cyrus,
Kincardineshire.
6th August 1926

Dear Mr Ogilvie,

I was greatly touched to receive your kind letter apropos *Penny Wheep* some weeks ago.

The death of one of Mrs Grieve's sisters, and a subsequent indisposition of my own, (from which I have now wholly recovered – I am really very robust despite my curious leanness) has prevented my replying sooner; these things, and the fact that I am up to the neck in proofs of *Contemporary Scottish Studies* and – worse – in rewriting, against time, (the MSS. should really have been in the hands of the publishers ere this) one of the main and most difficult sections of *A Drunk Man.* (Not, of course, to pretend for a moment that I am any better than ever – rather worse, alas! – in respect of my old difficulty of organising my affairs & replying to correspondence in any reasonable way. My conscience is pricking me with regard to Annand.[1] I should have written him months ago. I was so delighted with the Braid Scots number – and am so anxious that he and the others should keep to it and try it for all they're worth. But the old 'infirmity of will' – the curious inability to write – persists and worsens. It's really a side-result of far too-intense-preoccupation in other directions.)

I realise fully the importance of what you urge in regard to the

[1] J. K. Annand, see p. 361.

Drunk Man. It will either make or finish me so far as Braid Scots work, & Messrs Blackwood's are concerned. I dare not let them down with a work of such magnitude. As it now stands it'll be at least six times as big a book as *Sangschaw* – some risk for any publisher these days. I've let myself go in it for all I'm worth. My friend Scott, (the composer) and I afterwards went over the whole thing with a small tooth comb. But we both felt that the section I've been rewriting – which comes about midway in the book and should represent the high water mark, the peaks of highest intensity, could be improved by being recast and projected on to a different altitude of poetry altogether – made, instead of a succession of merely verbal and pictorial verses, into a series of metaphysical pictures with a definite progression, a cumulative effect – and that is what I've been so busy with. It's infernally intractable material: but I've spared no pains and put my uttermost ounce into the business. I'm out to make or break in this matter. There are poems in the book (which is really one whole although many parts are detachable) of extraordinary power, I know – longer and far more powerful and unique in kind than anything in *Sangschaw* or *Penny Wheep*; but that's not what I'm after. It's the thing as a whole I'm mainly concerned with, and if, as such, it does not take its place as a masterpiece – sui generis – one of the biggest things in the range of Scottish Literature, I shall have failed. Whole sections of it do go with a tremendous gusto and with a sweep over a tremendous range: but there are still a few movements that want supple-ing and accelerating and bringing into harmony with the others in this way or that. So you mustn't mind if I cut short this very egoistic letter.

I was glad to hear that you had again been fit, although you must have felt the strain of acting headmastership in Broughton (which I hope a happy holiday since has more than made good). I saw your name somewhere some time ago as having been placed on the list from which headmasters will be appointed and trust that ere long you will land a congenial billet. I hope Mrs Ogilvie and Agnes & John are all well. Please convey my compliments & regards to Mrs Ogilvie. I haven't had my holidays yet and do not propose taking them till the back-end when perhaps I'll go to London. In any case I'll be going down to East Lothian to my mother's for a few days and so passing through Edinburgh and will then look you up. I could fair do with a good long evening with you and a thorough talk. Each summer for the last three we've taken a house here at St Cyrus for a couple of months and, while it suits Mrs Grieve and, now, baby (who in a voracious and indefatigable little Monster) admirably it enables me to carry on my work in the doz. days with many of the effects of holidaying. But I am really feeling the need now, for divers reasons, of getting into a city and have during the past year tried to do so in all sorts of ways – but without success. I'm beginning to get desperate for I don't want to have to reconcile myself to Montrose – or the likes of Montrose – for good. But it's extraordinarily difficult. However, something may turn up – and probably most unexpectedly.

Again thanking you for your welcome and most encouraging letter, & with affectionate regards.

Yours
C. M. Grieve.

NLS   16 Links Avenue,
                                                        Montrose.
                                                        9.12.26

My Dear Mr Ogilvie

Many thanks for your kind and reassuring letter. I always suffer from reaction after putting out a book: and am ridiculously sensitive to what reviewers say – even when I know their incompetence and malice. I say to myself: what *can* reviewers be expected to make of a thing like the *Drunk Man* – yet I am horribly vexed when they make nothing of it or something utterly stupid. I set out to give Scotland a poem, perfectly modern in psychology, which could only be compared in the whole length of Scots literature with 'Tam O' Shanter' and Dunbar's 'Seven Deidly Sins'. And I felt that I had done it by the time I finished – despite all the faults and flaws of my work. (At the last moment I excised lyrics etc. which aggregated at least a third more than its published bulk.) The few people whose opinions I respect in regard to matters of this kind – i.e. who have the knowledge and understanding of poetry in general, and of Scots in particular – are all of like opinion to yourself, and they are isolated – scattered all over the country and not in touch with each other. Even making a discount for any particular partiality they share for me and my work, I think their unanimity in the matter almost proof positive that they are right. Even so the lack of interest in the book on the part of the public and the great majority of reviewers is dulling: and I am all the more glad to have a reassuring letter from yourself, and move forward again out of comparative dejection to the position that 'it is all right in its way, but will take a year or two in the nature of things to accumulate the reputation it deserves.'

I will send you a batch of cuttings in a day or two. Some of them make 'sair reading'. The sales, too, have been very disappointing so far. But then 7/6 is a fair sum and times are bad. So long as Blackwood's maintain their faith in me I don't care. It will be about a year at least before I ask them to publish *Cencrastus*, and it may be longer. It will be a much bigger thing than the *Drunk Man* in every way. It is complementary to it really. *Cencrastus* is the fundamental serpent, the underlying unifying principle of the cosmos. To circumjack is to encircle. *To Circumjack Cencrastus* – to square the circle, to box the compass, etc. But where the *Drunk Man* is in one sense a reaction from the 'Kailyaird', *Cencrastus* transcends that altogether – the Scotsman gets rid of the thistle, 'the bur o' the world' – and his spirit at last inherits its proper sphere. Psychologically it represents the resolution of the sadism and masochism, the synthesis of the various sets of antithesis I was posing in the *Drunk Man*. It will not depend on the contrasts of realism and metaphysics, bestiality and beauty, humour and madness – but move on a plane of pure beauty and pure music. It will be an attempt to move really mighty numbers. In the nature of things such an ambition cannot be hastily consummated. It will take infinite pains – but along these lines I am satisfied that, if I cannot altogether realise my dream, I can at least achieve something well worth while, ideally complementary to the *Drunk Man* – positive where it is negative, optimistic where it is pessimistic, and constructive where it is destructive.

Re your little joke you were of course – professionally – my English master. I never had a Scots master. But in what I say about Scottish schools in the *Drunk Man* I am (this is my line of defence – by means of reconciling the apparent inconsistency) thinking of the effects of our Educational System on Scottish psychology in general – in my own person I am partially (for alas! I had teachers of whom I have very different thoughts than of you and one or two others) one of the very few exceptions who prove the rule. Curiously the *Drunk Man* is addressed to another old teacher of mine, in my Langholm days – F. G. Scott – we never came into contact with each other as you and I did: I lost sight of him for years: I did not know he was a composer or in any special sense a Scotsman. It was only after I began writing my McD stuff that he got into contact with me – it seemed that McD was providing the very stuff he was at his wits' end to find anywhere – he didn't know then that McD was an old pupil of his . . . In any case, if the commentators etc. do ever descend in any measure upon my literary remains, they will find ample evidence and (so far as I can gauge them) all the hows and whys of my indebtedness to you and of your exemption from the criticism I have brought against your profession as a whole of (whatever else – arguably of more consequence from many points of view – they may have done) failing to stimulate the specifically Scottish qualities of their pupils.

You do not refer to the *Contemporary Scottish Studies*. I wonder what you think of it. Clear-enough-eyed to all its faults of temper and other things (and clear-enough-eyed to the necessity too of most of these very faults if the book was to affect its main purpose) I am in no way apologetic over it. It will do its work. There was a very understanding review of it in the *Glasgow Evening News*[1] – so understanding that I think Neil Munro himself must have written it. I'll send you the cutting with the others. In other quarters of course it has been either ignored or its faults have been concentrated on in a way that partakes of the worst nature of these same faults, to the exclusion of any reference to or comment upon the real values and intentions of the book.

I also recently did the Burns selection[2] with a provocative little preface in Benn's 6d. Augustan Series: and am to propose 'The Immortal Memory' at Cupar on 25th Jan, when I hope to give an address which will be the foundation of a monograph on the subject I have been contemplating for some time.

My apparent leanness is entirely due to my lack of teeth. I must really get a set of false teeth and set my friends at ease. As a matter of fact I keep wonderfully fit. I have not had a doctor since I left the Army in 1919, and no illness of any real consequence. I am frankly anxious not to die young. In many ways I am a late ripener. All my best work is still to come. I am only beginning to find myself. I have all sorts of things in contemplation – and in prose in particular I question if I will succeed in doing any justice to myself for several years yet. I have masses of stuff half-written or in rough draft that I simply cannot finish yet – at least in a fashion that will preserve my artistic integrity. But I know with the sort of intuition that guides me in these matters that it is only a question of time – I will do it yet.

You say nothing of yourself. I hope Mrs Ogilvie, Agnes, John and yourself are all well. It will be delightful indeed if you can contrive your holiday through here next summer. There is nothing I will enjoy more than a little succession of walks and sederunts and talks with you. Mrs Grieve and Christine (a very rumbustious little lady, indeed) are in splendid form, and join me in every good regard to all

---

[1] *The Glasgow Evening News*, 25 November 1926, published a review of *Contemporary Scottish Studies* which was hailed as 'a book likely to take an important place in Scottish letters'.
[2] *Robert Burns, 1759–1796* (London 1926) edited by C. M. Grieve.

of you. Be sure and remember me to any old friend of the Broughton days – and Mackie and Annand.

With every affectionate and grateful thought.

Yours,
C. M. Grieve.

NLS   16 Links Avenue,
                                             Montrose.
                                             8.1.28

Dear Mr Ogilvie

I am sorry to have had to let a week or thereby elapse before replying to your letter, which I was so delighted to receive. But I am having – and likely to have for some months yet – the busiest time of my life.

But first of all, let me congratulate you on your new appointment.[1] It is strange that I missed seeing any mention of it in the papers, or otherwise hearing of it. I am delighted that this long-overdue appointment has come your way at last – although Broughton without you is unthinkable. I am glad you are taking to the change not too badly and hope you will complete your career in all comfort and happiness and good health. You do not mention Mrs Ogilvie and the children (no longer children!). Mrs Grieve joins me in wishing all of you all possible good fortune in this New Year. We are all O.K. Hard work really agrees with me extraordinarily well: and I wouldn't mind if it were twice as hard if the paths I have chosen were not so desperately unremunerative – and yet I would not, and will not, change these paths one iota. The children are fair, fat, and flourishing.

As to wider issues, I am convinced that we are going to make a big issue of our Scottish Movement. The odds against us, culturally, politically, are tremendous – but a big change is taking place. For nearly two years I have been sending out three columns of propagandish matter to over 40 Scottish local papers weekly – and we are now beginning to appreciate the effect. But my biggest work has

[1] Ogilvie became Headmaster of Couper Street Primary School.

93

been correspondence. You would scarcely credit the amount of it – the affiliations I have made all over the world – the continuous effort to knit it all up into a definite and determined movement.

I had a splendid summer holiday which did me a world of good – over in Ireland as the guest of the Irish Nation at the quinquennial Taillteann Games. All the younger Irish writers are great friends of mine, and, above all, the two older figures – Yeats and A.E. You'd be interested in Yeats' opinions of my poetry. He has written to me about it in the most astonishing terms. It's curious how it is making way (except in Scotland) despite the linguistic difficulty. Robert Frost, the American poet, is one of the latest eulogists of the *Drunk Man*.

I had hoped to have had *Cencrastus* done ere this: but I have had too many other things to do – and besides it has developed too greatly. I have already more of it written than the bulk of the *Drunk Man*: and Edwin Muir, the only one who has seen any of it so far, is of the opinion that it is 100 per cent better than the *Drunk Man*. With luck I'll finish it this year yet: but I don't want to hurry it – it's worth taking time over.

In any case, I'll not get much more done till after the election. I've a Spanish novel[2] which I'm translating for Secker to finish: and I'm committed to a book on the National Movement I want out this spring before the election and to collaboration in another with Erskine of Marr, and I've meetings to address all over the place.

By the way I've just arranged to speak for Spence (along with Cunninghame-Graham, I think) at Dalkeith on Saturday first. I don't know what I may be doing on Sunday yet – I may be speaking again somewhere in the constituency – or I may go on to Inverness on the Saturday night. But if I stay in Edinburgh overnight I should like to run up on Sunday forenoon sometime and have a talk with you if convenient.

I'm interested in all your news. I wondered what had come over Mackie.

Excuse more in the meantime. Hoping to see you, if not this week-end, soon, and again with gratitude for your unfailing interest and every good wish.

Yours,
C. M. Grieve

---

[2] *The Handmaid of the Lord* (London 1930) by Ramon Maria de Tenreiro.

16 Links Avenue,
Montrose,
30.1.28

Dear Mr Ogilvie

I was delighted to hear from you again – but extremely sorry to learn of Mrs Ogilvie's condition. I sincerely trust that the operation was successful and that she may soon be entirely recovered. I have not had a moment to myself during the past ten days or so; or I would have written you ere this to express my concern, sympathy, and good wishes. But – busy as I have been – the matter has been constantly in my mind and I shall be glad if you can drop me a line to tell me how Mrs Ogilvie is. You do not mention yourself: but I know that this strain will have been telling upon you, and I trust you are fit.

Alas! The BBC are restricting travelling exes. to a minimum, I fancy. At all events my last broadcast was from Dundee. I hope you managed to hear me. I am speaking – from Dundee again – in about three weeks' time on 'Outstanding Qualities of the Scots Vernacular'.[1]

You'll have seen – or heard – of course about my attack on the Burns Cult. It has secured extraordinary publicity – and an analysis of press-cuttings etc. shows, to my surprise, about 50 per cent with me. I replied to Professor Bowman, Mr Rosslyn Mitchell and others in special articles in the *Glasgow Evening News* and *Glasgow Evening Times* last Thursday night.[2]

For the past year (since last May to be exact) I have been sending out special articles on Scottish issues and interests of all kinds at the rate of 5 columns per week through a special bureau[3] I formed for the purpose (in connection with the Scottish Home Rule Movement). These articles appeared in some 40 local papers weekly between Maidenkirk and John O' Groats – and I am satisfied that they are

[1] 'Outstanding Qualities of the Scottish Vernacular' was broadcast on the BBC Scottish Home Service on 14 February 1928.
[2] Speaking at a Burns supper organised by the Glasgow branch of the Scottish National Movement, Grieve dismissed Burns as an anachronism. *The Glasgow Evening Times* of 23 January began its report as follows; 'Strong criticism of the Burns Federation and Burns' worshippers was made by Mr C. M. Grieve ("Hugh M'Diarmid") on Saturday [and stated that the] best thing that could happen to Scotland in regard to Burns was that it should set itself deliberately to forget, for the next quarter of a century at least, that he ever existed.' Articles by MacDiarmid then appeared on 26 January in both *The Glasgow Evening Times* and *The Glasgow Evening News*. A. A. Bowman (1883–1936) was Professor of Moral Philosophy at Glasgow University.
[3] The Scottish Secretariat.

slowly but surely effecting a transformation of Scottish opinion. I have all sorts of things on the stocks. *To Circumjack Cencrastus* is shaping all right – but will be a tremendous book. I do not care though it takes me a year or two. I am also simultaneously working away at several volumes of lyrics – *Dimidium Animae Meae* (love lyrics); *Maidenkirk to John O' Groats* (purely objective lyrics – like 'Country Life', which, you may remember, begins

> Ootside – ootside
> There's bumclocks bizzen' by etc.

and 'Songs for Christine' – on the model of 'Hungry Waters'.

I have also been writing quite a number of lyrics in English.

At the moment I am putting everything else aside to finish as rapidly as possible a little book entitled *St Sophia: or the Future of Religion*[4] which is to appear in Kegan Paul's 'Today and Tomorrow Series'.

Albyn, (which has been selling well) I am not proud of. A curious story attaches. About a year before it appeared I had written to the publishers suggesting that I should do a vol entitled *Caledonia: or the Future of Scotland* for their series. They agreed – and then I found I wasn't in the mood. I was too much in amongst the stuff and simply couldn't write a statement in short compass. They wrote me for the MSS several times: but I kept putting them off. Finally a period of months ensued during which I heard nothing from them. Then I happened to hear that they were announcing a book entitled *Caledonia: or the Future of the Scots* by G. M. Thomson. I immediately wrote to them – but they said their acceptance of Thomson's book in no way prevented them accepting mine, written from a different angle – and would I send on my MSS at once? I didn't believe them – so hastily furbished up into a semi-connected form some of the stuff I'd sent out through the afore-mentioned Bureau – just a rough slapping-together of stuff written in a slip-shod and hurried fashion in the first instance. But they took it all right! And to make matters worse didn't sent me galley-proofs but only paged proofs – so the corrections I tried to make would have upset the pagination and cost too much. In the finish-up I had to leave it to them to make such corrections as they conveniently could. Needless to say they contrived to make precious few and failed to make some quite indispensable ones. So that's that.

Thomson's book gave me a chance for a journalistic grand slam. I had signed articles on it in over 30 different papers (all different

[4] This book never appeared.

96

articles) including *Irish Statesman, Forward, The Outlook, The New Age* etc. etc.[5] Quite a little feat!

I've been writing longish articles monthly too in such subjects as 'Neo Gaelic Economies', 'Anti-Intellectualism in Scotland Today', etc. in *The Pictish Review* and *The Scots Independent*.

I've been doing a lot of talking too and have a lot more in prospect – Leith on 16th Feb (reply to Lord Sands[6] & others re 'Synthetic Scots'). Edinburgh on 17th March (Outlook Tower Club when Mr & Mrs F. G. Scott and myself are supplying a real high-brow programme of the latest Scots poetry, music and argumentation).

You'll be interested to hear that Professor Saurat (who thinks I'm making a huge mistake in writing in Scots) recently read my 'Moment in Eternity' to 3 American Professors at London University and reports that they were literally astounded by its beauty and power!!

Bully for young Mackie![7] I'll let you know what train I'm arriving by on 16th Feb. – on the offchance that we might have tea together (and if Mackie can come along then too all the better). I had a long letter the other week from Mrs McCraig (Birmingham) – and will be replying to her this week for sure. Delighted to hear about Albert's new novel and will be on the alert for it.

Yes – I can quite imagine that the bulk of the inquiries will be unfriendly.

People who know nothing about me and haven't read a word I've written frequently astonish my friends (also a steadily growing body) with their extraordinary animosity towards me.

A Glasgow headmaster was to give a paper at a Burns Club the other month. Another headmaster called on him the previous week. Dialogue.

I see you're to be at — Burns Club next week. What's your subject?

I'm to be talking about a new poet – Hugh M'Diarmid.

(Quick as a flash) You'll be attacking him of course.

No. He's not a subject for attack or defence. It's a question of whether he has any significance. I think he has and it's that I want to discuss. – – – But have you ever read any of his stuff?

No fear!

And so the game goes on. I'm by no means tired of it.

5 For example, reviews by MacDiarmid of G. M. Thomson's *Caledonia* (1927) appeared in *Forward* on 5 November 1927, *The Outlook* on 12 November 1927, and *The New Age* on 10 November 1927.

6 Christopher Nicholson Johnston, Lord Sands (1857–1934) was Chairman of the Carnegie Trust for Scottish Universities from 1921.

7 This refers to the publication of Albert Mackie's *Poems in Two Tongues* (1928).

Love to all of you and every good wish; and may 1928 (however badly it has begun) prove a happy and prosperous year for you all.

Yours.
C. M. Grieve.

NLS

16 Links Avenue,
Montrose.
21/4/1928

Dear Mr Ogilvie

I was sorry to miss seeing you when I was in Edinburgh last – and to have been so long in writing you since. I hope that long ere this you have got rid of the troublesome 'screws' which were then afflicting you: and that Mrs Ogilvie has made an excellent and complete recovery. I have been desperately 'thrang' – with all manner of irons in the fire and a difficulty in manipulating them in the congested economy of my home which has not been eased by the arrival (a fortnight aft) of a son and heir.[1] Both Mrs Grieve and he are in splendid case. This is just a note, in passing, to show that the harassed husband and father is himself still to the fore.

I got an invitation to the Outlook Tower sent to Mackie too: but he was in Crieff and wrote me a long and interesting letter. I'm going to try to get him written today. I'd a note too – which I must answer – apropos the 'Majority' special number of the *Broughton Magazine*[2]: and will of course send something before the end of May (the time-limit allowed); but what? There's the rub.

I enclose a couple of pamphlets.

With kindest regards to all.

Yours,
C. M. Grieve.

---

[1] Walter Grieve was born on 5 April 1928.

[2] The 'Majority' number marked the twenty-first year of *The Broughton Magazine*; it appeared in Summer 1928 and contained seven MacDiarmid poems from *Sangs-chaw* and *Penny Wheep*.

16 Links Avenue,
Montrose.
Sat. 30th June 1928

Dear Mr Ogilvie:-

I am dashing off a note because I have just received the *Broughton Mag* (upon which all congratulations to all concerned. – I'd have been glad to have it if only for your photograph, but, as it is, there are heaps of things to make it treasurable to me and hundreds of others) – and my article does not appear? I am wondering if you ever received it. It's quite all right if you did – and did not think it suitable, or for any other reason. I sent it to you because I wanted you to tell me (as I said in my covering note) if it would serve the purpose – and, if not, if you'd any other suggestions to make. I wondered about receiving no acknowledgement: but thought it was just because you were busy. But I spoke of it several times to Mrs. Grieve and had meant to write you asking if you'd got it all right – but kept putting off doing so. I forget what I called it but it was a short essay in English and I was inordinately proud of the way in which I turned it and of suitability, I thought, for the end in view. Needless to say, I wrote it very much con amore – as to a tribute to you, and to Broughton, and to certain dead Broughtonian friends – but alas! I'm not worrying now of course about the thing itself but lest you should for a moment have thought me unmindful of your request. I sent it about 15th May. – In great haste, with every good wish to Mrs Ogilvie and family.

Yours,
C. M. Grieve.

16 Links Avenue,
Montrose.
18/5/29

Dear Mr Ogilvie

I was delighted to see your familiar script on an envelope again, but exceedingly sorry about Mrs Ogilvie. I do trust that she may speedily be all right again.

That you should not have had a look in, as you put, for the Broughton headship after all these years of splendid service is simply awful. Man's inhumanity to man − − − Scotland is simply rotten with hardship of this sort. It makes me boil − − −

I hope Leith school isn't too awful. But it is a great pity that without financial disadvantage at the end of the day you could not have finished your term at Broughton, but had to migrate to a different and less congenial atmosphere.

I resigned my Dundee candidature simply because, while I would have polled well, I could not have come near winning, and would have spent at least £200 to £300, which, ours being a young Party[1] − could be much more profitably spent in other directions. But my organisation will remain intact and intensive propaganda will be maintained, and on a future occasion the omens may be more auspicious. I run week-end schools there: 2 lectures, Sat. afternoon and evening: and 3 on Sunday, − forenoon, afternoon and evening.

Poetry, of course, remains my principal concern: and I am in the throes of a huge poem − *Cencrastus*. I have already written a great mass of it. But I am in no hurry. Be assured that however I may seem to be dissipating my energies, I am really working away systematically at it and fully alive to the passing of the years and determined to harvest timeously every grain that I possibly can.

I am only too willing to do what I can for the semi-jubilee issue: but what can I do? I am enclosing herewith a few new poems; I wonder if they will serve. If not, please just drop me a p.c. and I will do something else. Or perhaps you could suggest something − set me a subject as in the old days − and I will promptly do my utmost to score say 70 per cent of your always far too lenient marks.

The bairns are splendid: and Mrs Grieve and myself are in excellent fettle. John and Agnes will, of course, be grown up now; I trust they are both well and doing well.

Every kind regard.

Yours,
C. M. Grieve.

[1] The National Party of Scotland was formed in 1928.

100

NLS
TS

18 Pyrland Road,
London, N5.
6th January 1930

George Ogilvie, Esq, MA.,
67 Cluny Gardens,
Edinburgh.

My Dear Mr Ogilvie,

Many thanks for your note to hand this morning. I ought to have written you long before this but I have not become any less remiss in regard to correspondence than I have always been. My accident was a serious one and in fact I had an almost miraculous escape from death. I was thrown off a double decker motor bus and landed on my head sustaining severe concussion of the skull but fortunately no fracture. I have made an extraordinarily good recovery but must 'Ca' canny' for a while and avoid all mental stress and excitement, alcoholic stimulants, spicy foods, etc.

I came to London in the beginning of September and have (if all goes well with *Vox* as it promises to do) a very congenial and lucrative post here. Mrs Grieve and the children are with me and London is suiting all of them very well. I ought to have been here years ago and am glad that this opportunity presented itself when it did.

It may lead to still greater things. Senator Oliver St John Gogarty has been bringing special pressure to bear upon Lord Beaverbrook with whom he has been staying with regard to what he considers the 'Shameful way in which I have been frozen out' and I have just had an extraordinarily kind letter from Lord Beaverbrook in which he expresses the greatest admiration for my works and says that he is arranging for an early meeting. Gogarty in a letter to hand this morning, also refers to this and says that he feels that he has at last broken free 'the conspiracy of silence' which has hitherto surrounded my work.

I have all kinds of things on the stocks but the amount of work entailed in launching this new periodical and other things, have prevented my getting much done other than journalism. I am just arranging, however with the Porpoise Press to issue a new volume of my poems early in the spring[1] and my big poem *Circumjack Cencrastus* (which I have spent such a long time arranging and re-arranging) is

---

[1] The Porpoise Press did not bring out a new volume of poems but did publish a second impression, in 1930, of *Annals of the Five Senses*.

nearing completion at last and Blackwood's will publish it as soon as I can let them have the typescript.

With regard to journalism, I am busier than ever and, but for my accident, would have been appearing in all sorts of new waters. I have a special article on the Burns Cult in next week's *Radio Times*[2] (which has now a circulation of 1¾ million) and will send you a copy.

You say nothing of yourself, of Mrs Ogilvie and the children in your letter. I sincerely hope that this finds you all in the best form and Mrs Grieve joins with me (belatedly) in wishing you all the compliments of the Season and every happiness in the New Year.

This is a short and scrappy letter but I am not up to much writing yet. I will write you a long letter soon.

Ever yours,
C. M. Grieve.

NLS   357 Royal Liver Building,
                                                                   Liverpool.
                                                                   16.12.30

My Dear Mr Ogilvie

I am concerned to hear of your operation and subsequent weakness and – tho' you say little about it – gather that you are still far from robust. I wish I could take a run up to Edinburgh and see you: but, alas, that is out of the question in the meantime. I ought to have written you long ere this and have frequently had it in mind to do so, but I am a procrastinating creature, a bad correspondent in any case, and for most of the past year I have been having a very rough passage financially and otherwise. The year is closing in happier circumstances however and I have good grounds to hope that the incoming year will put me in more comfortable case. After a month or so's unemployment, following the collapse of *Vox*, I secured my present post as Publicity Officer to the Liverpool Organisation, a body run by the Corporation of Liverpool, Wallasey, Bootle and Birkenhead, to boost Merseyside interests of all kinds, and my function is to write leaflets etc. and maintain a steady flow of articles

[2] *The Radio Times*, 17 January 1930.

of all sorts to the home, Colonial & foreign press. It is really very interesting work and what I do is entirely dependent on my own initiative; I have to show results, of course, but apart from that I am almost entirely my own master, have an excellent office, etc. The salary was not too good to start with: but I have just had a substantial rise. I am still maintaining my London house and my wife and children are there – not an ideal arrangement: but I didn't know how I'd like Liverpool, I hoped to return to London, and I didn't want to bring my daughter away from the school in London. However, we may make some other arrangements soon now. In the whole I can congratulate myself in these difficult days; there are hundreds of thousands – through no fault of their own – in a far worse plight and without such compensating interests as I have in letters, politics and other directions.

Cencrastus has its qualities and looks like establishing my name far more widely than my previous books. *The New Statesman* gave a page to it; the *New Criterion* is doing likewise; Professor Denis Saurat and Gordon Bottomley are both writing about it in the next issue of *The Modern Scot*, and Yeats has been so moved that he is writing an essay on my poetry![1] I seem to be arriving.

But I did not do in it what I intended – I deliberately deserted my big plan, because I realised I had lots of elements in me, standing between me and really great work, I'd to get rid of – and I think I've done it. My next book will be a very different matter – with none of the little local and temporary references, personalities, political propaganda, literary allusiveness, etc. It is based on Goethe's *Faust* as Joyce's *Ulysses* was on Homer – i.e. takes *Faust* as its springboard – its framework – but it is to be cast in dramatic form and as straightforward and sun-clear as I can possible make it, with none of the experimentalism and ultra-modernist elements Joyce used. But we'll see. I'm working very hard on it and hope – although it's an enormous proposition – to have it ready for publication this spring!

My kindest enquiries regarding Mrs Ogilvie and your children – children no longer. I hope they are all well. Please remember me kindly to any other friends with whom you may be in touch. I see a good deal of Kerr here; he is very comfortably fixed, with a nice home, and a good Scots wife and a delightful little boy – and your

---

[1] *The New Statesman* Christmas Books Supplement of 6 December 1930 contained a long review of *To Circumjack Cencrastus* by G. M. Thomson. *The Criterion*, Vol X, No XL, April 1931, included an enthusiastic review of the same book by Edwin Muir. *The Modern Scot*, Vol 1. No 4, January 1931, published two reviews of the book by Gordon Bottomley and Denis Saurat. Yeats represented MacDiarmid in *The Oxford Book of Modern Verse 1892–1935 (1936)*.

name frequently crops up (always with great gratitude to you) when we foregather.

You may be sure that if and when I am in Edinburgh – or, more probably, Glasgow but with any chance of popping through to Edinburgh – I'll not lose the chance of seeing you; I would give a great deal for a long crack with you. May the opportunity come soon!

The best of Christmas wishes to you and yours and may 1931 be a happy year for all of you, and, – first and foremost – see you speedily and completely recovered from the after effects of your illness and operation.

Ever Yours,
C.M.G.

To Helen B. Cruickshank

Helen Burness Cruickshank (1886–1975), one of MacDiarmid's most devoted admirers, was a prominent figure in modern Scottish literature. As a poet she published work in both English and a dialect Scots that drew on her upbringing in Angus – her *Collected Poems* appeared in 1971 and her *Octobiography* in 1976. After leaving school at the age of fifteen she became a Civil Servant in London, staying there for ten years before returning to Edinburgh for another thirty years in her chosen profession. She first met MacDiarmid in 1924 at Ravelston Elms, the Edinburgh studio of the sculptor-poet Pittendrigh Macgillivray and was greatly impressed by his manner and appearance. She noticed, as she said in her 'Mainly Domestic' contribution to *MacDiarmid: A Festschrift* (Edinburgh 1962) 'a bush of silky hair above a high forehead and two deep-set eyes.' (Festschrift, 189)

As Secretary of the Scottish Centre of PEN (formed on 21 April 1928) MacDiarmid had to come to Edinburgh to attend meetings:

[He] always stayed with Helen Cruickshank and her mother over the Saturday night when the meetings were in Edinburgh, sleeping in the tiny front room at 'Dinnieduff' [at Corstorphine] with its sloping roof, which Mrs Cruickshank christened 'The Prophet's Chamber' after the story of Elijah and the pious widow who always placed her small 'chamber in the wall' at the prophet's disposal. Mrs Cruickshank was pleased to see C. M. G. as he brought news of Montrose and her nephew, Major William Wood, who also served on the town council.[1]

When MacDiarmid went to London – in 1929 to work on Compton Mackenzie's radio critical journal *Vox* – he persuaded Helen Cruickshank to take over his position as Secretary of Scottish PEN and she did this honorary work for seven years.

Helen Cruickshank was involved in the decision to move MacDiarmid up to Whalsay:

Robin Black [editor of *The Free Man*] consulted my opinion when Dr David Orr, then resident doctor on the island of Whalsay in the

[1] Gordon Wright, *MacDiarmid: An Illustrated Biography* (Edinburgh 1977, p. 45).

remote Shetlands, suggested that he could find a cottage for the poet and his family there to enable him to 'get on with his poetry' in peace and quiet. Seated on a sunny bench behind St John's Church in Princes Street, Robin and I debated the pros and cons of this idea throughout my office lunch-hour. I was gazing in the direction of De Quincey's tomb in the adjoining churchyard of St Cuthbert's when Robin said, 'And, of course, Whalsay is a dry island.' At which, I heard myself say firmly, 'I think he should go.' And go he did. I've often wondered whether we were wise in guiding the poet's decision to this exile. But looking to the output of work that flowed from the years in Shetland I think we were right. (Festschrift, 193)

She continued to give MacDiarmid moral and material support throughout his island exile and on hearing that he had been conscripted for National Service in 1941 used her professional influence as a Civil Servant to prevent the poet being employed as a manual labourer on the roads. Instead she arranged for him to undertake engineering work. The letters to Helen Cruickshank demonstrate the difficulties MacDiarmid faced at various times. Her loyalty to him was sustained until the end of her life and her attitude to his art is indicated by the closing stanza of her 'Epistle for Christopher Murray Grieve on his 75th Birthday':

> And sae I name ye a *releegious* poet,
> The foremaist ane frae John o'Groats tae Wamphray,
> Agnostic ? atheist ? pagan ? Deil a bit o't,
> Chief pillydacus o' the haill clanjamphrie!
> I mind o ane that bore in wind an weather
> A sacred load thro cataracts o' thocht.
> Na, CHRISTOPHER, yer faither an yer mither
> They didna wale *that* wechty name for nocht.

EUL

16 Links Avenue,
Montrose.
May 17th 1922.

Dear Miss Cruickshank,

Many thanks for your encouraging note. Letters are rolling in at a satisfactory rate. The leader in Tuesday's *Glasgow Herald*[1] was a great help. I shall know in a day or two how matters are likely to pan out. I do not expect to get quite the number necessary as a result of these letters: but intend to issue a circular to likely people, and my friends, the contributors to *Northern Numbers* and others interested will be able to bring sufficient personal influence to bear to rope in the requisite number. Running any periodical devoted to pure art these days even in England is lean and difficult work: and in Scotland the difficulties are greater. *Northern Numbers* succeeded wonderfully – but, as the shrewder reviewers noted, that was because of extra-literary considerations in the main: and the fact that I purposely included sentimental items which gave it a quasi-popular appeal.

In the *Chapbook*,[2] as *The Glasgow Herald* points out, there will be greater freedom of selection and room will be found for verses which, by reason of their departure from conventional standards will not readily find a public elsewhere.

As to *Northern Numbers* I intend to bring out a Third Series in the end of October or beginning of November this year, if humanly possible. Mr T. N. Foulis, the publisher, is in business difficulties however and I am not yet certain that he will be in a position to undertake this. If not, I shall either require to secure another publisher or become my own publisher. While then I am in no position yet to make promises of any kind, I should be happy to see any material you care to submit at your convenience.

I must warn you that I deal very faithfully indeed with my friends in regard to their MSS. *The Glasgow Herald* when reviewing the Second Series of *Northern Numbers* said that, unlike most Scottish poets (most even of the contributors to *N. N.*) I 'did not bleat and knew what I was after.' I certainly know that – but it is often very difficult to convince friends that there is such a thing or that it is at all

---

[1] Under the heading 'Modern Scottish Verse' *The Glasgow Herald*, 16 May 1922, welcomed Grieve's appeal for subscribers for a Scottish poetry monthly: 'It is encouraging to have [Mr Grieve's] assurance that Scottish poets are not lagging behind their English brethren in experimental vigour and in the devising of new forms of utterance.'

[2] *The Scottish Chapbook* which ran from August 1922 until December 1923.

desirable that my views should prevail. I must confess that I have little respect for most people's opinion of my own stuff. Happily I can add that I have found few contributors or would-be contributors who even remotely hinted that my criticisms and decisions were – however unfortunate – not utterly sincere, and I am sure that like these good people, if I do not accept the contributions you send me, you will nevertheless continue to support the venture and try again.

Northern Numbers had to sell – so I was to a certain extent out for names and included certain types of verse greatly admired by many people but to which I personally am utterly indifferent.

In the *Chapbook* commercial conditions won't weigh: and I'll be out for genuinely significant and experimental work wherever it is to be found.

I am interested to learn of your local connection. Do you know Mrs Violet Jacob?[3] She is one of the Kennedy-Erskines of Dun. Are you ever in Montrose? If so we might have a chat sometime.

I shall let you know if and when the *Chapbook* is to go on. I think it will all right. In the meantime I have pleasure in adding you to the growing list of prospective subscribers: and, apologising for my atrocious writing and hasty sentiments.

Remain,

Yours faithfully,
C. M. Grieve.

EUL
TS

18 Pyrland Road,
London, N5.
30th April, 1930.

Dear Helen,

I think I have located where, amongst my insufferable chaos of papers, there is every likelihood of the stuff I want for you about the Gaelic people being: but, owing to a variety of causes, I have been unable to comb through the accumulation in question. I will do it without fail by the end of the week at the latest and you will hear

---

[3] Violet Jacob (1863–1946), Scottish novelist and poet whose *Songs of Angus* (1915) enjoyed considerable popularity.

from me not later than Monday. Knowing as I do the amount of work and worry the PEN Secretaryship entails, I am exceedingly sorry not to have been able to be more – and more promptly – helpful in this matter, but my circumstances these days have been 'curious and harassing', apart altogether from the fact that I am striving might and main to complete *Cencrastus*, and trying to spatchcock poetry writing into a veritable maze of far more urgently necessary tasks is the Very Dickens. However, things are clearing up: and my most immediate and pressing worry has just been removed. I have received an appointment in Liverpool to write up all manner of articles and publicity matter in the interests of Merseyside developments. So that's that and will keep the pot boiling very nicely. I am not shifting my home – at all events in the meantime. Peggy and the bairns will remain in London: but I myself will go to Liverpool on 12th May.

You will appreciate that this is just a conscience-stricken note. I'll write more freely once I've been through the papers I speak of, and run the wanted cutting to earth. I wonder if you're at Blair Atholl. If so, I hope you and your Mother are having a very happy time, and both in splendid fettle. I hope the Dunbar Symposium goes off alright and will keep an eye on the *Record* for any report of it. There are lots of things I should write about – the egregious W. H. Hamilton,[1] etc., – but I mustn't today. Love from all,

Yours,
C. M. Grieve.

EUL   Royal Liver Building,
                                                                   Liverpool.
                                                                    14/6/30

Dear Helen,

I'd be very vexed about your going off to the islands on your own instead of synchronising with my own visit there, if the latter were by

---

[1] W. H. Hamilton contributed to the Third Series of *Northern Numbers* (Montrose 1923), to *The Scottish Chapbook* and to *The Scottish Nation*. He was editor of *Holyrood, a Garland of Modern Scots Poems*. In *The Scottish Educational Journal* of 16 October 1925 he took MacDiarmid to task for his 'abuse of writers of established rank'.

any means certain, unless something unexpected intervenes, Peggy and the bairns will spend August on Barra: but whether I'll manage – as I hope – a week or thereby with them there is still uncertain. It would have been nice to have forgathered there. But I hope you have a topping time in weather and all other respects, and that the funds hold out all right. If not, I'm afraid it's no use wiring me with your last bob. I'm still 'warslin' through'. I like Liverpool and what I'm doing here O.K.: but the financial side, while comparatively generous for this sort of appointment and likely to improve considerably as time goes on, isn't by any means adequate to my – or rather the Grieve family – needs; and free-lancing is a precarious way of keeping it up to the necessary level. Howsomever! I'm not going to give you a catalogue of wants and woes; I'm in fine fettle, and find it very amusing to write trade and technical articles on aspects of shipping, hardware exports etc. for journals like the London Chamber of Commerce one, the Overseas Issue of *The Ironmonger*, and the like and publicity matter of all sorts for American, Continental and Colonial papers and periodicals.

I'm afraid I won't manage up to the Bannockburn affair and I'm not caring much. Mums the word about *C. A.*[1] in the meantime. I'm earnest there: and having a deuce of a lot of correspondence thereanent with young people (for the most part) all over Scotland.

As to *Cencrastus* this is ready and typed all except a few odds and ends: but these are of a kittle character and I can't rush them, apart from the fact that I've been having a very busy spell and can't get the necessary conjuncture of time and mood.

I note what you say about *The Scots Observer*. It's been very good of you to keep sending it to me and I've found much to interest me in it. But I'll certainly have no earthly use for it under the editorship of the Rev. David MacQueen whom I'd have not the slightest hesitation in 'kiltin' in a tow' from the nearest lamp-post.

Re PEN, Grierson would make an admirable successor to Lady M.S.,[2] if he'd take it. I wish I'd been able to go to Warsaw too, but

[1] *Clann Albann*, the title MacDiarmid chose for the huge autobiographical poem he planned in the 1930s, was also applied to the political movement MacDiarmid hoped to generate at this time. In Octave Six (London 1967, p. 189) of his autobiography *My Life and Times*, Compton Mackenzie wrote: 'Ruaraidh Erskine of Marr and Christopher Grieve were both in sympathy with my fear of parochialism and we discussed [in 1929] the possibility of forming a society to be known as Clann Albain, the members of which would be pledged to do all they could to foster the Celtic Idea with a vision, on a far distant horizon at present, of rescuing the British Isles from being dominated by London.'

[2] When the Scottish Centre of PEN was formed on 21 April 1928 the three principal positions were filled as follows: President, Lady Margaret Sackville; Secretary, C. M. Grieve; Treasurer, Alexander McGill.

that's out of the question, although, if the London business hadn't gone awry, I'd certainly have done so. Failing Grierson I can't think of anybody, except, perhaps, Power.

I'm very sorry to hear about Barney's paw. Thus far away I can safely extend by proxy my tenderest solicitude to that doughty dog for whom – although we never got on to terms – I entertain no small measure of affection spiced with fear.

Every kind regard to your Mother. I am glad her Blair-Atholl visit set her up a bit and hope she'll have a happy summer.

Excuse this pencil scrawl. I've run out of ink and, most of the shops being shut, would have to go miles to buy a bottle. I'll write you again about the time I think you'll be back to Corstorphine. See and look after yourself.

Love,
Chris.

P.S. Peggy is weekending in Bucks with Bell, who wrote *Rip Van Scotland*[3] but I'm going to take a flat and she'll be up here for a week or two shortly.

EUL   Royal Liver Building,
                                                        Liverpool.
                                                        7/10/30

My dear Helen,

It is incredible – and ought to have been impossible – that I should have been so long in writing you. I certainly didn't mean to be and my prolonged silence means nothing whatever except that I am – have always been – a bad and am getting worse and worse correspondent. I'd as soon write a letter that isn't a purely and unavoidably business one as have a tooth drawn or join a Rotary Club or the Kirk nowadays. I'll soon have no friends left: and yet those who do not allow my remissness to make them remiss but maintain a one-sided correspondence with me can scarcely credit how glad I am to hear from them – to be kept in touch. If we are growing apart it may

[3] William Bell, *Rip Van Scotland* (1930).

be largely my fault but it is certainly not my desire. In extenuation I can of course always plead that I am excessively busy – plus for some considerable time back damnably (excuse me – but it should really be a cap D) worried in all my capacities as husband and father, as poet, as Nationalist. I'd certainly like to worsen the offence of my long abstention from letter writing by occupying the 'prophet's chamber' and giving you the whole tale of my trials and tribulations. But it 'ud have to be a long stay and I'd certainly consume all your whisky.

I have been delighted to have had news of you – from yourself direct to me or via Peggy or from others or via the press (Miss Lochhead[1] did you nicely and deservedly – I felt like hugging her – or both of you – and endorse every word she wrote). You'll have to publish that book of yours soon. I'm glad you're keeping writing and wish I saw more of your output.

I feel particularly guilty re the PEN but what can I do. I'll look forward to hearing what happened at the annual meeting. Power[2] as President would be O.K. He's been doing a power of good work recently – strong straightforward stuff that is building up the Scottish Movement. I'm glad the membership keeps growing and hope it will continue to do so and that I may foregather with you all again on some suitable occasion ere long.

I'm to be in Scot. (d.v. & w.p.) in the first week of December – but only for 2 days and I'm afraid they'll be confined to Glasgow. On Dec. 1st Kaikhosru Sorabji is giving a performance of his gigantic pianoforte composition, *Opus Clavicembalisticum* which is dedicated to me and I want to be there and on the 2nd I hope to address (sensationally) the Glasgow University Scottish Nationalist Assocn. of which I'm this year's Vice President, but I cannot prolong my stay because I'm to be addressing the Societé-Internationale de Unlologie et Beaux Arts in London on 3rd and want to see Professor Patrick Geddes (from whom I've just had a long letter – he enjoyed the PEN 'do') before he goes back to Montpellier. In other Scottish directions I am in eruption again – definitely getting on now with the organisation of Clann Albainn, and also with the Douglas Economic Proposals Enquiry Committee of the Scottish Nationalist Party – and of course you'll have seen in *New Statesman, Record* etc. with controversies of divers kinds.

Many thanks for *The Scots Observer* to hand today. I enjoyed seeing the article in print. Entre nous (as doubtless you've guessed) I wrote it and the *Daily Record* one and the *Glasgow Evening News* one and the

[1] Marion Lochhead, author of *The Scots Household in the Eighteenth Century* (1948).
[2] William Power (1873–1951), journalist and author of *Literature and Oatmeal* (1935).

Daily Express and several others still to appear – each different article; quite a little journalistic feat – and a valuable source of much needed augmentation of income.[3]

I expect *Cencrastus* will be out about 15th inst. The Porpoise Press also bringing out a very attractively got up new edition of *Annals* at 6/- very soon.

Enough of my deeds and projects! What of your mother. Give her my very best love. I'd like immensely to see her again. And do you ever see or hear from and about Macgillivray now? I've let him drop almost entirely out of ken – to my grief – but impotent grief. I just can't write letters. Hamilton[4] too I treated very shabbily – he meant exceedingly well – but his saccharine mentality finally scunnered me and his articles on Scottish poets in the Record were too dreadful for anything except perhaps Comic Cuts or *The Scots Observer* – which has undergone a feasible change for the worse under the perfectly Asinine McQueen.[5]

Forgive my violent language. If you can find the time give me a nice long letter soon and tell me all the literary chatter of the Capital of my 'own, my native' land and in particular of the PEN – the obese McGill[6] especially; another old pal with whom I've completely lost touch.

And (since after this patchwork of apology and invective and miscellaneous compunctions and grousings I'm in a generous mood – no; not for that reason but for his own sweet sake) give my love to Barney.[7]

And see and be a good girl until I see you again.

Yours,
Chris.

P.S. I've said nothing about Peggy and the bairns: but I think you're

[3] MacDiarmid prepared the public for the publication of *To Circumjack Cencrastus* by contributing polemical articles to various papers. For example he condemned the 'intellectual arrogance' of the poem in an article signed 'Pteleon' in *The Scots Observer* of 20 October 1930; and an anonymous article in *The Daily Record* of 21 September 1930 noted the 'blankly blasphemous' tone of the poem.

[4] W. H. Hamilton, a minister, came out in favour of *To Circumjack Cencrastus*. On 1 November 1930 *The Daily Record* printed two columns of letters for and against the poem; unlike his fellow churchman Very Rev Lauchlan Maclean Watt, Hamilton was impressed by the poem which he defended against 'the shabbiness of grudge in many of the earliest reviews'.

[5] Rev David McQueen, editor of *The Scots Observer*.

[6] Alexander McGill was associate editor of MacDiarmid's monthly *Northern Review* in 1924; his article 'Hugh M'Diarmid' in *The Glasgow Herald* of 4 April 1925 helped promote the reputation of the poet.

[7] Barney, Helen Cruickshank's dog.

hearing direct from her and have all the domestic news. I'm hoping –
if funds permit – to bring her to Glasgow in the 1st of December.

This is an execrable pen. I've every excuse for not writing letters!
Taylor too – please remember me to Taylor.[8]

EUL

Cootes,
Thakeham.
10/8/32

My dear Helen,

Many thanks for your long kind letter. I was over at Steyning
yesterday seeing Valda and James Michael – both of whom were in
excellent form – and Valda said she'd written you, so probably you
are in possession of more of the details than I transmitted. I do not
want you to send me anything either from Gibson's or elsewhere – I
know perfectly well that you have your own struggle to make ends
meet. Although I am in pressing difficulties that must be met
somehow or other at once, even the disposal of these will not help me
much; failing a regular job of some sort they will just keep on
recurring – you see I haven't any income at all; just occasional
cheques for articles and these do not cover our irreducible minimum
expenses – rent, grocer, etc, – let alone the arrival of a baby. I
appreciate the prejudice there is – especially at such difficult times as
these – against one regarded as a poet and erratic. I also know – and
in no wise repent – the extent to which I have made things difficult
for myself by my political and personal attitudes. But what I do
object to is the exaggeration of many of the rumours current about
me and the feeling in certain quarters that I am undependable,
unbusiness-like, etc. Now the fact is that (with the sole exception of
Liverpool) any drinking or other proclivities have never interfered
with the diligent discharge of my duties – I held my Montrose job,
for example, ten years. I'm not out now after any big post – all I want
is any sort of routine job bringing in £2 or over per week. That will
solve my difficulties and will entail quiet living and continued steady
application. It is not much to ask; and there is nothing whatever in
my past record to justify any fear that I would not prove an efficient

---

[8] The poet Peter Taylor who contributed to the Third Series of *Northern Numbers*
(Montrose 1923).

and trustworthy employee. I'd take any job I could do – clerical, journalistic, organising, secretarial – virtually anything that has nothing to do with selling things. This was what I wanted Sir Robert Bruce[1] to give me – or Anderson of the Record.[2] Either of them could have done it. And this – and not any other sort of financial assistance – was what I hoped for from Blackwood's too. But there isn't a ghost of a chance apparently.

Tom Henderson[3] has proved one of my staunchest friends. I'm in regular touch with him: and my articles are now appearing in the *Educ. Jul.* again practically every week – after a break of a month or two owing to pressure of other material on space – which 'break', however, and consequent failure of this small source of income too at this crucial moment helped to intensify my immediate plight.

Now, my dear, I am being absolutely frank with you. I must get a regular job somehow, somewhere – with a steady small wage that will enable me to keep a home of sorts going, I can carry on my work and supplement that wage with free-lance and other earnings. Any library job – organising secretaryship – or running a local paper like *The Montrose Review* again – would put me right: and I could struggle through another few years as I did that ten at Montrose. As matters stand I may be evicted from this house at any moment or have what little furniture we have seized. I'd sign an absolute teetotal pledge in return for any such job – and keep it.

MacGillivray thinks Johnstone's portrait of me 'very woggish'.[4] I've sent him my long article for the Edinburgh Rectorial campaign sheet. How are things shaping for the PEN Congress in Scotland?

I wrote Scott Harrison[5] and sent him a copy of 2nd Hymn but haven't heard from him.

Beaverbrook won't help me – regards me as a distinctly dangerous monomaniac – I do not trust Blake or Malcolm Thomson[6] at all; I'll be very pleasantly surprised if they do anything about your poems – though I wish they would.

46? – well, I'm not far off that myself; and my 40th birthday this week is the most perplexing and unpromising one I've yet encountered.

[1] Sir Robert Bruce, editor of *The Glasgow Herald*.
[2] David Anderson, editor of *The Daily Record*.
[3] Tom Henderson, editor of *The Scottish Educational Journal*.
[4] A drawing of MacDiarmid by William Johnstone was used as the frontispiece for *Second Hymn to Lenin* (Thakeham, 1932); Johnstone's oil painting 'MacDiarmid and the Horse Punchkin' was used as the frontispiece of *Tarras* (Edinburgh 1932).
[5] Henry Scott Harrison, a press photographer and artist friendly with Helen Cruickshank.
[6] George Blake and George Malcolm Thomson were both associated with the Porpoise Press.

I do appreciate all your kindness. See and look after yourself. Love to your mother and yourself.

Yours,
Chris.

P.S. I did a couple of hill poems for the suite[7] I mean to dedicate to you – but I'm not satisfied with them yet and am recasting them, besides having several others in the suite to do, so am not including these in *Scots Unbound And Other Poems* (which volume, by the way, is dedicated to Tom Henderson). But I'll send you copies as soon as I get them to my satisfaction.

I note what you say about Mr MacNicoll and his asking what my 'message', my philosophy was. One of the poems in this new book – one of the longest I have ever written, and one which F. G. Scott regards as one of my very best, is called 'Depth And The Chthonian Image',[8] and is designed as a perfectly clear and comprehensive expression of my whole aesthetic, political and general position – a complete statement of 'the faith that is in me'. Perhaps that'll help. It is in ten verses of 24 lines each – 240 in all – with an elaborate rhyme-scheme and little difficult Scots and only odd words of Latin, German and Greek.

EUL   [Whalsay]
                                                        3/7/33

My dear Helen,

There may be a letter from you this morning – unless you were too overwhelmed altogether by getting letters from Valda and I simultaneously last week – but if there is and it calls for any reply I will append that to this epistle which I must get off today to you in any case. From which you will infer, rightly, that there is something I want again. There is. For the past week or so we have been living in Brough Schoolhouse here and it is let as from Tuesday first to another party and we have to clear out. Other accommodation on

---

[7] 'Dìreadh I' (1163–74) is dedicated to Helen Cruickshank.
[8] 'Depth and the Chthonian Image' (346–53) was collected in *Scots Unbound and Other Poems* (Stirling 1932).

Whalsay is quite impossible to secure. Dr Orr's house is now finished and furnished but his sudden marriage upset all plans previously contemplated (the idea was that we were to run a joint menage and as he would have needed a housekeeper in any case Valda would act in that capacity) and the peculiar and unfortunate circumstances render it highly undesirable that if or when his wife returns our presence there should complicate an already exceedingly complicated situation and give her an avoidable *causus belli*. Now I foresaw something of this weeks ago and took the precaution – since there is an acute housing shortage here and cottages do not become available once in a blue moon – to snap up a cottage that happened to be vacant (took it for a year at the tremendous rent of 26/- plus 7/- rates). So we have a roof over our heads in prospect. But the place is unfurnished and we must get a workable minimum of goods and chattels installed into it immediately. I have written to have a table, five chairs, bedstead I have in Edinburgh sent up here; that can scarcely arrive by Friday however and we will stay at Orr's until they do arrive. Housekeeping on nothing but these will be no easy matter even temporarily; but my main object at the moment is to secure some bedclothes; we want you please to pick up two pairs of cheap blankets for us at the Army or Navy, or somewhere else – it doesn't matter if they are coloured – and send them on to us as quickly as you possibly can, together with a note of their cost, for, mark this, my lady, these are not to constitute another 'present by request'; we are to pay you for them. Seriously, will you please do this at once (or earlier); it is impossible to carry on without a bed at least. I want to stay on up here if I possibly can – especially as I have nothing to come back [to] & would I fancy find it practically impossible to get a job of any sort. The Shetlands are suiting me splendidly both physically and mentally; Valda likes them too but how the winters here will serve her I don't know – she'll find it damnably cold and dull I am afraid. However don't let us meet trouble half-way; at the moment we are all in excellent fettle. And this cottage is as cheap as anything I am likely to get anywhere – so is living here – so I am going to do my damnedest to hang on here over the winter, and get all the stuff written that is bubbling about inside me. The spate of composition has in no wise abated yet; I am keeping on turning out poems every day – I don't mean that I am just dashing them off, but working systematically at them and spending all my time brooding and labouring over them.

Excuse more at the moment. I have no news in any case. I see no papers and seldom get any rumour from the outside world at all, so I am inevitably short of matters to discuss and comment on. Please give my kind regards to all friends. I hope your mother is in good form and that you yourself were well set up again by your holiday and in much better care than when I saw you last. Valda and James Michael join me in best greetings.

Yours,
Chris.

EUL

Whalsay,
via Lerwick,
Shetland Islands.
23-12-37

My dear Helen,

You must have been having a great time again on my behalf – alas! I had hoped that these recurrent crises were over in my chequered career. Thanks to your kind offices, we have been deluged with unaccustomed delicacies of all sorts – your own kind gift of cake and shortbread, cakes from Jess Young, a box of groceries from George and Mary Dott, and another ditto from Dr Ramsay and a big Scotch Bun from Mrs McArthur.[1] If it had only been a matter of securing provisions for a week or so these gifts would have done the trick. Unfortunately – delightful though they are and very grateful, if remorseful, though they make us feel – they do not change the core of the problem, which, as I told you, is the difficulty in maintaining our credit accounts here for such daily essentials as milk, bread, and paraffin oil, until such time as I can get my books – or some of them – finished and sent in to the publishers, and draw the stipulated sums in respect thereof and square off our accounts. Even since I wrote you things have become much more difficult; we have had to cut down our daily milk supply by a half, and any day now may see us unable to replenish our oil-tin, no pleasant prospect at this time of year when there is only a few hours of daylight. However, the worst hasn't befallen us yet, we are hanging by our eyelids, and, thanks to your kindness, in the queer position of having honey, cakes, and all

[1] Jess Young and George and Mary Dott were admirers of MacDiarmid; as were Dr Mary P. Ramsay, author of *Calvin and Art* (1938) and Bessie J. B. MacArthur (see p. 457).

sorts of dainties, at the very moment when we are threatened with the loss of the most basic essentials.

I have written to thank the Dotts and am writing tonight to Dr Ramsay and Mrs MacArthur. So excuse just a short letter of thanks to yourself. If all goes well – i.e. if the main difficulty is overcome or staves off – I'll have a very busy time ahead. I expect the young fellow[2] who is going to act as shorthand typist to me up here about the middle of the month. I am putting as much 'copy' as possible ready for him. If he is as competent as he sounds, and nothing unforeseen intervenes, a month's hard work will greatly change the whole position. I'll have at least two of the books done and off by the end of February, and fees from two American anthologies and payment for a magazine contribution (also American) should come in by, or before, then. After that it should be plain sailing for a long spell ahead, and, given that, I trust I may manage to avoid dangerous snags for the future.

We are all O.K., though Valda has of course been worrying dreadfully.

All good wishes for the season, and for a bright and happy New Year, to all at Dinnieduff.

Again with best thanks.

Yours,
Chris.

P.S. I'm not sure if you meant to enclose Nan Shepherd's[3] letter to you in the last copy of *The London Mercury* you sent me. But I fancy it was; and of course I'm writing her. That reminds me, too – I have a formal application to make – will you please grant me your kind permission to include two of your poems – 'Shy Geordie' and 'Sea Buckthorn' – in the anthology I've been making for MacMillan's.[4] And which I have now in final shape. It is possible a fee may be payable to the writers of copyright poems I wish to include; if so, it will be a small one of 10/6 or at most £1.1/- per poem, but I'll let you know about that later, or, if that is decided upon, you'll receive payment direct from MacMillan's. But I must have a formal note giving me your permission to include these two poems – a separate note, as I'll have to send all such requisite notes on to MacMillan's, to vouch for the right to use such copyright material as I've included.

2 Henry Grant Taylor
3 Dr Nan Shepherd contributed an article on 'The Poetry of Hugh McDiarmid' to *Aberdeen University Review* 26 (1938–9).
4 In his anthology *The Golden Treasury of Scottish Poetry* (London 1941) MacDiarmid included Helen Cruickshank's 'Shy Geordie' as item number LXXVIII.

EUL

My dear Helen,

In reply to your letter asking for details to send to Mr. Lynd[1] – whose kindly interest in this matter I greatly appreciate – my position is as follows:-

I have, in addition to poems, the following books in hand for the publishers named, viz.

1/ a discursive history of Scottish doctors and doctoring from the earliest times to the present – Messrs Harrap.

2/ a book on the Islands of Scotland – for Messrs Batsford's British Heritage series.

3/ a Golden Treasury of Scottish Poetry – for Messrs MacMillan.

4/ an autobiography – for Messrs Victor Gollancz.[2]

I had hoped to have finished at least two of these in time for publication last autumn or at latest this spring. I over-estimated my strength, however; since my serious illness in 1935 my productive powers have not got back to their old standard. Besides all of these books have proved much more difficult to do than I anticipated – the first two because they involved a tremendous amount of reading and getting the necessary books up here involves delay; the third because my plan for it involves my making good English verse translations of the principal Scottish Gaelic poems, also the chief poems of our Scottish Latin poets, and that is not the sort of thing one can do to timetable.

Ever since I came up here five years ago my plan has been to get the household necessities on account from the local shops – to run such accounts until I completed books – and once I delivered MSS to publishers and secured payment to square the accounts and start the process again – generally from zero, because the type of book I write does not yield big advances, and because I have found it progressively impossible to secure journalistic work to keep the pot boiling, and have become almost wholly dependent on writing books.

[1] Robert Lynd (1897–1849), Literary Editor of the *News Chronicle*, was a committee member of the Royal Literary Fund which was (at Helen Cruickshank's urging) considering making an award to MacDiarmid.

[2] The history of Scottish medicine never materialised in print. The other titles are *The Islands of Scotland* (London 1939), *The Golden Treasury of Scottish Poetry* (London 1940), *Lucky Poet* (London 1943).

Owing to the delay then in completing above books, my local accounts have run on considerably longer than usual and my creditors are naturally anxious and restive – though all along these accounts have been restricted to bare necessities. They now amount to about £50 in all, and my other debts amount to about £25 – a total of roughly £75.

The position now is – that though I have recently been able to get voluntary secretarial assistance (which cuts out typing costs – but is balanced by additions to household expenses to cover my typist's keep), these books cannot now be ready for Spring – though they are all sufficiently advanced to ensure that the typing, etc., will be completed in plenty of time for Autumn, provided no unexpected difficulties arise in the interval.

But the question is whether I can keep going here until I complete them, There is a definite danger of credit being cut off – or unpleasant pressure to pay accounts applied before I can hope to be in a position to do so. Besides the longer period means that by the time I actually do complete these books, my accounts will have mounted until they absorb practically all I have to come in, and leave me at zero again.

It is a very difficult position, and it would be impossible for us to live more economically anywhere than we are living here.

I should also add that Messrs Covici-Friede are going to publish a selection of my poems in America,[3] but that has been delayed for various reasons unconnected with myself, and I have not received the stipulated payment (which in any case is small) so far.

Please thank Mr Lynd and Donald Carswell and other friends on my behalf.

As always,

Yours,
Chris.

[3] This project was abandoned.

Whalsay,
Via Lerwick,
Shetland Islands.
2-5-38

My dear Helen,

Very many thanks for the sweep ticket. One never knows. I've had tickets in a lot of the sweeps but no luck so far. Still, it's a long spell of bad luck that has no turning. Here's hoping. I was interested to note that the figures which comprise the ticket number tot up to 13, which used to be my lucky number.

We are still hanging on, but things are, of course, very difficult. Still the RLF meeting, if it's mid-May as you thought in your last letter, isn't long now. In several letters you referred to a possible balance from the fund you were so kind as to get up not long ago, and said you would send this in April. But perhaps it did not pan out as you hoped. I hate to mention the matter to you, but naturally your own references to it have led to hopes with each post that it might turn up.

I am afraid I am a hopeless individual. I ought of course to have concentrated first and foremost on what would quickest bring in money – but I felt in the mood for poetry, and concentrated instead on finishing and getting off to T. S. Eliot a huge new poem, *Mature Art* (over 10,000 lines – i.e. 100,000 words – i.e. over three times as long as *Cencrastus*). Which is all very well but if it finds a publisher (no easy matter with a poem of that size – not to mention the difficulties due to the kind of poem, sentiments expressed, language and etc.) of course there is absolutely no money in it.

But one way or another, I'll get all my books finished and then we'll see. Inter alia I've been having steady bad luck – anthology fees and payment for definitely accepted articles from America which I expected months ago have not come in yet – an incredibly long delay – and even a big essay[1] (10,000 words) I sent Eliot for the *Criterion* a couple of months ago (and thought might save our bacon by bringing in an extremely useful cheque for about £15 to £20) I have not yet had any word about (I've just learned Eliot has been away and won't be back to business till the middle of this month).

It's a great business!

However, the weather's improving – we've all had heavy colds but have now thrown them off – and on the whole we are feeling fairly fit and a little more optimistic than can be accounted for by any other

---

[1] Evidently Eliot was unable to use this contribution in *The Criterion*.

tangible reason than just reaction after a long stormy winter to the fact that the sun is shining gloriously again.

Love to you all: and here's to that £30,000 when it comes. I'll fly to Ireland to collect it – and thence fly somewhere outside British jurisdiction – to avoid having to give the Government any of it, despite the fact that that isn't perhaps too kind a way of showing my gratitude to the Government official who put me in the way of the windfall.

> Yours,
> Chris.

EUL

> Whalsay,
> Via Lerwick,
> Shetland Islands.
> 21-5-38

My dear Helen,

I am abashed by the extremely generous award of the Royal Literary Fund. This will enable me to finish all the books I have presently in hand all right, and what I receive from them will carry me on into 1940 – by which time I hope my affairs may be on a more regular basis. I have formally expressed my grateful thanks to the RLF in sending receipt to their Secretary, Mr Marshall, but I would be very pleased if you could personally express my deep indebtedness to Mr G. W. Blackwood for his very kind and helpful interest in this matter, and, through him, to his brother, Mr J. H. Blackwood, whose good offices, I imagine, have been largely instrumental in securing this most generous award. At the moment of writing, my wife has only secured a portion of the £75 from one of the shopkeepers here; they do not keep much cash in hand as a rule and the cheque was too big for them to cash all at once! As soon, however, as she receives the balance, my wife will pay the outstanding accounts, and I will a little later send the receipted accounts on to you, so that you may be in a position to assure Mr Blackwood that the money was duly expended on the purposes for which it was sent. As to the remaining £50, I too am anxious that this should last out as long as possible, and that it should be paid to me at the rate of £5 per month will suit me admirably and carry me on nicely until I complete the commissioned books on which I am now engaged. With warmest thanks to yourself, and all concerned.

Yours,
Chris.

EUL

Whalsay,
via Lerwick,
Shetland Islands.
21-5-38

My dear Helen,

I am amazed too. I also had thought £50 the most that I could possibly expect. I agree that should the need arise it will be difficult to know where to look for any assistance in the future; but the need simply must not be allowed to arise. This at any rate will certainly tide me over all right until I finish the books I have in hand, and what I get for them will carry me on for another year at least after that. Surely something will turn up in that interval – i.e. by 1940 – which will give me some regular income. I am afraid my literary work will not yield that in the absence of some journalistic or other job, or some regular arrangement for contributions to some paper or periodical; since my own work must necessarily become less and less likely to be remunerative, and, besides, more and more difficult to get published and past the law, on political grounds. On the other hand, my American edition is, I have just heard, going forward all right – my influence is increasing in the quarters in which I most wish it to increase – I will have no difficulty in securing more commissions for books of divers kinds, whatever difficulty I may have in executing these commissions – so on the whole the outlook is fairly good, tho' it is difficult to see far ahead and I expect that we'll have a deuce of an upheaval in Great Britain within the next year or so and that it will be exceedingly difficult, if not utterly impossible, for people of my kind to survive that Terror.

However, you have stood by me like a Trojan and it is high time that I ceased to look to you for any further assistance in this way.

I am sorry you did not have a longer holiday but glad you enjoyed

124

the little break you did have, and hope you have come back to find things no more worrying than they need be and have a somewhat easier time in front of you than has been your lot for some time back.

I enclose a separate letter dealing with the matters raised – very properly and naturally – in your letter to hand yesterday.

I was very sorry to hear of Macgillivray's death – ripe old age (and very lonely and in many ways unhappy old age) tho' he had reached. If you happen to have a copy of *The Scotsman* or any other paper in which a good full account of his life and work appeared, I'd be glad if you could send it to me.

You will of course understand that Valda and I were slightly misled by the references to a possible small balance from your previous kind effort in your previous letters; but naturally of course this RLF award disnecessitates anything of that sort (even if there had been any such balance) and we are glad we do not need that now – and sorry the Dotts[1] and others are having a difficult time too.

Accept our very best thanks for your wonderful help.

Love to all at Dinnieduff from all here.

Yours,
Chris.

EUL   Whalsay,
                                                                Friday.
                                                                [1938]

My dear Helen,

I'm not being the least bit nasty when I say that I'm not surprised to receive your clip on the lug re the Muir cartoon.[1] I'd heard it had affected quite a number of people in the same way; I even had an official wigging about it from the Communist Party! I am not only wholly impenitent, but I am going to carry the whole matter a great deal further. If it were only – as it is in part – a personal matter I would drop it right away! If in so far as it involves literary, and political questions it turned upon the importance or unimportance

[1] George and Mary Dott, a couple friendly with both MacDiarmid and Helen Cruickshank.
[1] Barbara Niven's caricature of Edwin and Willa Muir – see Plate Section – appeared in *The Voice of Scotland*, Vol. 1, No 2, Sept-Nov 1938.

of the Muirs' differences from my own standpoint, again it wouldn't be worth carrying further – indeed it wouldn't have been worth starting. But it does involve so much more that I am going to carry the whole thing to the very limit – in *The Criterion*, in my Autobiography, in subsequent issues of *The Voice of Scotland* – even though it alienates every friend I have and redoubles my own literary difficulties.

Of course I'm dedicating Dìreadh to you.[2] The fact that it is partly in Gaelic, German and Provençal won't make it unintelligible to you (since I supply translations of all such foreign elements). I believe it is a good poem – even as a separate poem, tho' it certainly loses to some extent by being divorced from its context in the longer poem of which it is part, and in which it has an important role. I have already passed the proof of it and hope to have copies shortly.

I'm certainly not going to quarrel with you no matter what you say or do – and even if you do give me an occasional clip on the lug or even feel moved to deal me still more drastic correction (as I imagine my autobiography at least will make you want to), I feel fairly confident that you won't really quarrel with me either no matter what I do or say.

Many thanks for your papers, etc. I do not know whether you know I'm to be in Glasgow for the Power[3] dinner, so I'll be seeing you. I shouldn't think it likely he's to be given the Freedom of Glasgow (tho' he well might be – only I fancy we'd have heard more about that if it had been on the cards) but I know there's to be a Civic Reception to which I and some others are going.

To revert for a moment to the Muir caricature business, I would point out that any objection taken to that cartoon on the core of its exaggeration of Willa's or Edwin's physical attitudes etc. involves not only a complaint against this particular cartoon but a condemnation of the whole art of caricature, which has always depended very largely on the exaggeration and deformation etc. of physical characteristics. Next the two figures were – or were intended – to be *like* Edwin and Willa in the photographic likeness sense; but so far from having only a modicum of truth, the fact is (no matter how you may be disinclined to recognise or admit it) that the real grievance against the cartoon is precisely the devastating and unanswerable truth of the essential point it makes – Willa's overpowering presence which has always been a nuisance to friends of Edwin's.

All news when I see you then! I have had a very nasty bout of 'flu

---

2 'Dìreadh (1163–74) was published in *The Voice of Scotland*, Vol 1, No 3, December 1938 and reprinted as a limited edition of 20 copies (Dunfermline 1938). This letter was written before its first appearance.
3 William Power.

this past fortnight from which I am now emerging – but, alas, weak as a kitten. It is appalling how a touch of this sort can take it out of one. And at this juncture I need every ounce of strength I can possibly muster.

I'd a letter from Cathie[4] the other day saying Donald was to be in Scotland, and with the good news about his play too![5] I'm extremely glad about that. I'm very sorry Flos[6] is having such a hard time. I haven't had any word of Mary Ramsay for a long time. I don't know what Dr Orr is doing yet – I had a brief note from him after he left here, and had occasion to write him, but I haven't heard again – I understand he'd gone off for a hike in the Highlands somewhere, but he's bound to [be] back to civilisation again since then – at any rate it's rather late in the season for roaming the wilds.

I'm looking forward to seeing you again after this long while. I'm very sorry Musmé and Harrison[7] have been having a difficult time with illness again. Love from us all to your mother and yourself, and kindest regards to Mrs Wilson.

Yours,
Chris.

EUL
TS

February 1939
Whalsay.
Wednesday.

My dear Helen,

I'm so sorry you've been off with laryngitis (though if it wasn't too painful or troublesome I've no doubt a week in the house, away from the worries of office-work was good for you in some ways – even if accumulated arrears on your desk to return to rather undid any little benefit accruing from the enforced rest). In any case I hope you are all right again now, and not faced with too much work.

[4] Catherine Carswell, see p. 419.
[5] In 1938 Donald Carswell's play *Count Albany* was placed first in the Drama League final in Glasgow.
[6] Flos McNeill, see p. 498.
[7] Henry Scott Harrison, the artist-photographer, was married to the Japanese artist Musmé Watanabe.

This can only be a very short note – to respond without delay to the requests in your letter. Yes: I have your Cathie's Burns,[1] and will return it by next post. I've kept it an unconscionable time, but I wanted to have it handy for something I hoped I'd get to do – that has never turned up. However, I've made from it the notes I wanted and have these if the need arises.

As to *Cencrastus*, all I can say is that Cencrastus, the Curly Snake, is a Gaelic (or Scottish) version of the idea common to Indian and other mythologies that underlying Creation there is a great snake – and that its movements form the pattern of history. In my poem that snake represents not only an attempt to glimpse the underlying pattern of human history but identifies it with the evolution of human thought – the principle of change and the main factor in the revolutionary development of human consciousness, 'man's incredible variation', moving so intricately and swiftly that it is difficult to watch, and impossible to anticipate its next moves. The poem as a whole therefore is a poem of Homage to Consciousness – a paean to Creative Thought. In so far as it is specifically a Scottish poem, and concerned in particular to glorify the Gaelic element in our heritage (which I believe underlies our Scottish life and history in much the same way that consciousness underlies and informs the whole world of man) the doctrine it is filled with is, to quote Count Keyserling, that 'the real goal of progress is on the one hand a total lived experience of the whole of the real, and on the other hand such a deeply rooted fixation in order that, thanks to it, man can by the function of comprehension and by spiritual initiative working through it, make the entire universe his own', and, of course, in my poem – I being a Scot – that fixation is the Scottish genius, or Scottish role in history. Or in other words the subject of my poem is World Consciousness which I believe to be the great function and destiny of Man – a historic mission of humanity in relation to the Cosmos in which we Scots can play our part in so far as we have that sharp awareness of our own nature in which, as in a mirror, we can see natures other than our own. I believe that this pursuit of World Consciousness is the phase of mankind's development upon which we are now entering. Materially we have conquered the world; spiritually we have scarcely begun to do so. Our Love must balance our Knowledge – the Physical Sciences have so enormously outrun our sciences of ourselves as to create a perilous disequilibrium – the goal up to recently has been 'when man to man shall brithers be for a' that' – the Parliament of Man and Federation of the World. But that is not enough. Our unique gift as human beings is the power to

[1] Catherine Carswell, *Robert Burns* (1933).

think (the great function almost everybody has all along evaded) and it is only by a realization and acceptance of that that we can give our Love the necessary fullness and guidance. In Russian religious thought (e.g. in Soloviev) man's destiny is through his consciousness to reconcile the lower orders of creation – animals, plants, minerals – to St Sophia, the Wisdom of God, who is the female hypostasis of the Deity. My poem envisages that reconciliation (and insists upon the part Scotland should, can, and must play in that great task) in purely intellectual – i.e. non-mystical and non-religious terms; and from the point of view of this devlepment of my own thought, it would be correct to say that the various aspects in which I have seen the Serpent, in addition to or alongside those aspects of it with which I dealt in the poem, are
1) The Caledonian Antisy[zy]gy
2) The Dialectical Process
which are of course all one and the same thing. The poem then is a praise of the power of conscious understanding and of our intellectual weapons, Dialectical Analysis and the employment of the Creative Faculty in Literature, and the careful keeping bright and clean of our linguistic weapons and our powers of mental alertness, assimilation, criticism etc. – all from the Scottish angle, since, as a Scotsman, that is the angle which is part of my nature and which I cannot get away from but can only use or abuse.

That's a rough statement of the thing, but I hope it may be serviceable to you. What such a theme for a poem means of course is that it becomes an attempt to box the compass – to envisage as far as one possibly can all the complex strivings and developments of human thought, and then, having done that, attempt to anticipate the upshot of the whole business (i.e. to 'circumjack' – or enclose – the Serpent) by using those attributes of the poetic faculty which transcend rational processes and carry one into the realms of gnomic utterance and prophecy.

The clearest statements of the theme are perhaps the last 2 lines on p. 9 and first 5 on p. 10, or, the first 8 lines on p. 12. Or the bottom verse beginning 'Man's the reality . . . ' and the lines 11–14 on p. 191 beginning 'A' men's institutions' down to 'the theme o' my sang'.[2]

But the poem is like its theme, fell ill to circumjack in a quotable piece that gives anything of the real gist of it. I may have missed something better suited to your purpose than what I've suggested.

[2] MacDiarmid uses the pagination of the first edition (Edinburgh 1930): The references are to the sections beginning 'Freedom is *inconceivable*. The word/ Betrays the cause' (185–6); 'And that is a' that I'm concerned aboot' (187); 'Man's the reality that mak's/ A' things possible' (282); 'A men's institutions and maist men's thochts' (285).

For until this moment it's a long time since I've looked the poem over and I've nearly forgotten all the ins and outs of how it goes. It certainly seems very crude and immature and jerky and unsatisfactory compared with *Mature Art*, which of course deals with essentially the same theme but with a far greater range of reference, a far greater degree of intellectual thoroughness, and the use of entirely different resources of imagery.

I'll look forward too to the very feminine thing you've done about some of my stuff for *The Glasgow Herald*. Good luck to it.[3]

Please excuse this very hasty scrawl. Have been off colour for some days with a horrid dose of the cold – we've all had it and still, alas, have it to some extent. So I'm not able to think or write very clearly.

Love to you all from all of us.

Yours,
Chris.

P.S. If you get *The Criterion* let me know how you like the Cornish Heroic Song section there.[4]

Valda says she hasn't written you for Christmas yet! But she will soon. She's had a bad time with the cold and you'll understand.

EUL   Whalsay.
                                                         Saturday 14/9/40

My dear Helen,

It was good to hear from you again, and to have bundles of papers again. As time went on I was becoming perturbed as to what had happened to you. I expected you were very busy, of course. But wondered if you were ill – or if the changed conditions at Dinnieduff had changed your mode of life – or what. We did not know you'd been on holiday. The letter you think you sent us before going off must surely have been an unfulfilled intention; in any case it didn't

---

[3] In a letter of 18 January 1938 Cruickshank told MacDiarmid 'I scribbled a fairly-feminine note on a few of your poems for the women's page of *The Glasgow Herald*. If it appears I shall send a copy to Valda.'

[4] 'Cornish Heroic Song for Valda Trevlyn' was first published in *The Criterion*, Vol XVIII, No LXXI, January 1939.

reach us. However all's well that ends well. I am sorry to hear however about our old friend Barney. Your present to Michael I am going to leave him to thank you for himself. He's not much of a letter-writer yet alas, but it's time he learned to express the gratitude he is still a good deal better at feeling than at acknowledging. His aunts down in Cornwall send him things every now and again but too seldom – and then only most tardily – hear from him in return.

What ails myself if I was wondering about you that I couldn't speir? Well, of course, this war has knocked everything endwise, and I find it very difficult to write letters. And get few. My roll of correspondents has almost got to vanishing point. Apart from letters I'm busy enough. *The Golden Treasury* should be out any time now. MacMillan's have not intimated my definite date. As you will see from the introductory notes and other critical apparatus it has involved a great deal of work. Worst of all was the need to cut it down greatly – it only amounts now to less than 1/3rd of my original selection. Paper shortage and other factors made this inevitable of course.

I've good cause to hope that a volume of my Autobio. is to appear ere long after all. I had been afraid that the War had put an end to any hope of this for the duration. This despite the fact that several publishers were enthusiastic and declared that but for War-time conditions they'd have been keen to publish it – despite too the continuing eagerness of several American firms. But it's really been a most difficult affair – for political and other reasons – but chiefly because the final MSS ran to 500,000 words! What has happened now is that this has been split into several parts which will in due course form separate books. These parts may be termed the Private Person; a Poet and his Friends – and the Quintessential Me. The former two elements – i.e. all the private, personal, domestic, psychological confession part on the one hand, and practically all my reminiscences and impressions of other people on the other, have now been shorn away and reserved for subsequent volumes (and with these have gone all my accounts of Scottish Politics, the Renaissance Movement, etc.) and what is left is myself purely qua poet, and my views on poetry. The publisher who has suggested this division is extraordinarily taken with the whole huge thing; and I have had no hesitation in acting on his suggestions. I have now given final effect to these, and believe the matter will now go through O.K. This first volume as it stands is unquestionably by far the best thing I have ever written, and altogether a unique sort of book. All this chopping and changing has of course involved infinite labour – merely handling a ½ million word MSS, trying to see it as a

131

whole, and then resolve it effectively into several different volumes is a deuce of a job.

And I've no sooner got rid of it than I'm tackling another at least as big – a huge survey and analysis of the whole field of Scottish personality throughout the ages. And besides that I have a vast amount of poetry on the stocks, a history of Scottish doctors and doctoring, a book on the Faroe Islands and a biography of John Maclean.[1]

So I'm not idle.

We are all well, but it's too long since we saw any of our friends, and the War makes us anxious about many of them, of course. But that's all I'm going to say about the War; there's really nothing else I could say that would have any chance of passing the Censor and not involving me in trouble with the Authorities. But I have no doubt you can imagine my attitude or at least the direction in which it lies.

War-time conditions here of course mean (only my work keeps *me* from this) irrepressible dullness. I scarcely ever see anybody to speak to at all except Valda and Michael – and with the few I do see the conventional things about the weather are all I ever exchange; I never discuss the War in any shape or form. Valda hears the Radio news from one house or another and transmits it to me; apart from that – and the occasional arrival of newspapers and periodicals (which I value almost solely for the literary *news* – not views – and with which I have seldom a particle of political sympathy or even interest in the issues with which they are concerned) – I might almost as well be on the Mountains of the Moon. But in most ways it is suiting me fine all the same and I'm certainly far from downhearted.

Love and every kind regard from us all.

Yours,
Chris.

[1] The books on Scottish personality, the Faroe Islands, Scottish medicine and John Maclean never appeared.

27 Arundel Drive,
Battlefield,
Glasgow S.
Tuesday 21/12/43

Dear Helen

How long ago is it since I wrote you – or you wrote me? Ages ago, certainly. You have probably as little time nowadays for letter-writing as I have – and that is next to nil. I have indeed practically no time or energy for anything at all except my engineering, which involves over and above the 47 hour week, a great deal of overtime and Sunday work. Work and sleep is practically all I can do – my reading is principally thrillers: all I am fit for in the hour or two after I come home and before I go to bed, and it has to be a jolly good thriller if I do not fall asleep over it at that. Valda is almost equally hard-pressed at her job, and the Christmas rush has been overtaxing her with overtime too. What a life! And yet both of us are fine and fit, and have been so ever since we came South except for occasional colds, touches of 'flu, etc. Michael, who has just arrived for his Christmas holidays, is a big boy now, sturdy and full of beans. What of yourself? Last I heard of you you were up to the eyes too in overwork at the office. I do not suppose that has abated – if it has in some ways, probably in others it has increased. I hope you are in good health and spirits nonetheless. I have scarcely encountered any mutual friends this last year or more – Flos MacNeill I had a talk with at an SNP Council meeting; Mary Ramsay I saw a couple of times in my first year here – but now I am almost finishing my second: and have not seen her this year at all. Nor does my mailbag yield me much, or in fact any, news of mutual friends – I hardly ever encounter or hear from any of my older acquaintances among the Scottish literati. F. G. Scott and I attended Willie Soutar's funeral. I was sorry to see no other Scot-tish authors there, except J. B. Salmond, Wm. Montgomery, George Bruce, and Alex. Galloway; the laurel wreath was sent, not by the Scottish PEN, but by John Middleton Murry. But perhaps I do wrong to blame either the PEN or Scottish authors generally – circumstances may not have permitted; in these difficult days it is not easy for anyone to get about much or keep up their peace-time interests.

I have contrived to do a bit of speaking, however – for the Glasgow University Poetry Society, the Scottish National Party etc. – and have been twice or thrice in Edinburgh actually – attending meetings of the SNP Council – but these were only flying visits, and were a case of going straight from work to the train, attending the meetings, and catching the last train back the same night.

I have always been very grateful however for the bundles of Times Lits., etc. you continued to send – as of course new orders are not taken for these, so I could not have procured them here, and not have the Times Lits. would be a sad loss to me.

But try if you can and write us a line and give us your news. This is just a hasty note to wish you all the compliments of the season, and every good luck in the New Year. Valda and Mike join in this, of course, with.

Yours as always,
Chris.

To William Soutar

The first important poet on whom MacDiarmid exerted a powerful influence was William Soutar (1898–1943) whose appalling predicament as a bedfast invalid for the last thirteen years of his life has been movingly recounted in Alexander Scott's biography *Still Life* (1958) and Soutar's own *Diaries of a Dying Man* (1954), edited by Alexander Scott. Soutar was an active young man who passed out of Perth Academy into the navy in 1916 then contracted an illness which, after an unsuccessful operation in 1930, permanently confined him to bed in his room of the family home at Wilson Street, Perth. Soutar, who was never given to public displays of self-pity, summed up his situation poignantly in his poem 'Autobiography':

> Out of the darkness of the womb
> Into a bed, into a room:
> Out of a garden into a town,
> And to a country, and up and down
> The earth; the touch of women and men
> And back into a garden again:
> Into a garden; into a room;
> Into a bed and into a tomb;
> And the darkness of the world's womb.

Soutar began his poetic career as a writer of juvenilia in English, poems collected in *Gleanings by an Undergraduate* (1923). While on holiday in Montrose in 1922 he twice (on 18 and 27 July) met C. M. Grieve who was about to launch *The Scottish Chapbook* and thus unleash Hugh MacDiarmid on to the world. The two poets quickly became friends and Grieve accepted Soutar's 'The Quest' for publication in the first number of *The Scottish Chapbook* (August 1922). On 20 September 1923, prompted by MacDiarmid's Scots poems in *The Scottish Chapbook*, Soutar wrote three poems 'in the Doric'. He greeted the publication of *Sangschaw* with the comment 'Good work, Christopher, my lad – but the big things which Scotsmen have yet to do in literature must be done in English.' Soutar was to change his mind radically on the subject. Just nine days after recording his rather dismissive opinion of *Sangschaw*, Soutar wrote 'Cock-Crow' which celebrates the coming of a saviour: 'His cronnie chaunticleer,/Wha blaws the bugill o' oor King/To lat the hale warld ken He's here'.

Penny Wheep did not impress Soutar as much as *Sangschaw* and he was, initially, so appalled at MacDiarmid's linguistic electicism in *A Drunk Man Looks at the Thistle* that he wrote a humorous rejoinder 'The Thistle Looks at a Drunk Man':

> Wi' booze o' a' guffs he wud droon
> That honest Doric, as a loon,
> He throve on in a bonnie Toun
> Whaur fowk still speak
> Nae hash o' German, Slav, Walloon
> An' bastard Greek.

Yet before long Soutar felt a Wordsworthian 'Bliss was it in that dawn to be alive' euphoria about the renaissance initiated by MacDiarmid. He was too magnanimous a man to continue to protest in the presence of what was clearly genius and became convinced that MacDiarmid had solved the Scottish language problem by combining the rhythm of oral Scots with the richness of literary Scots (as preserved in Jamieson's dictionary). In 1931 Soutar told MacDiarmid 'if the Doric is to come back alive, it will come first on a cock-horse'. His method of achieving a seminal impact on the Scottish people was to issue his *Seeds of the Wind* (1933), his first book of poems in Scots. By appealing primarily to children Soutar produced fresh, vivid verse. In 1935 his *Poems in Scots* appeared and it is on this volume that his reputation mainly rests. The most substantial poem in the collection is 'The Auld Tree' which was composed between June 1929 and October 1931 and dedicated to MacDiarmid. It gives a glowing verbal picture of a reborn Scotland whose prophets are a great patriot and two great poets: Wallace, Burns and MacDiarmid who makes a dramatic appearance towards the end of the poem:

> I heard a fitterin' fit; and turn'd
> And saw a man wha's twa e'en burn'd
> Wi' byspale glamer like he sklent
> On routhie years time yet maun tent.
> Word-drucken was he, but his words
> As the rambusteous lilt o' birds
> Wauken'd the thistle; and for lang
> I harkint while he sang his sang:
> But wi' his words I winna mell
> Sin he has screed them a' himsel'.

136

16 Links Avenue,
Montrose.
June 8th 1922.

Wm. Soutar, Esq.
Dear Sir:-

I am obliged to my good friend Kerr[1] for acting as the inter-
mediary through whom I am introduced to you and your promising
work. Of the three poems you send me (if, uninvited, I may presume,
not to criticise, but to jot down my impression) 'To the Holy Spirit' is
the most interesting and 'Amphitrite' the most finished. But in the
first of these you seem to be reaching out towards forms of expression
which I should be thrilled to see you master. The verses are unequal
– not, I mean, in form, but in quality of ideation and beauty of
utterance. Do not think me merely captious if I hint that God is none
the more divine for being chaired? *Oneness of concept, within the chosen
form whatever that may be, is an essential of great poetry, I think*. 'Nature
aching out her breath in the autumn rain' is more than a little forced.
I do not like the last line, 'Or silent, as the tired eyes' pray'. But the
four lines beginning 'Teach mine eyes' are the Real Thing.
'Amphitrite' is on a more commonplace level than 'To the H.S.' –
as is not unnatural since even the title is 1/3rd 'trite'. but of its sort it
is more than passing good – save the last three lines! It is in climax,
the magic of accumulation and triumph at the end, that you fail most
in these three. 'The Quest'[2] is slight – but I like it immensely, save
the last two lines.
But take courage, my friend! Whatever the faults of these verses
may be, the number of folk in Scotland today capable of writing as
good let alone better is very limited indeed: and it is something, is it
not, almost at first shot to come into the first half-hundred of
contemporaries in your country. I hope you will cultivate your gifts
assiduously. I shall certainly be greatly disappointed if splendid
work does not come from your pen. Your work has a bigness to begin
with, an originality of technique, a stature of conception, which
augurs most well.
As to *Northern Numbers* I am afraid that for a variety of reasons I
cannot invite further contributions to the Third Series to be published this autumn than I have already provided for – but the

---

[1] Roderick Watson Kerr (1893–1960) succeeded C. M. Grieve as editor of the
Broughton Magazine (1910–11), published his war poems in *War Daubs* (1919), and
founded the Porpoise Press in 1923.
[2] 'The Quest' was included in the first issue of *The Scottish Chapbook*, Vol 1, No 1,
August 1922.

venture is to be continued annually and I shall hope to induce you to join us yet.

But I have another matter in hand. Enclosed circular will explain.[3] The response to my appeal has been so far excellent but not yet quite adequte. But subscriptions continue to come in and I hope shortly to have the requisite number to enable me to launch this venture in August. Scotland is today almost the only country in Europe that lacks a periodical devoted to its distinctive culture, arts and letters. The majority of the contributors to *Northern Numbers* with some 30 or 40 other Scottish writers are associated with me in this enterprise. The emphasis here will be on experimental work – new forms – new ideas – new writers. I should be glad to have you as an occasional contributor to this. The standard will be as high as the available material permits – and the available material will be at least fully representative of the best Scotland is capable of today.

I am hoping that the men at the various Universities in Scotland will support this venture – both by subscriptions and by contributions. I am anxious to get into touch if possible with every young Scottish writer of any use at all. Banded together we can surely make a creditable display on behalf of this, at present, artistically moribund old country of ours. Don't you think so?

If you don't mind I'll keep hold of these three poems in the meantime. If you do anything to push the *Chapbook* I'll be most glad. In any case I hope you'll keep in touch with me and show me more of your work from time to time as you write it. If I can be of service to you at any time I shall be only too happy.

Believe me.

Faithfully yours,
C. M. Grieve.

NLS

16 Links Avenue,
Montrose.
6/12/22

My dear Soutar,

Sorry to have been so abominably slow in writing. Am including your 'Invocation', 'The Slayer', and 'Daphne' in fothcoming *North-*

[3] Grieve sent Soutar notice of his new monthly, *The Scottish Chapbook*.

ern Numbers[1] which I hope to have out just before Christmas. I hope this meets with your approval.

What about the Edinburgh University Supplement idea?[2] Are you going to give me someting special for that? If you see Kerr[3] tell him I am impatiently awaiting some contribution from him to the *Chapbook*, will you? I hope he hasn't been completely sucked under in the journalistic maelstrom.

By the way, I am also giving that Christmas poem of yours in the December *Chapbook*[4].

How do you like the *Chapbook* so far? I would like to have your views.

Mrs G. (who sends her kindest regards herewith) and I are hoping you are to keep that promise of yours: and give us a day or two here about Christmas time. Please notify compliance at your earliest convenience.

Excuse short note. Hope you are having luck all along the line. Every good wish.

Yours,
Grieve

NLS

16 Links Avenue,
Montrose.
Tuesday 7th August [1923]

My dear Soutar,

Everybody is on holiday bar me. I envy you chaps your carefree life – Malloch down in Cornwall, Jeffrey in Paris, Alasdair Alpin

[1] Grieve published, in January 1923, the third and final issue of *Northern Numbers* from 16 Links Avenue, Montrose (as the Edinburgh publisher T. N. Foulis was unable to bring the annual out due to economic difficulties). It included Soutar's 'Invocation', 'The Slayer', 'Daphne'.
[2] In *The Scottish Chapbook*, Vol 1, No 7, February 1923, editor Grieve ran a Supplement on Edinburgh University Verse, 1922–23. The issue included Soutar's 'Autumn', 'The Street', 'Ointment'.
[3] Roderick Watson Kerr.
[4] *The Scottish Chapbook*, Vol 1, No 5, December 1922, included Soutar's 'Christmas Eve'.

MacGregor in the Hebrides,[1] yourself in Orkney, Mrs Grieve for a month at Pitlochry and then another on the Borders – I could prolong the list indefinitely. I think I'll resign and go to Timbuctoo or Glasgow!

Excuse this pencil scrawl. Your June *Chapbook* (which contained your cosmic observations in re your prospective cadaver)[2] should be lying for you at your Edinburgh 'digs'. I'm sending another today to your hyperborean croft.

No sign yet of the public beginning to recognise my unquestionable genius. *Annals* has not sold enough to pay the binding – I never expected it would. But I'm not disappointed – it has appealed all right to the people I hoped it would interest and amuse.

Glad you liked the July *Chapbook*.

Am worried over the *Scottish Nation* – a stiff proposition to run in one's spare time apart from any difficulties other than literary. I'm having a job to keep it above water. But the Lord sparing me *I will*.

Hope you are in good fettle.

Always glad to hear from you. Any time you can possibly include Montrose in any of your comings and goings please do. Both Mrs G. and I will always be more than glad to see you.

Love,
Chris.

NLS   16 Links Avenue,
                                                Montrose.
                                              18th Nov. 1923

My dear Soutar,

Why this long silence?

You likes *that*! do you? Well I can't help it. I only write letters 'in deeficulty' – particularly to my best friends. I was delighted to receive the Doric triolets – splendid stuff. I hope you'll do more along

[1] George Reston Malloch, William Jeffrey and Alasdair Alpin MacGregor were (like Soutar) poets MacDiarmid regarded as part of the Scottish Literary Renaissance.
[2] *The Scottish Chapbook*, Vol 1, No 11, June 1923, contained 'Death' and 'Address To My Dead Body' by Soutar.

similar lines. John Buchan is compiling a Scots Anthology – Vernacular stuff only – and I sent him your triolets along with other stuff in response to a request from him for good stuff which he mightn't have seen.

Under what pseudonym if any does stuff of yours if any appear in *Scots University Verse 1918–1923.*[1]

And apart from all that *what* are you doing – and when are we to have you for that weekend. Soon I hope. The sooner the better. I'm getting anxious about you & Mrs G. has been in a chronic state of anxiety for a long time now – ever since you sent that photo in fact.

I say it flatters you. She says it doesn't but on the contrary——.

So there's nothing for it to preserve the peace of this household but to come down so that we can decide.

Write soon in any case and give me the news. How's Kerr and the Porpoise Press?

Writing's a deuce of a job – talking's so infinitely easier – Give me the chance.

Love from both (and the dog whom you've yet to meet).

Yours,
C. M. G.

NLS   Royal Liver Building,
                                                Liverpool.
                                                10/3/31

My dear Soutar,

I was delighted to get the page-proofs of our poems and since then two advance copies (one of which I have sent on to my wife) of the book and would have written you ere this thereanent and replied to your long and interesting letter but for the fact that I have been caught up in a special spate of work – and still am. Writing publicity articles for home, colonial and foreign papers of all kinds on abbatoirs, shipping services, hardware exports, and what not. But I can delay no longer.

[1] *Scottish University Verses 1918–1923: An Anthology of Verse from the University Magazines of Scotland* (1923), introduced by Neil Munro, contained nothing by Soutar.

First of all my heartiest congratulations.[1] I do not think the contents are by any means all of the same quality: but there is none I'd definitely wish omitted for the enhancement of the better ones. I am delighted with much that is in them and with the general development of your faculty. 'The Thoughts of God' is unquestionably a very fine poem and the best in the collection, but greatly though I admire it and would hope for further work of the same kind from you, do not imagine that I am insensible to beauties of very other kinds to its which are to be found on almost every other page. I am not going to attempt to 'distinguish and divide' here. I have done that in some degree in two articles[2] I have sent out – one to the Glasgow *Record* (tho' it is more likely to appear in the Glasgow *Evening News* perhaps) and the other to the *Scottish Educational Journal*. I'll get a review off to the *Scots Independent* in a day or two: and have asked to be allowed to do it also in *The Modern Scot*. (Whyte, the Editor, is seeing me here on Monday: and I'll mention it again). All good luck to the book; may it give you such a measure of recognition as will help to ensure the publication through the Porpoise Press or otherwise of the other stuff you have by you and encourage you to further efforts. I'll look forward eagerly to seeing how it is reviewed in various quarters. (Not that reviews matter much, of course. I hear that there's a 'bad one' – the phrase a correspondent uses – of *Cencrastus* in *The Adelphi*[3]: but I haven't seen it and have so secure – and adequately critical – a view of my own work and so complete an indifference to say the least of it for *The Adelphi* and most of the other English Literary organs that it won't worry me however condemnatory it may be. I say hard enough things about all sorts of people – and Middleton Murry and I had a very vicious set-to a year or two ago – and they're welcome to treat me in the same way. It'll all come out in the wash.)

As to what to say about Scots nursery rhymes, etc.[4] I agree that there is a very great deal in what you say but I think you are confusing two things – in both of which I am keenly interested: but

[1] Soutar's second book, *Conflict*, was published by Chapman and Hall, London, in 1931.

[2] In *Still Life* (Edinburgh 1958, p. 51) Alexander Scott noted that '*Conflict* was well received by the press ... while the Scottish newspapers, led by C. M. Grieve with a full-page review in *The Daily Record*, were almost rhapsodic.'

[3] Orgill Mackenzie's review of *To Circumjack Cencrastus* appeared on pp. 523–6 of *The Adelphi*, Vol 1, No 6, March 1931 with an inquisitive conclusion: 'That there is this fire in *Cencrastus* is certain. That is what angers one. Mr M'Diarmid is a poet, but has he not loaded his Pegasus so heavily with guidebooks to the stars that it amounts to cruelty to animals?'

[4] Soutar had written to MacDiarmid giving his opinion that 'if the Doric is to come back alive, it will come first on a cock-horse.'

on very different planes. Any revival of Scots among the people at large, in the schools, etc. has my strong support and I think that a re-vaccination of the children with it such as you suggest an excellent idea – but when I write or speak about a revival of Scots I am usually not thinking about that but about its effective resumption into literary practice and adaptation to the most modern expressive requirements. This latter is not necessary related to – let alone dependent upon – the former at all. If great poetry is written in any language it does not matter a hoot whether nobody can read it except the man who wrote it; that does not affect its quality: and I am not prepared to concede that the artist should be concerned with his audience or that art must subserve any social or other purpose except its own development. So far as I am personally concerned I am quite clear that I am not now nor likely to become – whatever potentialities I may have had in the past – the man to write these bairn-rhymes or repopularise Scots. I think you are wrong in your preference for *Sangschaw* and your description of my last two books as farragoes (or farragi or whatever the plural is) – tho' I myself described the *Drunk Man* as a gallimaufry. As a matter of fact it is far from that and is very closely knit throughout – much more so than *Cencrastus*. But in both cases I think you are misled by external appearance – the way I have put them together – while a very great part of the contents of both can be readily extracted as separate lyrics. I am quite sure that many people who have written or spoken to me along the same lines would have received a very different impression of both if this had been done. But in any case I cannot go back upon my tracks and, au contraire, am busy now with an immense work – a sort of Scots *Faust* – in which the general current of the whole will be tremendously stronger, the lyrical interludes relatively few and far between, the subjective eschewed for the objective and dramatic. . . .

But it's no use my going on like this, (giving – with characteristic egoism – three quarters of my letter to my own stuff and the fourth quarter to yours). I must dree my ain weird.

I haven't a photo by me at the moment but will get hold of one of you ere long. I was glad to receive that of Finlayson's drawing of yourself.

As to Branford[5] it is indeed a tragedy that he should have fallen on silence. I should immensely have like to meet him. Kerr is under the impression that his mentality has given way: he is supposed to be

---

[5] Frederick Victor Branford's collection of poems, *The White Stallion* (1924), impressed MacDiarmid who discussed it in *The Scottish Educational Journal* of 25 September 1925: 'Branford, however serious his inequalities, is unmistakably a major poet.' (Contemporary, p. 40).

somewhere on the Continent. The last I definitely heard of him (a year or two ago) he was with D. H. Lawrence at Capri but I've had no sure news since.

Every good wish.

Yours,
C. M. Grieve.

NLS
TS

321 High Holborn,
London, WC1
19th October, 1931.

William Soutar, Esq.,
27 Wilson Street,
Cragie,
Perth,
Scotland.

My dear Soutar,

Just a line to acknowledge safe receipt of 'The Auld Tree'[1]. It has just come in and I will read it and write about it to you in a day or so and then send it on to St Andrews as requested.

I am enclosing with this note a copy of a card we are issuing in connection with my new book[2] and have duly put your name down for a signed copy at (as you will see) £2.2.0. I think you will like the get up of the book which is by the best binder in London and has a half-binding of niger morocco with very attractive black and white modernist design for the boards. The poems in this book are all separable short items from *Clann Albann*[3], but that monster work will not be ready for a long time yet. I am hoping perhaps to get the first volume of it some time in the Spring, but there will be other four

[1] 'The Auld Tree' is Soutar's poetic vision of a reborn Scotland whose prophets are a great patriot and two great poets: Wallace, Burns and MacDiarmid. It appeared in *The Modern Scot*, Vol III, No 1, April 1932 and, with the dedication to MacDiarmid, in Soutar's *Poems in Scots* (1935).

[2] *First Hymn to Lenin and Other Poems* (London 1931). There was a limited edition of 450 numbered copies and a special large paper edition of 50 copies numbered and signed by the author.

[3] *Clann Albann* is MacDiarmid's projected and never-completed five-volume auto-biography in verse.

volumes each much bigger than *Cencrastus* to follow and consequently the whole cannot possibly be published until some time in 1932. In any case as you will be seeing from the papers shortly present conditions are (or rather have been) retarding my writing of it. It will take a little time after a domestic upheaval of that sort to get down again to a proper working basis.

I am sorry *Conflict* did not sell better, but publishing poetry is a desperate gamble. The main thing is that you should keep on writing it and find an outlet for some of it, as you have been doing hitherto, in *Adelphi* and other periodicals.

I hope you are keeping fairly well yourself. I note what you say about the Benn selection[4] but the difficulties were insuperable. You will have seen the announcements of the new miscellany of hitherto unpublished poems collected by Lascelles Abercrombie.[5] There are forty-seven poets represented, but so far as I can see I am the only Scottish one, with the exception of Lord Alfred Douglas. I expect the collection will be a pretty mixed lot, but I think there will be some interesting things in it.

With regard to the photograph you will have to wait a little while longer. My affairs are in chaos and I have not yet had my books and papers, etc., removed from home and brought down to my own flat, but I will not forget and will let you have a photo as soon as I can.

All the best to yourself,

Yours sincerely,
C. M. Grieve.

---

4 *Living Scottish Poets* (London 1931), edited by C. M. Grieve, was one of Benn's Augustan Books of Poetry.
5 *New English Poems: A Miscellany of Contemporary Verse Never Before Published* (London 1931), edited by Lascelles Abercrombie, contained (pp. 246–7) 'Charisma and My Relatives' and (pp. 248–50) 'To Lenin', footnoted as 'From "Clann Albann", a work in progress.'

NLS

321 High Holborn,
London, WC1.
26/2/32

My dear Soutar,

I ought to have written you long ago but for one thing expected 'The Auld Tree'[1] in last issue of *M.S.* and for another – as you may imagine – have been up to the neck in worries of all sorts. I wish I had time at the moment to write you at greater length – instead of being able to do little more than merely return your typescript – but if I once begin discussing the poem I'll not know when to finish. I appreciate its merits and am glad Whyte is going to publish it, but my own poetic is so radically different and my feeling about Scots so peculiar that I am probably not the best but the worst man to pass judgment on it. I do feel, that on the whole I have been in regard to Scots a thoroughly bad influence on you and others and that my own practice in regard to the synthetic business is so purely individual and inimitable that it justifies in my case alone – so far – what in other cases simply clutters up the verse with unvivified and useless words. But that of course is just being prejudiced in favour of my own work and methods.

However, all good luck to you.

Yours,
C.M.G.

P.S. My 'Second Hymn to Lenin' – about 300 lines – is appearing in the June *Criterion*.[2]

[1] 'The Auld Tree' appeared, without the dedication to MacDiarmid, in *The Modern Scot*, Vol III, No 1, April 1932, pp. 14–24.

[2] 'Second Hymn to Lenin' appeared in *The Criterion*, Vol XI, No XLV, July 1932, pp. 593–8.

Whalsay,
Shetland Islands,
Wednesday.
[5 July 1933]

My dear Soutar,

Many thanks for *Seeds In The Wind*[1] and your note. I hope – and believe – the former will help to bring about the overdue harvest of a new Scots poetry; some of the poems are not seeds but the genuine flower and fruit complete. I like especially 'Tam Tench', 'The Three Puddocks', 'Aince Upon A Day', 'The Gowden Ba', and 'Ae Summer's Day' – but above all 'Tam Tench', when it appeared in the *Free Man* I asked Black to tell you how much I liked it – it has a splendid gratuitousness. I also mentioned it to F. G. Scott, who had been taken with some of your work in various quarters. He spoke of setting some of them. Have you been in touch with him? In any case I'm going to put you, because (to save me the labour of writing it all out again) I'm going to ask you to send on to him once you've read it (F. G. Scott, 44 Munro Road, Jordanhill, Glasgow) the enclosed poem[2] which I solicit permission to dedicate to you. Let me know what you think of it. I hope *Seeds In The Wind* is getting the good reviews it deserves – so far I've only seen the Glasgow *Evening News* one – and is going well. Congratulations and every good wish to it and you.

As to Montgomery's[3] I hadn't seen it when you wrote me but some time after got a loan of it from Helen Cruickshank. I didn't write you or him partly because most of it was a kind of poetry for which (unlike most folk) I have no use and partly because it seemed to me too minor and derivative to give any indication as to what might or might not be his promise. He has obviously not found himself yet.

---

[1] Soutar's third collection, *Seeds in the Wind*, was published by Grant and Murray, Edinburgh, in 1933; a revised and enlarged edition (London 1943) and an illustrated edition (London 1948) subsequently appeared.

[2] MacDiarmid's poem 'Tam o' the Wilds and the Many-Faced Mystery' (368–79), which was published in *Scottish Scene* (1934), is dedicated to Soutar. The narrative leads up to a tribute to Soutar:

> I had written this and I suddenly thocht
> O' ane withdrawn frae the common life o' men
> Shut awa' frae the warld in a sick-room for aye,
> Yet livin' in what a wonderfu' world even then
> – The pure world o' the spirit; less kent
> To nearly a'body than Tam's interests even,
> And I saw in his sangs the variety o' creation
> Promise in a new airt mair than a' he was leavin'.

[3] William Montgomerie's *Via* (1933), his first collection of poems.

But from small pointers here and there I fancy he will – and that he has certainly something to find that is well worth having. But I did not feel that I knew him or his background well enough to warrant comment at this juncture. I shall, however, look forward with hope to his next volume.

As to myself, I am still in the Shetlands and mean to remain here over the winter if I possibly can. These almost uninhabited islands and lonely seas suit me splendidly: and I'm glad to be away from political movements, newspapers, and all the the rest of it for a while. Besides I have a heavy tale of work in hand for which this is an ideal atmosphere. In the interstices of leading the simple life of an island fisherman I have been able already to write more poetry than all my previously published stuff put together. The little pieces that have appeared here and there are not samples. On the contrary most of the stuff consists of poems too long for periodicals and I am satisfied is not only up to my best level but represents in several cases valuable new departures. I am hoping that a first volume of this may be out this autumn over the title *Stony Limits: and Other Poems*. It will consist of over fifty poems – nine or ten of which are as long as 'Tam of the Wilds', which I propose to include because it is quite unlike most of the others, unlike in theme, tone and technique and so helps to give that impression of variety which is one of the things I want. But most of the others are 'difficult' – indeed the title poem, and another long one, are in synthetic English – not Scots; I'm hoping that both these two will appear first in *The Criterion*; 'Stony Limits' is an in memoriam poem to Charles Doughty and the other an in memoriam poem to Rainer Maria Rilke. I'm also busy with my Autobiography of a Scots Poet. So I am not idle and enjoying life immensely – out with the herring fishers and all the rest of it.

Kindest regards to you all.

Yours,
C.M. Grieve.

P.S. I'm expecting Grierson[4] up here next week – his sister is wife of the laird to whom this island and some of the others belong.

---

[4] Herbert Grierson (1866–1960) was born in Lerwick.

Whalsay,
Shetland.
Tuesday. 20.2.34

My dear Soutar,

I was delighted to hear from you.

Your article[1] comes very near the bone and I agree with [it] entirely as a short description of the situation – taking your opening remarks on intellectualism as meaning factitious intellectualism, intellectualist posing, as distinct from intellect; poetry can never to my mind be over-intellectual and it is not the difficulty of poetry (or modernist poetry of the past) that comes between it and the people; it is mis-education and the debauching of the public mind by certain great interests – the public could readily appreciate far more erudite, elusive and esoteric poetry than our modern stuff in Elizabethan times, in ancient Greece, in still more ancient India and so on, and in Gaelic Ireland! Nor – though I know what you are striving at and essentially agree with you – would I use quite the same terms in certain other places; your linking-together, for example, of orthodox economics and endrocinal philosophy for the latter is a modern thing, with very other affiliations than orthodox economics with their 'sound' associations with 'Christian idealism', their historic relationship to the reformation, etc. But these are petty debating points: and only mean that I should be very glad to follow your article with another distributing the emphasis rather differently from my communist-nationalist standpoint. I hope the *Scots Observer* agrees; I believe they've gone down to a smaller size, and will therefore have less space. I'll send them an article following on yours immediately if they give me the word.

I am devilishly busy – busier lately (and likely to be for some time) than ever before in my life – and am trying to get my decks cleared a little as I expect to go to London early next month for a still busier time there. I sent some particulars to the *Free Man*[2] about new Scottish books – they may be in last week's which I don't get till tomorrow – but the gist so far as I am concerned is that Lewis Grassic Gibbon and I have a big book[3] coming out through Jarrold's; and I myself have a volume of essays[4] via Stanley Nott, and a

---

[1] Possibly a draft of Soutar's article 'The Poetry of MacDiarmid' which appeared in *The Free Man*, Vol III, No 10, 7 April 1934, pp. 8–9.

[2] 'Recent Books', *The Free Man*, Vol III, No 4, 24 February 1934.

[3] *Scottish Scene, or The Intelligent Man's Guide to Albyn* (London 1934) by Lewis Grassic Gibbon and Hugh MacDiarmid.

[4] *At the Sign of the Thistle: a Collection of Essays* (London 1934).

big volume of new poems via Victor Gollancz[5] – my biggest book, I think. Some of these poems, I think, show me approaching a solution of the problems which, as you say, I have been confronting. Perhaps you have seen my 'Genethliacon For the New World Order' in *New Atlantis*,[6] for example. But I think the best is a very long poem which has not appeared anywhere before: 'On A Raised Beach'. I hope to carry the whole business a good deal further with another big volume I have promised to have ready for autumn publication (and in the throes of writing which I am now labouring) – *Forty Songs* (Stanley Nott Ltd).

What of yourself? I see few papers – not even the *S. Observer* except when I've something in it – and do not know where you are appearing nowadays. No word of a new collection? You must have any amount of stuff. What is Montgomerie doing? Drop me a line now and again. Every kind regard to your mother, father, and sister; and to your nainsel!

Ever,
C.M.G.

NLS

Whalsay,
Shetland Islands.
12/3/34

My dear Soutar,

Very many thanks for your card and the copy of your epigrams[1]: These make a very attractive little book and I think one well worth putting out – there are certainly a number of these epigrams which express big ideas very effectively in the smallest compass and which, later on, should have their place in your Selected Poems. My only regret is that at least a proportion of them are not in Scots. I am feeling more strongly than ever the importance of carrying the use of Scots much further than we have already managed to do, and am all set for some intensive work in this direction as soon as I get through

[5] *Stony Limits and Other Poems* (London 1934).
[6] *The New Atlantis*, Vol I, No 2, January 1934, pp. 88–9.
[1] *Brief Words: One Hundred Epigrams* was published by The Moray Press, Edinburgh, in 1935.

my present programme – which, alas, is in arrears as I have been able to do little or nothing for about three weeks as a consequence of nervous and mental prostration following a severe chill. Most of the books I am busy on – a big book on *Scottish Eccentrics*, a biographical study of the Wolfe of Badenoch, a study of Scottish politics from the Communist angle – are or seem (though all on the lines of my general Scottish propaganda) little better than hackwork to one anxious to devote himself more to other forms of writing. But needs must, and in the meantime Poetry has had to take a back seat – apart from my translations of leading Gaelic poems, of which the Birlinn[2] in last issue of the *Modern Scot* was a sample. These latter I think are extremely useful and the Birlinn has certainly produced an astonishing crop of congratulations. The other afore-mentioned books are all due for delivery to the publishers now but I cannot finish them for a week or two yet owing to this untimely interruption of my activities. Once these are off my hands I will, if all goes well, have a month or two clear for my real Muse.

The lack of media nowadays I find a terrible nuisance. *The Free Man, New Britain, Scots Observer* in all going down the chute have practically shut up all my journalistic outlets. The new *Scottish Standard* seems to me perfectly hopeless but tho' superficially we seem in many ways worse off that we have been at any time since the old *Chapbook* and *Scottish Nation* days I think the leaven is working away steadily and surely enough – and in some very astonishing and important quarters. Otherwise why should I be asked all at once 1/ to speak at Manchester University on the new Scottish movement 2/ to allow someone to quote poems of mine in an article on Mac-Diarmid and Rilke which is to appear in the magazine of the London City Institute, and 3/ to send a poem to the magazine of the Oxford English Association. And these are only three straws taken at random showing in what far separated places the propaganda is asserting itself.

Things may, temporarily, be becoming more difficult for us in Scotland itself; they are steadily becoming easier outside Scotland. If the cessation of various periodicals has deprived me of journalistic outlets it must be having a like effect upon you. I see few papers or periodicals here; where are you appearing nowadays – apart from the *Educational Journal* in which I see you figuring every now and again? I hope at all events that you are working away steadily and have other books in the making.

Kindest regards to all of you. I'd like to have another peep in to see

[2] 'The Birlinn of Clanranald' by Alasdair MacMhaighstir Alasdair, translated from the Scots Gaelic by Hugh MacDiarmid, in *The Modern Scot*, Vol 5, No 4, January 1935, pp. 230–47.

you; we'll see how things go – I hope to go to Manchester early in May, and will then be in Glasgow for a few days (inter alia to get my eyes seen to) - so I might possibly then get a chance of visiting Perth. I'll certainly take advantage of any possible chance.

All the best

Yours,
C.M.G.

P.S. Regards to Montgomerie should you be seeing him.

NLS

Whalsay,
The Shetland Islands.
22/10/35

My dear Soutar,

Sorry to have been so long in assuring you of my safe acccomplishment of my long journey. This delay has been due to a painful and lamentably disabling accident I have incurred to my right arm. This is somewhat better, and I am again able to write. The accident had nothing to do with the essential illness which enhospitalled me at Gilgal;[1] despite the worst sea-tossing in my experience on my way home, and despite appalling weather conditions here which make the land almost indistinguishable from the sea, there has been no relapse in *that* and I think I have cleared the worst hurdle in my chequered career. Having you, and the opportunity of occasionally visiting your home, meant a great deal to me at Gilgal, and I am exceedingly grateful to you and your mother and father for the hospitality and kindness you gave me.

I was delighted to see your two poems in *New Scotland No I*;[2] my article therein was an old one sent in to *The Free Man* Black had by him – I did not know he was using it, or the poem either. It was, I thought, a deplorably weak No I, full of wretched printers' errors,

[1] Gilgal, a detached block of the Murray Royal Hospital, Perth, was opened in 1930 and intended for voluntary patients seeking psychiatric help. MacDiarmid spent seven weeks at Gilgal following his breakdown of 1935.

[2] *New Scotland*, Vol 1, No 1, 12 October 1935, printed 'The Happy Vennel' and 'The Murderer' by Soutar; and MacDiarmid's poem 'The Covenanters' (551).

beastly irrelevant snippets, and that abominable Naturopath stuff. It *could* – and should – have been so much better if only Black had taken pains to get decent fighting stuff from the folk able to supply it instead of rushing in where angels might well fear to tread with a sublime – or at least unearthly – reliance on his own incompetence. I am very anxious about the future development of the paper and will do my best to get it on better lines; alas! I am so out-of-the-way up here.

I hear from a chap Hendry[3] in Glasgow that he is shortly bringing out a new Scottish magazine, weekly or fortnightly. His letter indicated that he has the right militant hang of things. He wrote asking my help, and I've replied promising all the help I can possibly give.

My *Scottish Eccentrics* and *Red Scotland* have been postponed publication till January but my *Second Hymn to Lenin, and Other Poems* is just out.

Excuse this short letter at the moment; I've a devil of a lot more urgently requiring to be done than I can possibly tackle in the meantime. However, keep going as strong as you can – I'll be on the keen look-out for all you do.

Love to all of you.

Yours,
Chris.

NLS   Whalsay,
                                                                   Friday.
                                                               [13.12.35]

My dear Soutar,

Forgive me for being so long in acknowledging your poems in Scots, and the dedication of 'The Auld Tree'. I have been busier than I yet have the strength to be and cannot keep up to things in my jockeying between spells of desperate energy and the succeeding troughs of the waves in which I have to subside. It is a fine little

---

[3] J. F. Hendry (born 1912), Scottish poet and anthologist.

book[1] and a splendid contribution to Scots poetry – tho' I feel that your grip of, or dealings with, Scots so far only furnishes little poems of special interest at the present moment but does not token a comprehensive or radical grasp of it enough to essay the great tasks before it; that is to say that the latter require a different approach to the language, not only in degree but in kind. I feel this especially since I have been compelled to thoroughly reconsider my own whole position in regard to the language since my return here – as a preliminary towards far greater efforts in it than any I have already made. I do not know if you've seen Power's *Literature and Oatmeal* (if not you ought to – it's a splendid little book and, I think, far and away the best thing Power has done) but if you have you may have noticed what he says of me – viz. my non-realisation or only partial realization of my original declared purpose with the language. I agree with him – in that point. And I propose now to resume my task where I let that bigger task slide in order to accomplish what I have in the meantime accomplished. In other words, I am now addressing myself to epic in Scots and I hope that in this great venture I will have you with me – exploring the potentialities of Scots (a) in relation to major forms, (b) with an eye on the very greatest poetic achievements in other tongues, and (c) with a full view of the present and prospective conditions of poetry in a world perspective. You have made a splendid beginning. Go ahead!

I agree with you that we have reached a point where things are going to be, not easier, but far more difficult. A reason for, not discouragement but renewed and entire determination. The cessation of *The Modern Scot* is going to make it virtually impossible to secure periodical publication of Scots poems of any considerable length; and there is nothing on the horizon to take its place. *Alba Nuadh*[2] is worse than useless from this (and perhaps from any) point of view; and I scarcely think *The Scottish Bookman* will give us space enough to turn in – let alone to effect any real revolution in. Hendry[3] is projecting another Scottish magazine, but his infernal doggerel in *Alba Nuadh* gives me no hope that it will provide a platform for any first class work. However, we'll see. Perhaps we can break effectively into English organs – the December *London Mercury* is almost a Scottish issue, with 3 poems by me, an article on the Scottish Movement by Power, a review of Power's book by Malloch, etc.[4]

[1] William Soutar, *Poems in Scots* (1935).
[2] *Alba Nuadh/New Scotland*, a periodical incorporating *The Free Man*, contained several contributions by MacDiarmid in 1936.
[3] J. F. Hendry, the Scottish poet.
[4] *The London Mercury*, Vol XXXIII, No 194, December 1935, contained three poems – 'Veuchen' (1304), 'Glasgow, 1960' (1039), 'Larking Dallier' (1096–7)

The first photograph – taken in Carlisle in autumn 1892 – of Christopher Murray Grieve with his parents Elizabeth and James Grieve.

James Grieve, the poet's father, was a rural postman in Langholm. He died in 1911, at the age of forty-seven, from pneumonia.

The Post Office and Library Buildings, Langholm, in 1895. The Grieve family moved to a house on street level behind the post office where James Grieve was employed. Christopher Grieve had constant access to the library and used to fill a big washing-basket with books to be brought downstairs for long reading sessions.

Christopher Murray Grieve, second from left in back row, at a Sunday School picnic to Burnfoot, Eskdalemuir, in 1905. Grieve was a member of Langholm South United Free Church whose minister, Rev. Thomas Scott Cairncross, encouraged the literary talents of the young Sunday School teacher.

George Ogilvie (1871–1934), mentor to Christopher Murray Grieve. In 1904 Ogilvie was appointed Principal Teacher of English at Broughton Pupil Teacher Centre, Edinburgh. Grieve arrived at Broughton on 2 September 1908 and became Ogilvie's most promising pupil. When he left Broughton to embark on a career as a journalist, Grieve soon made contact with Ogilvie who was the recipient of some of the most revealing letters written by the poet.

c/o J. W. Storey,
55 Harcourt Street,
Ebbw Vale, Mon.
S. Wales.

—day. (Friday, I
think, or Saturday).

Dear Mr. Ogilvie:—

It's one in the
morning and I've just
transcribed my last sheaf of
notes.

I don't know why I feel
that I must write to you now
or never. I have tried to do
it a dozen times.

I will never return
to Edinburgh — to stay at all
events. Probably I'll never see
you again, but I feel that
you understand better than
anybody else I know — that you
will be glad to know that
it is all right, that I have
at last emerged from chaos
— from the hurricane of

of mental and moral anarchy
which has tossed me hither
and thither these last twelve
months.

I am in a good position,
earning good money, working
fifteen or sixteen hours
a day.

And I look back to you
as I look back to my dead
father, to my mother and one
or two others.

Enclosed you will
find a cutting — which perhaps
may interest Mr. Ross more than
you. I should be glad if you
would return it, as it is the
only copy I possess.

Yours Sincerely,
Christopher
Grieve.

P.S. Please let us keep up
a correspondence.

The first letter from Christopher Grieve to George Ogilvie, written in October 1911. In his postscript Grieve writes, "Please let us keep up a correspondence."

Grieve with his mother in Forfar in 1916, prior to his departure to Salonika where he served as a sergeant in the R.A.M.C. during the First World War. Elizabeth Grieve died in 1934.

Edwin Muir, Francis George Scott (with his eldest son George) and MacDiarmid in Montrose in 1924. Edwin and Willa Muir were then living in the High Street where Willa's mother had a shop. Scott, who taught Grieve at Langholm Academy, encouraged the poet when he was working on *A Drunk Man Looks at the Thistle*, the masterpiece he composed in Montrose.

William Lamb's bronze bust of MacDiarmid was sculpted in Montrose in 1925, when the poet was working on *A Drunk Man Looks at the Thistle*.

Peggy Grieve and Christine Grieve at 16 Links Avenue, Montrose. The poet married Peggy Skinner, in Edinburgh, on 13 June 1918 and the couple settled in 16 Links Avenue on 17 March 1922; their first child, Christine, was born on 6 September 1924.

On 23 June 1928 the National Party of Scotland was inaugurated at Stirling. MacDiarmid (*third from right*) was one of the founders and here he is seen with (*from left to right*) the Duke of Montrose, Compton Mackenzie, R.B. Cunninghame Graham, James Valentine and John MacCormick.

When MacDiarmid returned to Scotland in 1931, Helen B. Cruickshank held a party for the poet at her home in Corstorphine, Edinburgh. The photograph shows (*from left to right*) Mrs Cruickshank, MacDiarmid, Ann MacDiarmid, John Rafferty, Mrs Thomas Henderson, Professor Otto Schlapp, F. Marion McNeill, N. Jamieson, John Tonge, Peter Taylor, J.H. Whyte, W.D. MacColl, Helen B. Cruickshank, William Burt and (*in front*) Nannie K. Wells.

When Count Cedric de Montalk was imprisoned for publishing obscene literature in 1932 he asked MacDiarmid to look after his cottage, 'Cootes', at Thakeham in Sussex.
The photograph shows MacDiarmid revisiting 'Cootes' in 1974.

MacDiarmid and his second wife Valda (Trevlyn) – seen here with their son Michael, born 1932 – settled on the little Shetland island of Whalsay in 1933 and remained there until 1941. It was a time of severe economic hardship but also of great creative effort resulting in such poems as 'On a Raised Beach' in which the poet insists, "We must reconcile ourselves to the stones, Not the stones to us."

In 1933 MacDiarmid was a candidate in Aberdeen University's Rectorial Election and the photographs show him (1) addressing students in the university (2) taking the air in Aberdeen. The election was won by Rt Hon Walter E. Elliott, MP, with 307 votes; MacDiarmid came third with 158 votes.

MacDiarmid visited the Faroes in July/August 1933. Here he watches a football match; the men beside him wear the traditional dress of the Faroes.

In September 1935 MacDiarmid sustained a nervous breakdown and Francis George Scott arranged for him to be admitted to Murray Royal Hospital, Perth, so that he could receive expert treatment. After seven weeks the poet was able to return to Whalsay and is seen on board the Leith-to-Lerwick steamer.

In the summer of 1937 W.R. Aitken, subsequently the co-editor of MacDiarmid's *Complete Poems 1920–1976* (1978), visited the poet in Whalsay and took these photographs which show

(1) Valda, Michael and Christopher Grieve
(2) MacDiarmid
(3) Valda carrying fish, with Michael following

WILLA AND EDWIN.

Barbara Niven's cartoon of Willie and Edwin Muir. See MacDiarmid's letter of 1938 to Helen Cruickshank.

A bearded MacDiarmid in Whalsay in the summer of 1939.

In 1941 MacDiarmid was conscripted for National Service and reported to Glasgow. After completing a six-month government training course he qualified as a precision fitter and worked in the copper shell band department of Meechan's Engineering Company, Scotsoun, Glasgow. While at Meechan's MacDiarmid became friendly with Charles Nicoll, the engineer who took these photographs. The poet was badly injured when a stack of copper-cuttings fell on him and lacerated both his legs.

In 1950 the Duke of Hamilton offered the poet a house adjacent to his Lanarkshire mansion of Dungavel, near Strathaven. Shortly afterwards the National Coal Board bought the estate to establish a School for Miners; MacDiarmid then moved (in 1951) to Brownsbank Cottage.

In May 1957 MacDiarmid visited China with the British-Chinese Friendship Society. Here he is seen meeting Kuo-mo-jo, the Chinese poet and cultural leader.

MacDiarmid at Dungavel showing sleight of hand. In 'The Glass of Pure Water' he writes:
   Look at the ridge of skin between your thumb and forefinger.
   Look at the delicate lines on it and how they change
   – How many different things they can express –
   As you move out or close in your forefinger and thumb.

MacDiarmid speaking in Peking at
a gathering in honour of the poets Blake
and Longfellow.

MacDiarmid received an honorary LL.D. from
Edinburgh University on 5 July 1957 and is
here being capped by Sir Edward Appleton,
Principal of the University, at the McEwan
Hall, Edinburgh.

On 18 February 1961 MacDiarmid and Sir
Herbert Read took part in a rally, in
London's Trafalgar Square, to launch the
Committee of 100's civil disobedience campaign
against nuclear weapons.

MacDiarmid, seated beside Lady Russell, applauds as Bertrand Russell – instigator of the Committee of 100 – prepares to address the crowd in Trafalgar Square.

MacDiarmid, in Edinburgh in 1963, with Alan Bold, editor of *The Letters of Hugh MacDiarmid*. MacDiarmid subsequently wrote an introduction for Bold's first collection of poems, *Society Inebrious*.

Aba Bayevsky working, in Toronto in 1964, on his portrait of MacDiarmid: 'He works with great rapidity and assurance. It is a big painting of me, sprawled in an arm chair, and complete with kilt, sporran, tunic etc.' (MacDiarmid to William Johnstone, 22 June 1964).

Ezra Pound was one of the principal poetic influences on MacDiarmid who admired the American's radical manner and multilingual mode. In the autumn of 1971 MacDiarmid visited Pound at his home in Venice. The two poets had lunch together then walked in St Mark's Square.

MacDiarmid beside the Esk in his native Langholm.

One of the last letters written by MacDiarmid. MacDiarmid writes to Mary Macdonald (Fionn Mac Colla's widow): "I am terribly sorry, but I stupidly overestimated my strength when I wrote to you last."

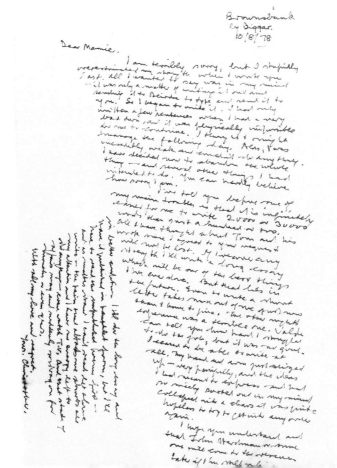

The last photographic record of MacDiarmid, taken on his 86th birthday – 11 August 1978 – at Brownsbank Cottage. MacDiarmid is seen, first, with his wife Valda (and the two dogs Tara and Clootie), and then, regarding the future philosophically, alone.

And so far as I am concerned I am putting all my affairs – journalism as well as books – into the hands of a first-class literary agent and in particular planning to put myself across in the American periodicals, while Barker Fairley – the Doughty man – is introducing me to Canada. I have no fewer than twenty new books – prose and poetry – on the cards and am devising my time-table to write them as and when my agent fixes contracts.

All this may sound (and of course is) very egotistic – but my object in jotting it all down here for your edification is simply as a way of saying 'Go thou, and do likewise'. I feel we who are interested in Scotland, Scots, and the Renaissance idea must all now redouble our efforts. We can make it – if we will.

Excuse more at the moment. If you haven't read Anne Treneer's *C. M. Doughty* (Cape) and Barker Fairley's *Selections From Doughty's Dawn in Britain* (Duckworth) may I strongly urge you to. I'll lend you them if you like. I expect to have an essay on them in next *Modern Scot*[5] and, a little later, 2 or 3 consecutive articles on Doughty in *The New English Weekly*. I am convinced that he is our line to take.

Now I've a lot of other long letters to write for tomorrow's mail, so must stop. Write me whenever you can and let me know what your plans and ideas are. Love and every good wish to your mother, father, sister, and your ain sel!

Yours,
Chris.

NLS

Whalsay.
16/12/35

My dear Soutar:-

It is all very well to remind me that the belly keeps up the back – but your splendid parcel of 'goodies' suggests that you think we here

– by MacDiarmid. William Power's article on 'The Literary Movement', in the same issue, described MacDiarmid as 'a man of undoubted genius and of consuming energy [who] ranks today with men like T. S. Eliot and Ezra Pound.' George Reston Malloch reviewed Power's *Literature and Oatmeal*.

[5] MacDiarmid's article 'Charles Doughty and the Need for Heroic Poetry' appeared in *The Modern Scot*, Vol 6, No 4, January 1936.

are dromedaries. Not so. Our backs are modest enough in size that the festive season is all too apt to finish by giving us the hump. And it is perhaps fortunate that in these latitudes we observe not only Christmas and New Year but Old Yule, etc., and so the orgy continues with us for nearly four weeks. In these circumstances the savouring of 'Himself' may well be held over until 25th January; all the other delectable items however are doomed to a very brief existence. Accept our warmest thanks.

I agree with what you say of the Epic – time and eternity; but so far as the linguistic medium and the question of proletarian literature is concerned I am not going to accuse you of petty bourgeois misconceptions of the latter, but simply suggest that you have missed the significance of the developments of minority languages and literatures in the USSR, and the relation of these developments to the whole Communist scheme of things. My poem will be planned to be an epic within the terms of your definition; it will – as you suspect – be wholly modernist in subject-matter (in *essential* subject-matter – tho' the actual framework or 'plot' is historical and legendary) and it will be in super-synthetic Scots. God help us all!

Every kind regard and good wish to you all.

Yours,
C. M. Grieve.

P.S. Mike was very thrilled with his 'stocking'.

NLS   Whalsay.
                                                              21/12/36

My dear Soutar,

I was glad to see Neil Gunn's short review of *A Handful of Earth*[1], tho' I detest the preciosity of Gunn's style. I was delighted to have the book itself, but sorry on the whole it wasn't in Scots. Muir's sabotage of our work – and all that Scots means – was an infernally dirty bit of work.[2] I was glad to see your effective little thrust at him.

[1] In his review of *A Handful of Earth* (1936) in *Outlook*, Vol 1, No 9, December 1936, Gunn called Soutar 'one of the two or three outstanding writers in Scotland today.'
[2] Edwin Muir, *Scott and Scotland* (1936).

I have of course broken completely with him and Whyte and the *Outlook*. Whyte and Muir were responsible for preventing the publication of *Red Scotland* – but it will come out yet and in greatly strengthened form. Thanks to Muir's influence in other ways I have been held up and frustrated but that will only be temporary. I have a very big programme of work in hand. But, apart from such difficulties as these, I have had to go much slower recently than I had hoped to do, for health reasons. I must not overdo it. I would be delighted to have a chance of visiting Perth again – but not, I hope, as a patient in Gilgal.

I hope you are in good form yourself. I think both of us this next year must take up Muir's challenge in no uncertain fashion and do big scale stuff in Scots. Others who seemed to be tending to reinforce us – like Hood, for example – have fallen away; so that if at all possible you and I must make redoubled efforts.

Please give my kindest greetings to your father, mother, and sister. I trust this finds them all fine and fit. My wife joins me in every good wish to you all for a happy Christmas and a prosperous New Year.

       Yours ever,
       C. M. Grieve.

NLS   Whalsay.
                                          31.5.37

My dear Soutar,

I've been desperately busy since I came back or would have written you sooner – and incidentally returned *Goodbye, Twilight*[1] which I like very well and would like to see a Scottish counterpart of. (Thanks, too, by the way for returning Gogarty.) I don't think I mentioned to you when I saw you – tho' I have had it in my head for a long time now – an idea in which I was going to suggest you and I might collaborate. A book of 400 or thereby lyrics (lyrics = short poems in this connection, not necessarily songs) – title *The Commons of Scotland* – the poems to be in Scots and for most part, to average 12 to 20 lines. The idea is that this collection should constitute a

---

[1] (Ed) Leslie H. Daiken, *Goody-bye twilight: songs of the struggle in Ireland* (1936).

comprehensive celebration of Scottish working class life, past and present (with the emphasis, i.e. the bulk of the pieces, definitely contemporary; and all from a strongly radical and republican angle). The poems, as I conceive the collection, would fall into two or three definite catagories:-

i.e.

1/ Purely political and militantly propagandist, such as tributes to Keir Hardie, John Maclean, John Murdoch, Thomas Muir, etc.

2/ Historical – dealing with crucial incidents and turning-points in the evolution of Scottish Democracy.

3/ Industrial and Agricultural – poems on all the most significant operations of human labour in Scotland, i.e. the building of the 'Queen Mary', a big casting in a Steel Works, a Pit Disaster, a Strike, the Crofters' agitation, a Land Raid, the Highland Clearances, and the whole host of such traditional ploys as 'Peat Casting', 'Out With The Herring Fishers', 'Building a Dry Stone Dyke', and (carrying on the tradition of the Gaelic labour songs, 'Cloth Waulking', etc.).

4/ Portraits of outstanding types of Scottish workers, a la (somewhat) Tennyson's 'Northern Farmer' or – better example of what I mean – Gerard Manley Hopkins's 'Felix Randal', about the death of a farrier, 'big-boned and hardy-handsome'.

It will not answer to my purpose unless about 70 per cent of the pieces are definitely urban and industrial as against 30 per cent rural: and the endeavour should be to distribute the subjects in such a way that all the main aspects of Scottish industrial and agricultural life are covered. The poems would have to be as straightforward and uncomplicated by linguistic, idealogical, and technical difficulty as possible – except in so far as a thorough use of Scots may be deemed to constitute a language difficulty. But what I mean is that it would be necessary to cut out purely intellectualist pyrotechnics and super clevernesses of any sort. The ideal – apart from a considerably greater use of Scots than we find on their lips nowadays – is the direct conversational sort of poem, that is not only readily intelligible to the workers themselves, but might almost have been written by them – so authentically capturing both the tone of their voices and their psychology. Also, there would have to be no defeatism – no turning back to the past but even where past events or habits of work are the themes, always a constructive and confident and forward-looking spirit – and, of course, whenever the subject allows, a definitely militant attitude. The Scottish Nationalist or anti-English or anti-Imperialist element would, of course, come in incidentally as it does in life, but would not be over-emphasized or definitely 'featured'.

Let me know what you think of this. I hope you may see your way to come in with me and try to realise the idea. I thought we could do about half the poems each. That would mean writing between 200 and 300 each – to allow a sufficient number of discards, because not good enough or not fitting well enough into a scheme of the book as a whole. We'd have to be very frank about each other's efforts. I thought I'd draw up a provisional list of contents and send this on to you – next week if possible. Then you could return it with comments, additions, etc. Then as each of us accumulated a good body of verse, we could send it to each other, and exchange detailed criticisms and suggestions. And in this way build up the whole thing.

I'm very much in a poetry-writing mood just now, but I cannot give any idea at the moment how rapidly I might be able to get them done, as I have several big undertakings in hand and must give most of my time and thought to them until I get them cleared out of the way. But when I'm in the mood I'm a pretty rapid worker – for example this past week I have written a volume of poems about as big as my *Stony Limits*, and am today sending it off to the publishers. That, of course, was just because I happened to strike a good vein and went at it hammer and tongs practically day and night continuously. But *The Commons of Scotland* is not a rush job anyhow; the main thing is to do it thoroughly well and embrace all the essential elements, I thought that – if you can see your way to joint in – we might (since it is always well to have a sort of time table to work to) hope to do it by the end of the year, and thus have it ready for publication in the spring. That all depends of course on what sort of progress we make since poetry can scarcely be written to order and poems turned out at so many per day like certain other products. It's a big job but I think tremendously worth doing. Let's!

However, let me know how the idea strikes you.

Kindest regards to your father, mother, and sister. I hope they are all well.

Love to yourself.

Yours,
C.M.G.

My dear Soutar,

Many thanks indeed for Haarhoff's lectures on Afrikaans.[1] I had seen reviews of it and noted it as a book to be got hold of, and indeed it is very good and much of it is equally applicable to the case for Scots. I wish in fact I – or preferably someone else with a more orderly mind and powers of more concise and concentrated expression than I have – yourself, for instance – would do a similar little book on the cause of Scots. But, later on, I think I'll probably do as you suggest and try to get an article in the Afrikaans quarterly, *Ous Eie Bock*. It's all very well Tommy Holland[2] almost wishing 'that Afrikaans could be made a compulsory part of the degree course in English literature'; it would say more for him if he showed some little concern to give Scots its due place at Edinburgh University.

I was greatly interested in what you said about Miss Monro's play[3] and wish I had heard it. I don't listen to it. I am afraid it'll be some little time yet before I 'revive you with something' either in prose or verse – tho' I have plenty of both in store. But, in the meantime, I am about to favour you with the sound of my voice again – broadcasting from Aberdeen on 16th inst. on 'The Shetlands and The Faroes: A Literary Comparison'.[4] I'm going on for a day or two to Edinburgh and Glasgow (I wish I could drop in and see you); but I want to get back here as quickly as I possibly can. I am in the throes of writing all sorts of books – so the autumn should see me flourishing again in the publishers' lists. And once I get them finished, I'm going to settle down to a long spell of Scots poetry in earnest. The immediate jobs include a big book on *The Islands of Scotland*, another (sort of companion volume to my Eccentrics), a discursive history of doctors and doctoring in Scotland from the earliest times to the present; and – if you please – nothing less momentous than my Autobiography. So I have my hands full. Happily I'm in fairly good form, but it's been a very difficult winter and both the first mentioned books have involved an enormous amount of reading which has had to be done before I could do much

[1] Theodore Johannes Haarhoff, *Afrikaans: Its origins and development* (1936).
[2] Sir Henry Thomas Holland (1868–1947) was Principal and Vice-Chancellor of Edinburgh University from 1929 to 1944.
[3] 'Greenside', Margaret T. Monro's historical play in six scenes, was broadcast on the BBC Scottish Programme on 19 March 1937.
[4] 'The Shetlands and the Faroes: A literary comparison', by C. M. Grieve, was broadcast on the BBC Scottish Programme on 16 April 1937.

actual writing. And I have also been working away at my monumental *A Cornish Heroic Song*, which is now I think about five times as
long as *Circumjack* and not yet completed.

What of yourself? I hope you too are busy and that we'll be seeing
the results ere long. It *is* a darned nuisance not having things like the
Modern Scot, Scots Observer, Outlook or anything to keep us in touch
from time to time with what each other is doing.

Love to your mother, father, and sister. I hope they are all fit and
fine.

And every kind regard to yourself from all here.

Yours,
Chris.

P.S. I can't promise anything definitely – but if possible I'll try to
break my journey either going or coming, and have a look at you in
Perth. Expect a stalwart **Highlander** in full war-paint.[5]

NLS   Whalsay,
2-8-37

My dear Soutar,

Though, being extremely busy, I didn't (as I should have done)
write again I was very anxious following your p.c. as to your eyes.
Your letter now – though you say nothing of them – seems to indicate
that all is well again in that quarter. I fervently hope so. And that in
every other respect you are in as good form as may be.

I read your letter with great interest. But I do not know that we
need to go into all this question of vicariousness – of responsibility for

---

[5] In his diary for 17 April 1937 Soutar noted 'About 3.30 C. M. G. came striding in,
resplendent in full Highland rig-out. He had been celebrating his descent upon
the South – but hadn't reached the blethering stage, so we had a hearty time, with
much loud laughter. He had a number of MSS with him and read part of his *Red
Scotland*, which sounded quite convincing. As he read, he supported himself at an
angle over my table, and the angle increased with the reading until he was literally
dropping cigarette-ash and dialectical materialism all about me. I thought it
might relieve the congestion if he removed his plaid – but discovered that it was
part of the regalia.' William Soutar, *Diaries of a Dying Man* (Edinburgh 1954),
edited by Alexander Scott, p. 111.

– at all. It is certainly not good Communism to dream of a state when everybody will come to their own perfect self-expression. Poets will always be rare birds and may – and indeed must – not hesitate to write and in so doing to undertake the responsibility of self-electing themselves (or being elected by their exceptional faculties) as the mouthpieces of their peoples. In any case the question does not arise just now; we are far from an achieved Communist State; we need not hesitate – indeed, it is our duty – to work towards it in our particular art any more than a Lenin or any other leader need hesitate to lead – and lead for – the masses. There is, or may be, a difference between writing *as if* the people wrote themselves, and the people actually making their own poems. The difference is likely to be in all respects enormously in favour of the former. That is what I propose – trying to do; i.e. as the aim to set ourselves. Even if we fall far short of it, we may yet be amply justified – not only relatively but absolutely.

I made my suggestion because the law of averages renders it highly unlikely that two such poets as we are will occur simultaneously in Scotland very often – either under Captalism or under Socialism. And it seemed to me that by some systematic comprehensive effort as I outlined we could best pull our weight and serve – if only as forerunners and to some extent models – for the more truly pro-letarian poets to come – the great causes we have at heart. In any case I consider it highly unlikely that any more integrally proletarian a voice than my own will be heard in Scottish poetry at all. So, for my part, I propose to go ahead with the scheme as outlined on my own; if – short of joining in with me as I suggested – you find you can do a poem or two suitable for such a collection I'll be very glad later on to have them.

One thing: I haven't time to go into it just now, but, though I suggested for this collection poems for the most part of a simple and straightforward sort (i.e. at least verbally) I do not agree at all with any plea of greater simplicity of expression, let alone subject-matter and idea, nor do I believe that that will be the course Poetry takes under achieved Communism – tho' it may have to for a while under the Dictatorship of the Proletariat and before the withering away of the State. Only for this particular collection I suggested poems that in language and substance should be so within the comprehension and sympathetic to the spirit of the Scottish working class that readers of that class might conceivably feel that they could almost have written them themselves.... But even that I qualified by insisting that they should be written in Scots.

However, I'll go ahead; we'll see what I turn out and later on we may rediscuss the matter on that basis.

I enclose a Canadian paper containing a poem of mine.[1]
All the best – and to your mother, father, and sister – from all here.

Yours,
Chris.

NLS   Whalsay,
                                          via Lerwick,
                                          Shetland Islands.
                                          1-12-37

My dear Soutar,

Very many thanks for your card and the copy of *Riddles in Scots*[1].
Many of them are delightfully turned and I have enjoyed going
through them. My little boy isn't quite at the stage when he can deal
with little mental problems of this kind, but he will enjoy them later
on all right. Surely there should be quite a decent demand for a book
of this sort even as things are. In a slightly healthier state of Scottish
affairs, of course, both it and your *Seeds in the Wind* should have been
taken up in schools all over Scotland. They are much better pabulum
for our young idea than the sort of stuff the schools are dishing up to
them. I hope at any rate you secure enough response to constitute
some reward.

I'm still up to the eyebrows in my own infernal muddle of multiple
composition, and finding it very difficult going indeed. Heaven only
knows what is to become of us all. The prospects are certainly bleak
and forbidding beyond parallel. And the mere idea of contemplating
the sort of works upon which I am engaged – let alone the further
enormity of expecting them, as I must, to yield me a livelihood – is
undoubtedly a species of singularly wild insanity.

I hope you – and your household – are all in good fettle. We are all
well enough here despite the extremely cold dull and depressing
weather which encompasses us and is likely, with little or no relief, to
continue to do so for another three or four months. If I succeed in the
interval in getting anything actually printed (and it is so long ago

---

[1] *The Canadian Forum*, Vol XVII, No 198, July 1937 contained 'The Glass of Pure
Water' (1041-3).
[1] Soutar's *Riddles in Scots* (1937).

now since I did that it seems almost beyond hope) I'll send you a copy. But I really seem nowadays only to be getting more and more deeply bogged in interminable enterprises of an extreme impracticality. And that in itself would not, of course, daunt my intrepid spirit very much were it not for the damnable obtrusiveness of the mere ways and means problem. But it is really very difficult to forge ahead to any effect when one's mind is divided between poetic and other works of a not remunerative kind and the acute pressure of the genial creditors upon whom one is dependent for the basic necessities of life. I live in the cheerful frame of mind of one who, probably just on the verge of writing really great poetry, incongruously finds the question of the continuance of even a minimal dietary thrust under his nose, and knows that it is futile to expect any consideration whatever on the strength of a possibly improved position discovering itself by some miracle once the great work is actually finished, and perhaps even published!!!

Wae's me! What a cheery letter! 'The troubles that afflict the just in number many be.' The only consolation – which really butters no parsnips – is that I could scarcely have so many troubles if I were not very specially and most excruciatingly just.

All the best.

Yours,
Chris.

NLS

Whalsay,
via Lerwick,
Shetland Islands.
23-12-37

My dear Soutar,

Many thanks for your card and letter and good wishes which my wife and I heartily reciprocate in regard to all at 'Inglelowe'. It is too good of you to threaten to jazz up our diet in this way. I do not know that lack of variety in food was really responsible for the unwonted melancholia of my mood when I wrote you last; I am afraid I had deeper worries. Since then other friends, like yourself, with a very welcome, though unflattering, reference of my troubles to my tummy, have come to the rescue with a range of Christmas fare of all kinds which has ensured for a good while ahead an adequate, not to say sensational, diversification of our Whalsay staples. But the absurd result, alas, is that now we are unusually well supplied with luxuries at the very moment when our basic essentials are in jeopardy – a certain quantum of milk per diem is a sine qua non; the same thing applies to paraffin oil and certainly in the long winter days and nights here when solar illumination is at a minimum the danger of not having the wherewithal to replenish one's oil-can one of these days is a prospect to make the stoutest heart quail. Bread too is a necessity which is scarcely offset by the presence in the house of cakes and biscuits. And there are one or two other things needed at regular intervals of a day or two, for which one must have a certain supply of ready cash. This is of course the core of my difficulty – and it has presented itself recently with unusual urgency for the simple reason that having taken on more contracts than usual I have been for a variety of reasons unable to discharge them as speedily as I had hoped and the various sums payable to me on each of these books are not payable until the completed MSS reach the respective publishers. I have been increasingly dependent on book-writing and no longer get much – or indeed any – journalism of the kind that up to a year or so ago used to bring in a modest flow of cheques and postal orders every now and again. The consequence is that our plan of life up here is to get commissions for books; write them and live while doing so by running up credit accounts with the local tradespeople; and then, once they are finished and off to the publishers – the pre-arranged advances come in, square off our accounts – and start the same Sisyphus-like course anew. Up to this year that has worked well enough since I came to Shetland. But this year I took on more books than ever, yet owing to the fact that they have taken me longer to do than usual, our credit accounts have had to run on longer and now the tradespeople are pressing for settlement – some of them – threatening cessations of credit which seem likely to make it impossible for us to procure absolute essentials such as I have named. The devil of it is that my difficulty, though acute, is temporary; I will finish 2 or 3 of the books by the end of February at latest and be in funds again then. But, although hitherto we have always squared off our accounts all right, the tradespeople here do not understand that sort of thing any more than sheep, and have of course a deep, if generally hidden, suspicion of a man who does not work for a living in any of the ways with which they are familiar, is evidently a gentleman and so (they argue) should never be short of money, and who, above all, is a dabbler in books and arts of which they themselves know – and can know – nothing and care less, a matter which outrages their amour propre and sense of the fitness of things, so that they dearly relish any chance of getting their own back and humiliating a 'superior'.

I expect all this was one of the main factors in colouring my last letter with such sombre hues. It is of course a devil of a worrying business even to a habitual liver on the edge of economic volcanoes like myself. But it may pass over without too excruciating difficult an interim. If it does – if I can tide over the next few weeks I'll be all right.

One of my main difficulties here has been that having to plan and do the research for and devise the form of words for the various books has been enough for one man, apart from the donkey-work of actually writing and then typing them. And this has restricted my output and taken up so much time to get one or two books done that the costs of living in the interval have barely been met by the proceeds, and so each restart, after a clearance of accounts, has been from zero.

To meet this difficulty my agent has urged that the only thing to do is to get hold of a competent secretary-typist who will do all the donkey-work, and thus enable me to do far more books in a given time, and so greatly increase my earnings. I have now arranged to do this. A young fellow[1] with the necessary accomplishments has volunteered to come up here and do all I need – for his keep, in the meantime, with a promise of some salary later on if and when my agent and I agree that the plan has resulted in the necessary financial betterment. He starts here about the middle of January. . . . The question now however, is if *we* will be here then; whether or not, in other words, we can hang on by our eyelids long enough to give the plan a starting chance.

Well, well, dismiss these lugubriousities for the time being, and hope for the best.

As to what you say re the Vernacular and our increasing literary isolation,

1/ things have certainly gone awry.

2/ nevertheless I am still confident of righting them and of going a great deal further than we've done yet with the whole Scots business and initiating a whole series of most vital and interesting new departures immediately I can lift my nose from the grindstone and readdress myself to Scots poetry.

3/ I am perhaps more favourably placed than you – there has been that isolating process so far as other Scottish writers and Scottish

---

[1] In his Acknowledgement to *Lucky Poet* MacDiarmid pays tribute 'to my honorary private secretary, Mr Henry Grant Taylor, M.A., for his most competent, careful, and painstaking labours'.

support in general is concerned, and particularly in the disappearance of organs like the *Scots Observer*, *Modern Scot*, etc. etc. But so far as I am concerned this has been more than made good by the better quality of new admirers of my work in other countries, and particularly in America, where I am having quite a vogue. Various articles have appeared about me recently in the USA; a lot of the younger American (Left-Wing) poets swear by me and are in regular correspondence with me; two firms of American publishers have approached me off their own bat to issue selections of my poems in America; I have sent new poems to several American periodicals; and I have within the past few weeks been asked for permission to give several poems each to two American anthologies projected for early publication – and both paying substantial fees on publication.

That reminds me. I want please to give three poems of yours in my own forthcoming Scottish Anthology for MacMillans – one of them 'The Auld Tree'. I'll let you know the other two I want shortly.[2] Please write me a formal note granting me permission if you will be so good – a separate note, because I'll have to send these notes in respect of copyright poems on to MacMillans to vouch that I've duly received permission. I expect fees will be paid – small fees of 10/6 or perhaps £1.1/- per poem; if so, you'll hear direct from MacMillans in due course. This is a huge Anthology – over or nearly 400 poems. I've done a lot of Gaelic and Latin translations for it.

Now all the best. I'll write again shortly, but in the meantime all of us are awaiting your far too generous gift with watering teeth.

Yours,
Chris.

The parcel has just come. It is of course far far too generous. Valda and Mike join me in best thanks.

I've just sent off a Vernacular Circle[3] article – attacking Muir – to the *Bulletin* (by invitation of editor).

[2] *The Golden Treasury of Scottish Poetry* (London 1941) contains three poems by Soutar: 'The Tryst', 'Song', 'The Gowk'.
[3] Every Wednesday the Glasgow *Bulletin* carried a column called 'The Vernacular Circle' in which linguistic issues of the day were discussed; it seems likely that this MacDiarmid contribution was rejected as being too controversial for the paper.

Whalsay,
Friday.
[14/1/38]

My dear Soutar,

Many thanks for your letters, and for the copy of Alan Hodge's letter[1] from the *Times Lit* my sub. to which ran out with the end of the year and hasn't been renewed yet. Hence but for you I wouldn't have seen it – which I'm glad to do. I had some correspondence with Hodge a year or two ago when he was editing *Programme*, an Oxford University students' magazine. He knew my work; but – nevertheless he was using pseudonymous initials – the enclosed article from that periodical (which please return sometime) was not actually by him, though he at least arranged for it. I am writing him since much of my recent poetry carries the sort of synthesis he seems to have in mind very much further than it has yet been carried by anyone else known to me, and draws in this way on out-of-the-way originals – Gaelic, Russian, modern Greek sources, etc. – which few, if any, of the other practitioners of what may be called 'the new plagiarism' cover at all. But if you haven't done so already, please do write him yourself along the lines you indicate in your letter to me – his apparent neglect of synthetic language, with, as you point out, the bearing of this on the trend towards classlessness.

I'm up the neck in anthologies – the latest being a request from Maria Manent, the distinguished Catalan lyric poet, for permission to include a Catalan version of a poem of mine in an anthology of poems by British poets translated into Catalan.

Excuse this short note too. I'm coping at the moment with an enormous poem[2] in MSS on huge unmanageable pages of grocery-paper – an effort running to several thousand lines, and leaving Joyce at the starting-post so far as the use of multi-linguistics is concerned (not only is it multi-linguistic but it is in praise of multilingualism in literature and all its practitioners).

Hope you're in good form – none the worse of the joys of the season. Love to you all.

Yours,
Chris.

[1] In *The Times Literary Supplement*, 1 January 1938, Alan Hodge announced he was doing a study of 'the synthetic elements in modern poetry'; he requested assistance from readers acquainted with 'the theory that "poetry is common property"' and aware of examples of synthetic poetry 'especially in the works of poets of Communistic sympathies'.

[2] *Mature Art.*

Whalsay,
via Lerwick,
Shetland Islands.
4-5-38

Dear Soutar,

Did I write you some little time ago re a new quarterly magazine of Scottish arts and affairs I am launching? It is to be called *The Scottish Republic*, and I am now trying to get the first issue together, with a view to publication either late this month or early next. To start with, it will be 32 pages, plus cover. And the point of this — necessarily brief — note is to implore you to send me something for it, if you possibly can. I think we'll have a rattling good first issue and I hope you'll be able to weigh in with something and preferably in Scots, which will otherwise be unrepresented. I'm itching to get back to Scots work myself, but can't manage yet, but in English — very multi-linguistic English — I've just completed, and got off to T. S. Eliot who is to read it with a view to possible production by Faber and Faber, a new poem, *Mature Art* (really a separable section of the 'Cornish Heroic Song') which is by far my biggest work yet, running as it does to 10,000 lines (i.e. thrice as long as *Cencrastus*) and, with notes, preface etc. totalling some 100,000 words (i.e. about twice the length of an average novel).

Hope you are in good form, and your father, mother and sister. How is the Party of the Picts[1] doing? I've heard or seen no more of them.

Do drop me a line.

All the best,
Yours,
Chris.

[1] Soutar's friend, James Finlayson the painter, earnestly advocated a form of Pictish nationalism which Soutar found comical. Soutar's pacifism offended Finlayson and so, as Alexander Scott writes in *Still Life*, 'during 1938 relations between the two men became increasingly strained. By the spring of the year Finlayson had promulgated an "Official Programme of the Pict Party", and when he visited Soutar at Easter the poet found him "quite assured of the infallibility of his political programme — but the party membership is still but 5." Perhaps it was his inability to convert unbelievers which was responsible for Finlayson's gloom on a visit later in April. . . . The last meeting between Soutar and Finlayson for several years took place on 29th August.' (pp. 98–9).

NLS

Whalsay,
via Lerwick,
Shetland Islands.
18-6-38

Dear W.S.,

I'm not sure if I ever acknowledged your note on the Vernacular question. Forgive me if I didn't; I've been badly rushed lately. I'm using it, of course.

And I'm glad to hear you are appearing in the little *Albannach*[1] anthology – as I am too. You and I and Ruthven Todd are the older men of the dozen; the rest are all newcomers (thank God!) to the Scottish literary field, and of most of them I know nothing. But J. F. Hendry is doing some excellent work – he'll be contributing to the quarterly, and I've got some really good stuff of his which I'll use in subsequent issues.

I don't know if you've seen our leaflet yet, so I enclose a copy.

I've just been reading a very useful article about your poetry by Peter MacCallum Smith, which is appearing in the July *Poetry Review*. The attitude to poetry is by no means mine; but the difference between his point of view and mine may be far more a difference in terminology than anything else, and our apparent differences might show themselves as really very slight if we could begin by a thorough definition of terms. That apart, however, I agree in essence with all the good things he says about you and your work and think it is high time they were being said in more articles here and there and am glad he has written this one.

Hope you are all in good form.

Love,
Chris.

NLS

Whalsay.
18/12/39

My dear Soutar,

It's a very long time since I hear from or of you. How are things? I hope you are about the bit and busy – and that your father, mother, and sister are all in good form.

---

[1] *Albannach: A Little Anthology of 1938 Scots Poetry* (1938), edited by C. J. Russell and J. F. Hendry, featured MacDiarmid's 'The Glen of Silence' (1310–12) and 'A Golden Wine in the Gaidhealtachd' (721–2) as the first two items – which were followed by Soutar's 'Scotland, The Unicorn'.

The Voice[1] is a temporary War casualty, but I think it'll resume publication very soon now.

As to myself:-

1/ The Autobiography is finished and in the hands of my agents. Gollancz are considering it. When Gollancz a long time ago now saw the first few chapters he said it was 99 out of 100 he'd publish, but he couldn't go the other 1 per cent till he saw what I said in the rest. Apart from the fact that it is 200,000 words long (and will probably need some cutting down) the book is by no means everybody's meat and there are only 2 or 3 British publishers who could conceivably issue it, since it is highly controversial throughout, involves legal dangers of diverse sorts, and is ablaze with Leninism from start to finish. However I hope for a good break with it. Several American publishers are keenly interested too. So we'll see. I should know soon now.

2/ *The Golden Treasury* is at the printers and will be out in the Spring all right.

3/ The big poem. I enclose prospectus.[2] It's the worst possible time of course for a huge project of this sort. There are never (let alone in war time) many people able and willing to pay a couple of guineas at one whack for a poem – even if its word length equals 3 novels! I must certainly round up every possible subscriber. I do not know if you know any such; if you do, I'll be very glad to send you – or them – additional copies of this prospectus. Even if the necessary number of subscribers is secured I don't know how the Obelisk Press people will manage since apart from the sheer amount of setting (and therefore expense) the thing presents all sorts of extreme typographical difficulties. Again, we'll see.

---

[1] *The Voice of Scotland* ceased publication with Vol 2, No 1, June–August 1939; it was revived in 1945.

[2] *Mature Art: An Exercise in Schlabone, Bordatini, and Scordattura* by Hugh MacDiarmid. The prospectus reads as follows: 'The Obelisk Press invites subscriptions for the above work by the famous Scottish poet. The price has been provisionally fixed at Two Guineas. This is his first long poem since he published *To Circumjack Cencrastus* in 1930. It is an enormous poem of over 20,000 lines, dealing with the interrelated themes of the evolution of world literature and world consciousness, the problems of linguistics, the place and potentialities of the Gaelic genius, from its origin in Georgia to its modern expressions in Scotland, Ireland, Wales, Cornwall, Galicia and the Pays Basque, the synthesis of East and West, and the future of civilisation. It is a very learned poem involving a stupendous range of reference, especially to Gaelic, Russian, Italian and Indian literatures, German literature and philosophy, and modern physics and the physiology of the brain, and while mainly in English, utilises elements of over a score of languages, Oriental and Occidental.' There are then quotations from T. S. Eliot's letters to MacDiarmid on the subject of *Mature Art* and an appeal for advance subscriptions.

But if I can get these three books out, and so off my mind, and win free to turn to other projects I have long had in view I'll be mighty glad. With a little luck I may even find myself 'in the clear' again, at long last.

I've no general news. Sort of marooned up here – cut off from books and papers and news of all sorts. But I'm in fine fettle, and Valda and Michael are both O.K. Love to you all and best wishes for Christmas and the Coming Year.

Yours,
Chris.

NLS

Whalsay.
8-5-40

My dear Soutar:-

It is eloquent of the conditions under which we are living that all these months should have elapsed before I could write you. And now it will cost me an additional contribution to the taxes! My affairs are more than ever what *Juno and the Paycock* calls in a 'state of chassis'. What is happening in Paris to the big poem I don't know. I fancy they got about enough advance subscriptions to justify their going ahead with publication, other things being equal – which of course they aren't; and, in present and prospective circumstances such a publishing project stands little chance.

Cut down by some 50,000 words to a net 150,000 Gollancz are still considering my Autobiography and will probably publish: but so far the matter has not been definitely arranged.

The *Golden Treasury* is in print, and proofs all passed: so it should be to hand any time now.

My immediate purpose in writing you today is to tell you that the Hogarth Press at my suggestion are willing to consider a selection by me[1] from 'Six Scottish Poets' for inclusion in their Poets of Tomorrow Series (while warning me that paper shortage and other difficulties may make it impossible for them to continue that Series.) The poets proposed are George Campbell Hay, Douglas Young

---

[1] Nothing came of this project.

Somhairle MacGill Eathain, Sydney Smith, yourself and myself. I have chosen 4 poems of Hay's, 4 of Young's, 2 of MacGill Eathain's, 2 of Smith's, 3 of my own and of yours I hope you will let me include

To Karl Marx
The Banner
Workers' Broadcast
Blood Sacrifice
Freedom
In Time of Tumult

These are only some of the poems in the latest book[2] I like best (as a whole I think it is probably your best book) but you will understand that I have selected these particular ones because they 'go with' the other poems in the selection especially well, making the book an impressive unity, and illustrating the points I make in a prefatory essay on 'New Bearings In Scottish Poetry'. If the thing comes off, as I hope it will, it will be a most interesting and valuable book.

Because I am anxious, if possible, to strike while the iron is hot, I have made typescripts of the poems I wish to include, completed my prefatory essay and had it typed, and am sending the whole thing off today to the Hogarth Press, pending hearing from you and MacGill Eathain and securing your consent. But I hope you will agree, and let me know to that effect as soon as possible. The thing may not come off of course, but I hope it does – and if it does I am satisfied that the selection is a thoroughly good one and will compare very favourably with any selection from any other six poets in England, or Ireland, or Wales, let alone Scotland itself, today.

I am, I supposed, pretty well marooned here for the duration now, and it's a dreich business. I can't keep myself in reading matter for one thing, and the outlook is in every respect the reverse of heartening. But I keep as busy as possible with one thing or another and am at least in good enough shape physically. I expect the whole thing is weighing on your spirit in much the same way: but I hope you are in about your usual good heart and busy too in all sorts of ways.

Kindest regards to your mother, father, and sister, and every good wish.

Yours,
Chris.

---

[2] Soutar's *In the Time of Tyrants* was privately printed and issued on 9 December 1939 in a limited edition of 100 copies numbered and signed by the author.

My dear Soutar,

I have had you on my conscience for a long time – with good cause, since I do not think I ever as much as acknowledged the parcel of books – Rocker, Levy, etc. – you sent me on loan.[1] I was more than glad to get them, have read them all very carefully, and will return them to you shortly now.

As you will understand present conditions have been immensely difficult for me, and with the difficulties in the literary and journalistic world, the inherent difficulties of the particular sort of things I have been writing during the past few years, and the immense mass of unpublished stuff that has been accumulating and weighing like a millstone round my neck, to say that I have been balancing on the verge of utter distraction is to put it very mildly indeed.

However, there are signs at last of a little loosening-up of the huge log-jam. The *Golden Treasury* should be out by now. I haven't heard a cheep about it from MacMillan's for a couple of months now. Final proofs had been passed then and the whole thing was *en train* and I expected to have copies in my mind by the beginning of October (MacMillan's last catalogue provisionally scheduled publication for the end of September!).

The trouble I have had with this anthology is, however, a mere flea-bite to that in which my Autobiography has involved me. That finally ran to $\frac{1}{2}$ a million words, and tho' various publishers reported on the MSS in the most enthusiastic terms, the thing was not a practicable publishing proposition in these times – and has been decreasingly so as war-time conditions have developed.

Finally the proposition emerged to extract from the whole some 150,000 words (the parts dealing with me *qua* poet, my poetic processes, and views on poetry) – leaving the remainder to form two other books to be negotiated later, viz. *A Poet and His Friends* and *Scottish Politics 1707-1940*.

This proposal, which has involved an infinity of dropping and changing, and been a regular heart-break owing to the nature of the material – the diverse interests of which were so closely woven together as to make any such reduction a most bewildering and infuriating problem – has now eventuated: and Messrs Methuen are to publish Vol I (at 15/-) – tho' that won't be to the spring now. And

---

[1] The books Soutar sent evidently included Rudolf Rocker's *Anarcho-syndicalism* (1938) and Oscar Levy's *The Idiocy of Idealism* (1940).

I am still horribly busy trying to tie all sorts of loose ends and make this some less lacunous in various ways. What a game!

The fall of France of course put an end to the Obelisk Press's proposal to issue my enormous poem. And I have consequently scores of thousands of lines of unpublished poetry on my hands and cannot find an outlet yet for any of it – let alone get rid of it and address myself to the many new themes which are clamouring for attention. The other idea of a selection of poems by some half-a-dozen younger Scots poets (in addition to yourself and myself) – about which I wrote you – is still on the tapis. Times are extremely unpropitious and prospects extremely uncertain. But if War complications ease off, the Hogarth Press will almost certainly publish this. In the meantime Messrs Methuen have it under consideration, and having sent it to them since they are a big and wealthy firm more able than a small concern like the Hogarth Press to surmount paper-shortage and other difficulties.

So that's how matters stand at the moment. Do write and let me know in turn what *you* are doing and how you – and your good people – are faring.

The immediate resumption of the *Voice of Scotland* is on the cards.

Do you see Miller's monthly (roneo'd) – *The Scots Socialist*.[2] This month's issue is to have the first of a set of three articles by me on John Maclean, to coincide with a memorial meeting to be held in the Central Halls, Glasgow, on Sunday first.

Despite the chaos of worries in which I am involved – and my extraordinary isolation here (for the past 3 to 4 months I have not even so much as seen anyone to exchange a word with at all, except my wife and son! – it is an incredible state of affairs) I am in good form, and trust this finds you in your usual cheery and busy condition, and that you too will have news of new books on the way.

There is another thing I remember just as I am about to close this epistle I specially wanted to ask you about. I wonder if you would mind telling me just exactly the sort of terms upon which the Moray Press are willing to issue a book like your *In Time of Tyrants*. i.e. what it costs the author, etc. I might be able to manage a similar-sized tome of some poems I want to see in print, and I'd like to know just in case ere long I do find it financially feasible.

In any case, please write me soon and give me your news. I am very sorry not to have been able to get to Scotland and see you all this

2 The *Scots Socialist*, edited by J. H. Miller, was the organ of the Scottish Socialist Party. No 5, Nov–Dec 1940, was a John Maclean 'Commemoration Number' and contained, on pp. 2–7, MacDiarmid's 'John Maclean, Scotland, And The Communist Party'. Part II appeared in No. 6/7, Jan-Feb 1941, p. 2. Part III appeared in No 9/10, April–May 1941, p. 4.

long time, but there is just a chance I may manage to do so before much longer now and if so I shall be extremely glad. It would do me a power of good to see your sonsie face again.

Love to you and all of you.

Yours,
Chris.

NLS

My dear W.S.,

Many thanks for your lovely card and letter received today. I expect you will have seen the *Golden Treasury* now. It is not quite the book it should have been – and would have been but for the War. MacMillan's are a very Tory firm and every pressure was brought on me to modify my Introduction and Notes, and in particular to excise the anti-English, anti-Imperialist, and too proworking-class elements therein. But I stuck to my guns and wouldn't, and, indeed, despite personal correspondence on the matter with Harold Mac-Millan himself who is an MP, junior Government post-holder, and son-in-law of the Duke of Devonshire, actually contrived to strengthen these offending elements. But at a cost! The book had to be reduced by over half, owing to paper shortage etc. I made some of the necessary excisions myself, but, owing to the impossibility of going into all the questions involved in correspondence with mails so delayed and uncertain I had finally to agree to MacMillan's themselves removing the very considerable balance necessary to bring the volume down to the required size. This had some disconcerting effects. Several friends of mine were eliminated altogether – Spence, Jeffrey, Montgomerie, and Branford[1] amongst them; my self-selection was restricted to, I think, the worst half; and both Mackie and you suffered (and the Anthology – and the arguments of the Introduction and Notes – suffered) by the cutting-out of your 'Auld

[1] Lewis Spence, William Jeffrey, William Montgomerie, Frederick Victor Branford.

Tree' and a longish poem of Mackie's, both of which I particularly wanted to retain. But of course I could do nothing about it. Apart from that, it will be very interesting to see what admissions in regard to Scottish Poetry this anthology compels some of the reviewers in the more important quarters to make, and perhaps other publishers, the Oxford University Press, for example, may be moved to give Scottish poetry a fairer deal in the future than they have done in the past, and thus other anthologists may have opportunities hitherto denied to redress the deficiences of my selection.

I have no word yet of the selection of recent poems by yourself, George Campbell Hay, Douglas Young, Somhairle MacLean, etc. but hope it may appear ere long, since apart from the, I think, very interesting contents, my long prefatory essay to it makes a splendid counterpart to my *Golden Treasury* Introduction, and would be very useful if it could appear just now and reap the advantage of the considerable volume of discussion and interest the *Golden Treasury* is bound to evoke. (I haven't seen any reviews yet.)

I am glad you've met Douglas Young. I haven't met any of these new chaps yet – haven't been off this island for a couple of years now. Young is a live wire in some respects and is doing good work for Scottish Nationalism etc. But his work in Scots has so far at any rate failed to ring any bell for me. Some of his verse in English is much better – but as wit-writing not as poetry. Hay is a much bigger man but in Gaelic – not in Scots. MacLean has done some very fine stuff, but, again, in Gaelic. You and I still have our chosen field to ourselves. There are a number of other young fellows with whom I am in touch, but tho' they juggle with Scots in various ways that interest me in different degrees, none of them, I think, have the root of the matter in them as poets.

In the second vol of my Autobiography – that to be entitled *A Poet and His Friends* – I am going to try, amongst other things, to give a bird's eye view of all your work and put my view of it on record. I think you will find that interesting; no doubt we will differ on divers points – as we should do. It is high time somebody who knows it all, and the Scots tradition as a whole, sized it up *in toto* in some such way as I intend, and as I have sized up and presented my own many-faceted productivity in this *Autobio*.

By the way, I note from your letter that I must inadvertently have conveyed a wrong idea to you; it is not Gollancz finally, but Methuen's, with whom I have now arranged to publish the Auto.

Many thanks for the sordid details re publishing finance. What I decide to do in this connection will depend on what is decided (I hope to hear any day now) about putting out a volume of my new poems in America. I'll let you know about this later.

177

I have only seen one or two short stories of Fred Urquhart's[2] and was not much impressed. But I'm glad you found him such a decent fellow and here's hoping his undoubted talents get on to effective lines.

I've no miscellaneous news to transmit but I'd be glad if you'd write again if you have any points to make about the *Golden Treasury*, and if you see anything in some of the papers (I don't see any newspapers nowadays) thereanent that calls for any reply - by the time cuttings reach me otherwise it'll probably be too late for me to reply effectively.

Love to you all and best wishes for 1941.

Yours,
Chris.

P.S. Glad you've had another spell of the Scots Muse – Other commitments are still obliging me to stall off a growing urge to invoke her myself too!

NLS   Whalsay.
                                                                       21-1-41

My dear Soutar,

Sorry to have been longer than I should have been, or meant to be, in writing to thank you for your all too kind parcel, but you must blame conditions here - the fact that I had a bad dose of lumbago, that with mail delays business worries supervened in a most annoying way, and that for the past week or so the weather has been of a kind that makes any effort save that just to continue living quite impossible – the worst snowstorm and blizzard, with very severe frosts, we've had during the seven years we've been here. Where I say 'worst' Mike would of course say 'best' – he's having a great time sledging – but for his mother and I it is amazing how desperately such weather complicates our routine of living until the inevitable

---

[2] Fred Urquhart (born 1912), whose *I Feel for A Sailor and Other Stories* (1940), laid the foundation for his reputation as one of Scotland's finest storytellers.

little daily chores swell out in the most monstrous fashion and consume just all the time there is.

However I smoked to you with great appreciation, and the books gave me a spell of most enjoyable reading – particularly the *Great Victorians*;[1] also Wintringham's *New Methods of War*[2] (I know Wintringham well personally, and had read other books and articles of his – but not this particular one). Eddington[3] I have barely begun yet: but I have several of his books and always enjoy his writings.

His mother and I have not lagged behind Michael himself in enjoyment of Lear; it was far too kind of you altogether to send Michael such a lovely edition, and it will certainly be a highly prized possession. He is already a great reader – particularly of history. Insatiable on the subjects of Wallace and Bruce especially. I enclose a note of thanks from Michael himself; what matter if there is a 'me' in limerick?

I hope you have now seen and like the *Golden Treasury*. The reviews so far (mostly from the English provincial press) are very favourable – all except the incredibly shabby one in *The Glasgow Herald*.[4] It is appalling to contrast the nasty grudging spirit of this with these English reviewers' insistence on how satisfactory it is that Scottish Poetry should at long last be recorded status of its own right in the Golden Treasury Series – their clear appreciation of the differences between the English and Scottish traditions – and their generous welcome of what is new to them (e.g. the Gaelic and Latin translations etc.). From what indications are as yet available to me I fancy it has been in considerable demand. I expect of course, to get trounced in the *Times Lit. Supp.* – and in *The Scotsman*!

I hope this finds you all in good form and that you had a happy Christmas and have entered with zest upon what will prove a fortunate New Year.

You must let me give you a copy, by the way, of my Autobiography when it comes. I'm not sure yet when it will be ready but it should not be so long, if all goes well.

Again with warmest thanks and good wishes to you all.

Yours,
Chris.

[1] *The Great Victorians* (1941).
[2] Tom Wintringham, *New Ways of War* (1941).
[3] Sir Arthur Eddington, *The Expanding Universe* (1940).
[4] *The Glasgow Herald*, 28 December 1940, p. 3. The review was fairly flattering but noted that the editorial introduction is partly 'devoted to a sparring match with Mr Edwin Muir on the question of the contemporary and future use of the Doric. It is interesting enough, notwithstanding certain unmeasured statements, but a "Golden Treasury" might have been spared the sound of battle.'

My dear Soutar,

Forgive my being so long in thanking you for the huge history book and the copies of *Labour Monthly* – or did I already acknowledge the latter and say how glad I'd be to have this? I forget. In any case I know I haven't written you since the History tome came for Michael. To say that he was overjoyed to receive it is to put the matter mildly. He asks me to give Uncle Soutar his best thanks. He'd have written himself but has been, and still is, confined to bed with a heavy cold of a type epidemic here just now; this, however, has enabled him to concentrate on reading and he has read a big part of the book (varying this with re-reading *Swiss Family Robinson* and the Penguin Illustrated *Robinson Crusoe*) and kept interrupting my own profound meditations with all sorts of questions and demands for elucidation on matters of which I am – perhaps reprehensibly but certainly – far more ignorant than he is himself. My glibness scarcely suffices to enable me to slither plausibly at all over these difficulties and he is not yet of course at the stage when I can explain to him that I have a different conception of history altogether to what informs these – and practically all – history books and that the matière of history to my mind wholly excludes the big battles, Black Princes, and such like events and people, in whom he has an inexhaustible interest.

I wish I could get down to Perth and have a long session with you. It is out of the question to attempt to even initiate in a letter any discussion of the present position and prospects: but we could perhaps talk things out. Alas, I am afraid that can't be just now – or, indeed, at any date determinable now. What a leeway we will have to make up when the opportunity does come? But I do wonder how you are faring and what you are thinking and writing these days?

I think I probably told you in my last letter that owing to the London blitzing the publishers had found it impossible to get my Autobio. out this Spring and had fixed publication for September. I hope the recent raids have not upset even this schedule. My book of poems publishing in America is now expected out in August. Originally this was to have been a selection of my previously published poems with one or two new ones; but now it is to be a new collection altogether. That is the Colt Press, San Francisco, book. Whether New Directions, Connecticut, are to put out a volume of my selected poems now is not definite, but they are to have about 1000 lines of new poetry of mine in the 1941 issue of their big magazine-book, *New Directions*, which comes out this autumn.

I'll send you copies of these in due course. Has F. G. Scott sent you yet a loan of my copy of Professor Southworth's *Sowing The Spring: Studies in British Poets from Hopkins to MacNeice*.[1] I sent it to F.G. to read, asking him (unless he heard from me in the interval wanting it back here for reference first) to send it on to you instead of straight home to me. But perhaps he hasn't sent it yet. After the Glasgow Blitz he and his family migrated to Taynuilt where they were to be until the end of this month. Perhaps in that migration he omitted to take it with him and so can't forward it to you until he returns to Glasgow. I think you'll find it very interesting. He has an admirable chapter on my own work, if written too much from an English angle, and so not doing anything like justice to my purely Scots significance or place in the Scots tradition. But the whole thing is very interesting. Southworth is a Professor at the University of Toledo (Ohio).

I am still very busy but have a period ahead now when I must abandon literature for other things, to wit cutting a supply of peat and getting it home and stacking it, collecting a supply of gulls' eggs for pickling (last season's yield has kept us going nicely all winter) and other chores; and already Valda has broken in on the even tenor of my book-and-paper half-buried routine with the first rude blasts of her Spring-cleaning operations. It is the onset of this many-sided and ineludible process of interruption that has delayed this letter: but bitter knowledge that it is only starting and must soon develop into an all-involving whirlwind of infernal irrelevance that has made me screw myself down to get this belated letter off to you by this mail at all costs, on the Now or Never principle. God bless us! What a life!

I hope all's well with yourself and your father, mother, and sister. And that somehow or other in the miraculous way you have you are managing to ride out the tempest and keep carolling above it.

Love from us all: and again warmest thanks for the huge book and the magazine.

Yours,
Chris.

---

[1] James G. Southworth, *Sowing the Spring* (1940). One of the Chapters is devoted to MacDiarmid.

My dear Soutar,

Your very varied parcel of reading matter was 'just what the doctor ordered' and it has given me some hours of great enjoyment. The *Fabulous Beasts* book and the King Pelican *British Birds* were in particular splendid discoveries. Bird-man Gould was quite new to me. His pictures are nearly as good as those of the American naturalist D'Audubon, a collection of which I saw a year or two ago.

I note what you say of Richard Church's reference in *John O'London* to Southworth's *Sowing the Spring* and my work. I haven't seen it of course but you are right in your surmise – I encountered Church some years ago when I was in a state of super-alcoholic lucidity and lofty scorn for the minor English muse, and gave him my opinion of his work, and that of some of his friends, with devastating frankness. I am not surprised that he nurses a bitter feeling.

I hope FG has now sent you Southworth's book. I had a line from him the other day – the first since I had asked him to send it on to you. He has now I understand hied him away to Taynuilt for 4 months' holiday. 4 months! These fellows do have the time!

I'm extremely sorry to hear you drew a blank with MacMillan's with your new Scots MSS. And much hope you've had better luck with Methuen. I'm afraid tho' it's going to be very difficult to get such things (I mean poetry particularly) published for a long time to come. For myself, my hopes lie with America. I'd certainly be glad to see your Scots MSS. Inter alia, I hope to do a long essay for an American review on Scots Poetry and I would like to refer to them in it and possibly find some quotes. But I won't get round to that for some months yet. Methuen's still have the typescript of the selection of poems by you, Hay, Douglas Young and myself, etc. – they've hung on to it for many months, without coming to any decision. I expect my Autobio. is all right for publication in September – unless worse befalls London, and British publishing generally, ere then. I'm certainly looking for proofs any day now. My collection of new poems via the Colt Press, San Francisco, is expectable in August, I understand.[1]

I have carried through and survived the peat-cutting business all right. But it is certainly hard work. I fancy convict labour is child's

---

[1] This book never appeared.

play to it. However, I've made siccar of an ample supply of fuel to last us another twelve months no matter to what fantastic level coal prices may rise. That is certainly a cheering thought. For coal is already 5/6 a bag with us here!

Since I completed this business of whittling away a mountain however I've fallen a victim to a very nasty form of 'flu which is rampant here. But for that I'd hoped to have completed and got away to the publishers this past week my book on the Faroes. However I haven't been able to do anything for about 10 days. I've all my material now, however, and about a week's hard writing will add that additional item to my bibliography, praise be!

I hope you have good news of Evelyn[2] and that she is enjoying la vie militaire d'une jeune fille en Angleterre very much indeed. F.G.'s Francise[3] is similarly engaged somewhere in England's green and pleasant land.

By the way, if I'm retaining any of your books longer than's convenient to you, please don't hesitate to drop me a reminder and I'll return them toute suite. I read things immediately they arrive, then lay them aside – read them again if and when they once more come to the surface – but I am habitually in such a state of what Sean O'Casey's Joxer calls 'chassis' that I am apt to overlook things.

You have already sent so much that I had not intended to take advantage of what you say about *Westward Ho*, *Coral Island*, and other possibilities of some forgotten bookshelf. But Mike, to whom I read that sentence from your letter when it came, knowing I am writing you, is consciencelessly insistent, so if you can really put your hands on copies of one or two such standbys of properly developed boyhoods as *Westward Ho*, *Coral Island*, and possibly *Kidnapped*, I am instructed to say that the Greater, and Lesser Shetland Gobblealls (a variety of the Shoveller) have their beaks open and their crops empty.

Love to you all.

Yours,
Chris.

---

[2] Evelyn was the girl adopted by Soutar's parents; she arrived from Australia in 1927. Soutar dedicated his *Seeds in the Wind* (1933) 'To Evelyn'.
[3] F. G. Scott's daughter Francise.

Whalsay.
28/7/41

My dear Soutar,

I am sorry to have been so long in writing to thank you for the parcels of books, etc. you sent to me, and to Michael (who is celebrating his 9th birthday today) but I have been having a strenuous time indoors and out (the great Peat effort is now over, praise be!) – and a worrying time withal, for, *inter alia*, – I learn that Messrs Methuen now fear that they are not going to manage to get my *Autobio* out this autumn after all owing to trade difficulties and the delays of the printers. Damn, damn, damn! Counterbalancing that to some degree, however, is the news that after all, not only the Colt Press vol[1] of my new poems is coming out all right, but that the New Directions, Connecticut, people are going ahead with a selection of my earlier lyrics made by Horace Gregory, also that they are publishing a long new poem of mine, 'The Divided Bird' in the issue of their book magazine, *New Directions*[2] which appears this Fall. (I must point out that this Divided Bird is no relative of your Undivided Bird, which stotted most vigorously in my reading to the delight alike of Michael and Valda and myself.) So I will not have an altogether barren hairst even if my damned Autobio *is* held over to the spring.

Palme Dutt's notes in his last two issues[3] you sent were, I thought, extremely good – also Ivor Montagu's article on American Imperialism – and the line propounded in these recent issues of the *L.M.* has my complete approval.

I note what you say about your new Scots poems and will look forward to reading them later. In this connection I am not only still busy with an essay for America as already mentioned, but have just been asked – and agreed – to contribute an essay on the outlook for, and requirements of, Scottish Literature to a symposium on Scotland After The War which is being got together for publication by the London Assocn. for Scottish Self-Government.

Michael, I should have mentioned, is not to blame for not yet having written to thank you himself for the far too handsome additions you sent to his growing library. He several times mentioned that he should be writing you, but I suggested he should wait

---

[1] Nothing came of this project.

[2] The projected New Directions 'selection of my earlier lyrics' never appeared; 'The Divided Bird' (712-20) appeared on pp. 220–8 of (ed) James Laughlin, *New Directions in Prose and Poetry* (Norfolk, Conn., 1941).

[3] The reference is to Palme Dutt's Marxist periodical *Labour Monthly*.

and send his letter along with mine – which latter I had meant to have had off to you several posts ago: and now tonight, when I *am* writing you, I have so many letters to write that he having been celebrating his natal occasion a little prematurely (thanks to an unusually extensive bout of baking his mother has indulged in) and having got a little above himself I have testily despatched him to bed (not before time anyway!) and he consequently can't do his share of the intended joint epistle on this occasion! You will please excuse him and understand him to be really most grateful, and anxious to write you, which he will yet!

I hope this finds you all in good case, and with good news of your Amazonian sister. Every kind regard to your mother and father, and again, warmest thanks and best wishes for the Muse's favours, and may you find a rich outgate soon.

Yours,
Chris.

NLS

Sudheim,
Whalsay.
8/11/41

My dear Soutar,

Just a quick note in reply to yours received today. I expect I'll get the books and mags. you mention on Monday: many thanks in anticipation from Michael and myself. Yes, I noted the *TLS* review of Vernon Watkins's book.[1] I know Watkins's work – in Wales, *Welsh Review*, etc. – and like much of it immensely. (Incidentally do you know David Jones's *In Parenthesis*? If not I can lend it to you.) Neither Jones nor Watkins nor I am confident any other poet in any 'civilised' country today confirms at all the idea that the time of 'difficult' poetry is past – or (save in Russia) really begun. I think it is all wrong to imagine that we have come to the end of a period of intense experimentalism and are about to enjoy a new simplicity and any abecedarian straightforwardness of expression. Bien au contraire! Lenin, Plekhanov, and other Marxists warned us insistently

---

[1] Vernon Watkins, *Ballad of the Mari Lwyd and other poems* (1941).

of the danger of anything of the sort. The great masses do not respond to the 'popular' in any healthy way, tho' they may be doped by it. The people who want that short cut to mass influence are the petty bourgeois 'interpreting class' – the teachers, ministers, and what not. It would simplify their work and consolidate their vested interests. Such hopelessly unscientific and non-dialectical and therefore dead things as dogmas, accepted opinions, established conventions of any sort alone can be expressed in that way – that is why the content of such expression in poetry, religion, etc. forms part of the stupendous millstone round the neck of human development. As in science so in literature, new developments (anything with life in it) must be difficult and its discoveries demand new terminology, experimentalism in expression, hazardous tentatives of all sorts in language, rhythm etc. I assembled in my Autobio a great mass of proofs (particularly in regard to music and abstract art) that the 'man in the street' responds readily enough to these whenever he gets a fair chance – responds more readily than the educated (i.e. miseducated) classes. This won't appear until my 2nd Autobio volume is published – but I give enough in the 1st volume to set out the whole position, and to validate it in terms of physiology, neurology, etc. This is no way denies the great possibilities of the ballad, of course (albeit it may be ballads transmogrified in form as Hopkins transmogrified the sonnet!). In America as you probably know there has sprung up in recent years a huge new ballad literature. I can't go into this at the moment: but I wish to goodness my Autobio were out – it goes into the matter all right and makes out a case that will be very difficult indeed for anyone to oppose. Yes: it has been held over until the Spring, damn it! So has my volume of poems per the Colt Press, San Francisco. Of the other volume which Laughlin, Connecticut, is publishing I have had no word these many moons – nor has the current *New Directions* which is to contain a long new poem of mine come to hand yet. All I have to report so far is that the American edition of the *Golden Treasury* appeared in the beginning of September: Norman Macleod's annual *Calendar*[2] just to hand contains in addition to poems by 18 American poets two poems of mine – 'A Golden Wine in the Gaidhealtachd' and 'One of the Principal Causes of War'. Scott mentioned in the only letter I've had from him for ages – received about a fortnight ago – that he'd been reading the MSS of 3 collections of yours. I'll look forward to them most keenly. He (Scott) objects to most of my new work for exactly the opposite reasons he advances, I understand, against much of your work – but I entirely disagree with the basis of his objection in

[2] (Ed) Norman Macleod, *Calendar: an anthology of 1941 poetry*, (1941).

each case, while warning you, in view of what you say in your letter, that if you develop the line of argument you lay down there you will not only rule out my latest work in the same way but your own too, and be forced on to the same uncomfortable (and soon quite untenable) fence-sitting middle position: and like Scott, find yourself to your annoyance, in the same camp as Jeffrey. Jeffrey has for some reason quite unaccountable to me his admirers in Dublin; I am not surprised Seumas O'Sullivan has published a Doric poem of his – I would be if Seumas published one of either yours or mine. Several Irish periodicals reviewing the *Golden Treasury* protested against Jeffrey's exclusion – I wish the writers in question had named any 'poem' of Jeffrey's I could possibly have included. Jeffrey, like Muir is no poet – they are both epigoni of the 'poetic' and 'accepted literary standards'.

There is one other recent manifestation that has cheered my meteorologically boisterous (but otherwise very boring) days – and that is a sudden crop of interesting letters anent my *Islands of Scotland* book. The last four are respectively from Dorset, Caithness, Canada, and New Zealand – all from people immensely delighted with that book and anxious to secure crofts in Shetland or (in two of the cases) in the Hebrides.

I keep hoping that economic forces will compel me ere long to visit my native country and in so doing allow me to descend upon you in Perth for a few hours and let us thresh out some of these matters in talk. That's the only way. Letters are hopeless. You and I could get somewhere I think in a good pow-wow; there is certainly scarcely anyone else in Scotland worth discussing such matters with at all – even Scott – they are all such sorry examples of the havoc of English-dominated education. Just as Sankhara, the Indian materialist, shows that Hegel (and all other Western philosophy) fails to bridge the gulf between thought and reality, because of defective premises at the very base of their systems, whereas for Sankhara himself there is no problem involved in doing so at all, so I feel that almost everybody is engaged with difficulties in regard to literature which do not exist for me at all, and which do not really exist at all except in the way in which their minds are corrupted from the outset by traditional delusions which result in it being impossible for me to discuss these issues with them at all since we are speaking different languages altogether. That is what I feel with Muir most of all – but with almost everybody else in some degree – that there is no opinion they can express of which I can make any more sense than if they spoke in Swahili or Red River Indian dialect. Ugh! What a mess!

Love to you all from all here.

Yours,
Chris.

NLS

Whalsay.
8-12-41

My dear Soutar,

The imperfections of Mike's enclosed note[1] are partially attributable to the fact that he wrote it while in bed, where all three of us have been spending most of our time lately under the influence of a species of 'flu which has been prevalent here. We're all nearly all right again, but I haven't let Mike go back to school yet (the local schools reopened on Monday after being closed for 14 weeks) and he has been dividing his time reading his books (including your latest gifts) and my own Wild West ones, and trying out a cycle which he has just acquired in those intervals of weather at all suitable for the purpose. These last have been few. We've been having a very stormy time of it this last 2 or 3 weeks, with 85 m.p.h. gales and the heaviest seas seen round these shores for 40 years. In this state of affairs, MacNeice's Yeats book[2] (which I found surprisingly good) and the *Labour Monthlies*, etc. have come in most opportunely. I'll return the Yeats book and Rodgers' poems (which I have found very disappointing – references in various quarters had led me to expect something a good deal better) in a few days time. This can only be the briefest of notes (but I don't want to miss tomorrow's mail boat with it – as we've had a period of very few and at that precarious mails in or out during this wild weather and I am fully conscious that it's high time you had an acknowledgement from me of these parcels etc.), and I am not going to say anything here of your typescript books, reserving what I have to say regarding these to a separate letter which must necessarily be longish and which I'll hope to get off later this week unless the weather worsens again. I hope this finds you all in good trim, and with good news of Evelyn. Every kind

---

[1] Michael's note thanks 'Uncle Soutar' for books he had sent.
[2] Louis MacNeice, *The Poetry of W. B. Yeats* (1941).

188

regard to your mother and father and Evelyn, and please once again accept my warmest thanks for all this reading matter, and in supplement of Mike's own blottesque gratitude for the books you sent him.

All the best.
Chris.

NLS

Whalsay.
9-1-42

My dear Soutar,

As, of your charity, you have doubtless understood my delay in writing you has been due to my involvement during this period in more than my accustomed tangle of personal difficulties of all kinds. I foresaw some time ago what the inevitable end of this must be if some miracle did not intervene – and of the possible miracles I had in mind in relation to the publication after all of my books in this country and in America there is unhappily still no sign. No news even; I haven't any idea what the position now is or when any of them will appear. Foreseeing this I warned F.G. some little time ago of the likelihood of my turning up ere long in Glasgow complete in boiler suit. That prognostication is now on the point of being fulfilled. I have been caught in a curious eddy of the industrial conscription. I leave here on Tuesday, expect to arrive in Aberdeen on Wednesday, thence to Glasgow, where I have to report for duty not later than Thursday afternoon. If all then goes 'well', I will be in Glasgow for some months anyhow. Valda and Michael will remain here in the meantime. I have of course no idea in advance what sort of circumstances I will be involved in or whether, for example, a run through to Perth will be at all possible. I had hoped that en route I might have stopped off and seen you: but the time-table prescribed for me rules that out. Still, we'll see a little later. In any case I am herewith with many thanks returning your MacNeice's Yeats and Rodgers' Poems[1] but I have not yet been able to put on paper what I

[1] Soutar lent MacDiarmid Louis MacNeice's *The Poetry of W. B. Yeats* (1941) and W. R. Rodgers's *Awake and Other Poems* (1941).

189

want to say about your own new poems and I am retaining these meantime (I hope this isn't inconveniencing you in any way) but will take them with me to Glasgow and if there is no early chance of seeing you and saying what I have to say instead of writing it, I will send you my promised epistle from there, along with your typescripts, as soon as I can. But I'd rather talk things over with you if at all possible. I can only say here that I read with horror what you said in your letter re publishing costs. These as I think you know have never troubled me; I have been one of the lucky beggars whose publishers have all undertaken the complete costs of publication without any financial contribution from the author. And I think it is simply hellish that work such as yours should not long ere this have put you in the same position.

On this score the only other point I have time to mention here (if indeed I did not mention it in a previous letter) is that the Chalmers Press, Edinburgh, produced Sydney Smith's *Skail Wind*[2] in excellent print, format, etc. and might do a book for you too. I know nothing about them, but if they too did require author's payment I cannot imagine that they would not be much cheaper than the atrocious proposal of which you give details or even than the Moray Press were. I'll find out exactly what the position there is from Sydney Smith and let you know. In any case I believe something may be able to be done in Glasgow with the printers of the *Scots Socialist*, or Aldred's *Word*[3], or Robert Thomson's firm; I'll spier at any rate.

And now in ending this brief and very blotty note, I have once again to thank you on behalf of all of us for your far too kind Christmas gifts. I am sorry to be so late in doing so, but you'll understand. I hope you are all well and that this year is good to you.

Anyhow, I'll write you again as soon as I can.

Yours,
Chris.

[2] Sydney Goodsir Smith, *Skail Wind* (1941).
[3] *The Word* was the organ of the United Socialist Movement, one of many radical publications associated with Guy Aldred (1886–1963), the celebrated anti-parliamentarian. When Sir Walter Strickland died in 1938 he left his fortune to Aldred who set up the Strickland Press, in Glasgow's George Street, to publish *The Word*.

c/o Donnelly,
35 Havelock St,
Glasgow.
28/12/42

My dear W.S.

I have just heard that you have been ill with pneumonia. I do hope you have made a complete recovery. Your name has headed a list of persons to whom I intended to write ever since I came to Glasgow – ten months ago. None of these letters, alas, has been written. I have been working the extremely long hours of the munitioneer and have had practically no spare time – and in what little I have had I have found myself too dog-tired to write to anyone. Besides this change of life to a man of my age entirely unused previously to any sort of manual labour – and it is very heavy labour I am doing from 8 a.m. to 5.30 p.m. daily and three Sundays out of four – involves psychological changes difficult to understand oneself or communicate to others. Not that I am unhappy or dislike the work – very much to the contrary indeed! – especially since now Valda and Michael have joined me here. And having recovered now from a serious accident I had some months ago when I disabled both legs and sustained other injuries I am in fact in excellent form and none the worse of my adventure into practical proletarianism.

I have intended however to write you at long last in time to wish you – and all of you – a happy Christmas: but did not manage, since what little leisure I have had recently has been wholly adscripted to reading the galley proofs of my Autobiography. This has been a heavy task – the lapse of time since I wrote the text has entailed many changes, the text itself is difficult and the book is very long – 300,000 words, it will run to practically 600 pages. Methuen's expect to publish it very soon after the New Year. I have practically finished with the proofs now.

Another matter on my conscience is that I still have the type-scripts of your books of poems – and in this connection too I have wanted to write you for some time. Wm. MacLellan, printer, Hope St, Glasgow is developing his business as a Scottish publisher. He has an excellent printing business with a thoroughly up-to-date and ample plant, prints very nicely indeed, has plenty of money behind him, and is a good fellow. He went to London recently to fix up some business relationships there and I was able to give him some useful introductions, which he profited by. Perhaps you have seen – or seen reviewed – a volume of poems he has just published with a long preface by myself, viz. *The Fury of the Living* by John Singer?[4] MacLellan also has in hand for early publication volumes of Douglas Young's and Sorley MacLean's poems. I am sure he'd be very willing to consider a volume by yourself. If you care to write to him thereanent and say you do so at my suggestion I think you'll find yourself able to arrange matters satisfactorily – and on better terms (i.e. without any question of paying yourself for the production of the book) than you have previously had. I do not know how matters finished up with you and the Moray Press but I was very sorry about the whole thing and do hope you were not too badly hit.

I heard the other week, just casually from someone I met that poor Victor Branford is dead. Do you know anything about this?

Please give my warmest greetings and best wishes for the New Year to your father, mother, and sister – all of whom keep well, I hope – and accept same for yourself. Valda and Michael join me in this.

Yours,
C.M. Grieve.

[4] John Singer, *The Fury of the Living* (1942).

To Neil M. Gunn

Neil Miller Gunn (1891–1973) was born in a village on the Caithness coast: Dunbeath, the setting of his novels *Morning Tide* (1930), *Highland River* (1937) and *The Silver Darlings* (1941). His father was a fishing captain – the heroic figure to whose memory *The Silver Darlings* is dedicated – but Gunn was encouraged to seek a safer career in the Civil Service. From 1923 to 1937 he was excise officer attached to Glen Mhor Distillery in Inverness where he set up home, with his wife Daisy, in their bungalow 'Larachan'. In 1937 Gunn scored a great popular success with his novel *Highland River*; elated by this triumph he resigned from the Civil Service and went, as the title of his next book explained, *Off in a Boat* (1938) with Daisy, sailing from Skye to Inverness. From 1937 to 1949 the couple lived at Braefarm House, near Dingwall, during Gunn's most creative period. Subsequently Gunn abandoned novel-writing, after publishing *The Other Landscape* in 1954, and went into a decline after Daisy's death in 1963. His story is sympathetically told in *Neil M. Gunn: A Highland Life* (London 1981) by Francis Russell Hart and J. B. Pick.

Gunn first made contact with MacDiarmid in 1922 after reading an appeal for contributions to *The Scottish Chapbook*. Delighted with Gunn's determination and sense of style, MacDiarmid published poetry and prose by Gunn in *The Scottish Chapbook* and *The Scottish Nation* and generally encouraged him to participate fully in the Scottish Literary Renaissance announced so eloquently in these two periodicals. When Gunn visited MacDiarmid in Montrose in 1924 it was the beginning of a friendship that eventually survived various crises over the nature of Scottish creativity. The two men especially enjoyed long all-night conversational sessions as Gunn recalled in 1957:

> Wondering if I could fix some sort of date, I looked up my copy of his *Contemporary Scottish Studies*, and beneath his signature on the flyleaf, he wrote: 'Inverness, 3 January 1927, 5.20 a.m'. Not a redundant word: precise, lucid and sober. So that night he must have been staying with me in the Highland capital. Probably

there was a good-going foray on. I suspect it had something to do with what we called the Gaelic aristocratic idea, which we were then hunting with all the ardent zeal our ancestors devoted to lifting cattle. Accordingly that Grieve should assume the name of MacDiarmid seemed perfectly natural. That he in particular used the name MacDiarmid when writing in Lallans was merely an instance of that higher logic which embraced all Scotland, and was then prepared to use all Scotland as a starting point for a good-going cattle raid into England, and after that it was the wide, wide world. By five in the morning all this was wonderfully clear. (Hart and Pick, p. 77)

When MacDiarmid's son Walter Grieve was born in Montrose on 5 April 1928 the poet asked two novelists to stand in as godfathers: Gunn, whose first novel *The Grey Coast* (London 1926) he had analysed in the *Scottish Educational Journal* (2 April 1926) as the work of 'Practically the only young Scottish prose-writer of promise manifesting himself today'; and Compton Mackenzie. The occasion has been memorably recorded in *My Life and Times, Octave 6* (London 1967, p. 134) by Mackenzie who found himself in enough pain to require the attention of MacDiarmid:

Grieve had been a medical orderly in Salonika in the war, and announced his familiarity with giving injections. Neil Gunn, whose novel *The Grey Coast* I had read with admiration, had just arrived to stay with the Grieves in Montrose, where at the Episcopal church he and I were to be godfathers of the Grieve baby at his baptism. Neil Gunn was standing by when Christopher put the needle into my arm. As it went in, the tall and distinguished figure of Neil Gunn went down on the floor full length in a dead faint caused by the sight of a minute drop of blood. When he became conscious Grieve was able to assure him that lots of men nearly collapsed when being given an injection.

MacDiarmid was anxious that the Scottish Literary Renaissance should be as broadly based as possible and wanted someone to attempt in prose what he had done in verse. Thus, after the publication of *The Grey Coast*, MacDiarmid took every opportunity – including the suggestion of collaboration – to persuade Gunn to renounce the gently philosophical manner he favoured and attempt something more experimental and extreme. In Gunn's work Scotland is remade in the image of the spiritually superior Gael in fiction that is full of archetypes and elemental symbols. A selfconsciously Celtic Innocent searches in the River of Life for the hazelnuts of Knowledge and the salmon of Wisdom and finds the Vision in the

194

Source. For MacDiarmid it was an art tinted by the dying defeatist light of the Celtic Twilight and he frequently rebuked Gunn for what he regarded as his escapism. When Fionn Mac Colla's powerful *The Albannach* appeared in 1932 MacDiarmid was ready to acclaim Mac Colla rather than Gunn as the truly representative novelist of the Highlands. This artistic argument between Gunn and MacDiarmid was reinforced by political division. After MacDiarmid's expulsion from its ranks in 1933, the National Party of Scotland merged with the Scottish Party to form the Scottish National Party in 1934. Gunn was an influential member of the NPS and very friendly with Sir Alexander MacEwen of the Scottish Party. Thus MacDiarmid saw Gunn, after 1933, as a man inclined to a safety-first political stance that was entirely appropriate to his artistic caution. Nevertheless the friendship was a close one and in later years the two men resumed contact on cordial terms.

NLS

16 Links Avenue,
Montrose.
14th June 1922

N. M. Gunn Esq,
Scaraben,
Lybster,
Caithness.

Dear Sir:-

I am sorry to have taken so long to acknowledge your encouraging letter of 15th inst.: but a consequence of my appeal was inundation with correspondence. The promotion of the venture proceeds satisfactorily: and I think the first issue[1] will appear in August all right.

I should be very glad indeed to have a 'read' of the work to which you refer which failed to find acceptance in the *G[lasgow] H[erald]*. My own work always fails to find acceptance there – although the reviewers of both volumes of *N.N.* in *The Glasgow Herald* paid me some extraordinary compliments.

N.N. (*Northern Numbers*) was launched in Nov. 1920. The contributors were Neil Munro, John Buchan, Mrs Violet Jacob, John

[1] *The Scottish Chapbook*, Vol 1, No 1, August 1922.

Ferguson and 7 others. The second series was published in Oct. 1921, with 19 contributors including Charles Murray, General Sir Ian Hamilton, Sir Ronald Ross, Dr Lachlan MacLean Watt, and 7 of the original 11. I am preparing the Third Series for publication this autumn: and intend to continue the Annual quite independently of the monthly.

The publisher of *N.N.* is Mr T. N. Foulis, 16 Frederick St, Edinburgh, or 91 Great Russell St, London. Each volume is 6/- net.

Hoping to hear from you again.

Yours faithfully,
C. M. Grieve.

NLS

The Scottish Chapbook,
16 Links Avenue,
Montrose.
26/7/23

Dear Mr Gunn,

I had meant to write you ere this (had I not been over exercised in regard to the *S[cottish] Nation*,[1] a tough job to run single-handed in one's spare time) to thank you for 'Visioning'[2] – a splendid piece of work! I don't know if you've written much prose yet: but you certainly should! I look forward with confidence to exceptionally fine stuff from you.

I am giving place of honour to your 'O Sun'[3] in our July *Chapbook*. The others I hope to use anon. I hope you'll like this Special Number. It'll be out tomorrow.

By the way, my brother and you knew each other didn't you? He's in the Inland Revenue Deparment – in Edinburgh now.

[1] MacDiarmid's weekly *The Scottish Nation*, edited by C. M. Grieve, ran from 8 May to 25 December 1923.
[2] 'Visioning' is an early short story by Neil Gunn; MacDiarmid published the following stories by Gunn in *The Scottish Nation*: 'Visioning' (July), 'Surfaces' (August), 'Down to the Sea' (September), 'The Hind' (December).
[3] Gunn's poem 'Oh, Sun!' appeared in *The Scottish Chapbook*, Vol 1, No 12, July 1923.

A. S. Grieve. We've a compositor here, too, just now, from Dingwall who knows you or of you – Macpherson's his name.

Have sent on 4 copies as asked of last week's *S.N.*, and 1 to Mr Ross. Many thanks.

Yours faithfully,
C. M. Grieve.

NLS

The Scottish Nation,
16 Links Avenue,
Montrose.
1/11/23

My dear Gunn:-

Many thanks for yours.

Circumstances have compelled me – without prejudice to subscribers who will duly receive 12 issues within the year – to lump September & October together in a single *Chapbook*! and that will be out tomorrow. Better late than never.

I'm very sorry about the 3 *N.N.'s*. You should have had them ere this. I have written off about them. It's too bad.

As to ordering *S.N.'s*, Menzies' people are to blame, I expect. They have hurt the *S.N.* in many ways and being monopolists leave us without redress. The only way to overcome that sort of thing is to order direct. Local newsagents doing so will find it more profitable to them in any case. They avoid wholesalers' commission. That is – they get it from us at same rate as Menzies' people do.

The *S.N.* has been in extreme difficulties: but – touching wood! – has again surmounted them, I think, and I am likely to get it on a very much securer basis shortly. But it's too much for me really – as a spare time job! I do all the correspondence, book-keeping, editing, proof-reading, despatching and a fair share of the actual writing, in an already severely-restricted leisure. However!

I'd have liked your comments on *Annals*. Commercially it's been still-born. But it's making headway in the right quarters, especially on the Continent – in France and Italy.

I follow your own work with keen interest. 'Down To The Sea' was a great piece of work – easily the best of yours I've seen. Quite a

197

number of friends wrote me anent it in high terms – people whose opinions are worth-while. Go ahead! You'll do. And your instinct's right. Chambers & the like are no good to you – except financially.

I've a confession to make. I'm Hugh M'Diarmid. Tell it not in Gath. I don't know of any handy dictionary – I use a big 6-vol Jamieson: Sir James Wilson's book on the Perthshire dialect: the Translation of The Scottish Dialects Cmmtee (Oxford); and a collection of glossaries and old Scots books.

Excuse this bald and scrappy note. I'm always glad to hear from you.

With every good wish.

Yours faithfully,
C. M. Grieve.

NLS

The Scottish Chapbook,
16 Links Avenue,
Montrose.
6/2/24

My dear Gunn,

Excuse pencil. I am up to the eyebrows in ink. This is my 40th letter tonight and I am ink-sick.

The Scottish Nation is reviving as an 80pp monthly[1] almost immediately – if I can get in all the money I got offers of. A mercenary but absolutely necessary proceeding! But I think we'll be on much likelier lines for commercial success (without any lowering – in fact with a market raising – of our flag) – as Rebecca West, William Archer, R. B. Cunninghame Graham & so forth are to be with us.

And you're one of the men I want the very best possible work out of. You're one of the few – with Muir, Branford, Malloch[2] & two or three more – who are really going to count.

---

[1] MacDiarmid revived the weekly *Scottish Nation* as the monthly *Northern Review* which ran from May to September 1924 and published three stories by Gunn: 'Adventure in Jealousy' (August), 'Uncashed Cheque' (August), 'Between Headlands' (September).

[2] MacDiarmid was anxious to swell the movement by adding Gunn to a group comprising Edwin Muir, F. V. Branford, George Reston Malloch.

Did you see the column leader *The Glasgow Herald* gave us on 31st Dec.?[3] If not you should.

I am determined by hook or crook to make *our* monthly equal to the Dublin Mag. – the splendid merits of which I concede. Your friend, Maurice Walsh,[4] has great stuff in him, too.

Excuse more just now. Do you read French? Saurat has an excellent article on 'The Scottish Lit. Renaissance' in the current *Revue Anglo-Américaine*.[5] I'll send you a copy if you care.

Yours with all good wishes.
C. M. Grieve.

NLS   16 Links Avenue,
                                                    Montrose.
                                                  5/1/2[5]

My dear Gunn,

Not my inveterate carelessness in such respects (which I frankly admit can go to intolerable lengths) this time – but the fact that I have been away from home and confined to bed with 'flu and certain of its accompaniments accounts for my non-answering to now of your last two letters at all events.

Of course I should have returned your MSS as soon as the *N.R.* ceased – but as you suggested I am indeed contemplating a very early renewal of that organ, and had hoped to have used some of your MSS.

I wish you had come down here that day you were in Montrose. I am 'snowed under' with correspondence of all sorts every second or third day and unspeakable agglomerations accrue. On one of these 'Caverned Echoes' lies. I have tried my utmost to lay hands on it

---

[3] *The Glasgow Herald*, 31 December 1923, devoted the first leader to the phenomenon of 'a genuine Scottish literary renaissance' and praised the work of both C. M. Grieve and Hugh M'Diarmid.

[4] Maurice Walsh (1879–1964), author of novels including *The Key Above the Door*; his friendship with Gunn is discussed in *Neil M. Gunn* (London 1981) by F. R. Hart and J. B. Pick.

[5] Denis Saurat, 'Le Group de "la Renaissance Écossaise"' in *Revue Anglo Americaine*, Première Année, No 4, April 1924.

tonight: but have so far failed. I shall however forthwith hunt systematically till I do find it again and you may depend upon receiving it before the end of the week.

As to 'Blaeberries' and 'Gentlemen' I enclose them herewith.

I am delighted to hear that you are contemplating a collection. You know my opinion of course – that these sketches of yours are by far the best work of their kind that are appearing in Scotland, or from the pen of a Scottish writer today. I am not surprised that they find ready acceptance in the *Cornhill* and elsewhere. It was extra-ordinarily good of you to let me have so many for my various publications: and that I did not use them all was not due to any fault of mine. If my papers had continued I would certainly have done so. 'Cavern'd Echoes' is, I think, the best thing you have done (so far as I have seen). I was greatly disappointed to have to deem it too long for the *N.R.* – but hung on to it with more than half a thought of, despite its length, chancing it in a later issue. It is well worth all the space it would occupy: and I am glad you intend to include it in the prospective volume, for which I shall certainly be on the look-out.

I am hoping to have my McDiarmid poems out ere long in volume form.

I have done little else: but have just had a short story (1,000 words or so) returned from *The New Age* (for which I have been for the past 9 months – and still am – acting as literary critic) on the score that it is far too strong meat even for that select reading-public. The Editor (who is my very good friend) tells me it made him literally sick. This I consider a feather in my cap. It is certainly the best thing I have ever written in prose.

Excuse this scrappy note.

It carries with it my sincerest apologies for what must have seemed a peculiarly wanton and ingrate delay. And every good wish for 1925 to Mrs Gunn and yourself.

Yours,
C. M. Grieve.

16 Links Avenue.
14th Oct. 1925

My dear Gunn:-

I've run out of ink. Never mind. Yes, *Sangschaw* came out a month ago. It has not been widely reviewed. *Aberdeen Jnl.* gave it a column of abuse. *Scotsman* was much better than I expected. Jeffrey reviewed it enthusiastically I believe in *Glasgow Evening Times*: A.E. gave it great praise in *Irish Statesman* (and wrote me personally – as have Professor Grierson and others). Muir is doing a special article on it for *Saturday Review of Literature* (America), which Saurat is translating for *Les Marges*. Tom Henderson is to review it in *Educ. Jnl.* So far *Glasgow Herald* hasn't touched it – tho' they print a McD. poem today.[1] Jessie Anne Anderson reviews it in annexed paper – which I send you for her article on myself. – But I'm satisfied that it will make good and achieve my purpose. I'm busy arranging a second volume for next year. – I'll be delighted to sign as you wish. Is it to be as C.M.G. or H. McD? By the way I took the liberty of inscribing one of the poems to yourself in the book.

Yeats's poem appeared in the Book of the Rhymer's Club in 1892. I don't know if that was its first appearance: but it was probably written that year.

How's *that novel* getting on?

I was speaking (and Scott was playing McD settings) to an Edinburgh audience under the auspices of Prof Patrick Geddes the other week – and I also gave poetry readings of McD, Muir and one or two others – including N. M. Gunn. Went off very well. Dundee next month; Falkirk in December. The blighters have simply got to wake up and I intend to hammer at them till they do.

Mrs G. undertakes to dispatch you Waldo Frank's stories *this week*.

I am to have one – perhaps 3 – articles shortly on Scots Renaissance in *The Irish Statesman*.[2]

Hope you are both well – and that your pen is busy. Be sure

---

[1] *Sangschaw* (Edinburgh 1925) was reviewed in the *Aberdeen Press and Journal* on 12 September 1925; in *The Scotsman* on 22 September 1925; in *The Glasgow Evening Times* on 24 September 1925; in *The Irish Statesman* on 3 October 1925; in *The Saturday Review of Literature* on 30 October 1925; and in *The Glasgow Herald* on 3 December 1925.

[2] 'Towards a Scottish Renaissance' by C. M. Grieve, *The Irish Statesman*, Vol 5, No 19, 16 January 1926.

and look us up whenever you get a chance. Mrs G. joins me in all kind regards to Mrs G. and yourself.

Yours,
C.M.G.

NLS   [November 1925]

My dear Gunn,

I have been going to write you for some time. I hope your copies of *Sangschaw* got safely back to you – but if they hadn't I'd have heard, I hope. I am still retaining your Magazine – because I hope to get my article on yourself done one of these days: and want to quote one or two sentences. I am tremendously taken with 'Half-light'[1] and have no fears of your novel if it is along these lines and if – as I confidently anticipate – you have been able to imbue your imaginative re-creation with an effective internal organisation, integrating the whole and transforming it from a mass of extraordinary suggestive words and incidents into an organic whole. I shall await further news of it with impatience. But impatient or not I have no fears of your eventual success – if you stick to it, and cease underrating your really remarkable abilities and the superior importance of their development to other pursuits which may be easier or more con-genial to you. I wish, in fact, that I had you in gaol – I'd be a rigorous and most exigent, however unconventional gaoler. I'm afraid I can't make you see the vital necessity of what I am driving after along so many different (and perhaps apparently diverse) lines – but there is no one else I know of, still outwith or merely on the fringe of this movement, whom I am more anxious to convert to a burning and insatiable enthusiasm for the concepts of a distinctive Scottish culture. You can – if you will – do a great deal.

Nor have I time here – apart from my aversion from letter-writing in any event – to discuss your *G.H.* article of last Saturday on 'New Forms'. But, God permitting, I will yet – vocally & vis-a-vis – if you do not advertently keep outwith the range of my tongue – which God forbid.

[1] Gunn's story 'Half-Light' appeared in the *Cornhill Magazine* in November 1925.

In the whole, however, I am satisfied with the way things are shaping.

The *G.H.* has ignored *Sangschaw* – so far. But I am in correspondence with Sir Robert Bruce[2] on the subject, & we'll see.

I enclose as you requested Muir's article:[3] Will you please return it soon, as I want to send it on to somebody else who proferred a like request & it's the only copy I have, or can easily get.

Muir is here just now and will be till after the New Year, when he is going to the South of France.

For myself I am busy – writing speeches for I am speaking at Falkirk, Dundee & Glasgow within the next few weeks – and making herculean efforts to knead into publishable shape a new prose work which will be a sort of Scottish complement of Joyce's *Ulysses*.

I have also another volume of McD poems ready for the publisher: and am adjusting my *Scottish Studies* which Leonard Parsons are to publish next Ocober at 10/6. Some book! You'll note how I reply to 'Theta' (Tom Henderson – Editor of the *Educ. Jnl.*) in this week's[4] article on Spence and Marion Angus. – I am afraid their criticisms of my style and arguments only divert me, however indignant or conceited, etc. I make myself appear for ulterior motives.

Now, there's a request I would make – but pay no attention to it if it presents any difficulty or if you do not wish to do that sort of thing for any reason. It is this – drinkable whisky, as I think I've told you before, is simply not procurable here – it is neither whisky nor Scottish: and the stuffie you gave me on two occasions was comparatively most astonishingly and delectably right. Can you procure me any against the forthcoming Xmas season, when I expect to have Muir & Scott & probably other visitors of a kidney to appreciate the genuine article – and to join with me in all the more delightful and soul-searching symposia under its benign influence. I do not want you, now, to make me a present. It is the fear that you will construe this request into a request of that kind that makes me hesitate to ask this favour. It isn't that at all, however – but simply that I can't get decent stuff & you apparently can. But whether you can in sufficient

---

2 Cf. 'The Two Bruces' (264) from *To Circumjack Cencrastus*:

    There were twa Robert Bruces.
    Ane edited 'The Glasgow Herald.'
    The ither focht for Scotland
    When it was *less* imperilled.

The Glasgow Herald reviewed *Sangschaw* on 3 December 1925.

3 Edwin Muir's review of *Sangschaw* appeared in *The Saturday Review of Literature*, 31 October 1925.

4 *The Scottish Educational Journal* of 27 November 1925 carried Grieve's article 'The New Movement in Vernacular Poetry – Lewis Spence: Marion Angus', collected in *Contemporary Scottish Studies* (Edinburgh 1976) pp 61–3.

quantity & with sufficient ease to enable you to accede to such a request is another matter – and, besides, it may be something you have to do sub rosa and can only do infrequently when circumstances favour. I don't know. The whole thing is 'wroft in mystery'. But if you can do it – and send me a bottle or two bottles – I shall be extremely obliged, and shall remit cost and carriage as soon as I know what they amount to. And I shall please want to know that simultaneously with their, or its, arrival. And you must please understand that I will not accept unless I am permitted to pay.

Now I must cease and be about my business. This leaves us all well. If you are knocking about near Xmas time be sure & look us up. I should like you to meet Muir, &, even more, Scott if he is here. And Mrs G. and I will in any case be always more than glad to see Mrs Gunn and yourself at any time. Baby is fat & flourishing. I trust Mrs Gunn and yourself are in the best of fettle. This carries with it our kindest regards to both of you.

In great haste.

Yours ever,
C. M. Grieve.

P.S. Muir's article got jumbled in 1st para. & was cut down into the bargain – quotes, etc, being excluded in latter half.

NLS   16 Links Avenue,
                                                                            Montrose.
                                                                       22nd Mar. 1926.

My dear Gunn,

Your book is fine. I return the proof-copy herewith. (By the way I assume that this is a duplicate proof and that you corrected and sent back another – because there are all sorts of mistakes – little misprints, typographical errors etc. uncorrected in this copy. I know how infernally difficult to spot such things are.) When I say your book is fine I mean that, as it stands, it is a good bit of work of which you have every reason to be proud. From a purely literary point of view I must, of course, admit that it doesn't 'make history' – but then you didn't set out to do that, which is precisely what you should have done. There is sufficient in this book to justify my hope that you will yet get right down to yourself. But you'll see by enclosed proof (which don't return) what I am about to be saying about you in the *Educational Journal*.[1] Good luck to your book – I hope it sells well – I hope it is the beginning of a prolonged and fruitful connection with the publishers – I hope you get enough money out of it (tho' here I'm doubtful) to pay for that new house of yours – and, once all that has happened, you won't want another house will you? – a bigger house – if so, it's hopeless – but I don't think so – I think you'll really begin to try your darnedest.

Your two plays – I like them both – in a way. Even in a literary sense, however, I do not think they're quite in final form – I think they can come through a great deal further. But what I've been mainly troubled about is with them from a purely producer's or actor's point of view. Technically they won't do – you say too much (drama can dispense with *so* much verbiage – gesture, posture, etc., facial expression, and so forth are all auxiliary means of expression which render so many words superfluous – how often in real life do we complete a sentence? – it is only necessary in 9 cases out of 10 to start a sentence, and it completes itself in our faces, etc.). You say too much – on the other hand (I'm thinking mainly of the three-act play) – you don't say enough – to clarify the intended underlying action – it doesn't transpire – clogged with words that do not advance it.

I have delayed writing sooner, however, for a variety of reasons. A sort of little 'palace revolution' is going on in connection with the Scottish National Players: and I've been waiting to see which side won. I'm not quite competent to criticise your plays from a severely technical standpoint – and that's what they need. So (despite my dissatisfaction with them in their present form – there's always a danger of blighters like me becoming hypercritical) I meant to try the plays on their Reading Cmmtee – if only that you might benefit by their report. But I'm not sure that an even better plan would not be to send them to R. F. Pollock[2] – and ask him to do for them just what some months ago (with tremendous benefit to it and permanent illumination in many directions to myself) he did to a play of

---

[1] MacDiarmid's review of Gunn's first novel *The Grey Coast* (1926) appeared in *The Scottish Educational Journal* of 2 April 1926 and is collected in *Contemporary Scottish Studies* (Edinburgh 1977). It contends that if Gunn 'can rid himself of his remaining inequalities – sustain himself wholly at the pitch of the best elements in this book – and bring the method by which he encompassed them to full maturity, he will rapidly take rank as the foremost of living Scottish novelists – a George Douglas Brown come to magnanimity and endowed with all the knowledge psychology has acquired since Brown's day.' (p. 98).

[2] R. F. Pollock, who worked with Dumbarton People's Theatre, was interested in developing an indigenous drama in Scotland.

mine. Pollock has been at 6s and 7s for private family reasons lately or I'd have done this ere now. I think it's the best plan – if you're really keen to learn (as, on the basis of what, in your technical ignorance, you have nevertheless contrived to do you jolly well should be). – In any case I'm not returning them yet.

'The Glog Hole'[3] verse came in splendidly. I'm extremely glad you've found such a use for it.

Busy myself – yes. *Penny Wheep* is coming out this spring yet – *A Drunk Man* in the Autumn, as also *Contemporary Scottish Studies*. The *Drunk Man* is swelling – I fixed him up with the publishers at 600 lines but now he's over 800. – Kindest regards to Mrs G. and yourself from Mrs G. and I. We are looking forward to seeing you ere long now.

Yours,
C.M.G.

NLS

16 Links Avenue,
Montrose.
22/6/26

My dear Gunn,

Splendid! Congratulations on your American settlement. You'll be eventually getting a certain number of copies of that American edition and I shall be glad if you can spare me one of these. I am making a little collection of American editions of works by friends of mine. I shall be keeping a keen eye open for reviews of *The Grey Coast* and hope to hear from you later on about how it has gone both here and in America, as to sales and as to expressed opinion. I hope you have had sufficient interest in the matter yourself to have instructed a press-cutting agency. The best way to do (if you haven't) is to give the press-cutting people a list of the papers, etc. to which review copies have been sent – which you get yourself from your publisher. You'd get 50 cuttings or so for about £1.1/-. And don't forget to send that photo of yourself, duly autographed.

---

[3] Gunn printed MacDiarmid's 'The Glog-Hole' (171) on the title page of *The Grey Coast*.

I'll be delighted to sign a *Penny Wheep* for you: and have no doubt I'll manage to furbish up a verse, too. It came out last week – delayed a bit by the strike. Perhaps you'd seen the *Aberdeen Free Press*'s article on it last Saturday. They've come round a bit. Along with all manner of vices it seems now that I *have* certain merits.

I've been deuced busy and am now ready for our St Cyrus hegira and some country walks, 'dooking' and general loafing.

Item I have got *Contemp Scottish Studies* in final shape for publishers – with preface, concluding chapter, index and what not.

Item I have *A Drunk Man*, etc. also ready – 2,600 lines in all.

Item I had an unexpected spasm which produced 25 poems for a new collection of lyrics (some of the best I've written) which I propose to call *The Luckybag*.

You'll have heard from Purves[1] about the Edinburgh University Women's thing.[2] And I hope you will and can give him something really good. Indirectly it'll be worth a good deal to you, as you'll represent Scotland in extremely distinguished cosmopolitan company – French, Italian, Spanish, English and American – e.g. Miss Colburn Mayne, Mrs Virginia Woolf. I'm contributing verse; Muir criticism; Scott, music.

Then Erskine of Marr and I (as co-editors) have definitely decided to go ahead with a new quarterly, on lines similar to those of the *Mercure de France*, to be called *The Scottish Review*. We've made arrangements with Edinburgh printers (the printers of the *Educ. Jnl.*) who will see to the whole of the business side – adverts, distribution etc. To mak' siccar I think we'll probably try to get 100 people to take up £10 bonds – not to be called upon unless audited accounts show a deficiency that calls for help. Bond-holders will get a free copy of the Review (which will include Music and Art) quarterly. But more of this anon. We're busy on the matter now: and will be issuing printed matter, securing publicity, etc., almost immediately. I'm hoping to have your help here again. All over we're going to pitch a higher standard than ever.

You'll be ensconced in your new house. Mrs Grieve joins me in hoping that Mrs Gunn and you may have all happiness and good fortune in it. This carries affectionate regards from us both.

I hope you've shown your appreciation of your good fortune in the

---

[1] John Purves was Lecturer in Italian at Edinburgh University and an enthusiastic reader of Scottish literature.

[2] *Atalanta's Garland* (1926), a book published on the occasion of the 21st birthday of the Edinburgh University Women's Union, contained work by Katherine Mansfield, Hilaire Belloc, W. H. Davies, Virginia Woolf, Edwin Muir ('On the Impoverishment of Language') and others. MacDiarmid's 'Hungry Waters' (52) was included alongside F. G. Scott's setting of the lyric.

only right way – i.e. that you've a second novel *ready now*; and a third well on the way.

I've been thinking that – since we understand each other pretty well, I think, and appreciate what each of us has that the other lacks and that is complementary – we might try a little experimental collaboration. My idea is to rough out a book in say 10,000 to 15,000 words (some really good tendenciously Scottish idea involving all kinds of Scots types, some of whom I know well, some of whom you know and I don't – ditto with settings in different parts of Scotland – technique of different occupations, touches of different dialects and so on). Then send it to you – to let your mind play over, bring out new aspects, introduce fresh characters etc. – bringing it up to 25,000 to 30,000 words. Back to me for another 10,000 or so: then to you for the same. And once we'd got to that stage we could meet somewhere and have a pow-wow and give it final shape there and then. How does that strike you? I'm in the mood for prose just now and have been doing all sorts of things. Along these lines we might complement each other in a way which would bring out a very remarkable book. In any case, I'd like to try out such a collaboration.

By the way, I'd like that *Irish Statesman*[3] as I want to try to polish off soon the little book of which it is to be the first chapter.

Excuse this hasty scrawl.

Yours,
C. M. Grieve.

NLS

16 Links Avenue,
Montrose.
14.12.26

My dear Gunn,

I was wondering what on earth had come over you. Expecially whether Mrs. Gunn was well or not. You do not say anything about her. So I assume no news is good news. Mrs. Grieve joins me in

[3] 'Towards a Scottish Renaissance' by C. M. Grieve in *The Irish Statesman*, Vol 5, No 19, 16 January 1926.

particular good regards to her. As for you – however, it's too soon in what I recognise must be a fairly lengthy letter to go into that.

First of all in case I forget once I get on to other things, since you want to be kept posted re my output.

1/ I enclose copy of my Benn's Series Burns.[1]

2/ 1/1½ will place an order for my 1/- pamphlet on *The Present Condition of Scottish Music*[2] which is due immediately – address, Proprietor, *The Border Standard*, Galashiels.

3/ P.O. for 3/6 is subscription for new series of Porpoise Press Broadsheets, one of which will be *The Lucky Bag*[3] by H McD. Porpoise Press is under management of Miss Spence now and deserves all support. Address Porpoise Press, Stafford St., Edinburgh.

Next – have you got a copy of Muir's new vol. of essays: *Transition*[4]. If not, I want to give you one. Please let me know as to this *by return*.

To polish off personal matters 1/ you've got right perspective of *Cont. Scot Studies*. I am very conscious of its faults – and just as conscious of the necessity of most of those very faults to enable it to effect its purpose which it undoubtedly will, no matter what anybody says about it or doesn't say. It is bound to tell enormously. In the Second Series I propose not to go on with similar personal studies at all – but to deal with the whole subject of Nationality, Future of Literature, Essence of Languages, etc. To write for Europe apropos Scotland instead of for Scotland apropos Scotland. And I don't care what anybody says about my English style. The only test of any style is its effectiveness for the author's purpose – and there is no mistake about mine for that! So there. Other people can chew over niceties. I want to win through and do things – and will!

2/ Thanks for what you say about *Drunk Man*. I am as satisfied with it too as is at all good for me. But my satisfaction is modified by my realisation of what *Cencrastus* will cost me. It'll be a very big book. *To Circumjack Cencrastus* is Scots for 'to square the circle', 'to box the compass': and I mean to do it in style though it costs my life.

I have just had a letter from an old English friend (himself a writer of parts) who has a most Un Sassenach-like appreciation of (inter alia) *my English prose style*, pace *Educ. Jul.* correspondents et sic. And in replying to his enthusiastic appreciation of *Contemp. Scots Studies*, I have just said after mentioning other things,

'You will be more interested to know that I am now feeling about ready to begin my frontal attack on English prose – so long

[1] *Robert Burns, 1759-96* (London 1926) edited by C. M. Grieve.
[2] C. M. Grieve, *The Present Position of Scottish Music* (Montrose 1927).
[3] Hugh MacDiarmid, *The Lucky Bag* (Edinburgh 1927).
[4] Edwin Muir, *Transition: Essays on Contemporary Literature* (1926).

meditated; and may do a great deal to it this incoming year, especially as my next McDiarmid book, which is to be a very big one, will be one which I can only develop very slowly. In the intervals I propose therefore to go ahead with prose. This has only been a matter of patience. I am not sure yet whether I am just mature enough in some ways for what I propose to attempt. We'll see. It's the sort of frontal attack which will, if it comes off, not only mean a great deal to Scottish literature, but will have a strong side-wind effect on English letters. I have a feeling in my bones that I'll be able to pull it off soon now.'

You know me well enough, and the English friend (who has seen far more of my English experimental fragments than you have) knows me well enough too, to appreciate that that is not idle swank but a tremendous intention which as soon as the psychological moment comes, will engage every cell of my brain with the most unsparing concentration. I quote it because it brings me to the question of your new novel. *The Grey Coast* was well reviewed and I presume sold well. In view of that (and the mediocre level of that vast majority of novels *which are published*), that Cape's have turned down your second novel *proves* that it must have very strong qualities. That they (or rather one man – Garnett)[5] has reacted unfavourably is not a bad sign; on the contrary it probably only means that you have done something another publisher coming fresh to your work from a different point of view, will snap up. It is as you remark unsatisfactory trying to write about this sort of thing. But while I recognise that such an experience entails certain effects of disappointment and doubt I am professionaly callous (or experienced) enough to know that, whatever your novel is, *it is an infinitely more promising phenomenon than if Cape's had jumped at it. It means at the least that you're not just repeating yourself*: but growing creatively. It may be that the growing pains still have you in their grip: and that you have not yet adequately emerged from the test. But from your letter I believe you have, and put it to you thus – Any author worth his salt *knows* whether he has done good work or not. He may not know *how* good. But if you are conscious that what you have done whatever it is has been done in a spirit of complete artistic integrity it is *infallibly all right* for its right public, and for yourself – which matters most. What you say of style modulation – altering to suit subject, mood etc. – is beyond a doubt right. Right in principle. All the best writers on the Continent are doing something along these very lines. Conservative critics hate it – it bewilders the general public – it is only a matter of time. Joyce in *Ulysses* has whole sections in which (as you will see from Muir's essay in *Transition* – I don't know if you've read *Ulysses*

5 Edward Garnett (1868–1937), publisher's reader and literary adviser.

itself) he does this very thing in a perfectly miraculous way. Go ahead with it for all you are worth. It is undoubtedly the prose method of the future. The old undifferentiated 'simple direct English' is as dead as a door-nail. I'm looking forward with the keenest of interest to reading it. I'd say send it on but you know what I am – and besides I've a better suggestion. What are you doing about New Year time? I get a couple of days then – and if you are to be at home would come up and have a go at it on the spot with you. If you're not to be at home I'll come up the very first possible week-end in the New Year. Or if you're free yourself why not turn up here about Christmas or New Year time. Let me know which of these three alternatives you prefer. And the Waldo F. book, and that American copy of the *Grey Coast* I want can wait till then.

You're wrong in one thing about that proposed collab. Behind everything else I have an intuition which assures me that what I'm doing is going to find a publisher all right; if I hadn't that intuition I'd never get through with it either. I'd have pressed the collab. business despite your objections had it not been for certain practical difficulties; but what I now propose is to leave it over until we get a chance of having a week or fortnight together: then we'll go at it and do it out of hand. Crockett wrote most of *The Stickit Minister* in 48 hours; Stevenson did *Dr Jekyll and Mr Hyde* in less than a week. We could certainly have a novel to show for a week together if we really got down to business. I shall be exceedingly surprised if I do not write one myself shortly. I have promised Blackwood's one by next autumn: and I have the most of it in my head now. There'll be no simple direct English of any kind about it.

Enough! The sense of all this is – Hurrah! Don't be discouraged. Keep on churning it out for all you're worth. So long as you know you're putting guts into it, it's worth while – even if you haven't yet resolved your experimental conceptions to reduce it to a form of maximum effectiveness. That'll come with practice.

Now, in conclusion, about these two plays, I've a hazy notion whereabouts they are: and will fish them out and re-read them and return them (honest Injun!) *not later than this week-end*. I can't say more.

Hoping to see you soon, and with every good wish, in which Mrs G. joins me most heartily.

Yours,
C.M.G.

P.S. Sorry for the execrable scrawl, but my pen's napoo. I'll look forward to your studied comments on *Drunk Man*. Such things help.

My dear Gunn,

A variety of unforeseen things has kept me much longer in writing
than I should have been – absence for a little while in Edinburgh,
then the sudden death of one of Mrs Grieve's sisters (involving
another, and longer, absence), a subsequent indisposition of my
own, and, as a result of these, arrears. You'll understand.
.... But I should have written at once to express our sympathy
with you in the loss of your mother. Although it has gone so long
unexpressed, it is none the less sincere – and our own recent loss has
accentuated our feeling for others.

We were very sorry to hear, too, that Mrs Gunn had been ill again
and through an operation. We trust that it was entirely successful
and that she is completely all right again by now.

And you're becoming a Big Man. I cannot tell you how much I
have enjoyed reading appreciative reviews of *The Grey Coast* in many
quarters – how much that enjoyment has been sharpened by the real
discrimination of many of them, the truth of what they said. But now
that you've had so much (deserved) encouragement – it's time you
were taken sharply to task: and probably I'm the man to do it. I'm
sufficiently at least a worker myself to have the right to do it – and
write sufficiently myself to know just what in sheer hard labour
inciting anyone to write more and better means. But it really is up to
you. I'd worry the soul into you (not out of you, I hope) if I was
anywhere within reach. With hard concentrated effort for the next
few short stories – and having an ultimate aim all the time, foreseeing the character of your eventual corpus as a whole, moving
systematically to create a real 'world of your own', there is every
likelihood that you would then rank as a representative Scottish
novelist – occupy a definite and high position in respect of the whole
cultural history of the country. That at any rate – and nothing less –
should be your aim: and the time to start to realise it – is not this
autumn or next year – but now and henceforth *all the time*!

This, of course, is pure preaching – and perhaps poor preaching.
Besides it doesn't say what – or only a comparatively unimportant
part of what – I want to say. It wouldn't really matter a fig to me if
you were to become a – or even *the* – representative contemporary
Scottish novelist, if I weren't interested in the *kind* of novelist you'd
be. Neil Munro is after a fashion representative enough and has a
solid body of work behind him. I appreciate him well enough: but I
wouldn't give two brass farthings for anyone who duplicated his
achievement. But it's because of the particular kind of thing which I

know you will do if you can be induced to apply yourself concentratedly enough to the task – the kind of thing which it is essential and inevitable that somebody should do in relation to Scotland soon, and which I think is the raison d'etre of your particular existence, your intended function – that I am inconceivably keen to know that work is going steadily and surely ahead at Inverness!

I've been hoping too – and haven't yet given up hope – that you've bought that car or motor-cycle combination, and that we may see Mrs Gunn and you soon. Failing that I've been seriously wondering whether we couldn't contrive a day or two in Inverness later on. I feel – I don't know if you reciprocate the feeling – that you are a person I must see more of, as much as I possibly can, in actual physical contact. Your splendid photograph (which otherwise I am delighted to have) aggravates this feeling – it's so like you that I almost involuntarily turn to it to open up a conversation – and then remember that despite its lifelikeness it's only a photo, damn it, and that it's useless talking to it.

I'm glad you like the collaboration scheme so far as it goes. I should probably have carried it a good deal further before this but for the deplorable way in which one thing and another has side-tracked my intentions during the past couple of months. I should really have done ten times the amount of writing I've been able to do. But I'll get on to the rails ere long and try to make up for lost speed. Don't be surprised some week if I send you 90000 words or so with the demand that (unless you can give good and sufficient reasons for regarding that either in subject or style as an unsuitable basis, I have other and better suggestions to make) you return it doubled in a fortnight's time!

I'm enclosing you a copy of Muir's latest.[1]

I'm writing this without reference to your last – buried somewhere under a pile of stuff – so you'll excuse me if I've forgotten any particular point to which I should have referred.

With affectionate regards from all of us to Mrs Gunn and yourself.

Yours,
C. M. Grieve.

[1] Edwin Muir, *Transition* (1926).

16 Links Avenue,
Montrose.
28/2/27

My dear Gunn,

We were extremely sorry to learn of the death of Mrs Gunn's father. I should have written sooner, because of this if for nothing else, but have been excessively busy, even for me. Belatedly, then, please convey to Mrs Gunn Mrs Grieve's, and my own, sincerest sympathy in her bereavement. We both trust that she herself is keeping better and that this latest sorrow has not reacted on her own health.

I needn't tell you I was disgusted beyond words over Blackwood's refusal of your novel. – And still more disgusted at the idea that you were discouraged, weren't going to 'see it through', and felt inclined to confine yourself to the kind of stuff you foreknow will be accepted.

The concluding paragraph of a very fine – 1½ page – appreciation of the *Drunk Man* by Senator Oliver St John Gogarty, which appeared in *The Irish Statesman*[1], is apropos:-
'Nationality in poetry will out, and the poet will be kept out from the great Encyclopaedia which has taken the place of Parnassus if he reveals the fact by dialect or sentiment that he is not an Englishman. Or, worse still, he will be ignored as Barnes, English though he is, is ignored, for writing according to genius and not grammar. Of course I am not unaware of the obvious corollary to this that no one except an Englishman can write English poetry. It is just as well: but it should comfort those whose aim it to bring beauty into words to realise that it matters not in what dialect she makes herself manifest: and Mr. McDiarmid can console himself (if he needs consolation) with the fact that he has written the most virile and vivid poetry that has been written in English or any dialect thereof for many a long day.' And, what's more, A.E. (Geo Russell) himself wrote me and said he'd read the *Dr Man* too and agreed with every word Gogarty said about it. So there!

So there you are – for it doesn't apply to poetry only, or to the outward forms of using dialect – it penetrates to the spirit behind: and that, too, I am more and more convinced is 'the matter' with your second novel.

And then Hergesheimer,[2] the popular American novelist, kept sending MSS. on their rounds for 14 years before he got a single

[1] *The Irish Statesman*, Vol 7, No 18, 8 January 1927, pp. 430–3.
[2] Joseph Hergesheimer (1880–1954), author of *Linda Condon* (1919) and *Balisand* (1924).

thing accepted. – But he didn't give in: and now they lap him up at his own valuation – and his own price.

You will appreciate why I conjoin these two things: and what advice to you lurks behind than.

So far as I am concerned I've made a little headway with my own novel (in English) but switched that to one side on a sudden impulse, deciding that my next book would be a collection of short stories in Scots. I've well over half the book written. One of the stories – 'The Common Riding' – will appear in the *Glasgow Herald* shortly.[3]

I'm busy now on an important series of articles for *The New Age*[4] (specially asked for) on 'Nietzsche and The Revival of the European Spirit' which is involving some hefty reading, and, what is worse, thinking! – a thing I detest – especially as this time I'll have to be careful, as I intend to have these articles republished in book form.

My Porpoise Press pamphlet[5] is in hand and should be out very soon now.

Perhaps you saw the *G. Herald* music critic's comments on my Music pamphlet in Saturday's issue.[6]

Muir had a good long review of the *Drunk Man* in *The Nation and Athenaeum*.[7]

My stuff (Blackwood's report) is now beginning to sell – slowly but steadily.

I haven't got McLeish written to yet. But I simply can't help myself in regard to personal correspondence. I haven't written to Mr Barron[8] either – or sent him the book I promised. But I think I will manage that this week. I am delighted Mrs Barron is doing your head. Did Paterson[9] show you McGillivray's comment thereanent? Paterson's been far too kind – sending me copies of these photos. I'm a bad hand at thanking folks – infinitely better at the asperities than at the amenities.

By the way, if these short stories are accepted (as I've little doubt they will be) for publication in book form I want to dedicate them to

---

3 *The Glasgow Herald*, 12 March 1927.
4 MacDiarmid wrote regularly for *The New Age* from 1924 to 1931.
5 *The Lucky Bag* (Edinburgh 1927).
6 *The Glasgow Herald*, 26 February 1927, carried a review of *The Present Position of Scottish Music* (Montrose 1927) by C. M. Grieve and commented: 'it is, unfortunately, merely destructive as a piece of criticism, and having laid bare all that is unsatisfactory in the present position in Scotland with regard to music, it leaves the unhappy reader wondering what Mr Grieve proposes to do about it.'
7 *The Nation and Athenaeum*, Vol XL, No 16, 22 January 1927, p. 568.
8 The Barrons, who lived at Oaklands in Inverness, were well-known figures on the local cultural scene; Mrs Gladys Caroline Barron was a sculptor who exhibited at the Royal Scottish Academy and other venues.
9 Andrew Paterson, the Inverness photographer.

Mrs Gunn and yourself – 'To J.G. and N.M. Gunn'? The title of the book will be *The Muckle Toon*.

Now I must stop. I've all sorts of other irons in the fire – but of these more anon. Mrs Grieve had the misfortune to slip or something and has a nasty bit of synovitis of the knee. But her mother came on Saturday: so she's getting a better chance to rest it now. Write soon, and give me your own news. I'm wondering if you've got Novel No 3 off yet?

Love to you both. Please remember me to the Patersons and the Barrons, and to McLeish[10] to whom *I will write yet*.

Yours,
C.M.G.

P.S. What about Saurat now?
Or has he put you in your pigeonhole?
I'm not just in a dead hurry for the book tho' – as *Cencrastus* is still hung up till I get these short stories and at least one other prose book off.

NLS   12/4/27

My dear Gunn,

Just a line to say that we shall be at home and more than delighted to see you when you come. But won't you stay here rather than at the Star? We can't offer you the comfort and facilities of Larachan: but there is a bedroom available and 'such as I have I give unto you'. However, whatever suits you suits me: please yourself without fear that I shall be offended if you don't choose to come here, or without imagining that this way of putting things in any way qualifies the readiness with which Mrs G. and myself shall welcome your decision if it goes against good Mr Amos in our favour. But let us know which it's to be: a p.c. will serve the purpose.

I'm not going to say anything more here and now – except that

---

[10] R.J. McLeish was a friend of Gunn's and an unattached officer on distillery duty at Fort William, Tobermory, Oban and Jedburgh. He wrote stories and poems in his spare time and enjoyed arguing with Gunn about MacDiarmid's poetry.

I'm delighted Mrs Barron's bust[1] of you has gone in. I don't know yet if McGillivray was at the choosing – he's been ill and prior to that away from Edinburgh and my correspondence with him is a bit out of gear. But we'll hear anon.

Love to both of you: and please remember me to other friends.

Yours,
C.M.G.

NLS
TS

16 Links Avenue,
Montrose.
16th May, 1927

My dear Gunn:-

Scotland is one of the few European countries in which a centre of the PEN Club has not yet been formed, although Sir J. M. Barrie, R. B. Cunninghame Graham and a few other Scottish authors are members of the London Centre. Some time ago Mr Galsworthy[1] asked Professor H. J. C. Grierson, of Edinburgh University, to try to form a Scottish Centre. Professor Grierson got in touch with me as the only member, I think, regularly resident in Scotland; but pressure of other work caused delay. Professor Grierson later asked me to go ahead with the arrangements along lines he had discussed with me, and I agreed to do so. I have since discussed the matter with the London Centre's Executive Committee (who are keenly desirous of completing the chain of international centres by establishing one in Scotland) and I am acting on their advice and with their support.[2]

The literary life of Scotland not being concentrated in any one city, it is proposed to do as has been successfully done in certain other countries and establish a national centre, with sections in Edinburgh and Glasgow. Membership of the Centre would carry with it membership of both sections – *and of all the other international*

[1] At the Royal Scottish Academy in 1927 Mrs Gladys Barron exhibited 'Neil M. Gunn, Esq', a bronze bust for sale at £105.
[1] John Galsworthy (1867–1933), the novelist, was first President of the London Centre of PEN.
[2] MacDiarmid became secretary of the Scottish Centre of PEN.

centres. But that, and all other matters including the appointment of office bearers, adoption of rules, and arrangements for meetings (the Club is of course purely a social one and not to be used for business purposes of any kind) can be discussed at an inaugural meeting which I propose to call at such time and place as may be convenient to the majority of those who agree to join; and at which I hope to have Mr Galsworthy, Mrs Dawson Scott (the Founder) or other representatives of the London Centre present to guide us.

I have pleasure in asking you to join. I enclose a leaflet giving some general information regarding the PEN Clubs. Membership will entail such annual subscription as may be determined at the inaugural meeting.

I shall be glad to give you any further information you desire. I am sending out some thirty of these circular letters in the hope of securing a sufficient nucleus of those qualified to be members to justify calling an inaugural meeting. A number with whom I have had an opportunity of discussing the matter verbally have already agreed to join. I hope you will do so too. Will you favour me with a reply at your early convenience?

Yours Sincerely,
C. M. Grieve.

P.S. Kindest regards from Mrs G. and myself to both of you. Trust you were none the worse of your flying visit here. Write soon and give me your news. I've none at the moment.

NLS   16 Links Avenue,
                                                       Montrose.
                                                       18/12/27

My dear Gunn,

I have, of course, been going to write you ever since your all-too brief visit. As you know I took it for granted you'd stay over the next day and got a nasty shock when you didn't − nasty because I'd arranged the previous night differently if I'd known there was no chance of having a talk with Mrs Gunn and yourself then; and − above all − because I was particularly sorry you (or rather Mrs

Gunn) went off without a fresh supply of books. This latter matter has been on my conscience ever since: and I've been hoping you'd run through to one of the PEN functions via Montrose and give me the chance to send you home with a load.

Apropos this PEN business, why can't you? I appreciate you can't come every month perhaps – but once in a while you could surely make a week-end of it. When I first broached the matter to you you said something along these lines yourself.

I haven't time to write a decent letter: so I'll take it for granted 1/ you've seen *Albyn* (and Thomson's *Caledonia*)[1] and my subsequent propaganda in *The Outlook, New Age, Scottish Home Rule, Forward*, etc.; 2/ my new 'Synthesis' articles in *Scots Independent*,[2] *Pictish Review*, etc. etc. and are therefore fully alive to all this is toward. I'm extremely busy and quite satisfied with the way things are going (despite the fact that Leonard Parsons[3] went phut! and did me out of all the royalties on *Contemp. Scots Studies*). I addressed the local Wesley Guild on Thursday night: presided over an area Trade Unions Conference on Friday; and have made arrangements to give a joint lecture-recital with Scott in Edinburgh early next year; to 'put Burns in his place' in Glasgow about 21st Jan; and to address the Dundee Theosophical people on 'Major Douglas and the New Economics' in March. Add to that fact that I've had my head done too (by William Lamb, the sculptor) – and I think I've put in a fair amount of work.

What about you? What *about* you? What about *YOU*! Not a cheep! Not a sign? (except that I saw you were having a story[4] in the *Scots. Mag.* – which I recently dealt with faithfully and in detail in a Dundee Socialist paper running in opposition to the daily paper proprietry who now own the *Scots. Mag.*).

But the novels – not a word; or even of a new one written along possible lines – although even Maurice Walsh has finally come up to the scratch and perpetrated a second story, about to be serialised in Chamber's to a great time of special advts, gossipy paragraphs, and a special advt of *Above The Door*[5] taken the form of a Benediction by Barrie. - - - What a life!

[1] MacDiarmid felt that G. M. Thomson's *Caledonia* (1927) and his own *Albyn* (London 1927) provided a theoretical foundation for a more enlightened stage of Scottish Nationalism and said so in various reviews and articles which led up to the formation of the National Party of Scotland the following year.
[2] C. M. Grieve's study of 'Neo-Gaelic Economics' was published in two parts in the *Scots Independent* (Vol II, No 2, December 1927, pp. 21–2; Vol II, No 4, February 1928, pp. 53–4).
[3] Leonard Parsons, the London publisher who brought out *Contemporary Scottish Studies*.
[4] Gunn's story 'Symbolical' was published in the *Scots Magazine* in December 1927.
[5] Maurice Walsh, *The Key Above the Door* (1926).

Seriously my dear man, I hope you're not going to let 1927 go to its unhallowed grave in this fashion – or, at least, without promulgating a very different state of affairs for 1928, and thereafter – but, especially, 1928. (I'm not to let you ride off on any mere thereafter.)

I can't imagine what Mrs Gunn is about letting you slack on in this way. I don't exactly blame her, of course; I appreciate you're a difficult case: but she should have called in expert advice long ere this. If something doesn't happen soon, Scott, Spence, myself and a few others will arrive in Inverness to conduct a public post-mortem.

I enclose a couple of books which I hope will interest Mrs Gunn and yourself respectively – and perhaps interchangeably – and they carry with them the best wishes of all here to both of you for a merry Christmas and a prosperous New Year.

I've never got McLeish written to; nor Mr Barron: but I'm thinking of them and of Mr Paterson with happy recollections of the good time I had in Inverness a year ago.

Yours,
C. M. Grieve.

NLS

16 Links Avenue,
Montrose.
16/4/28

My dear Gunn:-

I should of course have written long ago to tell you Higgins's *Dark Breed*[1] was safe – somehow left behind here. I have meant to send it to you ever since I got your note: and will in a day or two – just at the moment I want it for something that's cropped up. And I should have written more recently to thank you, and express my appreciation, of 'Defensio Scotorum'[2] (which the Aberdeen paper speaks of

[1] F. R. Higgins's collection of poems *The Dark Breed* (1927).
[2] In *The Scots Magazine*, Vol. IX, No 1, April 1928, Gunn appeared twice: first as himself with the opening episode of his new novel *The Lost Glen* (Edinburgh 1932); then under his Scottish Nationalist pseudonym of Dane M'Neil who contributed 'Defensio Scotorum: A Reply to W. S. Morrison' which drew attention to 'Hugh M'Diarmid, whose last long poem, *A Drunk Man Looks at the Thistle*, drew from an international critic the considered statement that nothing so great had appeared in English or any dialect thereof for years.' For MacDiarmid's reply to the *John O'Groat Journal* comment on 13 April 1928 see pp. 766–8.

as 'mostly noise' – make more of it!) and above all for the opening instalment of your serial with which I am thoroughly pleased and waiting for more. Good work! Go ahead!

But since I haven't written there have been reasons – the chief item being a son,[3] born on 5th inst – and it is about him I'm writing you. He's to be baptised in the Scottish Episcopal Church (Mrs Grieve's) and requires two Godfathers and a Godmother. If I were to say that Mrs Grieve is particularly anxious that you should consent to be one of the former I should be minimising the extent of my own concurrence in the invitation – we are both equally hopeful that you will see your way to accept this tripartite sponsoring. But there's even more in it than that. Godparents can act by proxy! and if you couldn't come we could get someone here to act for you. But we don't want to do this – because the other Godfather won't be here: and we don't want two proxies. Now the baptism is to be on Sunday 29th. Can you possibly come down for it? I am fully anxious of the enormity of this request – but *it won't happen again.* Do try – and relieve a harassed parent's mind. Both Mrs G. & the baby are O.K. Kindest regards to Mrs Gunn and yourself.

Yours,
C.M.G.

NLS   21/4/28

Dear Neil,

Mrs G. and I have decided to postpone the baptism till after the local Rector has his holidays instead of hurrying it in order to enable him to perform the ceremony before he goes on holiday. (Do not irreverently imagine that this is to enable him to summon up the necessary courage.)

Therefore – unless you have already arranged to come next week-end (in which case please continue the arrangement and wire us so that we can make the necessary other arrangements) – the function will take place sometime in May (towards the end); and it may be easier for you to take a run through then.

[3] Walter Grieve.

I enclose the latest.

By the way next PEN function is provisionally fixed to take place in Glasgow on 2nd June and we are trying to make it a grand rally. Gordon Bottomley is to be the Guest: and Compton Mackenzie is also likely to be there.

Mrs G. joins me in every good wish to Mrs Gunn and yourself.

A stupid attack on your *Scots Mag* article in reply to Morrison appeared in the 'John O'Groat Journal'; and I'm replying in this week's issue.

Yours,
C.M.G.

NLS   3.5.28

My dear Gunn,

What a pity! But for your disbelief in your ability to get down here for the date originally suggested for the boy's christening it would have gone ahead for then – and you'd have been able to come after all. And, alas, it can't be postponed till June 3 as you suggest (tho' I do hope you'll be able to be present at that dinner) because in the interval I heard that Compton Mackenzie was coming to spend the weekend May 12–14 with me and I took advantage of the opportunity to ask him to be the other godfather – and he agreed. Certain other difficulties in management I needn't detail have, however, prevented my writing you more speedily – but I do hope that you will come through by hook or crook for that date, and have a pow-wow with Mackenzie and me. I told him another novelist was to be his vis-a-vis in this important function: Mackenzie as you probably know has come all out on the Scottish Nationalist ticket. I have only one fact to mention in case you don't know – he's a Roman Catholic.

Now as to Eliot, I believe (vide *Drunk Man*) he's a Scotsman by descent – but it's a damned long descent: and mentally he certainly fills the role you seem to have cast him for in your papers. He is pure Boston – ultra-English classicist in criticism: that's what makes him so unintelligible to mere English conventionalists – they can't follow their own ideas to their logical conclusions well enough to recognise their own supporters.

222

This in great haste – Kindest regards to Mrs Gunn – Your Godson salutes you.

Yours,
C.M.G.

No dress function or any unnecessary requirements of etiquette.

NLS   16 Links Avenue,
                                                 Montrose.
                                                 20.6.28

Dear Neil,

Unless I write you right away heaven knows when I'll manage to. I don't know Compton Mac's address at moment – I'd a letter the other day dated 14th inst. from Harris: but he's on the move. However I'll be seeing him on Saturday, I expect, at Stirling[1] where we're both (with others) to be orating, and whence we go to Aboyne to weekend with Erskine of Marr, Hay of Seaton and other choice spirits. If you write him at once c/o Hon R. Erskine of Marr, Forest of Birse Lodge, Aboyne. You'll catch him there – on the hop, as it were.

I've meant to write you ever since you were here – partly to thank you for coming and standing by me so nobly in that grave crisis in the Grieve family fortunes: and partly just because I wanted to write in any case. But as matters stand this can only be the hastiest and scrappiest of scrawls. Walter R. is splendid but Kiteen[2] has had a tonsils and adenoids operation and Mrs Grieve was sick to death of the sound of the sea and pining for the hills – so about 3 weeks ago I

[1] The National Party of Scotland was inaugurated at a meeting held in the King's Park, Stirling, on Saturday, 23 June 1928. A poster advertised as speakers R. B. Cunninghame Graham, Hon. R. Erskine of Marr, Compton Mackenzie, Lewis Spence and C. M. Grieve. Seconding the resolution to establish 'Self-government' for Scotland, Grieve said, 'I rise to second the Resolution that Mr Spence has moved in the absence of my friend, Mr Compton Mackenzie. I know that Mr Mackenzie will be exceedingly sorry to miss this gathering today, and that the interest which he is taking in Scottish National Movement is a very genuine and a very deep one.'
[2] The poet's daughter Christine, born in 1924.

packed the lot off to Kirriemuir where they'll remain till the end of this month (I've paid them visits of inspection these last 2 week-ends).

For July I have taken a country cottage about 4 miles inland from Brechin – i.e. about 16 miles from here: so if (as I hope you will) you rush up here you'd better call at the *Review* office – any time between 9 and 5 daily except Saturdays – 9 to 12. And I'll guide you or direct you to our Arcadian retreat.

Compton Mac, Erskine of Marr, and myself have all been invited as 'distinguished guests' by the Tailltean Games Committee to attend that quinquennial function in Dublin in the 2nd and 3rd week of August: and intend to. Wish our visit had coincided with yours.

By the way you might when in Dublin call on
H. Robertson Christie
whom you'll find at Hodges Figgis & Co's place, 20 Naussau St, Dublin. He wrote me some time ago re the Scottish Movement (he's a Scot); joined the Nat. Party: and sent me author-autographed copies of books by Peadar O'Donnell and Liam O'Flaherty. It was on the latter's recommendations he wrote me. I fancy he's in touch with everybody and every thing worth knowing in Dublin. I'll be writing him this week and will mention you're to be over in July.

Your article in *Pictish Review*[3] was tip-top.

I've had *Courier* with J.R.'s[4] 1st article – and am eagerly awaiting more. I've devoted a paragraph on the series he's started in a thing I send out weekly to some 46 papers.

By the way – have you joined the Nat. Party? If not, why not?

I wish I'd time to say a great deal more but alas! Don't baulk me doing it sometime in July by word of mouth. Every kind regard to Mrs Gunn.

Yours,
C.M.G.

[3] 'Scotsman's English' by Nial Guinne, *Pictish Review*, Vol. 1, No 8, June 1928.
[4] John Macnair Reid worked, for some time, on the Inverness *Courier*.

16 Links Avenue,
Montrose.
27.8.28

My dear Gunn,

Home again after a splendid fortnight in Ireland during which I met everybody I wanted to meet and saw and investigated all that was necessary.

Item: Interview (Erskine of Marr and I) with De Valera and his chief henchmen.

Item: Tea with the Minister of Defence.

Item: A 6.30 to 1 a.m. discussion with Yeats, A.E., Higgins and others, after which Yeats and I perambulated the deserted streets till 2.15 a.m.

Item: A flight in an Avro-Anson 5-cylinder plane and about 1000 miles motoring with Gogarty (the 'Buck Mulligan' of Joyce's *Ulysses*).

Item – but why go on! I had the time of my life.

But this is just a hasty note. I'm sorry to have you sending them on: but I particularly want Higgins's *Dark Breed* and Valéry's *Serpent*.[1] Can you please book-post me them as soon as possible?

Pity you couldn't have a run down here just now. Montrose is literally buzzing with the Scottish Renaissance – Muir, Scott, Bain.[2]

Hope you are fit and fine and working like the devil – not at fishing!

The serial continues to go strong. Some splendid passages.

No time for more at the moment. My best regards to Mrs Gunn and to Reid.[3]

You'll know Compton Mac. is to preside at Mod. Concert in Inverness on September 20th. He's coming here later.

Yours,
C.M.G.

---

[1] Paul Valéry, *Le Serpent* (1924). A limited edition of 500 numbered copies, translated by Mark Wardle and introduced by T. S. Eliot.

[2] Robert Bain was poetry critic of *The Glasgow Herald* at the time.

[3] John Macnair Reid (1895–1954), the Scottish novelist, was friendly with Mac-Diarmid who dedicated the poem 'Depth and the Chthonian Image' (346–53) to him.

16 Links Avenue,
9.5.29

Dear Neil,

Yours to hand! I'm tremendously busy and can only send the merest note to comply with your 'by return' request. I don't think I'll really stand for Dundee. If I did I'd get a good vote and do not think there would be the slightest risk of forfeiting deposit; but the necessary funds are not available, and it is intended to build up a fund for next time instead. In any case Compton Mac. and others are against my standing – and I agree with them. The Movement is developing steadily and Westminster is not by any means an essential.

Will write you fully soon: but just at moment simply can't.

But good work is going forward in Dundee all the same. Have five lectures – week-end school idea – this weekend. Had F. G. Scott through giving concert the other week, etc, etc.

Am in great poetical vein just now: and wish to Heaven I could cut clear of everything else just for a week or two.

Looking forward eagerly to your vol of Short Stories.[1]

The North British News Agency stunt was a try-on – still in embryo stage – on part of few Scots Nats in Glasgow. It may develop yet.

Hope I *can* get to Inverness. The way is for the Branch to specially ask Headquarters for me.

I understand from the Dundee Comtt. you gave handsome donation to Election Fund. I regard this as largely – if not wholly – a personal tribute: and appreciate your kindness greatly. What money has come in – a substantial sum: but nothing like the £300–£400 which was absolutely necessary – will, I think, subject to consent of subscribers, be put into special account for contesting the constituency on future occasion.

Greetings to Inverness Branch and all good luck.

Mrs Grieve joins me in kindest regards to Mrs Gunn. Will eagerly look forward to July visit if I don't see you before then. Christine and Walter both in great form.

Yours,
Chris.

Hope you are writing like blazes!

[1] Neil M. Gunn, *Hidden Doors* (1929).

NLS

Vox,
10A Soho Square,
London.
23/9/29
Private Address:-
18 Pyrland Road, N5.

My dear Gunn,

I'm very sorry to be so long in writing you about *Hidden Doors*: but, as you will know, my affairs have been in what Boyle in *Juno and the Paycock* calls 'a state of chassis', and for the past week or two I have been busy transforming an ex-Wesleyan manse into a liveable condition and keying-in to my new job. But I didn't leave Scotland without reading the first reviews of *H.D.* and rejoicing to find them and the *Herald* one in particular, splendidly calculated to open doors to you. I hope the sales of the book have been in keeping: and that as a consequence there will be no further difficulty in the publication of your hitherto unpublished novels and ensuring a regular two-a-year from you in future. More power to your elbow! Go ahead and prosper.

As for me, I had come to the parting of the ways. Either I must cave in to some extent and 'be friends' where I didn't want to be, or clear out. I had absolutely made up my mind to break entirely with almost all those with whom I had been in any way associated, either actually or in the public mind, alike in the Scottish literary and political movements. And I have now taken that course at the price of expatriation. Needless to say this does not mean that I am going to cease my work for Scotland – it means that I am going to intensify it, in ways that I could not possibly do while I had to secure a modus vivendi in Scotland itself. Now I can afford to be absolutely ruthless: and will.

My lines have fallen in very pleasant places. I could not be associated with a more congenial lot of fellows. We've got a very nice house here and there'll always be a room and a welcome for you and/or Mrs Gunn if and when you care. I'm sorry it means a few pints of petrol more to reach me in future: but sincerely hope that won't affect your periodic visits, especially as the running expenses will mean increasingly less to a successful novelist, short-story-writer, playwright, and what not! I'm sorry I won't be able to hear the Aberdeen production of *The Hawk's Feather*; my portable here won't give me Scottish stations – a limitation I'll seldom regret.[1]

---

[1] Gunn's one-act play 'The Hawk's Feather' was broadcast from Aberdeen on 24 September.

Write soon and give me your news.
With kindest regards to Mrs Gunn and yourself.

Yours,
C.M.G.

P.S. Christine was speaking pure cockney within 48 hours.
The religious, etc. supervision of your godson calls for greater attention than heretofore. He has taken to London as a duck to water.

NLS   Royal Liver Building,
                                                      Liverpool
                                                   [June 1930]

My dear Neil,

I'd have been at Bannockburn (and rewarded your lifting eye) if I could possibly have managed it; and I'd be in London this next weekend – but alas! I have fallen on evil days: and my lot is to have illustrated articles on technical subjects in the Overseas edition of *The Ironmonger*, the London Chamber of Commerce Journal, the Hamburger Nachrichten, etc. – signed articles, damnie! You are quite right in feeling that I am not in some way doing myself justice – and I don't intend to! I refuse any sort of fitting in, any 'consent to a mutual relation', with my contemporaries; I'd rather be out of the game and done with altogether – but, though I have been having excruciating difficulties since I last saw you (and of course I should have written you long ere this – I so enjoyed your London visit, albeit conscious that circumstances prevented my giving you – or our having together – anything like the time I had hoped), I fancy I'll break out again all right, in unpredictable directions. That's as it may be; the point is – I'm not amenable to reason.

No. I can't manage London this weekend, bitterly as I'll resent not seeing you. I hope you've apprised Peggy. Poor kid she's been having a hard time – and doubtless she's said things she oughtn't: but in the circumstances she's to be forgiven. She's spending this week at the Nook, Blackness Road, Crowborough, Sussex, with the Muirs, but I think she'll be back in London on Saturday – or, at latest, Monday. She's none too well; highly neurasthenic. If you haven't done so, be sure and write her, and give her the chance of seeing you at least. For the matter of that whether she's in London or not there's a room and bed for you, if you want it, at 18 Pyrland Road, of course. Don't hesitate if this is convenient to you. I'm extremely sorry about Daisy's sister.

I needn't tell you I'm delighted the P.P.[1] (for which I personally have no use – nor it for me) are publishing your next novel, and I'll be all agog for that event. I've sent off *Cencrastus* to Blackwood's; and am very busy in other directions – intending, inter alia, and despite all my handicaps, to have a hell of a say – a much bigger say than ever – in Scottish affairs shortly. And don't you sniff about Clann Albainn – *it is going O.K.*

I would have liked a talk with you too, on many things, but apparently it's not to be – this time. Despite your melancholy mission I hope you have a thoroughly interesting and profitable time. Write me at length some time soon: and (d.v.) I'll reply in like measure. Every kind regard to Daisy and yourself.

> Yours,
> Chris.

NLS

357 Royal Liver Building,
Liverpool.
2.10.30

My dear Neil,

Heartiest congratulations! I cannot tell you how delighted I am – delighted on your own (and your wife's) account – delighted for the sake of the Porpoise Press[1] – and, above all, delighted for the sake of the Scottish Movement and the new literature we are trying to create. The only fly in the amber is the fact that I've to wait some months longer before seeing the book.

My own effort[2] will be out in ten days or thereby. No; I don't see

---

[1] The Porpoise Press published Gunn's *Morning Tide* in 1930.
[1] Gunn's novel *Morning Tide*, published by the Porpoise Press in 1930, had just been chosen as the Book Society's Choice.
[2] *To Circumjack Cencrastus* was published on 29 October 1930.

myself making any money out of it, but there's some good work in it, I think, and it is bound on various accounts to attract a considerable amount of attention.

How's the SNP going now in Inverness and the North generally? I'm beginning to be active again in this connection – am Vice President of the Glasgow University Scottish Nationalist Assocn. and will be speaking (in a sensational way which the press will splash) there on the 2nd of December (I want to be in Glasgow on the 1st Dec. because Sorabji's huge new composition, *Opus Clavicem-ballistieum*, which is dedicated to me, is to be played then). And I've also taken on the Presidency of the Liverpool Wallace Club. The SNP council have at last appointed the Douglas Proposals Inquiry Committee: and I'm deep in correspondence with the members.

Eric[3] is O.K. but I can't extract these drawings from him yet.

Kindest regards to Daisy and any other friends with whom you may be in touch – Macnair Reid, Patterson, Thomson, MacLeish and others.

Yours,
Chris.

P.S. The Porpoise Press are also issuing shortly a new edition of *Annals*.

NLS

357 Royal Liver Building,
Liverpool.
12/1/31

My dear Neil,

Glad to get your note. I should have written long ere this to wish Daisy and you all the best for 1931. But I do so now. I am afraid I won't manage to London while you're there. I wish I could; I'd like a pow-wow immensely. But I'm choc-a-bloc with work and Anderson is likely to be away for a while so I've to be on the spot.

I read *Morning-Tide* while in London. This is only to be the briefest of notes: but in any case there's no need for me to say more than that

---

[3] Eric Robertson, a mutual friend.

it delighted me immensely. It well deserves the Book Club's selection and is bound to be a huge success. Every hearty congratulation. It is a beautiful, moving, and historically important bit of work – definitely putting the new Scottish Literary Movement 'on the map', as the advertisement says. I'll await the reviews with confidence and every pleasureable anticipation.

You'll be seeing Peggy in London?

Excuse this hasty scrawl.

Love to you both: and please remember me to any friends you may be seeing.

Yours,
C.M.G.

P.S. And I hope you're up to the eyes in further work. I am. 1931 is going to be a great year.

NLS

[Liverpool]
13/3/31

My dear Neil,

Delighted to hear from you again.

Spence's[1] review of *Morning Tide* in the SMT Mag. was a vicious bit of work in intention but in effect negligible because the blighter has no standing and has lost any potentiality he ever had of doing useful work in a hopeless mixture of conceit, cant, venom and verbiage. His very physical appearance reminds me of a pig's carcase in a butcher's shop. I was disappointed in some of the other reviews I saw – notably the *Times Lit Supp* (tho' I needn't have been; it's a hell of a rag really) and the *Manchester Guardian*: but others were splendid: and I hope that the sales (and profits accruing to you) have been all that [you] could wish.

I'm very sorry you just missed the American choice. That would have been great going. But better luck next time!

That reminds me – a friend of mine here (whom you met) – Mrs. Sydney Merrill – is very anxious that you should autograph a

---

[1] Lewis Spence.

copy for her. Will you do this? I'll send one on for the purpose if you will. Let me know.

I'm very busy. Eliot (*Criterion*) has just accepted a 6000 word essay of mine on 'English Ascendancy and British Literature'[2] – really getting down to things and carrying the War into the enemies' camp. George Blake got it to read from Eliot and thinks it 'a first-class bit of work'. I've another long essay hitting out all round the wicket in next issue of *Modern Scot*[3] – editor of which, Murray McClymont Armstrong of the Liverpool Playhouse and others are seeing me tomorrow. Also I think the *Daily Express* are going to run a trenchant new series of mine on Scottish Development Problems. I'm going ahead too with the SNP Douglas Economic Committee: and hope to address Edinburgh and St Andrews University S. Nat. Societies towards end of next month – and possibly also Glasgow.

And I'm going ahead with my huge new poem.

Above all that I'm having a busy and amusing time here – tho' I've just recovered from a fortnight's illness. The children have both been ill: and so has Peggy but latest news shows improvement but they're going to Brighton for a holiday as soon as possible. I hope both Daisy and you are in good fettle.

Excuse this extremely hasty scrawl. Love to you both and regards to all friends.

Yours,
C.M.G.

Delighted at progress of Inverness Branch SNP. But intend shortly to put the 'cat among the pigeons'. Fed up with SNP policy altogether – and SNP personnel too. Nothing for it really but Clann Albann.

[2] *The Criterion*, Vol X, No XLI, July 1931.
[3] *The Modern Scot*, Vol II, No 1, April 1931, contained 'Scottish National Development, Civic Publicity, Tourism, And Other Matters' by C. M. Grieve.

18 Pyrland Road, N.5.
4/9/31

My dear Gunn,

I had gathered – I think from something Macnair Reid told Peggy – that you were to be holidaying in Ireland in August and would probably be turning up here about the month-end. But there's no word of you. I've had you on my conscience and been meaning to write you for long enough: but, as you probably know, I've been having a very towsy time. I got your note suggesting I should visit Inverness at Nat. Party Conference but my finances didn't permit. Since then I've been hunting in vain for a lucrative job and keeping the pot boiling by what free-lancing I could – though to tell the truth even in this emergency spending 99/100ths of the energy that should have gone in this way to a huge new poem which (just wait till you see) contains by far the best stuff I've done yet. Two biggish lyrics out of it are appearing in a miscellany of new poems edited by Lascelles Abercrombie[1] which Gollancz are publishing very soon – and Abercrombie thinks they are two of the most remarkable poems Britain has produced for long enough. (Talking of publishers' lists, my Benn Augustan Series *Living Scottish Poets* will be out in a week or so: and where the deuce are you anyhow in the autumn publishing announcements? I've been keeping my eyes skinned but haven't caught a flash of your scut anywhere.)

Then on top of all this Peggy took suddenly ill, had to be rushed into a nursing home, went through a touch-and-go operation, emerged a wraith, slowly recovered a certain amount of strength, and has been in Scotland for three weeks & will be till the end of this month. I've been a grass widower.

On top of all these troubles, something has developed which is the immediate cause of this letter. I got the offer of a directorship with post of literary adviser of a publishing firm.[2] It is a very good opening indeed – a chance of a life time – but it is contingent upon my putting in a certain amount of capital. Jobs of that sort aren't to be got otherwise. Indeed the advertisement brought any number of letters from ex public school and varsity men willing to put in the capital all right, but without the experience the firm needs and in most cases only willing to be ornamental but not to put their backs into the

---

[1] (Ed) Lascelles Abercrombie, *New English Poems* (London 1931). MacDiarmid's two poems 'Charisma and My Relatives' (301–2) and 'To Lenin' (297–9) appear on pp. 246–50 of Abercrombie's anthology and are footnoted as 'From *Clann Albann*, a work in progress.'

[2] The Unicorn Press, which published *First Hymn to Lenin and Other Poems* (London 1931).

business. The other 2 Directors[3] are business men – one looks after the printing, binding, relations with booksellers, etc; the other the financial side. The business is run on very economical lines. I have made thorough enquiries and have come to the conclusion that it is a tip-top proposition. My side would be to act as literary adviser, read the MSS, control translations, keep in touch with likely authors, etc. The other 2 Directors are both men I know I could work with all right. They have made the necessary enquiries too and believe I am the man for them. The trouble is the capital. I put the matter to a friend[4] the other day – an experienced business man. Business, of course, bad or he'd have had no hesitation in giving me all the accommodation I need: as it was, he has put up £250 for me. I need as much again – £150 at once in order to clinch the deal – the other £100 could lie over for some weeks at least. If I am able to clinch this I will have a secure job in London here, of a congenial kind, in which I will be my own master and have time enough for my own writing. I am satisfied that I will be able to pay back the bulk – or even all – the capital I require by the end of one year from now.

I don't think of you as a capitalist and somehow or other, while casting my thoughts round for someone to help me, you didn't occur to me. I haven't the slightest idea how you do stand financially as a matter of fact or what your commitments & liabilities may be. But I wrote an account of the whole business to Peggy in detail and to my surprise she wired back: 'Proposition good. Why not write Gunn. Sure he'd help you'.

I've taken 2 days since then to think over it – longer than I should have taken, for the matter must be clinched at once. (I must as a matter of fact be in a position to say 'yes' or 'no' by Monday; and to put in the £250 I have already raised plus at least another £150 by Tuesday or at latest Wednesday.) The man who has already come to my aid thought, despite the bad times, he might get a friend of his to come in too with £100, but was pretty sure he couldn't at the moment do more than that, if as much.

So I have finally decided to put the matter to you. If you can help me, it'll be of course on a purely business basis and I'll have a document duly prepared by a lawyer safeguarding your money in respect of that holding in this Company, plus security on my other assets, until such time as I repay you – and in the interval I will keep you posted periodically as to the position and prospects of the company.

[3] The other two directors were L. N. Cooper and J. F. Moore.
[4] William McElroy was a coal-merchant and a friend to various artists: he was, for example, Sean O'Casey's best man and the original of Poges in *Purple Dust*.

I need not stress by one word what all this means to me – and not so much me as Peggy and the children – nor say anything about gratitude etc.

There are only two points I need emphasise, in fact. 1/ That whether you can and do, or can't and don't, help me in this matter I want the thing to be a matter of absolute confidence between us.

2/ That you aren't to imagine for a second that if for any reason you can't see your way to help me that it'll make any difference at all to our friendship.

I'm calculating that, if you are at home, you'll get this letter tomorrow (Saturday) night or on Monday morning. That doesn't give you time to think really, but will you please wire me on Monday or at very latest Tuesday morning saying 'Yes' or 'No'. Wire me c/o The Unicorn Press, 321 High Holborn, London WC1.

I'll give you full details when I write again. Take it from me, it's a very good thing indeed and I don't mean to miss it if I can possibly help it – apart from the fact that there's damn all else offering, Fleet Street's a blasted Sahara, and I've been long enough unemployed now (apart from the costs involved by Peggy's operation) to know the feeling of being really down-and-out.

You'll appreciate both from the length – and the lacunae – of this letter how much I've been wishing this last day or two you'd turn up here. It would have been so much easier and more satisfactory to have talked the thing over in all its bearings.

As it is, I've left myself no time to say lots of other things, and ask lots of questions. If you've been in Ireland and are back home I can only hope you're both fit and fine, and have had a topping holiday, and that the silence surrounding your work will soon be broken by another publishers announcement.

Every kind regard.

Yours,
C.M.G.

MacDiarmid dedicated 'Charisma and My Relatives' (301–2) to him. When MacDiarmid's wife Peggy left him she lived with McElroy.

321 High Holborn,
London, WC1.
9/9/31

My dear Gunn,

In accordance with my wire I had meant to write you fully yesterday, but a rush of other work has kept me unexpectedly up to the eyes, and I question if I will manage to write you tonight yet. If not, I will without fail tomorrow, as I must definitely complete this work tonight. I need say nothing of my gratitude for your prompt response[1] (and my regret at having called on you at a less opportune moment than might have been). Re the amount I cannot quite see my way to yet, there is no hurry about that and I will manage one way or another – and tell you how and keep you exactly posted. I am not rushing matters – all the hurry meant was that I had to be in a position if need be to 'ante' up the requisite amount. The business is not a new one – it is over 100 years old but has been in abeyance for several years, and is now going to go forward on new lines, but with the benefit of the continuance of an established name. My two partners are both people (as I have carefully verified) of substance financially, good character, and thorough trade and technical (but not literary – that's where I come in) knowledge and connections. Re company law as you know I am certainly not versed in that but the other man who has come to my aid does – he's in a big way of business (as coal and iron merchant) himself and has thorough experience. I probably put what I meant loosely, but what is in process of formation is of course a private limited liability company. All the holding will be in the hands of the 3 of us equally. The main point is that our overheads are and will remain at an absolute minimum – we can scarcely even at the worst, for a time, lose any money at all – we see our profit clear in each item before we decide to

[1] On receiving MacDiarmid's request Gunn replied, on 6 September 1931, 'My dear Grieve, Why the deuce didn't you approach me earlier? I would have gone to London – for it was in my mind to go over another small business – looked into the whole thing and set up ways and means. A few weeks ago I got a good cheque for "royalties", but as I am myself bonded (big mortgage over house) at too big a percentage, I set arrangements going for cancelling bond. The advance I got earlier in the year I was tempted to invest in one of these "good things" that have proved anything but good. Thus at the moment my affairs are in a sort of happy state of equipoise! However, to come to business. I am enclosing a cheque for £100, dated for Tuesday to give me time to see my banker & arrange that it will be acknowledged. You seem to require a further £50 to put right by Wednesday. Well, if you can't get hold of it anywhere, wire me Tuesday forenoon and I'll fix it up somehow, I feel sure' (letter in NLS).

do it. But I will tell you all about this when I get a chance of writing fully tomorrow at latest. But please be sure that I am going very carefully – and fully aware of the deficiencies in my own exact knowledge of business, financial, and legal outs-and-ins. In any case as matters stand your money is intact and in my hands entirely until the thing is finally fixed up and prior to that you will have full details and time to advise me in return before final clinching. Awfully sorry I'm so desperately rushed at moment, but will write again tomorrow or later!

All the best to Daisy and yourself.

Chris.

NLS

321 High Holborn,
London, W.C.1.
24/9/31

My dear Gunn,

Since my last hurried note to you I have been very busy – not only in getting into this business here and getting it ship-shape and to my liking, but also 1/ coming to an arrangement with London Editorial Services Ltd whereby I will join that too and organise my journalistic interests on a proper and enlarged basis and 2/ going on with my various literary projects (The Benn *Living Scots Poets* is out now – Abercrombie's anthology will be out next month – Faber and Faber are considering publishing my *Hymn to Lenin* as a separate book, etc.). What a life! And beyond and that I have been moving actively in the inner circle of the Douglas School – seeing Orage himself and others. *The New Age* forecasts are all coming true – but the real crisis won't be for a year or two yet.

Now as far as this business is concerned I am satisfied (and friends of mine with sound business experience are with me in this). It only means I've found a pied-à-terre – what I make of it depends entirely on myself: but in any case by the end of next year (in addition to having had £5 a week, the use of an office, typist, etc., and plenty of time to do my own literary and journalistic work) we will not have risked more than a quarter of our capital. On that quarter we may or may not make much – but even if the worst came to the worst and it were all a case of dead loss, so far as you are concerned (as matters stand now) I'd only have lost £25 of your money – and if I cannot make that up in 12 months from now I must be a fool indeed. You see our overheads are extremely low and that, coupled with a cautious policy that would rather simply sit tight and wait for something to turn up than risk publishing anything we did not see from the outset covering its costs means that we are running practically no risk. What plans I have in mind are all along limited edition – signed copies – lines: and I fancy I'll have one or two good things here, because both Yeats and A.E. (who has a good American market of this kind) are going out of their way to help me, and this will give us a good start. But none of this will mature till the Spring and I can tell you all about it before that.

The Certificate is through and I have still £150 to find – £50 as quickly as possible; the other £100 not only can wait for a while but I know where I'll get it – it may be in a month or six weeks quite all right. But the £50 I must find at once. I don't know how you are fixed now – nor can I think of another source whence I can possibly get it soon enough. Once that is settled I'll feel very happy. I'd have written you sooner but it was no use until I saw finally how things were going to be. A little snag arose for example at the last moment over the question of whether the Unicorn was not a registered trade mark and we had to have the records searched. But now everything is in order and I have had time to get to know my two partners thoroughly and secure independent substantiation of their records and abilities and I am very well satisfied. The three of us will pull very well together – on general policy we see eye to eye – and our diverse qualifications complement each other splendidly.

There were some other matters I had in mind to write you about but I was interrupted by a caller and by a couple of 'phone calls when I finished the last paragraph. Besides which this is an infernally scratchy pen. So, whatever they were, they must wait. I hope all's going well with yourself – and that you're not affected by these infernal economy 'cuts'. There's almost certain to be a General Election within the next few weeks, I'm afraid – if so I'll be in Scotland, and am making arrangements to stand as S. Nat. either for Dundee or for one of the Edinburgh or Glasgow constituencies. It may be possible to work in a weekend at Inverness. All the best to Daisy and yourself.

Yours,
C.M.G.

NLS
TS

321 High Holborn,
London, W.C.1.
5th October 1931

Dear Gunn,

I have not time to write you at the moment but this is just a note to allay any anxiety you may be feeling. I quite appreciate your position and only hope that I have not unduly accentuated it. I shall find other ways and means without any question. As matters stand I am full of plots and ploys of all kinds for the present publishing season to a small extent and to a much greater extent for the Spring season. Of all these more anon.

I think I have some very good things in the offing. Apart from these you will be interested to hear that I have made arrangements with Douglas and Orage (whom I met recently and will be seeing frequently for some time to come) with regard to my taking over all the essential literature of the anti-banks movement. Cecil Palmer, who has hitherto been the publisher of Douglas books has been extremely unsatisfactory for various reasons into which I need not enter in detail here; suffice to say that Douglas and I came to a complete understanding and that I hope to carry through the entire business in the course of a few days. Allied to these – through the London Editorial Service and Combined Newspapers Limited – the directorates of both of which I have just joined – I have plans whereby we can not only effectively break through the grotesque position that has hitherto kept Douglasism out of American journalism and made it practically impossible to secure any book of Douglas even by ordering it from an ordinary bookseller in the whole of America – but also develop very quickly the existing position in regard to the New Economics in Canada and Australia.

With regard to these matters I will write you in detail as soon as I possibly can. In the meantime keep a 'calm sough' – or as calm a sough as the dreadful news about the extent of the cut affecting you permits. The prospects of an immediate election seem to have receded but it cannot be long delayed. As soon as it is actually on the carpet I shall be in Scotland and will hope to meet you and have a long pow-wow. I am not certain whether I will be standing for one of the Scottish constituencies myself or not but in any event my services will be available for the various national candidates and no doubt I shall be in Inverness to put in a word for McCormick.[1] What is happening with the Glasgow University Rectorial I have no idea. I

[1] John MacCormick, Secretary of the National Party of Scotland.

239

hear that the last issue of the GUM[2] contained tributes to Mackenzie from various other writers, but I was not approached in this connection.

Love to Daisy and yourself.

Yours,
C. M. Grieve.

NLS

321 High Holborn,
London, W.C.1.
[December 1931]

My dear Neil,

You'll have received your copy of *Lenin*.[1] Let's know what you think of it. Things are going all right with us here – that is, we've plenty of money on our books – the Lenin for example more than covered entire costs in the preliminary orders – but these are difficult days, and, not having paid up my full allotment, I'm in urgent need of £50 for a little while only – I and my partners can absolutely guarantee the return of this by not later than the end of January. We have a lot of money lying out but can't hope to get much in now till after New Year, while I'm tied up myself in various ways on account of these divorce proceedings. I know of course that January must be as much of a financial nightmare to you as to anybody & everybody else: and that you're probably in a bit of a pickle yourself, but if you can come to the rescue for this amount on a perfectly definite undertaking to have it back not later than the last day of January, please do – and in any case don't mind my asking.

I suppose there's no chance of your being down here about Christmas or New Year. I'd like to have one of our old 4 a.m. sederunts again. I've heaps of irons in the fire: and publishing schemes – as witness inter alia, the enclosed prospectus. But I'm too busy to write long letters.

How are things with yourself? And Daisy? Let's know what and

[2] Glasgow University Magazine.
[1] *First Hymn to Lenin and Other Poems* (London 1931).

how you're doing. McLeish sent in an order for *Lenin*: but I haven't managed to drop him a line yet.

All the best.
Chris.

Cootes, Thakeham,
Sussex. 14/6/32

My dear Neil,

I was extremely glad to get your letter – and I need not say how appreciative of its spirit. I wish I had known you were to be in London – I'd have found ways and means somehow of seeing you. I would give a great deal for a talk with you. Apart from anything else I'm disastrously cut off from Scotland and most of the activities that meant so much to me. But still living down here I'm getting a great deal done – I've done more poetry this last two months than in the preceding two years: and much of it – even to my severest critic, F. G. Scott – among my very best. *Clann Albann* will be some book. How about yourself? I haven't seen *The Lost Glen*[1] yet – nor heard how it has gone. Well, I hope; and hope too others are shaping and that you're in good form and forging ahead.

Now as to the Unicorn Press letter.[2] I'd like you to reply after some such fashion as this:-

Dear Sirs:-

I have to acknowledge your letter of — inst, which I was extremely surprised to receive. I felt it my duty to communicate at once with my friend Mr. Grieve and learn from him that your statement that

---

[1] Gunn's novel *The Lost Glen* (1932).
[2] On 28 May 1932 Gunn received a formal letter from The Unicorn Press whose directors were now listed as L. N. Cooper, J. F. Moore and W. P. Montgomery. The names of C. M. Grieve and S. C. Nott were scored out by L. N. Cooper who wrote to Gunn as follows: 'Dear Sir, We have reason to believe that you are holding a £100 Share Certificate issued to Mr C. M. Grieve, in the above Company. If this is the case, we would like to point out that this Share Certificate is not fully paid, and carries a liability of £24.8.0. We should be pleased to know if Mr Grieve has signed a transfer for this Certificate, as on our records the Certificate is still the property of Mr Grieve. We should be very pleased to hear from you on the matter.'

£24.8/- is due per £100 on his share holding is not true. He says he regards this as an attempt on your part to secure this sum from me by false pretences, and that he is taking legal proceedings against you forthwith. I shall be glad to have an explanation from you at once or I will put the matter in the hands of my own lawyers.

Yours etc.

Briefly, the point about The Unicorn Press is:

1/ All that was done for it was done by me – Orage, Sorabji, Douglas, Saurat, *Transition* etc. – and we had the makings of an excellent business, what we had already done having been successful but for the fact

2/ That owing to the quite unexpected default of Stanley Nott in paying up his share capital – through the collapse of his American interests – we ran short of capital, and

3/ In any case the business was handicapped by the other two partners each drawing £5 a week for work which was not essential at all to the enterprise & could quite well have been done by the typist in her spare time.

4/ These other two then started trying to induce fresh capital by false pretences (I am in a position to prove this) and finally succeeded in inducing a Mr. Montgomery to put up additional money, took him into directorship in my absence, and voted me out of it.

5/ I have reason to believe that their own share holdings are not paid up and that their actions are ultra vires.

6/ Nott and I had determined to get rid of them and would have done so but for his collapse through American slump.

7/ I am bringing actions against them and acting in this matter in concert with Peggy's lawyers and a firm of first-class accountants.

8/ To transfer the £100 shares to you at this juncture would weaken my position and not help you.

9/ Finally, the £100 shares should be a valuable property soon if the business gets half a chance.

I hope all this is clear. The immediate effect of all this has of course been to deprive me of any regular income or work and, in fact, I have not earned 10/- a week, for the past four or five months. The result is of course that I am – and so far as I can see, pending a satisfactory outcome of the Unicorn Press business or the very improbable contingency of a lucrative appointment or an Irish Sweepstake prize, likely to remain – up against the economic problem as excruciatingly as it is possible to be. I hope I can hold on here for a little longer in order to finish the books I am busy on, but it is exceedingly doubtful, and I may have to become a tramp in real earnest any day.

Kindest regards to Daisy, yourself, and all friends.

Yours,
Chris.

NLS

Cootes,
Thakeham,
Sussex.
24/6/32

My dear Neil,

Very many thanks for your letter and enclosure. I need say no more. My position is desperate and likely to remain so. However something may happen. I can hang on by my toenails a little longer – and with luck long enough to finish Vol. I of *Clann Albann* (which – at present rate of progress – won't take me more than another month).[1] I note what you say re violence; but my own conceptions of literary politics – as of Scottish politics – are extremely comprehensive and quite unshakeable. The leopard isn't going to change its spots. I agree with you, however, that certain forms of violence are too easy – weak – not really violent enough! And you can trust me to avoid these all right this time. My violent passages will be designed to kill. Did you see the second of my two poems to 'L.M.W.; An Apprentice Angel' (Lauchlan Maclean Watt) in Orage's *New English Weekly*?[2] That is the true stuff – bitter as Hell, but poetry! But the percentage of stuff that does not raise any personal or political issues and depends upon 'beauty' and 'music' in the more usual acceptations of these very misleading (and really meaningless) terms is very much higher. Instance – my 'Water Music' in the *Scots Observer* recently, which – if you haven't seen it – I'd like to send you a copy; and my 'Tarras' which is appearing in this week's *Free Man* (and again I'll send you a copy if you mention in your next that you haven't

---

[1] The poetry MacDiarmid published at this time was all conceived as part of *Clann Albann*. Both *Second Hymn to Lenin* (Thakeham 1932) and *Scots Unbound and Other Poems* (Stirling 1932) were described as 'separable items from the first volume of my long poem, *Clann Albann*, now in preparation.'
[2] 'An Apprentice Angel' (332–3), dedicated 'To L[auchlan] M[aclean] W[att]', is an attack on MacDiarmid's old enemy: 'I fancy your Presbyterian Heaven/'ll be haunted tae wi' a hellish leaven.'

243

otherwise seen it).[3] I think you'll agree that stuff like these is ample to offset a great deal more of my more questionable tricks than I propose to inflict upon the readers of *Clann Albann*.

I am much concerned about what you say of the disappointing reception – and stupid misprizal – of *The Lost Glen* (which I would have bought but for damned circumstances – and would like a copy of, yes thanks – signed), and especially your reference to Mackenzie. I'd like to know precisely what he did say. But it is satisfactory that men like Fausset and Bullett[4] – neither of whom are great or even good critics but both veritable giants to anything we possess in Scotland, including Mackenzie in this respect – came up to the scratch.

I've just had a letter from Orr,[5] of *Scottish Action* asking me for an article for their paper in support of MacGillivray and have written them a nice letter, agreeing, asking when they must have the 'copy' in hand, and how much space they want me to fill, and suggesting that they pass on my letter to MacGillivray himself so that he may give me a pointer or two as to the line I ought to take, in addition to keeping me posted themselves as to any developments which ought to affect the tenor of my article. In this connection I am of course 'lippening' to you and will follow your advice; I was extremely glad to hear from you that you'd satisfied yourself as to their 'strength' to run MacGillivray and that – tho' elections are little quantities – our splendid old man won't be let in for a wash-out.

As for the Unicorn Press, I had a letter from McElroy's accountants asking me to have a conference with Cooper (the Managing Director of the Unicorn Press) at their office, and promptly agreed – while pointing out that I did not think Cooper would agree. It was as I expected; I have just heard from them again – Cooper refuses to confer on the matter and threatens to proceed against me by the end of the month for the sums alleged to be due on the share-holding of which I am the registered holding. I wish he would; that would suit my book down to the ground; but it is only bluff – another attempt to extract £24 odds out of McElroy, as they have tried with you. I'll be glad to hear of any correspondence you have with them.

All the best to Daisy and yourself.

Yours,
Chris.

[3] 'Water Music' (333–7) and 'Tarras' (337–9) – which appeared in *The Free Man*, 25 June 1932 – are both celebrations of the landscape (and waterscape) of Langholm and obviously intended for *The Muckle Toon*, the autobiographical first volume of the projected *Clann Albann*.
[4] Gerald Bullet was a critic with the *New Statesman*.
[5] Presumably David Orr, the doctor who helped MacDiarmid find a home in Whalsay.

Cootes, Thakeham,
Sussex.
15/7/32

My dear Gunn,

Many thanks for *The Lost Glen*.

What you say about Macnair Reid and the Unicorn Press is of course purely damnable and of course I hadn't any knowledge of it whatever. Tho' it is just what I'd expect of Cooper who hasn't the remotest idea how to conduct himself in matters of the sort and is hopelessly crude and pigheaded. I have written to Reid – of whom I think a very great deal – lest he should have the faintest idea that I was in any way party to it.

In my previous letter to you I said how much I'd have liked a talk with you. I still would – and letters won't do instead. I am not going to go into the species of grievance you raise apropos what I said in *The Free Man*.[1] The quotation from your letter was not used in any disparaging way but simply to illustrate one point of view diametrically opposed to my own – though both are equally tenable by intelligent people and are on the same plane as a preference for apples to oranges in one man and the opposite taste in another. Our essential difference boils down to such an opposition – a radical psychological difference; the manifestations of which need not be taken 'personally' nor wound the amour propre of either of us. They are essentially incomparable. I have never done anything – nor do I now – than wish you well in any enterprise no matter how opposed that may be to what I think desirable. Beyond such differences upon which we can agree to differ there are of course further questions – or rather not questions since they are fundamentally undebateable, but rather questions of relative value which only the passage of time can put into proper perspective. I can afford to indulge in all manner of personalities because I proceed from an altogether abnormal basis of impersonality in regard to Scottish matters. Take Compton Mackenzie. I am sorry if he has been unfair to you in any way (as I am in the like case of *The Modern Scot* – whose dealings with you I was neither party to in any way nor did I know who reviewed *The Lost Glen*) but so far as I am concerned while he and I have been friendly

---

[1] In *The Free Man*, Vol 1, No 22, 2 July 1932, MacDiarmid replied to the manifesto on Scottish Nationalism in *The Daily Record*: 'a friend of mine writes to me this week apropos the Edinburgh Rectorial Election, "for any of us to rush in and tell everybody in Edinburgh that Colquhoun (now the Lord High Commissioner!) is a public danger might be to defeat the main end." Questions of tactics, however, do not affect relative values.'

enough and may still be or be again, I do not attach the slightest value to his literary work and I regard his bearing on the Scottish issue as wholly pernicious. Nevertheless pursuing my own tortuous and clearly enough comprehended course in certain contexts I would be prepared to eulogise his work. It is all a question of relativity; and if we come to that while not unduly overrating my own work as a poet I am prepared to hold (and many of my journalistic expressions of opinion are overcontrolled by that) that no fiction whatever matters a damn in relation to Scotland while any poem whatever above a very low plane matters a great deal. Here again this is not an arguable matter and need not affect our personal friendship. My reasons for attaching so much importance to Mac-Donald's book proceed directly from my conception of Scottish propaganda; and do not involve personal considerations of any kind. In other words behind all the complex network of my activities there is a definite irrationalism which will not be pinned down and which proceeds from the belief that I personally embody certain forces – I may do nothing of the sort but to construe that belief into a mere aspect of personal vanity or undependability in personal relationships is beside the mark. It is a spiritual phenomenon that lies outwith such considerations all together. All you have to say about tactics, my occasional sheer nonsense, etc., is not amenable to discussion in a mere letter; it must lie over until – if – we meet again.

The Macgillivray business (I have just written to Macgillivray) is of course in a different category and I will do exactly as you say and the article will be in the hands of Orr by about the middle of next month.

I'll send you copies soon of the pamphlet editions of *Tarras* and *Second Hymn to Lenin* and in the meantime enclose a page of the *New English Weekly*. Let me again regret that you too have found literary life a disillusioning and difficult matter, yet hope you will go ahead and do a great deal more – while carefully dissociating your personal reactions from other people's 'literary politics'.

Every kind regard to Daisy & yourself.

In haste.

Yours,
Chris.

P.S. Events are *moving my way* re Unicorn Press – do not do anything with them without telling me first – any question of £24 or anything else being due per £100 is now set and – I had a successful conference with Cooper and Moore the other week.

Cootes, Thakeham,
Sussex.
4/8/32

My dear Neil,

Many thanks for your letter – and your most penetrating and interesting remarks about 'sense of utterance' re my *Second Hymn*. I have been intensely preoccupied with this problem and its concomitants – bridging the gulf between poetry and the people, bringing poetry and practical power into effective relation again and so on: and have been debating some of the issues concerned with F. G. Scott, Gogarty and others. I wish we could have had one of our old all-nights together again to thresh it all out – them were the days! I cannot enlarge on the theme at the moment; I am up to my eyebrows, and higher, in the most desperate worries. This is just a note to tell you

1/ That I had a note last week from Orr wanting my article very quickly instead of in a few weeks' more time as originally suggested and p.c.'d him at once that he'd have it this week. I screwed myself down to a special spurt last night and have just posted it to MacGillivray for his approval, and, if so, immediate transmission to Orr. All my books went down the chute, of course, and I was handicapped by not having any of MacGillivray's stuff by me, nor even my own *Contemporary Scottish Studies*. But I did my very best – bearing in mind the questions of tone and line agreed between us – and sincerely hope it may suit the purpose.

2/ Valda had a son to me last Thursday morning.[1] Both are going on well now. But the confinement proved an altogether abnormal one and she will have to remain in the nursing home for at least a fortnight longer. Only her youth and exceptional vitality and the healthy country life we have been living down here pulled her through. I was at my wits end to get even the minimum charges together but we thought we could just pull through by the skin of our teeth, until this happened and of course upsets all calculations. Heaven only knows what's to happen.

3/ While though I have tried in every conceivable direction to get a job of any sort at any wage and it seems absolutely impossible – a £1 or £2 a week would make all the difference to us and while we would still have a desperate struggle, would at least give us a fighting chance – in other directions in which there is no, or no immediate, money I am finding myself as resourceful as ever and will not

---

[1] Michael Grieve was born on 28 July 1932.

contemplate defeat. I have fixed up my *Scots Unbound & Other Poems* for publication in a week or two; the limited edition of *Tarras* will be out next week; Wishart's have accepted two prose works – 'English Ascendancy in British Literature', and a study of 'Gertrude Stein';[2] Victor Gollancz has definitely decided (without fixing the date yet) to issue my *Selected Poems*[3]; Boriswood Ltd have under consideration a book or stories à la *Annals of the Five Senses*;[4] and the production of new poems goes on unabated. I enclose a proof of two which are appearing in the next issue of *The Decachord*.[5]

Not a bad tale for a fellow worried out of his wits. Oh, to hell with everything.

I wish you'd been a bit more communicative (I miss gossip down here) e.g. re the reason for the Carswells' refusal to help MacGillivray's candidature etc. Did you get a message from Naomi Mitchison and F. G. Scott? (Scott's present address is c/o Henderson, Beethoven Lodge, North Street, St Andrews).

Excuse this high pressure scrawl. Every kind regard to your wife and yourself.

Yours,
C.M.G.

NLS

Cootes, Thakeham,
Sussex.
16/8/32

Neil M. Gunn, Esq.
My Dear Neil,

My affairs are going steadily from bad to worse, mainly owing to the abnormality of Valda's confinement and consequent costs which have completely upset my calculations and resulted in my having to

[2] The essays on 'English Ascendancy in British Literature' and 'Gertrude Stein' were both included in the collection *At the Sign of the Thistle* (London 1934).
[3] Gollancz published MacDiarmid's *Stony Limits and Other Poems* in 1934.
[4] This collection never appeared but many of the stories intended for it are included in *The Thistle Rises: A MacDiarmid Miscellany* (1984).
[5] *Decachord*, Vol. IX, No. 35, September-October 1932, included 'Why I Became a Scots Nationalist' (339) and 'The Back o' Beyond' (331).

run into arrears with my cottage rent here and other things. As a result I may be evicted any day and have my few goods & chattels seized. In view of this, and the absolute lack of any prospects of a job or financial betterment, I recognise that I cannot hope to initiate the necessary proceedings to establish my rights in connection with the Unicorn Press and I am writing now to say that I think the best course is for you to write them and get a transfer form and send it on to me, when I will immediately fill it up transferring £100 shares to you, as I have already done in connection with Peggy and Mr McElroy. I will only do it provided there is no question of anything being due on these shares that they want you to pay. They tried that trick on with regard to Peggy and to McElroy but I made them climb down and I'll do it again if they attempt the same thing in your case. Will you get the necessary form sent me as quickly as possible, as I do not know now from day to day how I may be placed and it may be difficult if it is not done before I cease to have 'any fixed abode'.

The investment should be a good one – but I have every reason to have no faith in Cooper and Moore and they are likely to vote themselves all the profits as salary for services that are not only of no use to the Company but actually harmful – e.g. their action re 'Albannach' and MacNair Reid, and lots of other stupidities which have frittered away excellent prospects I secured for the Company. However, with McElroy, Peggy & yourself as substantial shareholders you may be able to make common cause and have the Company put on a better basis. Properly run, it ought to be – and can be – a very good business.

Kindest regards to Daisy & yourself.

Yours,
Chris.

NLS

c/o Dr. Orr,
Island of Whalsay,
Shetland Islands.
19/5/33

My dear Neil,

Excuse pencil.
I was delighted to hear from you. I had felt that we had got

249

completely – perhaps irreparably – out of touch with each other, as, in certain respects and these incomparably the most vital to me, I am out of touch with everybody else in Scotland: and, indeed, I cannot even yet move about with any confidence, or produce effective work, in this new world of my spirit. But I am gradually finding myself – a new self. That is why I am here – have been a fortnight, I will be, I hope, for many months. I am rowing about on lonely waters; lying brooding in uninhabited islands; seeing no newspapers and in other ways cutting myself completely away from civilised life.

I had thought you might be in Edinburgh during the months I was there and that I might see you again. I should have written you. But apart from the fact that I was having a hell of a time and wholly obsessed by my own spiritual and material problems, I kept expecting to hear from you. You never acknowledged *Scots Unbound*. (I hope you received it all right?)

I knew of the Unicorn Press developments, but have been unable, since it would be a costly business, to bring the necessary actions to secure redress there. As matters stand I still hold the shares, but have never had any statement of profit and loss, nor any royalty on my own *First Hymn to Lenin* nor even any statement of sales.

I have just had a final communication from that nitwit, McCormick, intimating that the National Party Council have resolved to exclude me from membership. Much good may it do them. It can do me no harm. I feel regarding them as a man may feel about a troupe of gibbering lunatics; and, of course, they feel the same about me – and I don't care which is right.

I hear you've a new novel – *Sun Circle* or some such name – coming out soon. Be sure and send me a copy of it. All good luck to it. And write me at greater length and give me your news and views. I expect Gollancz will publish my selected poems this year – also a new longish separate poem (about 900 lines) I've written since I came up here.

I hope you're in fine fettle and working hard. Every kind regard to Mrs Gunn, and yourself.

Yours,
C.M.G.

P.S. This damned island is of course, dry, Water, water, everywhere and not a drop to drink.

My dear Neil,

I was very glad to get your letter; and the copy of *Sun Circle*[1] for which my best thanks. I thoroughly enjoyed reading it; please give due weight to this confession; for I have read very little fiction for years and have reduced my reading of fiction and all the other popular forms of writing to an irreducible minimum these many moons. His high-and-mightiness made an unusual exception in your case and I hope you are duly grattered and flattified – especially since I was very much surprised at the degree of unexpected pleasure I got out of this – not to be taken as a precedent – deviation from my rule. I have tried to discount it as being largely the inevitable result of my prolonged abstention from 'light relief' of this – or, apart from my own journalisic irresponsibilities, any other – kind! But the effort has not been very successful – horribly unsuccessful in comparison with your novel itself; and a disgustingly overwhelming balance of credit accrues to the actual merits of the book itself – despite its fictional form. My objections to the latter remain; briefly stated, I prefer the practice of following thoughts to their extreme limit, a limit which is undeniably outside the range of popular fiction!

To leave these arid altitudes and descend to the more appropriate 'between friends' level, I was delighted, for reasons quite apart from any personal predilections and views on the novel as an art form, to find *Sun Circle* so good: because – though you may not have suspected it (or your suspicions may have run at times in other directions altogether) – I have been seriously worried about you. I conceived that *Morning Tide* had left you with a very real difficulty; I think *Sun Circle* shows you have surmounted it all right: and I shall be surprised (and I am not saying this condescendingly or inferring that *Sun Circle* runs any risk of popularity in a derogatory sense) if it does not prove commercially a better proposition than you imagined when you wrote me. I hope it has been well received.

I ought to have written you earlier: but have been extremely busy myself: and have now completed a body of new poetry which amounts to at least as great a bulk as half of all I have published. Not a bad six weeks' output. As to quality I have no doubt that some of the items will *add* considerably to whatever reputation I already have with those whose opinions weigh with me, while the bulk of the work is up to my usual standard and similar in kind – or kinds –

[1] Gunn's novel *Sun Circle* (1933).

although this new world of the Shetland Isles is reflected throughout in subject matter, etc. But it is the first category – which are new in kind and form – I am concerned about.

Well, what about this true inwardness of the Scottish Nationalist Movement? You know, of course, that the Party have finally excluded me[2] – and I am perfectly satisfied that they can't afford to. I don't know whether you see *The Free Man* regularly, but if you do you will be to that extent *au courant* with my views. My coming up here is no retirement from the fight – it is on the contrary a reculement pour mieux sauter. My influence is steadily increasing in influential quarters; if there is any further to the left I can possibly go I am going it – and not only politically but culturally. In other words, if I am not already literally an impossible person I intend to become one. You know the action I took about MacLeod's Recent Scottish Exhibition in Glasgow[3] – that is only a slight foretaste of what I will do in all sorts of other connections. Take the question of next year's PEN Congress in Scotland, for example: how tactfully do you imagine I am likely to act in relation to all the nonentities who will expect a share of the limelight and whose money and social influence will, I admit, be essential to the success of the gathering? I am utterly irreconcilable and in that and in other connections – e.g. the Universities – I will pursue a course calculated to the last degree to give me opportunities for 'making things difficult' to say the least of it. No considerations of personal prestige or any favours that may be bestowed upon me will induce me to hold my hand a moment longer than I think the most effective moment for striking; I will 'hit below the belt' in the matter either of 'personalities' or leading people on to the ice by not disclosing what I intend to do or say until what I judge to be the psychological moment or unscrupulously saying one thing to one person and the opposite to another, etc. In short – whatever other people or parties may do in Scotland – my own course at all events is perfectly clear and insusceptible of the slightest deviation and if health and harness hold I will have an amusing time during the next few years. The shots in my locker are far from spent and it will become increasingly difficult to bottle me up in any way.

Now there's a confession for you. Give me yours in return.

Shetland is my best discovery yet: I'm in the pink of condition – or rather the peat-brown – and having a splendidly simple and enjoyable time of it. I hope Mrs Gunn and you are in the best form too;

[2] MacDiarmid was expelled from the National Party of Scotland in 1933.
[3] In January 1933 *The Glasgow Evening News* and the booksellers W. & R. Holmes mounted an Exhibition of Modern Scottish Books in Dunlop Street, Glasgow. R. D. Macleod, consulting librarian to W. & R. Holmes prepared *Modern Scottish Literature: A Popular Guide-Book Catalogue* (1933).

Heaven only knows when we'll meet again – I won't willingly come back to Scotland at any time except for the express purpose of making some 'unfortunate scene' and then getting out of it again as quickly as possible. But let us keep in some sort of touch at any rate by the occasional interchange of letters.

Every good wish to both of you.

Yours,
Chris.

P.S. I certainly never got your letter re *Scots Unbound*.

NLS

Whalsay,
Wednesday.
[25/11/33]

My dear Neil,

Delighted to get your letter on my return here last Friday. I am afraid I could not have managed by hook or crook to get to Inverness much as I would like a night with you again, after this long interval. The sort of issues you raise could only be talked out – no use starting to write about them. I do not admit your analogy of A.S. Neill, etc. as applicable to the Scottish situation; but I may be wrong – the proof o' the pudding must as always be in the preein' o't; let those who think like you fire ahead and give us even the first tiniest instalment of satisfactory results – you have the field pretty well to yourselves, and do not seem to me to be doing anything worth while with it. On the contrary all such little manifestations and manoeuvres of a more accommodating spirit as I have yet seen have in my opinion been demonstrably harmful, not beneficial, to the cause. It's no use trying to tell a modest fellow like me that my single stand in the opposite direction nullifies all your efforts; if you are all pulling together except me I must automatically become a negligible factor in the proceedings – and I am quite prepared for that. I shall bear none of you any ill-will – if the results are there, albeit got by methods I completely distrust. But as long as those of you who believe in other tactics than mine fail to achieve the results, then I must keep exerting myself along my own lines. And – modest as I am – I cannot

253

shut my eyes to the fact that I not only remain (little as that is) by far the most powerful non-Conservative personal force in Scotland today, but that (and I can only attribute this to the growing recognition of the futility of the other policy) my personal influence is again becoming markedly stronger in all sorts of directions.

Yes, considering the platform on which I stood and other factors, and the rapidity with which the whole thing was arranged – I did very well at Aberdeen.[1] What is of more consequence is that the Aberdeen group are not only not disappointed but determined to carry on the fight, and that they are linking up with similar groups in the other Universities. I am going down to Edinburgh again on Friday (probably you heard all the story about the suppression of the issue of *The Student*[2] at the time of the Sept-Jubilee celebrations) to lead a Union debate on the subject of Scottish Renaissance next Wednesday – catching return boat the following day.

We put out a Magazine at Aberdeen, but it was hastily written by the students themselves; my own contribution, sent by return of post in response to telegram, only arrived in nick of time for it, but my suggestions of others who might send messages – yourself included – there was no time for the boys to follow up.

Hope you're in good form and full of work. I'd been having a particularly productive spell myself before this jockeying to and fro cut in on it; I don't suppose I'll get settled down now till after New Year. But I'm hoping for a hard spell of work all Spring.

Every kind regard to Daisy and yourself.

Yours,
Chris.

---

[1] At the Aberdeen University Rectorial Election, 1933, votes were cast as follows: Rt Hon. Walter E. Elliot, MP (307), G. K. Chesterton (220), C. M. Grieve (158), Aldous Huxley (117).
[2] The Edinburgh University student newspaper.

Whalsay,
Shetland Islands.
21/12/34

My dear Neil,

Just a line to wish Daisy and you all the compliments of the season and every good luck in 1935. I hope you are both fit and fine. I am delighted to see everywhere splendid reviews of *Butcher's Broom*[1]. I saw it at Carswell's but only had time to read (and greatly enjoy) a few chapters before leaving London and it. But I'll get a copy. For the nonce I can only say that I hope the sales will be as good as the reviews. I was also glad to hear that Schalit is translating *Lost Glen* into German. Hope with all this you are busy with all sorts of new irons in the fire – including the Whisky book[2] for Routledge's (I'm doing Lenin in the same series.) I'm up to the eyes myself. I hear little or nothing now (and of course don't want to) of the Scottish Nationalist Movement (tho' they'll be hearing a great deal of and from me they will hate like Hell this next year), but I saw the other day an announcement re the *Scottish Standard*[3] and will no doubt see an issue or two of that when it starts.

Drop me a line sometime and give me your news. Letter-writing from here is a difficult business; there is nothing to write about, and I don't get much oil of outside news to keep my epistolary wick burning.

Yours,
Chris.

---

[1] Gunn's novel *Butcher's Broom* (1934).
[2] *Whisky and Scotland* (1935), the title Gunn contributed to the Routledge Voice of Scotland series.
[3] The monthly *Scottish Standard* began publication in February 1935; it was subsequently incorporated with *The Modern Scot* into *Outlook*, the first issue of which appeared in April 1936.

My dear Neil,

I was delighted to get your letter which, forwarded here, reached me in Glasgow. I only got back here on Monday after three weeks' absence – in Manchester, where I was speaking, Glasgow, and Edinburgh. I was delighted to hear you'd finished your Whisky book which I am looking forward to with keen anticipation, and would gladly have accepted your invitation and hied myself North to crack another bottle (or two) of that excellent stuff to which you introduced me of old and my memory of which has never dimmed. But, alas, after a day or two on any one of which I thought I might wire you to say I was coming I found I couldn't manage it – the oculist and the dentist kept me in Edinburgh a few days longer than I anticipated, and so I had to come straight back here since I have a good deal to polish off yet before the end of June. I've had a hefty winter's work and have no fewer than four – and probably five – books appearing this autumn; but I had a bad winter in respect of health; hence the need to have my teeth and eyes attended to, and a general overhaul, which, having been had, and since I have now only a few odds and ends to complete during the next few weeks, I am hoping to have a decent summer in which to pull myself properly together again.

I would greatly have liked to have seen you again and talked things over, all the more so as I am very unlikely to be South again this year. It is a long time since we met last and a great deal has happened in the interval and it would be good to compare notes over a drop of decent stuff. I will certainly miss no chance of foregathering with you. I think often of the Montrose days when I was so active and constantly in touch with you and others. Now I am more and more on my own, except for Scott, and even letters are few and far between while I go months at a time without seeing a newspaper. Save for an occasional recounter with yourself and one or two others I would not have it otherwise. Any relation I could strike up or renew now with almost any of my compatriots would necessarily be on personal grounds or based on past rather than present or prospective ties. I have almost nothing in common with any of them intellectually or emotionally. I have gone very far along a road from which there is no turning back and upon which one cannot have more than an irreducible minimum of company at any time. I have no idea how you stand now – in relation to Scottish Nationalism and in your general outlook and cultural conclusions; but I personally am implacably opposed to everything I have yet heard voiced in regard to any of these matters by any of my compatriots and striving incessantly to find means of expression for ideas at the utmost remove from all they can entertain or express. And I am confident alike that I shall yet succeed in doing so and that my doing so will be an extremely important matter for Scotland and for far more than Scotland. What can anyone do with a fellow like that?

I hope you've a splendid time in Ireland and that both Daisy and yourself are in splendid fettle. I'd like to have a while in Ireland again myself but that is out of the question at the moment. I'll be here all this year now unless something quite unforeseen happens (though there is one contingency I know of which may possibly take me to Oban in October and keep me there for a month or longer) – and that being so, and you being relatively a free agent, why don't you take a trip up here instead? We'd be awfully glad to have you and have ample (if somewhat barely furnished) accommodation. Any time that suited you would suit us – and the fact that this is a dry area can be got over, you know!

Every kind regard to you both.

                    Yours,
                    Chris.

NLS   Whalsay.
                                                           17/2/36

My dear Neil,

I was glad to get your last letter and should have replied sooner. But what with the weather and one thing and another!

I'm in good form again now and very busy. I expect my *Scottish Eccentrics* this week but *Red Scotland* is hung up owing to certain elements allegedly seditious which I refuse to excise or moderate; I expect I'll transfer it to other publishers.

I'm to be in Aberdeen shortly broadcasting and – desiring to see your face again (and further stimulated thereto by having procured from our mutual friend Mr Patterson a copy of that fine photographic study in which I am seen in the very act of biting your ear!) –

I had thought of 'spiering' whether you couldn't run down there and let me (and possibly my wife also) spend a night or a couple of nights in Inverness. I didn't do that because I have also to be in Edinburgh debating: and in any case this is all to be the most hurried of visits, since we are taking up our abode again in Edinburgh about the end of March. I am hoping that may mean a better chance of seeing you now and again (since I entirely agree with you – and with F. G. Scott who has recently been writing me in like strain – that 'Them were the days' – when we were all full of eagerness and hope.) I am not surprised that you have become tired of the Scottish Nationalist Movement in all its phases. So am I – and yet my chief reason and main hope in again returning to Scotland is precisely to put a jolt into the whole business again. What's the betting that I don't succeed?

Don't hear anything about more books from you. Have you put your threat to cease awhile from literary production into effect? I hope not.

Love to you both,

Yours,
Chris.

P.S. Just about forgot one of my chief reasons for writing you tonight.

I don't know if you are in touch with any of Inverness County Council members – or if, perhaps, your own post as a civil servant precludes you from any activity in matters of this sort; but my friend here (the reason for my originally coming here) Dr David Orr is applying for the post of MD to the Parish of the Small Isles (i.e. Eigg, Rum, Muick & Canna). And as you know canvassing is almost a *sine qua non* in regard to such appointments. I'd be glad if you could drop a word on his behalf into any relevant ears to which you may have access. He is fine fellow – greatly esteemed here – and likely to do particularly well in the Gaelic isles being himself a fine specimen of the Gael and very keen on the life, language, and culture of the Gaels. He's a jolly good doctor too – and young and of splendid physique while the four or five years' experience he's had up here will stand him in good stead in the Hebrides. If you could just whisper here and there (it's regrettable that these tactics are so necessary, of course, but . . . .) that you've a friend in the Shetlands who knows this applicant, Dr Orr, well and speaks very highly of him, I'd be very greatly obliged. Attaboy! Up Guards and at them!

Whalsay,
Via Lerwick,
Shetland Islands.
21-10-37

My dear Neil,

I caught a chill on the way back about a fortnight ago – or I'd have written you sooner. I didn't get back by Inverness after all. After a wonderful time in Eigg, Skye, South Uist, Barra, and finally Mull and Iona, I discovered, in Tobermory, that the direct boat back here was from Aberdeen and not, as I had thought, from Leith, so McColl and I cut across to Dunblane (where we saw Angus Clark), Woodside where we saw Hugh Patterson, and Perth, where we saw Soutar – and there we parted, he to London, and I to Aberdeen and thence home – to such an infernal programme of book-writing under unfavourable conditions as would appal even you.[1]

Well, well. It was a great time; the weather was extremely kind, and we saw everybody we wanted to, I think – Compton Mackenzie, MacNair Reid, Father John MacMillan, Donald Sinclair's brother Neil, my friend Sam Maclean and his brothers at Raasay, etc etc. and, after all these years, it was great seeing Daisy and you again – quite like a breath of old times.[2] Queer that I should have been in at the beginning of your sojourn in Larachan, and in again just at the end of it.

I wonder if your 'flitting' is over. If so, I can only hope that it did not take too much out of you, and that you are now comfortably settled in, like your new abode, and are both in the best of form.

I have no news – though I should add (as perhaps you have heard already) that in addition to the various people I've already men-

---

[1] In a letter of 6 June 1983 to the present editor, Sorley Maclean recalled that 'It was in September 1937 that Christopher and W. D. MacColl made the trip. I was then teaching in Portree School. They came first to Raasay and stayed with my family, then stayed for a hectic week-end with me in Portree and then went I think to Barra. The trip was for Grieve's Islands (Batsford) book.' W. D. MacColl was a Scottish Nationalist and Gaelic revivalist; he was involved in the publication of Sorley MacLean's *Dàin do Eimhir* (1943). Angus Clark, whose father had slate quarries at Ballachulish, was likewise a Scottish Nationalist activist. Hugh Patterson was a Scottish Nationalist who lived in Lochalsh for some time.

[2] Father John MacMillan was a priest in Barra; Donald Sinclair was a Gaelic poet much admired by MacDiarmid who wrote a poem 'Donald Sinclair' (1259) in his memory.

tioned I also met Sir Alexander McEwen[3] – on the boat, he going to Lochinaddy and I to South Uist – and had a few words with him.

Write me sometime and tell me how you've got fixed up in your new home, and give a poor creature virtually cut off from the world altogether and living in a little limbo of his own the benefit of your news of the human species to which he once belonged but seems, on the verge of the depths of another Shetland winter, to be now expelled from for good and all.

And above all, do send me the books you so kindly promised. Books are a serious matter up here I can tell you – we are always at the last gasp for something new to read. And I was so thoughtless as to mention, in a letter I sent her from Arisaig, to Valda that you were sending on a couple of books – and the creature has been at me ever since. Besides, I really want them.

With every good wish and affectionate regard to Daisy and yourself.

Yours,
Chris.

NLS

Whalsay,
Via Lerwick,
Shetland Islands.
1-12-37

My dear Neil,

Very many thanks for the two books.[1] I am glad to have them. I seem to gather from your letter that you suspect me of regarding you as one who has sold his soul for financial success. I think nothing of

---

[3] Sir Alexander MacEwen (1875–1941) was a prominent Liberal and provost of Inverness from 1925 to 1931. He was friendly with Gunn and shared his interest in a revival of Gaelic culture in the Highlands. In 1932 Sir Alexander MacEwen and the Duke of Montrose formed the Scottish Party. Gunn disliked the splitting of the movement and saw that nationalism would be vitiated if divided between a leftist National Party of Scotland and a moderate Scottish Party and so he tried to bring both sides together. They were united in 1934 when the NPS and the SP merged to form the Scottish National Party.

[1] One of which was Gunn's novel *Highland River* (1937) whose success encouraged him give up his job in the Excise.

the kind; what I do in certain connections think is that no mere mercenary motive or submission to the mercenary machinations of others, but much more complicated causes involved in the contemporary organisation of the literary and publishing world and in the agencies that shape our cultural conceptions and predilections have come between you and the maximum services you could have rendered to Scotland and to literature (and in this connection the two are indistinguishable.) I cannot – and you would not want me to – go into the whole question here; but my view is only my view and is amply offset by the totally different views of a great multitude of others, and you have the further satisfaction of knowing that if I (from my Marxist standpoint, boldly confronting precisely those issues in aesthetics which Marx and Lenin and other leading Marxist writers left well alone) cavil at your work in certain respects what I cavil at is not only or particularly *your* work but the work of the vast majority of writers everywhere. Only I come closer to grips with your exemplification of a very general sentimentality because in your case it happens to be applied to Scottish subject-matter – which least of all in my opinion requires it, and in relation to which at all events other issues altogether seem to me to be infinitely more important – and by a Scottish writer – of whom the historical situation requires in especial the repudiation of anything of the sort. But bless me, I may be wrong. In any case, I have never had an opportunity yet of arguing out the matter in a set form – either in my own writings or in conversation. My 'quarrel' with you goes far deeper than any question of accusing you of being mercenary; and it is not a 'quarrel' of a sort that blinds me to the very high qualities of much of your work in both of these books, or prevents me enjoying them, or blemishes in any way my genuine delight in the measure of success and repute you have achieved, or leads me to question at all your integrity as an artist, or your deep concern and patient and skilful grappling with Scottish issues. I do not even, when I fancy that ten or more years ago we stood closer to each other spiritually, believe that our subsequent divergence could or should have been averted. Yet I regret that the divergence took place and admit that I had coveted other things for you and that I wish both for your sake and my own that we might have kept in closer contact intellectually. My cavillings therefore arise almost wholly on scarcely arguable grounds upon which the passage of time alone can decide. We will see what we will see. These statements are all evoked by your remark that at the time you wrote me you were not feeling much in sympathy with me. Well, since then I have read these two books and I am feeling more in sympathy with you than perhaps at any time since the Montrose days if sympathy means – not agreement with the

261

shapings and angle and directions of your spirit, but renewed and intensified interest in your development and keen desire to see you achieve the very best of which you are capable. But, as you will appreciate, that does not mean that our directions are not diametrically opposed or that – without any question of varying integrity or ability between us – if matters were threshed out completely in set debate between us, we would not find a single point of fundamental artistic or political agreement.

To turn from these difficult issues to a practical aspect, be sure that nothing I have said in the foregoing paragraphs, leaves me in any doubt whatever as to how I should reply to your query as to whether – if that is possible – you ought to stick to less remunerative lines or seize any opportunity that may present itself to do work of a more lucrative sort which would enable you to buy a bigger boat and venture into Shetland waters. Without any hesitation whatever I advise – I might even say enjoin – the latter; and my wife asks me to say that she is emphatically, and most hopefully, of the same opinion. So go ahead, old man. We'd be more than delighted to see you up here next summer – even if that had entailed your perpetration of a best seller!!!

As a matter of fact, of course, the elements in your work I question most are not those which have given you such measure of popularity as you have won, but those but for which you would probably have done even better commercially, as well as, in my opinion, artistically.

However, this is just a letter and not a critical excursus. I only wish that in lieu of either the one or the other of these I could see you more frequently and talk with you in no set but a random fashion on these and other matters. I was very happy indeed to see Daisy and you again after all these years. And I hear from MacNair Reid that you are very nicely ensconsed in your new home, delightfully situated in a wide valley, he says. I can't gather from his letter exactly where it lies. I think I told you that one of my earliest recollections is of a holiday I spent near Dingwall and Garve. But that is a long time ago, and I'm not sure of the lie of the land at all. But I hope you are most comfortably fixed and liking it and going ahead with the good work for all you are worth.

Blessings on both of you. My wife joins me in every friendly sentiment.

Yours,
Chris.

P.S. I note what you say about remembering you if I come across

262

anything specially good. So far as my own work is concerned I'll certainly send you a copy if I have anything printed that seems to me worth while. But so far as others are concerned, though I keep fairly well posted, I do not see nearly as much here as I'd like to. I lent MacNair Reid a very remarkable novel – I think the most important thing in English fiction since Joyce's *Ulysses* – It is *Nightwood* by Djuna Barnes (Faber and Faber.) If you haven't seen it I think it is particularly worth your attention, and if you care I'll gladly send it on to you after I get it back from Reid.

NLS

Whalsay,
Via Lerwick,
Shetland Islands.
21-2-38

Dear Neil,

I'd have replied right away to your welcome letter[1] – and the challenge it contained re defining myself exactly in regard to your work – only you said in it you were off in a few days later to Ireland. So I thought I'd wait till you'd be back. Now I can't lay my hands on your letter. But in any case I don't know it's a matter to try to thresh out in letters. I'd rather have a good night's talking with you sometime e.g. when you come up here with your boat (as my wife and I *do* hope you will). At the same time I'm not shirking the matter by any means, and I've just dealt with it in a longish poem I've taken the liberty of dedicating to you. It is called 'Good-Bye, Twilight',[2]

[1] On 3 December 1937 Gunn wrote a long letter justifying his own artistic approach and challenging MacDiarmid to be more precise in his criticism: 'You see in my work evidence of the sentimental. I, in yours, evidence of the romantic-sentimental. So there may be some point of common vision! . . . Yet I am sure you will have your own definition or exposition of these elements [you dislike in my work], and until you care to define them with some precision I might merely waste time in first assuming and then analysing. So get down to it!' (letter in NLS).

[2] 'Good-bye Twilight' (1124-6), here projected as part of *Mature Art*, is inscribed 'For Neil M. Gunn' and issues an ultimatum to artists lurking in the Celtic Twilight:

> Out from your melancholy moping, your importance, Gaels,
> (You stir the heart, you think? . . . but surely
> One of the heart's main functions is to supply the brain!)
> Back into the real world again. . .
> – For the true spirit is still living here and there, and perhaps

and is part of a very long poem – about double *Cencrastus* – I'm just having typed out to send to Eliot. I'll send you a copy of 'Good-Bye, Twilight' soon. I've got a very able chap[3] up here now as secretary-typist and had begun to hope we might make rapid progress with some of the many books I have on hand: but he has been ill for a week, and now, alas, comes the news that his mother has died, so he's going South tomorrow and I'll be without him again for a week or ten days at least. A great pity – it may make all the difference between a couple of books of mine catching Spring publication or being held over until Autumn. However, it can't be helped.

I greatly enjoyed the instalment of your account of your voyage in the *Scots Magazine* and will look forward eagerly to the publication of this book.[4]

I hope you had a nice holiday in Eire; and that both Daisy and you are fine and fit, and the good work going ahead like billy-O!

Are you taking to the water this summer again? If so, do think of doing these Shetland seas.

Love to you both.

Yours,
Chris.

Whalsay,
Via Lerwick,
Shetland Islands.
9-5-38

My dear Neil,

A thousand thanks for *Off in a Boat* which – despite all the splendid things in all your books and the undoubtedly greater literary importance of some of these, I have enjoyed more completely – more entirely without reservations of any kind – than any of your others.

The day is not far distant when the Scottish people
Will enter into this heritage, and in so doing
Enrich the heritage of all mankind again.
[3] Henry Grant Taylor.
[4] Gunn's *Off in a Boat* (1938) describes the trip he and Daisy made in the summer of 1937.

Here again I think what gets me is the fact that it is not fiction – and that the others are. But I am not going to argue about that just now. It is a most delightful book – some of the photographs too are really wonderfully fine – and I hope it scores even half the success it deserves.

What about the coming summer? Are you going to venture into Shetland waters? We'd be extremely pleased to see Daisy and you. I do not expect to be away at all this year. I'm still up to the neck with all sorts of books – and likely to be for months ahead – and apart from that I'm just about to launch a new quarterly of Scottish arts and affairs, called *The Scottish Republic* and devoted to the advocacy of Scottish Republicanism and the Leninist line in regard to Scotland of the late John Maclean, and the detailed analysis of Scottish issues in the light of dialectical materialism.

But while my other books are dragging their weary way towards, one hopes, eventual completion, I have at least completed and sent off an enormous poem[1] – over 10,000 lines (i.e. thrice the size of *Cencrastus*) and, including preface, notes, etc., amounting to over 100,000 words. Heaven only knows if I'll get a publisher. But at least this poem is (mainly) in English, so that may help.

I hope you are both fine and fit. Write and give me your news one of these days. As I said in my last letter I've mislaid yours and can't remember your new address, so I've no option but to send this one too to your old address.

Again, warmest thanks, and every good wish.

Yours,
Chris.

NLS   Whalsay,
Via Lerwick,
Shetland Islands.
6-7-38

My dear Neil,

I don't know whether you are home from Germany yet or not (or perchance languishing in one of the dungeons of the Gestapo): but

[1] *Mature Art.*

265

MacNair Reid mentioned in a letter the other day that Daisy and you were going there about (I took it) the end of the month, so you are perhaps home again. I am writing because your last letter did not give me time to reply before your departure for Munich (where I hope you had a splendid time) – and the news it contained of the Tait Black award[1] called for immediate cheers of which I was thus denied any chance of delivering myself, and which I have had rumbling about inside me ever since like thunder in the hills. So here goes – I must emit them at last! Heartiest congratulations – and many happy returns! I was delighted to hear the good news, and hope it – and your subsequent European trip – may have kindled you to triple-strength determination to go ahead with still more and better books. Dorothy Parker, the American journalist, has a 'crack' about a lady friend who periodically alarmed the neighbours for a long time about an infant she was going to produce first in May, then in August, then in November. It finally did arrive – and Dorothy Parker's telegram, among the host of congratulatory telegrams received by the happy if belated mother, read: 'Congratulations. We all knew you had it in you.'

I feel sure I'll feel called upon to hail the book of yours I'm really looking for (and in so saying I am not casting any 'asparagus' whatever at anything in your fine tale of work done up to now) with a similar telegram one of these days. In the meantime my message is: 'Grow old along with me – The best is still to be.'

Hope you are both fit and fine.

Love from us all.

Yours,
Chris.

P.S. You'll have heard of my new paper[2] perhaps. I'm enclosing a leaflet – but the first issue will be out this week anyhow.

P.S. Poetry is quite another matter of course. Eliot found *Mature Art* 'very interesting and individual and indeed a very remarkable work' which 'undoubtedly ought to be published' – but came to the conclusion that it was outside the scope of his firm, must entail a heavy loss to the publishers (which – as he pointed out – is not only no adverse criticism of a poet but may be a compliment) but he went on to say that if I submitted it to another firm he would give it his 'personal support, for what that may be worth'. That was good of

[1] Gunn won the James Tait Black Memorial Prize for 1937 for *Highland River*.
[2] *The Voice of Scotland*, Vol I, No I, June-August 1938.

him and may mean a great deal. MacMillan's now have it under consideration. But it's such an enormous thing – and (hopeful as I am by nature – and necessity) I am not very hopeful that such an undertaking is likely in these difficult days to commend itself to them or any other firm (and certainly only a firm like theirs – old established, wealthy, wide ranging – could tackle it; and there are only one or two such firms in Great Britain). However! We'll see. Two nieces (I think) of yours – Marjorie and Elma Robertson – are to be here next week for a week or so, with a couple of male friends of theirs – and mine.

NLS

Whalsay.
3-11-38

Dear Neil,

You were down in Glasgow about the time Valda and Michael were there. Valda was sorry not to see you.

I think my last letter to you asked if you couldn't send me on for a little a copy of the German review containing your article on Scottish Literature. Perhaps you hadn't a copy handy or something. In any case you did not reply.

My purpose in writing now is to ask if you are going to the dinner to Power in Glasgow on 3rd December. I intend to be there and, all being well, thought I might call in by Dingwall and we could go down together. In order to be sure of getting there in time I'll require to leave Lerwick on Monday 28th inst. I travel by Kirkwall and Scapa to Scrabster. How precisely the railway goes from Scrabster and whether Dingwall is on the direct line or where I cannot remember – if I ever knew. But it should be possible to pick you up on the way South (that is to say, if you are at home and travelling thence to Glasgow.) I reach Scrabster sometime early on the afternoon of Tuesday 29th inst. If the idea appeals to you – and the thing fits in and you haven't other plans yourself – perhaps you will let me know and tell me how one gets from Scrabster to Dingwall. You need not be alarmed at the prospect of my appearance in your civilised purlieus; it is true I have these days a very shaggy beard – but whether I retain that or not is a matter of contention here at the moment. Valda is all for its complete removal. Taylor wants the side-bits, etc. excised and only some sort of goatee or imperial left.

Personally I want to keep the whole thing but to dye it a vivid red – at present it is a sort of teased rope colour with numerous strands of grey. However we'll see.

I hope all is going well with Daisy and yourself in every way and that you are not given over too completely to the joys of idleness. (The only thing of yours I've seen recently is your *Scots Magazine* article on Leslie Mitchell.) I am still in the throes; but despite its inordinate length and inconceivable complication have now renewed hopes of securing publication for my long poem after all. Incidentally a longish swatch of it (about 500 lines) is appearing in *The Criterion*:[1] but whether in the next issue or the one following that I'm not quite sure yet. And I'm publishing a long poem[2] in the next issue of the *Voice of Scotland* too, and having a small edition of it struck off as a separate pamphlet. And I'm having my 10,000 word essay: 'Modern Scottish Politics In The Light of Dialectical Materialism' printed as a pamphlet too and hope to issue copies of it to each subscriber along with the 4th issue of the *Voice of Scotland*, just as I am issuing copies of the CP pamphlet on Scotland with the next (the 3rd) issue (which will be out about 10th December). There are a lot of other things I'd like to mention but I mustn't let myself run on. If we meet about the end of the month, as I hope, we'll aiblins have a good crack. In the meantime love to you both from all here.

Yours,
Chris.

NLS

Dungavel,
By Strathaven,
Lanarkshire.
3-3-50

My dear Neil,

Many thanks for the message you sent me in connection with the

[1] 'Cornish Heroic Song for Valda Trevlyn', projected as the 'opening section of an extremely long unpublished poem [*Mature Art*]', was first published in *The Criterion*, Vol XVIII, No LXXXI, January 1939.
[2] 'Direadh', one of the 'shorter separable lyrics' from *Mature Art*, appeared in *The Voice of Scotland*, Vol I, No 3, December 1938.

recent Election,[3] in which, as you know, save for a few Liberals, all the minority elements were blotted out by the neck-to-neck campaign of the two big parties.

I am in favour, as always, of Scottish Independence and stood strictly for that. What we will – or should – do with it once we have it is another matter into which my campaign speeches did not require me to divagate. So I could honestly accept and use your message (several newspapers paragraphed it). But of course we both know that while we can go so far together in our political ideas there is a point a little further on at which we sharply divide. I am a Communist – not a member, just now, of the CP, but hand in glove with and working actively for all the 'Communist-dominated' movements in the country – the National Peace Committee, the British-Polish Society, the Scottish U.S.S.R. Society, etc. etc.

The campaign was great fun. I think I addressed over 50 meetings in a fortnight – mostly in the open-air. Despite the miserable showing so far as votes go, 'it's coming yet for a' that'. While not reflected in the voting, the awakened interest in and attention to Scottish affairs of all kinds is most marked everywhere I have spoken – and I am speaking continually all over the bottom half of Scotland. And elsewhere. On Sunday I am off to Birmingham en route for Aberystwyth where I am to address the Arts Society of the University of Wales on 'A Scotsman Looks at English Literature'.

In the interstices of spouting I am writing a great deal again. The next volume of my Autobiography should be out soon; also books via the Grey Walls Press on 1/ Burns and 2/ Dunbar.[4] And I have an enormous amount of unpublished poetry; it is a bad time for poetry publishing. But bits of these huge poems do keep getting into print in American and Italian periodicals; and no doubt will find book publication yet. Lately I have recurred to Scots, and have a great deal in preparation there, carrying the whole thing which gave me my initial impetus to fresh levels.

Yes. I do hope we can meet and have a good pow-pow in Edinburgh at the Festival/International PEN Congress time. As I have told you before I have always greatly regretted that I have seen so little of you in the last twenty years! I hope you – and Daisy

---

[3] In the General Election of 23 February 1950 the results for the constituency of Kelvingrove were as follows: Rt Hon. Walter Elliot (Conservative: 15,197), J. L. Williams (Labour: 13,973), S. J. Ranger (Liberal: 831), C. M. Grieve (Independent Scottish Nationalist: 639).

[4] (Ed) Hugh MacDiarmid, *Robert Burns: Poems* (London 1949); (Ed) Hugh MacDiarmid, *Selections from the Poems of William Dunbar* (Edinburgh 1952).

– are in good form. I had heard you'd moved,[5] and gathered from somebody who'd seen you (Eoin O'Mahoney, perhaps?) that the need to do so had come unexpectedly. It must have been a great nuisance. I hope you are comfortably re-established in your new home, and in good working fettle. Are you still in touch with John MacNair Reid? I haven't seen hint or hide of him for years, nor even heard anything about him.

I myself – tho' no doubt more battered and disreputable than ever – retain as I approach my 60th year unabated energy, and, failing to get a house in Glasgow, Valda and I are for the nonce comfortably ensconced in a house given to us on his Dungavel estate by the Duke of Hamilton – a fine commodious house in the middle of a pine wood, where for once I have room to dispose even all my books and papers in a reasonably orderly and get-at-able way.

I don't know that you got a copy of my Election Address, so I enclose one – decorated with, I think, a photograph of myself which gives a really accurate view of what I actually look like nowadays.

With affectionate regards to you both.

Yours as ever,
Chris.

NLS

Brownsbank,
By Biggar,
Lanarkshire.
10/12/54

Dear Neil,

I have been away from home or I'd have received and replied to your letter[1] of 27th Nov. ere this.

[5] In May 1949 Gunn Settled into Kincraig, a house near Dingwall, after living for twelve years at Braefarm House.

[1] On 27 November 1954 Gunn wrote to MacDiarmid: 'Dear Christopher, Put it down to curiosity, but I should like to know just what you meant in the recent broadcast discussion when you placed my work in "the nineties". It was obvious to any listener that your criticism was meant to be damaging, if only from the way Edwin Muir and Douglas Young at once countered you. . . The nineties surely stand for an ultra-sophistication, for men like Beardsley and Oscar Wilde, for an aspect of urban civilisation that must be about the very antithesis of the country which I have tried to evoke in a score of novels'.

The broadcast[2] was unscripted. We talked 1¼ hours, and that had to be boiled down to 3/4 hour. All the meat was taken out of it. No wonder the *Scotsman* radio critic – and other commentators – complained that the Chairman had intervened whenever we seemed like getting into any real discussion and prevented it. Certainly all I really wanted to put across was cut out.

I was really concerned in all I said to stress the materialist (i.e. the Marxist) case against Edwin Muir – and to a lesser extent against Douglas Young. The 'Nineties stood not only for Beardsley, Wilde, etc. – but also for the Celtic Renaissance (i.e. the Celtic Twilight stuff), e.g. Patrick Geddes with his Celtic Renascene, the early Yeats poems etc. That was the point of my reference so far as you were concerned.

My criticism was, of course, not meant to be damaging, nor I think capable of being so, since you have an immensely larger following than I and the differences between our points of view are likely to be perfectly well known to most of either your readers or mine. I was simply concerned to dissociate myself from romantic idealisations of Gaelic 'spirituality', etc., and a non-scientific attitude to Nature, in accordance with my own Marxist tenets. I do not believe there is any future in anything else. Also I have little or no use for novels of any kind – except detective stories. But I did go on and admit (a most damaging admission from my viewpoint) that you were by far the best living Scottish writer of imaginative prose in the English language.

No, Neil, I have, I think, read everything you have written and never without appreciation of many elements in your work. But we are at opposite poles in all our ideas. In expressing mine, I am only carrying on the 'propaganda of ideas' which I have always done – but without any personal ill-feeling against my political and aesthetic opponents.

Alasdair Borthwick was Chairman of our discussion. No doubt a full recording is available. If so, you would realise that I did you no injustice but only emphasised that your work and mine represented entirely opposite tendencies. You must remember that what we were discussing was the reality or otherwise of what has been called the Scottish Renaissance Movement. There have been a great number of essays on that in American, Canadian, French, German & other reviews & books lately and all these writers, taking as their basis the proposed basis for such a renaissance as laid down by me at the outset in the *Scottish Chapbook* and elsewhere, omit your name

[2] 'Heritage' was broadcast on the BBC Scottish Home Service on 25 November 1954.

271

altogether – I think rightly in this context, since you stand for something entirely different.

As far as I am concerned I think this Renaissance Movement – as defined by me – is only the beginning and will be carried a very great deal further politically & otherwise in the next year or so.

I hope you, and Daisy, are well, I have scarcely heard a cheep about you since I saw you last at the International PEN Congress in Edinburgh, but I was told recently that you were having further trouble with your eyesight. I do hope this is not true – or, if true, not serious trouble.

Every good wish to you both.

Yours,
Chris.

NLS

Brownsbank,
Candymill,
Biggar,
Lanarkshire.
14/12/61

Dear Neil,

It was good to see your hand-o'-write on an envelope again, and I am glad you liked the brief remarks I made – all too brief; what the devil *can* one say in two-three minutes. However the programme[1] came over very well – I had no difficulty in hearing it tho' I am very deaf nowadays.

For some reason I've always thought of you as younger than myself – due, I think, to your early association with my younger brother in Cupar.

Glad you're nicely situated now on the Beauly Firth[2] and inclined (at times anyhow) to envy you 'a freedom that positively seems to expand'. My cottage here is splendidly situated in prospect of low

[1] 'Neil M. Gunn: An appreciation for his seventieth birthday' was broadcast on the BBC Scottish Home Service on 18 November 1961. MacDiarmid was one of five speakers.
[2] In 1959 Gunn sold his house Kerrow, in Glen Cannich, and bought Dalcraig, a house facing south over the Beauly Firth, some two miles from Kessock Ferry.

272

round Border hills: but recently advancing age has made my wife and I less able to cope with the exigencies of living in a primitive way without 'mod cons' so for some months now the cottage has been under reconstruction. Electric light, bathroom, etc. etc. have all been installed and once I find out again where the deuce all my books and papers are now located we'll have an easier time.

Actually, however, I'm busier than ever – addressing a constant succession of meetings under all sorts of auspices, taking a weekly University Extra-Mural class in Lanark, – and I have no fewer than 4 books and 2 pamphlets[3] due out. They should have been published ere this but the printing and publishing trades seem nowadays as vexatious in their delays as the Law. They can't be long delayed now, however, and include 1/ my Collected Poems 2/ a long poem 3/ translation of a Swedish epic poem in 27 cantos by the leading contemporary Swedish poet, Harry Martinson.

Norman McCaig (my source of occasional news of you) tells me you've stopped writing: also – more ominously – that you very strictly limit your intake of whisky. I hope that neither of these precautions means that there's any real need for you to ca'-canny. And that this finds both Daisy and you in good fettle.

I remember the occasion you refer to very well, en route to St Cyrus: but have had cause to wish other drivers to whom I've entrusted myself were as expert as you were then. Both my wife and I were involved in a very serious accident two years ago – missed death by a miracle and sustained injuries from the consequences of which we still suffer. And more recently a car in Edinburgh struck me a glancing blow and I recovered consciousness in the Out Patient Dept. of Edinburgh Royal Infirmary with the back of my head all stitched up.

Anyhow I wouldn't mind a run with you again today or any day. Here's my warmest regards, and every good wish for Christmas and New Year to Daisy and you from Valda and

Christopher.

---

[3] The four books are: ('A long poem') *The Kind of Poetry I Want* (Edinburgh 1961); *Collected Poems* (New York 1962); the fourth edition of *A Drunk Man Looks at the Thistle* (Edinburgh 1962); *Aniaria* (London 1962) by Harry Martinson, adapted from the Swedish by Hugh MacDiarmid and Elspeth Harley Schubert. The two pamphlets are *The Man of (Almost) Independent Mind* (Edinburgh 1962) and *The Ugly Birds Without Wings* (Edinburgh 1962).

To R. E. Muirhead

Roland Eugene Muirhead (1868–1964), sometimes called the Father of Scottish Nationalism, was born heir to a fortune associated with the family business of Gryffe Tannery at Bridge-of-Weir. Throughout his long lifetime he used his position and his wealth to support a variety of nationalist activities. In 1906 he co-founded (with Tom Johnston) the Scottish ILP journal *Forward* and in 1918 he re-founded the Scottish Home Rule Association, transforming the predominantly Liberal prewar SHRA into a pressure group able to exert an influence on socialist organisations. Muirhead was Secretary of the SHRA until he left in 1929 whereupon the SHRA collapsed.

Determined to create a nationalistic consciousness in Scotland Muirhead set up, in 1924, the Scottish Secretariat as a publishing concern for the distribution of Scottish material. As Jack Brand writes, in *The National Movement in Scotland* (London 1978, pp. 198–9),

> Most of the writing was done by Hugh MacDiarmid either anonymously or under the pseudonym of 'Mount boy'. It was used to spread Home Rule and Scottish propaganda under the name of an apparently neutral body when articles would not have been accepted had they come from an identifiably political source. The whole operation was financed by R. E. Muirhead from 1924 until his death. Up to 1928 it was carried out on behalf of the SHRA and thereafter on behalf of the NPS and SNP although after 1945 Muirhead used the Secretariat to publish independent nationalist pamphlets.

Muirhead encouraged the formation of the National Party of Scotland in 1928 and was Chairman until the NPS merged with the Scottish Party to establish the Scottish National Party in 1934. His Scottish Secretariat issued the *Scots Independent* (founded 1926) as an independent monthly until 1939 when the SNP took the paper from Muirhead and made it an official party publication. Muirhead was President of the SNP in the 1940s and lost his faith in parliamentary action when he saw Robert MacIntyre win Motherwell for the SNP

274

in a by-election of April 1945 then lose it two months later at the General Election.

Saddened by this spectacle Muirhead began to advocate extra-parliamentary action and founded Scottish Congress in 1950. It was a non-violent body dedicated to Gandhian principles; as such it published the *National Weekly* and supported Michael Grieve, the poet's son, when he refused to be conscripted into the British army in 1950. MacDiarmid said of R. E. Muirhead (in the programme of the Presentation of the Andrew Fletcher Award to Muirhead on 11 September 1956):

In any other country in the world he would have been recognised as a Grand Old Man of his people. In Scotland if he has not been able to compete for the regard of his compatriots with royalties, film stars, golf champions, English carpet baggers and all the other riff-raff on whom the spotlight concentrates, I have no doubt that he will be fittingly recognised in time as a salutary force at the roots of our national existence, as one who in a time of sad distortion of all Scottish interests and values kept a way open for a return to our true tradition, and as a human being who in his gentleness and generosity and unselfishness sums up in his own character all those qualities which however they may be dis-counted by 'smart Alecs' are nevertheless essential to the ultimate achievement in our country of anything really worth while in any field of endeavour.

EUL

16 Links Avenue,
Montrose.
2/2/23

R. E. Muirhead, Esq.
Dear Sir:-

Excuse a brief scrawl!

I am just off to London where inter alia I am to address the London Burns Club; but my principal object is to make final arrangements re the new Scottish weekly, which will be a Scottish equivalent of *The New Statesman* or *Nation*,[1] predominantly a literary

---

[1]   *The Scottish Nation* which was published weekly from 8 May 1923 to 25 December 1923.

and artistic review, devoted to Scottish life, letters, and arts in general; but, also, an attempt to fuse all sorts of Scottish interests into a keener nationalism; and, in particular, designed to foster the demand for Scottish Home Rule.

I hope to have a regular column or so devoted to SHR Assocn. affairs in addition to weekly articles of high literary quality dealing systematically with the various aspects of the case for Scottish Home Rule.

In these circumstances I hope to secure the active support of all Scottish Home Rulers.

Prospectuses, etc., will be issued as soon as I return from London.

Can I count on your co-operation? Needless to say such a venture will require all the support it can possibly get in the intial stages.

Yours faithfully,
C. M. Grieve.

EUL

16 Links Avenue,
Montrose.
29/3/23

R. E. Muirhead, Esq.
Dear Mr Muirhead:-

Further investigations since my last letter make me absolutely certain that the proposed weekly can be made a huge success along the lines I intend to take.

As I said when I quoted you estimated figures I gave advt. revenue at an absolute minimum as guaranteed by advt. agents. I have, however, been exceptionally fortunate in securing the best man possible to get in London in that connection. And his pro- visional bookings are already such that the paper will be self- supporting – independent of any revenue from sales at all – for the first few weeks at all events. He is already booked up for the whole of the space allocated to advts. in the Dummy copy – and all with first-class firms – while if I accept any Scottish advts. at all I shall have to increase the number of pages beyond the 24 projected.

I think you will agree that this is a good omen. It is seldom that such a venture can begin so heavily advertised – and with advts. of such exclusive quality.

I would be less sanguine were it not that I know that, not only will we begin so well, but that we can absolutely depend upon considerably more than the minimum I quoted as probable revenue from English advts., for a sufficient length of time to ensure us a splendid chance to acquire an adequate permanent circulation.

In these circumstances I hope you will not consider me importunate if I ask you to let me know at the earliest possible moment to what extent you and any of your friends are prepared to help me in securing the necessary initial capital and in proceeding to form a private company.

I must complete all my arrangements within ten days from this date at the very outside: and I am confidently relying upon your assistance.

I am also anxious to know whether the suggestion you made with regard to the Assocn. *News Sheet* is likely to come to anything.

I am hoping to be in Glasgow one of these days but am (like yourself) up to the eyebrows in all sorts of work, and will therefore be glad if – pending my hope of seeing you shortly and talking matters over – you can let me know at your very earliest what practical assistance I can count upon.

> Yours faithfully,
> C. M. Grieve.

EUL

16 Links Avenue,
Montrose.
26/4/23

R. E. Muirhead, Esq.
Dear Sir:-

Your last letter greatly disappointed me. The offer of practical assistance came from yourself in the first instance and, while counselling delay, you expressly re-iterated that if I decided to go on you would help me to some small extent at any rate. The suggestion that the Assocn. News-Sheet and the new paper might in some way be conjoined was also thrown out by you.

However I know that you are eager, too, to see such a paper as I proposed launched and I believe, and earnestly hope, that you will give it all the help, other than financial, you possibly can. I have succeeded in overcoming my difficulties and (delaying the whole question of forming a company for some time until we see how it goes) the new paper will be duly launched on 8th May as arranged.

Substantially it will be as per dummy, with the exception that it will consist of sixteen pages instead of twenty-four (for purely technical reasons – we cannot handle a 24-page without introducing new machinery).

I am therefore anxious for all the help you may care to give me in bringing the matter prominently before all the members of the Scottish Home Rule Assocn. and soliciting their active support. I do not wish subscriptions: preferring that orders should be placed with local booksellers and stationers.

I wonder if it is too much to ask if you would be so good as to circularise all the branches drawing the attention of members to the new paper and asking them to support it? I will also esteem it a great favour if you will give the matter as much publicity as possible in the next News-Sheet. I am arranging for the distribution and display of preliminary bills throughout Scotland in the beginning of the week. Descriptive leaflets will also be broadcast.

In regard to the space provided in the dummy under the heading 'The Scottish Nationalist Movement' and 'Branch Reports', this will still be available if you wish to make use of it. Branch reports will be few and far between of course during the coming summer months. But notes and news as to the development of the S.H. Assocn. and other relevant matter, will be welcome. Can you arrange for me to receive at least 4 or 500 words every week for this feature?

I hope to have the solid support of the Assocn. in this difficult undertaking and in return the new paper will do its utmost to serve and further the movement in every way.

Thanking you for all the trouble you have already taken in connection with this, and hoping to hear from you with reference to above points at your earliest convenience.

I remain,

> Yours faithfully,
> C. M. Grieve.

EUL
TS

16 Links Avenue,
Montrose.
17th July, 1923.

R. E. Muirhead, Esq.
Dear Mr Muirhead,

What must be must in regard to *The Scottish Nation*? Believe me intensely appreciative of all you have done. I quite understand your position: and, even if I could, would not do anything to press the claim of *The Scottish Nation* if help accorded to it meant any diminution of help to the political side of the Scottish Home Rule Movement.

At the same time I am writing today to Sir Daniel Stevenson[1] in the hope that he may now be home. I shall be very grateful indeed if you can do anything to back up my appeal to him. If I knew he was at home I would come through to Glasgow immediately and see him personally as you suggest. But I am afraid that he may not be at home, and in that case it may be too late before my letter reaches him.

Whether the *S.N.* ceases or continues believe me heart and soul, now and always, with you in your propaganda. I shall do anything I possibly can in any direction and if there is anything you would like me to do I shall be only too happy to try to discharge in that way part of the debt I owe you for your goodness to me.

If the *S.N.* ceases I shall be much freer, and will devote a considerable part of my time to propaganda, in the shape of articles on various aspects of Scottish nationalism, initiating newspaper controversies, etc. and doing all that one man can do to intensify interest in the questions at stake.

Again thanking you.

Yours faithfully,
C. M. Grieve.

[1] Sir Daniel Stevenson, Lord Provost of Glasgow from 1911 to 1914, was a Liberal whose nationalist sympathies drew him to the Scottish Party.

EUL

16 Links Avenue,
Montrose.
25/10/23

R. E. Muirhead, Esq.
Dear Sir:-

The Scottish Nation completes its first half-year with next issue. It has had an uphill fight: but it has been well worth it. I have many scores of tributes to the paper. I know that a large number of readers will be extremely sorry if the paper is discontinued. These are the advance-guard of the Scots people – they already have that national consciousness upon the wholesale development of which the future of distinctive Scots nationality rests. No one is more keenly conscious than I am of the imperfections of the paper – I know a score of ways in which it could be strengthened and improved. That is only a question of time and money. In the meantime, it has to be remembered that I am doing the whole of the work connected with it – collection of materials, reading of proofs, conducting of correspondence, dispatch of papers, book-keeping, etc. – in my spare time: as well as a great deal of the actual writing.

We have had the disadvantage of being unable owing to lack of finance to advertise the paper as we should have done – as it would have paid a hundred times over to have done. We have not even been able to engage any one in Edinburgh and Glasgow, let alone elsewhere, to canvas the retail newsagents, seek additional subscribers, ensure a fair display of posters, etc. We have been prejudiced because of our stand for Scottish national self-determination and our sympathetic attitude to labour. Nevertheless, we have kept going. The influence of the paper is increasing gradually but surely. The literary standing of the paper is improving. It is providing an outlet for an increasing number of Scottish writers. It is doing incessant propaganda work for Scottish nationalism that I am persuaded cannot fail to have a great effect in the long run. The ring of hostility amongst the publishers is being broken. My London friends are confident of our ultimate success – if we can only hold out a little longer. Six months has not been long enough to give us a fair chance. It would be a thousand pities to let the effort lapse now. I should be glad to have your opinion.

I do not know whether you saw Sir Daniel Stevenson. I had a brief note from him and from the wording of it I felt that he had not understood my letter to him. It simply said that he 'was connected with too many Associations as it was, at present, and could not see his way to assist another'.

As matters now stand I must have additional capital – or discontinue the paper. I do not want a great deal. I have every reason to believe that if we can keep going for another six months we shall have found our feet. So I am endeavouring to raise £3-400. I already have a number of promises of sums of £5 and £10 – contingent upon my being able in this way to raise not less than £300. Some time ago you were good enough to offer £5 a week for 6 weeks provided I was able to secure a number of others to do likewise. I do not know whether you will still be willing to help. But you will forgive me if I seem to be importunate. I must exhaust every possible source of help at this juncture. You may know a few friends who would be willing to give £5 or £10, provided others are prepared to do likewise up to the necessary amount. Or if the matter were properly put before him Sir Daniel Stevenson might now be willing to give us the little assistance necessary to enable us to carry on until we turn the corner.

I know you will help if you can: and if you can't it can't be helped. May I ask you to let me know at your earliest convenience? Thanking you in anticipation.

Yours faithfully,
C. M. Grieve.

P.S. I have written to as many others as I think might help and am now awaiting replies.

EUL   16 Links Avenue,
                                                                     Montrose.
                                                              14th Jan. 1924.

Dear Mr Muirhead,

Many thanks for your last letter. I am now happily in a position to take advantage of Sir D. M. Stevenson's kind offer. I have in fact got rather more than the £500 stipulated – albeit mostly in £10 and £20 lots. But I have gone into the whole matter very thoroughly with advt. agents and others, and with John Buchan and others well able to advise and assist. And I find that the best plan is not to go on as a weekly: but to reappear as an 80 page monthly at 1/- per month. I am making arrangements along these lines and already the indications are that we shall be much better off for advts. With this £500 odds and a guaranteed monthly revenue from advts. which will go a considerable distance towards meeting the costs of publication, I have already letters indicating that we shall get a sufficient number of subscribers to throw us on the right side – slightly: but still that gives us a splendid fighting chance. I have been fortunate too in enlisting the help of certain big writers whose names alone in the first two or three issues will help our sales and our advts. From a literary point of view this magazine will take a much higher level – or rather a more uniformly high level – than did the weekly: and will have a much broader scope. I have been enheartened by the number of letters I have received deploring the stoppage of the weekly: and expressing hopes that it will be resumed. I am going to make exhaustive efforts to secure a solid list of subscribers for the first year of the monthly, and have various plans to that end well advanced. I shall spare no effort to make it a magazine worthy of Scotland in every respect.

The *Glasgow Herald* leader of 31st Dec. on 'The Scottish Literary Renaissance' greatly encouraged me. The admission that 'even for the sake of English Literature, literary devolution is necessary' carries the unavoidable implication that that equally applies in the political sphere. I have great hopes of seeing Scottish Home Rule a fait accompli this year.

Continental indications are good too. I have just been reading a most able article extending over eight pages on 'Le Groupe de "La Renaissance Écossaise"' in the *Revue Anglo-Américaine*[1] which clearly points out the political objective which is inseparably part of the goal which the movement I have been seeking to stimulate has set for itself. And I myself am busy writing a longish article through Professor Aloysius Brandl of Berlin University for an important German review in which I am even more strongly stressing the extent to which a Scottish Literary Renaissance in full depends upon the restoration of Scottish Independence.

Will you please communicate with Sir Daniel – and tell him that I have now succeeded in fulfilling the condition he made and am in a position to carry on as a consequence.

With every good wish and my best thanks.

Yours faithfully,
C. M. Grieve.

[1] Denis Saurat, 'Le Groupe de "la Renaissance Écossaise"', *Revue Anglo Américaine*, Première Année, No 4, April 1924.

16 Links Avenue,
Montrose.
26th April 1924

Dear Mr Muirhead:-

I sent on Montrose paper containing Marquis of Graham's Speech: and devoting considerable space to the Draft Bill.

I would have given a great deal to have been able to attend the Demonstration tomorrow: but am up to the eyes in arrangements for the above.[1] Things promise well: and I think we've provided a bumper shillingsworth.

If you have space, will you please alter the advt. in *Scottish Home Rule* which you have been so kindly giving, to the following in next issue:-

A Creative and Critical Magazine.
The Northern Review
(The Organ of the Scottish Renaissance)
Edited by C. M. Grieve
Poems, Plays, Short Stories, Essays,
Critiques, Book Reviews, etc. etc.
80 pages   1/- net
First Issue Ready May 3rd
The contributors include:-
John Buchan, R. B. Cunninghame-Graham,
Lady Margaret Sackville, Dr G. P. Insh
Walter de la Mare, Edwin Muir,
Hugh M'Diarmid, Alexander MacGill, etc.
The Magazine For the Thinking Scot
From all the leading booksellers and
Newsagents,
or, direct, from
The Northern Review,
c/o The Darien Press, Bristo Place,
Edinburgh.
I shall be eager to hear what you think of it once you see No I.
Yours, with every good wish.

C. M. Grieve.

---

[1] The letterhead on this letter reads '*The Northern Review*/A Progressive Monthly Of Life And Letters/Edited by a Group of Scottish Writers'.

EUL

Dear Miss Milne,[1]

I got your letter all right: but did not understand you wanted me to begin sending in articles, before I heard from you as to what papers etc. were going to take them. Otherwise I would have seen to it long ere this. I'm sorry about the loss of time through this misunderstanding. But I will see that you receive a supply this week and regular batches of articles thereafter.

I should have written you ere this, but have been awaiting results of my efforts to secure a publisher for the suggested book. (My idea all along was to get a publisher in the ordinary way – without any expense to the Socy. or any one else.) I approached Messrs Benn's first but they have finally decided not to undertake it. I am in negotiation with other firms: and will let you know as soon as I hear from them. I think I will manage to fix it up.

In other directions I have not been idle. The *Scots Observer* has a set of 3 articles on 'Scottish National Politics' from me, apropos the Draft Bill, which I think will be appearing very soon now, and I have also sent articles to *The New Age* and one or two other papers. As and when these appear I'll send you cuttings: and follow up correspondence on the subject through the papers in question.

Many thanks for the poems you sent in a recent letter. I wish I had a medium in which to use them. I'm always glad to note your occasional appearances in the *Herald*.

I will be writing again in a day of two.
Every good wish.

Yours sincerely,
C. M Grieve.

---

[1] Miss Milne, one of Muirhead's secretaries.

EUL

Mayfield, Hillside,
by Montrose.
30 June 1927.

to
The Scottish Secretariat,
30 Elmbank Crescent, Glasgow.

Dear Sir:-

Will you please reply to *Dundee Free Press* – regretting error in regard to their requirements and saying that there will be no difficulty in giving them the Local Special Service exclusive, as articles sent out under that arrangement are in all cases sent only to one paper and are specially written for it and for the area it serves. Further, that in view of the character of the *Dundee Free Press* and the wide area it caters for you are not sending them any set list of subjects, but have arranged with a contributor (whose articles will be signed A.K.L.) who is specially familiar with Dundee and the adjoining counties to send them two specimen articles viz. Tayside Topics I The Rural Community Council II A Giant in Bank Street (which they will now have received). You hope these specimen articles will prove suitable and if so that they will use them as the first two of the series. Others of varying nature, and dealing as occasion suggests with literary and other topics with a local bearing, will follow regularly each week-end. Payment, at the rate arranged, should be made to the Secretariat Office, and any correspondence relative to the series should also be directed thither.

If you reply in above strain at your earliest convenience, your letter will follow on the receipt by the *D. Free Press* of my specimen articles in question which, sent direct to them (without disclosure of my own identity but signed A.K.L. and franked 'Scottish Secretariat Special Service') will reach them on Saturday evening (2nd July).

Will you please tell Mr Muirhead that I hope to send him two or three specimen articles for the *Forward* in the beginning of the week?

Yours sincerely,
C. M. Grieve.

Mayfield,
Stillside,
by Montrose.
16/7/27

R. E. Muirhead, Esq.
Dear Mr Muirhead:-

Through the courtesy of the publishers Messrs Kegan Paul I have just had an opportunity of reading in proof-form an essay which they are publishing shortly in their well-known Today and Tomorrow Series entitled *Caledonia: or the Future of the Scots* by G. M. Thomson. A little later the same publishers are publishing an independently-written but largely complementary essay by myself entitled *Albyn: or the Future of Scotland.*

Mr Thomson and I agree entirely as to the present condition of Scotland and its cause. Where we differ is that while he recognises that nothing but a timely revival of Scottish Nationalism on an adequate scale can avert the calamity of the complete de-Scoticis-ation of Scotland, he does not believe that will happen – he thinks the time already past. I think otherwise.

Apart from that Mr Thomson's essay is an extraordinarily valu-able one for our purpose; it is the most compact, comprehensive, incisively-written unanswerable demonstration of the need for Scot-tish Home Rule that has yet been penned. And the essays in this series (which are cheap – 2/6) are selling tremendously not only in this country but all over the English-speaking world, and are usually reviewed at considerable length in most papers. I think every effort should be made to secure the maximum amount of publicity and discussion of these two books – Mr Thomson's and, later, mine. And to this end I intend to devote myself to the utmost during the next few weeks. I have already written to a whole string of editors; and I am preparing thoroughly good, well thought-out, and trenchant articles with regard to Mr Thomson's book for Secretariat issue.

My own idea in securing Kegan Paul to publish *Albyn* was to provide the Scottish National Movement with an effective bit of propaganda literature: and I had also a good deal to do with the genesis of Mr Thomson's book which will serve the same end. I am sure you will agree when you see them both that at least that object has been secured.

I am writing you in order to see if you can accept a special page-article from me reviewing Thomson's essay for your September issue of *Scottish Home Rule*[1]: as that will give me an opportunity of meeting certain points Mr Thomson raises which I have not dealt with in my own essay – written, as it was, without seeing his or consultation with him.

I was also to ask whether you did not know the Editor of the *Scottish Co-operator* (Mr Murray has left it, hasn't he?) and if so whether you could not approach them, as you approached *The Forward*, to put in a weekly article. What I would suggest in this case is that my series should be entitled 'Scotland Today and Tomorrow' and that each article should deal succinctly and comprehensively with one given aspect; i.e. in succession

1/ Population and Social Conditions.
2/ Industry
3/ Agriculture
   etc.

thus systematically covering the field and, in effect, making a complete and thoroughly up-to-date restatement of the case for Scottish Home Rule, without obtruding that phrase itself too much but rather letting the logic of the facts themselves indicate it as the only solution. Each article would occupy about a page of the *Scottish Co-operator* – no more.

I feel that we must do our utmost in every possible direction during this next autumn and winter and am making all the arrangements I can personally to that end.

I have not heard yet from Tom Johnston:[2] but sent him cuttings etc. and wrote him in full detail.

With best wishes.

Yours sincerely,
C. M. Grieve.

---

[1] 'The Future of Scotland' by C. M. Grieve, J.P., *Scottish Home Rule*, Vol 8, No 5, November 1927.
[2] Tom Johnston, who was to become a junior member of the minority Labour government of 1929–31, had co-founded *Forward* with Muirhead in 1906.

EUL

16 Links Avenue,
11/1/28

R. E. Muirhead, Esq.
Dear Mr Muirhead:-

Many thanks for your kindness in regard to the Aldred-Miss Lennox[1] business. I am greatly indebted to you. I thought I had said in my original letter that it was a dispute with the *Forward* people that was the trouble – but I did not know the details. All I know now is that Aldred sticks to it that the accounts – or some of them – were paid, and that Neil Docherty lost some of the receipts, but that he has others to produce. I understand the case is going on.

But I am quite certain that you satisfied yourself that the case was hopeless and advised Miss Lennox wisely. There is no use throwing good money after bad and I hold no brief for Aldred personally – however interested I may be in the maintenance of certain kinds of propaganda. In any case all I wanted you to do was to find out if the security available was sufficiently good to get a loan on the strength of. I have since heard from Miss Lennox and the initial amount of money to fight the next stage of the case has apparently been raised by one means and another.

I am afraid I put you to a considerable amount of trouble and I greatly appreciate your help in this matter. Miss Lennox tells me that you offered her a cheque but that in the circumstances she felt obliged to refuse it.

I did not get to the Kilmarnock Conference. My motion – through Montrose ILP – through unfortunate negligences on the part of the local Secretary was not forwarded in time for the Agenda and it became a question as to whether the Standing Orders Committee would strike a point in favour of it. I see from the newspaper reports that they did not succeed in dealing with all the Agenda business even. But when I found last Thursday that there was no definite word from Willie Stewart regarding the matter and that it was very problematical whether the motion would come up, I did not feel justified in attending – though I would have made a point of being present had I been sure it would come up.

[1] The Antiparliamentary Communist Federation, founded by Guy Aldred (1886–1963) had headquarters in Bakunin House, Burnbank Gardens, Glasgow and a Bakunin Press bookshop in Buchanan Street. At the end of 1927 an action by *Forward* against the Bakunin Press meant that Aldred had to raise £50 to save himself from bankruptcy. Miss Helen Lennox, a friend, asked MacDiarmid to intervene and he contacted Muirhead to see if he could help Aldred.

288

I am delighted to hear from Balderstone[2] of the progress being made with the bringing into being of a National Party, and am keenly looking forward to the tea at Balderstone's house on the afternoon of 21st inst. at which, I understand, you are to be present.

Again with thanks and every good wish.

Yours sincerely,
C. M. Grieve.

EUL

16 Links Avenue,
Montrose.
26.2.28

Dear Mr Muirhead:-

It was exceedingly good of you to accede to my request in the Aldred matter. I am quite sure that you are not in the least prejudiced against Aldred and, of course, I have no idea as to the information you have since received on the subject of his action against *Forward*. As to the rights and wrongs of that matter I myself have no opinion. It seems an extremely complicated question. On the Sunday following our Burns Supper in Glasgow I had a long talk with Aldred and he gave me the whole of his side of the story. I was greatly impressed – but did not lose sight of the fact that I had not heard the other side of the story. But from what I do know of Aldred himself and his career and his attitude to the *Forward* case I feel very strongly how unfair it is that legal costs should render it difficult for him to fight out his case. He may be right or he may be wrong – but to determine which should be a matter for justice and not for the longest purse.

I would on these grounds alone have had no hesitation whatever in lending Aldred money if I had had it to lend. Unfortunately I had to make it clear to him that he need not look to me for aid in that way. But on Friday I had a long wire from him asking for £10 as a loan and definitely promising repayment in two or three days. And I decided to take a risk and appeal to you on that understanding. I have not

---

[2] H. Balderstone was one of the founders of the National Party of Scotland.

heard from Aldred since but, of course, I hold myself responsible for repaying you.

I could have sent him a pound or two myself but not £10, and I gathered from his wire that he urgently needed the latter sum and that nothing less would suffice.

I hope you may see your way to be present at our debate on Saturday. Mr G. M. Thomson (author of *Caledonia*) is also to be present. We are to meet somewhere in the afternoon and to have tea together. I have left it to Thomson to fix a time and place. I'll let you know what he arranges, on the off-chance that you may be able to join us.

Again thanking you.

Yours sincerely,
C. M. Grieve.

NLS

16 Links Avenue,
Montrose.
15.5.28

Dear Mr Muirhead:-

Mrs Grieve and I can only thank you for your gift to our baby boy.[1] It was far too kind of you. As to his staunch Scottish character, he will certainly as he grows up understand who among all the people I know I esteem most highly – and why.

Scottish Secretariat

I was not forgetting about the *Scottish Co-operator* and shall be glad if you can now take this up with them again and fix it up. I can do it all right. The reason why this is relatively easy as compared with special localised articles for the 'Orkney' paper and the 'Kelso' paper is simply the latter involve research into subjects which I have not 'on tap', as it were, and necessitate special reading, etc. for which in the meantime – do what I will – I simply cannot find time; whereas the former will be quite in line with what I am doing anyhow and can be written straight out of my head.

---

[1] Walter Grieve, born 5 April 1928.

290

National Party

As I think he told you I had Compton Mackenzie down here over the weekend, and had long and thorough discussions with him – and one or two others who happened to be here, too (including Neil Gunn, the Inverness novelist, who wrote the recent 'Defensio Scotorum' article in reply to W. S. Morrison's in the *Scots Magazine*, and J. B. Salmond, the Editor of the *Scots Magazine*).[2]

The main point I wish to take up in the meantime is the question of Parliamentary candidatures.

I know your position. And you know also that Compton Mackenzie has been approached to stand as Labour Party candidate for Ross and Cromarty by Ben Shaw:[3] and purposely deferred seeing him on the matter and coming to a definite conclusion until he had talked it over with me. Then I, too, am on the ILP panel of prospective candidates and just at the moment have some hopes of being selected for Dumfriesshire in room of Mr Richard Lee who has had to withdraw. I had a letter from Willie Stewart the other day about this and am awaiting further developments.

Now, on reading the National Party Constitution, Compton Mackenzie and I construe the relative clauses to mean that
(a) no candidate will be put up by the Party except he (or she) stands exclusively as a Scottish National Party candidate.

but
(b) this does not debar members of the National Party – not put up by it as candidates – standing under other auspices.

If this interpretation is correct it means
(a) That the National Party will put up as many exclusively Nat. Party candidates as it can;
(b) but may also benefit by having other members whom it cannot afford to finance as a Party and who cannot afford to finance themselves standing under other auspices.

Both Compton Mackenzie and I would of course immensely prefer to stand as exclusively Scottish Nationalist candidates, but in view of the imminence of the next General Election, and, I am afraid, the unlikeliness of the SNP fighting funds being sufficient to promote many candidatures by then, it seems to us that it would be to the direct advantage of the SNP if some of its members allow themselves in the meantime to go forward as ILP or Labour Party candidates – while in their election addresses, speeches, etc., stressing the national issue as well as their party one. Otherwise (a) it seems that

---

[2] W. S. Morrison's 'Defensio Scotorum', *Scots Magazine*, Vol VIII, No 6, March 1928, was refuted in 'Defensio Scotorum' by Dane M'Neil (pseudonym of Neil Gunn) in the following issue of the magazine.

[3] Ben Shaw was Secretary of the Scottish Labour Council.

the party will be seriously limited in the number of candidates it can put forward, and (b) these may be practically confined to those who happily can finance their own candidatures.

We would like a definite ruling on this immediately.

As matters stand, Compton Mackenzie is anxious when he sees Ben Shaw (he – Compton – is returning to Glasgow on Thursday) to arrange:

(a) to stand in the Labour *and* SNP interest (i.e. insisting upon the fact that he is standing in the dual interest);

(b) to arrange a swap of prospective constituencies with J. M. M'Diarmid[4] – i.e. Compton to stand for the Isles, M'D. for Ross & Cromarty. From a SNP tactical point of view I strongly recommend this if it can possibly be worked.

Compton Mackenzie wonders whether the best way in the interests of the SNP would not be to try to arrange with the Labour Party and ILP to compromise and run in certain constituencies joint candidates as suggested, while undertaking – as a quid pro quo – not to oppose or contest an equivalent number of other constituencies in the meantime. This provision, it seems to me, should be readily agreed to, as the SNP cannot possibly be in a position to contest more than a few constituencies by next General Election – while the ILP and Labour Party might readily to recognise that although certain Socialist members may not be willing to come out as Nationalists, others can do so without being any the less Socialistic and even on the grounds that Scottish independence is a short cut to Socialist Government in Scotland, and that therefore a group of candidates who are definitely Nationalist-Socialists is quite a reasonable proposition, likely to be helpful to both parties at the present juncture.

I'd be glad to have your views on this. You will recognise that I am arguing purely on grounds of practical expediency as matters stand – and that my argument in no way runs counter to my conviction that we need a S.N.P. exclusive of all existing parties. The only question is whether to achieve that we are to take a line which will curtail the number of our members who can contest constituencies – until such time as the Party is financially strong enough – or whether, in view of the Party's financial weakness we should not take what advantage we can of increasing our influence by other means.

[4] J. M. M'Diarmid was Labour and Home Rule candidate for the Western Isles. In *My Life and Times, Octave Six 1923–1930* (London 1967, p. 134) Mackenzie writes: 'From Montrose [where I had acted as godfather to Grieve's son Walter] I went for the first time to Iona, where I met J. M. Macdiarmid and told him definitely that I was not prepared to contest a seat for Labour because Home Rule was obviously not going to be a main plank on their platform at the next General Election.'

Mackenzie thinks you might discuss this with Ben Shaw & Stewart and so prepare the way for him before he sees them on Thursday or Friday.

Yours,
C. M. Grieve.

P.S. Mackenzie will be staying at the Central Hotel, Glasgow.

EUL

16 Links Avenue,
Montrose.
24.5.28

R. E. Muirhead, Esq.
Dear Mr Muirhead:-

Unfortunately, I cannot be in Glasgow on 28th inst: but hope to be there on 1st and 2nd June. I have a PEN function on the evening of 2nd June: but shall look forward to having a talk if possible during the afternoon. Compton Mackenzie will also be in Glasgow at that time: as he also is to be at the PEN dinner in question.

The very last thing in the world I want to do is to weaken the policy of the Party in any way; and so far as I am personally concerned, of course, whether I agree with it or not, I shall loyally abide by whatever the Party decides and do my utmost in every way to further the agreed-upon policy.

But I think that at this juncture the suggestion I put forward as a result of my talks with Compton Mackenzie should be very carefully considered. I wonder if I put it quite clearly in my last letter. Let me recapitulate it thus:-

1/ The Party should only be responsible for purely Party candidatures and should promote as many of these as possible.

2/ But since it is – to all appearances – impossible for the Party at the next general election to put forward candidates in every constituency, or even sufficient to attempt to win a majority of the Scottish representation, it is not desirable that the Party should debar members of the Party whom it cannot afford to put forward and who cannot afford to put themselves forward from standing in the interests of any of the other three Parties.

293

3/ Provided they stand in each case not as Tories, Liberals or Socialists but definitely as Tory-Nationalists; Liberal-Nationalists; or Socialist-Nationalists as the case may be.

4/ Failing to secure a reasonably large number of candidates standing purely as Nationalists, it would be in the interests – not of the Party as a Party perhaps – but of the real objectives of the Party if it could have little groups acting as Nationalist 'caves' in each of the three existing Parties: and endeavouring to insist, each with their own Party, that Scottish Conservatism, Liberalism, or Labour, as the case was, should disassociate themselves from their English equivalents and re-orient on a Nationalist basis.

5/ Such action would be complementary to the work of the Party and would anticipate the position that would be reached were Scottish Self-Government re-established in so far as the three existing parties are concerned.

With every good wish.

Yours,
C. M. Grieve.

P.S. Of course you will appreciate that so far as I am concerned I hope for a condition of affairs – once a Scottish Parliament is established – when we will not merely have Scottish Liberalism, Conservatism or Socialism: but the political embodiment in an effective party of certain ideals and principles outwith English politics altogether and shared by none of these three parties.

P.P.S. My idea is also of course that by some such means we can retain in active association with the Party men like Kinloch and M'Diarmid, and like Ed. Scrimgeour.[1]

EUL

16 Links Avenue,
Montrose.
26.10.28

Dear Mr Muirhead,

I note, in today's *Glasgow Herald*, an advt. for a reporter for the *Scottish Co-operator*, for which I am applying. I think you know some

---

[1] At the General Election of 1922 Edwin Scrymgeour defeated Winston Churchill at Dundee.

of the people connected with this: and, if so, if you can put in a word
on my behalf I shall be very grateful indeed.

> With best wishes,
> Yours sincerely,
> C. M. Grieve.

EUL   16 Links Avenue,
                                                        Montrose.
                                                        1.11.28

Dear Mr Muirhead,

I am in a somewhat tight corner, and while I hesitate to bother
you again and have certainly no claim on your kindness I can think
of nobody else to whom to turn at the moment. As you know, I have
had a difficult time keeping my head above water for various reasons
for the past year or two; but, while matters are improving in this
respect and I am hopeful of getting squarely on my feet ere long, I
have certain obligations to meet in about a week's time which I
cannot meet unless I secure a loan.

Several things upon which I was counting have failed me – or, at
least, are not now likely to materialise in time to enable me to meet
my obligations. One of the most important of these is a commission I
have secured to translate a Spanish novel – *La Esclava del Senor* – for
Messrs Martin Secker.[1] I am to receive £50 for this. But I had hoped
that the matter would have been settled last August in which case
the translation would have been done and the money in my hands
ere this; it has dragged on until now – mainly owing to copyright
difficulties – and I have only now succeeded in getting the thing
definitely arranged. I will not be able to complete this translation for
4 or 5 months: but will get payment of about £20 to account when I
finish the first section, and the balance on completion.

Now (apart from the fact that I am anxious to get away from
Montrose – mainly because it is suiting my wife's health worse and
worse the longer I stay here) I should be able to meet my obligations

---

[1] Ramon Maria de Tenreiro, *The Handmaid of the Lord* (London 1930). The
translation appeared anonymously and was first listed as one of MacDiarmid's
works in *Second Hymn to Lenin* (1935).

and get clear of my difficulties if I could get a loan of £50 for six months[2] – that is to say, repayable, at latest, in May (by which time I will have completed the translation and received payment).

If need be, however, I could pay it back at the rate of £1 per week until such time as I received payment for my translation, when I could complete the repayment of the balance of the loan.

I can offer insurance policies: or a lien over furniture, books etc., worth between £3-400 as security.

It may turn out if other things materialise that I can pay back the loan more quickly than by May next; and of course, if I could do so, I would.

It goes against my grain to have to seek help in this way at all, and especially from you, who have been so good to me already, but in the circumstances I have no alternative. It is an old story this of poets finding it extremely difficult to get modus vivendi: but I think the worst of my difficulties are behind me and being in a position to definitely guarantee repayment of this loan as soon as my translation is completed makes it possible for me to ask your assistance as I certainly could not ask it if I had not the ability to repay at an early date so clearly in view.

With best wishes.

Yours sincerely,
C. M. Grieve.

NLS   16 Links Avenue,
                                                          Montrose.
                                                          5/11/28

Dear Mr Muirhead,

I need not attempt to thank you for your great kindness in acceding to my request, and for your very kind letter. I had the Scottish Movement foremost in my mind too when I ventured to ask your help – because (apart from personal and domestic aspects) I was afraid that circumstances would so develop as to disfranchise me and prevent my doing what I can to help either by standing as a

---

[2] On receipt of this letter Muirhead sent £50.

candidate or otherwise publicly advocating our aims. The fear of bringing a species of disgrace on the Party in this way has literally haunted me for some time – although I kept on hoping some of my numerous irons in the fire would (to mix my metaphors) turn up trumps in time to avert that, and only wrote you when the time was coming too near and no way out was appearing. My plight is directly due to my Scottish Nationalist activities, too, – I should have gone bankrupt a few years ago, instead of seeking to pay off debts incurred in connection with my ventures (*Chapbook*, *Nation* etc.) which were too much altogether for the very narrow margin my wage here allows after meeting my necessary domestic requirements. But instead of doing so I took the course of paying off these debts! and it seemed hard that after doing that systematically for these years I should have to go under just as this psychological moment when in the shape of this Spanish translation, and, I hope, other things, a gradual improvement in my position appears to be within early reach; and, above all, just at the moment, when I want to help to strike when the iron is becoming hot and carry the Movement which has consumed so much of my energies forward into the sphere of practical politics. In the latter connections I do not exaggerate my own importance; I am not indispensable – but I am heart and soul in this business, and, while I know how much you are doing and wondered if I was justified in asking you to help me personally when the Movement is needing so much from you, I felt that in helping me you would be still helping the Movement, perhaps to as great an extent as you could have done by devoting the same sum of money in any other direction. It will certainly be my aim to prove it so.

I have a feeling – no, not a feeling but absolute knowledge – that owing to the adverse conditions under which I have been working I have not got down yet under the very surface of my passion for Scotland and for freedom (they are mutually indispensable and complementary in my life) but that given better conditions I will do so, and correspondingly contribute more to the Movement than I have yet been able to attempt or imagine. In this connection it must be remembered that all my work hangs together – my poetry and my general propaganda are parts of each other: and I am unquestionably doing far more for Scotland when my activity issues in poetry rather than in any other form. Only that cannot be controlled; the spirit blows where it listeth. I have no silly personal pride; I do not write poetry – I am merely the vehicle for something far greater than myself. Without egoism therefore I know that Yeats, Mackenzie and others are right when they tell me that I am by far the greatest Scottish poet since Burns. After all what does that amount to: I may be that and still relatively negligible to Burns. In any case I know that all the best poetry I have in me is still to write. And it will take some writing – and this, too, makes me more defenceless in many ways than people not burdened with such a mission. Nor can I blame people for not recognising my quality as a poet. I stand at the very opposite pole of Scottish poetical genius from Burns: he was a great popular poet – I am essentially, and must be, an unpopular one; a poet's poet. Burns was so great in the one direction that Scotland needs a great poet now of precisely the opposite cast, and, if I am not that one (time alone can tell: my work will take another quarter of a century to estimate fairly) I shall at least have done a great deal towards preparing the way for him.

My task is to be unpopular – a fighter – an enemy of accepted things; not in any captious fashion but out of profound conviction, and while I may often mistake the promptings of my heart and be merely factitious, I have reason to know that the best of my work at all events is proving a powerful influence because it springs from the deeps of the destined.

But the nature of my task multiplies my difficulties: and this has prevented my securing remunerative work in many directions than would otherwise have been open to me.

Withal, things are improving and will improve and your aid now will, I feel confident prove the turning-point in this respect. It has taken a great load off my mind and I go forward to intensified struggle with fresh determination.

Yours sincerely,
C. M. Grieve.

P.S. I shall be at the Conference on Saturday. We had a very good meeting in Dundee: but (in case you got a cutting) the Dundee *Courier and Advertiser* report was hopelessly garbled and seriously misrepresented what I said. I have written correcting it.

16 Links Avenue,
Montrose.
Wednesday 29th May 1929

Dear Mr Muirhead,

I sincerely hope that tomorrow will see you returned to West-minister as Scottish Nationalist MP. This is just a note to wish you all the luck of the Poll. I am sure that if a good cause, a splendid record, and thorough hard work can do it you will romp home. I do not know the constituency myself – and can only live in hope, nourished by such grains of comfort as the papers furnish from time to time.

But (and I do not want to be a Job's comforter and to prematurely offer consolation where the event will show that congratulations are due) even if you do fail, at this first time of asking, to be returned, you have certainly done magnificent propaganda work, and the whole question of Scotland is in a far more live and oncoming condition than ere before.

I only wish I had been able to go forward to the vote along with McCormick and yourself. I would certainly have polled well in Dundee and my withdrawal afforded great relief in quarters where I was by no means anxious to oblige. But, as circumstances would have it, there was nothing else for it. We are a young party and – ill though it may be to thole, in view of Scotland's desperate needs today – we must 'creep afore we ging'.

Every good wish then. I trust you have not been overdoing it yourself: but are fine and fit. I shall impatiently await the verdict, and in victory or defeat remain

Yours very sincerely,
C. M. Grieve.

8/8/29

Scottish Secretariat
Dear Sirs:-

I have just received your wire. It came to St Cyrus and Mrs Grieve took it in my absence but couldn't reply. She was expecting me home on Monday, but I went elsewhere and only got back today. I can't understand non-arrival of last week's articles: they were duly posted on Friday.

This week's articles I will not be able to post until tomorrow (Friday). My arrangements are all upset at the moment unfortunately, as I am leaving Scotland permanently in the beginning of next month and going to London. But I will carry on as well as I possibly can. Sorry for any irregularity and inconvenience but that is unfortunately unavoidable in the circumstances.

Yours sincerely,
C. M. Grieve.

EUL
TS

Whalsay,
via Lerwick,
Shetland.
8–2–39

R. E. Muirhead, Esq,
Scots Independent.
Dear Mr Muirhead,

Many thanks for your letter. I hope that the note I have now added (on a separate page of typescript) to page 1 of the article will make the points you raise clear. I note what you say about Scottish Nationalists fighting each other. I agree of course that it would be well if we could all concentrate all our powers against the common enemy. But I note that whereas recently Mr Edwin Muir has spoken from Scottish Nationalist platforms both in Scotland and in London, the New York *Times Literary Supplement* rightly construes his last book (*Scott and Scotland*) as a blast against Scottish Nationalism! I am afraid that in pursuing this great cause we cannot exempt ourselves from the need to fight not only the Enemy outside but also the enemies in our own ranks, and that whatever casualties we suffer in the affair we must expect to receive our most painful wounds in 'the house of our friends'. I accept these things as inevitable, and, distressing and dangerous as internecine strife may be, feel that even that is a small matter compared with the dangers of a spurious unanimity which turns blind eyes to real and deep-seated differences and seeks success by any pretence of 'Peace, Peace', when there is no real peace.

With kindest regards,

Yours sincerely,
C. M. Grieve.

NLS

Whalsay,
Shetland.
21/4/41

Dear Mr Muirhead,

I was extremely sorry to hear of your brother's death[1] and would have written to offer my sympathy to you and the other members of your family had it not been that I did not hear of it until a good while after it took place. I am very much isolated here nowadays and see few papers and then as a rule only very belatedly.

I write now to give my small contribution to the Nationalist Mutual Aid Committee. I regret greatly that I cannot give a larger amount. I do hope you secure an adequate response to your appeal in these times which are not only difficult but likely to be very much more difficult yet in the near future and for long enough ahead. Nothing seems to me a more clamantly deserving cause than this just as nothing seems to me more hopeful for Scotland's future than the stand many of these young Scots have taken before the Tribunals. The violation of the safeguarding clauses of the Union in this matter is so flagrant that I cannot understand how the whole business cannot be brought to trial by Petition of Right or some other procedure; and it is certainly incredible that some at least of the leaders of the Scottish Bar do not rally to defend the integrity and autonomy of Scots Law. Apart from the question of national principle one would think they would be jealous to defend their own professional interests.

[1] Dr R. F. Muirhead (who knew William Morris and Peter Kropotkin) ran, in Glasgow, a Tutorial College mainly for electrical engineers. He played a prominent part in the Highland Land League and organised Home Rule demonstrations in the 1920s.

I hope you keep in good form yourself. With every kind regard, and best wishes to all your Committee in their work.

Yours for Scotland,
C. M. Grieve.

EUL

Dungavel,
by Strathaven,
Lanarkshire.
16/3/50

R. E. Muirhead, Esq.
Dear Mr Muirhead,

After the election[1] I had to go down to Aberystwyth to address the Welsh students on Scottish Literature but came back on Friday in order to be able to attend the meeting in the Secretariat on Saturday. Although I am not a member of that Committee I thought I might be allowed to attend. Unfortunately while away I contracted a bad dose of 'flu, which worsened on the Friday so that instead of getting into Glasgow to the meeting on Saturday I had to stay in bed. I asked Mr Goldie to let you know. I have not yet heard how the meeting went, but trust it was promising and that the idea of a Scottish National Congress may develop.

As to the election, I have not yet seen the final accounts and do not know just how Mr Goldie now stands in regard to getting in the various monies promised in event of my deposit being lost. But according to the figures I have, the position should be (even allowing for one of the promised guarantees of £25 not materialising) that all the accounts can be discharged and £125 repaid to you, as arranged.

I will see Mr Goldie in the beginning of the week and find out precisely how matters stand, and arrange that you be repaid as soon thereafter as possible. I trust this is satisfactory to you.

I need hardly express my thanks to you again for coming to our assistance in the handsome way you did. The result – not only in Kelvingrove, but in almost all the other constituencies contested by

[1] In the General Election of 23 February 1950 the result for Kelvingrove was: Rt Hon Walter Elliot (Con: 15,197), J. L. Williams (Lab: 13,973), S. J. Ranger (Lib: 831), C. M. Grieve (Ind. Scot. Nat: 639).

Scottish Nationalists – must have been very disappointing to you, as to me; but none of the smaller parties had any chance in this Election which was simply a neck-to-neck race between the two big Party machines. Even so I think we Scottish Nationalists might have done better but for the Covenant Committee's directive to Covenant signatories not to make the matter an election issue. Indeed the Covenant Committee went further and actually prejudiced the Nationalist candidates in the eyes of Covenant signatories. This was definitely harmful to us in my opinion.

Nevertheless I feel that matters will be very different next time, especially if the Covenant Committee then do make the matter an election issue, as they have indicated they will.

Apart from that I think we had a rattling good campaign in Kelvingrove and made the most of it from a propaganda point of view. I have no doubt that was true also in the other Nationalist-contested constituencies.

With my kindest regards.

Yours for Scotland,
C. M. Grieve.

NLS

Brownsbank,
Biggar.
9/7/52

R. E. Muirhead, Esq,
Dear Mr Muirhead,

I understand Michael[1] has shown you David Watson's[2] letter in which he advised him that it was useless to go ahead with the Stated Case, as the pass had been sold by Parliament, and since the Court

[1] In December 1950 the Edinburgh Appellate Tribunal rejected Michael Grieve's application to be registered as a conscientious objector although he expressed his objection to the imperial war being waged in Kenya and argued that conscription was a violation of the Act of Union which safeguarded Scots from being sent overseas by a Westminister parliament. During the legal struggle that followed Muirhead appeared in court as witness to Michael's integrity. In June 1952 Michael Grieve was sentenced, at Glasgow Sheriff Court, to six months' imprisonment.

[2] David Watson was Michael Grieve's Counsel.

303

can neither make nor unmake the Law but simply apply it no good could come of further proceedings, and the only way in which the evil could be undone was to fight it out on the political plane. Mr Watson therefore advised Michael simply to concentrate on his own personal position and try to secure a re-hearing by the Tribunal on his plea to be registered as a Conscientious Objector. In other words, he advised him to abandon all idea of fighting on the political and moral principles involved, and simply seek in his own personal case to get off as lightly as possible.

This advice was of course an enormous disappointment. I thought it desirable to secure another opinion, so I wrote fully to Dr Mary Ramsay[3] and asked her to get in touch with Mr Gordon Stott[4] and secure his opinion. I did this because she knows Mr Stott personally and because when Michael's case first came up Mr Stott wrote me and expressed his readiness to do anything he possibly could to help.

I have not heard yet from Dr Ramsay or Mr Stott, but in the meantime it seems that Mr Watson's advice is entirely wrong. The Lord Chief Justice has decided that the Criminal Justice Act does not apply to CO s. That means that the proceedings already taken in Michael's case, including the sentence passed on him, cannot be sustained, and that if he proceeds with his appeal he must win.

In these circumstances however Mr Watson cannot represent him and it will be necessary to secure Mr Stott or someone else to do so.

This is a very important issue not only for Michael but for all COs.

I need not tell you how grateful my wife and I are to you for all your help in this matter. With every good wish.

> Yours for Scotland,
> C. M. Grieve.

NLS

Brownsbank,
By Biggar.
10/7/52

R. E. Muirhead, Esq,
Dear Mr Muirhead,

Since I wrote you a few days ago on the question of whether – and if so how – Michael should go on with his Stated Case in view of Mr

[3] Mary P. Ramsay, author of *Calvin and Art* (1938).
[4] Gordon (later Lord) Stott, a senior Counsel, had been a conscientious objector.

Watson's disappointing attitude, I have heard from Mr Gordon Stott that it will be quite in order for him, as he is a senior counsel, and Mr Watson a junior, to be consulted by us – i.e. our solicitor – and that he would not want any fee. So if Mr Stenhouse will apply to him he will do all he can. He says, if I understand aright, that in any event the Stated Case can be dropped later, even if we go on with it now, if we change our plan of campaign. It is clear of course that legal technicalities can never win the case for fundamental principles and that it is the business of the Courts at this stage just to administer the law, not to go down to fundamental principles.

Mary Ramsay showed Mr Stott a quotation from Forbes of Culloden, in the Porteous Riots Case, viz;- 'My Lords, we acted in that affair, as our consciences directed us, and there is no power on earth that dare call our actions in question', and Mr Stott asked to keep a copy of that quotation.

The whole point is that we as Scots must find a way to bring into public and open discussion this violation of Scottish principles of freedom of conscience, which are in Scots Law *legal* principles, as Forbes of Culloden claimed, and as our older writers showed also. There is no way in which we can do this unless in the Courts in actions such as Michael's. It may well be that Michael must face prison, as that may be the only way. The 'law' (without the dignity of a capital letter, for I mean only the technical and anglified institutions, not our Scots principles as Law) is vengeful and spiteful as any other precarious and temporary institution inevitably is. So it may be that if it comes to a struggle over technicalities, the 'established order' authorities will have a pull over us. But what we must do, it seems to me, is to concentrate on finding and relentlessly and unremittingly sustaining a method of resistance to all this. We have betrayed Scotland and our Scottish principles too long and sacrificed lads like Michael – but it won't be in vain in the long run.

So, if you agree, will you please tell your solicitor to write at once to Gordon Stott, (his chambers are at 32 Dundas Street, Edinburgh), and he will certainly do all he can to advise and help, and he is as sympathetic to our fight for freedom of conscience as anyone could be. I do feel we have to find a way to take the whole question back to its fundamentals and Michael's case may give us our opening even if not in quite the way that at first seemed to offer itself. The main thing is to apply to Mr. Stott officially now – i.e. for Mr Stenhouse to do so.

With every good wish.

Ever yours for Scotland,
C. M. Grieve.

To Herbert Grierson

MacDiarmid always had a high regard for prominent academics and admitted 'if I have been a collector of anything it has been Professors' (LP, 47). During MacDiarmid's most creative period Herbert Grierson (1866–1960) was probably the best-known literary academic in Scotland, a man closely associated with Edinburgh University where he was Professor of Rhetoric and English Literature from 1915 to 1935 and, after being knighted in 1936, Rector until 1939. Grierson was fascinated by MacDiarmid's experimental use of Scots and continued to have a high opinion of his talent. *A Critical History of English Poetry* (1944), by Grierson and J. C. Smith, applauds his energy and ambition:

> Conceiving that a century of Whistlebinkie had left Scots unfit for high poetry, Grieve has ransacked the makars and the dictionary for material out of which to frame a new poetic diction for Scots. His critics scoff at his 'synthetic Scots'; but there is really nothing absurd in attempting to do for Scots verse what Spenser did for English; *solvitur* – or *solvetur* – *ambulando*. (p. 487, Peregrine edtn).

Eventually it was John Buchan, not Grierson, who wrote the introduction for *Sangschaw*.

NLS

16 Links Avenue,
Montrose.
30th April 1925.

Dear Professor Grierson,

It was exceedingly good of you to reply from Holland to my last letter. I was notified a few days ago that my name had not been included in the short leet for the appointment:[1] and I am writing now

[1] MacDiarmid had unsuccessfully applied for the post of Keeper of the National Gallery of Scotland.

to tell you how grateful, none the less, I am for your efforts on my behalf. Something else of a suitable nature may turn up and, difficult as my circumstances have been in ways that conflict with my desire to devote myself more fully to the exploitation of the creative faculties of which I feel myself possessed, I am by no means going to allow myself to be discouraged or to give up the good fight.

I know that you will be sorry that your efforts were unavailing: and for that reason I have the less hesitation in asking another favour from you. Messrs Blackwoods have accepted for publication this autumn a volume of my Hugh McDiarmid poems – some 26 in Braid Scots, one in English, and one (dedicated to Professor Saurat) in French. Of the Scots poems – most of which have not been hitherto printed and, carefully selected, are, I believe, much better than most of McDiarmid's that has – the majority are quite short: but there are two longer poems, 'Ballad of the Five Senses' (30 verses) and 'I Heard Christ Sing' (20 verses). I enclose a copy of the latter (I have not the former by me at the moment) and, if you think well of it, I should like to inscribe it to yourself in the volume. The 'Ballad', which I have dedicated to Sir Robert Bruce in esteem of his efforts to revive the Vernacular, is a purely metaphysical poem which I am hoping you will like.

Now, if I am not asking too much, I would esteem it an exceedingly greater favour if you would furnish my book with a little introduction. Whether volumes of poetry should have such introductions is perhaps debateable: but in the Scottish succession in which I am fain to have a part – Hugh Haliburton, Charles Murray, and Mrs Violet Jacob and others – there have usually been introductions: Andrew Lang's to *Hamewith*[2] and John Buchan's to *Songs of Angus*[3]. Besides I have a vivid recollection of your excellent remarks on the subject of the Revival of the Scots Vernacular when I addressed the Historical Assocn. and I believe it would be extremely useful to our Movement, such as it is, to have your views on the general question so given. My own point of view I think you know: but I am enclosing herewith a copy of an article I had in the *Scottish Educational Journal*[4] some time ago, as also copies 1/ of Saurat's articles[5] and 2/ of an article that

[2] Charles Murray, *Hamewith* (1909).
[3] Violet Jacob, *Songs of Angus* (1919).
[4] 'Reviving the Scots Vernacular' by C. M. Grieve, in *Scottish Educational Journal*, Vol VIII, No 6, 6 February 1925, pp. 128–9.
[5] Denis Saurat, 'Le groupe de "la Renaissance Écossaise"' in *Revue Anglo-Americaine*, Première Année, No 4, April 1924.

appeared in a recent *Glasgow Herald*[6]. The latter I should be glad if you would return at your convenience as I possess no other copy.

You will forgive me for making this request – I am afraid of becoming importunate – and I hope you will see your way to accede to it, as a great deal may depend upon the success of this first volume of McDiarmid's work and I am anxious to have it given as good a send off as possible – I am sure that I could not be introduced to the public under better auspices than yours. If this first volume is sufficiently successful – and, judging by the unusual interest McD's work has already created in many, and some very unexpected, quarters, I think it will be – the same publishers have an option on two succeeding volumes.

You will understand, of course, that I wish no hint given that McD is a pseudonym.

If you can see your way to do me this great favour (perhaps you will be so kind as to let me know that, and as to whether you will accept the dedication of 'I Heard Christ Sing' or not at your early convenience), I shall either arrange to let you have early proofs of the poems, or send you copies of them in typescript.

Again thanking you for your efforts on my behalf in re Keeper's Post, and with every good wish.

Yours faithfully,
C. M. Grieve.

P.S. I find that I have not a copy by me of the *Scots Educ Jnl* containing article – in which I explained my attitude to Braid Scots fairly fully – but I will ask the Editor to send you one on.

---

[6] *The Glasgow Herald*, 4 April 1925, carried an article by Alexander M'Gill which claimed that 'Apart from Charles Murray, John Buchan, and Mrs Jacob, the only poet who has attempted to use the [Lowland] speech in a manner worthy of appreciation by the broad-minded, non-insular critics of the Continent is Hugh M'Diarmid . . . He is ever experimenting with a new Scottish literature both as to form and content, and these endeavours are justifying themselves.'

16 Links Avenue,
Montrose.
12/5/25

Dear Professor Grierson,

Your letter filled me with compunction. It is too bad that I should have worried you when you are otherwise so busy, and so indisposed at that. I am afraid that I ought not to have done it, and I cannot express my gratitude for the wonderful considerateness of your letter in the circumstances.

I wrote at once to Blackwood's and have their reply stating that complete proofs will be available this week. I shall accordingly send you a set of proofs which will be better even than typescript – apart from the fact that I have not retained copies of some of the poems. I also asked when 'copy' for the introduction would require to be in their hands, but they have omitted to reply to this. I'll write again and let you know.

I hope you'll have received the *Scottish Educ. Jnl.* with my article by the time you receive this.

> 'There was nae reek i' the laverock's hoose
> That nicht - and nane i' mine'

is not really translated by Saurat. The first line is an old Perthshire saying meaning simply: 'It was a dark & stormy night' so the two lines really mean: 'A dark & stormy night succeeded that wet forenight and my heart was similarly dark & stormy.'

I am greatly indebted to you for your suggestion re Verse 4 of 'I Heard Christ Sing' (which – the dance of the disciples & Christ's singing in the centre – is founded on an incident narrated in a recently discovered portion of Syriac Apocrypha). Apart from the point re Mark and Luke the excision of that verse as you suggest *does* greatly strengthen the poem and I shall therefore cut it out.

McDiarmid's poems only partially illustrate Grieve's esoteric propaganda with regard to the Vernacular – for some of them are in particular dialects – not standardised Scots – and others are so little in Scots as to be quite intelligible to any intelligent Sassenach. McDiarmid is by no means committed to Grieve's position. So please express your own views without any tenderness for my theories. I have no objection to your expressing even diametrically opposed opinions. The main thing is the poetry – as poetry: then as a contribution to Scottish literature in particular: and lastly as a contribution to the present efforts to revive Braid Scots of which my ideas are only one aspect. What you call the element of imaginativeness is the main thing: that *is* what I am trying to reintroduce into Scots verse. Dunbar is my favourite poet – as he was W. P. Ker's.[1] I detest most of Burns & all Kailyard stuff. My protest is primarily against 'prosaic poetry'. As Sir George Douglas[2] has pointed out 'in reading a collection of Scottish poems, identical situations, identical trains of thought, will be found to recur with an iteration which only poetic beauty of an uncommon order can save from becoming wearisome' – and that is seldom if ever found. I am trying to break this vicious circle – and recapture a range and a tone compatible with national pride and comparable to that of the literatures of other nations.

My programme is:-

1/ to use the resources of Scots more fully than they have been used since Dunbar.

2/ to seek a deeper intellectual content than has generally characterised Scots verse.

3/ to eschew the popular and the hackneyed.

4/ to align my work with what I regard as the most significant tendencies emerging in welt-literatur – (e.g. in thinking of the Ballad form I have been influenced by Carl Spitteler's[3] theories, & I may follow him with regard to the epic too) – and those most incompatible with English traditions, tastes and tendencies.

5/ to widen & vary Scottish technique which has got into a deplorably narrow groove.

Enclosed long poem 'Braid Scots' (which is not in the volume) at least illustrates my tendencious intromissions with foreign literatures.

The translations of Stefan George & Merezhkovsky are going in – without the foot-notes.

I quite see your point about the dedication: and can only hope to have the privilege of dedicating to you a little later something worthier.

I feel sure that what you say in the preface – the mere fact that you evince an active interest in what is being attempted – will have far-reaching consequences, and that although you may not be specially interested in this particular question, to have you introduce my poems will give them the exact 'cachet' I (perhaps presumptuously) covet for them.

Again thanking you and apologising for this long letter.

---

[1] W. P. Ker (1855–1923), the Glasgow-born medievalist.

[2] Sir George Douglas (1856–1935), author and lecturer in Scottish Literature.

[3] Carl Spitteler (1845–1924), the Swiss poet whose Nietzschean epics *Prometheus und Epimetheus* (1881) and *Olympischer Frühling* (1900 ff) utilise the climbing imagery MacDiarmid was also to develop in his poetry.

310

With every good wish.

> Yours faithfully,
> C. M. Grieve.

P.S. In another recent article I have said:-
'I have elsewhere expressed the view that Braid Scots is now likely to realise some of its tremendous latent potentialities, if only because of that flux of which Oswald Spengler writes in his *Downfall of the Western World* between Apollonian (in this case English) and Faustian (equivalent here to Scottish) elements, whereby submerged and neglected elements (e.g. Braid Scots) come with their own at the expense of those dominating elements which have completely fulfilled themselves and are bankrupt of any reserve of impredictable evaluation. I have found my surest indication of this in the alignment of the principal qualities of Braid Scots which have hitherto failed to find effective outlet – and to which the stream of English cultural tendency has been overwhelmingly antipathetic – with the significant tendencies emerging in "advanced" art and thought all over Europe.'

To Pittendrigh Macgillivray

James Pittendrigh Macgillivray (1856–1938) was King's Sculptor in Ordinary for Scotland from 1921; his principal works were the colossal Burns Statue in Irvine; the Dean Montgomery Memorial, St Mary's Cathedral, Edinburgh; the colossal statue of the Marquis of Bute for Cardiff; the Byron Statue, Aberdeen; the John Knox Statue, St Giles' Cathedral, Edinburgh. An expansively romantic figure, Macgillivray was also a poet who privately printed the collections *Pro Patria* (1915) and *Bog-Myrtle and Peat Reek* (1922). Macgillivray believed in dialect Scots, not Synthetic Scots, and MacDiarmid represented him in *The Golden Treasury of Scottish Poetry* (London 1941) with 'The Return', an English poem whose conclusion makes characteristically patriotic gestures:

> Och, then, for the bonnet and feather! –
> The Pipe and its vaunting clear:
> Och, then, for the glens and the heather!
> And all that the Gael holds dear.

Strongly attracted by Macgillivray's energy and force of personality, MacDiarmid made large claims for his friend's seminal significance for the Scottish Literary Renaissance. Writing in *The Scottish Educational Journal* of 31 July 1925 he devoted a eulogistic article to Macgillivray:

> Macgillivray, in fact, is by far our best complement to Burns as a vernacular poet: he essays many of the kinds of poetry which were outwith Burns' range, and, to an infinitely greater degree than most, eschews mere imitation of Burnsian models and the Burnsian spirit . . . [also] let him be seen as the founder and fountainhead of a truly national school of sculpture and as one of the most delightful, versatile, bracing and vital artists Scotland has ever possessed and lamentably misprized, despite a certain amount of lip-service, and as a giant among pigmies so far as all his self-conceived rivals in the Art of Sculpture in Scotland today are concerned. Pittendrigh Macgillivray – the very name is a guarantee and a slogan! He will assuredly come into his own yet!

NLS

16 Links Avenue,
Montrose.
10th Feb. 1925

J. Pittendrigh Macgillivray, Esq, RSA, LLD.

Dear Dr Macgillivray,

My ventures were all (in a material sense) unsuccessful as you know – that is to say, they did not pay their way; I never expected them or wanted them to do more. But they were all insufficiently financed. I was not out to make money – but I lost money. They have, however, done their work to some extent. Of that I am assured. My main regret was that running them singlehanded in my scanty spare time and as economically as possible I was unable to develop as I should have liked to do – as the interests of the movement I was trying to create demanded – the various acquaintances that came my way as a result of them. It was physically and financially impossible for me to reply to half the letters I received. My only excuse was my entire disinterestedness – I sacrificed all I possibly could to keep them going. I even sacrificed my own career – staying so long down here on a little local paper, simply because it gave me more leisure for my efforts on behalf of Scottish nationalism and letters, that, now that my ventures have all come to an end, I find that I cannot get a suitable post anywhere. I have put myself out of the running. And now more than ever it is necessary that I should secure a more renumerative appointment of some kind.

You will excuse this preamble, I am sure, to an appeal for your help in a direction in which it occurs to me that you may have some influence. I have applied for the vacant keepership of the National Galleries advertised in Saturday's *Glasgow Herald*. The appointment lies with the Trustees and the advertisement makes no disqualification of canvassing. I am therefore assuming that canvassing is permissible and seeking to enlist what influence I can. I shall be extremely grateful if you can do anything to help me in this connection. The advertisement states that applicants under 40 may be preferred, so that may give me a better chance.

Please forgive my importunity,

And believe me,

Yours very sincerely,
C. M. Grieve.

P.S. As you probably know the present trustees are:-

313

NLS

Gibson Place,
Roadside,
St Cyrus.
3rd Aug. 1925

My dear Macgillivray,

I was immensely touched by the sheer kindness of the letter you wrote me apropos the circular about my *Educational Journal* articles: and *meant* to write and thank you forthwith and try to explain why I had not written again to you in connection with the Academy Keepership (for which – thanks to yeoman efforts on the part of Professor Emerson and John Buchan – I had a close if finally unsuccessful run). But somehow I couldn't. I get tangled up into all sorts of knots in regards to correspondence. I do not have any silly pride in being an unconscionable sort of individual: I simply am – and can't help being – as long at any rate as economic and other circumstances compel me to drudge all day and then crush all my other activities into the fag end of my evenings. Regardless of all other claims I feel compelled to organise my leisure in such a fashion as to devote it as wholly as ever I can to original writing.

Space in the *Educational Journal* doesn't allow me to do justice. I ought to have had room for quotations, etc. Besides I need a pretty big canvas to develop my ideas about anyone in a way that satisfies me. In these articles I can only put forward one or two points from a special angle – I haven't time to go all round the people – and even then what I say is often not clear enough owing to being insufficiently developed. Buchan was greatly pleased with my article on himself.[1] Naturally I have not heard from any of the others. But I

---

[1] The first article of the 'Contemporary Scottish Studies' series in *The Scottish Educational Journal* was a tribute to John Buchan, published on 19 June 1925.

314

feel I have said some things that wanted saying: and I know that the articles are creating a considerable amount of interest. They are to be published in book form next year by Messrs Leonard Parsons Ltd.

I do not remember whether I told you or not – I have not told many, and am exceedingly anxious to keep the pseudonymity a secret otherwise – that Hugh McDiarmid is one of my pen names. A volume of his Braid Scots poems under the title of *Sangschaw*, with an introduction by John Buchan, is being published this autumn by Messrs Blackwood.

I should immensely like to come and see you, and will miss no opportunity of doing so. In the meantime unfortunately opportunities are few and far between – I have to keep my nose pretty consistently on one grindstone or another. For months I have been trying to get a chance to run down to Dundee to see Stewart Carmichael[2] but haven't managed yet. But one never knows. I may strike it sufficiently lucky yet to have more time to myself and for my friends than I can at present by hook or crook contrive. And Mrs Grieve will certainly be extremely anxious to accompany me. But – this is another of the complications with which I have to contend – we have a little daughter, not quite a year old, to think of now.

But if you should on your part ever be in this airt we shall – all three, not to mention the little Cairn terrier – be more than delighted to see you.

With every kind wish.

Yours,
C. M. Grieve.

NLS

16 Links Avenue,
Montrose.
11th Aug. 1925.

My dear Macgillivray,

I was delighted to have your kind letter again: and to know that you have put another collection of poems in order. I shall look

2 The painter Stewart Carmichael was the subject of an article, in the 'Contemporary Scottish Studies' series, on 25 December 1925.

eagerly forward to seeing it. Force of habit has made me give my home address above: but we are still at St Cyrus and will be till the end of the month.

I had a letter yesterday from Stewart Carmichael. He is going off to Belgium and wants me to run down to Dundee and see his stuff before I write on him. So, as this is the only chance I have, I am just writing him too to say that I will go to Dundee for Saturday afternoon if that suits him.

Mrs Grieve joins me in every kind regard.

Yours,
C. M. Grieve.

NLS

Gibson Place,
Roadside,
St Cyrus.
30th August 1925

Dear Macgillivray,

I do wish I could get into the habit of replying to letters at once. It would save me some conscience-stricken periods. But any chance I have of writing a letter is always literally snatched from the jaws of competing circumstances. It is extraordinarily good of you to want to give me the *Scottish Nation*[1] you had bound. I simply do not know how to thank you. There is something horribly graceless in the modern Scot. I am always in my element if anyone does me an injury – but a kindness finds me helplessly gauche. Your verses greatly pleased me, too. They 'loup' out like a mountain spring – perfectly pure and apparently effortless – but what a pressure is behind them really, from what depths do they rise so clear and leaping so highly.

We go back to Montrose tomorrow. We've had a fine holiday – Baby is brown as a berry – but work here is done under doubled difficulties: I have a hefty winter's programme and shall be glad to be back to all my books and papers.

Mrs Grieve joins me in every good wish.

[1] *The Scottish Nation*, a weekly edited by C. M. Grieve, ran from 8 May to 25 December 1925.

316

Again with thanks.

Yours,
C. M. Grieve.

I had a delightful time with Mr & Mrs Carmichael. 'Dundee is dust'[2] I have said but S.C. if not a trumpet in the dust is at least an elfin horn – a redeeming note!

NLS

16 Links Avenue,
Montrose.
28th Oct. 1925

My dear Macgillivray,

Yes, Mackenzie[1] is a 'slythy tove'. His grouch is because I dropped him. He knew my intentions in regard to *Northern Numbers* from the outset: his only complaint was that I put him near the end of the first book – behind whom he considered his inferiors. I have gone through the *Chapbooks*: I never advertised him as a contributor to them. I suspect him of writing an anonymous letter which appeared in *The Scotsman* some time ago – stating that he and another contributor had refused to contribute again to *Northern Numbers* after the first issue – a lie. He needn't pride himself on my having asked him to contribute to start with. I have learned a lot since: and were I starting afresh the contributors would be a very different set.

Your last letter interested me more than I can say. Of course you appreciate that I am so much younger – brought up in so much less Scottish an atmosphere than yourself – finding myself in regard to Braid Scots and the Auld Makars only after a long hegira in foreign literatures, and in their most ultra-modern and 'high-brow' aspects at that. All this complicates my case. You are right in many ways – my psychic hasn't fully emerged yet from obsessions of technique alien to the true direction of my M'Diarmid work. – But I am looking forward to having a long talk to you on these matters yet. I know of no other man in Scotland who can teach me anything along these

2 'Dundee is dust/And Aberdeen a shell.': from 'Edinburgh' (1204).
1 Donald A. Mackenzie (1873–1936), Scottish poet and folklorist.

particular lines but yourself (tho' I agree with you that perhaps Spence[2] is another of what must be at best the very little handful who have a glimmering of the true spirit), and I am eager to learn what I may 'while it is yet day'.

I am deeply touched by what you say of your possible intentions in regard to your books, papers, etc. I can only say that I shall esteem it a very high and precious honour to be permitted to do anything for you in anyway at any time.

I enjoyed – as you would know I would – your Corstorphine 'outburst'. Would that the *Chapbook* had been alive! – I should have loved to have published it there.

Excuse this hasty note. I may be in Edinburgh one day ere long again. Professor Grierson[3] has undertaken to form a Scottish Branch of the PEN Club, and as the only member of it living in Scotland (I belong to the London Centre) we've been corresponding: and a meeting in Edinburgh soon will probably ensue.

Mrs Grieve joins me in every good wish.

Yours ever,
C. M. Grieve.

NLS

16 Links Avenue,
10/6/26

Dear Macgillivray,

I have just discovered that stupidly somehow I forgot to enclose proof of preface etc. in my last letter. It has been lying in my pocket mixed up with an miscellaneous collection of papers. I am now sending it on. Do not return it. I have altered it somewhat. I have added a sentence dealing with the way in which the poem should be pronounced – to save altering 'I'm's to 'am's, etc.

Your last letter with proofs gave me a bad time. I considered the matter very thoroughly: and took the views of other friends too. I quite saw all your points and agree that the excision of certain passages would make the work more harmonious, etc: but it would be a false harmony – not true to my intention – depending upon the ignoring of essential elements and aspects of experience which are

[2] Lewis Spence (1874–1955), poet and Scottish Nationalist campaigner.
[3] Professor Herbert Grierson, see p. 306.

318

compatible to the psychology of the hypothetical toper (putatively identified with myself). My own first idea was the one you suggest of the Drunk Man waking up in the glory of the morning. I deliberately abandoned it as untrue. I cannot give that sort of happy ending. Nor, with all respect to your judgement, can I delete the passages you suggest. If I did I would from my point of view falsify the whole thing. But what I feel is perhaps best put in what another friend writes, and you may be interested in seeing how just what you object to is valued by him. He says:-

'You have completed in my opinion the greatest poem ever produced by a Scotsman. I am not excepting Burns whose work in comparison with yours gives one a sense of restriction (and consequently power) that is bound eventually to become less and less congenial as man develops consciousness and intelligence. I'm perfectly satisfied with the architecture of the boat. I've had doubts at times about certain passages, but I can't now find a word to say against them. *I* mightn't have included them but then I'm not *you* and it's exactly for this reason, that the whole thing bodies forth the living image of C. M. G. that I have come to see it as the masterpiece it is, for what man in ten generations succeeds in getting outside his own skin. Now I feel that you have in this poem. You have limned yourself – the Scottish terrier in excelsis! The feature will become more and more clear to the generations yet to come.'

Perhaps – and perhaps not. But determined things must be left to hold unbewailed their way to destiny. At the same time I am grateful to you for your interest and the close reading you gave the proofs, and the many little suggestions you made – some of particular value which I am glad to have had – e.g. thingum for mummy and the query about blate which I had used quite erroneously.

I'm writing in a hurry. I'm off to Glasgow this weekend to lecture to the New Education Fellowship and am excessively busy. I am glad to hear what you say of Blackwood's and hope matters will arrange themselves. I am eagerly looking forward to that book.

Mrs Grieve asks me to thank you for the delightful poem, so kindly inscribed, you sent her the other day, and, on my own behalf, I thank you for sending it to her, too. It was a 'very gentle, perfect' thought.

I'm hoping to see you ere long and talk matters over. It's so difficult writing letters about things.

I hope you are well and that all is going well with you in every way. Please present my compliments to Miss Macgillivray. All here join with me in every good wish.

Yours,
C. M. Grieve.

319

Avondale,
St Cyrus,
August 13/26

My dear Macgillivray,

I have had rather a harassing time or you would have heard from
me sooner, and regained your MSS more quickly. Shortly after my
return from my delightful week-end with you, one of Mrs Grieve's
sisters – the one between Ina and her – died very suddenly, and we
had to go to her home for the best part of a week. I probably caught a
chill travelling but I had a bad time for a while after I got back – a
narrow squeak for a recurrence of a kind of kidney trouble that gave
me a fright over a year ago; and – to complete the tale of troubles –
Christine took ill too and we were kept very anxious about her for
several days. However, Christine recovered as quickly as she succumbed, and I am feeling quite fit again – as, faith, I'd need to do for
I'm in deplorable arrears with work of various sorts that ought to
have been completed ere this. Especially my *Drunk Man*, which I
have promised to deliver to Blackwood's by the end of the month.
However I'm going to have an intensive fortnight at it, for Mrs
Grieve (whom these divers ills have brought a bit under the weather
too) Ina, and Christine are going off to Selkirk and East Lothian for a
fortnight tomorrow.

I do not know if you are still following the *Scot. Educ. Jnl*: but if so
you'll see Donald Mackenzie[1] is flourishing in longer letters than
ever. I didn't see last week's, but, judging by this, Spence must have
replied to him in it. I'm to take no notice in the meantime or in fact at
all – unless and until he gives me an opening for a 'killer'. Two bards
are 'on my top' in this week's too. So it is becoming more and more
'Grieve's Weekly' – a grievious state of affairs!

I've enjoyed both these poems – 'Jazz' is 'all there', not an
essential detail missed, a complete criticism reproducing in the most
extraordinary way the whole appearance and feel and effect of the
thing criticised and damning it out of its own mouth, as it were.
'Quid Pro Quo' also hits its bull's-eye; it's a very compact and
effective little transcript from life.

I trust all's well with you. (By the way, I keep hoping to hear that
you've been able to arrange about your new volume of poems. I've
been re-reading Spence's article in the *19th Century* and feel even less
satisfied with it than I felt when you read the proof – and especially

---

[1] *The Scottish Educational Journal* of 13 August 1926 printed a long letter from Donald
A. Mackenzie defending his right 'to protest against the literary heresies of
Grieve, Spence and Co'.

with his dismissal of you in a couple of sentences and his silly exclamation over Rachel Annand Taylor's ballad and Thomas Sharp's stuff.[2] I'm going to seize the first possible opportunity I have to deal exhaustively and in detail with your poetry and put it in its proper place. I'll probably be able to get a really well-written article of some 5–6000 words on it accepted by one of the reviews: and arrange for its subsequent publication in brochure form.)

Please give my compliments to Miss Macgillivray.

Mrs Grieve joins me, as does Ina and, I am sure in spirit if she is too young yet to do so actually, Christine in kindest regards and every good wish.

Yours,
C. M Grieve.

NLS

16 Links Avenue,
Montrose,
6th Sept. 1926

Dear Macgillivray,

At last! Many thanks for all your delightful letters. I owe you apologies for being so long in responding: but I have been unable to help myself. I have simply been in such a condition of mind and body recently that I have had to restrict myself in every direction to doing only what I could in no way avoid. The fact is that I seem to have overdriven myself badly. The final stages of the *Drunk Man* took every ounce out of me. Since then I have been very much in the trough of the wave – in the grip of a species of impotence bred of pure exhaustion. I must take things easy for a little to regain my energy.

I need not tell you that both Mrs Grieve and I were greatly disappointed that things turned out in such a fashion that your week-end at St. Cyrus did not materialise. We were both looking forward immensely to having the pleasure of your company there. But nothing turned out as we hoped. I had intended to give myself a 'good breather' – have plenty of walks, and lying in the sun, and

---

[2] Rachel Annand Taylor (1876–1960) published volumes of poems and a study of Dunbar; Thomas Sharp published *New Poems* (1925).

sea-bathing. Alas! I only got into the water once. My nose was kept on the grindstone almost all the time. But we do hope that you will take the first available chance of giving us a visit now. Both this month and October happily often have spells of splendid weather here. Indeed as I write the sun is shining beautifully and I wish you were here to talk to instead of my having to write to you.

Your poem affected me greatly. I am not going to try to say here anything of what I feel about your having to leave your house and studio – and the position generally. You will know quite well how I do feel. To secure effective expression of that may take time – but it will come. I know from the nature of the emotions it has aroused in me that my impressions – so poignantly reinforced during my week-end with you – will ultimately come from me, in their mature form, in certain pages of literature of a not unworthy order.

Your mention of Miss Cruickshank[1] jabs my conscience again. I have treated her abominably. I am really a perfectly hopeless fool in personal relationships.

I should have valued it immensely if I had been able to go over the *Drunk Man* with you before I sent it off. But until the very last moment it was a hopeless jumble of scraps of scribbled and cross-scribbled MSS. I sorted it out by a last effort into some kind of order (re-writing no more of it than I could possibly help) – the comps. will curse: it is just barely an intelligible MSS. However, I hadn't a scrap of strength left. – But it is a big thing. It is me in every way – satire, lyricism, and all the rest of it: beauty and fun and savagery and objectionable elements all mixed just as they are in me. It is a real achievement, I know, and once I have had a rest I shall feel immensely stronger and more mature for having written it.

I had no knowledge of the Stewart letter at all.[2] I had art nor part in it. I missed some of the letters – I only get the *S.E.J.* sent me on those weeks when I've articles in it. Intervening issues I miss. So I didn't see either the beginning of the business nor the end of it. But on the whole I agree with you. I hated Spence's last letter. It was very weak and futile. I am certainly going to eschew any tendency in future to merely personal slanging and recrimination – and go for the ideas behind the men for all I am worth without condescending to the individuals at all.

This is a mixed-up epistle. When I began talking about the *Drunk Man*, and wishing I could have had the advantage of going over it

[1] Helen B. Cruickshank.
[2] Presumably this refers to a letter, published in *The Scottish Educational Journal* of 27 August 1926. It was signed 'Lover of Justice' and attacked Donald A. Mackenzie. The Editor of the journal published two more letters in the same issue then closed the correspondence.

with you, what I meant to have gone on to do was to thank you for your offer to help me with the proofs. It is exceedingly good of you and I shall certainly be greatly relieved and proud to accept your offer.

Excuse more just now. Be sure and come down any chance you can get. You will be more than welcome any time. I have Mrs Grieve and Ina and baby back now and we are home from St Cyrus again. Mrs Grieve was so sorry arrangements would not permit her to avail herself of your kind invitation when she was passing through Edinburgh on her way North again.

Please give my compliments and kindest regards to Miss Macgillivray.

With love from us all.

Yours,
C. M. Grieve.

NLS   16 Links Avenue,
                                                              Montrose.
                                                              23/9/26

My dear Macgillivray,

Excuse a short note. I am enclosing the first batch of *Drunk Man* proofs to hand – about a fifth of the total. They are sending me the proofs in instalments in this way to expedite matters and I've promised to return them as quickly as possible. Any radical alter- ations – or anything that would involve any avoidable cost – is of course out of the question. I have just run them through and corrected a few literals that leapt at my eye: but I am taking advantage of your kind offer and sending them to you to read over in the hope that they will not be an inconvenience to you. I hate giving you any bother: but I'm hopeless at reading what I've written – my memory outruns my eye. No doubt there are typographicals you'll spot much more quickly than I would – and there may be an exchange of a word here or there which would be an improvement or some other little suggestion which will occur to you. Be sure I shall be only too glad to have these – and I know that if for any reason I do not act on any such you will forgive me – it will not be for want of any consideration. In fact as I have already told you I greatly regret that my involved methods of working – and the difficult circumstances that further involved me this summer – prevented my having the opportunity of going through the whole thing with you before I sent it off and availing myself of your experience. It would have been a great help to have had someone who *knew* to discuss matters with before finally committing myself. However, as matters turned out, that was impossible and now it's too late for recasting and only very minor adjustments, if any, can be made. The main thing is to have the text free of either typographical or literal errors.

Sending proofs like this doesn't of course give you a chance of considering the parts in relation to the whole, at all and all the main elements of the book are still to come – as he gets more vertiginously fou!

It was really good of Blackwood's to undertake this volume at all – *Penny Wheep* sold very badly. The industrial troubles completely upset the spring book sales.

I am sorry to hustle a kindness in any way: but will you please let me have these proofs back as soon as ever you can – as I (and Blackwood's) are anxious to have the book out as soon as possible now.

My *Contemporary Scottish Studies* is practically ready – I've read all the proofs except of the Contents List and Index. It reads a great deal better as a book than I had expected – despite some repetitiveness (none the worse of that: I wanted to reiterate and hammer home some things). Of course I trimmed up things here and there and gave it a good introductory chapter, and a wind-up one.

I hope your big casting is going (or has gone) all right: and that this finds all well with you, and with Miss Macgillivray. I'll write soon again. I'm hurried tonight. There're one or two things I wanted to ask you about. I'm thinking about that article on your own poetry. But if your new book is coming soon I'd rather wait for that. The trouble with illustrating points by reproductions of your art-work is where to place such an article. Otherwise it's a splendid idea and one I would certainly act on. It would be all right, of course, for the subsequent reproduction in monograph form. However, I'll see. I'll do my best. I'm going to settle down and re-read all I have of yours – and rethink-out the whole position. I have several things on the stocks – one a short book on *The Scots Lyric Since Burns* which would involve a good deal about you; and another on *Braid Scots* approached from a subjective autobiographical sort of angle which again would give me a good chance of trying to do justice to you and your work.[1] I'm feeling fitter again. Unfortunately I'm 'pretty sair haud'n doon' with a plethora of pure drudgery that recurs at this time of year – local directory compiling work, etc. – I wish to Heaven I could get a decent job somewhere – on the literary staff of a paper; or in a decent library – where the work during my working hours would be comparatively congenial and not a pure waste of time, and where whatever leisure I had would be more secure and less liable to interruption than my evenings here. However . . . !

Love from all.

Yours,
C. M. Grieve.

NLS

16 Links Avenue,
Montrose.
28/9/26

My dear Macgillivray,

Many thanks for your most kind and encouraging letter. I agree with most of the small corrections you suggest, and am giving effect to them. The change of title is not possible. As a matter of fact I do not agree with you in preferring *In Vino Veritas* although I quite see your point with regard to the existing title of which I am not specially enamoured either. I would however have deferred to your advice but for the fact that the book has been advertised already in various quarters under this title, parts of it and paragraphs regarding it have already appeared giving it that title, and to effect the alteration now would mean quite an amount of extra setting too. Your point about the Chinee[1] affects me differently. Theoretically I would defend my verse – you say it is beneath me – well, drunk men go beneath themselves; i.e. to deny representation to this element in the general 'drunk' wd be a species of camouflage. Practically, however, I believe you're right – that the verse goes over the score and would be better out or modified. But the trouble is my brain isn't working just

[1] Neither of these books was published.
[1] At the beginning of *A Drunk Man* there is a reference to 'some wizened scrunt o' a knock-knee/Chinee' (84).

325

now. I couldn't devise a substitute verse or think of a happy modification for anything. But I may yet. I will if I can.

The thing as a whole is really a trial run. I shall do better next time. I have a big programme in front of me and all my deepest difficulties to solve. I have devoted a great deal of thought to the business of becoming a Scottish poet on a big scale, and I am conscious that I have not yet penetrated into the necessary dimensions – and (if I may say so) that I am *over*burdened in many ways rather than *under* equipped. My intention in the *Drunk Man* was to try out various kinds of poetry – to run a gamut from pure doggerel to 'high' poetry. I do recognise and agree with you as to the tremendous power of simple statement, with your analogy from sculpture – but, on the other hand, I claim that purely decorative work, specialised effects, etc. have their own values, not necessarily lower – though very different – than those of the other. The first reaches a large public; the second a select few. But the artist is not concerned with his public. I never write with any thought of the potential reader. But simply to realise the effect the spirit prompts me to attempt to secure.

One of the projects exercising my mind is to dig down to my own rockbottom conclusions (not those of any hypothetical *Drunk Man*) in regard to a series of things – Scottish National issues (not opinions, but fundamental intuitions and convictions), organic apprehensions, the definition of the spiritual affirmities we have in common etc. – and to express these in a set of poems as bald as lightning, in the guise of a reverie on, or series of confessions to, yourself – i.e. as prompted by a consideration of your life and work, your kindness and advice to myself, the general position in which you and I have found ourselves – and if I pull that off to ask you to let me dedicate it to you, as a thanks offering for the privilege of having known you – one of the only two real oases I have found in Scotland, apart from my wife. I hope I can do it ere long. The lines I want to go upon are very clear to me now, and in such poems I will not be playing about with words – I will be getting there; there will be power in every syllable – devoid of recrimination, arrière pensées, personalities, of every kind.

The sort of poetry I mean is a great deal above the three bits you mark on the proof as good. There is one example of it in *Drunk Man* – the poem beginning 'O Jean, in whom my spirit sees'.[2] I am sure you will agree with me as to the qualities of that poem. But, at the same time, though I recognise its tremendous power (and note that in achieving it my utterance becomes absolutely simple, straight-

[2] 'O Jean, in whom my spirit sees' opens an eight-quatrain section (146) of the poem.

forward and devoid of decoration) I personally still prefer (for other ends at all events) the different kind of poetry, caviare to the general, which depends upon subtle word-play. My own favourite in the *Drunk Man* is the one about the fork in the wa' and the Seecund Comin'![3] But I do not expect many to share my taste.

While I agree with you in the main as to writing to be understanded of our own day and generation, I also think that a poet is entitled to demand of his public that they accompany him to any plane upon which he can secure the effects he wants to secure. But I recognise that few will acquiesce in his request unless he first of all proves his power on easily accessible levels and thereby gains their confidence that if they put themselves to the trouble he asks – i.e. to understand the precise significance of out of the way terms for example – he will have something to show them that he cannot otherwise reveal. (NB. The percentage of out of the way words in *D.M.* is really small and bits of mystification, and leg-pulling and conscious cleverness are defensible in the context. Instabilities and confusions alternate with clarities in a real drunk.)

It may interest you to know that of my own list of the 'high lights' of the *Drunk Man* three were in this first part of the proof you return – and only one of them was amongst those you singled out as good. That was the 'Blue Saltire' one.[4] Of course I know that the three you marked just struck you at first reading – and I quite understand the appeal of their straightforward statements. But my other two were the one with the word 'hwll' in it and that about 'Harns like seaweed'.[5]

You'll have read the rest now and before I see your comments I enclose the list of my own preferences:[6] it may amuse you to compare

1 The long one about Dostoevski beginning 'What Earthquake chitters oot'.
2 The long verse libre one about the chitterin' knottit stang.
3 The one about the Cavaburd.
4 The one about the ship-fratt on the air – cross-brath'd cordage.
5 Fork-in-the-wa' – Seecund Comin'.
6 Jean.
7, 8, 9, Bits of three other long poems.
10 Like stars the thistle's roses flooer.
   The sterile growth o Space ootour.

[3] This refers to the two quatrains beginning 'I'm fu o' a stickit God.' (134)
[4] 'Or this or that anent the Blue Saltire' (95).
[5] 'The devil's lauchter has a *hwll* like this . . . My harns are seaweed' (95).
[6] The passages itemised by MacDiarmid occur as follows: 1 (137–42), 2 (147–50), 3 (151–2), 4 (155–6), 5 (134), 6 (146), 10 (166), 11 (166–7), 12 (156–7), 13 (156), 14 (128–9), 15 (82), 16 (110).

11 O I ha'e Silence left.
12 Then let me pit in guid set terms.
   Oor quarrel wi th'owre-sonsy rose.
13 Grugous Thistle, to my een.
14 Returnin' tide can never fill.
15 The Dedicating Poem.
16 My Belly on the gantrees – a piece of mystification. I haven't an idea of what I was after – or rather of what the words mean – what matters is the sound – shout it out loud and don't bother about the sense and I think you'll find it fairly comes off.

However! Excuse this long farrago. I'm tremendously obliged to you for the care you've bestowed on these proofs and your great helpfulness. I enclose last few pages of proofs (rather first pages). The Dedicatory Poem is a case in point – pure aesthetic play, depending precisely on the strangeness of the words – but, I think, coming through their unfamiliarity with complete success. At least Scott thinks so – I could not have struck a vein that would have pleased him better – and that's what mattered most in regard to it.

Love from all,

Yours,
C. M. Grieve.

Many thanks in particular for 'thingum'[7] instead of 'mummy', also for querying *blate* in the first stanza. That was a stupid and quite unaccountable use of the wrong word altogether. I can't imagine how I've passed it so long without noticing it.

NLS   8/10/26

My dear Macgillivray,

We're all at sixes and sevens. That's the worst of trying to do things by correspondence. Especially with me. I'm a rotten letter-writer. My last letter seems to have given you totally wrong ideas so I must have been even more maladroit than usual. It was written in a hurry: but I wasn't angry with *you* – but with *myself*. I hated not being

[7] 'Am I a thingum mebbe that is kept/Preserved in spirits in a muckle bottle' (92).

able to agree to your suggested deletions. I thought and thought over them, and tried alternative verses and poems copies of which I will send you. I am scribbling this in a hurry as I am off to Glasgow in about an hour's time. I didn't quote my other friend's comments with any view to setting them up *against* yours – but to show or indicate for your consideration another point of view nearer in some ways to what I instinctively hold but had not time to elaborate. I can't just tell you why I feel that I can't end on a happy note for instance – why I must 'stand in my own light as it were' – why I find it easier to be at enmity than at peace – why I feel that I must always do something to counterbalance the pleasure people can derive from my work – but there it is. I must. As to 'Scottish terrier in excelsis', you have picked it up wrongly. I ought to have explained. The reference was to the verse about the terrier (Territorial) with nothing on below his kilt who landed on the thistle.[1] My friend thought I had expressed to the Nth the sensations of a naked soul landing on the thistle. I am not deceived in regard to some of his other remarks. They were his opinions – not mine. But I agree that it was asking too much to dump such a piece of stuff on you for one night – one reading. And behind it all is regret that circumstances didn't allow of going over it thoroughly and discussing it with you. Do not imagine that I do not value your opinion. I do – and my other friends. My friends as you suggest *are* few – and I fancy well-chosen (not that I have chosen them any more than they have chosen me, or *Fate* has chosen *us* rather). Any perturbation I have had has not been as between your opinions, his opinions, and my own: but has rather arisen from 'a guilty conscience' in regard to my work itself – the consciousness that it, or parts of it, were done under circumstances which did not allow me to see 'all round it'. My haste wasn't due to want of artistry either. I have other causes for hurry and I am afraid they will not allow me to ease off as, I agree entirely with you, I ought to do.

Your previous letter received yesterday was a precious document I shall treasure all my days.

Excuse this hasty scrawl. I shall write you as soon as I return from Glasgow.

Yours,
C. M. G.

---

[1] 'I kent a Terrier in a sham fecht aince,/Wha louped a dyke and landed on a thistle./He'd naething on ava aneth his kilt./Schönberg has nae notation for his whistle.' (96).

329

16 Links Avenue,
Montrose.
1st Nov. 1926

My dear Macgillivray,

I have been worrying over not getting you written to since I came back from Glasgow. This cold weather simply paralyses me – and I have needed all the energy I could command to discharge my unavoidable tasks. Besides the 'shades of November' and the approaching term-time always involve me in specially tortuous labyrinths of worry. But behind all these considerations have lurked the unsolved perplexities of the mess of misunderstandings into which our correspondence so unexpectedly landed. Blackwood's were so long in sending 'revise proofs' that I got hopelessly 'nervy' – imagining all kinds of things, ie that they had decided not to publish after all – and finally I wrote and then they came: two copies. I made a few corrections on one of them and have returned it. The other I have kept by me a few days longer: and have been reading and re-reading it, and, along with it, your letters, I am now sending it to you: and you will see that I have made several alterations and have acted upon many of your suggestions, while others of them are covered by the phrase in the preface about pronunciation – I was unwilling to make all the alterations (not all of them by any means marked by you) your several suggestions in this connection involved, partly because I wished to add the very minimum to the cost of producing the book, and partly because the true effect could only have been got by the thorough phonetisation of the whole thing – and where the same word (perhaps with a different shade of meaning altogether) is used in English and in Scots with a difference in pronunciation I am as averse on many grounds from spelling it phonetically in Scots as I would be from spelling it so in English. But as to your major suggestions – deletions, the question of switching the things back into normal by having the 'Drunk Man' waken up in the sunshine of the morning, and the idea of giving a page or two of notes or a concise statement of what I was after – I had to turn all of these down (not without anxious thought) on the score, first of all, of expense (they would have substantially upset the book as set), second, of inability in my then exhausted mood to give effect to them, and, third, because they either did not represent an intention that I could at all harmonise with what I had already done, or, if they did, an intention that would require for its realisation and incorporation a virtual remaking of the whole thing. You will appreciate how, seeing things in that way, I was worried and will, I believe, have excused long ere this any shortcomings in my hastily-written 'per contra' notes. But behind all these things, at the heart of our respective attitudes to the poem (or to certain elements in it) – along with all that we have in common – there is an entire difference of conviction on certain crucial issues. It may be an element of the Classical – Romantic quarrel (we are all both, but we are not all both in precisely equal proportions nor do our appearances in the one aspect and then in the other always synchronise) – or it may be due to the relative immaturity of my art, or my knowledge of life, or simply to the difference of the kinds of life we have led or of the current influences on our psychological conditions. I do not know. But I was tremendously touched by what you said when suggesting that I should end with a Sunny Morning Epilogue – the *real* beauty of the thistle – and turn to enjoy life again with my wife and baby. And this was subtly and strongly reinforced by the beautiful note and prayer and poem on Mrs Macgillivray's death which I herewith return as requested. It has been a great privilege to be vouchsafed this glimpse, this intimacy with you. It must be a wonderfully sustaining thing – a great privilege – to be able, upon an occasion, to accord such a privilege. I cannot tell whether or not the like may ever be mine. In scores of directions I find two very different impulses animating me –1/ to avoid coming to any conclusions on certain fundamental matters: i.e. moral and ethical problems; and 2/ to experiment with the artistic expression of every different attitude to them I can conceive, i.e. to make every different attitude as wholly mine at a given time as I possibly can and find to what extent I can make a 'convincing' poem of it. In other words I do not agree with you that the true view of the thistle after all is that seen in the sunny morning or that the love of woman or child has compensations outwith a very limited sphere. Nor am I yet committed to the contrary position. But you will see that I am in no case yet to accord intimacy-candour on such intimate matters as my view of my relationship to my wife or child – on such a plane as yours. This was what I meant when I spoke of getting 'right down to my basic positions' – i.e. putting myself in a position to meet the future on that plane, or, in other words, to take sides in regard to such questions instead of, as so far I have done, playing with them or watching them playing with me. And yet I suspect that I really have made up my mind – that under an appearance of play I have all along been in deadly earnest – and that all that remains is to discover the conclusions I have long ago come to and acted upon. How else explain my inability to adopt some of your suggestions? But once I do discover these subterranean conclusions and drag them forth to the light I may be able, if need be, to alter them. I do not know. But I

331

tried (although admittedly I was not in a good state for versifying and, if I had had time, your idea of an Epilogue might have come to something satisfactory) to give expression to the Epilogue idea: and here's the utmost I was able to make of it.

> And yet gin I could fa' asleep
> To wauken here at fresh o' morn
> Hoo bonnie micht this thistle seem
> Wi' jinglin dew on ilka thorn!
>
> Fu' weel I ken that frae sic thochts
> As mine the nicht a'e side o' truth
> Is wantin', when it needs a'side them a'
> To see things richt – altho' forsooth
>
> They're ill to see thegither and
> Compared wi' a' I'm seein' noo
> The pink and green at brak' o' day
> Micht seem owre bonnie to be true
>
> Yet a' that maist men dinna see
> – Or winna see – is needs worth mair
> Than a' they wull or aiblins can
> Gin use – or *that* – gars't seem maist fair!
> Or Gin that sae seems mair true and fair!

On the other hand it would take too long here to tell you the things that I myself would fain delete, or rather alter – get a better means of expressing – in the *Drunk Man*. There are many of them – the conditions under which I work preclude my seeing all round things, but it is hopeless to say 'do less then – but do that better'; I have to do as I can – and the conditions that make my work no better in some ways than it is make it no worse in others.

I don't know when it'll be out. I expect very soon, unless the coal shortage etc. is interfering with things. I expect little kudos, and less cash, from it. Graves[1] and others are astute enough to know they can hurt me (i.e. damage me with my publishers, restrict my sales, etc. – they can't hurt me personally) better by ignoring it rather than by condemning it or damning it with faint praise.

I expect my 'Contemporary Scottish Studies' book will be out this week.

I have also done a Burns selection with a provocative little preface which Benn's are publishing in their Sixpenny Series this month (November). I'll send you a copy as soon as it's out.

[1] Charles Graves was on the staff of *The Scotsman* and a director of the Porpoise Press.

I've been wondering about your own poems. I saw the note on the envelope about the arrangement with Blackwood's being off. Have you decided upon something else?

Excuse this rough scribble which doesn't say half what I've tried to say. It carries with it kindest regards from all here. I trust it finds you well. Please make my compliments to Miss Macgillivray.

Yours,
C. M. Grieve.

To William Blackwood & Sons Ltd

In the 1920s William Blackwood & Sons Ltd was a prestigious and powerful publishing house whose imprint carried great authority. The firm was associated with such great names as George Eliot and through 'Maga' – as the long-lived monthly *Blackwood's Magazine* (1817–1980) was called – brought to the attention of the public such exciting new Scottish fiction as *The Thirty-Nine Steps* (1915) by John Buchan (who was to contribute a perceptive introduction to *Sangschaw*). The four books containing the great Scots work MacDiarmid composed in the 1920s were all published by Blackwood: *Sangschaw* (1925), *Penny Wheep* (1926), *A Drunk Man Looks at the Thistle* (1926) and *To Circumjack Cencrastus* (1930). After *Cencrastus* Blackwood's declined to publish any more MacDiarmid books so the poet began the confused bibliographical career that continued until the publication of *Complete Poems* in 1978. In her essay, 'Mainly Domestic', in *MacDiarmid: A Festschrift* (Edinburgh 1962 p. 191) edited by K. D. Duval and Sydney Goodsir Smith, Helen Cruickshank provides an interesting anecdotal account of MacDiarmid's relationship with his famous publisher:

> On one of Chris's visits [to my home in Corstorphine, Edinburgh] it occurred to me to ask whether he had ever met his publishers, Messrs. Blackwood. He told me that they had accepted the MacDiarmid MSS 'out of the blue', but they had never met. I rang Mr George Blackwood and received a cordial invitation to call. We had a pleasant chat in their famous old Saloon, with its round polished table and warm red walls hung round with mellow portraits. I felt that Christopher Grieve was not out of place here in the company of Christopher North, the Ettrick Shepherd and others of the *Noctes Ambrosianae*.
>
> On learning that another MacDiarmid volume was in the making, Mr Blackwood asked Chris to send it along when ready. Some time elapsed, however, before *To Circumjack Cencrastus* reached that stage ...

NLS

16 Links Avenue,
Montrose.
7th April 1925.

Messrs Wm. Blackwood & Sons,
Publishers.

Dear Sirs,

   To enable Professor H. J. C. Grierson to supply a preface to my
volume of poems, I wonder if you would be good enough to tell me
when proofs will be available. My idea, if possible, is to let Professor
Grierson have a set of the proofs by him when he is writing his
preface – if you do not require to have his introduction in hand before
that. Should you, however, desire to have the 'copy' for his preface in
hand before such time as proofs can be ready, I must try to send
Professor Grierson copies of the poems.
   Will you please let me know at your early convenience, so that I
can make the necessary arrangements?
   And oblige.

                    Yours faithfully,
                    Hugh M'Diarmid.

NLS

16 Links Avenue,
Montrose.
16th April 1925

Messrs Wm. Blackwood & Sons,
Publishers.

Dear Sirs:-

   I enclose a cutting of an article from *The Glasgow Herald*[1] of
Saturday 4th inst. with reference to my Braid Scots poems. Other

---

[1] Alexander M'Gill's article 'Hugh M'Diarmid' in *The Glasgow Herald* of 4 April
1925 enthusiastically endorsed the experimental Scots of MacDiarmid: 'He has
discarded the regular newspaper dialects, and out of a great and thorough
knowledge of Scots words and idioms he has fabricated, wilfully, a Scottish
literary language which is rooted in old Scots and in the unsleeping soul of the
Scottish nation. He has eschewed merely Burnsian Scots and gone back to the
language spoken and written by the Makars before the decay set it.'

articles having recently been devoted to them in *The Scotsman* by Dr Geo. Kitchin,[2] *The London Mercury* by Mr D. Cleghorn Thomson,[3] *La Revue Anglo-Américaine*[4] and other French periodicals by Professor Denis Saurat, the well-known authority on Blake & Milton. I have also had very appreciative letters from Mr John Buchan, Mrs Violet Jacob, & other well-known authors; while I have had numerous letters asking where copies can be had. It seems curious that so much interest should have been aroused as I have only so far published a few of them in various now-defunct periodicals.

There is obviously a demand for a volume and I have reason to believe that it would sell well and score a succes-d'estim. May I ask if your firm would consider the publication of quite a small volume containing some 25 of my best poems – of each of which very flattering things have been said by competent and well-known critics? I am not in a position to pay myself for publication, otherwise I should have done so already: but I could help by giving the names of at least 200 probable purchasers known to me. Perhaps subscription forms could be issued, in which case I could, I am sure, do a good deal. In the event of your firm undertaking publication I think I could obtain a short introduction from my friend, Professor H. J. C. Grierson of Edinburgh University.

If desired I shall be happy to send you cuttings of the other articles to which I refer.

Hoping to hear from you at your convenience.

Yours faithfully,
Hugh M'Diarmid.

---

[2] George Kitchin's article on 'The "Scottish Renaissance" Group', in *The Scotsman* of 3 November 1924, was critical but conceded that 'there are certain pieces of [MacDiarmid's] which raise him above the common level of writers in dialect'.
[3] In Vol XI, No 61 of *The London Mercury*, November 1924, David Cleghorn Thomson praised C. M. Grieve's editorial initiative in 'affording publicity to the Doric poems of . . . Hugh MacDiarmid and others'.
[4] Denis Saurat, 'Le groupe de "la Renaissance Écossaise"' in *Revue Anglo Américaine*, Première Année, No 4, April 1924.

16 Links Avenue,
Montrose.
30th April, 1925.

Messrs Wm. Blackwood & Sons,
Publishers.

Dear Sirs:-

I have to thank you for your letter of 28th inst, and for the proposals[1] you make with regard to my poems, which are entirely satisfactory to me. I have much pleasure in accepting, and hereby do so, and undertake to offer you, in accordance with your stipulation, my next two books at the same terms.

I am writing to Professor Grierson tonight with regard to an introduction.

The specimen pages are very pleasing both as to the type used and the size of page. Since I wrote to you friends have suggested that *Sangschaw* would be a better title than *Penny Wheep*. I am inclined to agree with them, but I will leave that to yourselves.

With compliments and best wishes.

Yours faithfully,
Hugh M'Diarmid.

16 Links Avenue,
Montrose.
1st June 1925.

Messrs Wm. Blackwood & Sons,
Publishers.

Dear Sirs:-

I now enclose corrected proof of *Sangschaw* together with 'Copy' for Mr Buchan's preface.

Professor Grierson has suggested that by the excision of the verse I

---

[1] Blackwood's offered to pay MacDiarmid a royalty on all sales of 10 percent on the first 750 copies sold, 15 percent for the next 750 copies, and 20 percent on all sales beyond 1,500.

have marked 'delete' on page 6, the poem[1] greatly gains in force. I am inclined to agree with him and as the poem is inscribed to him I should like if possible to fall in with his suggestion. This, however, would have the effect of making the poem terminate at the bottom of Page 9, and leaving Page 10 blank. I therefore enclose another short poem for Page 10. The contents page would have to be altered accordingly.

Mr Buchan pointed out that the Glossary was perhaps not quite so full as was desirable. I have therefore deleted one or two unnecessary items and added a few others. I trust this will not cause much trouble.

With every good wish.

Yours faithfully,
Hugh M'Diarmid.

NLS

16 Links Avenue,
Montrose.
14th August 1925

Messrs Wm. Blackwood & Sons,
Publishers.

Dear Sirs:-

Progressive tendencies in Scottish Arts and letters have at present no distinctive medium and I have recently been discussing with many friends the possibility of establishing one on a modest scale. Past effects have, I think, failed mainly because they did not attract the right men and took too low a level. I believe that really first-class work – equal, while distinctively Scottish, to the best that is being produced by the younger schools in other countries, cannot fail to find its public. To work from the bottom upwards is surely the wrong method. I and my friends have thoroughly thrashed this matter out recently with a wide circle interested in London, Glasgow and elsewhere. There is every sign that a Scottish Literary Renaissance is imminent and we would like to make an effort to crystallise it.

[1] 'I Heard Christ Sing' (18–21) is dedicated to H. J. C. Grierson; it is followed by 'Moonlight Among the Pines' (21–2).

338

I wonder if your firm can be interested in this matter. If so, I feel sure that with your name and organisation you can set this movement on its feet, giving it an international standing and making it a paying proposition.

What I would venture to suggest to you is that you might consider the publication of a small quarterly devoted to Scottish letters, Art & Music, entitled *Scots Art* and comparable in size to, say, *The Scots Magazine*, but admitting only work of first-class creative value calculated to give international consequence to contemporary Scottish culture.

To do this a little group of contributors of outstanding quality, fully abreast of contemporary world-art, is necessary, and I think I have these now in the following, who are prepared to collaborate along with me along definite lines:-

Art and Creative Art-Theory	Professor McCance.	Art-Critic of *The Spectator*. Himself an ultra-modern artist of exceptional quality – as is also his wife, whose work along with his is shortly to be on exhibition in London. Both are well known in London and Parisian art and literary circles. Both are Scots and definitely interested in this question of a Scots Renaissance.
Aesthetics & Poetry	Edwin Muir.	Well-known in America as contributor to *New York Nation*, *The Freeman*, *The Dial*, etc. Translator of Hauptmann. Formerly literary editor of London *New Age*. Critic at present on *Nation & Atheneum*. Contributor to *Calendar of Modern Letters* etc. Poems recently published by Hogarth Press.
Philosophy and International Criticism	Denis Saurat	Professor of University of Bordeaux. Directeur de l'Institut Français in London. Authority on Blake and Milton. His

339

		Milton: Man and Thinker recently published by Jonathan Cape. Well known in France, Sweden & America as literary critic and philosopher of outstanding ability. His Philosophical Dialogues will be published in America & Britain in October. His function will be to relate our activities to tendencies in world-art – to supply an adequate rationale, and suggest a technique of inspiration.
Imaginative Prose & Poetry.	C. M. Grieve.	Author of *Annals of the Five Senses*. Member of PEN Club. Present literary critic of *New Age*. Contributor to *Les Nouvelles Litteraires* etc. His *Contemporary Scottish Studies* are to be published next year by Messrs Leonard Parsons Ltd.
Music	Francis George Scott	Assistant Lecturer in Music at Jordanhill Training College, Glasgow. The only living Scots composer of international calibre. Pupil of Ravel and Roger Ducasse. Engaged in creating a Scottish national idiom in music, setting Dunbar, my own poems, etc.
Poetry & Drama	Hugh M'Diarmid F. V. Branford	Braid Scots writer. Contributor to *London Mercury*, *The Dial*, *Neuve Gids* (Holland), etc. Two volumes published by Messrs Christopers.

I suggest that the group be limited to these seven for the first year

340

unless under special circumstances – the offer of work of first-rate quality by presently unknown writers. Each of them in these first four issues is prepared to give the very best work he can, and work, definitely Scottish, except Saurat's, in each number, bearing upon that of the others so that each issue will create a homogenous whole moving into a definite direction through the separate fields of music, art and literature. Each issue will thus be self-contained and a complete work of art in itself. The contents will be purely artistic – i.e. non-political, etc. Each of the seven have a certain following already, and their friends would be a good nucleus of a body of subscribers apart from the general public of whom we believe a sufficient number would be attracted to make the venture moderately profitable to you.

For the first year, then, I would be prepared to act as editor, and I and the others would contribute, without remuneration, and at the end of the first year the matter could be reconsidered on the basis of the results achieved.

So far as you are concerned the matter reduces itself to an offer for your consideration of a four-volume miscellany, each volume to include three or four illustrations and a piece of music, and publishable perhaps at 5/- each.

All of us have discussed this matter – and the whole question of the possibility of a Scottish Renaissance – with many well-known writers, musicians & artists in London & Paris, and find that they are agreed that it is a most promising idea and – provided that a publishing house of high reputation takes it up – by far the most likely method of encompassing our objective.

I sincerely trust that you may be able to give the matter your favourable consideration.

Yours faithfully,
Hugh M'Diarmid.

NLS

16 Links Avenue,
Montrose.
20th August 1925.

Messrs Wm. Blackwood & Sons,
Publishers.

Dear Sirs:-

Many thanks for yours of yesterday's date. Your list is a very full one, so far as the leading British and Colonial papers and literary periodicals is concerned. I am afraid that the special nature of *Sangschaw* as Braid Scots work makes it scarcely worth-while sending copies to the *Bristol Times*, *Exeter Gazette*, *Portsmouth Times* and *Plymouth Mercury*. For personal reasons I do not think the book would receive fair treatment from *The Poetry Review* or *The Scots Magazine* – with both of which periodicals, as a critic and reviewer elsewhere, I have been at complete variance. I would suggest that these six might therefore be left out. On the other hand I think copies could profitably be sent to:-
Thos. Henderson Esq. B.Sc. Editor, *Scottish Educational Journal*, Moray Place, Edinburgh.
Alex. McGill, Esq. c/o 'Columba', Clyde Street, Glasgow.
W. Sorley Brown, Esq. Editor, *Border Standard*, Galashiels.

I hesitate to add to such a large list: but other papers included might perhaps be left out (I confess I know little of the value of the Colonial papers) to make room for the following:- *The New Statesman*, *The Calendar of Modern Letters*, *The Criterion* (quarterly), *The Adelphi*, and *The Irish Statesman*.

I shall myself send copies to Col. Buchan, Professor Grierson, Professor Saurat, Herr Kjersmeier and other foreign litterateurs and editors of Continental organs with which I am connected.

It is good of you to include in your list three of the friends I mentioned in my letter of 14th inst. to you. Their addresses are as follows:-
Edwin Muir, Esq., Penn, Buckinghamshire.
C. M. Grieve, Esq. c/o Scott, 103 Woodville Gardens, Langside, Glasgow – or c/o *The New Age*, 70 High Holborn, London W.C.
F. V. Branford, Esq. Ardguy, Ross-Shire.

With many thanks.

Yours faithfully,
Hugh M'Diarmid.

P.S. Muir will review it in American *Saturday Review of Literature* at editor's special request.

342

16 Links Avenue,
Montrose.
12th Feb. 1926.

Messrs Wm. Blackwood & Sons,
Publishers.

Dear Sirs:-

In accordance with our arrangement that you should have the option on my next two volumes, I propose to submit for favour of your consideration two new collections of my poems.

The first of these, which I have named *Penny Wheep* is a collection of some 45 poems in Braid Scots and 3 in English. Most of them are short lyrics, and of various kinds similar to those in *Sangschaw*. My hope is that you may see your way to publish this as a companion volume to *Sangschaw*.

I write, of course, in ignorance of how *Sangschaw* has sold. But I imagine that it will continue to have a certain sale for some years, and it may well be that a maintenance of interest, and perhaps growth of reputation, by succeeding volumes will react favourably upon it too and keep it in demand.

I do not know whether you would be prepared to publish *Penny Wheep* before the end of the spring publishing season. If you would care to consider it with that in view I should be happy to send you the MSS. now. If, however, you would rather consider it for autumn publication I will keep the MSS by me a little longer.

The other book is a long poem of over 600 lines: but divided into several sections, and having within the sections a great variety of manners and measures of verse, including lyrics, humorous and satirical verse, translations from the French and the Russian etc. I have named this collection *A Drunk Man Looks At The Thistle*: and friends who have seen it regard this as by far my best work to date. Sir Robert Bruce, of *The Glasgow Herald*,[1] is publishing six shorter extracts from it shortly in the columns of that paper. It may be in

---

[1] *The Glasgow Herald* of 13 February 1926 carried an article and six poems from 'a gallimaufry in Braid Scots, entitled *A Drunk Man Looks at the Thistle*. It is a complete poem, in over 600 lines, deriving its unity from its pre-occupation with the distinctive elements in Scottish psychology which depend for their effective expression upon the hitherto unrealised potentialities of Braid Scots; but it is divided into various sections, affording scope for a great variety of forms, including lyrics, nonsense verse, verse libre, and translations from modern Russian, German, and French poems. The intention here has been to show that Braid Scots is adaptable to all kinds of poetry, and to a much greater variety of measures than might be supposed from the restricted practice of the last hundred years.'

tomorrow's issue – if so, I will enclose a cutting with this letter. I hope that you may consider this for autumn publication – that is why I venture to suggest *Penny Wheep* for this spring instead – and, if so, perhaps you will let me know when you would like to have the MSS sent to you. I am anxious to keep it by me for a little yet, at any rate, for final revision.

Trusting to hear from you, and with best wishes.

I remain

Yours faithfully,
Hugh M'Diarmid.

NLS

Avondale,
St Cyrus,
Kincardineshire.
9/7/26

Messrs Wm. Blckwood & Sons,
Publishers.

Dear Sirs:-

Will you please be so good as to send on my behalf copies of *Penny Wheep* to Edwin Muir, c/o *Nation and Atheneum* London and Thos. Henderson, Esq. B.Sc., *Educational Institute of Scotland*, 47 Moray Place, Edinburgh?

I hope the book is going well. I have only seen one or two reviews so far but these have been very flattering, and I have had quite a number of congratulatory letters.

I had hoped to have sent *A Drunk Man*, etc. to you before this: but I am very conscious, if I may say so without immodesty, that this is or has all the makings of being one of the biggest things in the whole range of Scottish literature and I am determined not to let it out of my hands until I am absolutely certain that I can make no more of it. I think I shall be able to send it to you by the first week of September, however. I am anxious if possible to have it published this autumn and hope that this may be possible if the MS reaches you not later than the week mentioned.

In conclusion, I must say again how delighted I was with the production of *Penny Wheep*. I do not think any format could have pleased me better.

With compliments best wishes.

> Yours sincerely,
> Hugh M'Diarmid.

NLS

> Avondale,
> St Cyrus,
> Kincardineshire.
> 6th August 1926.

Messrs Wm. Blackwood & Sons.

It was good of you to send me the cuttings which I now return. I am sorry to have kept them so long. But I was called away South soon after receiving them owing to a family bereavement and since then have had an indisposition, due to a chill caught when travelling, I think. I have now recovered, however, and am making up arrears of correspondence. I am sorry if my retaining these cuttings so long has caused you any inconvenience.

Reviews of *Penny Wheep* seem slow to appear. In particular I had hoped to have seen notices ere this in *The Manchester Guardian* and *The Times Literary Supplement*.[1] I hope a review copy was sent to the latter. You will remember that with regard to *Sangschaw* a copy was sent to *The Times* but not to the *Literary Supplement* until later. A friend of mine on the editorial staff of *The Glasgow Evening Times* tells me that he has written an article on *Penny Wheep* but that it cannot appear until a review copy is received, copies sent to the *Glasgow Herald* apparently not sufficing to embrace the *Evening Times* too, so will you please be good enough to send the latter a copy. And on my behalf will you please also send:-
I copy each of *Sangschaw* and *Penny Wheep* to
Professor Lascelles Abercrombie,
The University, Leeds.
and 1 copy of *Penny Wheep* to
Gordon Bottomley, Esq.
The Shieling, Silverdale, Carnforth.
with my compliments.

[1] *The Times Literary Supplement* reviewed *Penny Wheep* on 24 March 1927.

I am now almost ready with *A Drunk Man* and will forward the MSS very shortly.

With thanks and best wishes.

Yours sincerely,
C. M. Grieve.

NLS   16 Links Avenue,
                                                                               Montrose.
                                                                         6th Sept. 1926.

Messrs Wm. Blackwood & Sons,
Publishers.

Dear Sirs:-

On 28th ult. I sent you the MSS of *A Drunk Man Looks At The Thistle* per registered post. I trust you safely received this. You will excuse my anxiety as I have no other copy of a very large part of the poem.

With best wishes.

Yours faithfully,
Hugh M'Diarmid.

NLS   16 Links Avenue,
                                                                               Montrose.
                                                                         9th Sept. 1926.

Messrs Wm. Blackwood & Sons, Ltd.,
Publishers.

Dear Sirs:-

Many thanks for your kind letter of 7th inst. I am very sorry about the extremely disappointing sale of *Penny Wheep*.[1] No doubt the Strike

---

[1] In a letter of 9 February 1927 Blackwood's described the sales of the first three MacDiarmid books as follows: '*Sangschaw* (during 1926) – 106 copies, *Penny Wheep* (from April to end of 1926) – 117 copies, *A Drunk Man Looks at the Thistle* (from November to end of 1926) – 99 copies.'

and bad trade is largely responsible. I hope there have been more sales since the end of June. Reviews have been appearing very slowly. I see *The Irish Statesman* review only appeared on 14th August and there is a long one in a Kirriemuir paper of last week. So far I have seen more in either *The Manchester Guardian* or *The Times Literary Supplement*.

I hope *A Drunk Man* will make up for it, and revive sales both of it and of *Sangschaw*.

The sample page you enclosed is very nice, I think, and will make a fine compact book. I am hoping to go on holiday in October but if proofs do not come before then I shall keep you posted as to my address to obviate any delay.

With every good wish.

Yours sincerely,
Hugh M'Diarmid.

NLS

16 Links Avenue,
Montrose.
1st Oct. 1926

Messrs Wm. Blackwood & Sons,
Publishers.

Dear Sirs:-

I herewith return corrected proofs of *The Drunk Man*.

I have made two small changes for p. 26, and p. 96 respectively and enclose 'copy' for these. I hope that this will not cause much trouble.

I can't remember whether you gave me a second proof or not before printing off my two previous books, but I should be glad if you could do so in this case. I would let you have it back by return of post to avoid delay.

My address from Friday night (8th inst.) to the following Monday will be c/o Scott, 103 Woodville Gardens, Langside, Glasgow.

With best wishes.

Yours sincerely,
Hugh M'Diarmid.

NLS

16 Links Avenue,
Montrose.
25/11/26

Messrs Wm. Blackwood & Sons,
Publishers.

Dear Sirs:-

Many thanks for the six copies of *The Drunk Man*. I trust that the
sales have made a satisfactory beginning. I am again greatly pleased
with the way in which it has turned out. So far I have seen no reviews
but they will not be long now. I understand that there is to be an
article-review of it in this week's *Scots Observer*.[1]
Will you please send one copy of *Drunk Man* to each of the
following with my compliments?-
1. Professor Denis Saurat, Professor of French, London University.
2. Edwin Muir, Esq. c/o *The Nation and Athenaeum*, London (Marked
'Private & Personal' and 'Please Forward').
3. Professor H. J. C. Grierson, Edinburgh University.
And oblige.
Now that you have published the two subsequent books on which
you stipulated for the option when you accepted *Sangschaw* – and all
three having been poetry and poetry of a kind which may take years
to secure due recognition and from which, at the best, comparatively
little profit can accrue either to writer or publisher. I have been
anxious to offer you a prose work and have begun to put together in
final form a big mass of notes for a volume of biographical and
critical studies. I have also a novel in preparation but cannot say
when I shall be in a position to complete and submit it for consideration. The volume of essays, however, which I propose to call *At the
Sign of the Thistle*, I intend to go straight ahead with now and will, if
you care to publish them, be able to deliver the complete MSS by the
beginning of March. The total number of words will be about 80,000
to 85,000 – that is to say, the essays will average about 2,500. I
enclose a list of the subjects.[2]

[1] Robert Angus, in *Scots Observer*, Vol 1, No 14, 1 January 1927, described *A Drunk
Man* as being 'in the best sense revolutionary; it is creative destruction, voluntary
destruction, pled for with fierce vigour, scathing satire, and intellectual force; for
it contains the Scottish interpretation of the cosmos in all that cosmos's baffling
complexity. It is also noble and impressive poetry, which makes Mr M'Diarmid of
more than national importance'.
[2] The outline for the book reads as follows:
At the Sign of the Thistle.
by Hugh M'Diarmid
1. John Davidson

With best wishes.

Yours sincerely,
Hugh M'Diarmid.

NLS

16 Links Avenue,
Montrose.
5.2.27

Messrs Wm. Blackwood & Sons,
Publishers.

Dear Sirs:-

Will you please send me one copy of *Sangschaw*, and oblige?
I expect you have seen *The Irish Statesman*[1] review of *A Drunk Man*.
As you probably know, *The Irish Statesman* is edited by the Irish poet
'A.E.' (George Russell) and I was so intrigued by the evidence of
knowledge of the Scots tradition in this review that I wrote to 'A.E.'
to find out who had written it. It is so curious a thing that one has to
go to Ireland for a competent review of a Scots poem. A.E. replies
that the writer of the review was Senator Oliver Gogarty (himself the
writer of many fine lyrics). 'A.E.' says he would have reviewed it

2. Robert Buchanan
3. 'Fiona M'Leod'
4. David Gray
5. John Barlas
6. George Macdonald
7. S. R. Crockett
8. 'Ian Maclaren'
9. 'Hugh Haliburton'
10. William Archer
11. W. P. Ker
12. 'J. B. Selkirk'
13. Patrick Geddes.
14. Andrew Lang
15. George Douglas Brown
16. Thomas Common
17. James Moror
18. James Murdoch
19. Principal Caird.
20. James Cooper
21. Duncan M'Naught
22. Abbot Hunter Blair
23. Theodore Napier
24. Hector Macpherson
25. Walter Smith
26. William Alexander
27. Roger Quin
28. J. M'Dougall Hay
29. Herman Melville
30. W. A. Mackenzie

[1] 'Literature and Life: A Drunk Man Looks at the Thistle' by 'Gog' (Oliver St John
Gogarty), *The Irish Statesman*, Vol 7, No 18, 8 January 1927, praised MacDiarmid
'because in the wonderfully flexible and containing form he has chosen he has
managed to become, as it were, a frenzied mouth letting the present-day soul of
Scotland speak out with its metaphysic, its politic and its poetry'.

himself but found that Gogarty had a knowledge of the Scots Vernacular. He himself ('A.E.') however, thinks just as highly of it and says he considers it by far the best of my books and far superior to anything he has come across in contemporary English poetry. This is great praise from such a man and leads me to hope that the book will still make good, if slowly, despite the stupidity and incompetence of so many of its reviewers. You would also see Edwin Muir's review in *The Nation and Atheneum*[2] and I understand – though I have not seen it – that Robert Bain again deals with my work in a review of the Scottish poetry of the year in the *Burns Chronicle*.[3]

I am hoping that these notices have led to some increase of sales. I do not know when you issue statements: but I do not appear to have had any except in respect of *Sangschaw* in the beginning of last year, i.e. only a month or two after it was published and before some of its best reviews appeared.

With best wishes.

Yours sincerely,

Hugh M'Diarmid.

P.S. I have since had a long letter from Senator Gogarty. I thought you might like to know this.

NLS

16 Links Avenue,
Montrose.
18/4/27

Messrs Wm. Blackwood & Sons,
Publishers.

Dear Sirs:-

I am sorry that inadvertently I have forgotten to post you receipt for the cheque on account of royalties received a month ago. I now do

<hr />

[2] Muir's enthusiastic review appeared in *The Nation and Athenaeum*, Vol XL, No 16, 22 January 1927.
[3] Robert Bain's survey of recent poetry in the *Burns Chronicle* of 1926 asserted that 'the most signal event of the year, and of many years, has been the appearance of Hugh M'Diarmid's *Sangschaw*'.

so. I thought I had sent it off at the time, and certainly meant to do so, and trust that my delay has occasioned you no inconvenience.

I am very glad to see that the books continue – if very slowly – to sell: and am inclined to believe, with some of my friends, that at least in a few years' time on a republication perhaps of a selection of the best things in the previous books a sale will be secured which will compensate for the poor sales previously. This, at any rate, was the case with Murray's *Hamewith.*[1]

I had hoped to have sent you a prose MSS ere this: but neither the novel or the volume of essays I previously mentioned to you are yet completed. In the meantime, however, I have practically ready a volume of short stories,[2] several of which have appeared during the past six weeks in the *Scots Magazine, Glasgow Herald, Scots Observer,* etc., and would seem likely to prove considerably more popular than my poetry has yet done. I hope to forward this to you for the favour of your kind consideration in the course of a few days now.

With best wishes.

Yours sincerely,
Hugh McDiarmid.

NLS

16 Links Avenue,
Montrose.
3rd October 1927.

Messrs Wm. Blackwood & Sons,
Publishers,
Edinburgh.

Dear Sirs:-

Many thanks for your cheque for £4.9.6 in respect of royalties accrued.

A Glasgow gentleman is desirous of lecturing shortly to a well-known Burns Club on the *Drunk Man* and to that end he has requested a sight of the cuttings of reviews received.

Unfortunately I find that my collection is not complete lacking, in

---

[1] Charles Murray, *Hamewith* (1900).
[2] These stories are collected in *The Thistle Rises* (1984).

particular, *The Manchester Guardian* review and Mr Edwin Muir's notice of the book which appeared in the *Nation and Athenaeum*.

I wonder if you have a complete collection and will be so good as to lend it to me for a little. I will see that it is duly and safely returned to you.

Thanking you in anticipation.

Yours sincerely,
Hugh M'Diarmid.

NLS
TS

18 Pyrland Road,
London, N5.
5th April, 1930

Messrs Wm. Blackwood & Sons,
Edinburgh.

Dear Sirs,

I was, of course, very disappointed when you decided not to publish the last collection of poems *Fier Comme un Ecossais* I submitted to you. I felt that it contained some of my best work, and wondered why you did not like it, especially as my little public has been steadily growing and it was likely to sell at least as well, if not better than its predecessors. You did not specify your reasons for refusing it nor give me any indication of the lines along which, as my publishers, you would prefer me to develop, but your letter suggested I should wait until I had a larger collection of work to draw from. From this I have ventured to hope that you meant that you would be prepared to consider other work from me, and that I need not conclude that my connection with your firm, which I value so highly, is at an end.

I think I suggested when I wrote you last that a volume of my selected poems – drawn from the volumes you have already published, and from *Fier Comme un Eccossais*, and elsewhere – might be published now, and that, if you thought of this, I could probably get an introductory essay for it from W. B. Yeats, or from A.E. Your reply did not refer to this suggestion, and I should be glad to hear from you now as to this.

My big poem – *To Circumjack Cencrastus* – is now nearing comple-

352

tion, and is, in my own and my friends' opinion, the most important thing I have yet done – quite different in kind from *The Drunk Man*, I hope I may send it to you soon, and that you will be willing to consider it for autumn publication.

Yours sincerely,
C. M. Grieve.

NLS

The Liverpool Organization,
Royal Liver Building,
Liverpool.
30.6.30

Messrs Wm. Blackwood & Sons,
Publishers,
George Street, Edinburgh.

Dear Sirs:-

I am sending you herewith two-thirds of the 'copy' of my poem, *To Circumjack Cencrastus*. There are several little things I want to do to the final third yet, but I will forward it to you soon. On the basis of the material I am now sending, however, you can perhaps decide whether you will publish it or not. I am anxious to have a quick decision as I am particularly set on having this book published this autumn. You will see from the structure of the poem, and its length that in the event of your deciding to publish it, it will be desirable to have a longer page than in my previous books, i.e. a page that can accommodate 40 to 50 lines, as some of the verses (where lyrics in italics are interposed) run to about that, and it would be very awkward and confusing to have such verses broken up over 2 or 3 pages.

I hope my other books continue to have occasional sales. I had expected a statement from you about this time, but I may have miscalculated when that is due.

With every good wish,

Yours sincerely,
C. M. Grieve.

353

NLS   The Liverpool Organization,
                                        Royal Liver Building,
                                                  Liverpool.
                                                   8/7/30

Messrs Wm. Blackwood & Sons Ltd.

Dear Sirs:-

Many thanks for your letter of yesterday's date intimating that
you are willing to publish my poem, *To Circumjack Cencrastus* this
autumn, provided I can let you have the rest of the 'copy' without
delay. I will send you this within ten days' time at the most. I trust
this will be satisfactory to you.
With best wishes.

                              Yours sincerely,
                              C. M. Grieve.

NLS   The Liverpool Organization,
                                        Royal Liver Building,
                                                  Liverpool.
                                                  23.9.30

Messrs Wm. Blackwood & Sons Ltd.,
45 George Street,
Edinburgh.

Dear Sirs:-

Many thanks for your letter of yesterday's date. I have tried hard
to hit upon a satisfactory sub-title – but cannot.[1] The incomprehen-
sibility of the title will perhaps have its own publicity value and in
any case I believe that a very extensive press campaign[2] in connec-

---

[1] The title 'To Circumjack Cencrastus' is Scots for 'to square the circle'; the subtitle
adopted, 'The Curly Snake', emphasises the serpentine nature of Cencrastus and
honours a path in Langholm.

[2] In the *Daily Record* of 21 September 1930 an anonymous article appeared under
the lurid heading 'A Poet Runs Amok – Noted Men in The Pillory – Bitter
Invective'. It drew attention to the poem's 'violence of expression' and concluded
'Many of its passages would be characterised by any section of the Christian

tion with the book is being organised by some of my friends and that this will have the effect of concentrating public interest on it. This is apart from normal reviews altogether and will be principally concerned with some of the more sensational elements of the poem – its 'attacks', for example, on Mr Ramsay MacDonald, Sir Harry Lauder, and others and its political and satirical features generally. If the 'stunt' press take these up effectively and make a 'splash' of them, the book should get a big popular advertisement which will quite get over the difficulty of the title. But if – in the next few days – I can think of a suitable sub-title I will suggest it to you at once.

I do not know whether (as in my previous books) you intend to have a 'Jacket', but if so – in partial explanation of the title – the following paragraph might go on it.[3]

With best wishes,

Yours sincerely,
C. M. Grieve

Suggested Paragraph
Writing to the author a year or two ago with regard to his previous poems, Professor Lascelles Abercrombie said: 'We'll hear more of you. You have a serpent in you which will eat up everything else.' This is the author's attempt to deal with the serpent (Cencrastus) in accordance with the ancient Gaelic saying: 'It's a big beast there's no room for outside.'

Church as blankly blasphemous.' MacDiarmid himself orchestrated this press campaign. Writing as 'Pteleon' in the *Scots Observer* of 2 October 1930 he warned readers of the offensive nature of *To Circumjack Cencrastus* (published on 29 October 1930): 'There is much in Hugh MacDiarmid's new long poem, *To Circumjack Cencrastus* (Messrs Blackwood, 8/6), which most people will deplore and a great deal that, surely, no one can justify. There is a super-abundance of needless personalities – scurrilous vilification of great Scotsmen past and present with whom the poet happens to disagree for political or other reasons or for none to all appearances except gratuitous ill-will . . . Anti-English sentiment of the most virulent kind abounds, and along with it violent depreciations of British Imperialism and a rank hatred of America. This element culminates in an inexcusable attack on the Royal Family.'

[3] This paragraph duly appeared on the dustjacket of the book.

NLS

The Liverpool Organization,
Royal Liver Building,
Liverpool.
25.9.30

Messrs Wm. Blackwood & Sons,
Publishers.

Dear Sirs:-

I have thought of an appropriate sub-title after all, viz. 'The Curly Snake'. Will you please therefore give the title as *To Circumjack Cencrastus, or, The Curly Snake*.

Probably you have seen copies of yesterday's *Evening News* both of which contain lengthy advance articles about the book.

I note you are sending me revised proofs.

With best wishes.

Yours sincerely,
C. M. Grieve.

NLS
TS

321 High Holborn,
London, WC1.
11th January 1932.

Messrs Wm. Blackwood & Sons,
George Street,
Edinburgh.

Dear Messrs Blackwood,

Ever since I published my *Contemporary Scottish Studies* (1926) I have had repeated requests that I should follow up that book with further essays of the same kind.

In the interval I have written a good deal in many periodicals and newspapers – articles in many cases which have had considerable influence and have contributed considerably to the growth of the New Scottish Movement in politics and literature alike. I am now writing to ask you if you would care to consider the publication of a book, under the title of *At the Sign of the Thistle (1st Series)*[1] containing

---

[1] *At the Sign of the Thistle* (London 1934) as eventually published, by Stanley Nott, contained eleven essays: 'English Ascendancy in British Literature', 'Gertrude Stein', 'The Purpose of the Free Man', 'Donald Sinclair', 'Problems of Poetry

many of the most important and controversial of these, including my long essay on *English Ascendancy in British Literature* (from *The Criterion*), my Defence of Synthetic Scots (from *The 19th Century*), my article on *Braid Scots and the Sense of Smell* (from the *Scottish Nation*), my *Confessions of a Scottish Poet* (re-written from articles contributed to the *Glasgow Evening News*), notes on *Burns and Baudelaire, Byron as a Scottish Poet*, etc., and extracts from my regular contributions on *Welt-Literatur* to the *New Age* over a period of four years, including my critique of Gertrude Stein. The book will also contain much new matter specially written for it.

I should be extremely glad if you could consider an early publication of this book and in view of the letters which I have received, I think it ought to find a very good sale. In the event of your being willing to publish it, I could put the material together in the course of a very few days and send it on to you, but I should like a small advance payment (of say £25) on account of royalties.

As you have probably noticed my poems have been receiving increasing attention and in the opinion of many friends it would be a good idea now to put out a small volume of selected poems, drawing upon the four volumes you have published, *Annals of the Five Senses* and the *Lucky-Bag* (Porpoise Press) and my *First Hymn to Lenin and Other Poems* (published by the Unicorn Press) and Mr A. R. Orage, the former editor of *The New Age*, is anxious to write a detailed study of my work which could be used as a prefatory essay to a book of this kind. I am satisfied that if he did so, it would add considerably to the importance of the sales of the book in this country, and more particularly have a valuable effect in putting over my work in the United States of America, where Mr Orage is well-known and has very considerable influence as a critic. I should be extremely glad if your firm could see their way to put out a book of this kind and I can make the necessary arrangements with Mr Orage. Failing that I should like to come to an arrangement whereby the Unicorn Press can publish such a book, with an agreement for the paying to your firm of a certain commission in respect of those poems I should include which are derived from the four books of mine you have published.

I am enclosing a separate sheet[2] giving extracts from the opinions

---

Today', 'Faroese Holiday', 'Life in the Shetland Islands', 'The Burns Cult', 'The Case for Synthetic Scots', 'The Present Position of the Scottish Nationalist Movement', 'A Plan for the Unemployed'.

[2] The tributes were as follows:
Ever since I first heard of your poetry from Edwin Muir, and first dipped into *A Drunk Man* I have been keenly aware that you are one of the small number of poets of the European world. In particular – though this is but a detail – your

that have been expressed with regard to my work recently by three very well-known writers.

With best wishes,

Yours sincerely,
C. M. Grieve.

NLS
TS

321 High Holborn,
London, WC1.
27th January 1932

Messrs Wm. Blackwood & Sons Ltd,
Publishers,
George Street,
Edinburgh.

Dear Sirs,

I wrote you a week or so ago with regard to two matters. First, a question of putting out a volume of essays under the title of *At the Sign of the Thistle*, and second, with regard to a selected volume of my poems, culled from the various volumes published by you and from other sources as well as from unpublished material.

I hope you received the letter in question, but I should be glad to have your earliest possible reply in regard to these two matters. Circumstances necessitate that I must move as quickly as possible in these matters and get them fixed up as I must plan an intensive programme of work for a few months ahead and I cannot do so unless I come to a definite understanding with publishers and secure a certain small advance on account of royalties.

In addition to these two matters I have now in hand a new volume of poems to be entitled *Alone with the Alone*. This will consist for the

translation of Blok and Hippius are the only real re-creations of Russian poetry in England.
Prince D. S. Mirsky.

There are few living writers who can send me anything I am so keen to see.
Gordon Bottomley.

A poet of genius with wide intellectual interests. I find hardly any character in contemporary poetry so intellectually exciting.   A. E. (George Wm. Russell)

main of a single long poem,[1] prefaced by a prelude of some fifteen lyrics, the whole to be slightly smaller than *A Drunk Man Looks at the Thistle*. The fifteen lyrics in question I have now got and could send for your consideration as soon as you care. The long poem I have on the stocks, but if I can concentrate on it (and that all depends upon whether I can afford to do so for a week or two at this juncture) I can complete before the end of February.

If you care to publish this would the end of February be in time to enable you to issue the book this spring. I am very anxious it should appear this spring if possible and so follow up the publicity I have received in various quarters apropos my *First Hymn to Lenin* and other matters. I am sure that you will appreciate that just as in the case of *The Lucky Bag* (Porpoise Press) the fact that I had *The First Hymn to Lenin* published otherwise than by your firm, was simply because I regarded it as an interim work instead of a substantive production and felt that your firm had already done so much for me that it was to our mutual advantage in regard to minor works to divide the responsibility to some extent.

Kindest regards.

Yours sincerely,
C. M. Grieve.

CMG/JB

NLS   'Cootes',
Thakeham,
Sussex
16/7/32

Messrs Wm. Blackwood & Sons,
Publishers.

Dear Sirs:-

I appreciate very greatly the spirit in which you wrote to me some months ago with regard to my idea of putting out a volume of my Selected Poems, but although Messrs Victor Gollancz were prepared to do so I finally decided that it would be unfair to you since – as you pointed out – it would probably kill any further sales of my

---

[1] The long poem 'Depth and the Chthonian Image' (346–353) contains the phrase MacDiarmid intended for the title of this projected collection: 'You are at aince the road a' croods ha' gane/And alane wi' the alane.' It appeared in *Scots Unbound and Other Poems* (Stirling 1932).

books published by you.[1] I was also influenced by feeling that such a volume would be premature in view of the fact that during the past year I have written very considerably more poetry than all my previous work put together. The great bulk of this has not been published in periodicals or otherwise yet, but good judges who have seen parts of it regard it as far and away my best work. It is all part of a huge scheme[2] which I am steadily working out but I am not yet in a position to seek publication even for the first volume of this – although that already amounts to over 8000 lines. I am anxious however to issue a small book containing the very best of the short separable items from this mass of writing this autumn and I should be extremely glad if you are prepared to consider publishing it. The selection in question will consist of some twenty poems – two or three of them fairly long but the remainder short lyrics. All of them stand by themselves without reference to the big structure in which they will finally find their place; and unlike perhaps my *Hymns To Lenin* and other things which for political and other reasons you might not wish to issue, all these poems are free from politics and other questionable matters. The volume, which I propose to call *Scots Unbound, and Other Poems*, would be about the size of *Sangschaw* or *Penny Wheep*, and if you care to consider it I can send you the complete MSS at once.

With best wishes.

Yours sincerely,
C. M. Grieve.

P.S. On second thoughts to aid your judgement and give you an idea of the quality of the contents of the proposed volume I enclose herewith cuttings of the two of the poems which would appear in it, and also send you a photograph of the bronze head of me by William Lamb[3] which is in the current Royal Scottish Academy – and which I would propose to use as a frontispiece for the volume. (You may also find use for it for advertising purposes.)

[1] On 28 January 1932 Blackwood's wrote to MacDiarmid regretting that they could not accommodate his proposals: 'We think, therefore, that you should be free to handle your works in the way you suggest, making use of such portions of the volumes we have published as you may desire, although we fear that will mean practically the extinction of the sale of the books in our hands.'

[2] *Clann Albann*, MacDiarmid's projected autobiographical poem.

[3] As published, by Eneas Mackay of Stirling in a limited edition of 350 signed copies in 1932, *Scots Unbound and Other Poems* reproduced as a portrait frontispiece Lamb's bronze head of the poet. An Author's Note stated: 'The poems in this volume, like those in my *First Hymn to Lenin and Other Poems* (Unicorn Press, 1931) and *Second Hymn to Lenin* (Valda Trevlyn, Thakeham, 1932), are separable items from the first volume of my long poem, *Clann Albann*, now in preparation.'

To J. K. Annand

James King Annand (born 1908) was editor of *The Broughton Maga-zine* in 1925–6 and warmly welcomed MacDiarmid's *Sangschaw* in the December 1925 issue:

> Broughton has reason to be proud of her son and former Editor, C. M. Grieve, who, writing under the pseudonym of Hugh M'Diarmid, has just published a volume entitled *Sangschaw* . . . M'Diarmid's work, although an experiment in a new type of Scots poetry, is a complete success at the first venture. He has shown us that Scots is still a suitable, and a highly successful, medium of expression for all kinds of verse.

Annand then planned the Summer 1926 issue as a Braid Scots number in honour of *Sangschaw*; MacDiarmid, as the following letters show, was delighted to contribute to his old school magazine. Annand went on to make a reputation as a distinguished writer of Scots verse for children in his collections *Sing It Aince for Pleasure* (1965), *Twice for Joy* (1974) and *Thrice to Show Ye* (1979). He also edited *Early Lyrics* (Preston 1968) by Hugh MacDiarmid.

NLS

16 Links Avenue,
Montrose,
13th April, 1926

Dear Annand,

I was delighted to hear from you again, having had you (and Mr Ogilvie) pretty severely on my conscience for some time. Mr Ogilvie, of course, has long known how inexplicably hopeless a correspon-dent I am. In my usual way I allowed time to slip by before setting to to acknowledge the Xmas 'Mag' when I ought, of course, to have written per return to say how much I appreciated it and your great kindness to me. Especially should I have written to say how gladly I would do anything I could to help in the idea of a Broughton Poets' Number you mooted. Finally I did screw myself down to do these things but thereafter I carried my letter to you unposted in my pocket for weeks until it fell to pieces. Belatedly then let me thank you for the far too kind things you said of my own work and express my pleasure in finding in Broughton such an interest in the Scots Literary Movement we are trying to create.

You suggested in your last letter that I might send you something for the Summer issue. I have a new volume of lyrics coming out through Blackwood's almost at once – *Penny Wheep* – a bigger collection than *Sangschaw*. I enclose proofs of one or two poems[1] from it which have not appeared yet in any other periodical. You can use any of them if and as you care. My *Drunk Man* is coming out in the autumn. But it has grown greatly even since the quotations appeared in the *Herald*[2] and now stands upwards of 1200 lines. I enclose herewith also one poem from it which has not appeared anywhere else.

The Editorial[3] question is a difficult one. Any success I am having in Scots is due to my development of a flair for discovering the inherent & otherwise unsuspected capabilities of Scots terms for readaptation to vital uses – a knack of hitting upon ways of utilising them which is somehow indefinably but very clearly in accordance with their own nature. Mere wrenching – catechesis – or the inartistic employment of them (that is to say any use of them which does not justify itself completely in the result and make them somehow the inevitable media of whatever is effected through them) is hopeless. It is wonderful what a weight of out-of-the-way terminology one can carry along successfully in the current of a genuine poetic impulse or overcome by sheer concentration of effort towards finding its ideal use. It is along these lines and no other that Scots can be profitably used and no one should attempt to use it unless he finds English incapable of expressing what he wishes to express. At the same time, while this applies to any serious attempt to use Scots for literary ends, it is different with experimentation in a School Magazine & it is only by such experimentation as you propose probably that the profitable literary use of Scots can be renewed to any extent.

[1] 'Somersault' (47–8) and 'Parley of Beasts' (54) – both from *Penny Wheep* (1926) – appeared in *The Broughton Magazine*, Vol XIX, No 2, Summer 1926.

[2] The *Glasgow Herald* carried, on 17 December 1925, a note on *A Drunk Man Looks at the Thistle* and, on 13 February 1926, an article and six extracts from 'a gallimaufry in Braid Scots, entitled *A Drunk Man Looks at the Thistle*'.

[3] When Annand decided to have a Braid Scots number of *The Broughton Magazine*, to celebrate the publication of *Sangschaw* (1925), he felt he might have difficulty with an adequate Scots vocabulary of terms for literary criticism and asked Mac-Diarmid to direct him to a source. Annand accepted MacDiarmid's first suggestion.

The vocabulary or source such as you ask for exists, however. One has to acquire an adequate vocabulary by fitting in little bits from one quarter & little bits from another, with an eye open all the time to justifiable extensions of the previous use of terms of all kinds. The only thing I can suggest to get over the difficulty of the Editorial is the following alternative:-

1/ that you should write your Editorial in English and let me translate it for you into Scots

or

2/ that you should write it in Scots, and let me correct it.

I shall be happy to do either of these.

Both the little German translations[4] you send me are of interest. That is the way to train yourself to write in Scots – but keep your ear wide open all the time to make sure that you tolerate no avoidable incongruities. Pay at least as much attention to surety (dynamic inevitability) of movement as is paid in poetry in better-established media; don't let unconquered terms stick cacophonously out of the context – overcome them, make them pliable and responsive to your purpose. Save as a means to acquiring a knowledge of the language you can afterwards fuse with inspiration and make instinctive – capable of reflecting your psychology instead of obstructing the flow of meaning in anything you write like a lump of unlovely agglomerate – translating English or other poetry into Scots is hopeless if the method is only to hunt out terms in Scots which have some correspondence in *mere meaning* to those in the poem in question. In other words you must master the language *first*. Poetry cannot be written in any language save by a master of it. . . . And yet your translations are as good as a big percentage of the translations into English even of continental poetry. But you will not be discouraged, I know, or take it amiss, when I say that nevertheless they are not *really* good. To achieve poetry in any degree at all in Scots is extraordinarily difficult – to translate (i.e. reproduce) foreign poetry in Scots almost impossible. But I hope that to you & others as to me that very difficulty will prove a tyrannical incentive.

Accept my thanks & every good wish, & please convey the same to Mr Ogilvie who I trust is keeping stronger.

Yours,
C. M. Grieve

P.S. My *Contemporary Scottish Studies* are also appearing in book form in the autumn – through Leonard Parsons Ltd.

[4] Annand's translations, of Heine's 'Ein Fichtenbaum steht einsam' and Goethe's 'Der du von dem Himmel bist', appeared in the Summer 1926 issue of *The Broughton Magazine* over the initials K. B. R.

NLS

16 Links Avenue,
Montrose.
25/5/26

Dear Annand,

I should have written you some time ere this, too, but for the General Strike. I think you know my political position. Nothing ever so shook me to my foundations as this Strike – and the hellish Betrayal of its Collapse. I have been unable to think of anything else. Inter alia I have incorporated in my *Drunk Man* a long 'Ballad of the General Strike'[1] which I think will rank as one of the most passionate cris-de-coeur in contemporary literature. . . . Congratulations to yourself and the other FPs. on their Strike action, and, in particular, to Mackie.

I'll do the translating of the Editorial this week-end and let you have it in the beginning of next week. I hope that'll be in time for you. I can't manage earlier. As a matter of fact I scarcely know where I am or what to tackle first. I just let everything slide during the strike and now I am wallowing in accumulated arrears.

Yes. The *Herald* used the 'Hanging Judge'[2] after all. I had not expected them to do so. *Penny Wheep* should be out any day. It was all but out when the Strike started. It'll be good of you if you get in touch with Blackwood about a review of it, as you suggest – it'll be out long before 23rd June, & indeed I shall be surprised if the advance copies are not being distributed before you get this. The three poems[3] you mention will do splendidly: but if you would care for a hitherto unpublished poem to go along with them or instead of one of them just let me know and you'll have one by return – one of the *Drunk Man* ones. The *Drunk Man* is now almost in final shape, and runs to well over 2000 lines.

I'll be writing to Mr Ogilvie today or tomorrow too. He wanted me to suggest a longish poem for Verse Reading in Scots – but there is absolutely nothing yet in the least suitable – unless Nicholson's 'Aiken Drum'[4] – that I can think of. Another instance of the

---

[1] The ballad (119–22) anticipates MacDiarmid's passionately political poetry of the 1930s.

[2] 'The Hanging Judge' is the section of *A Drunk Man* beginning 'Grugous thistle, to my een' (156).

[3] Two of which were 'Somersault' (47–8) and 'Parley of Beasts' (54) which appeared in *The Broughton Magazine*, Summer 1926.

[4] MacDiarmid is probably thinking of William Nicholson's long poem *The Brownie of Bludnock* rather than the same poet's ballad 'Aiken Drum'.

innumerable lacunae in our corpus which I'm looking to see Mackie
& you & others helping to fill yet.

Yours,
C. M. Grieve.

NLS

16 Links Avenue,
Montrose.
2nd June, 1926

My dear Annand,

Herewith translation, and your original. I am very sensible of
your kindness to me in all this, and am looking eagerly forward to the
issue. Be sure and keep aside a number of copies for me. There are
several people to whom I shall want to send one.

No more just now! I'm just scrawling this off in haste, as I've been
too long in letting you have this already. But I've been living in an
awful rush these past few weeks.

I enclose a poem just written[1] in case you *do* want one to the
Magazine's very own cheek. But, if not, or if it's too late, or otherwise
unsuitable, never mind.

Best wishes,

Yours,
C. M. Grieve.

[1] The poem was 'Yet ha'e I Silence left, the croon o' a'' (166–7), the conclusion of *A
Drunk Man Looks at the Thistle*. It arrived too late for inclusion in the Summer issue
of *The Broughton Magazine*.

NLS   Brownsbank,
                                                             Biggar.
                                                             17/12/69

J. K. Annand, Esq

Dear Jim,

   I've sent off the letter[1] as requested to RAMC Records – but with
some dubiety as to the wisdom of doing so. For I demobilised myself
– and Records won't have any note of that, I think. In any case
during the last 9 months of the War I was detached from the RAMC
and attached to the Indian Medical Service. Still, we'll see what
RAMC Records have to say. I'll send on their reply to you.

   I need not tell you I'll be very pleased to answer any questions re
my chequered career you wish to ask – in so far as I can. There are
certainly plenty of errors current about various points – and as you
say I'm not too reliable myself about some of them. However we'll do
our best.

   I'm keeping all right physically but still quite unable to make up
the really hopeless arrears in my correspondence or address myself
to the various books I should have written and delivered to the
publishers weeks, or months, ago and have in fact hardly begun yet.
I've developed an extreme allergy to paper and ink! The trouble, I
think, is simply I have far too many things going on in my head at
once and can't find outlets for them.

   We'll see what 1970 brings. I hope this finds Paddy[2] and you both
O.K. and Valda joins me in wishing you both a Merry Christmas
and a happy and prosperous New Year.

                              Yours,
                              Christopher Grieve.

[1] When preparing his article 'Hugh MacDiarmid: Some notes on the poet's early
   career' for *Akros 14* (April 1970) Annand wanted to clear up conflicting statements
   about MacDiarmid's army career, especially the date of demobilisation. Annand
   typed a letter requesting information from Army Records and asked MacDiarmid
   to sign and post it in the sae supplied. Annand adds, in a letter of 20 August 1982
   to the present editor, 'He agreed to sign and post, but in spite of the statement in
   his letter of 17/12/69, I do not believe he did so.'
[2] Paddy, J. K. Annand's wife.

NLS

Brownsbank,
Biggar.
6/1/70
new 'phone number:- Skirling 255

J. K. Annand, Esq

Dear Jim:-

Many thanks for copy of your *Akros* article[1] rectifying some of the particulars re my chequered career.

The *Monmouthshire Labour News*, run by the South Wales Miners Federation, ceased publication. That was the reason I left Ebbw Vale and returned to Scotland. My services were not dispensed with.

My next job was on *The Clydebank and Renfrew Press* – one of a group of local papers (*The Southern Press*, *The Govan Press* etc) published by the printing firm of Cossar, Govan, but the one I was on was run from Clydebank and I was located there. I contributed to the other papers of the group but my reportorial duties were confined to the Clydebank area. My brother had nothing to do with getting me my next job – in Cupar Fife, where Messrs Innes ran *The Fife Herald*, the *St Andrews Citizen*, and the *Fife Coast Chronicle* for all of which I was chief reporter. My brother was in the Inland Revenue Office in Cupar, but he and I never got on together.[2]

Then came *The Forfar Review* and – after I was demobbed – *The Montrose Review*.

I had been in the RAMC (Territorial) which I joined in 1908, so it was natural that on joining the Army in 1915 I joined the RAMC. I got rapid promotion and was successively Sergt, Staff Sergt, and Quarter-Master-Sgt. But on being sent to Aldershot for posting overseas I had to revert to Sergeant, which was my substantive rank, the QMS being only an acting rank. I went out to Salonika with a complete General Hospital, the 42nd General Hospital, all the doctors, nurses, and most of the rank-and-file being Scots.

I was invalided home in 1918, served as depot Sergts' Mess Caterer at Blackpool in August 1918, and had married my first wife in June 1918 while on convalescent leave. She died in July 1962.

The trouble about service in Italy arises from the fact that I was in

---

[1] Annand's article, 'Hugh MacDiarmid: Some notes on the poet's early career', appeared in *Akros 14*, April 1970.

[2] In a letter of 20 August 1982 to the present editor Annand comments: 'His remarks about his brother do not tally with his account in letters to Ogilvie. His brother Andrew did a great deal for him. I had confirmation of this from an old lady who lived in Cupar at that time. Andrew was in a civil service job in Cupar. It was at Cupar too that he met his future wife, Margaret Skinner.'

charge of a company of 1000 soldiers from Salonika invalided home. That is, technically, while in Italy I was 'on active service'. As you remark my memory is not too good in certain respects, but I must have been in Italy again since I certainly visited Genoa and Faenza, and that was not on my invalid train passage through: but I can't for the life of me remember how I got to these places. Incidentally, the invalid train took 13 days and nights to carry us from Taranto in Italy to Le Havre, as we were shunted into sidings and left there for hours and occasionally whole days.

As to demob. I was in camp at Dieppe when the Armistice was declared, and then I was attached to the Indian Medical Service and posted to Sections Lahore Indian General Hospital at Chateau Mirabeau, Estaque, Marseilles where I spent the next nine months – finally as I told you demobilising myself. I ought to have gone to Ripon for demob. but at that time there were proposals that married soldiers who had had malaria should not be demobbed for a year or so, and some of us were determined to get out of it by hook or crook. I went to St Andrews where my wife was living and that is probably why I thought I'd been demobbed in 1920, for I was certainly only a very short time in St Andrews before I got the Montrose job.

The Kildermorie Side School (that is what it was officially called) job was under the Ross and Cromarty Education Authority and subject to Inspection. I had four pupils – two, as you say, children of the Head Stalker, and the other two children of other stalkers. Boath, the nearest village, was eleven miles away.

Most of *Annals of the Five Senses* was written in Salonika and only put together – and finally published – after demob.

All the best to Paddy and you for 1970, from Valda and I.

Yours,
Chris

P.S. I'm returning the typescript in case you need it.

Brownsbank
11th Sept. '70

Dear Jim Annand,

Many thanks for your letter re the Ogilivie correspondence.[1] I have no objection to your going ahead and having these letters published – but I must see them first and know what exactly is in them. There may be things in them I would find embarrassing or that are liable to misunderstanding without explanations by myself. All my affairs are now being gone through with a small tooth comb by all sorts of people in this and other countries, and many of these people have a point of view not at all compatible with my own. A case in point is that David Craig and John Manson – the editors of the forthcoming Penguin paperback of my *Selected Poems* – have been busy digging out from old periodicals etc all sorts of uncollected poems of mine which I purposely did not include in my *Collected Poems* or *More Collected Poems* for the simple reason that I consider them far below the standard of the best lyrics in *Sangschaw*, *Penny Wheep*, and *A Drunk Man*. They made a big collection and have certainly put a great deal of work into their self-imposed task. I have now obtained from them the text of all these poems – and I am simply appalled. It will do me, or any one else, no good whatever to have this stuff reprinted, and I must refuse. In the *Times Lit* and elsewhere Craig and Manson have already proclaimed that these poems belong to the same vintage as my best Scots lyrics which is absolute rubbish, and they contrast them with the very different kind of poetry I have been writing during the past 30 years and prefer them immensely. This is a matter that will of course be debated for years – but I prefer that happens after my demise and does not complicate my present position. I have no idea what the bearings of anything I say in these letters to Cholly[2] may have in such connections, but I think you will understand I must make sure before anything is done. As matters stand I am in arrears with all manner of books I have to write and I am much more concerned with expressing things from my present standpoint than with the reprinting of things written years ago from a standpoint I have long since completely abandoned. Also in addition to all the work I am saddled with – and that will certainly take me several years now to do: if I do manage to do it all – I have imminent visits to Italy,

---

[1] Annand quoted from the letters to Ogilvie in his informative introduction to his edition of MacDiarmid's *Early Lyrics* (Preston 1968) and intended for some time to do an edition of the Ogilvie letters.
[2] Cholly, Ogilvie's nickname.

Israel, and Canada to cope with so my time is very badly mortgaged.

So, please, before you do any more, can you let me have the complete text of the letters in question and once I have read and considered them I will be able to tell you what I think. Do not misunderstand this. I appreciate all you have done and the amount of work annotation, etc. must have entailed.

I hope you are O.K. again so far as health is concerned. I had a nasty time recently. The lower parts of my legs became very badly and painfully inflamed and broke out into sores and swellings. I got the doctor and the first thing he asked me was if I had been in long grass recently. Now I do not go tramping about and am in fact little outside at all. Then I remembered that Isabel McCaig[3] drove me home one night from Edinburgh and in parking her car missed the cindery patch and got into long grass. It had been heavy rain and the grass was very wet, so the car stalled and she could not get it off. I went out to help, i.e. try to shove the car. Apparently I was allergic to something – the Doctor thought some small insect in the grass. However I got some tablets and some ointment and the thing cleared away.

All the best to Paddy and you from Valda and I.

Yours,
Chris

NLS

Brownsbank,
Biggar,
4/10/71

Dear Jim,

Many thanks for the copy of the *Elegie*[1] – most attractively produced and bound. The Scots of your translation reads very well indeed. This is, indeed, a very worth-while bit of work. It tak's mony a meikle to mak' a muckle, and this opusculum will go to build up the

[3] Isabel MacCaig is the wife of the poet Norman MacCaig.
[1] Annand's translation of Ronsard's *Elegie on the Depairture o Mary Queen o Scots on her retour til her Kinrick o Scotland* was produced on a duplicating machine; twenty copies were bound in cloth boards by Annand who distributed these in 1971. The translation is reprinted in Annand's *Poems and Translations* (1975).

revived interest in Scottish history and literature. Congratulations and best wishes.

These prostatectomy operations such as I had can't be got over in a hurry. All the doctors say that very often men who undergo them have a new lease of life, and the last medico I had here said that I might well live to 100. You should have heard Valda's jaw drop when she heard that. After all the poor woman has put up with me for 40 years – and the prospect of another 20 was a bit too much for her!

As I think you know I've cancelled all my American and Canadian programme and for some time ahead won't be taking on anything I can possible avoid. I'm well enough in general, but some of my organs are still reluctant to resume their proper functions, so I've to ca' very canny indeed.

Every kind regard to Paddy and you from Valda and I.

Yours,
Chris.

NLS

Brownsbank,
Candymill,
Biggar,
4/12/73

Dear Jim,

Many thanks for the Lallans magazine and for your latest book of poems.[1] We have been away – in London, Ewell, Oxford, and since returning to Scotland, in Glasgow, and are going off in a day or so to Ireland, where I have engagements in Dublin and Cork.

I greatly enjoyed my visits to Firrhill and Broughton Schools.[2]
The Lallans magazine has made, I think, an excellent beginning.

---

[1] *Lallans* was launched in 1973 as a periodical, edited by J. K. Annand and published by the Scots Language Society, devoted to the study of Scots writing. The new book of poems was Annand's *Twice for Joy* (1974).

[2] Annand taught at Firrhill School from 1962 until 1971. In 1973 he chaired a meeting at which MacDiarmid addressed Firrhill pupils. In the same afternoon Annand took MacDiarmid down to Broughton School to meet the headmaster, staff and senior pupils.

The only thing I personally objected to was Dr Templeton's insistence on Scots as it is spoken.[3] She seemed to belittle my 'synthetic Scots' as artificial. It is the old business of folk-song revivalists regarding the folk-lore song originals as somehow more natural and more desirable than art-song. This is, of course, rubbish. All literatures evolved by moving away from the grass roots and evolving higher forms of literary expression. I know no literature of any value that uses the language in which it is written as that language is used by the man in the street. All living languages add to their vocabularies by importing words from other languages, or from scientific and other specialised vocabularies, or by inventing new words. And certainly I myself have no interest whatever in writing for the minimally literate, and I would not be associated with the Lallans Movement if, as Dr Templeton claims, its chief, if not its only, concern is with Scots as it is spoken.

I enjoyed meeting you again in Edinburgh and was glad to find you looking so 'chuff'!

Valda joins me in kindest regards to Paddy and you – and to your clever granddaughter[4] who drew the illustrations for you.

Christmas will be on us before we get back from Ireland, so here's wishing Paddy and you and all your children and grandchildren, a happy Christmas and good New Year.

Yours,
Chris

P.S. I was sorry I couldn't accept the Ramsay Head Press's invitation to the function marking their publication of Albert Mackie's two books[5] – which, of course, I'll buy. I hope the affair went off well and that Bert is in good form.

---

[3] The first issue of *Lallans* contained an article by Janet M. Templeton asserting that 'It is natural, grass-roots Scots that the Lallans Society aims to encourage.'
[4] Annand's grand-daughter, Claire Mutch, illustrated *Twice for Joy*.
[5] Mackie's two books are *The Scotch Comedians* and *Scotch Whisky Drinker's Companion*.

To Oliver St John Gogarty

Like James Joyce, who portrayed him as 'Stately, plump Buck Mulligan' in *Ulysses* (1922), Oliver St John Gogarty (1878–1957) was born in Dublin but whereas Joyce chose 'Silence, cunning and exile' Gogarty acquired status, success and respectability. His wealthy parents sent him to Trinity College and, like Mulligan, he studied medicine and stayed in the Martello Tower at Sandycove, near Dublin. Because of his financial advantages he tended to patronise Joyce and encouraged him to drink heavily; yet he sensed that Joyce's literary talent was greater than his own. After Joyce left Ireland, Gogarty pursued a distinguished career as a surgeon. In 1922 he was made a Senator of the Irish Free State but the same year *Ulysses* appeared and Gogarty grew to resent Joyce's international celebrity. When his country adopted the name Eire in 1936 Gogarty expressed his disapproval of new political developments and three years later he moved to the USA. His own works include the witty prose of *As I Was Going Down Sackville Street* (1937) and *Tumbling in the Hay* (1939) and the verse of *Collected Poems* (1952).

Gogarty was an enthusiastic champion of MacDiarmid's poetry and his eulogy of *A Drunk Man Looks at the Thistle*, in *The Irish Statesman* of 8 January 1927, greatly encouraged the embattled Scottish poet. As one of the organisers of the Tailltean Games, Gogarty invited distinguished writers such as MacDiarmid to Ireland. MacDiarmid wrote (Company, p. 192):

> I owed a very great deal indeed to Dr Oliver St John Gogarty and to A.E. (George W. Russell). Gogarty took me round the pubs in Dublin he and Joyce used to frequent when they were medical students. I stayed when in Dublin at Gogarty's house in Ely Place, and through him met Walter Starkie, Eoin McNeill, and many others . . . It was through Gogarty and A.E. that I met Yeats, at A.E.'s house.

373

ECB

16 Links Avenue,
Montrose.
7/3/28

Dear Senator Gogarty,

Many thanks for yours of 4th inst. – a tonic to a man recovering from a dose of 'flu and inclined to feel that he had never done anything worth doing and never would. A flight to Paris[1] would do me a world of good – only I wouldn't want to come back – for a while anyway. I've been too long in Scotland without a break and am staled with hack-work. But the possibility of a trip to Dublin ere long is a stimulating notion. To meet A.E., and F.S. Higgins and yourself and one or two others would take me out of myself for a little with excellent effect. In the meantime (although I am at the stage when I am so concentrated on doing infinitely better that I cannot tolerate anything I have already written) it is thoroughly encouraging to find my work so extraordinarily appreciated in such unexpected quarters. Compton Mackenzie, the novelist, for example, in the *Pictish Review*[2] the other month said that he had so high an opinion of Mr Grieve's poetic genius that he thought it might even encompass the feat of recreating the Scottish nation yet!! I haven't been able to write a line since. The responsibility is too great!

I haven't seen Wyndham Lewis's book on Villon yet: but I will certainly be on the look-out for it – not because of his regard for M'Diarmid in itself but because it is just the type of man who would write a good book on Villon that I would expect to like some of my work and to help me – even through what he says of Villon – to understand myself a little better.

But the most revivifying thing in your letter is the compliment of suggesting that I might 'distinguish and divide' your *Wild Apples*.[3] I do not feel at all competent to undertake the duty in question. But I

---

[1] In a letter of 4 March 1928 Gogarty told MacDiarmid: 'I flew to Paris on last Saturday week back and there I met D. B. Wyndham Lewis the *Daily Mail* contributor who has recently written a fine book on Villon. When we were speaking of Scots Poetry he said of Hugh McDiarmid "He is greater than Burns."'

[2] In the *Pictish Review*, Vol 1, No 4, February 1928, Compton Mackenzie's article 'Towards a Scottish Idea' responded to Grieve's cultural programme for Scotland.

[3] Gogarty's collection *Wild Apples* was first issued in a limited edition by the Cuala Press of Dublin in 1928. On 4 March 1928 Gogarty wrote MacDiarmid: 'I have a book for the Cuala Press *Wild Apples* which requires weeding out and I have no one to prune me. I want 50 copies privately printed. If I can get it into type probably you could select 20 or so and send them back soon.'

shall, of course, be delighted to render you any service I possibly can and to give you my frank and reasoned opinions. And you may be perfectly certain that I shall take no umbrage whatever if you disregard my advice entirely. You shall simply have my best attention to the matter in question for whatever it may be worth: and you can rely upon me to return the poems promptly.

For myself – although I may prefer this one to that – I anticipate a treat, and a hard task, not in preferring these but in discarding those. With every good wish.

Yours,
C. M. Grieve.

ECB   16 Links Avenue,
Montrose.
22.5.1928

Dear Senator Gogarty:-

It was extremely good of you to include me in the happy half-hundred.[1] Your *Wild Apples* certainly make almost all the verse I have encountered for ages intolerably tame and insipid. How glad I am I did not require to try to do any picking and choosing amongst such fruit! It reminds me of the saying that there is no bad whisky – only some better than the rest (i.e. 'The Crab Tree', 'Corn from Syracuse', 'Portrait with Background' and 'To George Redding'). But I have enjoyed them all. They are true fruit of the tree depicted – so perfectly – in the first: and have a most distinctive – sharp and health-giving – savour. To vary the metaphor, they are the salt which the porridge of modern poetry so greatly needs: original, brave, picturesque and eminently lovable stuff – 'a man speaking'.

I am sorry to have taken a week or two to acknowledge them. As a matter of fact I read them through on arrival (as repeatedly since): and they induced a set of verses, which I had intended sending you long ere this, but cannot now lay my hands upon – or remember. I am in a state of chaos: very busy with all manner of things I'd fain not have to do, and, at the same time, up to the eyes in a huge new

---

[1] MacDiarmid was sent one of the copies of the limited edition of *Wild Apples*.

poem[2] which will knock the *Drunk Man* into a cocked hat. I'd give anything to be able to do nothing else but let it rip for the next six months: it needs getting down to far more systematically and concentratedly than I can manage. However, the vexatious thoughts and delays of external circumstance may not be all to the bad – if I could only get the effect the one is really having upon the other into proper perspective. Over and above these conflicting aspects of a dual life domestic affairs have had an important place – thanks to the arrival of a son and heir, to whom Compton Mackenzie stood godfather the other Sunday. He spent the week-end here and is now off to Iona. We were talking of your poems – he also having received a copy of your book – and were at one in a very keen and high appreciation of them. How curious that two of your fifty readers should foregather in this insignificant little Scots burgh!

I owe to you, too, the invitation, received yesterday, to attend the Tailltean Games, and mean by hook or crook to do so. I shall look forward to my birthday on 11th August with a very unusual keenness this year.

> Every good wish.
> Yours,
> C. M. Grieve.

ECB   16.11.28

My dear Gogarty,

I am sorry to have been so long in writing: but as you've probably seen there has been a saltatory development of Scottish Nationalism,[1] and what with the Glasgow Rectorial, big meetings in Glasgow, Dundee, Perth, etc. I have been absolutely up to the eyes in it. The Scottish papers are full of it – scarcely one of them 'll mention my name, and none of them 'll print even a letter to the Editor from me on any political matter (all the main ones boycott even my literary articles or poems): but they all know that I am the fons et origo of this whole business and that the Movement has now a

[2] *To Circumjack Cencrastus* (Edinburgh 1930).
[1] MacDiarmid was one of the founders of the National Party of Scotland which was inaugurated on 23 June 1928.

headway on it nothing can stop. But even to all but a little group inside the Movement itself I'm just selling spectacles to the blind – all the rest are in it for hopelessly wrong ideas or the lack of any. However – it'll all come out in the wash.

I needn't tell you how grateful I am to you – and to Mrs Gogarty and 'A.E.' – for your efforts via Rothermere[2] and subsequently Jeffries on my behalf. It would have been amusing if it had come off. It may yet – but now, I'm not sure I want it to. You'd see perhaps that in today's *Daily Mail* a column is given to a Scottish Woman Poet (a friend of mine, Miss Angus)[3] and after that my monstrous egoism feels that an article on Hugh M'Diarmid in the same quarter would be as if – dealing with contemporary Irish Poets – they'd done Miss Letts[4] and then Yeats: or (a better parallel) as T. S. Eliot or Sacheverell Sitwell would feel if an article on them had succeeded an equally eulogistic one on, say, Ella Wheeler Wilcox or Alfred Noyes. I'm not feeling jealous or peeved – it's only a question of relative values. Miss Angus is a friend of mine: and I gave her her first 'boost' and several subsequent ones – but she is not an original poet, and her work is very small and thin. However – once again – it'll all come out in the wash.

But I am very conscious of your kindness and the great trouble you have put yourself to in this matter. I owe a great deal more than that to you; but for your *Irish Statesman* review of the *Drunk Man*[5] I don't know that I would have 'continued poet' at all, and certainly it was the great treat of my Dublin visit that gave me the necessary impetus to go forward with my new big poem *Cencrastus*, which is developing splendidly. I don't care a rap what the *Daily Mail* or any other paper or periodical – or public opinion – says or doesn't say, good or bad, about me and my work really: I only respect the opinion, and care for the pleasure of a few friends. And it isn't 'boosting' I want – except in so far as that might conduce to give me what I really need – viz, slightly better economic conditions in which to continue my work. I am really just hanging on by my eyelids. There isn't a paper in Scotland which would give me a job as a reporter even, let alone on the literary side; they won't even give me a little book-reviewing to augment my income by an occasional

2 Harold Sidney Harmsworth, Lord Rothermere (1868-1940).
3 Marion Angus (1866–1946) whose Scots poems, in *The Lilt* (1922) and *The Tinker's Road* (1924) for example, represented the sentimental style of vernacular verse that obtained before MacDiarmid.
4 Winifred M. Letts was a minor Irish poet whose *More Songs from Leinster* appeared in 1926.
5 Gogarty's review of *A Drunk Man*, in *The Irish Statesman*, Vol 7, No 18, 8 January 1927, praised the poem for letting 'the present-day soul of Scotland speak out with its metaphysic, its politic and its poetry.'

guinea. And as a reporter on any of the dailies I'd have almost double what I have here as an editor-reporter-and-general-knockabout, and far less work and far more time to myself. It is almost incredible. I feel myself as if I were living in a bad dream and that all my preposterous monetary worries will suddenly vanish and leave me in at least as secure and well-paid a position as some hundreds of other Scottish journalists with no pretensions to any brains – and no brains to pretend to. But, of course, that won't happen and I must just 'warsel on': and – in my better moments – I am conscious that that has its advantages too (for me – if not for Mrs Grieve and the bairns).

How about 'Transatlantic Winds'?

Remind me to 'A.E.' and all friends

I enclose a couple of snapshots: I'm afraid they're not very good: but they're all I can lay my hands on at the moment.

Yours,
C. M. Grieve.

The other man in one of the snaps is F. G. Scott.

ECB

16 Links Avenue,
Montrose.
30.5.29

My dear Gogarty,

I have a recollection in my mind that you were going to Germany about this time to do some flying. Perhaps it was earlier? But I'm writing, because I'm going to the International PEN Congress in Vienna (June 24th to 29th) via Ostend, Cologne and Wurzburg: and if you are in Germany might have a chance of half-an-hour with you.

The Vienna programme is very attractive – includes trips to Semmering and Rax Mountains, and to the Wachau, returning by steamer down the Danube: also an aeroplane trip over Vienna which (since you whetted my appetite) I'll take care not to miss.

How about the Atlantic Flight poem? I've always been hoping it would come to hand. I've written piles of stuff myself and am hoping to get my *Cencrastus* into final shape for autumn publication.

I've translated a Spanish novel too – *La Esclava del Senor*[1] by Ramon Maria Tenreiro (the one I spoke to Dr Walter Starkie about at your house), which Martin Secker will be publishing almost immediately.

I trust you – and Mrs Gogarty and your son and daughter – are all happy and well.

Yours,
C. M. Grieve.

ECB

'Vox',
10A Soho Square,
London, W1.
30.12.29

My dear Gogarty,

This is just a belated note to hope you and yours had a happy Christmas and – perhaps in time even yet – to wish you all happiness and prosperity in the New Year.

And not the letter I owe you and have been intending to write for ages.

My new job here kept me so infernally busy for a while that I kept on postponing writing, and then, about four weeks ago, (as A.E. may have told you) I was hurled from the top of a double-decker motor 'bus and sustained severe concussion. I have made a wonderful recovery. Happily my skull was not fractured, largely owing to my great cushion of hair, I fancy, and to the fact that

it takes a lot
to rattle a Scot.

But it was a narrow squeak and I am told that I must avoid mental stress and excitement, alcoholic stimulants, spiced foods, and even tobacco (but the latter I disregard as a mere General Practitioner's convention) under penalty of risking brain fever or a cerebral haemorrhage, for some considerable time to come.

A pleasant prospect and me eager to put my new poems into final shape and start to others.

[1] Ramon Maria de Tenreiro, *The Handmaid of the Lord* (London 1935).

But there it is, and these are the reasons why I've been so long in writing you.

I hope this finds you in the best of form and all going well with all of you.

Yours,
C. M. Grieve.

ECB
TS

'Vox',
10A Soho Square,
London W1.
3rd January 1930

My dear Gogarty,

I need not tell you either how vexed I was to miss you on Wednesday or that to have seen you again would in itself have given me the happy New Year you wished me. But the year has a long time to run and I shall hope in the course of it to see you yet. My wife was disappointed too; she has heard so much of you and thought she was going to see you at last.

But my vexation was increased when I got back to *Vox* office. You must have thought me curiously disjointed and incoherent on the 'phone; the trouble was 1. that I got a bad line in a perfect pandemonium of a big printing works, and 2. that my silly head is still very easily rattled. Consequently I could only catch bits of what you were saying. But if you had got through to me the first time you had 'phoned I could have popped into a taxi and got round to you in a few minutes, and easily have had half-an-hour or so with you without prejudice to seeing the current issue of *Vox* safely to bed. So I have added the fact of your first call not finding me to the list of grudges I have against telephone people, as the crowning enormity of them all, and been cursing with vigour ever since.

And to think of you having a cup of tea for your lunch on New Year's Day! It doesn't bear thinking of – tho' I was in the same sad straits myself, all alcoholic stimulants being strictly forbidden me still!

I was greatly interested in what you said about Lord Beaverbrook – for his Scottish *Daily Express* gets most of its articles on Scottish subjects from a group of pet enemies of mine; nit-wits like Rosslyn Mitchell and Hugh Roberton[1] and the like, churning out the stupid old Scotch fudge. On the other hand, papers like *The Glasgow Herald* and *Scotsman*, which shook in their shoes when the *Express* entered the Scottish field, are thereby greatly relieved. They knew that in re specifically Scottish subjects they had nothing to fear – and need not attempt to improve their own fatuous handling of them – so long as the *Express* was only drawing upon the same stale idea-less old clique of contributors. With all due modesty I flatter myself the situation would have been very different if I had been contributing regularly to the *Express* on such topics; it wouldn't have been just the same old thing hashed up once more.

Messrs Bumpus sent the books yesterday and I autographed them and dispatched them to Lord Beaverbrook. I sent a note to him saying that at your request I had done so, with great pleasure, and, being not unmindful of his own Scottish connections, wondered if he would care to accept from me copies of my *Contemporary Scottish Studies*, pamphlet on *The Present Condition of Scottish Arts and Affairs*[2], etc., which I thought might be of some little interest to him as bearing upon current Scottish issues in view of his admirable Scottish edition of the *Express*.

You asked about my poem. The big poem[3] ought to have been finished ere this but I have kept re-arranging it, and am not yet satisfied. It is a whale of a thing and I am anxious to manipulate it in the most effective final form. But I don't think it'll be long now; and as soon as I have it ship-shape I'll have it typed in duplicate and send you a copy.

I have another volume of poems of various sizes; but Blackwood's wouldn't publish it – mainly I think because certain poems in it offended that very conservative old firm a. politically b. morally. But it contains some of my best work, and I'm trying to arrange with the Porpoise Press (another Edinburgh firm) for its early publication, and also for the publication of a small volume of short stories and plays.[4]

---

[1] Rosslyn Mitchell was a Scottish journalist whose *Passing By* (Edinburgh 1935) collected articles contributed to *The Daily Record*. Hugh S. Roberton, (1874–1952) the founder (in 1906) of the Glasgow Orpheus Choir, was also a journalist whose contributions to *The Daily Express*, *The Daily Record*, *Glasgow Evening News* were collected in *Curdies* (London 1931).

[2] *The Present Condition of Scottish Arts and Affairs* (Dalbeattie 1928) was issued as an anonymous pamphlet by the Committee of the Scottish Centre of the PEN Club.

[3] *To Circumjack Cencrastus* (Edinburgh 1930).

[4] Although Porpoise Press did not issue MacDiarmid's projected 'volume of poems of various sizes' – provisionally entitled *Fier Comme Un Ecossais* – the firm did print a second impression of *Annals of the Five Senses* in 1930.

How about yourself? I'm hoping something more of yours will be coming along soon. I've been trying to arrange to do an article about you for the *Bookman*, but the Editor has been on holiday and while they have just taken another article of mine I haven't heard from them about my suggested article on you yet.

I'm doing a hefty amount of journalism of all kinds for a score of different papers and periodicals (in addition to *Vox*) and at the moment am in the throes of doing a special batch of Burns' articles in readiness for the 25th. One of these will appear in *The Radio Times*[5] (which has a circulation of 1¾ million), and I'll send you a copy.

All success to the hotel which I am confident will be one of the most delightful 'howffs' imaginable.

Once again every good wish for the New Year to Mrs Gogarty, your son and daughter, and yourself.

                    Yours,
                    C. M. Grieve.

ECB   18 Pyrland Road,
TS   London, N5.
                                          7th January 1930

My dear Gogarty

I have your two kind letters. I mentioned about the reading or reciting of Dr Bridge's poem, as requested, to Major Stone and, when writing to Mackenzie yesterday, quoted the portion of your letter in question.[1]

This is just a note to say that I do know Maxton and practically all the Scottish Socialist MPs and leading workers in the Labour and Socialist Movement throughout Scotland and am very friendly with many of them still despite my differences of opinion, and certainly in a position to get all kinds of exclusive inside information, and meet any of them personally at any time under intimate conditions. As you know, I was for several years a very active Socialist propa-

[5] C. M. Grieve's article on Burns ('Scotsmen Make a God of Robert Burns') appeared in the *Radio Times*, 17 January 1930.
[1] Christopher Stone was London Editor of Compton Mackenzie's magazine *The Gramophone*.

gandist and a Socialist member of Town and Parish Councils and other public bodies. But my views have changed very considerably and on the whole I think I can now best be described as a 'crusted old Tory'. I have had, in any case, sufficient experience of political movements not only to understand your attitude to politics and exonerate you, but I am afraid to share it myself.

The Porpoise Press are, I think, going to publish in the early spring a new volume of poems of mine (mostly short ones but including one considerably lengthy one) under the title of *Fier Comme un Ecossais* and I am having the MS typed to send on to them this week. While doing so, I shall have it done in duplicate and send you the other copy.

Excuse this hasty note. I will write you again very soon. In view of what you say with regard to the need for caution and avoiding stimulants &c., I shall certainly be cautious for some time yet. Love to all.

> Yours,
> C. M. Grieve.

ECB
TS

'Vox',
10A Soho Square,
London W1.
16th January, 1930.

My dear Gogarty,

Many thanks for yours of 14th inst. What you say of the 'Great mirth which must be behind the Jest of Creation' and the 'laugh not the logos' you will find repeated curiously enough, in my own way, in some of the poems in *Another Window In Thrums* e.g.

'That great hippodrome Hereafter . . . .
Wi' Lauder's kilt and Chaplin's feet
Supernumerary to the Paraclete' . . . .

and

'Owre nice for Lauder, and for God.'[1]

---

[1] The lines (248) appeared in *To Circumjack Cencrastus* (Edinburgh 1930).

Another Window in Thrums as it appears in this typescript is an extract from a much bigger mass of verse which constituted an early draft of my big poem, *Cencrastus*. But I found a much better (and far more direct) way of dealing with *Cencrastus* and as it ultimately appears it will bear no resemblance whatever to this early draft. I will send you a typescript of *Cencrastus* in its new form – as far as I have gone with it – very soon.

Let me know what you think of this lot.

That reminds me. You will see I've dedicated the little collection to Compton Mackenzie and yourself. Please may I?

Yours,
C. M. Grieve.

P.S. *Vox* is doing (everything considered) very well – but not well enough to carry our heavy overhead. There is no question but that it will make good if only it can hold out till we turn the corner and are getting an adequate advertisement revenue – but the question is whether we can hold out or not. I'm worried about it, for if we can't and *Vox* has to cease publication, I'll be in a fix right enough that'll take all my fighting spirit. And the trouble is that I've had a stiff fight for too long as it is: and want an easier time (i.e. not easier so far as work and responsibility goes, but so far as security goes). That's why I am hoping so much that Lord Beaverbrook will take a fancy to me.

ECB

18 Pyrland Road,
N5.
17/3/30

My dear Gogarty,

I have been wondering what has happened to you: and whether you saw Lord Beaverbrook or not. Perhaps he has been too entirely 'wrapt up' in politics to have any concern with the details of journalism. A very promising opening influential friends discerned for me – to do the London letter for the Aberdeen *Press and Journal* – was shut with a bang as soon as the matter was referred to the Aberdeen editor, solely on account of my reputation as a Scottish Nationalist. John Buchan and others had been so sure of my getting

384

this that they had ceased efforts in other directions: but they are resuming them again. There is very little offering, however. I do hope something will emerge soon or I shall be in Queer Street with a vengeance. I had a very nice meeting with Mr Cape[1]: and, on his suggestion, wrote a first chapter of my Burns' book and a full plan of the remainder. But I have just heard from him that he cannot see his way to commission the work but if I care to complete it and submit it to him will 'consider it with every prejudice in its favour'. I am going to go right ahead with it: but I do not work well under conditions of difficulty and uncertainty. However, we'll see.

I have had the pleasure recently of introducing several discriminating friends of mine to your poems – to their great delight in every case. Amongst them were Edwin Muir, the critic, and his wife, and they were tremendously taken with 'The Plum Tree by the House' (to the exquisite beauty – and the 'great deal more in it than appears on the surface' – of which I have not already testified but do so now with my heartiest congratulations), and, of course, 'Golden Stockings'.

The *Everyman* people haven't published my article on you yet, but it will be in any week now.[2] It should have appeared before this, of course, but that's the worst of free-lance work – it's so infernally precarious.

Every good wish and kind regard.

Yours,
C. M. Grieve.

P.S. I haven't had a final decision yet from the Porpoise Press people about my *Fier Comme Un Ecossais*. The remodelling of the firm, under new control, isn't complete yet but I should have definite word very soon now.

I have been working very hard on my big *Cencrastus*: and think I am pulling it off all right.

[1] Jonathan Cape, the publisher.
[2] MacDiarmid's article on Gogarty – 'The Wit Turns Poet' – eventually appeared in *Everyman*, Vol 7, No 180, 7 July 1932.

ECB

My dear Gogarty,

I have dug it[1] out from the chaos of my papers at last, and now send it on to you, with apologies for my unconscionable delay, and renewed expression of my delight in it. There are some splendid verses – quite in your best vein: and, above all, the last – a magnificent ending. I hope for more of the same ever and again.

How are the reminiscences going? I am anxious to have 'copy' as soon as ever you can manage it now. Our spring list is pretty well fixed up now: and I am hoping to put your book in hand very quickly.

Did I ask you – or forget to ask you – in my last letter if you'd be good enough to ask the Hospitals Sweep people to send me 12 books of Irish Sweep tickets? Please do. Various friends of mine asked me to get them books and I promised to do so.

The lady with the pheasant-coloured hair is quite a figure in Bloomsbury circles.[2] We have had some most amusing times together – and would have had more but for the horrible tangle of my own affairs (the divorce went through last Saturday).

Every kind regard to yourself, A.E., and all other friends.

Yours,
C. M. G.

[1] Gogarty had sent MacDiarmid a copy of his poem 'Leda and the Swan' which appeared in *Others to Adorn* (London 1938). On 1 December 1931 Gogarty wrote to tell MacDiarmid: 'Send me if you haven't lost it the only copy I had left of Leda.'

[2] On 26 December 1931 Gogarty wrote to MacDiarmid: 'Has Pamela Travers delighted you? What wit! But possibly she was shy or didactic, another form of shyness with her, in the presence.'

To Compton Mackenzie

Compton Mackenzie (1883–1972; knighted 1952) is probably the most celebrated novelist to be associated with Scotland this century. He achieved bestsellerdom as early as 1912 with *Carnival* and the following year *Sinister Street* made such an impact that Henry James wrote to tell the young author he had emancipated the English novel. Although Mackenzie is best known for his hugely enjoyable farces set in the Highlands and Islands – for example *The Monarch of the Glen* (1941) and *Whisky Galore* (1947) – he has some serious reflections on Scotland and nationalism in his huge fictional master-piece *The Four Winds of Love* (1947). Mackenzie's decision to support the National Party of Scotland in 1928 was welcomed by Mac-Diarmid who was also delighted when Mackenzie, standing as a Scottish Nationalist, won the Glasgow University Rectorial Election of October 1931.

Writing in *The Pictish Review* (Vol. 1, No. 4, February 1928) Mackenzie called for a new spirit to lift Scotland and concluded: 'Fuse thought with action and recreate a nation. I have enough faith in Mr Grieve's poetic genius to believe that it might effect even as much as this.' Mackenzie never deviated from this opinion as witness the references in his ten-octave autobiography *My Life and Times* (London 1963–71). For example, in Octave Six (p. 133), he quotes what he wrote after his first meeting with the poet in Glasgow in 1928:

> I found Grieve the poet very remarkable – a little like D. H. Law-rence, but with a harder intellect and, I think, a richer genius. I hope that between us we shall be able to steer the [Scottish Nationalist] movement out of any kind of parochialism.

Mackenzie played a crucial part in MacDiarmid's life when he persuaded him to leave Montrose to go south as London Editor of the radio-critical journal *Vox* which Mackenzie had set up as a potentially successful companion to his magazine *The Gramophone*. While in London MacDiarmid suffered severe concussion after falling from an open-deck bus then sustained a more traumatic shock when his wife Peggy left him to live with the cultural coal-

387

merchant Billy McElroy. *Vox* was under-capitalised and folded after fourteen weeks. Although faced with the prospect of coping with economic hardship and personal distress MacDiarmid did not, as the letters show, bear Mackenzie any grudge on this account.

HRC   16 Links Avenue,
                                                     Montrose.
                                                      14/4/28

Dear Mr Compton Mackenzie,

I need not say that I was delighted to receive your letter. Absence from home and domestic circumstances have prevented my replying sooner. I lead, as you may imagine, an extremely busy and difficult life. For a journalist of my type and with my tendencies to manage to carry on at all in Scotland literally involves hanging on by one's eyebrows all the time. Every effort is made to freeze one out. However (though it *is* cold) I am inured to it now and quite insusceptible of being really frozen out, I fancy – though my powers may at times be numbed in many directions in which I would fain be active. You'd understand my position better if you knew how few were the encouragements such as yours which I have received from my fellow-countrymen. (I have had better luck with folks in Ireland, France, etc.) The sales of my poems are, of course, negligible: and I'm not sure that the fact that I write poetry at all does not lessen the influence I could otherwise exercise in other directions. People don't trust poets.

However, our general propaganda is making real headway at last. The country is wakening up: and a new sense of nationalism is becoming very wide-spread and manifesting itself in all manner of promising ways. To gather them up and direct them to a goal is the task now: and I believe that the National Party now in process of formation will succeed in doing that. I do hope you will see your way to announce your candidature for a Scottish constituency. As I have just written to Erskine,[1] even as a gesture it will be invaluable at this

---

[1] Hon. Ruaraidh Erskine of Marr, who died in 1964, was in MacDiarmid's opinion 'one of the most remarkable personalities of modern Scottish history, the very core and crux of the *Gaeltacht*.' (Contemporary, p. 89) He was President of the Scots National League (founded 1922), one of the founders of the National Party of Scotland, and founder of the periodicals *Guth na Bliadhna*, *The Scottish Review* and

juncture – i.e. even if you did not really decide to go forward when the General Election comes. A great deal will depend in the immediate future on the evidence of return to Scotland of men of your prestige. If the old tendency of holding South is reversed – if people see that distinguished Scots are impressed by and in active sympathy with the New Nationalism and returning to take a personal share in the work – it will be half the battle. I do not think the two factors you mention will militate in any way in modern Scotland against your candidature. After all half the candidates for Scottish seats are always 'Carpet-baggers' from the South, without being real Scots as you are. The fact that your work and reputation have not hitherto been specifically identified with Scotland will not matter as against a definite stand now. And as for being a Catholic – the sectarian issue cuts little or no ice really. The anti-Irish propaganda of a few Protestant Zealots has had no practical political effect. There are quite a number of constituencies which are predominantly Catholic. There are very few in which the fact of your being a Catholic will prejudice any considerable section of the electorate.

I am delighted at your decision to transfer to the Scottish PEN. This, too, will help us immensely. Anything that will enhance our prestige in any way is of vital importance. I haven't yet heard from Ould re your transference: but my Committee (all of whom are strong Nationalists) will be as pleased as myself.

I note you hope to be in Scotland in May and June. We are arranging a PEN Dinner in Glasgow – provisionally so far fixed for June 2 – when our guest is to be Gordon Bottomley.[2] It would be splendid if your arrangements fitted in to enable you to be with us on that occasion.

But, in any case, I shall be most eager to meet you. Could you come to Montrose? Mrs Grieve and I would be most happy if you could. But if you do, I warn you you must take pot luck. I am a working journalist with all that that implies of limitations in the way of living, and style of hospitality I can offer. And besides, Mrs Grieve has just presented me with a son:[3] and, in a small house a baby is apt to be distractingly vocal at times. But if you care to risk these discomforts and inconveniences, we shall be delighted.

If Montrose is not convenient for you let me know your arrange-

The Pictish Review. Encouraged by Erskine and MacDiarmid, Mackenzie took an active part in the North Midlothian Election in 1929; Lewis Spence, the National Party of Scotland candidate, lost his deposit (polling just over eight hundred votes in a seat easily won by Labour).

2 Gordon Bottomley (1874–1948), whose play Gruach was performed with great success in 1923 by the Scottish National Players.

3 The poet's first son, Walter, was born in Montrose on 5 April 1928.

389

ments and we will fix something up between us. I shall look forward very keenly to a meeting with you and it is so much easier to talk over things than to write them – especially in hand writing such as this.

With every good wish.

Yours,
C. M. Grieve.

16 Links Avenue,
Montrose.
27.4.28

Dear Mr Compton Mackenzie,

Yes. It will suit us splendidly, and Mrs Grieve and I will be delighted to have you here from 10th or 11th May as you suggest. We are having a glorious spell of weather at the moment (after a particularly long, grey, wet winter), and we trust that it may last and let you see this part of Scotland at its best.

I am particularly interested in what you say about Ben Shaw and the invitation to you to stand as Labour and H. R.[1] I have been a member of the ILP for over 20 years – and have taken and still take an active part hereabouts – JP, former Socialist Town and Parish Councillor, etc. A year or so ago Willie Stewart said they were going to put me up for a constituency – preferably a rural one (as I was a member of the Fabian Land Inquiry Committee in 1912 and responsible for all the Scottish information in the book on *Rural Reform* subsequently published through Constable), but I have heard nothing more about the matter since. I know most of the Glasgow Socialist MPs, etc. and cordially detest them. I thoroughly agree with you as to the danger of the Scottish Socialist and Labour movement trying to use the new Nationalist feeling merely for party political ends. Writing recently in *Forward*, Cnclr. John S. Clarke expressed the view of the whole Glasgow group when he said: 'As a

---

[1] Ben Shaw, Secretary of the Scottish Labour Council, tried to persuade Mackenzie to stand as a Labour and Home Rule candidate for a suitable constituency; Mackenzie eventually decided not to 'contest a seat for Labour because Home Rule was obviously not going to be a main plank on their platform at the next General Election.' (Octave Six, London 1967, p. 134).

question of political expediency I am sympathetic to Scottish Home Rule, but I do not want the tin-can of Scottish Nationalism tied on to the Home Rule puppy's tail.'

I enclose a proof of my reply to Clarke as it will appear in the May *Pictish Review*.[2]

The dinner to Gordon Bottomley has now been definitely fixed for June 2, and I am delighted that you, too, are to be present.

As to other younger Scottish poets, do you know the Porpoise Press publications? All the three first-mentioned books on this list contain excellent, if unequal, work.[3]

There is another matter. Mrs Grieve and I are anxious to have our young son baptised on Sunday, May 13. Mrs Grieve belongs to the Scottish Episcopal Church: and two godfathers are required. A great friend of mine, Mr Neil Gunn, author of *The Grey Coast* (perhaps you know it) has consented to be one of them: but he may not be able to be present in person. I wonder if you would care to do us the very great favour of being the other?[4] We would esteem it a very great honour, indeed. But do not let us seem to be trying to take any undue advantage of your visit in this way, and if you would rather not you will, of course, just say so. But there is no one Mrs Grieve and I would rather have and – as although I know hosts of people I have exceedingly few real friends whom I can ask for such a favour and none within easy range – the fact that your visit was to coincide with the Sunday in question (we are assuming you will at least stay over the Sunday) seemed a way out of our perplexity quite beyond our expectations. Will you be so kind as to drop me a line as to this?

Yours,
C. M. Grieve.

---

[2] *Forward*, the Scottish Socialist paper, carried two articles by John S. Clarke: 'The Fraud of Nationalism' (24 March 1928) and 'Nationalism v. Socialism' (31 March 1928). MacDiarmid took Clarke apart in *The Scots Independent*, September 1928, and the May issue of *The Pictish Review* (Vol 1, No 7) where he wrote: 'The practical effect of Mr Clarke's utterances – if utterances so stupid can ever have any practical effect – is simply to prefer English Nationalism (or that variant and projection of it, British Imperialism) to Scottish Nationalism.'
[3] The Porpoise Press, founded by Roderick Watson Kerr and George Malcolm Thomson in 1923, included volumes of poetry in its first series such as Frederick Victor Branford's *Five Poems*, Alister Mackenzie's *Poems*, William Ogilvie's *The Witch, and other Poems*.
[4] Mackenzie agreed to be one of Walter's godfathers and wrote amusingly of the event, see p. 194 of the present edition.

HRC

16 Links Avenue,
Montrose.
31.5.28

Dear Compton Mackenzie:-

I am coming through to Glasgow tomorrow (Friday) and understand that we are both to be at the meeting of the National Party Policy Committee at 7 p.m. I put the matter along the lines we agreed upon very fully and very strongly to Muirhead,[1] and I am glad that we are going to have this opportunity of going into the whole question round a table. It would be exceedingly unfortunate if the Party started business with any sort of ill-thought-out and half-baked policy: and, while I appreciate their many good qualities, I 'ha'e my doots' as to the amount of brain-power that is yet available amongst us. I'll be in Glasgow all Saturday and part of Sunday: but must return here by Sunday night.

Both Erskine and I have received invitations from the Tailltean Games Council: and both of us intend to accept. I hope you may yet see your way to go too (you were doubtful whether you could when you were here): we would have a good time together.

You suggest that it might be possible to try on a Manifesto or Circular letter signed by some of us – with a view to giving much-needed publicity to Scottish nationalist aspirations – on the Press Association people. I think something of this kind is very urgently desirable. The English papers have practically boycotted all reference to the National Party.

For the July issue of the *Scots Independent*[2] I am wanting a number of prominent Scots to write short articles hailing the formation of the National Party. Will you write one of these – and will you do me the further favour of inducing Cunninghame-Graham to do likewise? 'Copy' must be in hand by about 12th June. What about Sir Ian Hamilton in this connection? Do you think you could induce him to give us his blessing?

Delighted to hear you had such a good time on Iona: and hope your sciatica has been comfortably quiescent the while.

Am looking forward to a further talk with you: and to hear the final impressions of the position your visit has led you to – together

---

[1] R. E. Muirhead, see p. 274.

[2] In *Scots Independent*, Vol. II, No. 9, July 1928, C. M. Grieve enthused over the prospect of Mackenzie identifying himself with the National Party of Scotland: 'He has a great deal to give our Movement; and the future of our Movement will depend to a very great extent upon its capacity to accept the sort of thing he has to give.'

with any suggestions for getting forrader. Your Godson is progressing very nicely, and Mrs Grieve joins me in every kind expression.

Yours,
C. M. Grieve.

P.S. In case I forget to ask you about it in Glasgow, please remember to give me Lawrence's address so that I can make sure of getting a copy of the magnum opus of which you spoke.[3]

HRC

16 Links Avenue,
Montrose,
11.4.29

My dear Compton Mackenzie,

I was extremely disappointed you didn't get to Dundee last night for the National Campaign meeting. Head-quarters didn't warn us and you were duly advertised. We had an excellent meeting, McCormick[1] and I talking. We are at Kirkcaldy tomorrow night and at Edinburgh next Tuesday. We are not setting the heather on fire, but things are slowly but steadily developing and I am much more hopeful than I was some time ago. The party is being steadily remodelled on effective lines – we are increasingly attracting clever young people and getting rid of the old fogies. The National Conference on 27th inst. will put everything on a much better basis. The party is steadily eliminating the moderatist, compromising,

---

[3] In Octave Six (p. 131) Mackenzie makes a reference to the fact that 'Lady Chatterley's Lover was privately printed some time in 1928' and MacDiarmid, a connoisseur of erotica, is probably referring to D. H. Lawrence's sexual magnum opus.

[1] John McCormick (1904–61) who founded the Glasgow University Scottish Nationalist Association in 1927 and helped found the National Party of Scotland in 1927. A moderate opposed to MacDiarmid's radicalism he was instrumental in forming the Scottish National Party in 1934; when he left the SNP in 1942, because of opposition to his plan to withdraw from elections and cultivate all-party support for home rule, he founded his Scottish Union (later Scottish Convention).

democratic, element, and all the young people are coming round to the realisation for the need of – and readiness to institute – a species of Scottish Fascism.[2]

I couldn't ascertain from McCormick whether you are still ill – or have recovered but were precluded from coming North just now by arrears of work due to your illness. I sincerely hope at all events that you are again in good form, and that we will see you up here by next month.

So far as Dundee is concerned, I know that I would get a good vote – and have a sporting chance of actual return – if the necessary money is forthcoming, but, while various things are being done to raise a proportion of it in Dundee and amongst my personal friends, time is getting short and unless there is a prospect very quickly now of the money – or most of it – being available I will most reluctantly have to stand down. Unfortunately I cannot help financially myself, and Dundee is such a whale of a place to tackle – 120,000 electors. But I am still confident that, with its 25,000 Irish Catholic votes and the fact that it is a two-seat constituency, it is by far our best chance – remembering too that I am well known there and persona grata with the bulk of the influential labour people. Such a coincidence of favourable elements makes it a pity to have to back out but I am afraid there is no other way. McCormick told me definitely last night that at most only Camlachie and Dundee – and West Renfrew where Muirhead is of course financing himself – are to be contested: and that Headquarters still hopes to be able to help in financing the first two. Camlachie has already raised or has prospects of raising most of what is required there. But I question very much if Headquarters will be able to come to the rescue in time to enable my candidature to go forward. All kinds of essential preliminary work – e.g. the addressing of 120,000 envelopes, itself a big task – are hung up; we cannot commit ourselves till we see at least an off-chance of raising the bulk of the necessary cash – but if we delay too long we won't be able even if the money comes in at the last moment to get the necessary work overtaken in time.

All this is due to our failure to seize the opportunity after the Rectorial and the big Glasgow Conference to sweep through the country with meetings in every important town.

---

[2] In *The Scottish Nation*, 5 June 1923, MacDiarmid wrote an article 'Plea for a Scottish Fascism' which asked the following question: 'Is it not time for a Scottish Fascism to oppose the anti-national forces which are robbing Scotland of the finest elements of its population – and at one and the same time denying the Scottish people access to millions of acres of the finest scenery in Scotland, and setting the sport of English plutocrats before the vital needs of the country?'

I'm in fine form again, and as busy as usual, only more so.
With every good wish.

Yours sincerely,
C. M. Grieve.

HRC   16 Links Avenue,
                                                Montrose.
                                                17.6.29

My dear Compton Mackenzie,

Mrs Grieve has had an intuition all along – a 'hunch' – that you
would pull it off all right: and if I failed to cherish quite such a lively
confidence it was through no lack of confidence in you, but because I
know rather more of the difficulties of launching such a project.[1] I
cannot tell you how delighted I am at the good news, and the
prospect held out to myself; I need not tell you that (apart from my
own interests altogether) you have my best wishes in whatever you
attempt. We shall naturally be on the 'heckle-pins' until we hear
further.
  I am delighted to gather from the news of the furtherance of this
project, and your reference to the Gallipoli Reminiscences,[2] that you
have got through the gruelling time you have been having and are in
better form again.
  This is just a short note. I am busy clearing my decks, preparatory
to leaving on Thursday first for London and then, on Saturday
morning, for Vienna to attend the PEN Congress there.
  In case you should happen to be in town either as I am going or
returning the particulars of my movements are as follows:-
  Arrive London early hours of Friday morning (21st). Stay overnight with Edwin Muir (The Nook, Crowborough, Hants). Leave
for Ostend 10 a.m. Saturday morning.
  I shall probably leave Vienna on 28th arriving in London on night
of 29th and spend the Monday and perhaps the Tuesday in London.
I must be back here on the Wednesday.

[1] The launching of *Vox*, Mackenzie's radio critical journal which employed Mac-
  Diarmid as London Editor.
[2] Mackenzie's *Gallipoli Memories* (1929), war memoirs of the Dardanelles.

I'm glad to be getting clear away for a while. This Scottish business is on my nerves. A horrible botch has been made of the first real chance we've had of creating a big National Movement and we have now a perfect mess of stupidity to clear away again.

My poem[3] is developing splendidly. But I've a good deal to do yet if I'm to have it ready for autumn publication, as I'm hoping. I don't want to hurry it, though; it's by far the biggest thing I've done yet.

Muir's dedication of his *John Knox*[4] to me has put the fat in the fire again. It's another smashing bit of work in the right direction.

Every good wish.

Yours,
C. M. Grieve.

HRC

16 Links Avenue,
Montrose.
7th July 1929

My dear Compton Mackenzie:-

I arrived home in good form last Wednesday forenoon. My holiday has done me heaps of good. I have not been in better condition for years. Accept my warmest thanks for your hospitality on Jethou.[1] It was a great treat to see you again and to visit your beautiful island home. But I am afraid my coming was partly responsible for the bad time you had last Monday. Miss Boyt[2] told me you had been doing a little extra in order to leave you freer to talk with me. I do hope you had a good sleep on the Tuesday forenoon and have since been in much better form and making good progress

---

[3] *To Circumjack Cencrastus* (London 1930).
[4] Edwin Muir, *John Knox: Portrait of a Calvinist* (1929).
[1] Mackenzie leased the Channel Island of Jethou, for £100 per year, from 1923 to 1930. 'It was some time [in 1928] that a story by D. H. Lawrence appeared in the *London Mercury* called "The Man Who Loved Islands". I told Charles Evans of Heinemann's that if he included it in a forthcoming collection of Lawrence's short stories I should injunct it [because] if Lawrence used my background of a Channel Island and an island in the Hebrides for one of his preposterous Lawrentian figures the public would suppose that it was a portrait.' (Octave Six, p. 131).
[2] Nellie Boyt, Mackenzie's secretary.

with the remainder of your Gallipoli book[3] to the completion and publication of which I will eagerly look forward.

Naturally the thought of *Vox* has been foremost in my mind. I am as fully convinced as when I was talking with you of the thorough excellence and promise of the idea, and ready as soon as you give the signal to come South and do my very utmost. Peggy is, of course, wildly excited (and just as persuaded as I am that an opportunity has presented itself which must be seized with both hands). We are in touch with people about getting a house in London, and making all such other arrangements as will enable us promptly to instal ourselves there as soon as we get the word.

Please excuse a short letter. I have been thinking continuously about *Vox* and all your plans for it and the position, prospects and problems of Radio generally since I left Jethou: but I need say nothing about that here. Suffice it that I am with you up to the hilt and will do everything I possibly can to prepare myself and make sure that I do not let you down in any way. It is a big thing – the biggest thing since the New Journalism – and bigger; an inspiring cause to work for under an ideal leader.

I am busy clearing my decks. I have done a good deal of writing since my return: and am keen to finish *Cencrastus* before you call me South. I do not think I will have any difficulty in that. I feel like a new man somehow.

Peggy joins me in gratitude and every good wish. Again thanking you for all your kindness and hospitality – and with kindest regards to Miss Boyt and Miss MacSween,[4] who were both so good to me.

Yours,
C. M. Grieve.

P.S. I shall look forward to hearing when you are coming North so that I may run through to Edinburgh or Glasgow and have a talk again with you.

I had Neil Gunn here on Thursday night. He was in great form. They want you and I to speak in Inverness. But they will be writing you about this. The Bannockburn demonstration seems to have been a wash-out. Spence[5] appears to have been particularly egregious.

[3] Mackenzie's *First Athenian Memories* (1931) was the second volume of his war memoirs.
[4] Chrissie MacSween, who assisted Nellie Boyt on secretarial work for Mackenzie on Jethou.
[5] Lewis Spence (1874–1955), poet and Scottish Nationalist.

The Wynd,
Kirkton, St Cyrus,
Kincardineshire.
28/8/29

My dear Mackenzie,

I should have written you long ere this – to congratulate you on your success in finally arranging for *Vox*, and to thank you on my own behalf. Not that I really needed to do the latter. You know my position and feelings. I have been as obstinate and ill to move as I know how; but my position here, and in Scotland generally, was becoming quite hopeless and, but for your intervention, must soon have ended in disaster; I am unfeignedly glad that you have thus cut the Gordian knot for me.

I was, of course, looking for your letter, and hoping to see you in Glasgow or elsewhere: but I guessed what had happened, and knew that you must have completely overtaxed yourself in finishing the Gallipoli, and concluding the *Vox* arrangements. I am delighted you managed to cut clear away to the islands and recuperate.

I have been extremely busy myself. Uprooting myself has been a rather more intricate process than I anticipated – even if it has been more a matter of liquidating liabilities than anything else. However, I am well forward with my arrangements now, and will arrive in London, with wife, and family, goods and chattels all complete on the morning of Tuesday 10th Sept. We haven't definitely settled on a house yet, but will have done so ere then – in Highgate or Highbury. Peggy is looking forward to London with unmitigated pleasure, and is as grateful to you as I am myself.

I note you have made other arrangements in some respects than were in your mind when I saw you in Jethou – taking offices (instead of carrying on from Firth St) and making it 6d instead of 2d etc. But I'll be keen as mustard to hear all the details when I get up, and to start in. My confidence in the project and in you are absolutely unqualified. All the folks I've spoken to about the matter think *Vox* should go all right. One thing is certain. You won't be able to overwork me; I'm more than ready for all the work that there possibly can be, and the keener the fight the better I'll be pleased.

I'll write you again next week, when I've definitely fixed on a house, and tell you what my address will be.

Every good wish from all here.

Yours,
C. M. Grieve.

398

P.S. Above address only means we've been living in the country all this month (although, of course, I've been going back and forward daily). But Peggy and the bairns are in splendid fettle as a result, and should have a good basis to carry them through their opening months in London. But we'll be back to Links Avenue, for packing up, etc., at the end of this week.

HRC   'Vox',
TS   10A Soho Square,
London, W1.
11th February, 1930.

My dear Mr Mackenzie,

I was very sorry to hear that you were ill again and hope that by the time this reaches you, you may be much better.

I need not tell you how sorry I am for your sake, and for Barrow's and Maclaurin's,[1] that things have not gone better with *Vox*, but 14 weeks did not give it a chance – at least a year should be allowed to get a weekly on its feet – and I feel it has largely 'gone by default'. I have not heard anything of what you may have felt and said about the Directors' decision a week ago, with regard to the monthly – failing more capital, it was the only way out – but I fancy that when you consented to the monthly you scarcely expected, any more than the rest of us did, that things were so bad as to necessitate the dismissal of the *Vox* staff and an attempt to carry on the monthly with the *Gramophone* staff under Major Stone.[2]

One of the difficulties here has been the continual 'excursions and alarums'. Last Tuesday – the Tuesday prior to the meeting – Barrow and Maclaurin 'phoned me to go up to their room. They were in a great state about a letter Major Stone was said to have written, advising you to stop *Vox* altogether except for the issue of a small

[1] Togo Maclaurin and Jack Barrow persuaded their fathers to put up the capital to form a company to publish *Vox*.
[2] Christopher Stone was London Editor of Mackenzie's magazine *The Gramophone*: 'The editorial office of *The Gramophone* was to be moved from 58 Frith Street to share with *Vox* the much ampler quarters of 10A Soho Square. Christopher Stone never liked the idea of *Vox*, but he agreed to the move and also to *The Gramophone*'s investing £1,000 of the £10,000 of capital for the new venture.' (Octave Six, p. 178).

paper with your Causerie from Guernsey. I said that I had not seen it; but they asked me if it was put through, not to publish it in that week's *Vox* but to let them know, and expressed the opinion that Major Stone had always been antagonistic to *Vox*. Similarly, yesterday (Monday), Mr Maclaurin told me that Major Stone had himself, to their surprise, volunteered the new arrangement, provided he got complete control, and that that was what he had been working for all along.

I put these things frankly before you (not as expressions of my own views) because my position has been a difficult one where such crosscurrents were at work, and, while I know *Vox* was in a bad way, I should feel very differently if I thought I had been jockeyed out of my post and that, in a little while, the necessary additional capital to keep the venture going will be put up all right.

However, these things may be, I need not tell you again how grateful I am to you for the opportunity you gave me. Nothing of this kind can affect in any way my regard for you. London has presented me with all kinds of problems of its own – apart from those incidental to my accident – but I like being here, and shall do my utmost to stay here, while it has done Peggy an immense amount of good even in this short while and banishment to a provincial routine again would break her heart. I am very worried too at the possibility of my having to withdraw Christine from the Convent School.

I have put out feelers of all kinds to try to get another post as quickly as possible and hope that something will come of one or other of these very soon. But the sudden cessation of my connection with *Vox* has put me in a tight fix – apart altogether from my feelings on being thus unceremoniously displaced. Bringing my goods and chattels down here involved considerable expense and I had to take on pretty heavy responsibilities here – which would have been all right given a fair amount of time, but, as things have turned out, leave me with 'the baby to hold'. As you know, I came here without any contract though, as I explained to Major Stone (who said he would leave the matter to you) I was prepared to sink or swim with *Vox* but regarded it as quite a different matter to have *Vox* going on while I was given notice (and superseded with scant ceremony). That prejudices my position in regard to getting another post, and, while I do not want to be troublesome in any way, I do not see why, if the Directors were pusillanimous, they should use the remainder of the capital to put things on a new basis without due regard to the position of those whom the new arrangement displaces. In the absence of a contract, I can always fall back upon the custom in regard to such matters, and, in the case of one holding a responsible post as editor, the usual thing is at least a payment of three months' salary. As you probably know I am a member of the National Union of Journalists. I would, of course, have been infinitely happier if I had been in a position simply to snap my fingers and walk out.

Beyond indicating to Major Stone that I regarded sinking or swimming with *Vox* as one thing – and being dismissed while somebody else ran it as a monthly, as quite another thing, I said nothing whatever of my own position, and acquiesced in his suggestion that he should write you, although he did not indicate the lines along which he intended to write nor am I sure that he appreciates the position at all from my point of view. I did mention Mrs Callis, however, and Miss Skinner.[3] Mrs Callis has done splendid work and spares no effort, and I think Major Stone has now come to an arrangement with her. At all events she is doing various things for the monthly for him and is, I believe, to run the Women's Page. Miss Skinner, as you know, I brought down from Scotland, and both Mr Jordan and Mr Wright say she is by far the most competent typist in the office. I hope Major Stone can retain her. In any case, none of the girls so far have got notice.

This is the curious thing up to now. We were told that all the *Vox* staff were to go; but everybody else seems to be carrying on as usual except Mr Jordan[4] and myself.

It is too bad worrying you with this long letter, when you are ill and have no doubt all kinds of work and worries of your own to contend with, but I feel you will like to have a perfectly frank statement of my attitude.

To turn to other matters, I have not heard again from the Porpoise Press people, but should do so soon, and believe they will put out the book all right. It contains some of the best work I have done, and several of the poems will, I think, please you particularly – dealing as they do with Gaelic themes.

The Scottish Educational Journal have been an unconscionable time in publishing my article on your *Gallipoli Memories*,[5] but they have to give precedence to professional matters and most of their space recently has been taken up with one or two big issues of that kind. I heard from the Editor, the other day, however, and understand that the article will be in very soon now.

Again wishing you a speedy recovery, with every good wish to

---

[3] MacDiarmid's wife's maiden name was Peggy Skinner: when the poet met her in 1918 she was a copyholder in a newspaper office in Cupar.

[4] Philip Jordan, sub-editor on *Vox*.

[5] MacDiarmid's review of *Gallipoli Memories* appeared under the title 'The Art of Compton Mackenzie' (by 'A. L.') in *The Scottish Educational Journal*. Vol XIII, No 12, 21 March 1930.

Mrs Mackenzie and yourself, and to Miss Boyte and Miss MacSween.

Yours,
C. M. Grieve.

12/2/30
Many thanks for your note just to hand. I knew you had not received Major Stone's letter telling you exactly what had been done.

HRC

10A Soho Square,
London, W1.
3.3.30

Dear Compton Mackenzie,

Many thanks for your note. I am delighted to hear you have contrived – Heaven only knows how – to do no fewer than 60,000 words of your novel: and hope it will be speedily finished. Every good luck to it and to you.

I haven't got fixed up but am still hoping to do so all right with the Allied Newspapers. I will know definitely in a day or two. I had dinner the other night at the Caledonian Club with Mr Wm. Will – one of the directors, and really the lynch-pin of the whole concern on the business side. Amongst other things he said he would speak for me to get some reviewing etc. to do for *The Daily Telegraph* and suggested that I should ask you to reinforce his effort in that direction by writing on my behalf to Sir Gomer Berry. I said I would ask you to do so. I would be very grateful if you would be so kind as to do this. You could mention in your letter that perhaps Mr Will had already suggested me in this connection and that at all events, if the matter were referred to him, Mr Will would support your appeal on my behalf.

Peggy and I are anxious but not dispirited. It will be all right if I get into a new post soon but our margin is distressingly narrow and in settling up Mr Pollard[1] gave me less than I expected. I had understood that, like Mr Jordan and Mrs Callis, I was to get a

---

[1] Cecil Pollard, business manager of *The Gramophone*.

month's pay but that the balance of the advance made to me when I arrived in London was not to be deducted. You will remember – on your own kind suggestion – I got prepaid £48, which came in very handy owing to costs of removal here, etc. I afterwards drew only £48 per month instead of £52 – thus repaying the advance at the rate of £4 per month. So £20 was outstanding: and Pollard deducted that from the month's pay. I had understood that this was not to be done, in the circumstances, and was correspondingly disappointed. Pollard said he would take the question up, but I don't expect he will. I loathe these mean economic neccessities.

Every good wish from Peggy and myself.

Yours,
C. M. Grieve.

HRC

321 High Holborn,
London WC1.
7/9/31

My dear Mackenzie,

Congratulations on your *Daily Mail* venture (it should of course be the *Daily Mail* who should be congratulated).[1] I'm looking forward to your break-off tomorrow and thereafter to a weekly treat. I hope you are fine and fit these days. You're to be in London shortly, aren't you. I'd like to see you. It's been too long since I did. Peggy has been in Scotland for several weeks and will be for several more. She had a very serious operation – touch-and-go – but is picking up now though still far from well. I've got fixed up here now[2] – indeed one of my first tasks brought me up against your contribution (I wish it were longer – it's a bit short compared with Maugham's, Novello's, and others) to Frederic Bason's *Gallery* book which we are issuing shortly. I'm enclosing a copy of our first book. I know it's not the sort of thing you can say much about in the *Daily Mail* – unless you use it as a peg for something about Maugham and the theatre generally – but if you can make some sort of reference to it in the by-going we'll

[1] Mackenzie contributed regular reviews to the *Daily Mail*.
[2] The Unicorn Press.

403

be glad. Am making great headway myself with the Scottish *Faust* –
two long separate poems from it are being used by Lascelles
Abercrombie in a miscellany of hitherto unpublished poems Victor
Gollancz are putting out shortly.[3] It's certainly the best stuff I've
done yet. And Benn's are putting out this month my selection from
Living Scottish Poets in their Augustan series.

My compliments and regards to Mrs Mackenzie and to Misses
Boyte and MacSween. I hope they are all well.

As ever yours,
C. M. G.

HRC   Whalsay,
                                       Shetland Islands.
                                               3-12-37

My dear Compton Mackenzie,

I wonder if you can give me a little help. I am in a very difficult
position. The circumstances are these:-

Since I came up here 4–5 years ago I have lived by writing books –
running up accounts for the necessities of life with the local tradespeople while writing them, and then squaring these off, and starting
afresh, whenever I received cheques from the publishers. The two
things of course have never done much more than square – the
amount received by way of advance on a book on signature of
contract, delivery of MSS or actual publication, just serving to cover
the costs of living for us during the period spent in writing it and
leaving us with a little in hand. We have been content enough as long
as things even panned out in that way – precarious as it has always
been.

This time, however, for one reason and another, I have been
longer in completing books, the accounts have run on longer, and the

---

[3] When MacDiarmid's poems 'Charisma and My Relatives' (301–2) and 'First
Hymn to Lenin' (297–9) appeared in Lascelles Abercrombie's anthology *New
English Poems* (1931) they were footnoted as coming 'From *Clann Albann*, a work in
progress.' This reference suggests that MacDiarmid conceived this autobiographical project as a Scottish *Faust*.

tradespeople are becoming pressing – I suppose they are having greater difficulties of their own these days, too.

I took on too much, the books have proved more difficult to do than I anticipated and have involved much more preliminary reading etc. I cannot finish any of them before the end of February at earliest. But if I can keep on working steadily I can certainly finish my book on the Scottish Islands[1] for Batsford by then, and my book on Scottish Doctors and Doctoring[2] for Harraps by about the middle of March. There are substantial advances to come on both of these books. On the Islands book I get 100 guineas – half on delivery of MSS and the other half on publication. I have also money to come from Covici-Friede in America who approached me to let them put out a selection of my poems there.[3] I agreed – but I don't know yet when exactly they will publish or when exactly I'll receive their Cheque. As to my Autobiography,[4] Gollancz will probably publish this – he said it was 99 to 1 probable, but that the highly controversial nature of the book made it impossible for him to decide definitely until he had seen the whole MSS (of which he had only seen the first two or three chapters).

My agent in London wrote me some time ago urging a speed-up and increase of my output. He said he had no difficulty in getting me contracts – if I could discharge these more speedily he could get me all the more – with the result of greatly increased earnings. To this end he advised me to get hold of a secretary typist without delay.

I replied that I was willing enough but that while it was true I could not speed up and increase my output without secretarial help it was also true that I could not get secretarial help without first of all completing the books I am working on and receiving the stipulated payments.

Since then, however, he has got in touch with a young fellow[5] who is eager to come to me as secretary-typist simply for his bed and board, until we see after 6 months or a year whether increased output so improves the financial situation that I can afford to pay him a certain wage.

I wrote accepting the offer – the chap to come here about the middle of January – but I told my agent that, while I agreed that it might pan out O.K., circumstances in the meantime were such that in agreeing I was taking all my courage in my hands.

Since then, however, it has become clear that if I cannot get help I

---

[1] Hugh MacDiarmid, *The Islands of Scotland* (London 1939).
[2] This was completed but never published.
[3] An unrealised project.
[4] Hugh MacDiarmid, *Lucky Poet* (London 1943).
[5] Henry Grant Taylor.

may not be here to take advantage of secretarial assistance by mid-January. The tradespeople are increasingly pressing and I am afraid that if they do not get some satisfaction they will at least stop credit and thus cut off our necessary supplies, and make the whole situation impossible.

I am therefore under the necessity of trying to find somebody who will advance me £50 or thereabouts (I might manage on £30 to stave off the most pressing people) – to be repaid by me as soon as I complete my Islands book and receive the £52.10/- then payable to me, which, as I say, will be towards the end of February, or beginning of March at latest.

I wonder if you can possibly do this for me. I would be tremendously grateful. If I can get over this difficulty, until I get that book done, then my way will be clear for a year or more ahead, as I'll have the money coming in from the Doctors book shortly after, the Covici-Friede payment, payments for some poems 1/ in an American anthology and 2/ in an American magazine, *The Partisan Review*, and finally, whatever is agreed upon once I get the Auto-biography finally fixed up.

I hope I've made the position clear. It's useless to try to explain this sort of thing, of course, to the local tradespeople. They do not understand anything except regular weekly wages – any one like myself who gets lump sums at irregular intervals and who obviously has no regular job or does no real work in their sense of the term, is a gentleman and ipso facto wealthy, and thus at once an object of servility and suspicion. I've paid the blighters off periodically all these 4 to 5 years, and they ought to know that if they exercise a little patience I'll do so again. But no! I've been a little longer this time than usual – and perhaps they themselves are finding business a bit more difficult; I don't know – and so, as a stranger, and as a person who engages in activities incomprehensible to them and doesn't earn his living in any of the ways with which they are familiar, I am turned upon at once. – – –

Please give my kindest regards to Miss Boyt and Miss MacSween.

I hope you are in good form yourself and free again of that infernal sciatica.

Every good wish,

Yours,
C. M. Grieve.

Whalsay,
Via Lerwick,
Shetland Islands.
24-9-38

My dear Compton Mackenzie,

It was extremely kind of you to send me – and inscribe – the copy of your *Windsor Tapestry*[1] which I have read with very great interest, admiration for the skill with which it is woven, and sheer joy in the wit displayed. Beyond that, I am of course in complete agreement with all you say in your devastating analysis of Lord Baldwin, of the Archbishop of Canterbury, of *The Times* and the ductile press generally, even of Attlee and his *sans-culottes* – but, on the other side, I need not tell you that I have no enthusiasm or even respect for the ex-King or the present King or any of their forbears, relations, or personal friends, and am an out-and-out republican – and not a bourgeois republican but a Communist one.

When I wrote you last, I had not heard that the question of the publication of the book had been arranged and did not know how matters stood about it. I have since read various reviews and was glad to see somewhere that the book had been selling well. And I trust that you have had a thoroughly satisfactory return for the immense task you must have had, and the worries the various difficulties about it all entailed.

You were ill too. I sincerely hope you are fine and fit again now.

I think I sent you a copy of my new quarterly.[2] The second issue is almost ready and I will send you a copy when a supply reaches me. There is a better chance now than ever of a sort of Celtic Front[3] – a co-operation and policy of mutual support between the younger writers of Ireland, Wales, and Scotland. And I think a bigger group of such younger writers of better calibre than ever before. Keidrych Rhys's paper, *Wales*, has just had a Celtic Front issue with groups of Irish and Scottish contributors. I am following suit in *The Voice of Scotland*. Norman MacLeod, the American poet, (whose grandfather went out from Raasay), writes me that he thinks the younger British

---

[1] Mackenzie's *The Windsor Tapestry* (1938) was a sympathetic biography of the life and abdication of Edward VIII, Duke of Windsor.

[2] *The Voice of Scotland* which initially ran from June 1938 to August 1939 and was twice revived after the Second World War.

[3] Mackenzie and MacDiarmid were both interested in the possibilities of a Celtic Front and considered (as Mackenzie says in Octave Six, p. 189) 'forming a society to be known as Clann Albann, the members of which would be pledged to do all they could to foster the Celtic Idea with a vision, on a far distant horizon at present of rescuing the British Isles from being dominated by London.'

school (i.e. Auden, Spender, MacNiece, etc.) have been boosted far beyond their desserts and the younger Irish, Welsh, and Scottish poets neglected, so he is arranging an anthology of the latter to be published in America.[4] Another step in the same direction is the fact that T. S. Eliot is publishing in *The Criterion* the opening section (about 500 lines) of my *Cornish Heroic Song*, and the MSS of some 20,000 lines of that huge poem – forming a separate book – is now being considered for publication by MacMillan's, to whom Eliot has warmly recommended it.[5] The whole *Cornish Heroic Song* – most of which is now finished – runs to about three times that. I think it contains a lot of my very best work. But of course, in times like these, a poem of that magnitude presents a very difficult publishing problem indeed. However, we'll see.

Please excuse this short letter, as I *must* get off both my Scottish Islands book and my discursive history of Scottish doctors and doctoring by the end of this month and have still a great deal to do.

I am hoping a little nearer the end of the year to migrate to a cottage in Eigg for a few months – not permanently (even if the Eigg cottage were available for more than a short let), since I intend to keep my home here. But I will be glad to be among Gaelic people for a while; the people here are so utterly without any cultural traditions or taste – so destitute of any knowledge of or love for poetry and music.

My wife, who is (or during the crisis that led to the abdication was, and I think, unabatedly remains) a keen supporter of the Duke of Windsor's, is deep in your book, and asks me to conjoin her thanks with my own for sending it to us.

With kindest regards to Miss Boyte and Miss MacSween, and every good wish to yourself.

Yours,
C. M. Grieve.

[4] (Ed.) Norman Macleod, *Calendar: an anthology of 1940 Poetry* (Prairie City, Ill., 1940).

[5] Eliot included 'Cornish Heroic Song for Valda Trevlyn' in *The Criterion*, Vol XVII, No LXXI, January 1939; and took a great deal of interest in the epic poem which MacDiarmid usually referred to as *Mature Art* and occasionally as *Cornish Heroic Song*. See pp. 446–9.

To Albert Mackie

Like MacDiarmid and J. K. Annand, Albert Mackie (born 1904) attended Broughton School and (in 1922–3) edited *The Broughton Magazine*. He became one of Scotland's best-known journalists, editing the *Edinburgh Evening News* from 1946 to 1954 and contributing humorous poems to that paper under the pseudonym 'Macnib'. His Scots work in *Poems in Two Tongues* (1928) was well received as a genuine contribution to the Scottish Literary Renaissance initiated by MacDiarmid. Mackie's poem 'To Hugh M'Diarmid' describes how 'a deid M'Diarmid turns/Tae form a Twae-in-Yin wi Burns.' MacDiarmid included Mackie's poem 'Molecatcher' in *The Golden Treasury of Scottish Poetry* (London 1940).

NLS

16 Links Avenue,
Montrose.
2/7/28

Dear Mackie,

Just a hasty line to congratulate you on *Poems In Two Tongues*. Somehow or other I missed seeing any announcement of this (it doesn't seem to have been reviewed yet in *The Glasgow Herald*, *Scots Observer* and other papers I'm in the habit of seeing). The first I saw of it was J. M. R. (i.e. James M. Reid, author of *The Sons of Aethne*) in *The Bulletin* – a stupid line or two – but that needn't worry or disappoint you; Reid doesn't know the difference between a poem, a philosophical treatise and a police report. He dismissed my *Drunk Man* as an egregious instance of a man who probably couldn't write anything worth while in English making himself deliberately unintelligible in an invented language of his own. And then the following day I saw a review in *The Weekly Scotsman* and immediately wrote to the Darien Press for a copy: and have since read it several times with very considerable appreciation and pleasure. I haven't time – nor is it perhaps desirable – to enter into any friendly little arguments here. 'Elegy' and 'Pease O' My Banes' – tho' more in the Violet Jacob strain than most of your poems – are, technically, the best things in your book, I think. From that point of view both are extraordinarily good. At the same time I prefer those less 'finished' and successful poems – which are more numerous – in which you are cutting clear of Kailyaird 'content', – particularly (but here I may not unnaturally be prejudiced) the poem you dedicate so generously to myself, and yet I am not sure that 'Molecatcher' doesn't come nearest being a great poem. I say this despite the fact that humanitarian sentiment cuts precious little ice with me. But you set the whole thing in an extraordinarily appeal angle. All the same the poem doesn't quite come off – it is difficult to put a finger on the cause of its failure – it comes so near being a really great poem and just fails. In these matters such little things – unponderables – make all the difference. There are, of course, just little personal points – not reasoned criticisms. I shall look eagerly forward to your future work – particularly big poems: we've had a surfeit of little poems vignetting all sorts of personal and particular impressions. If I may stick to the egotistic pose generally accredited to me, I have no hesitation on the strength of what you give us here in saying that, next to Spence and myself, you are already the best of living Scots poets outwith the Kailyaird school. I am hoping to have an opportunity of saying a little about your book in *The New Age* and elsewhere.

I had meant to write in reply to the welcome letter you sent from Crieff some months ago: but I am a hopelessly off-putting correspondent.

Although I am addressing this from Montrose, Mrs Grieve and family and I are really living in a cottage some miles beyond Brechin just now (I am busy with a tremendously long Scots poem[1] which I fancy will knock the *Drunk Man* into a cocked hat) and won't be back into Montrose till the end of August – but, after that, if you've ever a week-end to spare we'd be delighted if you cared to take a run up. A good talk over things might be useful to us both.

Again with best thanks and every good wish.

Yours,
C. M. Grieve.

[1] Hugh MacDiarmid, *To Circumjack Cencrastus* (Edinburgh 1930).

Whalsay,
Shetland.
3/1/41

My dear Mackie,

The top of the New Year to you and your good lady.

I was delighted to hear from you – and in such a generous and encouraging strain. Thanks too for the preliminary pars. which I saw first as reproduced in my own old paper, *The Montrose Review*, and then in a cutting from *The Evening News* itself. I am more than pleased to hear about the 1000 line Scots poem and will be eager to hear further thereanent – or perchance see it and your versions of the Birlinn and Praise of Ben Dorain if and when I get to Glasgow again. I value especially your remarks on my renderings of these – I agree entirely with you about the Ben Dorain one: but believe I could now rework it a bit and bring out the three movements.[1]

I haven't seen any reviews yet from the Scottish papers, or any of the leading English papers or periodicals – most to hand so far are from the English provincial press, but some of these are very good, and quite a number express satisfaction that Scottish poetry should at last have been accorded independent place in the Golden Treasury series instead of being a mere subsidiary element in Palgrave. So it will be interesting to see how this affects the Oxford University Press, etc. which have hitherto refused Scotland such autonomy. I am very conscious of the defects, omissions, etc. of my book, but as a pioneer effort it will do its job.

When I used the adjective 'generous' above I had specially in mind the fact that the 'Molecatcher', much as I like it, did not give you due representation and that you might well have been disappointed to find your poem on myself not included, as I had intended. But my initial selection had to be drastically reduced and after cutting out a certain number myself I had (owing to the delays and difficulties of corresponding back and forward with London in wartime conditions) simply to let Macmillan's effect the remainder necessary to reduce the book to the requisite proportions themselves.

[1] In a letter, of 10 July 1983 to the present editor, Albert Mackie writes: 'My review would be late in 1940 in the *Glasgow Evening News* . . . The reference to the two Gaelic poems is explained by the fact that I was busy translating *Moladh Beinn Dorain* when *his* translation [587–600] came out. I then busied myself on MacDonald's *Birlinn Chlann Raghnaill*, but he beat me to that also [515–32]. . .The "1,000-line Scots poem" was my *Big Music for Alba*, which William MacLellan, the publisher, retitled *Sing a Sang o Scotland* (1944). I had largely completed it by 1941 but could see little hope of publishing it.'

This had some disconcerting effects – on your poem, on a long one of Soutar's, on several of my poems, and eliminated various people altogether, e.g. Wm. Jeffrey and Lewis Spence. But there was alas! nothing else for it.

I note what you say about 'an overworked journalist': but I myself found the interstices of an overworked journalist's time my most productive, and up here I frequently wish I had not all my time to myself, but a job to tie me down and concentrate my powers. I would fain in fact be back in journalism again, especially as my own particular lines are all hopelessly unremunerative, and I have indeed made all sorts of efforts since this War began to get a post – but in vain. The Scottish press are all fairly good to me in giving me publicity; but I think it would do more for Scottish literature if one of them would give me a billet.

Of course I know what it is and temperaments differ and you must be kept busy enough in all conscience. Yet I have a hunch that you'll come away all right yet so far as our Vernacular Muse is concerned and amply redeem the indubitable promise – and indeed performance – of your first book yet. (Speaking of younger men following up, I wonder if you see Douglas Young's roneo'd periodical, *The Auld Aberdeen Courant and Neo-Caledonian Spasmodical*, with translations into Scots verse from half the literatures of Europe and prose articles in Scots too. It's worth a write-up.)

I haven't been off this chuckie-stone for over two years now and may not be for long enough yet – that depends on how the War goes – but I certainly reciprocate your wish that we might see more of each other. I'll not lose any chance of doing so you may be sure.

My next book will be my Autobiography, *Lucky Poet* which Methuen's are publishing this spring. I wrote over ½ million words but just finished and sent it to my agents on the eve of the War, which of course made a book of such a size out of the question. But for paper shortage and other war-time difficulties Victor Gollance told me he'd have been glad to publish the thing *in toto*. As things were, the project ultimately suggested itself of cutting it into 3 books of about 150,000 words each. The first dealing with myself *qua* poet, my poetic processes, ideas on poetry, etc. is that which is now coming out. The others *A Poet And His Friends* (dealing with Yeats, A.E., A.R. Orage, T.S. Eliot, etc.) and *Lament for the Children* (dealing with my domestic life, divorce, etc.) will appear later, the first of these probably in the autumn. In any case they are all written and ready.

Even more serious has been the effect of the War in holding

back publication of poems. The huge poem[2] of which enclosed leaflet gives some account would have been published before this, but the Fall of Paris, etc. has of course quashed the project. Another long poem on the Spanish War,[3] in reply to Roy Campbell's *Flowing Rifle*, can't be published just now for political reasons. It runs to 4000 lines and contains a great deal of the best poetry I have written.

Ah, well, what are difficulties for – but to overcome.
All the best.

                    Yours,
                    C. M. Grieve.

[2] *Mature Art.*
[3] Hugh MacDiarmid, *The Battle Continues* (Edinburgh 1957).

To William McCance

William McCance (1894–1963) was born in Cambuslang and in 1919 moved to London where he participated in the Vorticist movement and became art critic of *The Spectator* from 1923 to 1926. He exhibited sculpture and painting at James Whyte's gallery in North Street, St Andrews; contributed (as did MacDiarmid) prose to Whyte's *The Modern Scot* magazine; and drew cartoons for *The Free Man*. From 1930 to 1933 McCance was Controller of the Gregynog private printing press in Newton, Montgomeryshire; his first wife, Agnes Miller Parker (1895–1980), produced wood engravings for the press. McCance was lecturer in typography and book production at Reading University, from 1944 to 1959; when he returned to Scotland he married Dr Margaret Chislett, in 1963, and lived and painted in Girvan. At the time of the Richard Demarco Gallery's retrospective exhibition of McCance's work, MacDiarmid wrote (to Demarco on 24 November 1971) that McCance 'was always immeasurably ahead not only of the mass of his fellow Scots but of practically the whole body of his (saving the mark) fellow artists'.

NLS

Vox,
10A Soho Square,
London, W1,
7.1.30

My dear McCance,

A line to say how much we enjoyed Friday night's gathering.

It has since occurred to me – apropos what you were saying about somebody to do the secretarial work for the Group – why not my wife. That is just her line and you would find her thoroughly efficient, and I know she would just love doing it; she is at a bit of a loose end and eager for something to take up her energies and enlist her enthusiasm. She is a shorthand writer and typist and could take down anything to dictation, and she can use one of the typewriters in my office. And, of course, we are on the 'phone here.

Another advantage is that I could help her in regard to press-work and other publicity. What do you think?

By the way I am wondering if you have a copy of my *Drunk Man*. If not, I want to give you one. Or if you have one – but would like a copy of either *Sangschaw* or *Penny Wheep* – I'll send you either of these instead.

I'm just arranging for the early publication of a new collection under the title of *Fier Comme Un Ecossais*. Your Piper would make an excellent decoration for the cover. I wonder if we can arrange this.

Kindest regards to both of you, and to Mr Aaronson.

Yours,
Grieve.

NLS

The Liverpool Organisation,
Royal Liver Building,
Liverpool.
5/9/30

My dear Mac,

I was down in London from Friday night to last night and quite disappointed not to see Agnes and you. I understand you've been – and still are – holidaying in Yorkshire and hope you've been having a splendid time and better weather than has been prevailing in Liverpool here where it has been unusually cold and wet. When are you going to Wales? I am afraid I'll not be down in London again before you flit but may see you at your new place. One thing I particularly wanted to see you about this time in London and that is to ask you to do a drawing of Peggy for me before you leave town. I'm not a millionaire of course and can't afford fancy prices but I always had it in mind to ask you to do this for me and postponed asking you in the forlorn hope that my bank balance would improve sufficiently to make me offer you a commission rather than make a request. What a hope! Seriously, if you can spare an hour or two, will you phone up Peggy and arrange a time and do me something of her. I'd like to have it as a souvenir alike of artist and subject.

Kindest regards to both of you. Drop me a line sometime and give me your news. All the best.

Yours,
Chris.

NLS

Royal Liver Building,
Liverpool.
[1930]

My dear Mac,

Your time in London is now running short and I expect Agnes and you are 'thrang' saying goodbyes to all your friends. I do not know whether you've been able to make any drawings of Peggy yet or not; she hasn't mentioned the matter but her letters have been pretty scrappy recently what with Walter being unwell and her employment with Mr Phillips (whose affairs I hope are on the upgrade). The purpose of this brief note is with reference to the George Douglas Brown[1] things in the possession of Mrs Mansbridge's father. I'd give a good deal to get dealing with these, either for writing about them in the press or editing them for publication in book form, or, preferably, both. I could make a bit of money on the business if I got the handling of it and that happens to be a matter of some concen to me at the moment. I'd be very glad if you could use your good offices in this connection, and let me know what's what. I'd be very glad to run down and discuss matters in London with Mrs. Mansbridge or her father.

Looking forward to seeing you after you're installed at the Gregynog, with every kind regard to you both (and to Aaronson, Donaghy, and other friends).

Yours,
C. M. G.

[1] George Douglas Brown's novel *The House with the Green Shutters* (1901) is generally regarded as the most seminal Scottish novel of the twentieth century; Brown died the year after the publication of his book and left behind papers indicating his plans for future works of fiction.

416

NLS
TS

The Unicorn Press,
321 High Holborn,
London, WC1.
1st October 1931.

Wm. McCance, Esq,
Gregynog Press,
Newton,
Montgomeryshire.

My dear McCance,

I ought, of course, to have written you ages ago and no doubt you arrived at all kinds of conclusions as to why I had not. I have been having a very unsettled time in many ways, but have now found *pied à terre* on lines not dissimilar to your own. I observed that you (I take it) or some one else connected with the Gregynog Press had noticed the intimation, as I received a notice regarding some of your forthcoming publications addressed to me here.

I am writing you at the moment not to enter into lengthy details but mainly to tell you that (apart from hoping that Agnes and yourself and Blair Stanton and Gertrude are having a pleasant and prosperous time) I have not forgotten about certain drawings of yours I thought might be used in certain ways provided appropriate poems could be fitted to them.

In connection with the Unicorn Press it will be specialising mainly in bibliographical works and finely printed limited editions, etc., but there is a possibility that we may see our way to initiate a series of small books of poetry on the lines of Faber and Faber's 'Ariel' series. In his connection I am very anxious at the moment, if possible, to have another look at your 'Transparent Charlestown' and some of the other drawings of that set. I wonder if you would care to send these to me and let me have a look at them again and then write you certain definite proposals. Of their safe custody once I receive them you can depend, and naturally I will not use them in any way until we come to a mutual arrangement regarding their use.

I am not going to write you any more at the moment but hope to hear from you in return in the course of a post or two. Should you be in London shortly I hope we would not fail to arrange a meeting. Please address any correspondence to me at the above address and in the event of your being in London phone me here *and not at Pyrland Road*. There are reasons for this requisition which can be explained later.

Love to you and Agnes and the rest of you.

Yours,
Chris.

417

Whalsay,
Shetland Islands.
4/1/34

Dear Agnes and Mac,

Glad to get your card. What's been happening? Haven't had any news of you for a long time. Did the Kingdom of God finally become impossible? I hope you've made an advantageous move and are both in the best of fettle. We've been up here – next to the North Pole – for nine months, and have quite gone native. Write sometime and 'gie's your news', and I'll reciprocate – too busy at moment with commencement locally of annual binge which they hold on and including – not the new Christmas and New Year – but the Old Style Ones 5th to 12th Jan. Every good wish to you both.

Yours,
Chris.

To Catherine Carswell

MacDiarmid's relationship with Catherine Carswell (1879–1946) began in acrimony (over the subject of Burns) and developed into mutual admiration. Catherine Roxburgh Macfarlane was born in Glasgow, experienced an unhappy first marriage (annulled in 1908), and made a reputation as dramatic and literary critic of *The Glasgow Herald* from 1907 to 1915 when she married Donald Carswell, a barrister who had taken up journalism in Glasgow. When the couple moved to London she wrote for *The Observer* and formed a close friendship with D. H. Lawrence who encouraged her to complete her Glasgow novel *Open the Door* (1920). Lawrence also urged her to do justice to the passionate nature of Robert Burns in her book on *The Life of Burns* (1930). It was the national poet who brought Catherine Carswell and MacDiarmid together since both had a vested interest in the revision of his reputation. In his introduction to *Lying Awake* (London 1950, pp. xii-xvi), his mother's unfinished biography, John Carswell writes of his parents:

> It was a happy marriage, both of talent and temperament, even though the talent and temperament brought by each partner were so different . . . [After the publication of *The Tranquil Heart* in 1937 the] expenses of living were now less, and my father, after many years of literary hopes and disappointments had a regular post in the Home Office . . . The war broke out, and a few months later my father was killed in a motor-car accident in the darkness, as he left his work. Not very long afterwards I was sent to the East on military service.

10A Soho Square,
LONDON W1.
14/2/30

Mrs Catherine Carswell.

Madam,

I have made repeated efforts during the past ten years to get
various publishers to put out (not under my editorship – nor under
yours!) such an edition of Burns's letters as you so typically accuse
me in your *Radio Times* article[1] of being blind to the need for. It would
be child's play for me to take the feet from you in matters of this kind,
by detailing what I and others have actually done for Scottish letters
that you know nothing about, or have attempted to do and might
have succeeded in doing but for the insensate jealousy of people like
you. To seize on a printer's error with regard to a Gaelic name in my
Everyman article, while your own gave 'Langellier' for 'Angellier' –
not to mention the appalling gaffe of '*Mr MacMaster*' (for Mac-
Donald) – is typical of your methods. But the people I care about do
not need to have these things pointed out to them and you are
welcome to the others. It will all 'come out in the wash'.

C. M. Grieve.

Grand Hotel,
Lerwick.
30/1/1934

Dear Mrs Carswell,

Many thanks for your letter of 25th inst. I drafted the appeal for
The Free Man, but only suggested a few names of fairly wealthy
people, tho' I knew that in addition to these Black[1] would send
copies to all the people whose names and addresses he had whom he
thought likely to help. So I had no idea really who received it. I

---

[1] Catherine Carswell's article, in the *Radio Times* of 14 February 1930, began: 'I do
not propose to score off Mr Grieve on debating points. It would be so easy that it
would be a shame to take the money.'
[1] Robin Black, publisher of *The Free Man*.

420

haven't heard the result yet but had a wire from Black a week ago indicating that the crisis had been staved off, but not absolutely averted, tho' results were coming in. I hope he has received enough now one way and another to ensure continuance. But literary people are definitely the worst to appeal to just now in matters of this sort, and I hope he had not many of my friends of that sort on his list, for as far as I can make out they are almost without exception having a very lean and harassing time. Certainly I am no exception myself; I have been living up in Whalsay for nine months now, and it would have been absolutely impossible for me to have lived anywhere else except in a poorhouse or prison. But these Shetlands are a wonderful place for people like me. My 4-roomed cottage, standing by itself on a hillside and looking over a wonderful view of islands and voes, has a rental of only 27/- a year, and a fair proportion of our feeding – fish, potatoes, etc. – is gratis. With these advantages one can contrive to make ends meet. London, alas, is a very different proposition and I earnestly hope some windfall – some lucky and lucrative 'hit' of one kind or another – may come your way shortly. I am not in the way of getting much news of my friends nowadays and had not heard anything of Donald or you for a long time. I keep an eye on *The Times Literary Supplement* and publishers' announcement of course, but had not seen anything about any work of yours or Donald's since your Duckworth *Burns*.[2] It is possible that I may be in London for a week or so within the next couple of months, and I will drop you a note in the hope that you may be in town and that we can foregather somewhere and have a meal together. I have lots of irons in the fire myself at the moment – a big illustrated book[3] of a miscellaneous character (poems, plays, essays, etc.) in which Lewis Grassic Gibbon and I have collaborated, which Jarrold's are publishing shortly; and a very big volume of new poems of mine Victor Gollancz is putting out. My projected London trip is in the hope of fixing up one or two other things at which different publishers are nibbling a little too long without getting firmly and finally hooked.

Every good luck to you both and to the boy.[4] I hope that a year that has not opened too promisingly may speedily transform itself into a very fortunate one and bless you both with some of the success you richly deserve.

Yours,
C. M. Grieve.

[2] Catherine Carswell, *Robert Burns* (1933).
[3] *Scottish Scene* (London 1934). The book was published without illustrations.
[4] John Carswell.

My dear Cathy,

So sorry to hear you're off colour and trust it may ·be a very temporary indisposition. Thanks for your note – the line you took in your Burns Nicht debate – and the *Glasgow Evening News* cutting. I expect Blake hasn't forgiven my *Modern Scot* lines[1] anent his beefy brow; in any case he has always been opposed to me. Qu'importe?

I am sorry I won't see Donald & you before we go off. I must write you shortly. As Valda will tell you I've not only landed a good contract for Routledge's but they are going to develop a Scottish section and are paying me a nice retainer to introduce Scottish authors and suggest Scottish books to them, etc. And in this connection I have suggestions to make to Donald and you – and, once I do so, which will be soon, if you do not fancy them, you may have alternative proposals for books to put forward yourselves. In any case it's a wealthy and well-established firm and we must do what we can to improve the shining hour. Please do not say anything about this in the meantime at least to others of our mutual acquaintance; I can't open the door to them all.

Best wishes to all of you: and renewed thanks for all your great kindness.

Yours,
Chris.

Whalsay.
19/7/35

My dear Cathie,

I too have been baffling my pressing difficulties a great deal lately by a flat refusal to have anything to do with them.

[1] MacDiarmid's poem 'Welcome to the PEN Delegates' (1299–1302) appeared in *The Modern Scot*, Vol V, Nos 1-2, June 1934 and contained the following reference to George Blake:

> The changing shapes of clouds
> Before a gale are nothing to the crowds
> Of novelists who, in huge remainders, now
> Stampede the scene behind Blake's beefy brow . . .

I had a pretty rotten winter with eye and other troubles which made it difficult to get my work done, so on the way back from Manchester I saw an eye-specialist and got glasses, and also had myself equipped with a new set of dentures (having been toothless for over two years) and arrived back here looking and feeling a new man. It didn't last long. I got a severe chill and sequelae in the shape of acute rheumatic pains and stomach and abdominal troubles. Since then – 3 or 4 weeks – I've done little except lie about half-sleeping – utterly exhausted.

Yes. I had a most interesting time in Manchester. But the job offer is only one of those intelligent anticipations of one's most secret desires – desires practically debarred from fulfilment because I'd need close on £1,000 p.a. and the guarantee that I'd be free to have 2 or 3 months here every year. Happily, tho' the weather has been diabolical, Valda made up for my collapse; she had a much better winter and is more robust than she's been for a very long time. James Michael too is in great fettle – an appalling concentration of noise and activity.

The Essex Cottage is a great find, and we hope you have a splendid time there. Trust Don and John are both in good form. John wouldn't like to come up here, would he – the voyage is cheap – and the Shetlands would be something quite new to him in the scenery line?

Yes, I knew about *The Scots Week End*. I thought it a splendid idea and was extremely glad Routledge's took it up. You are very welcome to the three items[1] you mention, and as to the cut in No 1, that doesn't worry me – it belongs to my earliest period and is the sort of poetry I've now lost all notion of. I'll look forward to the collection keenly – it should be great fun.

But damn the making of books! I've published 1 this year already and have other 3 and parts of other 2 as well as the Grieve-Wells joint work – and perhaps a volume of short stories too – coming out this Autumn. I'm very tired of the whole business – only the thought of even trying to do anything else makes me tireder still.

Love from all here.

Yours,
Chris.

[1] *The Scots Week-End* (1936), edited by Donald and Catherine Carswell, contains five items by MacDiarmid: an abbreviated text of 'A Moment in Eternity' (3–8); 'The Poet's Passing', subsequently entitled 'Skald's Death' (482); 'Wheesht, Wheesht' (45); 'Thoughts on my Boss', comprising the six lines beginning 'Curse his new hoose, his business, his cigar' (235), from *To Circumjack Cencrastus*; and 'Up to Date', comprising the quatrain beginning 'Christ wha'd ha'e been Chief Rabbi gin he'd lik't' (85) from *A Drunk Man Looks at the Thistle*.

Whalsay.
Friday.
[1935]

My dear Cathie,

Glad to get yours today and to know you are better. Trust this will continue and that both the Markets book and the Abbey Theatre one will get nicely off your hands. The reason why A. J. B. Patterson of Routledge's hasn't got in touch with you is that both his partners have been away – one in America (the one you ask for name of – Frederick J. Warburg) and the other involved in nasty motor smash in which his 18-year-old daughter was killed; so Pat has had to hold off – unable to commit himself in their absence. I have just written him again on a variety of matters and you'll be hearing from them all right in a day or two now, I expect. We're all well here except myself; I got a nasty chill about a fortnight ago and it has resulted in complete nervous and mental prostration – just at the worst possible moment, too, when I was working day and night to finish certain books. So, alas, my time-table of work is all upset. I'm a great deal better than I was but only able to pick at work for very short periods in the day yet. Fortunately a spell of better weather has set in and this will help to buck me up – the incessant rain and constant howling winds were becoming utterly unbearable.

Excuse this hasty note to catch tomorrow's mail-boat. I quite agree with you – Edwin would have been better with Knox;[1] I was greatly surprised and sorry when I heard he'd fixed on Scott because I had thought Donald would be approached to see if he'd do that. If you see Flos MacNeill please give her our love; I'd a letter from her the other day but can't manage to reply for this mail yet – and there isn't another till Monday.

Valda joins me in love to John, Don, and yourself

Yours,
Chris.

---

[1] Edwin Muir's contribution to the Routledge 'Voice of Scotland' series was *Scott and Scotland* (1936).

Whalsay.
26/12/35

Dear Don & Cathie,

Many thanks for your card. I have been wondering how things were with you. As for myself I have not yet been able to pick up all the threads where they broke so suddenly in July – tho' despite the truly infernal weather that has prevailed without intermission since I got back from hospital in October I have had a fairly satisfactory convalescence and am getting down to work again. We are delighted to hear of the production of Don's play[1] next autumn and will hope to see you then – but Valda (who badly needs a holiday after the strains entailed first by my collapse and then by Mike's illness) is likely to be in London (on the way to, or returning from, Cornwall) ere long. How is the 'sort of Scottish week-end book' (Routledge's) progressing? Trust this and all your other ploys are shaping nicely and that you are all in good trim.

Love from all here and every good wish to a bright and prosperous New Year.

Yours,
Chris.

Whalsay,
Via Lerwick,
Shetland Islands.
15/8/36

My dear Cathie,

Just got yours of the 8th, from Calais. You do not say when you'll be back, but I take it you were a bird of passage at the Hotel Sauvage, so I'm writing this to Keats Grove. I am delighted to have such a long and most interesting letter from you; and to know you've managed a holiday somehow or other. Hope it thoroughly rests and

[1] Catherine Carswell had written MacDiarmid about possible productions of Donald Carswell's play *Charles III*.

refreshes you. I am very sorry about the way Don's been let down and do hope Brandon Thomas makes up for it all later, I'll look forward to your *Boccaccio*: and am glad there's a woman's paper in the wind, what's happened about the Scottish week-end book? Do hope you are all well and wish you a real spot of luck – a thoroughly good break – soon.

As to myself, I've twenty books on the stocks – four done, and the rest in active preparation. There *is* a method in my madness. I am really as excitable about ideas – take them as personally – as most people take everything but ideas. But if I go in for personalities I do it for the same reason that Marx and Lenin and others – Burns: Blake – did. They are vitally necessary; the only way. One must get right down to brass tacks. Politeness – the deprecation of personalities, etc. – is an evasion, a short circuiting, of the dialectical process, just where it needs most rigorous application. Communists may be too interested in Greece, Spain, etc. to trouble about Scotland – but Scotland needs to be troubled about too – I'm in Scotland and regard that as my job. Marx's and Lenin's 'personalities' were vitally important in their own countries and times; and I am convinced that mine will have a shrewd bearing on things in Scotland. Besides the 'personal' is vitally important – it is a mistake to think that Communism has no use for it or can slur over it, and I am desperately anxious that the Communist Movement – and particularly in Scotland – should not develop any avoidable blind spots – which is precisely what Scotland has been to most Communists so far. Malraux is right; Communism is a great fertilizer of personality.

I quite understand that my letter[1] was not very clear or important to you, nor was what I was trying to achieve by it. I did not mean it to go out alone – I had intended following it up with copies of two essays on 'Modern Scottish Politics in the light of Dialectical Materialism' and 'Scottish Culture and Imperialist War'. But a typist failed me. These essays and others I have now added to my *Red Scotland*; they will clear up matters for you all right and show you that I only used Muir's references to me as a pretext – that I am intent upon a reorientation of the Scottish Nationalist Movement and a definite opposition to the proliferation of pseudo-Fascist Boards in Scotland which, inter alia, the *Outlook* has been advocating and which have gone uncriticised elsewhere owing to the fact that Scotland is the blind spot of even the Social Democratic and Communist elements in Scotland. The letter is also connected with my Edinburgh Rectorial Campaign as United Front Candidate. It is

[1] MacDiarmid's open letter to James Whyte, see pp. 850–4.

only intelligible in the light of these things, and of other things with which I am concerned in some of my new books, but I could not bring out the relationship either in that letter or (for lack of time, since it is a very complicated matter and would take much space) in this. But I at least gained one of my immediate objectives – which was to alienate some of the younger writers, like Soutar and S. C. Hood, from the *Outlook* and initiate an attack on the Muirs whose influence I regard as thoroughly pernicious in every way. (I told F. G. Scott and others over a year go that I would have to fight Muir if he came back to Scotland – my seizing on his sentences about myself was only a pretext; I'd have made one if he hadn't given me one.) I am out for a big cultural fight – and, above all, for an *International* United Front in Great Britain, with the achievement of an autonomous Scottish Workers' Republic as one of its definite objectives. I am not unaware that I may have to fight this matter right through to the final court of appeal in Moscow itself. But I have been doing a course of very thorough and comprehensive political reading and feel fully equipped (while under no illusion as to the magnitude of the fight – or the probability that I may be thrown overboard too like John Maclean) – on whatever grounds I may be beaten at least it will not be able to be said that my line is not consonant with dialectical materialism. I can't go into the matter here, however. You'll see the essays in question later. And also roneo'd copies of my speeches in connection with the Edinburgh Rectorial and at an Inter-University United Front (Socialists, Communists and Nationalists) Conference in, I expect, October, which will also express the elements of the same programme – the *Red Scotland* line. This is an old issue – the Socialists and now the Communists have always dodged it, – dodged any consideration of Scotland *separately* – against them and this neglect – this insistence on the need to take England and Scotland as a unity – is dialectically indefensible.

Muir's opinions of my poetry, etc. do not matter to me and have never mattered to me. I do not regard him as fit to judge – I have no use whatever for his own pretensions to creative artistry either as a poet or as a novelist, and I have seen nothing of his 'critical' writing for years that did not simply disgust me. But it is one thing to be angry at his remarks on my work – and quite another to insist on pointing out that he had said precisely the opposite in print a few weeks earlier – the latter affects the questions of his credibility as a witness and his personal motivation – and while it may seem that my letter was prompted merely or mainly by wounded amour propre I am confident that the upshot will prove that I was at least as much concerned to prevent him exercising an influence I regard as harmful on our younger Scottish writers. And I have no doubt at all that I will prevent his doing so and discredit him completely – he is playing into my hands in the most delightful way – it would have made matters much more difficult for me if he had come away at this junction with an eulogy of my work. Thank God he didn't do that.

We're all in good form. Valda and Mike got back about a fortnight ago. In time to enjoy some of the splendid weather here which has been better all summer than any available in Cornwall or elsewhere in the South.

Love from all here to Don, John, and yourself.

Yours,
Chris.

I have heard nothing more about the Association For Defence of Culture Conference – I thought there would have been an official report. Of course I don't see things here – I only get the *Left Review*, Left Book Club News, and Left Book Club books of the month.

Whalsay,
Via Lerwick,
Shetland Islands.
5/10/36

My dear Cathie,

Many thanks for your most interesting letter. I'll look forward eagerly to the Boccaccio which will be a magnificent bit of work if it is better than your Burns – also to the Scots week-end book shortly. I enclose a couple of leaflets (*not* by way of soliciting a subscription) but just to let you see what I'm up to. Muir and Whyte were partly instrumental in stopping my *Red Scotland* book with Lawrence and Wishart, but I'd heard prior to that – in YCL circles, etc. – about the Scots issue of the *Left Review*[1] and that of set purpose I was not to be asked to contribute. The Muirs and Whyte figuring in it as the Scottish bourgeois left writers of importance in Scotland today

---

[1] The Scottish issue of the *Left Review*, Vol II, 1936–7, contained articles by Neil Gunn, James Barke, J. H. Whyte, Edwin Muir, Catherine Carswell, Willa Muir and a poem by William Soutar.

makes the thing a laughing stock to anyone who knows what's what in Scotland. The Scottish question has always been the blind spot alike of the CP and of the Social Democratic parties, and their attitude to it – and to the questions of Scots and Gaelic Literature – is indistinguishable from that of die-hard Imperialists. The CP have the wind up – and with cause – about my forthcoming biography of John Maclean (in which I'm collaborating with his daughter) since this is the very issue upon which they betrayed Maclean with the disastrous results which Gallacher admits in his autobiography. My *Red Scotland* is the only analysis yet made of these issues and of all the relevant phases of Scottish History, in terms of Dialectical Materialism. And when you read my discussion along these lines of Muir's nonsensical *Scott and Scotland* I can promise you some splendid fun.

I know Muriel Rukeyser's work through the *American Nation* and will send you some cuttings with this letter if I can lay hands on them. I would very much have liked to meet her.

Barbara Niven is a Manchester (professional) artist – daughter of a former MOH for Manchester. I am very fond of her and her work. She also did an oil painting of me of which I'll try to send you a photograph. Professor Barker Fairley also did a portrait of me which has *at least* all the wildness the absence of which you note in Miss Niven's drawing.

Many thanks for your good wishes in Edinburgh Rectorial. I'm putting out a big pamphlet (40 pp.) on 'The Betrayal of the Scottish Universities', and will send you a copy when they are issued.

Glad John had such an interesting time in France. I hope he'll have a good year. And that he'll manage the Sorbonne or some other French University all right later on. I wish he'd penetrate to the Shetlands on one of his holidays. We'd be very glad to see him here, and these islands are undoubtedly a new experience.

Valda joins me in every kind regard & good wish to Don and John and yourself.

       Yours ever,
       Christopher.

Whalsay,
via Lerwick,
Shetland Islands.
19-1-40

My dear Cathie,

Valda and I are horrified to hear of Donald's tragic death. Will you, and John, please accept our deepest sympathy?

Mails here are very belated, infrequent and uncertain. That is why we have been so long in writing you. We did not get newspapers containing notices of Donald's death until a couple of days ago, and this is the first mail out since.

I feel this loss very keenly myself. We were late in making each other's acquaintance and I did not see a great deal of Donald and you. But there are very few among the host of my literary friends I like as well as I liked Donald.

Behind the fact of his sad death I cannot but wonder how, in these terribly difficult times, you and John will be affected. I do hope that it will not affect the continuance of John's time at the University, and, though I know how extremely hard things are just now for many writers, I hope that you are, for once, among the luckier ones in this respect, and have enough in hand of a remunerative sort.

Our kindest thoughts are with you both.

I was afraid when the War broke out that things would just become absolutely impossible for me here right away. But they have turned out not so bad as I feared and if they do not get much worse we will manage to hang on – since we have no option; it is apparently impossible for me to get anything down South. I tried everything I could just after the War started, but did not get a nibble at all. Not that I want to go South if I can possibly help it – but Valda needs a change badly, and this place isn't giving Michael much chance either.

However I mustn't grumble, to you of all people, and in a letter occasioned so sadly; and whatever the hard cash situation and the outlook (or want of outlook) may be, I have a good deal in hand at the moment. My Autobiography is finished; Gollancz is keen on it, but my agents haven't finally fixed up yet. And Macmillan's are publishing my *Golden Treasury of Scottish Poetry* this spring, while the Obelisk Press in Paris are taking in advance subscriptions for my huge poem[1] – longer than 3 novels! – at £2.2/- per copy. But what a proposition in times like these!

---

[1] *Mature Art.*

With love to you both and every warm regard.

Yours,
Chris.

P.S. You will understand of course that though we understand how terrible a shock to you Donald meeting his death in that way must have been we are without details – only the bare newspaper statement, – and do hope the details do not worsen the sufficiently terrible fact, and that both John and you were in a state of health which enabled you to bear your tragic loss with no more than the unavoidable (and that all too sufficiently great) shock.

c/o Black,
2 Park Terrace,
Glasgow.
19/9/42

Dear Cathie,

It is a very long time since I heard from, or even of, you. I hope things have been well with you and am anxious to know how John is fairing.

As you may have heard I have been working in Glasgow as an engineer(!) since the beginning of this year. A few weeks ago I sustained a serious accident at work, disabling both legs. I have since been confined to bed and am only now beginning to be able to hobble round again. However, I hope to resume work shortly and to be able to get a flat here and get Valda and Michael down, as I expect to be here until the end of the War at any rate.

This is not a real letter, however, but just a brief note to introduce my friend, William MacLellan, head of a Glasgow printing business, who is striking out now as also a publisher of Scottish books and has in hand for early issue volumes by several young Scottish poets, also an opera by Dr Erik Chisholm, etc. I am sure you will agree with me that in these very difficult times an enterprise of this sort deserves every assistance. While on this visit to London, Mr MacLellan is eager to explore trade avenues, and make personal contacts, so that he can have as effective a selling and publicity organisation behind his prospective publishing list as possible. I will be very grateful if you can have a talk with him and put him in touch with people likely to be useful.

Please write me sometime when you have a moment to spare and give me your news.

Every kind regard and good wish to John and yourself.

Yours,
Christopher Grieve.

To T. S. Eliot

MacDiarmid regarded himself as a modernist who had as much in common, stylistically, with the innovatory trio of Joyce, Pound and Eliot as he had with the Scottish tradition. Coincidentally, Mac-Diarmid and Eliot share an important date in the calendar of modernism: the pseudonymous Hugh MacDiarmid made his poetic debut, with 'The Watergaw', in *The Scottish Chapbook* of October 1922 – which was the same month *The Waste Land* appeared in the first issue of Eliot's periodical *The Criterion*. MacDiarmid greatly admired Eliot's intellectual approach and critical prestige and was proud to be associated with *The Criterion* (which ran from October 1922 to January 1939). Eliot praised MacDiarmid's *Mature Art* and paid tribute to his inventive use of Scots. In *The Company I've Kept* MacDiarmid includes Eliot in two separate lists: first he names him in a list of his 'best friends – A.E., Will Dyson, T. S. Eliot (whose first wife was a Scotswoman from Glasgow)' (Company, p. 74) then subsequently cites him in a catalogue of poets ruined by religion as witness 'the recent deplorable cases of T. S. Eliot, Edwin Muir, and W. H. Auden' (Company, p. 174). MacDiarmid's most celebrated reference to Eliot (1888–1965) occurs in *A Drunk Man Looks at the Thistle*:

> T. S. Eliot – it's a Scottish name –
> Afore he wrote 'The Waste Land' s'ud ha'e come
> To Scotland here. He wad ha'e written
> A better poem syne – like this, by gum! (94)

TS

18 Pyrland Road,
London, N.5.
December 9th, 1930

T. S. Eliot, Esq.,
Editor,
The Criterion,
c/o Messrs Faber & Faber.

Dear Sir,

Would you care to consider an article on 'English Ascendancy in British Literature'[1] – discussing the way in which, instead of pooling their resources, or at least acting and reacting freely upon each other (and a common bilingual or multi-lingual public) and giving British literature far more variety, Irish, Scottish Gaelic, Welsh, and, to a lesser extent, Scottish Vernacular, and even English dialect literature and a case like the late Charles Doughty have been practically excluded from the knowledge of most British people – and consequently have had their potentialities inhibited – by the English ascendancy tendency. It seems to me that this article will fit in with your series on nationalism announced for 1931. Apart from anything else it is absurd that English readers who would be ashamed to be found unfamiliar with what any significant writer in European literature 'stood for', if not with his works, should know nothing of such great poets of our own islands as Aodhagan O'Rahaille in Ireland, Alasdair MacMhaighstir Alasdair in Scottish Gaelic, and William Dunbar in the Scots Vernacular.

You may know of my own work as a Scots poet over the pseudonym of Hugh M'Diarmid; and, over my own name I have written a considerable number of books on Scottish and allied cultural and political topics, while, as the former literary critic of *The New Age* I have a very wide knowledge of most European literatures, and more particularly of modern movements in thought, arts, and letters.

Yours sincerely,
C. M. Grieve.

[1] 'English Ascendancy in British Literature' appeared in *The Criterion*, Vol X, No LXI, July 1931 and was subsequently collected in *At the Sign of the Thistle* (London 1934) and again, by Kenneth Buthlay, in *The Uncanny Scot* (London 1968).

TS
                                18 Pyrland Road,
                                London, N.5.
                                16th December, 1930

T. S. Eliot, Esq.,
The Criterion,
24 Russell Square,
London, W.C.

Dear Mr Eliot,

Many thanks for your kind letter of 10th inst. As you may know, I am at present working in Liverpool, but I hope to be in London ere long and nothing would please me better than to have an opportunity of accepting your kind invitation to lunch with you. I will let you know in advance when I am to be in town. I am having my essay on 'English Ascendancy in British Literature' typed and will send it to you in the course of a week or thereby.

                        Yours sincerely,
                        C. M. Grieve.

                                321 High Holborn,
                                Liverpool.
                                5.1.31

T. S. Eliot, Esq.

Dear Mr Eliot,

A very happy New Year to you, and heartiest congratulations on your Harvard appointment – mitigated by regret that the latter will involve, I suppose, your absence from London for some months and correspondingly diminish one's chances of seeing you. But I hope we may meet before you go.

By the way, when we met at your Club, you very kindly promised to put in a good word for me with Mr Richmond[1] of *The Times Literary Supplement* with a view, if possible, to securing me a little reviewing

---

[1] Bruce Richmond (1871–1964) was editor of *The Times Literary Supplement* from 1902 to 1937. He was knighted in 1935.

there. I should be very greatly indebted if you could. I must secure additional work somehow or other.

Every kind regard.

Yours,
C. M. Grieve.

357 Royal Liver Building,
Liverpool.
12/2/31

T. S. Eliot, Esq.,
Editor: *The Criterion*

Dear Mr Eliot,

Many thanks for your note. You would have heard from me long ere this, and received my article, had I not been off with influenza, etc. I had written the article and had it typed but finally was not satisfied with it and busy recasting it when I had to lie off. But I will send it on in the course of a few days now. I hope to get down to London soon, too, and to have the pleasure of meeting you. Every kind regard.

Yours sincerely,
C. M. Grieve.

TS   18 Pyrland Road,
                                        London, N.5.
                                    26th February, 1931.

T. S. Eliot, Esq.,
Editor, *The Criterion*,
c/o Messrs. Faber & Faber,
24 Great Russell Street,
W.

Dear Mr Eliot,

I am sorry (owing to illness and what not) to have been so long in
sending this essay in to you. I hope it will now prove acceptable. It
may be too long for your purposes but 'cuts' may be made if need be,
and there are one or two rather lengthy 'quotes' which might
perhaps be given in smaller type.
  With best wishes,

                        Yours sincerely,
                        C. M. Grieve.

TS   Royal Liver Building,
                                        Liverpool.
                                    9th March 1931.

T. S. Eliot, Esq.,
Editor: *Criterion*,
24 Russell Square,
London, W.C.1.

Dear Mr Eliot,

Many thanks for your letter of 6th inst.
  I am very pleased that my essay has interested you and that you
are in agreement with some of its contentions. I was afraid when I
sent it to you that it was on the long side and will be very glad to
make the necessary cuts to bring it down to the number of words you
require. Your suggestion to omit the discussion on the Gaelic poets
seems to me the best way to effect this but I do not know that that will
be sufficient to reduce the essay to the limit you require, and it may

be possible for me to effect certain other cuts and compress one or two of the passages. If you will send me the essay back here, I will go over it and return it to you as quickly as possible.

With kindest regards.

Yours sincerely,
C. M. Grieve.

18 Pyrland Road,
London, N.5.
17/7/31
Phone: Clissold 5263

T. S. Eliot, Esq.

Dear Mr Eliot,

I'm in town (and likely to be for some time now) and if you are too and have the time to spare I would like to take belated advantage of your kind invitation and meet you somewhere. I am free all next week with the exception of Monday.

With compliments and every good wish.

Yours sincerely,
C. M. Grieve.

18 Pyrland Road,
London, N.5.
22-7-31

T. S. Eliot, Esq.

Dear Mr Eliot,

Many thanks for your letter of yesterday. I shall be very glad to lunch with you on Friday 31st inst, as suggested, at whatever time and place you arrange later.

With best wishes.

Yours sincerely,
C. M. Grieve.

TS

321 High Holborn,
London, W.C.1.
8th October 1931.

T. S. Eliot, Esq.,
c/o Faber & Faber,
24 Russell Square,
W.C.1.

Dear Mr Eliot,

I had a letter yesterday from Donaghy.[1] He is in the Down County Mental Hospital, Down Patrick, and he says that he is now very much better. He only sent me a short letter but promised to write me fully in the course of a day or two.

I was talking to Major C. H. Douglas[2] last night and discussing the relation of his economic ideas to Nationalism and the idea of atomisation as against the acceptance of any convention. Your name cropped up and Douglas said that he had never met you and would like very much to do so. I wonder if you would care to meet him and if so if we might arrange to meet together for lunch somewhere soon.

I have found Daniel Corkery's book *Hidden Ireland* of which I was speaking to you and will send it on. I promised to send you copies of my first two McDiarmid books of lyrics. I cannot remember at the moment, however, whether I mentioned this when I was writing to Blackwood and asked them to send them to you or not. They sent me a set here the other day and I am rather puzzled as to whether these were the ones I intended for you, or whether you have received copies yourself independently, though I rather fancy if the latter had happened you would have dropped me a line, unless perhaps you are

[1] The Irish poet John Lyle Donaghy contributed to *The Criterion*; in his poem 'Grotesque', from *Wilderness Signs* (1942), he says 'I presented myself as a pathological case/but my extreme sanity put out the psycho-analysts.'
[2] C. H. Douglas (1879–1952), the Social Credit theorist, was an economic influence on both MacDiarmid and Pound.

too busy at the moment. But I would like you to have them so please let me know.

Every kind regards,

Yours sincerely,
C. M. Grieve.

TS

321 High Holborn,
London, W.C.1.
30th October, 1931.

T. S. Eliot, Esq.,
Messrs. Faber & Faber,
Russell Square,
W.C.1.

Dear Mr Eliot,

I have been hoping to hear from you on two accounts. I am anxious if you care to arrange an early meeting at which I might have the pleasure of introducing you to Major C. H. Douglas. Please tell me if you agree to have lunch with us one day next week. I am going off to Ireland on Friday and will be away for several days and if we can possibly arrange it mutually before then I shall be very glad. In lieu to replying in writing to this note, perhaps you can phone me up on Monday or Tuesday.

I am also wondering in the absence of any reply to my last letter whether you have yet received these two early books of lyrics of mine. If not I am anxious to send them to you as soon as possible.

Every kind regard.
Yours sincerely,
C. M. Grieve.

TS

321 High Holborn,
London, W.C.1.
3rd November, 1931.

T. S. Eliot, Esq.,
c/o Faber & Faber, Publishers,
Russell Square,
W.C.1.

Dear Mr Eliot,

I shall be back from Ireland on Tuesday evening and either *Wednesday* or Thursday would suit Major Douglas and myself for lunch. I hope one of these two days will be suitable to you. Will you please ask your secretary to phone me up to say which you prefer and I will then arrange with Major Douglas and fix a place and let you know.

I presume that 12.30 or 1 o'clock would be convenient.

Yours sincerely,
C. M. Grieve.

TS

321 High Holborn,
London, W.C.1.
5th November, 1931.

T. S. Eliot, Esq.,
c/o Faber & Faber,
Russell Square,
W.C.1.

Dear Mr Eliot,

Many thanks for your note. I am glad that you will be able to come to lunch with me and meet Major Douglas at 1 o'clock on Wednesday of next week (11th inst). I hope the Holborn Restaurant at the corner of Kingsway and Holborn will suit you.

I have written to Major Douglas by this post and if this suggested place is agreeable to him and to you we will take that as the arrangement. If I hear from either of you to the contrary I will get on the phone and suggest another place on Wednesday forenoon.

Kindest regards.

Yours sincerely,
C. M. Grieve.

TS   321 High Holborn,
                                                 London, W.C.1.
                                              16th November, 1931.

T. S. Eliot, Esq.,
c/o Faber and Faber, Publishers,
Russell Square,
W.C.1.

Dear Mr Eliot,

When I lunched with you some time ago at the Royal Societies Club you mentioned that you would like to meet Mr. Whyte of *The Modern Scot* when he came to town and I promised that I would let you know and try and arrange a meeting. I saw Mr Whyte here on Friday and he is to be in town all this week. I wonder if you could lunch with us either on Tuesday or Wednesday. If so perhaps you would ask your secretary to phone me up here either on Tuesday morning or Wednesday morning so that I can get in touch with Mr Whyte and arrange it.

Kindest regards.

Yours sincerely,
C. M. Grieve.

321 High Holborn,
London, W.C.1.
12/1/32

T. S. Eliot, Esq.

Dear Mr Eliot,

This is just a note by which to introduce you to my friend, Mlle Millig Garten (a friend, too, of 'A.E.'s', Gogarty's etc.) who carries with her the typescript of a French essay by Puis Servien whose other work you may know. I am much interested in this particular essay and think that you possibly may be too. Many thanks for your letter of the other day. I am glad to know you aren't going to be away from London until September.

Every kind regard.

Yours,
C. M. Grieve.

TS

321 High Holborn,
London, W.C.1.
18th February, 1932.

T. S. Eliot, Esq.,
The Criterion,
c/o Messrs. Faber & Faber,
24 Russell Square,
W.C.2.

Dear Mr Eliot,

Many thanks for your letter of yesterday's date. I am delighted that you like my 'Second Hymn to Lenin' and wish to publish it in your June issue.

I quite see your point about the quatrain to which you take editorial exception and I am, of course, quite prepared that it should be omitted from the poem as it appears in *The Criterion*.[1] I also agree

---

[1] 'Second Hymn to Lenin' (323–7) appeared in *The Criterion*, Vol XI, No XLV, July 1932. Eliot retained the disputed quatrain:

with you with regard to the personal criticism you make of the phrase 'win through' and am greatly obliged to you for the useful suggestion that it might be put in quotes with the implication of being used sardonically. I have been thinking about this and failing anything more effective occurring to me in the way of altering that first line I will certainly adopt your suggestion when I restore the stanza for any subsequent publication of the poem in book form.

I have been making an intensive study for some time past of all the poetry of Charles Doughty and am planning to write a short book about it at an early date.

> Every good wish,
> Yours sincerely,
> C. M. Grieve.

P.S. I wonder if you have already arranged for Doughty in your Poets on Poets Series; and, if not, whether the idea would appeal to you.

TS

321 High Holborn,
London, W.C.1.
17th March, 1932.

T. S. Eliot, Esq.,
c/o Messrs. Faber & Faber,
24 Russell Square,
W.C.2.

Dear Mr Eliot,

With reference to my 'Second Hymn to Lenin' which you have accepted for *The Criterion*, I am writing to ask whether the type for this can be kept standing so that I can subsequently issue the poem in pamphlet form.[1] I should be willing to pay for the rent of keeping

> *Gin I canna win through to the man in the street,*
> *The wife by the hearth,*
> *A' the cleverness on earth 'll no' mak' up*
> *For the damnable dearth.*

[1] *Second Hymn to Lenin*, published over the imprint of Valda Trevlyn, appeared in a limited edition of 100 copies in 1932.

the type standing and perhaps you will advise me about this at your earliest convenience.

Thanking you in anticipation and with every kind regard.

Yours sincerely,
C. M. Grieve.

'Cootes',
Thakeham,
Sussex.
5/4/32

T. S. Eliot, Esq.

Dear Mr Eliot,

Many thanks for your letter. I note the type can be kept standing and I will write to the printers (who, as you say, will of course print the pamphlet) giving particulars of what I want done with it, and asking them for their estimate. If you are agreeable I should propose to publish the pamphlet a month, or, if you prefer, two months after *The Criterion* appears. The publishing date can be fixed later; the pamphlets can be got ready as soon as *The Criterion* has been run off.

Things have gone badly with me financially & otherwise recently and I am very anxious to obtain additional literary or journalistic work of any kind or any sort of job whatever. Alas, either is excessively ill to find these days. I have meanwhile 'parked' down here in a cottage where I can live very cheaply and am working hard to finish several new books, including a novel and my big poem (of which the Lenin hymns are separable short items) – which is, I think, making good progress.

Every kind regard to yourself.

Yours sincerely,
C. M. Grieve.

P.S. I find that in the draft of the Second Lenin poem I sent you I omitted 3 verses, which I now enclose on a separate sheet. But I will leave it to you whether you care to include these in *The Criterion* version – tho' the 3rd of these 3 verses seems to me important to the poem.

Whalsay,
via Lerwick,
Shetland Islands.
4-2-38

T. S. Eliot, Esq.,
c/o Messrs. Faber & Faber,
London,

Dear Mr Eliot,

I have just completed what I believe to be an important long poem – between 4,000 and 5,000 lines – entitled *Mature Art*.

I define it as a 'hapax legomenon of a poem – an exercise in schlabone, bordatini, and prolonged scordatura' and it is, I am very safe in saying, a very advanced example of 'learned poetry', much of it written in a multi-linguistic diction embracing not only many European but also Asiatic languages, and prolific in allusions and 'synthetic poetry', demanding for their complete comprehension an extremely detailed knowledge of numerous fields of world-literature. At the same time the logic of the whole is quite clear, and most of the poem should be understood by almost anyone who reads while he runs – if he runs fast enough.

I write to ask if I may offer this work for publication in the first place to Messrs Faber and Faber. If you wish I can send you the typescript immediately. It has not been submitted elsewhere, and only two very small portions of the poem have appeared as separate poems in American and Canadian periodicals. I remember with pleasure my meetings with you in London six or seven years ago, and I need not say that apart altogether from whether Messrs Faber and Faber can see their way to undertake the publication of this poem, I should esteem it a very great privilege to have you personally glance through the MSS, and would be very vitally interested indeed in any comments you might care to make.

With compliments and high regards.

Yours sincerely,
C. M. Grieve.

P.S. I also hope to submit in a few days for favour of consideration for *The Criterion* an essay on what may be called the British Question in the light of dialectical materialism. Socialist thought has sedulously avoided the British Question – paying lip-service to Scottish, Welsh, etc. autonomy, but in practice doing nothing to further these causes, and in fact steadily supporting British Imperialism. While the essay is written from the Dialectical Materialist standpoint and I am a member of the Communist Party, it is, of course, severely critical of Communist Party policy, and is full of very important, and little understood, implications in view of recent developments in Ireland, the growth of the Welsh movement, and the changing situation in Scotland. The article is a political counterpart to the article on 'English Ascendancy in British Literature' I contributed to *The Criterion* a few years ago.

Whalsay,
Via Lerwick,
Shetland Islands.
18-6-38

T. S. Eliot, Esq.,
c/o Messrs. Faber and Faber.

Dear Mr Eliot,

Many thanks for your very kind letter with regard to my poem, *Mature Art*.[1] I was afraid that your reply with regard to the possibility of publication by Messrs Faber and Faber would be as in fact it is; I know well enough the difficulties of publishing such a big work in verse, and how unpropitious the times are for such an undertaking. But my disappointment is greatly mitigated by your very great kindness in saying that you would be willing to give the book your personal support if I submitted it to another firm. I wrote to Messrs Macmillan & Co Ltd for whom I have other work in hand at present and who published my *Selected Poems*, and I have just heard from them expressing their readiness to consider this poem too. So I will be greatly obliged if you will be so good as to send the MSS round to them. I enclose four additional typescripts – three Appendices and a

---

[1] On 8 June 1938 Eliot wrote to MacDiarmid: 'You will have understood that my delay in writing to you about *Mature Art* was due to my absence abroad. I tackled it on my return, and I must say that it seems to me an extremely interesting, individual, and indeed very remarkable piece of work. There can be no doubt that it is something that ought to be published, but the question is how, and by whom. For in the first place, any publisher who undertook it ought to have the courage and conviction to be prepared to publish the whole poem when it is complete. I am sorry that I cannot get my colleagues to consider undertaking a work in verse of this size. I cannot afford to lose much money for them on poetry.'

batch of miscellaneous additions which can be fitted into their proper places in the MSS later on. Perhaps in the meantime you will kindly add this material at the end of the MSS I sent you and pass on the lot to Messrs Macmillan's. I would be glad, however, if you could spare the time to read the First Appendix before passing it on, and consider whether you would not care to use it, as a separate poem, in *The Criterion*. Apart from anything else, it may, however, be on the long side for that.

I understand that work must have accumulated during your absence abroad, and it may be for this reason that I have had no word from you yet with regard to the essay: 'Brief Survey of Modern Scottish Politics In The Light of Dialectical Materialism' which I ventured to submit some months ago in the hope that it might prove acceptable for *The Criterion*.

Again thanking you, and with my best wishes.

Yours sincerely,
C. M. Grieve.

TS   Whalsay,
                                                                via Lerwick,
                                                                  Shetland.
                                                                  17-9-38

T. S. Eliot, Esq.,

Dear Mr Eliot,

Very many thanks for your kind letter. I was afraid that, owing to its length and for other reasons, the essay would probably not commend itself to you as suitable for *The Criterion*. But I am delighted that you wish to publish the 'First Appendix' (Cornwall)[1] section of *Mature Art*, and I accordingly enclose a copy of it herewith. I have restored the full title to it, with a little explanatory footnote, as 'First Appendix' has, of course, no meaning out of the *Mature Art* context.

I note that you have sent on *Mature Art* to Messrs Macmillan with

---

[1] 'Cornish Heroic Song for Valda Trevlyn' (704–12) appeared in *The Criterion*, Vol XVIII, No LXXI, January 1939.

your warm recommendation, and I am greatly indebted to you for that.

I shall think over very carefully what you say about dealing with aspects of the wide-ranging theme of the essay on Scottish Politics,[2] and thus bringing a more detailed forensic to bear on specific matters; and it may be a little later I will be able to submit one such shorter essay for your kind consideration.

With compliments and best wishes.

Yours sincerely,
C. M. Grieve.

P.S. I do not remember if I sent you a copy of my new quarterly.[3] So I enclose one now.

TS

Whalsay,
via Lerwick,
Shetland Islands.
20-9-38

T. S. Eliot, Esq.,
Editor, *The Criterion*.

Dear Mr Eliot,

Many thanks for your letter of 16th. inst. re Mr Keith Henderson's *Burns By Himself*.[1] I knew this book was coming out but have not seen it yet; I expect little so far as Mr Keith Henderson is concerned, but, since the book brings together a lot of Burns' own self-criticism and literary views I will be very glad to have an opportunity of reviewing it for you, all the more so as I have been reading extensively and otherwise planning a book on Burns for a

---

[2] In an undated letter Eliot wrote to MacDiarmid: 'I must say I think this Appendix will be very much more impressive and effective in *The Criterion* than your article on Scottish Politics in its present form. For one thing, the article is about twice as long as it is convenient to publish. For a second point, I had much rather have a contribution which you could sign with your own name, than a manifesto from the Red Scotland Committee.'

[3] *The Voice of Scotland* was launched with the June-August 1938 number.

[1] MacDiarmid's review of Keith Henderson's *Burns – By Himself* (1939) appeared in *The Criterion*, Vol XVIII, No LXXI, January 1939.

long time. I wonder, incidentally, if I could not do this for Messrs Faber & Faber's 'Poets on Poets' series – if that series (to which I can recall no recent addition) is still a live element in your publishing programme. Perhaps you will be so kind as to let me know what space you can afford for an article, which is only a review in the sense that I can use this book as a convenient peg for some concentrated expression of my own considered opinions regarding Burns. Since Burns's historical setting and his relationship to his predecessors is so important to any understanding of him, I hope you may be able to allow me to have a fair amount of space (provided of course you approve the article I subsequently submit). I will be glad if you will send me Mr Keith Henderson's book.

Mr John Lindsey also wrote a book about Burns lately. Have you had this for review? – – I do not remember it being reviewed in *The Criterion*.

I would also greatly welcome the opportunity to review for you – if you have not already allocated it elsewhere – Sir H. J. C. Grierson's new biography of Sir Walter Scott, on which I think I could give you a really thorough piece of criticism.

With best wishes,

Yours sincerely,
C. M. Grieve.

TS   Whalsay,
                                                         via Lerwick,
                                                            Shetland.
                                                             20-1-39

T. S. Eliot, Esq.

Dear Mr Eliot,

I read your 'Last Words'[1] with the deepest sympathy, and in agreement generally with what you say of the present position and prospects and the difficulty with which – only by a very few and in obscure little periodicals – the continuity of culture and a platform for original writing will almost certainly have to be maintained, if it

---

[1] The last issue of *The Criterion* was published in January 1939.

can be maintained at all, for probably a long time ahead. I need not tell you either how deeply I regret the cessation of *The Criterion*, how very great (and, at the moment and doubtless for long enough, irreparable) I consider the consequent loss, or how keenly I appreciate the increasing difficulties the maintenance of such a review must have entailed on you. I am not surprised that it has gone down; I only marvel at the courage which has maintained it so long at such a high level. But my own experience tells me also of the dangers attendant upon the relinquishment of a long-borne burden, and I sincerely hope that in becoming relieved of this strain you will not in turn be saddled with the equal or greater burden of missing too paralysingly all the work in connection with *The Criterion* you have had for these sixteen years.

It was very kind of you to write me and to return the Scott review typescripts. I regret that I did not contrive in good time to say what I felt needed saying about Grierson's book – and about Scott – in practicable space. I am hoping now to do it for *Scrutiny* (Dr Leavis was kind enough to say he greatly liked my *Criterion* review of the Burns book). But where in the world, now the *Criterion* is gone, am I to find publication – let alone a market! – for poems like the *Cornish Heroic Song*?

If, however, Roy Campbell abandons the idea of doing a book on Burns for the 'Poets on Poets' series, I would greatly like to have the chance of doing it.

Again with compliments and thanks and every kind regard.

Yours sincerely,
C. M. Grieve.

TS

T. S. Eliot, Esq.,
c/o Messrs Faber and Faber,
Publishers.

Dear Mr Eliot,

    I wonder if Messrs Faber & Faber would be willing to consider a selection of a few hitherto-unpublished poems of mine as a volume in your Sesame series.[1] I know of course something of the difficulties of publishing just now, and realize that you may not be able to continue with this series. So far I have seen no new addition to it announced.

Nevertheless I trust that you may find it possible to go on with it.

    If you cared to consider these poems I should be very happy to send you the typescript.

    With every good wish.

Yours sincerely,
C. M. Grieve.

Whalsay,
Shetland Islands.
17/3/41

T. S. Eliot, Esq.,
Messrs Faber and Faber Ltd.
Dear Mr Eliot,

You will remember the huge poem of mine you read a year or thereby ago. It was to have been published by the Obelisk Press,

---

[1] Eliot replied on 13 June 1940 explaining that the Sesame series 'is meant to consist only of selections from authors' previously published work . . . So I am afraid that a volume of unpublished verse would break the continuity of the series, and would have to be considered separately.'

Place Vendôme, Paris; but the Fall of France quashed that project. I have now adapted a small portion of it, dealing with linguistic matters and the limitations of the human mind, and called this (which is complete in itself) *In Memoriam James Joyce* and I wonder if you could consider it for publication. I think it would appeal to all Joyce enthusiasts and probably become a 'collectors' piece'. And as a separate thing this portion of my huge poem is, I think, a practicable publishing proposition, though of course it still makes 'a poem of some length'.

I have sent the MSS to my literary agents, Messrs Gilbert Wright (London) Ltd, 45 Frognall Court, Finchley Road, London NW3. (Telephone – Hampstead 1572) and told them I was writing to you in the first instance and that they were to hold on to the MSS in the meantime until we heard whether or not Messrs Faber and Faber could consider it.

In this remote island I hear little news and I do not know what the position is in London, but I hope you are safe.

With best wishes.

Yours sincerely,
C. M. Grieve.

Sudheim,
Whalsay,
Shetland Islands.
12-5-41

T. S. Eliot, Esq.,
c/o Messrs Faber and Faber.

Dear Mr Eliot,

Many thanks for your kind letter. I was sorry to hear from your Secretary in acknowledging receipt of my MSS that you were off ill, and while your letter indicates that you are back at work again I hope you have made a good and complete recovery.

You must be having a terrible time in London these days. On this remote little island I am very isolated and hear very little news. While I knew that publishers etc. were carrying on under increasing difficulties I had not realized how serious the paper shortage is.

Otherwise I would probably have understood that there was little hope of getting such a poem published just now. Probably my best chance in the meantime is in America. The Colt Press, San Francisco are publishing a volume of new poems of mine this autumn, and *New Directions* are having some poems of mine (extracted from my long poem) in their next annual miscellany which also comes out in the Fall.

I should have liked Messrs Faber and Faber to have published this *In Memoriam James Joyce*[1] all the same, but your kind letter goes far to compensate me for my disappointment, and the kind things you say about the poem make me feel that I can afford to wait and that it will yet come into its own.

Again thanking you, and with compliments and every good wish.

Yours sincerely,
C. M. Grieve.

---

[1] On 24 April 1941 Eliot wrote to MacDiarmid: 'I have read with great interest the part of your long poem which you sent me and wish that we could publish it. It is, incidentally, a very fine monument to Joyce though I am afraid that it gains no advantage from the association until such time as Joyce's later work is properly appreciated. I not only enjoyed the poem but there is a great deal in it that has my sympathy as well as admiration, but in this time when we are really being starved for paper it is works like this which must suffer. I hope that you can find a publisher who will venture on it and I am sorry to relinquish it, but it is works which could gain only slow appreciation that must suffer during this immediate crisis.'

27 Arundel Drive,
Battlefield,
Glasgow S.
2/9/45

T. S. Eliot, Esq.,
c/o Messrs Faber and Faber,
Publishers.

Dear Mr Eliot,

I am sorry the paper situation is not much improved.[1] Nevertheless I am grateful to you for your note, and am taking advantage of your 'somewhat chilly encouragement' to send you the MSS of my Joyce poem.

With every kind regard.

Yours sincerely,
C. M. Grieve.

Brownsbank,
by Biggar,
Lanarkshire.
25/12/54

T. S. Eliot, Esq.

Dear Mr Eliot,

Mr Wm. MacLellan, the Glasgow publisher, who is publishing my long poem *In Memoriam James Joyce*, has forwarded to me your

---

[1] On 28 August 1945 Eliot wrote to MacDiarmid: 'I am afraid the paper situation is not appreciably better now but if you are willing to take the trouble to send me the poem again on such very chilly encouragement, I should like very much to have an opportunity of reading it again now!' After reconsidering the poem Eliot wrote on 4 February 1946: 'I have had your Joyce poem for a long time. I found my Board indisposed to take it on but I am afraid I have been hanging on to it and brooding over it by myself from time to time to try to think whether anything could be done. It is a magnificent tribute to language and even the least sympathetic critic could not deny that it is an astonishing piece of work. I don't believe that more than very few people would read it because I don't think that more than very few people have the right infatuation with language. But I still don't see what can be done and I at last reluctantly return it.'

letter of 21st December.[2]

I regret that the quotation relative to this poem from yourself was printed without your express permission, but that was because I wrongly thought it was from the very kind letter[3] you sent on the occasion when the younger Scots poets presented me with a portrait of myself several years ago. I have since consulted the text of your letter and find that the quotation in question is from the letter you sent me in the Shetland Islands prior to 1939 when you had read the typescript of the poem. I can assure you that that letter is accurately quoted, but I have not yet put my hands on the original, and immediately I do so I will send you a copy of that letter.

I realise of course that you have not seen the text as it is now being printed but it is not substantially altered from the typescript you read – only tightened up in places – and I sincerely hope that when you do see it your opinion of it will be as good as that you so kindly expressed in the letter in question.

I am very sorry, of course, that a letter of yours should have been quoted in this way but that was due to the mistaken impression that it came from the letter you sent on the other occasion – which letter was published in various papers at the time.

I trust you are keeping well and ask you to accept all the compliments of the season and my best wishes for your happiness and prosperity in the coming year.

Yours sincerely,
(C. M. Grieve)
'Hugh MacDiarmid'

[2] In promoting *In Memoriam James Joyce* (Glasgow 1955) the publisher, William MacLellan, cited Eliot's encouraging letter of 24 April 1941, see p. 454. Eliot wrote to MacLellan, on 21 December 1954, objecting to the unauthorised use of his words on the back of a leaflet advertising the book. On receiving MacDiarmid's letter Eliot replied, on 29 December 1954: 'As you recognise fully that the permission should have been asked and as you account for the omission, there is nothing more to be said, except that I can see no reason why the permission should not have been given if asked. Any statement I have made about your work I will take the responsibility for. Wishing you and your publishers all success with the sale of the new book and with its reception.'

[3] On 15 August 1948 Eliot wrote to Albert Mackie: 'I very much regret that I shall be unable to attend the lunch to be given in honour of Hugh MacDiarmid, and the presentation of his portrait, on the 28th of this month . . . As I cannot be present, I should like to send my greetings to Hugh MacDiarmid and to the Makars assembled to do him honour. There are two reasons why I should have wished to be present on this occasion. The first is my respect for the great contribution of the Poet to Poetry – in general – in my time; the second is my respect for his contribution to Scottish Poetry – in particular . . . It will eventually be admitted that he has done more also for English poetry, by committing some of his finest verse to Scots, than if he had elected to write exclusively in the Southern dialect.'

To Bessie J. B. MacArthur

The Scots poet Bessie J. B. MacArthur, whose publications range from *The Clan of Lochlann and Silis: two Celtic plays* (1928) to the poems in *From Daer Water* (1962), was friendly with leading figures in the Scottish Literary Renaissance such as MacDiarmid, Soutar and Helen B. Cruickshank.

NLS

Royal Liver Building,
Liverpool.
25/2/31

Dear Mrs MacArthur,

How kind of you to write me! I am very glad you like *Cencrastus*. It has certainly brought me far more appreciation than any of my previous books. As a whole I do not think it is so completely achieved as my *Drunk Man*: nor did I succeed in working out my intention – indeed I deliberately departed from it, realising that I was not yet capable of that task, and that it was necessary first of all to get rid of all kinds of elements (not without their own values) which have been standing between me and my real job. I believe I've done that now; and can go ahead to a far bigger task. That's what Bottomley and Saurat both mean in the last *Modern Scot*[1] when they indicate a sort of

---

[1] *The Modern Scot*, Vol 1, No 4, January 1931 contained two reviews of *To Circumjack Cencrastus*: Gordon Bottomley concluded that 'If [MacDiarmid] ever finds a human and Scottish figure on which to focus [his gifts], they are of the right kind and fulness to enable him to do for his country what Ibsen did for Norway in *Peer Gynt*, De Coster for Belgium in *Tyll Ulenspiegel*, Cervantes for Spain in *Don Quixote*'; Denis Saurat argued that 'it is in Hugh M'Diarmid to become the great national Scottish poet, if the Scots will have him. He cannot do it without them, but an intense condemnation of him might be of as much use to him as praise . . . There is, I should say, already perhaps too much of himself in *Cencrastus*. I take it that *To Circumjack Cencrastus* is to expel the self, which stands and bars the threshold into real epic poetry.'

national epic – perfectly clear and straightforward and without cheap personalities, highbrow display, etc. – as what I'm obviously in training for: and that in fact is what I am tackling now – a vast business. Goodness only knows if I can pull it off; but I think I can and have already put an enormous amount of labour into the preliminary work to ensure a design that will be four square, we'll see. Letters such as yours certainly encourage one.

I'm so sorry I was remiss about you and the PEN – it was to my loss, too, for otherwise we might have met, as I hope we may do yet. But I'm glad you joined all the same and delighted to hear that you enjoy the little functions it runs.

What of your own work? Are you still writing? I am afraid I am not so closely in touch with Scottish matters as I was some time ago.

Again thanking you, and with every good wish.

Yours,
C. M. Grieve.

NLS

Whalsay,
via Lerwick,
Shetland Islands.
5/11/37

Dear Mrs MacArthur,

Many thanks for your kind letter and the copy of Reid's[1] poem, which I am delighted to have. I like both his use of Scots and the subtlety and exactitude of his descriptive faculty. It is nearer to my own kind of work, I think, than almost anything else I have seen in Scots.

It was all the kinder of you to write me again in that I have had you on my conscience (a faculty – if only intermittently operative – I still retain) since you wrote me a very kind letter indeed some years ago when I was in London wasting my substance (or my lack of substance) in riotous living, and recalling me to Scotland and my duty there. I ought to have replied to that letter. But I am very wayward and difficile – and didn't. Nevertheless it was not without

---

[1] Possibly Alexander Reid (1914–82), the Scots dramatist.

its effect and if I stupidly jibbed at it at the time sense repossessed me in due course and I was very grateful.

I had a glorious time in the Hebrides and Western Islands – Skye, South Uist, Barra, Mull, Iona, Eigg, and all round about Glenfinnan, Loch Shiel, and Arisaig. It was a perfect revelation to me – and has meant a kind of rededication of myself to Scotland. I think it will bear good fruit ere long, though things (and I do not mean merely material circumstances) are still almost inconceivably difficult for me. I ought of course, to have gone to one of the Hebrides – not to the Shetlands. The difference is between islands with a cultural background and islands with none – a delightful people, interested in music, dancing, subtleties of speech and spiritual things, and a boorish people with no more intellectual interests or spiritual perceptions than their own grice. And yet I love this desperate emptiness of life – this stony restitution and last ditch of the world sort of feeling.

Were you at the Mod? I almost ran down from Perth, where I was seeing Soutar, but I had been away from home too long, so I didn't. But all over the islands and in Inverness, Dunblane, and elsewhere I had the pleasure of looking up old friends and making new ones – McNair Reid and his wife in Eigg, Gunn in Inverness, Compton Mackenzie, Annie Johnston, and Father John MacMillan in Barra, Angus Clark in Dunblane, Hugh Patterson at Burrelton, and so on.[2]

But you know – magnificent as the Highlands and Islands are – my heart is always in the Borders, which, for one reason and another, I have not revisited for just on twenty years.

Barring colds, Mrs Grieve and Michael and I are all very well. Trust you are in good form too. Are you writing at all nowadays, and how is the Clarsach?

Again with thanks and best wishes, and every kindest regard to you and yours.

Yours,
C. M. Grieve.

[2] The authors John Macnair Reid, Neil Gunn and Compton Mackenzie, Annie Johnston, Angus Clark and Hugh Patterson were activists in the cause of Scottish Nationalism. Father John MacMillan was priest at St Munn's, Ballachulish, and the original of Father James Macalister in Compton Mackenzie's *Whisky Galore* (1947).

Whalsay,
Via Lerwick,
Shetland Islands.
25.2.38

Dear Mrs MacArthur,

Many thanks for sending me these poems.[1] I am keenly interested in your impulsion to write in the Doric now and anxious to encourage it all I can. But when it comes to commenting on your poems I feel I am hardly the person to be fair to them – as my own entire tendency has been to get as far away as possible from the traditional alike in subject-matter and in vocabulary. At the same time I must agree that your poems are· quite effective – especially, I think, 'The Lowe' and 'Sternies'. The best of the lot to my mind is 'Smoort' but here I have a suggestion to make which I feel would clinch it and raise it to a higher dramatic level – but which at the same time I fancy may not consort with your notion of poetry in the way it consorts with mine. It is a very simple matter, but very simple matters make all the difference of course in the art of poetry. It is simply that the last word should be not 'will' but 'fill'.

Apart from that, however, I would strongly urge you to experiment more outside the beaten track alike in sentiment, subject-matter, and vocabulary. To restrict yourself to the traditional themes not only gives a number of poems a certain unfortunate sameness, but it has two even worse effects – it throws them into unnecessary competition with the best that has been done in the same style on similar subjects, and it perpetuates an unfortunate divorce between one's thematic and verbal material and the sights and sounds of contemporary life absorbed and appreciated at first hand. Please do not feel that I am being in any way at all patronising in making these comments, or special-pleading for my own school of poetry.

I will look forward in any case, I hope, to seeing further poems of yours later, and I hope your Doric impulse holds, and carries you further and deeper.

Perhaps you saw my articles in the *Bulletin* recently in defence of Scots as a modern literary medium.

Yes. We have been having a towsy time here too with gale-force winds – and here we have no trees or heights to protect us from the full violence of the blasts. But, apart from occasional colds,

---

[1] Bessie J. B. MacArthur, *Scots Poems* (1938).

460

owing to too much wet, we are all well. Trust this finds you all in good form too.

With every kind regard from Valda and myself.

Yours,
C. M. Grieve.

NLS

c/o Scott,
44 Munro Road,
Jordanhill,
Glasgow.
12.7.42

Dear Mrs MacArthur,

I am still in Glasgow, you see – despite many ups and downs since I wrote you last. I finally got a good job with Mesrs Mond Nickel Coy Ltd in the new factory they are running for the Ministry of Supply, and was all set to have my wife and Michael come down, when I suddenly lost the job, simply because the Ministry of Labour had issued a decree that jobs of the kind I was holding in Government factories were thenceforward to be filled by women. Followed a desperate search for another job, and, pending that, I had to postpone the coming down here of Valda and Michael. However, I'm all fixed up again, this time in a genuine engineering job, as a fitter with Messrs Meechan's Ltd, Scotstoun, and Valda and Michael are ready to come down now just as soon as I give the word.

It is in this connection that I am writing you. I am hoping to send Michael after the summer holidays to Kilquhanity School, near Castle Douglas, but in the meantime his mother and I are anxious to fix him up somewhere in the country until we ourselves get a place in Glasgow. So his mother suggested in a recent letter that I might write you and find out whether you could not possibly take in another little evacuee for a while. If you could that would not only make things easier for Valda and I until we get some sort of home fixed up here, but it would be far better for Michael himself instead of a violent break with the country life he has always had up to now, especially as, until we do get fixed up, his mother would have difficulty in looking after him properly in Glasgow, and I could hardly help her in doing so, as I work very long hours – 8 a.m. to 8.30 p.m. 3 nights a week, 8 a.m. to 5.30 the other three, and three Sundays out of every four, so that I have virtually no time to myself whatever, except Saturday afternoons. And extremely hard physical work it is. But I am getting used to it now and like it well enough.

Please let me know then if you could take Michael for a month or so on the same footing – and for similar payment – as you took your little evacuees.

Incidentally he has a dog (a collie) which he is desperately anxious to bring down to Scotland with him, and for which, of course, his mother and I have no use whatever in a city like Glasgow. If you could take him for a while, could you take the dog too?

What sort of summer have you had? I trust you are all well and your sons safe and sound. Every kind regard.

Yours,
C. M. Grieve.

To Naomi Mitchison

Born in Edinburgh in 1897, the daughter of the Oxford physiologist J. S. Haldane, Naomi Mitchison (whose brother was J. B. S. Haldane, the controversial geneticist) has led an active life that reflects her background of economic privilege and radical unrest.

She became an upper-class rebel, espousing feminism and socialism; in 1916 she married the Labour politician G. R. Mitchison, later Lord Mitchison. Her novels express her abiding interest in the social dynamic of history and she tends to treat the past as an adumbration of the present. Among her historical novels are *The Conquered* (1923), *Cloud Cuckoo Land* (1925) and *The Corn King and the Spring Queen* (1930).

NLS
TS

321 High Holborn,
London, WC1.
27th January, 1932

Mrs Naomi Mitchison,
River Court,
Hammersmith,
W. 1.

Dear Mrs Mitchison,

How can I thank you for your references to me in Edinburgh the other night. I would not attempt to do so if I did not feel that they were in a measure justified. They certainly represent my constant appreciation of the need for a poet to grapple with the problems of his age (not perhaps that I have achieved this in anything like the measure you suggested, but that I have certainly felt it to be urgently necessary and consistently striven to achieve it). I have a great body of other work on hand and feel that speeches such as yours in clearing away a great many of the misapprehensions which have hitherto thwarted my efforts in Scotland and elsewhere must, to a large measure, simplify my task in attempting these.

When you return to London I should like to have the opportunity of coming to see you again.

You probably appreciate from my last book *First Hymn to Lenin* the profound effect upon me in certain directions of the book you gave me, viz. Gerald Heard's *Social Substance of Religion*[1] and I feel that I have been thinking so largely since then along certain lines of interest that we have in common that we could very profitably (or at least I could) take up our previous conversation where it was left off.

I hope all your own work goes well and that you and your children are fit and fine.

Again thanking you and with every kind regard.

Yours sincerely,
C. M. Grieve.

CMG/JB

NLS

Whalsay,
Shetland Islands.
17/1/34

Dear Mrs Mitchison

It was nice to get your Christmas card, forwarded on from Edinburgh, away up here in our Polar retreat. And we heartily, if belatedly, reciprocate your greetings and good wishes.

I do not know if you got the message I sent via Whyte (knowing you were to be in St Andrews about that time) apropos the portion of your novel which appeared in *The Modern Scot*.[1] I was immensely taken by it – by the novelty and efficacy of the technique, and have been haunted ever since by the prose rhythms of your marvellous description of the Hebridean seas. Has the book not been published yet? I fancy it can hardly have come out without my hearing of it and

[1] Henry Fitzgerald Heard, *Social Substance of Religion* (1931).
[1] *The Modern Scot*, Vol. IV, No. 2, July 1933, included 'Interlude', an extract from Naomi Mitchison's political novel *We Have Been Warned* (1935).

contriving somehow or other to lay hands on a copy – but it may have; I am almost completely cut off here from news of all kinds (tho' I always get *The Times Literary*).

We have been up here for over nine months now and, in fact, I have gone almost completely native. I like it immensely and it is suiting my work – or rather has been; it has involved very rigorous disciplines I was undoubtedly needing, but I feel that having nothing else to do but write is now beginning to make writing far more difficult than it would be if I was occupied all day with other work and had only – as I used to have – a little leisure at night to write in. That makes for concentration and – in my experience – better work. But I can't get a job of any kind anywhere so I'll have to stay here.

I have a big book – *Scottish Scene*, a miscellany of poems, plays, essays, short stories etc., written in collaboration with Lewis Grassic Gibbon coming out through Jarrold's this spring; and Victor Gollancz has just decided to put out a big collection of my new poems, *Stony Limits, and Other Poems*.

You'll be thinking I am very slow about repaying my debt to you. But that has been unfortunately utterly impossible yet – during the past fifteen months my total earnings have averaged less than 30/- per week, and I have only been able to keep going at all because life up here is extraordinarly cheap – e.g, I have a 4-roomed cottage the rent of which is only 27/- a year! But I have been working very hard and I have several other books in hand the issue of which may, I am hoping, put me on my feet again and enable me to discharge my liabilities during the current year.

Living the simple life of a fisherman-crofter, out on land or sea in all sorts of weathers, has certainly set me up again physically, and both my wife and baby are in excellent form, tho' the conditions here and the absence of all company and entertainment in these stormy months where there is only a few hours' daylight presses more hardly on them than on me.

I trust you are well and have many projects in hand. Wishing Mr Mitchison, yourself, and the children every good luck this New Year.

Yours,
C. M. Grieve.

465

To William Johnstone

William Johnstone (1897–1982) was probably MacDiarmid's closest friend among visual artists. Like MacDiarmid, he was a Borderer (from Hawick); like MacDiarmid, he was closely associated with the composer Francis George Scott (who was Johnstone's cousin). He was one of the first important Scottish painters to exploit the emotional possibilities of abstraction, using expressive areas of intense colour to suggest quintessentially Scottish qualities. After studying at Edinburgh College of Art he went to Paris in the 1920s to train in the studio of André L'Hôte. He then worked as an influential teacher of art in London becoming Principal, successively, of Camberwell and the Central School of Arts and Crafts. His first wife, Flora Macdonald, was an American sculptor he met in Edinburgh and married in Paris (in 1927); when this ended in divorce he married Mary, who had been one of his students at the Royal School of Needlework. He had two daughters, Elizabeth and Sarah; one by each marriage.

He was closely associated with MacDiarmid after being introduced to the poet by Francis George Scott. In his autobiography *Points in Time* (London 1980, p. 72) Johnstone said that Scott encouraged poet and painter to regard themselves as part of a Scottish Renaissance:

> We three were to be the core of this Renaissance. [Scott] felt that if we all pulled our weight together and tried, Christopher with his poetry, I with my painting, and Francis with his music, all having a revolutionary point of view, we could raise the standard of the arts right from the gutter into something that would be really important. He thought that it was a great coincidence that there were three of us, all from the Borders, interested in a great resurgence of art in Scotland – three, like the Pre-Raphaelites.

MacDiarmid and Johnstone were associated in several projects. The limited edition of *Tarras* (Edinburgh 1932) has a frontispiece 'Macdiarmid and the Horse Punckin' from an oil painting by Johnstone; the limited edition of *Second Hymn to Lenin* (Thakeham 1932) has a cover drawing of the poet by Flora Macdonald and a portrait frontispiece by Johnstone. MacDiarmid dedicated the poem 'Water Music' (333–7) to William and Flora Johnstone and provided poems for two of the painter's projects: *Poems to Paintings by William Johnstone* (Edinburgh 1963) and *Twenty Poems by Hugh MacDiarmid With Twenty Lithographs by William Johnstone* (Crailing 1977). Johnstone's own writings on art education were far-sighted and influential: *Creative Art in England* (1936) which was republished as *Creative Art in Britain* (1950); and *Child Art to Man Art* (1941).

NLS

'Cootes',
Thakeham,
Sussex.
5/4/32

My dear Johnstone,

I had meant to write you before this. To attempt to get you down here over Easter was out of the question; we are only getting the place into livable order now. It has involved carpentry, ironwork, plastering, colouring, window-glazing and the Lord knows what else. But it is a delightful place and we'll soon be in a fit state, to house friends. Keep it in mind for your summer holidays – all of you – but I hope you'll come down before that, and, in fact, first possible chance.

Re cash I'm desperately sorry but I'm temporarily hard up against things myself. Furnishing this, etc. has been an expensive process. But I'm getting my nose hard down to work and will be in a better state ere long. The business – the Unicorn Press – is still in critically difficult straits. But as I said I'll be personally responsible for the fee for your jacket. The Press can't possibly pay you anything at the moment, nor can I personally but I'll remit as soon as I get anything fixed up.

There is one way out of the difficulty. A friend of mine is willing to guarantee an overdraft of £50 on my behalf. The trouble is that I have not at the moment an operative personal account, and Valda's account with the Midland Bank is too new an account for this purpose. My friend's guarantee – which would be backed by her bankers (Coutts & Co) – would be accepted by any bank. If you have a private account it could be done through that. The modus operandi would simply be that you went to your branch manager

467

and said you wanted an overdraft of £50 against the guarantee of so-and-so (I'll supply you with the name, and reference to my friend's bankers before you do that if you agree to do it). Then it'll be arranged in a day or so; your a/c will be credited with £50 - or you'll be allowed to draw on it to that extent – and I'll draw on you as required for some £42 and you'll be in immediate possession of the £8 balance of the fee for your jacket. Please let me know by return if you're willing to do this, or, better, wire me, and I'll write at once to my friend, and, to you again by return. This would involve you in nothing and would help you – and help me very considerably.

I'll write again soon. I'm just making arrangements for publishing my next book with your portrait as frontispiece & Flora's on cover.

Have just got some new poems of Robinson Jeffers.

Hope all of you are in good fettle. Valda joins me in all love. Sursum corda.

Yours,
Chris.

NLS

Whalsay,
Shetland Islands.
June 3/1935

My dear William,

Your letter of 11th ult. has been lying here awaiting my return from a three weeks absence in Manchester, Glasgow, and Edinburgh; and I have only just received it. I am delighted to learn of your show, and trust it has been a great success. I would have been only too glad if I could have helped with publicity in any way, but nowadays I am cut off from all journalism – none of the Scottish papers have any use for me, or I for them. And living away up here on this lonely little North isle of the Shetland group I go for weeks at a time without seeing a paper – I never buy any and only now and again some of my friends send me one or two, which, of course, are a week old or more before they reach me. The consequence is that I am not in a position to see any of the notices of your show which may have appeared in the London press or elsewhere. I'd be glad therefore if you'd send me on cuttings of any good notices you've received to read – and return to you.

I've often wondered how you were getting on and thought of writing you – but one gets out of the way of letter-writing. As for myself I am as busy as ever – but confining myself these days to writing books. I published five last year and have already published one this year and have four more coming out this autumn. Life up here suits us very well and is certainly conducive to work. Valda and I are both O.K and our boy is growing big and strong. We have a nice cottage here, looking out across the islands and the waterways to the Atlantic. Life here is very simple and free and easy – with very long wild black winters, but from now for a month or two the full benefit of the midnight sun, so that one can read out of doors without difficulty at two or three in the morning.

I spent a day or two with F.G. in Glasgow. He is in fine form and doing splendid work.

Glad Flora and you are well and the child thriving: and hope things have greatly improved for you generally. Do let me know soon how the Show went. I'll be keen to hear and only wish I could have seen it.

Love from us all.

Yours,
Chris.

Remembering an exploit of ours, you'll be amused to know I'd a letter the other day from Richard Church – wanting to put a poem of mine in one of Dent's Anthologies.

NLS
TS

Whalsay,
Via Lerwick,
Shetland.
28-10-39

My dear Johnstone

Excuse just a very brief note. The War of course played havoc with the *Voice of Scotland* printing office, but I had a letter from the

Manager a few days ago saying the issue was almost ready. So it should come to hand very soon now.

Up here of course I am virtually marooned – today I got the first newspaper to reach the island for a fortnight – and mails are very belated, infrequent and uncertain. I had no idea till F.G. told me how drastically the War had affected schools like yours – staffs sacked; number of pupils down to zero, etc. It must be an infernal state of affairs. I hope that your job is secure enough.

Barbara Niven[1] wrote you off her own bat about these poor artists – I only gave her your address in connection with your show. But she is always busy with all kinds of charitable and political movements. She is a splendid girl. I hope you meet her.

I'm glad to hear your show is coming off yet, and hope it is a big success. What about your Macmillan book?[2] Is that out yet? I'll see the blocks are sent on just as soon as possible now to the address you give.

I'm just completing my Autobiography – I think it's a good book; I hope to get the typescript off to the publishers this week. Also I think the Obelisk Press, Paris, will be publishing my big new poem – *Cornish Heroic Song for Valda Trevlyn*[3] (over 20,000 lines) – ere long, if I can get sufficient advance orders on the strength of a prospectus they are just printing for me.

We are all in good enough form here though the winter weather has set in and it's damnably cold. Hope despite your worries and the circumambience of sandbags and other evidences of militarism this finds Flora, Elizabeth, and yourself in good trim too. All the best. We'll meet again some day.

Yours,
Chris.

[1] Barbara Niven (1896–1972) was a painter and prominent member of the Communist Party.
[2] William Johnstone, *Child Art to Man Art* (London 1941).
[3] MacDiarmid occasionally referred to his *Mature Art* project under this alternative title.

NLS

Wm. Johnstone, Esq. O.B.E.

Dear Willie,

Yes. We got back a fortnight ago – after a magnificent holiday in Canada where we enjoyed an abnormally early heat-wave and absorbed more sunshine than we are likely to encounter in Scotland in an equivalent number of years.

I was in Edinburgh and saw Collocott.[1] I think I know the drawing you consider 'the only one worth using'. But there is another one which is better for reproduction. Duncan Glen, the author of the book,[2] had chosen it, and I agreed. Anyhow I am greatly indebted to you for it.

While in Toronto, some of my friends at the University suggested I should let an artist called Ab. Bayefsky[3] paint me, and assured me that if he was on form he would very probably do *the* painting of me. He did. He works with great rapidity and assurance. It is a big painting of me, sprawled in an arm chair, and complete with kilt, sporran, tunic, etc. That was a busy 2 or 3 hours, for in addition to sitting for Bayefsky, I also made a tape-recording of the whole of the *Drunk Man* for the present Professor of German there, and it turned out a splendid recording.

Naturally since I came back I've been infernally busy, dealing with accumulated correspondence, demands for lectures, etc. etc.

Will be glad to see you any time you can manage up. Hope all is going well with the proofs, lay-out, etc. for the poems.

Kindest regards to Mrs Johnstone and Sarah.

I met an old pupil of yours the other day – Ruari MacLean, the typographer who was co-editor, I think, with Tony del Reinzo of some periodical.

All the best.

Yours,
Christopher.

[1] T. C. Collocott of W. & R. Chambers who published Duncan Glen's *Hugh MacDiarmid* (Edinburgh 1964).

[2] Glen's book has a frontispiece portrait of MacDiarmid by Johnstone – drawn especially for the book. The drawing Johnstone originally favoured is probably the one executed in 1936 and reproduced opposite p. 113 of the artist's autobiography *Points in Time* (London 1980).

[3] Aba Bajevsky's portrait of MacDiarmid is reproduced on p. 132 of Gordon Wright's *MacDiarmid: An Illustrated Biography* (Edinburgh 1977).

NLS

Brownsbank,
Biggar,
Lanarkshire.
3/9/65

Wm. Johnstone, Esq. O.B.E.

Dear William,

It is a long time since I heard or saw anything of you. I trust you –
and Mrs Johnstone and Sarah – are well. As you will know I've been
here, there, and nearly everywhere, and horribly busy as usual. But
I'll be at home now except on 10th and 11th inst., when I'll be in
Glasgow, until – I hope – the end of the year. Heaven knows I've
plenty to do – one book of 100,000 words to deliver to the publisher
by the 1st October and I've hardly got the thing begun yet. I wish I'd
been a farmer too. The sheep and I would have made excellent
company for each other.

Kindest regards to you all from Valda and I.

Yours,
Christopher.

P.S. Sorry to learn the Stone Gallery in Newcastle was to be closed.

NLS

Brownsbank,
Biggar.
10/8/69

Dear William,

We got down to Langholm for the Common-Riding all right, and
had a nice quiet week there in excellent weather, which did me a lot
of good. With care I should be all right now. I haven't quite got into
harness again but am managing – more slowly than I'd like – to
make up some of my arrears of work.

What's this nonsense of yours about taking things easy, and
getting on with my writing instead of travelling about all over the
world? That wouldn't do at all. I've always done my best work in the
interstices of being active in all sorts of other directions. I need that

sort of stimulus. But my energies are certainly reduced and I'm cutting out all manner of less important engagements.

It was nice of you both to come and see me in Chalmers Hospital. I cannot gather from either your letters or from what Valda tells me of your 'phone conversations just what the position is now 1/ with regard to the poems you wanted or 2/ with the preparations for your big Show later on.

I hope you are all well and enjoying yourselves. There doesn't seem to be much, if anything, of any particular interest in the Edinburgh Festival this year and I don't think I'll bother going in, tho' I have a couple of Poetry Readings in the first week of September.

With love and best wishes from Valda and I.

Yours,
Christopher.

NLS

Brownsbank,
Biggar.
25/3/74

William Johnstone, Esq. O.B.E.

Dear William,

I am sorry to have been so long in writing to you – if only to explain what happened when I refused to speak to you on the 'phone. I hate the 'phone and never use it if I can possibly help. It is Valda's 'phone – and in at least 99 per cent 'phone calls are for her, and either something to do with dogs, or just gossips with her cronies. In any case on that occasion the 'phone had been ringing every now and again and Valda was yattering away. So I was fed up. I was trying to concentrate on something I was writing, and I just could not bear the thought of speaking or being spoken to on the 'phone.

You must have thought me incredibly churlish, but I am sure you will understand from the above explanation.

I've been away a lot in London and elsewhere, and have a lot of engagements in the near future – in Wales, Oxford, etc. etc.

As you will have seen I have become an Honorary RSA[1] – titularly

[1] Royal Scottish Academician.

473

the Academy's Professor of Literature. I do not for a moment imagine you will approve of my acceptance of this appointment, but the fact remains that if you will only become an Academician too we might well join forces, and working within that August body have some effect in securing the changes in it which we both agree are vitally necessary.

I hope your health is keeping up. I am in good fettle myself, but somehow or other incurred a bad back last week and was scarcely able to move for a day or two. Then the damned thing disappeared as suddenly and inexplicably as it had come about – and I am all right again.

Love to Mary, Sarah, and yourself, from Valda and I.

Yours,
Christopher.

To Francis George Scott

Francis George Scott (1880–1958) is one of the most important figures to feature in MacDiarmid's career: the fact that *A Drunk Man Looks at the Thistle* is dedicated 'to my friend, Francis George Scott, the composer, who suggested it' speaks for itself. Unfortunately in later years Scott tended to exaggerate his part in the making of MacDiarmid's masterpiece and claimed, in the Autobiographical Letter of 1946 reproduced in Maurice Lindsay's *Francis George Scott and the Scottish Renaissance* (Edinburgh 1980, p. 56), 'I'm pretty certain I supplied the last two lines to bring the thing to some kind of conclusion.' MacDiarmid himself said (Company, p. 96)

> I had got to the point [in the shaping of *A Drunk Man*] when I had ceased to be able to see the forest for the trees. I found the necessary imaginative sympathy in F. G. Scott and handed over the whole mass of my manuscript to him. He was not long in seizing on the essentials and urging the ruthless discarding of the unessentials. I had no hesitation in taking his advice and in this way the significant shape was educed from the welter of stuff and the rest pruned away.

Scott was born in Hawick and went to Edinburgh to qualify as an English teacher. At Langholm Academy one of his pupils was C. M. Grieve who was greatly impressed by his teacher's intellectual energy and force of character. In 1923 another former Langholm Academy teacher, William Burt, drew Scott's attention to the MacDiarmid poems in *The Scottish Chapbook*; contact was re-established between teacher and pupil since these Scots lyrics were exactly what Scott the composer wanted. As Scott said, in the Autobiographical Letter:

> From [the reunion in 1923] to the publication of *Cencrastus* in 1930, I should say that practically every poem Grieve wrote was sent to Glasgow for my consideration . . . During this spate of creative activity, Christopher spent as many weekends in Glasgow as he could manage, and the Scott family took its month's holiday in Montrose . . .

Scott's home at 44 Munro Road, Glasgow, thus became one of the central stations of the Scottish Renaissance. It was a lively family home – for Scott's wife Burgess and the four children Malcolm, George, Lilias (known as Lovey) and Francise (known as Sancise) – as well as a haven for fellow-artists like MacDiarmid and Scott's cousin William Johnstone. To that address, as Scott says, MacDiarmid sent poems for criticism and comment. Yet the poet refused to accept the composer's purely musical criteria. Scott, who lectured in music at Glasgow's Jordanhill Training College, deplored MacDiarmid's move from lyrical achievements to epic aspirations and told him so in a letter of April 1940 with reference to the *Mature Art* project:

> I often wanted to ask you how you came to switch over to your irregular rhythms of recent years. Quite recently I went through *Sangschaw*, *Penny Wheep* and the *Drunk Man* looking for some explanation, but what came out most clearly was that the success of these books was largely the natural forcefulness of the poetic rhythm they contained. How you came to lose or throw away this sense of rhythm is a mystery to me. You may not think so, but I can assure you not much of your stuff since these books has any musical vitality.

According to MacDiarmid (Company, p. 98) Scott 'became increasingly reactionary in the last decade of his life' and the poet left the composer's house after hearing him express 'the most violent anti-semitic opinions.'

Scott's magnificent settings of MacDiarmid lyrics are contained in *Scottish Lyrics set to music* (5 vols, Glasgow 1922–1939) and discussed in Maurice Lindsay's book on the composer. Some of the songs are performed – by Isobel Buchanan, Malcolm Donnelly and Lawrence Glover – on *Francis George Scott: A Centenary Song Recital* (Scottish Records). Neil Mackay's edition of *Songs of Francis George Scott 1880–1958* (Glasgow 1980) contains forty-one songs including fourteen MacDiarmid settings.

EUL

Cootes,
Thakeham,
Sussex.
22/7/32

My dear F. G.,

The best thing in your letter is the hint that you are thrang with what promises to be an exhilarating addition to Scots musical

476

achievement. I wish you'd told me what sort of thing you're on. I'll be keen for more news of this and for God's sake don't let my mixed mails distract you. In this connection, is there any more news of Whyte publishing more of your setting? I don't suppose you've had a chance to wring Balderstone's neck yet re Scots Wha Hae?[1] And to jump about alarmingly from topic to topic, thinking over all your settings of stuff of mine, – and allowing for its 'obscenity' (and thus perhaps impossibility for public purposes) – I still wonder you've never been moved to do that *Drunk Man* thing – 'O Wha's been here afore me, lass, & how did he get in'.

I'm enclosing a cutting of *N.E. Weekly* with 'The Oon Olympian'.[2] Busy with an article for *The Dublin Magazine*[3] on poetry & politics with special reference in England, Scotland, Ireland and Russia – which deals with some of the issues that have been raising their noses in our letters recently. That reminds me – did you see last year my long article in *Criterion*[4] on 'English Ascendancy in British Literature' or not. If not, I'll send it on to you. My shorter recent poems, – those in some measure approved by you – 'Back O' Beyond', 'Dytiscus', 'Milk Wort & Bog Cotton', 'Lynch Pin', etc. are to be appearing weekly in *Scottish Educational Journal* under general title of 'A Kist o' Whistles'. I expect you know same useful organ is serialising my 'Course of Scottish Poetry' (over pseud of James MacLaren) – Chapter III appearing this week, I think.[5] I'll offer Whyte 'Depth & Chthonian Image' but doubt if he'll take it owing 1/ length 2/ idea being assiduously disseminated in certain quarters that since I became a Bolshie I've ceased to do good work. I did send you one of my lamb's head photos, didn't I?[6]

Am busy for a few days with domestic affairs but fancy I'll have a

[1] H. Balderstone was one of the founders of the National Party of Scotland. On 28 June 1932 Scott wrote to MacDiarmid: 'Over a fortnight ago Balderstone was going to put across at Bannockburn my setting of "Scots Wha Hae" ... Balderstone who was to bring along a singer to rehearse the song setting on Friday 17th failed to turn up as arranged [which was] a bit of the most hellish rudeness I've met with for many a long day.' Scott's version of 'Scots Wha Hae' appeared in *The Free Man*, Vol I, No 48, 31 December 1932.

[2] 'The Oon Olympian' (354-61), *New English Weekly* , Vol 1, No 14, 21 July 1932.

[3] *The Dublin Magazine*, October-December 1932, contained two poems – 'Lynch-Pin' (332) and 'Milk-Wort and Bog-Cotton' (331) – by MacDiarmid but no prose. 'Milk-Wort and Bog-Cotton' is dedicated to Seumas O'Sullivan, editor of *The Dublin Magazine*.

[4] 'English Ascendancy in British Literature', *The Criterion*, Vol X, No LXI, July 1931.

[5] 'The Course of Scottish Poetry' by 'James MacLaren' ran in eleven parts in *The Scottish Educational Journal* from 1 July 1932 to 14 April 1933.

[6] William Lamb's bronze head of MacDiarmid was sculpted in Montrose in 1925 and can be seen in the William Lamb Museum, Montrose.

good bag to send you next week – including some more of that set of 20 lyrics I promised to confine to things you approved. I've a devil of a lot on the stocks but not just ready yet for putting on a moving platform under your eagle eye. But I'm enclosing here two old poems 'The Crown of Rock' and 'The Summit', I came across hunting through some papers; I fancy you may have seen them before. Also enclose short poem on 'The Scott Centenary' which – in the scheme I have in mind – 'would appear immediately after 'The Oon Olympian.' Can't remember if I sent you 'Two O'Clock In The Morning' before.

Think I will 'get' 'The Lost Pigeons' all right; also have doing 'Parley of Beasts' along lines you suggested in full view. Don't worry about 'On Bare Hill Tops' – I'll rise to them yet. What I'm finessing for is a hill done on a par with the bog in 'Tarras' – and I want the Langfall or Kernigal ditto. Also I've a really big religious poem on the go – an attempt to really do, in Scots, what I partially did in 'A Moment In Eternity'. I expect you saw the useful review of my *Living Scottish Poets* in yesterday's *Times Literary Supplement*.[7] I've also a 'Plea for Synthetic Scots' article appearing shortly in *Scots Observer*.[8]

I'll adopt your splendid idea of re 'The Monument'[9] – and get the thing severely-graven and final enough.

Meant to say other things, but duty calls. In any case I'll be writing again in a day or so. Hope you're all O.K. My compliments to Madame. Let's hear how your own work shapes.

Yours,
Chris.

P.S. Please send back 'The Point of Honour', 'On Coming Home': and 'Crown of Rock' and 'Summit' after perusal please – I haven't copies.

---

[7] *The Times Literary Supplement*, 21 July 1932, said of the anthology *Living Scots Poets*, edited by C. M. Grieve, 'The little book is worth any man's reading; but the Scottish upper school that fails to make use of it is missing a valuable opportunity.'

[8] 'A Plea for Synthetic Scots' appeared in the *Scots Observer* of 1 September 1932.

[9] 'The Monument' (386) appeared inside a monumental design in *The Free Man*, Vol I, No 48, 31 December 1932.

My dear F.G.,

I was very glad to get your letter, and the copy of your new vol. of songs,[1] for which many thanks indeed. I had been hoping, as I think I had told you, to be in Edinburgh and Glasgow this month addressing meetings of the Verse Speaking Association: also a Scottish Parliament of Youth under the auspices of the Nationalist Society of St Andrews University. So I was looking forward to seeing you all and talking things over. But, of course, all these engagements have been cancelled by the War. Up here we're absolutely marooned – I see few papers, hear no wireless, know little or nothing of what's going on. I had no idea of course of such things as you mentioned – re Bill Johnstone's College,[2] for example, or your own situation at Jordanhill. I hope things have panned out better there than you were afraid they might do, as far as *you* yourself are concerned at all events.

I thought my own position was going to be quite impossible here: but now I think I can manage to keep going – unless, of course, things get very much worse with rising prices, shortage of foodstuffs, etc., as they probably will. In any case I think we are in for a very long War and that it hasn't really started yet and that all the false issues will have to be cleared away before the real issue emerges. I thoroughly approve of Russia's policy in any case; I haven't seen Saurat's idea on International Police, etc. to which you refer, but have no use in any case for anything of that sort.

I have been principally occupied myself with 1/ my Auto-biography, which I am just finishing now and hope to get off to my agents this next week. Several American publishers have been inquiring keenly after it, so I'm hoping it goes well. My *Islands*[3] book has been quite a success.

Also I'm busy with my long poem[4] of which you saw a duplicate. I've altered it a lot since then. A firm in Paris were going to publish it, if I could get a fair number of advance subscribers, but the head of

---

[1] Scott's *Scottish Lyrics set to music* appeared in five volumes (Glasgow 1922–39).
[2] William Johnstone, Scott's cousin, was appointed Principal of the Camberwell School of Arts in 1938. On 21 September 1939 Scott had written to MacDiarmid: 'Here's the tale as it affects Willie Johnstone – Camberwell Art School – formerly 1200 pupils and 86 teachers, 8 of whom were part-timers, has now become 30 pupils with six full time teachers and all the others sacked . . . What will come of it I don't know; the college is going to continue at Jordanhill.'
[3] *The Islands of Scotland* (London 1939).
[4] *Mature Art.*

the firm died[5] and I thought this meant that the project had fallen through. But it hasn't; the dead man's son[6] is now carrying on the business, and he has got into touch with me again and is printing some prospectuses on the strength of which when they come I'll try to get the necessary number of advance subscribers.

The War too has held up the Johnstone Number of the *V. of S.* This hasn't been so important of course since his Show was off anyhow. But it should be ready very soon now.

I had hoped to have got going long ere this with a lot of new Scots lyrics I have in mind. But it has been just impossible. Life is a hellish queer business nowadays, and I can't get the necessary grip of myself at all. Probably the whole situation in which I am involved will be clear to you when you read my Autobiography which I think is by far the best book I have written and really puts me on paper – and incidentally may solve some of my problems by exact definition. Of course the War may hang it up too, though not in America maybe. I can't see it getting out in this country just now – it pays no regard whatever to the Disaffection Act, Libel Act, or anything of that sort, but is an out-and-out revolutionary document ablaze with Leninism from start to finish and by far the most radical statement of the Scottish Case yet made – or, I fancy, imagined by anybody else. It will certainly create a sensation if it gets printed.

I am longing to see you: and indeed would do almost anything for a chance to be in intelligent company again. It's a devil of a business being stuck up here all the time and never seeing anybody one can possibly discuss anything that matters a damn with.

Barring seasonal colds, etc. we are all in good shape physically. Valda's mother died recently and she should have gone down to Cornwall and should go now as soon as possible: but that's out of the question in the meantime. In other respects than curtailment of steamer services and infrequency and belatedness of mails the War so far has made little difference to us. We have to 'black out' of course, but otherwise things here go on just as before, with no sandbag references or gas masks or anything about the place at all.

I hope the boys are all right at Selkirk and that you are all well. I was glad to hear your rheumatism had eased off again. I get occasional spells of that too nowadays.

I wish I could get hold of someone to play me your setting of

---

[5] Jack Kahane was head of the Obelisk Press, the firm that intended to publish *Mature Art*.
[6] Maurice Girodias.

Hay's poem:[7] but I'll have to wait for that till I see you, I suppose. I had been looking forward to meeting Hay too if I'd got South just now as planned – and I'd promised to look Burt[8] up also in his new Edinburgh home: but these hopes must go by the board too. I have no other news. I'm not seeing enough to read or hearing intelligent talk to keep my brain moving: so I'm afraid that until the situation clarifies I won't be able to tackle any poetry-writing. I'm glad however to have got this infernal Autobiography off my chest. It has not been an easy business by any manner of means. I'll probably have to cut it down a bit – I imagine as it now stands it runs to at least 150,000 words – and I'd rather have it a third less. However, we'll see. It's an extremely readable document in any case, I think; and like the *Islands* book will, I fancy, go well.

Valda and Mike join me in love to you all.

Yours,
Chris

EUL   Whalsay.
                                                                       20-11-39

My dear F. G.,

I would unload the whole of my Autobiography on you if I had a duplicate. It runs at the moment (it may have to be cut down) to nearly 200,000 words, and is quite unlike any autobiography ever written – full of poetry, and imaginative prose rather after the fashion of *Annals of the Five Senses*, but giving all the facts too, naked and unashamed, and a real unity as a book from beginning to end despite all the impredicable variations – and with a steel core 'stalk of carl hemp'[1] right through it! Here's hoping!

The Golden Treasury of Scottish Poetry (Macmillan's) is to be pub-

---

[7] On 30 June 1939 Scott wrote to tell MacDiarmid he had set 'To a Loch Fyne Fishermen' by George Campbell Hay, a poet he regarded (as he said in a letter of April 1940 to MacDiarmid) as 'the next star in the Scottish firmament'.

[8] William Burt, like Scott, had been an English teacher at Langholm Academy when Grieve was a pupil.

[1] 'Come, firm Resolve, take thou the van, /Thou stalk o'carl-hemp in man!' Robert Burns, 'Epistle to Dr Blacklock'.

lished in the spring. I've regrouped the poems so that they are not in chronological order but that poems are grouped together which have something in common as in Palgrave. The apparatus of glossary, notes, etc. – and long critical prefatory essay – have involved endless work.

I'm just as eager to turn out some lyrics of the right sort for you as you can be to have them, and if the Autobio finds publishers all right my way should be clear ahead now for some time, with the necessary peace of mind, or absence of worry in the mere mechanics of living, my lack of which has been responsible for my long absence from this field. It is impossible to soar and sing when one is bogged in the sort of infernal mess I have been in so long. But I've a whole notebook of likely themes, etc. upon which I'll be very happy to set to work whenever I can now.

An excellent 1,000-page anthology of literature in English since 1914 has just appeared from an American firm. With really good critical essays, etc. It gives all the cream of modern English and American writing (poetry *and* prose) – and with an excellent full page write-up about me, and five or six poems I'm there in grand style – the only Scottish writer who is, or, frankly, (bowing to Mr Edwin Muir and Mr James Bridie) possibly could be. I don't know what the thing costs – it is beautifully produced. But if you can get one of the Glasgow libraries to get it, or if Jordanhill runs to this sort of thing (the book is designed for advanced student use in America and has all the necessary academic fit-ups in the way of notes, etc.) I can recommend it to you as by far the best anthology I've encountered – besides it's a compendium bringing together significant material which to get hold of otherwise would entail the consultation of several hundred volumes. And it brings out in the most impressive way what is really going on in the literary world and shows the tremendous swing of the most significant literature to the Left. It is called *This Generation* and is edited by Professors George K. Anderson and Eda Lou Walton, and published by Scott, Foresman and Co. Chicago under the aegis of the English Department of Brown University.

Very sorry indeed to hear of your head cold. Trust it will soon pass and neither lead on to anything bigger nor leave troublesome sequelae.

Hope the Saltire Concert goes well with you and Lamond and Chisholm and Davie.[2] Wish I could be there.

[2] The sentence refers to three prominent figures on the Scottish musical scene: Frederic Lamond, Glasgow-born pianist and composer; Cedric Thorpe Davie, pianist and composer; Warwick Braithwaite, the New Zealand conductor who conducted the Scottish Orchestra from 1940 to 1946.

We're O.K. here despite truly infernal weather, war-time rations, absence of news, and general abominableness of everything except ourselves.

Please give our salutations to Mrs Scott and the boys when writing.

I've no doubt that Francise and Lovie[3] are spoiling you all ends up and that grass widowerhood for a spell under their auspices is suiting you just as well really as a like diet suited our old friend Nebuchadnezzar.

All the best. Love to you all.

Yours,
Chris.

P.S. I see I've forgotten just why I was dashing off this letter in such a hurry – i.e. to enclose copy of review-article I've just done for the *New Alliance* of your Vol V. 1/ so that you may see it in case it doesn't appear or only appears in curtailed form, and 2/ in case I've come a cropper which may be corrected in time, s'il vous plait.

Taylor[4] is still here and doing all right. He's an absolute Pacifist and hasn't been tribunalised yet – he is 27.

Whalsay.
Saturday 7/9/40

My dear F.G.,

Please excuse pencil.

I do not think I sent you before a copy of enclosed poem,[1] which I am confident you will agree is one of the best I have written; and far and away the most completely achieved poem of mine you have seen for a long time.

I've been having a very hectic spell. I think I told you in my last the position now re my Autobiography, out of the vast MSS of over

---

[3] Scott's daughters Francise and Lilias (known as Lovie, or Lovey).
[4] Henry Grant Taylor, MacDiarmid's honorary private secretary in Whalsay.
[1] MacDiarmid enclosed 'Auld Reekie' which he later retitled 'Edinburgh' (644-6); the final seven lines of 'Auld Reekie' were subsequently detached and entitled 'Dante on the Edinburgh People' (647).

350,000 words (500,000 originally) I have now extracted a book of about 150,000 (confined to the elements in the original which present me *qua* Poet – leaving aside me the Private Person and me the Politician for other books to be made out of the discarded 2–300,000 words later on.

This I have just accomplished and sent off to the publishers and you can take my word for it that it's the goods – the quintessential Me at the top of my bent, a rip-roaring irreverent series of variations on my personality and contemporary Scotland, full of the most outrageous humour and packed with interesting material, curious observation and sound common sense.

Desperately hard work though it has been, I have thoroughly enjoyed going through and working upon the mammoth manuscript again, and – better test perhaps! – so has Valda; coming again on all sorts of choice bits has kept us both in roars of laughter.

So you have a treat coming all right.

Here's to it.

Love to you all.

Yours, Chris.

P.S. Rush work on above job has kept me from getting Saurat's typescript read, but I'm clear now for a little, and will read it and return it to you in a few days.

EUL   Whalsay.
                                                   Saturday 26/4/41

My dear F. G.,

Glad to have your letter – to know you are all O.K. – and to hear about the 7 Deidly Sins.[1] Splendid. I'm wondering now what is going to be done about it – i.e. if and where and how it is going to have its premiere and whether or not publication is on the cards.

I wish I'd good news – of things attempted and done – to set beside yours. But I've been having a very sticky time, and can't get

[1] Scott's Ballet Suite *The Dance of the Seven Deidly Sins* had been offered to Sadlers Wells. It was not, however, produced by the company.

down to my new big poem yet – tho' I will very soon now, unless some other damned intrusion of circumstance, through the War or what not, knocks my plans agley once more.

What I'm really very annoyed about is the matter referred to in the enclosed letter from my agents. I've told you in previous letters I think about the reduction of the Autobio to 1/4 of the original MSS, and the plan to make two other volumes out of the material not used in Vol I. Amongst that discarded material was a very long chapter – the second of two such chapters – about my friends and acquaintances Orage, Cunninghame Graham, Compton Mackenzie etc. That was discarded from Vol I. But the other of these two chapters I retained – in part at least; the part dealing with yourself, Saurat, Sorabji, and Gogarty. And that, to my great regret and disgust, is the part that has to be sacrificed now. I've just wired agreeing to Methuen's suggestion. I had no option. The 2nd Vol is to be called *A Poet And His Friends* – and they are quite right; this material will be more in place there although they themselves as you will note agree that it was germane to this 1st Vol. – and as a matter of fact there are certain things in it, more especially in the passages dealing with you, that powerfully illustrate and bear out the positions I am most concerned to establish in this book, and I hate like Hell losing them, even temporarily. I ought to have learned patience by this time – yet I am incurably impatient in such matters, tho' I know that my time will come and the matter isn't perishable. Still when one has been at pains to present far-reaching and subtle cases, and has taken the trouble to secure first-class illustrative material which in such matters is not easily come by, it is a damnable nuisance to be precluded in this way from unmasking all one's batteries at once. I say nothing of the personal side; you will understand that – besides the question of giving a good show to yourself and some of the others, I was very much alive too to the effect that would have on readers in, at once, discounting the concentration of the volume on my single self and reinforcing my arguments in terms of others as well as myself. Still, it may be all for the best in the long run. Without the thing by me I cannot quite gauge the effect of leaving this chapter out on this Vol. I as a whole; it is far too big and various a thing to hold in one's mind's eye. We'll see how the book goes when the proofs come. That shouldn't be long now – unless some new catastrophe overtakes London in the interval. But however this Vol as a volume of shapes now after all these choppings and changings I do particularly regret the elimination from it of the material about yourself – you will not quite understand why until you get the proofs (and with them the typescript of this omitted chapter) and can then see what the effect of the inclusion of the latter would have had on the book as a whole.

485

However, that's the sort of infernal worry this War has bogged me in. Otherwise matters are going better than I should have hoped. In America especially. And that reminds me. Now you're back at No 44, I wonder if you can please dig out and send me a copy of the 'Two Memories' poem – the one about the weaver's hide and the white swans in the blue October heights. I can't find a copy here and I want it quickly for one of my American ventures.

Also I wrote Soutar the other week and said I'd be arranging with you to send him on the Southworth book: so he'll be looking for that when you're ready.

I have Lehmann's *New Writing in Europe*[2] (as well as the 1st 3 of his Penguin *New Writing*); it is as you say (less politely phrased than in the words you used) a hell of a production.

Please send me back the Gilbert Wright letter too sometime: also enclosed cuttings which (though there isn't much in them – the most interesting being Naomi Ryde Smith's) may interest you. In any case all over the Golden Treasury continues to be very favourably – and extensively – reviewed. There hasn't been time yet under present conditions to get the Dominions and Colonies or the American reviews: but they should be arriving soon now.

We're all O.K. here. The annual curse of Spring Cleaning is on. A kind of blitz too – hardly more supportable in some ways though less dangerous than the other. And I've a strenuous time just looming ahead. – of cutting, drying and getting home and stacking our fuel supply (of peat) for next winter, and also doing a lot of dangerous rock-climbing to collect gull's eggs for pickling – our last season's supply saw us nicely through the winter and we used up the last of them (in perfect condition – and jolly good: worth three or four hen's eggs each) only a few days ago.

But here it keeps horribly cold and grey yet.

Love from us all to Lovey and yourself. And please give our kind messages when you write to Mrs Scott and the boys. Also to Sancise. I hadn't heard she was in the WAAFs and trust she is in good form and liking the life.

Yours,
Chris.

[2] John Lehmann, *New Writing in Europe* (Harmondsworth 1940, p. 130), cited 'Hugh MacDiarmid, whose *First Ode to Lenin* (sic) preceded all the other literature of outspoken revolutionary sympathies and remained in a place by itself with its eloquence and straightforward vigour.'

My dear F.G.,

I'm tremendously glad to have a letter from you again at long last: and, to signify same, am replying per return as directed.

I need hardly point out that it has not been the fact that two letters of mine to you remained unanswered that prevented my writing you again, or, if need be, several times again during this long hiatus. But simply that I have been having a difficult time myself in many ways and have been so beset with worries that I was in no letter-writing mood – apart from the fact that I had no news to give you. I thought some months ago all was hunky-dory, that 2 and probably 3 books of mine would appear this autumn, and that I would then be free to turn to the stream-lined dramatic poem, and other projects. Alas, in these times more than ever, the best laid schemes gang aft agley. The Autobio had to be held over to the spring. Also, owing to increasing paper shortage, the question of further 'cuts' therein arose; there have been all sorts of difficulties. Then the months passed and no word came from America. I was afraid my arrangement there had come unstuck too. But just last mail I heard finally from San Francisco. That book's[1] all right, but is to be more comprehensive i.e. to include selected poems from previous volumes, as well as new poems. But it should have been out in August, now it is scheduled for early in the New Year. I have still no word about the other (New Directions: Connecticut) volume, nor have I heard about, or received any copy yet, of the current *New Directions*[2] which is to contain a long poem of mine, and is due out this Fall. I am busy on my Faeroes book, etc. and still not free to turn as I want to the great spate of new poems which will win through all right as soon as the channel is cleared.

I note what you say about Materialism and Idealism: but we are quibbling about words, I fancy. If by materialism you mean – not the philosophical significance of the term, but just greed, money mania, etc. then of course I am with you all the way. But idealism has never opposed that – the two have gone hand in hand all the way. The vast majority of money-grubbers, mindless opportunists, 'practical people' also believe all the old idealistic and religious stuff – the real out-and-out materialists, anti-God, anti-all supernaturalism, are few and far between – it is to these I belong. It is a misuse of terms

[1] The projected Colt Press selection of MacDiarmid poems.
[2] 'The Divided Bird' (712-20) appeared on pp. 220–8 of (ed) James Laughlin, *New Directions in Prose and Poetry* (Norfolk, Conn. 1941).

to call us anti-or non-idealists, however, if by idealism is meant a concern for the things of the mind, a selfless devotion to great causes, etc. The vast majority of people are idealists: it is they who have involved us in all the mess – and will keep on doing so by hook or crook if we cannot extirpate the religious superstition. Consider the role of the Churches in Spain and in all the countries involved in this War, including, not least, our own – consider how these black reactionaries are using the present war to get a new stronghold on popular education in Scotland and elsewhere.

So far I am concerned the question you ask about looking back over my 50 years (not quite – till next August) is not relevant. Because I have held precisely the same position since my early teens; all that has happened since has simply been that my life-experience has confirmed and reconfirmed it, and that I am very much better equipped to argue the matter with professional philosophers, divines, etc., than I was. But if your question implies a connection between the changes in my earlier and my present work as a poet and what you suppose to be my abandonment of idealism and religiosity, and my intensified Dialectical Materialism, then you are wrong because so far as my stand is concerned as between Materialism and Idealism, both my earlier poetry and my latest have been produced by a mind entertaining precisely the same ideas.

Nor do I share your pessimism. Neither in the masses of humanity involved directly or indirectly, the casualty rate, the damages, the abundance of cruelty and treachery, is this War on any unparalleled scale: nor does it seem to me that there is much, if anything to choose between any of the protagonist Powers: nor do I believe that civilisation is menaced, nor that the thing particularly affects the progress of the Arts in one way or another: nor that the Arts or Literature or the level of human consciousness and sensibility is other than in a far higher and more hopeful position than it has ever been before.

All this, with a wealth of wit and humour, and a higher satirical power than I have ever shown before, conjoined to a great deal of beautiful poetry and lovely evocations of aspects of the Scottish landscape and seascape and phases of Scottish history and elements of Scottish psychology, is fully set forth in my Autobiography – and for every position I take up in regard alike to my political views and my aesthetic position, literary doctrines and attitude to the language question in Scotland, etc. etc. I adduce overwhelming scientific and other support – the book is not only exciting but encyclopaedic and goes far beyond anything ever produced in Scotland before in its astonishing revelation of personality, on the one hand, and sheer knowledge, both in mass and in detail. So look out! And I need hardly tell you it is absolutely uncompromising – 'Christless Bobbie' applied to the entire present position and prospects with a vengeance.

I have been watching Saurat's manoeuvres with immense sympathy for Saurat himself and none whatever for his pronouncements.[3]

I am exceedingly sorry to hear about Johnstone.[4] I saw a paragraph about him in *The Scotsman* a week or so ago, but gathered from it he was busy with the proofs of his new book. It was an extremely laudatory paragraph, and I imagined from it all was well with him. If you see him or are writing please give him our warmest regards and best wishes, and also to Flora and the child.

Please also give my very belated (since I did not know of course till I got this letter of yours) and heartiest congratulations to Lovey on her graduation. I am delighted to hear she is 'through' and now undergoing practical training under your eye up there. Love to Sancise too. I am glad she is enjoying her work and trust she keeps fine and fit.

I have left to the last my congratulations on the 7 Deidly Sins. This is indeed great and glorious news. I expected it. I heard some while ago that there had been a paragraph to that effect in some paper and by today's mail The Saltire Society's newsheet comes to hand and reproduces the paragraph in question from the *Glasgow Herald*. I need not tell you how delighted I am and how entirely confident of the quality of the work in question. I hope Braithwaite[5] seizes the opportunity with both hands and if he does – and I hear in time – I'll

---

[3] Saurat had become closely involved with General de Gaulle's political activities in London.

[4] In *Points In Time* (London 1980, pp. 189–90) William Johnstone writes about the war years: 'My Junior Art School was at once evacuated to Chipstead, near Sevenoaks, where we found an empty mansion house in a beautiful park. Flora and Elizabeth went to Selkirk to stay with my mother, and here they were joined by Francis George Scott's family who had been evacuated from Glasgow so that the little house could hardly contain them all. A decision regarding my family had to be made. As Flora retained her American passport, and many of our American friends had left Britain already we decided that Flora and Elizabeth should go too.' In *The Scotsman*, 23 September 1941, A Scotsman's Log reported, under the heading 'Noted Scottish Artist', 'Mr William Johnstone, the distinguished Scottish artist, has been spending a few weeks in Selkirk, not painting, as is his wont, or lecturing, but "loafing around in the sun" – so he words it – and reading the proofs of an important new book in art education.' The book was Johnstone's *Child Art to Man Art* (1941).

[5] Warwick Braithwaite conducted the Scottish Orchestra from 1940 to 1946; in fact the first public performance of *The Seven Deidly Sins* was not given until 6 June 1946 when Ian Whyte, of the BBC, conducted it. The second performance, in 1954, was conducted by Alexander Gibson.

489

do my very damnedest to inflict myself on Scotland again at that time and attend the concert in question, in the company, I hope, of the Composer and his good lady! It's time I had a look at Scotland again. Orr was very keen for me lately to go down and have a holiday with him at Leith; but I wouldn't. It takes something to move me nowadays. But where the 7 Deidly Sins are concerned I'm certainly ready to make an 8th.

Like yourselves (as I gather from your letter) we here are also O.K. Mike is just back to school after the Tattie Holidays, and during that fortnight off he has inter alia kept us in plenty of fish with his rod. Valda is in fine case too, and despite all the infernal difficulties of my own position, I am hard as nails and fit as a fiddle – not only physically but psychologically, including *qua* poet!

I'll write again soon and hope then to fill up any gaps in this hasty epistle (e.g. I note what you say re Soutar – but defer comment). My regards please to Burt when you see him. Hope the boy does O.K. in the R.A.F.[6] How are George and Malcolm? I hope George isn't in line for any calling-up.

Love from us all to you all.

Yours,
Chris.

EUL

Dungavel.
Saturday. 20/10/50

Dear F.G.,

I had hoped to have got into Glasgow and out to 44 Munro Road before I got off to Russia on 26th inst. But now it is unlikely I can manage. As Valda probably told you when she met you the other day I have been extremely busy. I addressed about 15 meetings in Fife – Kirkcaldy, Dunfermline, Buckhaven etc. – and before that University College, Newcastle, and a big public meeting in the City too. I am due back from Russia to London on 11th Nov. and will be

---

[6] Billy Burt – William Burt's son to whom MacDiarmid's poem 'Hungry Waters' (52) is dedicated ('For a little boy at Linlithgow') – was killed in 1942 when serving as a Pilot Officer in the RAF.

just in time to get to Sheffield on 12 Nov. for the World Peace Congress. I expect to be a week in Sheffield.

On top of all this there is the infernal worry of 'flitting' – once we find somewhere to flit to. We haven't yet – but expect it'll all be fixed up, and the translation effected, before I get back. For weeks now all our stuff has been packed up – ready to move at a moment's notice. This has meant I haven't had access to my books and papers. The need to leave here came at a particularly bad time. If I'd been left here another 2 or 3 months in peace I'd have completed two big new books. As matters are they have had to be set aside sine die. I was also making excellent progress with a huge body of poetry – and in particular with a whole host of new Scots lyrics. When I can get back to these Heaven only knows. In any case I am quite unwilling to write an occasional lyric. I must be able to write to my own satisfaction the complete sequences I have in mind – or nothing. But despite all the difficulties I am more assured than I have ever been.

You and I both know Saurat's endearing little ways, but I feel he was sincere – and right – when he told me in Edinburgh that apart from my poetry all together my reputation can safely rest on *Lucky Poet*. I have constant proof, from readers of a calibre I have reason to respect, of the remarkable fashion in which that book continues to make its way and of the eagerness with which its successors are being looked for. The second volume, *A Scottish Poet And His Friends*, is a far greater monster than the first. I have no doubts whatever of its effect.

I know you do not approve my political position – or rather that you do not think it matters a great deal, and certainly not compared with my best poems. But I think you are wrong there. Sir Reginald Coupland[1] is shortly to publish his study of British intra-national politics. It does not surprise me that he has come to the conclusion, that I am the only political thinker in Scotland today who matters – just as for Wales he has singled out my friend Saunders Lewis: and he has given us a chapter each. For Young, McCormick, etc. etc. he has no use whatever. Sir Reginald's reputation in his field is the highest of any English expert. I do not know him personally. His interest in my political position – and his thorough knowledge and understanding of all my work – came to me as a bolt out of the blue.

---

[1] Sir Reginald Coupland's *Welsh and Scottish Nationalism* (London 1954) was, in fact, critical of MacDiarmid: 'When he published his two books of lyrics in 1925 and 1926 it seemed to many of those who read them as if Scotland had at last produced another great poet. But he failed to reach the heights which seemed at that time to be within his grasp. Was it the Depression and the shadow of the Second World War? Whatever the reason, it was as if politics had taken control of his poetry . . .

Incidentally I should add that of all the people I respect you are the only one I know of who in any way disapproved my action at the PEN Congress. The great majority of the foreign delegates were certainly whole-heartedly with me – as was shown by the fact (not reported in our 'free' press) that the resolutions proposed by the International Executive backed by UNESCO were defeated and a motion embodying my views carried instead.

So I continue to dree my weird. What of yourself? You know, I think, that if it had been a matter of will I would have set aside anything and everything else to furnish you with other lyrics of a kind you could have set. But with all the good will in the world that is not how things worth doing can be done. I realize that I may well have seemed to have gone off the rails and wantonly wasted myself in profitless ecentricities. But the end is not yet. I am convinced – more than ever – that my wild divagations have been essential, and that the time is near now when their fruit will be reaped.

The other books (i.e. in addition to the successive volumes of my autobiography) I have in hand are a huge study of Scottish national characteristics – not as imagined by people who have 'notions' about these but as revealed on the basis of a sufficient number of actual lives (say, ten to twenty thousand – and that is probably an underestimate). The whole thing is based on indisputable facts and the conclusions, revolutionary as they are, are incontestable. Secondly, I have put together a big volume of my essays on Scottish literary topics. I have just heard too that my *Selected Poems of William Dunbar* in the same Grey Walls Press Series as my Burns won't (owing to the London Printers' troubles) be out now until spring.

Also, Oliver & Boyd have now published their *Poets' Quair*, an anthology of Scots Poems for schools.[2] I wonder if you've seen this? I haven't got my copies yet but will send you one when they arrive on Monday or Tuesday.

I have just received *Marsyas*[3] with Lillias' poem in Scots, English, and French. Please give her my heartiest congratulations. I would like to have seen her before she goes to America. I wish her all the best.

Now I must wind up. If there is time before 26th I'd greatly appreciate a letter from yourself telling me what you have in hand and how you are keeping. And Mrs Scott and the boys.

My essay on 'Aesthetics in Scotland' – part of which I am to

In later years he drifted into a sort of revolutionary pessimism which has frozen the springs of poetry he drank from in his younger days.' (pp. 389–90).

[2] (Eds) David Rintoul and J. B. Skinner, *Poets' Quair* (1950).

[3] *Marsyas*, the Provençal paper associated with Saurat and his group.

deliver in the spring as a public (Glasgow Corporation) lecture will be published in pamphlet form in April or May.[4] I finished it a month or so ago. I have also four or five Burns Suppers to do in January – in Doune, Edinburgh, and Glasgow – and a lecture on Contemporary Scottish Literature to give in Coatbridge to the Annual Meeting of the Scottish Library Association. So I'll be busy enough when I get back. In the meantime I'm looking forward to meeting all the leading Soviet Union writers and having great 'plane flights from London to Moscow and back. All the best.

Yours,
Chris.

P.S. Did you hear D. G. Bridson's talks on 'Written and Spoken Poetry' on the Third Programme recently?[5] I have just had a long letter from him. He intends to make great changes now he is in charge of all the poetry reading on the 3rd Programme – and in particular to give far more scope to Scottish work. If you haven't heard his talk I'll send you a copy of the script. It is important. He is particularly interested in a lot of my later poetry which he finds especially suitable for the radio.

EUL

The Cottage.
Brownsbank,
Skirling,
by Biggar,
Lanarkshire.
26/1/51

My dear F. G.,

As you have probably seen from references in the press I have been continuously on the move since my return from the USSR – speaking at meetings all over the country. I have also had to do a great deal of writing on the subject. I have an article on it appearing in the

---

[4] *Aesthetics in Scotland* was not published in 1951. Alan Bold's edition of the work was published, by Mainstream Publishing, in 1984.

[5] D. G. Bridson, 'On Spoken and Written Poetry', BBC Third Programme, 27 September 1950.

February *Scots Review*[1]; another I've got to do for *The British Weekly*, a third for *Russia Today*[2] – and so on.

At the moment I am just concluding my Burns observances – the last of them in Edinburgh tomorrow, for the National Council of Labour Colleges.

I was delighted to hear some of your Burns settings juxtaposed in Herbert Wiseman's broadcast[3] on Thursday night – and especially glad at the broadcasting of birthday greetings to yourself. I hope you are in good form, also Mrs Scott – long since well recovered from her illness – and all the family.

We finally migrated to this new abode about three weeks ago – under handicaps, since Valda had the current 'flu, and the snow etc. was in full blast. Amongst other things our water supply was frozen up underground and until yesterday it has been necessary to carry milk-churns full from the nearest farm.

It is a very nice place, away up in a fold in the hills – yet handy for the main bus route. Actually handier for Edinburgh than Glasgow – since I can get to Edinburgh in 1½ hours: but going to Glasgow means changing buses in Biggar – with ½ hour's wait – then a long ride via Lanark, Carluke, Wishaw, and Motherwell.

Valda has been much better since we came here and I am as usual – though steadily getting more grey and wrinkled.

The cottage is too small unfortunately. We had to store a good deal of our stuff. But we've got dug in fairly comfortably now and will be all right when we've everything finally settled and the right routine devised.

You have probably seen from *The Scotsman*[4] that I've bitten off a very big bite in my usual regardless way. I criticised the very short time allowed for the Scottish Poetry competitions for the Festival of Britain, and the panel of judges – Sir Herbert Grierson, Sir Alex Gray, James Bridie, etc. Douglas Young then published a challenge to me in which he said that if I would submit about 8 Scots lyrics (hitherto unpublished and unbroadcast) to a like-sized panel of my

---

[1] 'Impressions of the USSR', *Scots Review*, Vol II, No 12, March 1951.
[2] 'A Poet Who Knew the People', *Russia Today*, January 1952.
[3] Herbert Wiseman, 'Songs of Burns', Scottish Home Service, 25 January 1951.
[4] *The Scotsman* (5 January 1951) carried MacDiarmid's letter protesting against the Scottish Committee of the Arts Council's Festival of Britain competition for Scots and Gaelic verse: he objected to the time limitation and condemned 'the incompetency of the panel of judges' comprising Sir Herbert Grierson, Sir Alexander Gray, Professor J. D. Mackie, William Power and Douglas Young. In *The Scotsman* of 10 January 1951 Douglas Young replied by challenging MacDairmid to submit 'at least eight [superior] unpublished Scots poems by himself' to a panel of his own choosing. MacDiarmid's letter accepting the challenge appeared in *The Scotsman* of 24 January 1951.

own choosing – and if that panel decided that my lyrics were better than the lyrics which were accorded the prize in the Festival Competition, he would 1/ eat his blue bonnet 2/ publish my poems at his own expense. Subject to settlement of details I have published in *The Scotsman* my acceptance of this challenge. So I'll have to woo my long-neglected muse to some effect.

I have no other news I think, though I have all sorts of writing in hand and – while ostentatiously not entering the Scottish Festival of Britain Poetry Competitions – I did enter the English one for a long poem (300 lines). I hear a broadcast of my poems is to be given on the Third Programme[5] very shortly – don't know exact date yet.

Drop me a line sometime soon and give me all your good news in return.

Valda joins me in every kind regard. Michael is down at Kilquhanity until such time as he goes to gaol.

Yours,
Chris.

EUL

Brownsbank,
Candymill,
Biggar,
Lanarkshire.
15/3/57

Dear F.G.,

I had hoped to have seen you long ere this, indeed, as I told her, soon after I saw Mrs Scott at the Saltire lecture – incredibly long ago that seems now. But it was not to be. I thought I'd have an hour or two in Glasgow, and be able to run out to Jordanhill, when I came back from the lectures I gave in Inverary and Campbeltown several weeks ago. But I had no sooner arrived at Renfrew airport than I was collared to give an address of welcome to a Chinese delegation and then I had to hurry through to Edinburgh to preside over a gathering addressed by a Jugoslav artist.

[5] 'Hugh MacDiarmid', BBC Third Programme, 6 February 1951. The poems were read by James McKechnie, Dermot Cathie and Molly Weir.

And now I'm in a worse plight than ever. I'm giving a series of lectures in South Wales in the beginning of April – Swansea, Ammanford, Ystradynglais and elsewhere – and then I'm going to China. I'll be 4 weeks in China, flying via Brussels, Warsaw, and Moscow, and 6 to 7 weeks out of Britain in all.

As you probably know I've been getting a tremendous press lately – long articles, and public lectures, about my poetry in USA, Latin America, Poland, France, Germany and elsewhere, and in the current issue of *Encounter*[1] a 14-page study of my poetry. The Joyce poem[2] sold out completely and a second edition is due out any day now and is already well ordered up. It has been by far my most successful work not only in sales, but in the extent, and quality of the reviews. The second volume of the huge poem of which the Joyce is the first (first of four) I am still wrestling with the final section of. You perhaps heard the selection from it given some months ago on the Third Programme.[3] I called it then *Impavidi Progrediamur*, but when it is published I'll probably change the title to the Scots, *Haud Forrit* which means practically the same. The China trip is too great a chance to miss, but if it had been anything less irresistible I'd have turned it down and got on with my writing instead. For in addition to finishing *Haud Forrit* I have in hand an enormous poem on Glasgow which – if the *Drunk Man* is my equivalent of 'Tam O'Shanter', will be my equivalent of Jolly Beggars.

My Spanish War poem[4] – in reply to Roy Campbell's *Flowering Rifle* – will be published before I get back from China, with the title, *The Battle Continues*. It is longer than the *Drunk Man*.

I have just rejoined the Communist Party and that too will entail a lot of work – reviewing for *The Daily Worker*, etc. And my duty to the Party – especially in these days when Communists and Communist sympathisers are only too apt to be victims of the witch-hunt – has compelled me to alter my intention in another important matter. Edinburgh University has offered me the LLD to be conferred at a Graduation Ceremonial on 5th July, and tho' I do not believe in honorary degrees, despise most of the people who get them so such that I hate to be bracketed with them in any connections, and have little or no regard for our Universities which I regard as over-Anglicised, anti-Scottish, and bastions of reaction, I

[1] Burns Singer, 'Scarlet Eminence', *Encounter* Vol VIII, No 3, March 1957, pp. 49–62.
[2] *In Memoriam James Joyce* (Glasgow 1955).
[3] 'Impavidi Progrediamur, BBC Third Programme, 19 December 1956. Readings from the poem by James McKechnie, Ewan McColl and Seamus Ennis.
[4] *The Battle Continues* (Edinburgh 1957).

have felt obliged to accept in order to put myself in a stronger position to fight for the causes I have at heart.

The immediate cause of this letter is one I have just had from a friend of mine in Edinburgh, Mr H. A. Scott. His daughter[5] is an old friend of mine and is now a lecturer at Brno University in Czecho-Slovakia. I stayed with her last time I was in Prague. Mr Scott has received a number of copies of this brochure on Janacek, translated by Mrs Milner,[6] another friend of mine. He asks me to send you a copy, which he thinks will interest you. He is a great admirer of your songs.

I enclose too – since I am afraid you must almost have forgotten what I look like – a photograph of a bust of me sculpted by Lawrence Bradshaw last time I was in London.

We are all well and trust this finds all of you in good fettle too. Valda will be in Cornwall while I am in China. I'll seize the first opportunity I have of seeing you after I get back. In the meantime, love to you all.

Yours,
Chris.

[5] Jessie Kocmanová.
[6] Jarmila Milner.

To F. Marian McNeill

Florence Marian McNeill (1885–1973), a perceptive folklorist and prominent cultural nationalist, was born in Holm, Orkney, where her father was a minister. She graduated from Glasgow University, did social work in London, then worked on the staff of the Scottish National Dictionary in Aberdeen. Her interest in Scottish traditions resulted in a variety of books beginning with *Iona: A History of the Island* (1920). *The Scots Kitchen* (1929) is a popular collection of Scottish recipes; *The Silver Bough* (1957–68) a sustained study of folklore and national festivals. Her first contact with MacDiarmid was on the basis of a common interest in achieving political independence for Scotland.

NLS

1 India Buildings,
Victoria St.,
Edinburgh.
22/11/32

Dear Mrs McNeill,

It has just been put to me that it is important (and that you feel aggrieved) that I ventured to speak on the Communist issue while speaking for you at the Municipal Election: and that I actually lost you hundreds of votes. I sincerely hope that the latter is a misinterpretation of the situation and that I did not really effect the opposite of what I intended to do. I was particularly glad to have a chance of trying to help you, and do very greatly regret if it panned out otherwise.

Yours sincerely,
C. M. Grieve.

My dear Flos MacNeill,

   The top of the year to you! Valda joins me in every good wish for
1934. So, lucky woman, you are in the 'fold of the sunbeams' (though
at this time of year it can hardly seem that). A place I have always
wished to see. Our thanks for your too-kind thought – the chocolates,
and, above all, *The Scots Kitchen*. What a book! It is a real treasure
from cover to cover. I do wish you could follow it up soon with the
one about the local festivals. But the main thing is – we hope you are
well and that all is going well with you. The Scottish Movement
seems to be in the doldrums: never mind – the time will come yet.
   Love from us all,

                    Yours,
                    C. M. Grieve.

My dear Flos McNeill:-

   It was too good of you to 'remember' Valda with the exceedingly
'dinky' handkerchief – she'll write you herself soon; please excuse
her at the moment – but we were both very glad to get your address.
You were on our list to write to, but we couldn't lay hands on your
whereabouts. I am very sorry indeed to hear you are having such a
poor time of it still and very sincerely reciprocate your wish that 1936
will prove kindlier than 1935 has done.
   I am still far from well and must be exceedingly careful – which
doesn't suit my temperament at all, especially as I came back from
hospital with ideas for still greater adventures in poetry than any I
have attempted yet and all agog to get on with them. I have some
twenty books on the tapis, and to have to ca' canny is far from my
liking.
   When any of us will be in Edinburgh again there's no saying. I'm

to be broadcasting early in March – probably from Aberdeen – but think I'll be in Edinburgh then too. Valda needs a holiday very badly; my illness and the incredibly bad weather here for the last three or four months has completely played her up, and if possible I hope she may go down to Cornwall soon, with Mike, who is now nicely recovered from his alarming and painful illness.

I hope you will regain all your health and strength, and have more than a spot of good luck soon. I keep hoping to hear that the Festivals book is coming out.

Love and every good wish from us all.

Yours,
C. M. Grieve.

NLS   Whalsay.
                                                                 21/12/40

Dear Flos,

I do not know if I have, old friends as we are, presumed before, to address you by the name I have been accustomed to hearing Helen Cruickshank and others using: but 'Dear Miss MacNeill' would be altogether too chillingly formal.

This is just a hasty line to say what a great pleasure it was to get your card by last mail and to reciprocate on behalf of all of us here your good wishes for Christmas and the New Year.

I am so glad you are enjoying the *Golden Treasury*. It isn't the book, alas, it should have been – or would have been but for this War. It had to be cut down by more than half, and that eliminated much I would fain have kept. Macmillans are a very Tory firm and I had great difficulty in getting my Introduction and Notes through; they wanted me to modify them in various ways – in particular, to excise the anti-English and anti-Imperialist elements. But I stuck to my guns. So there we have it. It is too early yet for me to have seen any reviews. No doubt there will be a good deal of soreness and opposition in many quarters.

But it's coming yet for a' that – the new autonomous progressive Scotland, I mean. The real forces that will carry it through are coming to the fore at last. I expect you see all the elements in the developing situation even more easily than I do. What I mean are such things as Arthur Donaldson's *Scottish News and Comment* and Harry Miller's *Scots Socialist* – the out-and-out stand quite a number of young men have taken on Scottish Nationalist grounds against the illegal conscription – and the fine brairding of new literary talent in men like Douglas Young, George Campbell Hay, and Somhairle Mac Gill Eathain.[1]

I wonder what you are doing yourself – what writing, etc. you have in hand? I trust this finds you in the best of fettle. Apart from minor ailments and a bout or so of 'flu Valda, Michael, and I are in fine form. None of us have been South – or indeed off this island – for a couple of years now, but one of our petitions to Santa Claus is for an intermission of our exile, a holiday in Scotland, and a chance to see our friends again, in this New Year.

Every kind regard and good wish from all of us.

Yours,
Chris.

NLS

The Carlisle Journal,
60 English Street,
Carlisle.
Tuesday.
[1945]

My dear Flos McNeill,

Sorry I delayed a little replying to your welcome letter and thus necessitating a second letter from you. But I have been much away and extremely busy. My job here takes me all over the South of Scotland and the whole of Cumberland and part of Westmorland. I like it very well (after all it is my own birth ground – and part of Scotland Irredenta!), and I expect I'll have more spare time for my own writing once I'm in better possession of all the ropes here.

I am, of course, delighted to hear of your *Anthology of Iona*,[1] and will be very proud to have you include the two extracts from my *The*

[1] Somhairle Mac Gill Eathain is the Gaelic spelling of Sorley Maclean.
[1] (Ed.) F. Marian McNeill, *An Iona Anthology* (1947).

Islands of Scotland. (It is so long since I saw that book I can't remember what the passages are.) I note Aeneas Mackay will be writing Messrs Batsford's.

I'll look forward to seeing the Anthology in due course: but here's wishing it – and you – the very best of luck.

With every kind regard.

Yours,
Chris.

To Maurice Wollman

Maurice Wollman edited the following anthologies all of which included contributions by MacDiarmid: *Modern Poetry 1922–34* (1934), *Poems of Twenty Years* (1938), *Selections from Modern Poets* (1939).

SUNYB

Whalsay,
Shetland Islands.
8/9/33

M. Wollman, Esq.,
34 Cranbrook Rise,
Ilford,
Essex.

Dear Sir,

It is very kind of you to wish to include some of my poems in your Anthology,[1] and I gather from your letter that you are a friend of my good friend, Mr John Gawsworth. I have been obliged however to make a rule of charging 10/6 per poem for inclusion in anthologies and do not depart from this except when there is special cause to make an exception. I do not know whether there is any provision for such payments in this case. Please do not imagine that I wish to make difficulties of any kind, but there are two other matters which affect settled principles of mine – the first is the question of publisher and the second of fellow-contributors. There are certain publishers whom I would not allow to put out any work of mine upon any consideration, and in just the same way there are many writers with whom I could not allow my name to be in any way associated. I should therefore require to be satisfied on these three points before I

---

[1] (Ed) Maurice Wollman, *Modern Poetry 1922–34* (1934).

could endorse the permission which subject to my consent has been given by Messrs Blackwood and Messrs Aeneas Mackay.

As to the usage of the word *cheville* in the last line of my poem,[2] I imply that any attempt on the part of man to ascribe anything of which he is conscious to a divine source is, in view of his limitations, no more than equivalent to a misuse of words, a fumbling after a term which in the nature of things he is incapable of finding with a consequent falling-back upon an approximation which is hopelessly wide of the mark.

With best wishes.

Yours sincerely,
C. M. Grieve.

SUNYB

Whalsay,
Shetland Islands.
26/1/34

Dear Mr Wollman,

Many thanks for yours of the 20th just to hand. It is very good of you to suggest substituting 'Milk-Wort and Bog-Cotton' for the 'Farmer's Death' in your anthology, and if that will not cause you too much trouble, please do so. I would greatly prefer it. There is no need for you to apply to Aeneas Mackay for permission; the copyright is mine and he will have no objection. You are right about C'wa[1] – it means come away. We similarly use G'wa meaning go away. The poem is addressed to the Earth – a personification of the Earth. The milkwort however is not the harebell, but a very tiny, very beautiful, moorland flower. Milkwort is its correct English name; I do not know of any special Scots name for it. I don't know what you call bog-cotton in England – the English Dictionary gives canna (which we also use in Scotland – it is simply our Gaelic name for it, cannach) and defines it as cotton-grass, so that may be what you call it in English. It is just a straight grass stalk or small red

[2] MacDiarmid's poem 'Cheville' (353) ends with the poet 'Seeing, and sorry for, all drowned things, sorry/Yet with, *cheville*, a sense of God's glory.'
[1] MacDiarmid's lyric 'Milk-Wort and Bog-Cotton' (331) begins 'Cwa' een like milk-wort and bog-cotton hair!'

which at the flowering season has a tassel of silky white stuff flying from its top.

Every good wish.

Yours sincerely,
C. M. Grieve.

SUNYB

c/o Woodhead,
12 Petherton Road, N.5.
20.7.34

Dear Mr Wollman,

Many thanks for yours of yesterday's date. I got my copy of the Anthology all right and have greatly enjoyed going through it. It is a delightful collection, and the grouping of the poems – or, rather, since they are happily not divided off into certain groups but given an unobtrusive sequence and ordering – is very effective. I saw Sélincourt's[1] rather captious comment on the splitting-up of certain poems owing to the turnovers, but that certainly did not detract from my pleasure and I like the entire planning and get-up of the volume very much. I hope it meets with the success it deserves.

As to your two queries:-[2]
1/ 'Forenicht' is accurately enough given as 'the interval between twilight and bed-time' but personally I prefer simply 'early evening'.
2/ The second one is much more difficult. The lines run:-

> There was nae reek i' the laverock's hoose
> That nicht – and nane i' mine.

literally translated this runs:-

> There was no smoke coming from the lark's nest that night –
> and none from mine,

which of course makes no sort of sense in English.

Actually the first line is a metaphor which means: It was a dark and stormy night.

---

[1] E. de Sélincourt, Wordsworthian scholar and critic.
[2] The two queries refer to MacDiarmid's lyric 'The Watergaw' (17).

505

But the trouble with simply giving the line that gloss is that it does not explain the actual words of the original, and, also, makes nonsense of the second line:-

> It was a dark and stormy night
> That night – and none in mine.

The end of that is, of course, exactly contrary to what I am really saying viz.

> It was a dark and stormy night
> That night – and my heart was dark and stormy too.

In view of these difficulties, perhaps the best gloss would be:-
The first line reads 'There was no smoke coming from the lark's nest that night', a proverbial figure of speech meaning that it was a dark and stormy night, while the second line must then be read as meaning 'and my heart was dark and stormy too'.

This is a good example of the virtual untranslateability into English of many highly-concentrated Scots phrases.

Another even more impossible instance is the first verse of one of my very best poems, 'Moonstruck':-

> When the warl's couped soon' as a peerie
> That licht-lookin' craw o' a body, the moon
> Sits on the fower cross-win's
> Peerin' a' roon.

Attempting a straight translation we get:-
When the world is dozed like a top at the height of its spin, *that light-looking crow of a creature*, the moon, sits on the four cross-winds, peering all round.

The line I have underlined is nonsense in English – light-looking and crow seeming a contradiction in terms, and crow a most inapt epithet to apply to the moon. I can find no passable equivalent for the phrase in English at all – no means whatever of conveying its quality – but in Scots it is (if I may say so with all modesty) a marvellously effective description.

With every kind regard.

> Yours sincerely,
> C. M. Grieve.

506

To British Broadcasting Corporation

MacDiarmid's relationship with the BBC was characterised by the occasional confrontation, especially as he was deeply suspicious of the cultural credentials of Melville Dinwiddie. When Dinwiddie was chosen (by Lord Reith in 1933) as Controller of the BBC in Scotland, he was minister of St Machar's Cathedral in Old Aberdeen and a man with a military background. In MacDiarmid's view this was the wrong sort of Scot for a job with immense artistic implications. MacDiarmid worked amicably enough with producers such as Robin Richardson, a familiar figure in Edinburgh's literary pubs. George Bruce, poet as well as producer, became a close friend.

BBC

Whalsay,
Shetland Islands.
24/11/33

Scottish Regional Director,
British Broadcasting Corporation,
Queen Street,
Edinburgh.

Dear Sir:-

I am informed that on Sunday, November 19th, on the Daventry National Programme, in the item at 2.40 p.m., viz. 'Poetry and Prose II Extracts from Scottish Literature (from Glasgow)', the broadcast included Copyright poetry of mine. No permission was sought to do this, nor any arrangement made for payment to me of a fee, and the matter therefore resolves itself into a question of breach of copyright. It affects my reputation in another way for I have recently had occasion to state in print why I could not consent to broadcast under the present regime and conditions of the B.B.C. and the unwarranted use of my work must have seemed inconsistent with my declared attitude; I should therefore in addition to adequate payment require a proper apology and explanation broadcasted to make it clear that I was in no way whatever a party to this use of my work.[1]

I shall be glad to have any observations you care to make at your earliest possible convenience.

Yours sincerely,
C. M. Grieve
('Hugh MacDiarmid')

BBC
TS

1 India Buildings,
Edinburgh 1.
11th December, 1933.

Hamilton Marr, Esq.,
Programme Services Executive,
British Broadcasting Corporation,
Broadcasting House,
London, W.1.

Dear Sir,

Reference your letter AS/HM dated 30th November, this has been forwarded and has just reached me here. I have noted contents of same, but the letter dated 16th November, addressed to my previous Sussex address by you has not reached me. In any case you will appreciate that the fact that I gave permission for the broadcasting of certain works on previous occasions in response to applications, and on the understanding that certain fees should be paid, in no way mitigates the flagrant breach of copyright involved in

[1] As a result of this protest the BBC eventually made the following 'Scottish Announcement' on 2 January 1934 at 6.22 p.m: 'We have to make a short announcement with reference to the broadcasting of Mr Hugh MacDiarmid's poem "A Herd of Does" on Sunday, November 19th, 1933. Owing to a misunderstanding, this poem was read without the permission of the author, which, we are now informed, will be witheld for the future in regard to any of his works. We take this opportunity of apologising to Mr MacDiarmid for any inconvenience he may have been caused.'

taking it for granted that I would be equally willing in respect of the broadcast of 19th November. Without prejudice to the action I must raise in respect of this I again ask you to broadcast a clear statement that the poem in question was broadcast without my permission, and that I have subsequently stated that I have definite objection to any of my work being broadcast in the future.

Yours sincerely,
C. M. Grieve
(Hugh MacDiarmid)

BBC

Whalsay,
Shetland Islands.
19th Dec. 1933

Hamilton Marr, Esq.,
(for Programme Services Executive)
B.B.C.

Dear Sir,

I have to acknowledge your letter (AS/HM, 12th inst), also cheque[1] received here yesterday for 10/6 in regard to the broadcast poem in dispute. I herewith return the cheque in question; it is scarcely for the BBC, having violated my copyright, to determine what sum they will pay in respect thereof, and the fee of 10/6 is far too small. This may be the fee you agree to grant when you solicit and receive permission to broadcast a poem, but I would point out that in this case no such permission was given, nor, had I received your letter of 16th November addressed to Thakeham, Sussex (which has never reached me), would it have been given.

That after sending that letter you proceeded with the broadcast in the absence of any reply from me shows that there was no question of a mere accident or misunderstanding here, but, on the contrary, a deliberate breach of copyright. You had applied for permission and

[1] In the original manuscript of this letter the word cheque has been ringed with reference to the following note written at the top of the page by a BBC official: 'retained for cancelment – Payee has written the following on back of cheque "Returned to BBC by post on 20th Dec 1933 with letter refusing for grounds stated to accept this small payment. (Sd) Hugh MacDiarmid."'

had not received it; nevertheless you proceeded to act as if you had – and now tender me the usual ridiculously small fee as if I had, in fact, acquiesced. In these circumstances, and in the absence of any apology and reasonable tender from you, I have only to intimate that I have now no option but to proceed against the BBC for breach of copyright.

My demand that a statement shall be broadcast intimating that the poem was given without my consent is a different matter altogether – and that was why I made it, as my letters bear, without prejudice to any claim I might make for breach of copyright. As my original letter shows I asked for this explanation to be broadcast because in view of the attitude I have found it necessary to take up in recent published articles to BBC policy, and, in particular, Rev Melville Dinwiddie's appointment, I have apparently allowed my own work to be broadcast (as has been the natural deduction from the fact that it was broadcast) has seemed a rank inconsistency and has done my reputation real harm in quarters I respect. I again ask that such an explanation be broadcast without delay but do not agree that this settles the matter and relieves you further liability; on the contrary I ask that this shall be done without prejudice to the claim for £50 compensation for breach of copyright your attitude now obliges me to raise.

Yours sincerely,
Hugh MacDiarmid.

BBC

Whalsay,
Shetland Islands.
4/1/34

Programme Services Executive,
British Broadcasting Corporation,
Broadcasting House,
London W.1.

Dear Sirs:-

Your ref/ AS/RJFH dated 29th Dec. I have to thank you for above letter, with copy of short announcement you propose to broadcast. The latter is satisfactory from my point of view, and I beg to state that if it is broadcast, and if, as you propose, the sum of £5-5/- is paid to me, I shall accept these two actions as full and final settlement of this dispute.

Yours sincerely,
'Hugh MacDiarmid' (C. M. Grieve)

BBC

c/o Carlisle Journal,
60 English St.,
Carlisle.
30/7/47

To
Talks Director,
B.B.C.,
Glasgow.

Dear Sir:-

I am not sure whether Mr Robin Russell[1] is still in charge of the Arts Review: but some time ago he asked me to submit suggestions for other talks I might care to give.

Sydney Smith, the Edinburgh poet, has just published *Carotid Cornucopius*,[2] a Rabelaisian, Joycean, adventure in words, puns, and verbal fun and fantasy generally, about which I would very much like to say something in an early Arts Review.[3]

I should also like to have a short talk on 'Recent Developments of Scottish Poetry', based on work by Maurice Lindsay; Hamish Henderson, W. J. Tait, and others – a short, say 7 minute, talk.

And if it could be arranged I would like to do a bi-centenary tribute to Susanna Blamire,[4] the poetess in the Cumbrian and Scots dialects, who wrote some of the finest Scots verse ever written by any non-Scot, and fully equal in its own kind of lyric and song to all but

[1] Robin Richardson had in fact replaced Robin Russell.
[2] Sydney Goodsir Smith, *Carotid Cornucopius* (1947).
[3] MacDiarmid contributed a five minute feature on 'Essays on Literature' to Arts Review, Scottish Home Service, 18 February 1948.
[4] MacDiarmid's 'Susanna Blamire: a bi-centennial programme in honour of the Cumbrian poetess' was broadcast on the Scottish Home Service, 27 November 1947.

511

the very greatest work of the same sort ever achieved by any Scots poet. Could this possibly be a longer talk – say 10 or 12 minutes?

If you approve of these – or any of these – suggestions please let me know, and I will prepare and let you have scripts for consideration at once.

With best wishes.

Yours sincerely,
C. M. Grieve
(Hugh MacDiarmid)

BBC

32 Victoria Crescent Road,
Glasgow, W.2.
11/11/48

Alastair Dunnett, Esq.,
Talks Producer,
B.B.C., Edinburgh.

Dear Mr Dunnett,

Many thanks for your letter of 8th inst. re *Vedanta For The West*.[1] The book is now out (Messrs Allen and Unwin. 16/-).

The line taken in regard to bridging the gulf between Eastern and Western Thought in this country by Aldous Huxley, Gerald Heard, and others is one that I have followed very closely, on the basis of a very thorough prior knowledge of the Vedas and Commentaries thereon; and I am au fait with the principal European writers on the subject too – especially the French, German and Russian. As I think I told you in my previous letter, the Huxley-Heard development was preceded by, and stems from, an increasing interest in this matter manifested by several important British writers, notably my friends W. B. Yeats, A.E. (G. W. Russell), and T. S. Eliot. My own point of view is different from theirs; I am equally anxious to see an East-West rapprochement – but I think it ought to be based on other elements than those that appeal to Huxley, Heard, etc., and have formed the basis of Theosophical Thought – my own preference (and the more likely, I think, to be useful to the West) is for the

[1] (Ed.) Christopher Isherwood, *Vedanta for the Western World* (1948).

Sankara philosophy. I have written a good deal about this in my autobiography *Lucky Poet*, and elsewhere, and my ideas on this matter have excited a considerable amount of interest not only in this country but in the USA, and in India itself. Incidentally it is at this point that the whole matter has a special bearing on Celtic thought, literature, and, above all, music.

My attitude then is one that qualifies me to suggest an alternative to the Huxley-Heard line, which I can discuss in the light of adequate knowledge and fully appreciate, while I disagree with it in some important respects but not to the extent of denying the extreme importance (which they affirm) at this turning point in human history of bringing about a better mutual understanding between Eastern and Western Thought.

I feel sure I can give a very good – and probably important – talk on this subject, apropos this book.[2] There is implicit or/and explicit in most of the essays in this book a depreciation of Western Thought (as materialistic) compared with Eastern Thought (as more 'spiritual'). My attitude holds a balance which can reconcile a considerable draught of Eastern Thought without in the least degree repudiating our Western heritage. What I feel is that these writers have concentrated on certain elements of Eastern Thought but without due knowledge of, or regard for, certain other elements which are much more compatible with our own traditions, i.e. that an effective and useful fusion of Eastern and Western Thought can take place much more easily at a different point than the particular *point d'appui* these writers have chosen. Not only so: but Asia is in the melting pot, and I feel that the elements in Eastern Thought these writers base themselves upon are old and declining elements, whereas the alternative elements I suggest are on the up-grade today throughout the East and far more likely to be those upon which the future will rest – and therefore the ones to be reckoned with in any attempt to bridge the gulf between East and West in the light of the actualities and probabilities of the conditions which obtain today.

As you probably know the book (edited by Christopher Isherwood) has as its contributors:-

From the West. Aldous Huxley, Allan Hunter, Gerald Heard, John Van Druten.

From the East. Swami Prabhavanda, Swami Yatiswarananda, and Swami Adbutananda.

[2] On 14 December 1948 Donald Boyd, Chief Producer, Talks Department, BBC, wrote a Memo to the Scottish Home Service: 'We have discussed this proposal with Third; who do not feel sufficiently confident to book it as a talk. But Third ask me to say that if you put it into your programmes they would be interested to see the script.' That seems to have been the end of the matter.

The thesis of the book is that in a time of doubt, scepticism, and self-searching, a group of intelligent leaders have found faith and belief not in the dogmas of any one religion but in the philosophy based upon the Vedas – a philosophy that postulates an acceptance and understanding of all religions and which they have found in themselves.

Vedantic philosophy is based on three propositions 1/ that the real nature of man is divine 2/ the aim of human life is to realise this divine nature 3/ that all religions are essentially in agreement.

Each principle is examined in turn by a group of scholars from East and West.

I trust this will help you. I will be extremely interested if I can undertake this talk.

With best wishes,

Yours sincerely,
C. M. Grieve.

BBC
TS

Brownsbank Cottage,
Candymill,
By Biggar,
Lanarkshire.
10:5:52

To
Officer i/c Third Programme,
Broadcasting House,
London.

Dear Sir:-

Some seven or eight months ago a programme[1] about the Scottish Lallans Poets was recorded with a view to production in the Third Programme. The script was by Ewan MacColl and amongst the

---

[1] 'The Lallans Makars. An account of some Scottish poets by Ewan MacColl' was pre-recorded on 26 September 1951 and broadcast on the Third Programme on 23 June 1952. MacDiarmid's poems were read by John Laurie, Alex McCrindle, Norman MacCaig; other poets represented were Sydney Goodsir Smith, Douglas Young, Alexander Scott, Robert Garioch.

readers were Messrs Alex McCrindle and Norman McCaig. This feature has never been broadcast.

I understand that the reason for this is that an official of the Scottish Region of the BBC objected on the grounds 1/ that if they broadcast this the Third Programme would be trespassing on what was properly the province of the Scottish Region, and 2/ that those responsible for the script were mainly Left-Wingers, and that as a consequence there was too much Communistic poetry in the script and this gave a lop-sided and unfair view of the state of Scottish Poetry today.

The truth is that while I and several others concerned are Left-Wingers politically, there was no political element at all in the poems chosen or in the accompanying comments. Poems of mine have been previously broadcast in the Third Programme and that brought me a large appreciative mail, without any adverse comments on political or other grounds. I have reason to believe that the real ground for the objection to the script was jealousy, and prejudice against my personal politics (although my political views were not reflected in the actual script at all). None of the other poets drawn upon in the script belong to the Left politically, and there is a consensus of critical opinion in this country and abroad which regards them collectively as the best poets in Scotland today, so the selections from them did not afford any lop-sided view of the condition of poetry in Scotland.

It is a very serious matter if my political enemies are to prevent my non-political poems being broadcast in this way by advancing such false reasons for their action and I am writing you now to ask if you will be so good as to favour me with an explanation.

Thanking you in anticipation.

                    Yours sincerely,
                    Hugh MacDiarmid.

BBC

Brownsbank,
By Biggar,
Lanarkshire.
2/10/52

Robin Richardson, Esq.,
B.B.C.,
Broadcasting House,
Queen St.,
Edinburgh.

Dear Robin,

The death of Major C. H. Douglas, of 'Social Credit' fame, announced in yesterday's papers, prompts me to suggest that a talk about him should be given by the Scottish BBC.[1]

As you probably know I was closely associated with him for a good few years and, indeed, published some of his books. His ideas have already been put into partial practice by the Governments of Alberta and British Columbia, but his influence has been far wider than this suggests. It has indeed been world-wide. Douglasite Movements have been established in almost every civilised country, and a vast literature has grown up about his theories. The relation of these theories to those of other currency reformers and advanced economic thinkers is extremely interesting and important, but I am not thinking of a talk about that – it would be too technical. What I have in mind is a personal tribute to the man as I knew him – probably the only Scotsman who has inspired a world movement.

Perhaps you will let me know if the BBC would care to consider a talk along these lines, and if so I will be glad to submit a script.

With every kind regard to yourself.

Yours,
C. M. Grieve.

---

[1] Aidan Thomson, Assistant Head of Scottish Programmes, replied on 28 October 1952: 'I am writing about your letter of 2nd October addressed to Robin Richardson on the subject of C. H. Douglas. We considered this at once in view of the topicality but came to the conclusion that we would not be able to find a place for a talk. We generally feel that by now the interest in Scotland would be limited to specialists and that other material which was knocking at the door at the time had a greater claim.'

BBC

Brownsbank,
By Biggar,
Lanarkshire.
23/4/53

To
Programme Director (Talks),
Scottish Home Service,
B.B.C.

Dear Sir:-

My long poem *A Drunk Man Looks at the Thistle* – first published 27 years ago and long out of print and unobtainable – is on the point of being republished by the Caledonian Press, 973 Argyle St, Glasgow C3. It is generally agreed that this poem has had a very marked effect on modern Scots poetry. A review copy will be sent to you, but because of previous quite incompetent comments on my work and *unsatisfactory readings* of Scots poems of mine, I write to say that in this case I cannot grant permission for any of the poems in the *Drunk Man* to be used or quoted in any review of or talk about this poem unless I am consulted in advance and agree in writing.

Yours sincerely,
'Hugh MacDiarmid'
(C. M. Grieve)

BBC

Brownsbank,
By Biggar,
Lanarkshire.
16/7/53

Melville Dinwiddie, Esq.,
Scottish Regional Director,
B.B.C.

Dear Sir:-

I write to protest against the denigratory references to me made by several of those who took part in the Arts Review feature in the Scottish Home Service last night.[1]

[1] 'Arts Review', Scottish Home Service, 15 July 1953 included a review of Scottish periodicals including *Scottish Journal* to which MacDiarmid was a frequent contributor. John Wilson said 'I think also that in a magazine attempting to crystallise all that is thought and said, etc. about Scotland – in a magazine attempting

Scornful reference was made to the claim advanced in certain quarters that I am the most important Scots writer since Burns, and mention of my name in this connection was greeted by one of your contributors with an asinine hee-haw.

This claim however has been repeatedly made by men like the late W. B. Yeats, Mr Sean O'Casey, Mr T. S. Eliot and many others infinitely better qualified than any of the Arts Review contributors.

Not only so, but I have twice been presented by large bodies of Scottish and other writers with testimonials making that claim on my behalf, and two successive Prime Ministers have secured Royal Pensions for me for my distinguished services to Scottish literature. No other Scottish writer has been accorded such recognition.

All the signatories to these testimonials and all the British and foreign critics, anthologists, etc. who have applauded my work may of course be wrong, and Messrs John Wilson, Robert Kemp, Pete Westwater etc. right but it seems very unlikely.

Even if those I have just named are wrong they are, of course, entitled to their own opinion and I have no objections whatever to the most savage criticism, provided I am allowed to reply. I have myself subjected Mr. Kemp and others to very severe criticism, but I have done so in journals in which it was open to them to reply – and not over the BBC reaching an immensely larger, if less interested, public, where it is possible to subject a man to the most spiteful attack without his being able to defend himself at all.

In this case I have not the slightest doubt that Messrs Kemp and others were 'getting their own back' for adverse criticisms of their work published elsewhere by me, and that Mr Robin Richardson who was responsible for the programme was similarly actuated since I had been constrained in recent correspondence with him to withdraw permission for any quotations from my poems to be broadcast as part of any 'critical' talk, since my experience is that such talks are almost invariably given by people with no qualifications whatever while people like myself who have devoted their lives to Scottish literature are excluded. The people to whom I refer have established no reputation in this field and have no substantive original work to their credit. Why the Scottish BBC prefers the inferior in this way and fails so conspicuously to give contemporary writers of value anything like the sympathy and support young English writers are given on the Third Programme and elsewhere is a mystery to many but I do not think it can be dissociated from the fact that a virtual monopoly of the talks, book reviews etc. on such

such atask in 16 pages – two signed articles and a poem by one author, Hugh MacDiarmid, is a bit too much of a good thing. In fact, with Mr MacDiarmid in this mood, it's a bit too much of a bad thing as far as I'm concerned.'

matters is given to a small group of men of no personal distinction or qualifications in this (or any other) field. It is at any rate a fact that my own work has never been adequately dealt with on the Scottish Service, but only on the Third Programme. Nevertheless in the talks in the Fabric of Scottish literature Series in 'Scottish Life and Letters', the speakers who broadcast both on poetry in Scots and poetry in English by contemporary Scottish poets accorded me first place. In view of this I think I am justified in protesting against the way in which in last night's Arts Review I was subjected to personal spite in remarks which so far as their critical content went were on no higher than the 'Get your hair cut' level of gutter exchanges.

Yours sincerely,
C. M. Grieve
('Hugh MacDiarmid')

BBC

Brownsbank,
By Biggar,
Lanarkshire.
29/8/53

Melville Dinwiddie, Esq.,
Director, Scottish Region, B.B.C.

Dear Mr Dinwiddie,

I am sorry to have been so long, owing to absence from home and other causes, in replying to your letter[1] in answer to my complaint about the vicious and quite unjustifiable attack made on me by several speakers in 'Arts Review'.

Your letter, however, did not supply any acceptable reason for

[1] In his letter of 29 July 1953 Meville Dinwiddie said: 'I have now heard the recording of the programme and cannot agree with you that the mention of your name in the quotation from the slip enclosed in the current number of *The Scottish Journal* was greeted with a sneer or a "hee-haw" as you term it. One could have deduced from the emphasis of the reader that he did not altogether agree with the statement on that slip and neither did John Wilson entirely agree with your contributions to that Journal but surely those taking part in "Arts Review" have as much right to their opinion and may express it as definitely as *The Scottish Journal* has to say what it did about The Saltire Society and the other aspects of Scottish culture with which it dealt.'

this attack. My place as an important Scottish poet – and in the opinion of many distinguished critics the most important Scottish poet since Burns – has been attested by a great number of important literary critics at home and abroad and by leading contemporary poets in this and other countries (e.g. T. S. Eliot, the late W. B. Yeats, Dylan Thomas). It has also been attested in signed public testimonials by nearly all our contemporary Scottish authors of any consequence. And finally on the recommendation of two successive Prime Ministers (Sir Winston Churchill and Mr Attlee) the late King and the present Queen conferred honours upon me in respect of my 'outstanding services to Scottish Literature'.

Why then should the Scottish BBC disregard the opinions of all these qualified people, and prefer to subject me to the denigrations of a bunch of pip-squeaks of no consequence whatever?

Even so the incident might have been defensible if these broadcasters had subjected my work to serious and reasoned criticism. But they did nothing of the sort, nor were they qualified to do anything of the kind. They attacked me on grounds which showed clearly that any stick was good enough for them to beat me with. There were several points on which as I told you I had deemed it necessary to refer to my lawyer, and these matters have now been referred to counsel. They include the fact that part of the attack was based on the assumption that an article in *Scottish Journal*[2] attacking the Saltire Society was written by me. The article in question was an anonymous one and there was no justification for assuming that I wrote it. Then it was also said that far too many contributions from my pen were used in that *Journal*. Even if I had written the whole of every issue your broadcasters had nothing to do with that. All they had any conceivable right to do was to criticise the quality of my actual contributions. What they did say was a base attempt to cut down my market i.e. to interfere with my source of livelihood; and I am advised that this is actionable. You say that anyone who attacked the Saltire Society as that article did was entitled to expect a

---

[2] The *Scottish Journal*, No 7, May-June 1952 contained an anonymous article on 'The Saltire Society Conference' claiming 'The real trouble is that in relation to Scottish culture [the annual conference of the Saltire Society] presents *Hamlet* without the Prince of Denmark, since the gathering, if not the whole membership, was conspicuously lacking in practically everybody who really matters in relation to Scottish culture. It comprises, instead, only a lot of, no doubt very well-intentioned, nonentities, hardly any of whom have made a substantive contribution of any kind to any of the arts, or even to such possible auxiliaries as education and journalism. Having no creative gifts themselves they have no insight into the creative process and its lets and hindrances. They nevertheless expect to have their opinions taken seriously. The result is a lot of talk that simply succeeds in saying nothing to the point at all.'

counter-attack – but I have still to learn that the BBC has any brief to defend the Saltire Society or regards it as one of its duties to reply to critical articles in periodicals in this way. Articles in newspapers and periodicals can generally be replied to, but the BBC affords no chance to a writer attacked as I was attacked to defend myself.

You may be surprised to learn that this attack on me by a group of nonentities was widely resented and that I have received a letter signed by over 50 well-known Scots protesting against it, and protesting also against the way in which Scottish writers of distinction such as myself are virtually excluded from the microphone in favour of lickspittles of no substantial achievement at all. The Scottish BBC in its infatuated pursuit of the Lowest Common Denominator has restricted Scottish Literary broadcasts to a sorry level and failed completely to do for Scottish poets and other Scottish writers of quality anything like what the English BBC does for English writers. The reason for this is that those in charge of Scottish broadcasting have no creative talent worth a rap themselves and resent it in others, while their whole attitude to Scottish literature, is anti-national and defeatist. So naturally they take the readiest and cheapest means of attack without consideration of probity.

Of that letter with over 50 signatures I am having copies made and these I will send together with a short statement of the way the Scottish BBC has treated me and treated Scottish Literature generally to our MPs and others. I will also publicise the matter in papers at home and abroad, and in many of the lectures I am delivering this winter.

As a protest against the attack on myself, and against the ill-treatment of Scottish Literature generally, I have now to say that whereas I had stipulated that in future copyright work of mine must never be broadcast except by express written permission from me, in future I will give no such permission at all, and have taken steps to debar any broadcasting of my work in Scotland for the whole period of copyright, i.e. for 50 years after my death. The only exception to this rule is with song-settings by Francis George Scott to lyrics of mine. I have nothing to do with these. That is a matter entirely for Mr Scott. When such are broadcast I receive no renumeration at all.

Burns protested against Edinburgh's treatment of Robert Fergusson; Burns himself was badly treated by the Edinburgh literati. It is common for Burns Club speakers nowadays to say that that sort of thing could not happen in Scotland now. But Mr Walter Elliot MP, the late Mrs Catherine Carswell, and the late Mr 'James Bridie' have all declared in print that I have been as badly treated by contemporary Scotland as Fergusson and Burns were in their day. And certainly the Scottish BBC will go on record as having carried on the shameful tradition of the traducers of Fergusson & Burns.

Yours sincerely,
C. M. Grieve.

BBC

Brownsbank,
Candymill,
By Biggar,
Lanarkshire.
4/9/53

Melville Dinwiddie, Esq.,
Director, Scottish Region, B.B.C.

Dear Mr Dinwiddie,

As you know a month or so ago I intimated that none of my copyright poems must be broadcast in future without my written permission in each case; and in a subsequent letter to you I went further and said that it would be futile to ask for such permission as I not only would never grant it but had taken the necessary steps to ensure that no poems of mine would be broadcast by the Scottish BBC during the whole period of the copyright (i.e. for fifty years after my death.)

In these circumstances I am surprised to find that copyright poetry[1] of mine was included in the broadcast, 'A Seat In The Sun', by John Lindsay at 8 p.m. in the Scottish Home Service on 1st September.

I will be glad to have your explanation.

Yours sincerely,
C. M. Grieve.
('Hugh MacDiarmid')

[1] An extract from *Dìreadh*.

BBC

Brownsbank,
Candymill,
By Biggar,
Lanarkshire.
17/9/53

Melville Dinwiddie, Esq.,
Controller, B.B.C.,
Scotland.

Dear Mr Dinwiddie,

Your Ref. 11/MD of 16th Sept. '53

I have to thank you for above letter. Since I wrote you on 4th inst. I have discussed the matter with several friends of mine who have strongly urged me not to enforce the ban on the use of my works in radio on the ground of public interest. They urge that I have no right to deny poetry-lovers in Scotland opportunities to hear poems of mine in this way from time to time. For that reason I feel obliged to reconsider my decision as you suggest, and I beg now to withdraw it so far as the broadcasting of poems of mine is concerned. I must however continue to refuse to allow poems of mine to be broadcast in talks or accompanied by critical comment of any kind. The sort of concerted attack on me by several speakers in the 'Arts Review' of which I originally complained is, I think, unprecedented – at any rate I can recall no previous occasion on which anyone has been subjected to this sort of thing – and as I pointed out in my letter to you contained two very dangerous and quite unwarrantable elements, namely, the ascription to me of an anonymous article in *The Scottish Journal*, and the statement that that periodical contained too much work by me, a statement calculated to affect my source of livelihood.

Yours sincerely,
C. M. Grieve
('Hugh MacDiarmid')

523

BBC   Brownsbank,
                                                       Candymill,
                                                       By Biggar,
                                                       11/3/54

Robin Richardson, Esq.,
B.B.C., Edinburgh.

Dear Robin,

Just a line to let you know that your suggestion re Macbeth is
bearing fruit. I have been working steadily on it since I saw you and
hope to send you a few hundred words summary in the course of the
next few days. As I am doing it, it will be a full-scale poetic drama. In
the real story – as compared with the Shakespearian story – there are
some magnificent opportunities for poetry and song.

In view of the various broadcasts arranged in connection with the
centenary of Sir J. G. Fraser recently I am wondering if any similar
arrangements have been made or are in contemplation to mark the
centenary of Sir Patrick Geddes, whose range as a polymath and
influence in many directions in various countries East and West was
certainly not less than Fraser's. He was undoubtedly one of the
greatest Scotsmen of modern times and has never got his due in his
own country. I knew him well for many years and would welcome an
opportunity to pay tribute to his many sided genius in a talk.

Every kind regard.

                              Yours,
                              C. M. Grieve.

BBC   Brownsbank,
                                                       By Biggar,
                                                       Lanarkshire.
                                                       24/7/54

Roderick C. MacLean, Esq.,
Talks Producer,
B.B.C., Glasgow.

Dear Sir:-

Many thanks for return of my Geddes script. I note what you say
regarding the arrangements you are making for covering this cen-

tenary. I understand only too well that criticism of the Scottish Universities, and a whole-hogging detestation of the *ethos* of Scottish life, and of bourgeois culture generally, are not welcomed by the Scottish BBC, and that an occasion such as this is apt to be taken to allow as many people as possible to say nothing worth saying rather than have one person give a forthright and controversial talk. I can imagine how Geddes himself would have abhorred the sort of thing that is likely to be said about him now by the smooth types who would have been his unscrupulous enemies while he was alive but are quite prepared to give him meaningless praise now he is safely dead.

So far as I myself am concerned I will have other opportunities of publishing my views of the man and his work – and of criticising what the Scottish BBC may do about the matter. But I am not prepared to take part in such a discussion as you suggest along with a number of speakers. Time wouldn't allow anything worth saying to be said, and I loathe these exchanges of fatuities which the BBC prefer. Indeed the whole point of my approach to you was to see if 15 minutes or so could not be secured to deal with the Geddes case effectively instead of the 3 to 5 minute sort of thing which is of no use except to morons to whom nothing is of any use anyhow!

Yours sincerely.
C. M. Grieve

BBC

Brownsbank,
Biggar.
6/5/60

Dear George Bruce,

One of the most interesting Scots I have known (incidentally an old friend of F.G.'s too) is William McCance, to whom I devoted a chapter in my *Contemporary Scots Studies*. Incidentally he is the husband of Agnes Millar Parker, the etcher, wood-cut artist, and book illustrator, whom the late George Bernard Shaw singled out as a sheer genius in these media.

Well, McCance, whom I have known for forty years, has latterly been lecturer in typography and book-production at Reading University, and the Reading Museum and Art Gallery is holding a large, comprehensive retrospective exhibition of his work, paintings, sculpture, drawings, water-colours, graphic work, and some of the books he designed when he was controller of the Gregynog Press in Wales. John Wain has written a foreword for the catalogue.

You know it has frequently been pointed out that literature and the Arts in Scotland have always been singularly lacking in innovators. Well, McCance is an exception. He has always been away out ahead in all his work. Withal, he is passionately Scottish.

I wonder if you could find space in Scottish Life and Letters, or in Arts Review – or as a separate talk – for a feature about this remarkable exhibition of over 40 years work. It ought to be much better known in Scotland, and claimed for the Scottish Renaissance to which it undoubtedly belongs.

The exhibition opens on 11th June, and I want to go down for it. I am lecturing to the Doughty Society in Cambridge University on 20th May, and going on to Cornwall, but I expect to be back in London in time to get down to Reading before the opening of McCance's show. So if there is any chance for a script[1] please let me know before 18th inst. if possible as I am travelling down to London then.

With best wishes.

Yours,
Chris.

BBC   Brownsbank,
                                                                Biggar.
                                                                3/9/60

George Bruce, Esq.,
Features Producer,
B.B.C.,
Edinburgh.

Dear George,

You may remember I spoke to you some time ago about my idea of a Macbeth play – based on the real story of Macbeth, since as you

[1] The BBC did not commission a script.

know, Shakespeare's play is quite false to history. Not only so, but Shakespeare seems to me to have opted for a dramatically much inferior story compared to the real one.

My idea has been to write a poetical play in Scots and in the Scottish poetical tradition, but pressure of other commitments has prevented my really getting down to it, though I have devoted a lot of thought to the matter and done most of the necessary research.

I am now however anxious if possible to go ahead with the idea, especially as the leader in the current *Times Literary Supplement* puts me on my mettle with the following remarks:-

'But the Scottish writer whom one would really like to see turning his hand to drama is the foremost living Scottish poet and man of letters, Mr Hugh MacDiarmid. Mr MacDiarmid's work in prose and verse, in Scots and English, has been full of what the Scots call "flytings" but it is more deeply, in a long poem like *In Memoriam James Joyce*, for instance, a long argument with, and sometimes a "flyting" directed against, himself. Mr MacDiarmid should persuade himself to turn some of the episodes of a career so full of arguments and conflicts, so sturdy and sometimes so solitary a struggle against injustice and philistinism, into a chronicle play.'

It is a play of this kind I have in mind, or, as the *TLS* leader says – and I agree – 'Can these gifts [i.e. the gifts of the distinctive Scots genius] be harnessed to the drama? Not, perhaps, to the drama in the older sense. But they could, very well, be harnessed to drama in the modern Brechtian tradition, drama whose pattern is epical rather than tragic or comic, drama concerned with the opposing attitudes, and contrasting arguments, that arise from a complex and apparently insoluble social situation, rather than from individual character.'

The trouble is that if I am to work on this it would have to be commissioned. Otherwise I could not afford to give it the time and concentrated effort required. I do not know whether the BBC might be willing to consider this, or indeed how they should be approached in such a connection. But perhaps it is within your province to put the suggestion forward? If so, I would be glad if you could do so. Naturally I would require to work to a time-limit, and I do not think I could undertake to complete the task in less than nine months from the date of being commissioned.

With best wishes.

Yours sincerely,
C. M. Grieve.

527

BBC   Brownsbank.
                                                             10/10/60

George Bruce, Esq.,
B.B.C.

Dear George,

   I am not forgetting about the outline of my Macbeth play, which I
had hoped to send you before now. Other pressing matters have
intervened, however, and monopolised my attention in the interval.
I now find too that there are one or two points I must check up in the
Mitchell Library in Glasgow before I commit myself finally to the
way in which I treat the issues to which they relate in the play.
Otherwise I think the thing is shaping well and I am confident I'll be
able to make quite an amount of good poetry out of it. I'll write you
again as soon as I possibly can and send you the outline of the course
of the play. This is just a note in passing to account for the delay in
case you have been expecting a synopsis from me before now.
   All the best.

                              Yours,
                              Chris.

BBC   Brownsbank,
                                                             3/12/60

George Bruce, Esq.,
B.B.C.

Dear George,

   Many thanks for your letter re Macbeth. Alas, Foot and Mouth
Disease on this farm has held me up for a week or two; police
restrictions on all movements here, all cattle and sheep destroyed
etc. And now I am obliged to apply myself exclusively for the next
few days to the huge Swedish translation I have in hand. Nevertheless I think I will be able to send you either – or both – synopsis and
instalment of actual text by next week-end. I am sorry I cannot
manage sooner but I have not only bitten off a great deal more than I
can chew in various connections but as the purely poetic possibilities

of the Macbeth have emerged in the course of my work I have had to recast my plan entirely. I had originally conceived the thing as a historical play – now I am concerned to make it a dramatic poem, and a major work at that. How quickly I can get it written now depends entirely on how free I can get to concentrate on it. It is unfortunate that I have so much else in hand at the moment – and with date lines to meet. But I think I will be able to get down to it in real earnest very soon now, and I am so full of it that I feel sure the actual writing will not take me long. The difficulty will rather be to keep pace with the flow, which has been bottled up too long.

I hope this unfortunate delay will not hamper your own arrangements. I am very grateful to you for your interest and anxious to put you in possession of sufficient to go on without any avoidable delay now.

With best wishes,

Yours,
Christopher Grieve.

BBC

Brownsbank,
Candymill,
Biggar,
Lanarkshire.
3/6/61

George Bruce, Esq.,
Features Producer,
B.B.C.

Dear George,

Many thanks for your note. *Aniara* is being published by Hutchinson (London) and simultaneously by Bonniers (Stockholm) and Knopf (USA). The publishers have had the complete typescript for a couple of months now but I haven't heard yet by what date the book is likely to appear.

I've been having a very busy time and consequently have had to shunt the Macbeth drama on to a side-line. But I hope to restore it to the main track shortly and propel it then without further diversions to its terminus.

In the meantime I have four books[1] appearing this year – i.e. *Collected Poems* (Macmillan, New York); *Selected Poems* (Chosen by Norman MacCaig); *The Kind of Poetry I Want* (Bodoni, Italy); and the *Aniara* translation. Also the David Hume lecture I gave recently is being published as a pamphlet. So I haven't been idle!

Trust all's O.K. with you. Kindest regards to Mrs Bruce and yourself.

Yours,
Chris

BBC

Brownsbank,
Biggar.
3/11/61

George Bruce, Esq.,
Features Producer,
B.B.C., Edinburgh.

Dear George,

Many thanks for your letter re Neil Gunn's 70th birthday. I would certainly hate not to be one of those paying tribute to him in the programme[1] you are devising. It is quite true that much of his work is not of a sort I care for, but the man himself is a different matter. I saw a great deal of him in the '20s and there are few, if any, of my compatriots of whom I have been – and am still in recollection – fonder. It has been a grief to me that our ways have lain so far apart in the last two or three decades. He is a grand fellow and I will be very happy to do a short script about him.

I'll think about it today and tomorrow, and let you have the 500 words on Monday. Recording on the evening of the 16th will suit me all right.

[1] The MacCaig selection never materialised in print. The other books appeared in the following order: *The Kind of Poetry I Want* (Edinburgh 1961), *David Hume, Scotland's Greatest Son* (Edinburgh 1962), *Collected Poems* (New York 1962), *Aniara* (London 1962).
[1] The tributes to Neil Gunn were assembled in 'Scottish Life and Letters', BBC Scottish Home Service, 18 November 1961.

It's a long time since I saw you. I hope this finds you in good form. With warmest regards to Mrs Bruce and yourself.

Yours,
Chris.

BBC

Brownsbank,
Candymill,
by Biggar
1/7/64

George Bruce, Esq.,

Dear George,

Many thanks for the script of the discussion on Walter Keir's review of Buthlay's book.[1] What you say in your note in expansion of Alex Scott's remark re my being 'the worst poet' I of course understand perfectly. The necessity of being honest with oneself – i.e. exhibiting one's weaknesses as well as one's strengths – is not generally understood. Alex Scott is quite right – but it is part of the image I have always tried to project that it should be so. It would not have suited my book at all to be faultless. My job, as I see it, has never been to lay a tit's egg, but to erupt like a volcano, emitting not only flame, but a lot of rubbish.

All the best.

Yours,
Chris

[1] 'Arts Review', Scottish Home Service, 14 May 1964, included a discussion following Walter Keir's review of Kenneth Buthlay's *Hugh MacDiarmid* (1964). George Bruce, producer of the programme, explained the circumstances in a letter to the present editor (5 July 1982): 'Chris was in Canada during the Arts Review in which Kenneth Buthlay's book on MacDiarmid was reviewed. In the discussion which followed Norman MacCaig commented that MacDiarmid, to say the least, was the best poet in Scotland today, to which Alex Scott added, "And also the worst". Thereafter he added some qualification to his quip, but since the comment to that point had been a paean of praise, and since I had to cut something from the programme for time, I cut the qualifications. Chris asked to see the script, which did not exist, but I had a transcript made of the spontaneous discussion, which I sent him along with a letter in which I said I was to blame for the blunt comment made by Alex Scott on account of the cut I had made. Naturally I was apprehensive about the outcome, but how fortunate it turned out.'

531

To Routledge

MacDiarmid's relationship with the publishers George Routledge (later Routledge and Kegan Paul) began with the publication of *Albyn* (by Kegan Paul, Trench, Trubner) in 1927, led to *Scottish Eccentrics* in 1936 and was resumed in the 1970s with *The Hugh MacDiarmid Anthology* (1972), edited by Michael Grieve and Alexander Scott, and *The Socialist Poems of Hugh MacDiarmid* (1978), edited by T. S. Law and Thurso Berwick. The crucial period, covered in the following letters, is the mid-1930s when MacDiarmid was retained by Routledge for a while and then rejected over his political testament *Red Scotland*, a book that has never appeared as the manuscript is missing.

UR

12 Petherton Road,
London, N.5.
17/9/34

Messrs Kegan Paul,
Publishers.

Dear Sirs,

I have been engaged for some time in the British Museum and elsewhere collecting material for a book on some famous Scots Eccentrics, a contents-outline of which I enclose; and I am writing you now in the hope that you may care to consider the publishing of this.

As you probably know a considerable cultural movement has developed in Scotland during the past decade, and Scottish books of all kinds are in increasing demand. I have taken a leading part in promoting this movement; the last issue of *The Bookman*,[1] a special

---

[1] *The Bookman*, Vol 86, No 516, September 1934.

Scottish number, was largely devoted to my work. I am best known as a poet, having published many volumes of verse, anthologies, essays in literary criticism, etc. My more general works on Scottish matters, however, in addition to my early pamphlet, *Albyn* in your Today and Tomorrow Series, include a big volume of *Contemporary Scottish Studies*, and a book which created widespread interest this spring, *Scottish Scene* (published by Messrs Jarrolds) of which I was joint author along with the novelist, Lewis Grassic Gibbon.

Scots Eccentrics should prove a very popular volume. All the individuals dealt with had extraordinary personalities and most of them were important people in their diverse fields. Most of them have not been dealt with in any volume for many years, and in each case first-hand research has brought out masses of new information which give a basis for entirely fresh and unconventional accounts.

I live in the Shetland Islands and having now collected all the necessary material I am anxious to return there as soon as possible and settle down to my winter's writing. I shall be in London however for another week or ten days and if you are interested in this proposal I could call and see you at any time you care to appoint. I could contract to deliver the complete typescript (80,000 to 90,000 words) by the first week in March.

Yours sincerely,

C. M. Grieve.
('Hugh MacDiarmid')

UR   12 Petherton Road,
                                               London N.5.
                                                  22/9/34

Dear Mr Warburg,[1]

Many thanks for your letter of yesterday. I have pleasure in returning the agreement form[2] with my signature appended. I am very proud to have formed this connection with your firm, and you

[1] Frederick Warburg was joint managing director of Routledge; he left in 1935, bought Martin Secker's company and sold it to Heinemann. See his *An Occupation for Gentlemen* (1959).
[2] For *Scottish Eccentrics*.

can rely upon me to do a book worthy alike of the rich material this subject matter places at my disposal and of your firm's distinguished traditions.

Yours sincerely,
C. M. Grieve.

UR   Whalsay
                                                                     30/10/34

My dear Pat,[1]

We had quite a nice passage up for a wonder, just managed to slide through between gales, – even Valda wasn't sick – but since then the weather has been simply hellish (a cold hell!), torrential rain, hurricane winds, and at the moment for the sake of a little variety, snow. I am glad to be back; our cottage, after our seven months' absence, is being put in order and once that is done and we are comfortably ensconced in it again I'll gladly settle down again to a steady winter's work the fruits whereof you will see anon; but just at the moment (it being lunchtime) I cannot resist a twinge of envy as I think of you no doubt lifting a nice pint or two in the Chapter House and would fain be at hand in case your strong right hand should prove unequal to the task!

I am making my remarks on Mr Maitland's proposal[2] in a more formal letter which accompanies this one.

I will write you again in a few days' time but in the meantime I have just bethought me of Ezra Pound's book of essays[3] published by Faber and Faber a copy of which you thought you could wangle for me and which I'd greatly like, and I have looked up your catalogue and find that the two language books I had in mind are;-

[1] A. J. B. Paterson, Routledge's sales manager, known for his enthusiasm for Scottish writing and his love of conviviality. MacDiarmid dedicated *Scottish Eccentrics* to 'my friend and fellow-countryman A. J. B. Paterson with gratitude and affection.'
[2] Maitland, an Edinburgh bookseller, proposed an anthology of prose and verse from *The Free Man*, the Social Credit weekly in which C. M. Grieve contributed a causerie 'At the Sign of the Thistle'. In his report MacDiarmid thought the suggestion sound but the plan rather vague.
[3] Ezra Pound, *Make It New*, (1934).

534

Richards' *Mencius on the Mind*[4]
Downey's *Creative Imagination*.[5]

I read a bit of *Butcher's Broom*[6] while I was staying with the Carswells,[7] and agree with all you say. Gunn has gone completely off the rails and I do not think he is likely to get back on to them again. It is a great pity as he has real ability. But a Book Club success is nearly always fatal; as F. G. Scott says there is no more weakening kind of light in the world than limelight.

Valda joins me in all the best.

Yours,
C.M.G.

UR   Whalsay.
                                                               Friday.
                                                               n.d.
                                                       [November 1934?]

My Dear Pat,

Yours of 11th just to hand. Excuse a brief note in reply; will write you at greater length in a day or two. Many thanks for the issues of *The Week*;[1] will be particularly glad to receive this regularly. I note the books are coming on; sorry you are having trouble getting the Pound essays out of Faber's – don't bother: you have enough to do. I hope the 'flu hasn't left any after-effects. It's good news Gunn has come in on the Whisky idea[2]; he'll do a good thing on it. About this

---

[4] I. A. Richards, *Mencius on the Mind* (1932).
[5] June Etta Downey, *Creative Imagination* (1929).
[6] Neil M. Gunn, *Butcher's Broom* (1934). Paterson had written to MacDiarmid (25 October) saying, of Gunn's novel of the Highland Clearances, 'These rapturous rhetorics of his are going to damage him completely as a natural writer, and he is just not great enough to carry them off.'
[7] Donald and Catherine Carswell lived at 17 Keats Grove, Hampstead, London.
[1] 'Claud Cockburn's roneo'd *The Week*. . . literally kept me alive in the Shetland Islands. I subsequently met Cockburn in London and he is one of the most delightful, well-informed, and wittiest men I have known.' (Company, p. 271).
[2] Neil Gunn was, from 1923 to 1937, excise officer attached to an Inverness whisky distillery; he agreed to write *Whisky and Scotland* (1935) for the Meanings In Scotland series.

series by the way (I think I mentioned it in my last letter) the contract specifies the payment of half the agreed advance, viz. £20, on publishers' signing contract, so – being like most writers and all poets chronically hard-up – I was confidently expecting cheque in question ere this, the signed contract having come to hand about a fortnight ago. What's the reason of this thusness? I haven't spiered the firm, of course; but that cheque would be particularly useful at the moment and it is clear enough from the terms of the contract that it should have been paid on signature of that.

Remember me to Richardson.[3]

Valda joins me in every kind regard,

Yours,
Chris.

UR   Whalsay,
                                                         Shetland Islands.
                                                                21/11/34

Dear Sirs:-

Many thanks for your letter (GR/FJW) of 16th inst., enclosing form of agreement respecting my book: *What Lenin Has Meant To Scotland*[1] for your forthcoming series, which I have much pleasure in returning herewith with my signature attached.

With best wishes.

                                              Yours sincerely,
                                              C. M. Grieve.

[3] Maurice Richardson was Routledge's publicity manager. As a Communist in the 1930s he told the Party newspaper, *The Daily Worker*, that Routledge were publishing Sir Walter Citrine's *I Search for Truth in Soviet Russia* (1936) and had sold 20,000 copies to a steel company for them to give to their workers. The order was consequently cancelled and Richardson was dismissed; later he worked as editor of *Lilliput*.

[1] In 1934 Routledge asked Lewis Grassic Gibbon to edit a series of books on 'Meanings In Scotland'. MacDiarmid was contracted to write the title on Lenin and also (from 28 September 1934) retained by Routledge, at the rate of £1 per week, to advise the firm on Scottish subjects. On 19 July 1935 Routledge gave MacDiarmid six months' notice that the retainer was to be terminated.

Whalsay.
10/1/35

My Dear Pat,

I am utterly astounded and disgusted at Gibbon's letter,[1] copy of which you sent me (and which, of course, I regard as absolutely confidential). Many of us who have been interested in his work have feared that his potentialities would be drastically restricted by this incredible coarse strain under his veneer, and, indeed, his money-grabbing propensities were discerned and discussed by us when the present arrangements were first mooted. They are bad enough in themselves but when they are conjoined to such impudent express-ions towards Mr. Warburg the matter is, of course, insufferable.

As to matters of fact, I do not know how the idea of this series first arose, you and Gibbon had broached the matter before I joined you, but thereafter we all took a part and the final set of titles, authors to approach, etc. were the result of a pooling of our various suggestions – in particular, the Whisky one for Gunn, the Sex one for Willa Muir,[2] and the Lenin one for myself were my own suggestion. If Gibbon threw off the initial suggestion that was about all he did.

As to payment the £100 is much more than adequate. I am afraid Gibbon is inclined to think in terms of best-seller novels – which are not applicable to other types of books. In any case, in my own experience, I know that in Benn's Augustan Poets Series[3], – where the editor had to do the actual selection and provide preface, notes etc. – he got a fixed sum of £12.10/-; and again in their new 1/- Series of Poets[4], Messrs Macmillan only pay an advance of £5. Compared with these, and taking into consideration that Gibbon's editorial work would be little more than nominal, your terms are very generous indeed.

You may recall that, so far as I am concerned, while in view of the circumstances we agreed that it would be better for me to stand aside

---

[1] On 18 December 1934 Gibbon asked Routledge to increase his editorial fee, for the Meanings In Scotland series, from £100 to £200. On 4 January 1935 Paterson sent a copy of Gibbon's letter with the following comment: 'Here's a letter from that bloody impossible – Mr Lewis Leslie Grassic Gibbons Mitchell. Is he quite compos mentis or is this an inverted form of Marxian Nationalism run riot and gotten itself mixed up with a peasant inferiority complex?' On 8 February 1935 Paterson wrote: 'My dear Chris, I see that poor old Mitchell died last night.'

[2] Willa Muir's contribution to the Routledge series was *Mrs Grundy in Scotland* (1936).

[3] For the Augustan Books of Poetry, published by Benn, MacDiarmid edited *Robert Burns, 1759–1796* (London 1926) and *Living Scottish Poets* (London 1931).

[4] MacDiarmid was represented in Macmillan's Contemporary Poets series by *Selected Poems* (London 1934).

in Gibbon's favour in respect of this series, I should have regarded the work as coming within the terms of my arrangement with you without additional payment. In any event, while one must live, money is by no means the first consideration in relationship to a firm of the standing of yours, and I do not believe that it will be to Gibbon's interest in the long run to think exclusively of LSD and have no regard to questions of status and good tradition, let alone standards of simple politeness.

Finally – to dispose of this very disagreeable matter – let me say emphatically that I do not think you need have the slightest fear that anything Gibbon says or does will spoil the contacts you have already secured with Scottish writers. If anything of that sort is attempted please let me know immediately and I will pull every conceivable rope to prevent it.

What with the Christmas season, etc., mails are late. I had hoped by this to have had several letters which have not yet come to hand and as a result of these to have had various things to lay before you. But they cannot be long now. If letters prove too slow and uncertain a way of getting things to business point, I'll try to have a run down (early next month) and see various people in Edinburgh and Glasgow.

I noticed *The Week* was deferring issue for a few days at Christmas time; but please don't forget to send me the issues as they come in.

Hope you had a good time at Southport. We had a quiet time here but then the island folk only started on Monday (since they adhere to the Old Calendar) and their celebrations now continue till about the end of the month. The men go in batches round the houses – every man with his bottle of whisky. And when I tell you that about 7 p.m. on Monday there were no fewer than 25 men in my cottage here – and that it is a point of honour that every man must sample every other man's bottle – you can imagine the hectic splore that was therewith inaugurated. Wish you'd been up here this week!

Valda joins me in every kind regard to your wife and family and yourself – and Mr Richardson. I'll write you again in a few days' time and hope to have some news for you by then. Believe me exceedingly sorry that you have had this disgusting affair to cope with – but only thereby made all the more anxious to do whatever I possibly can, both in my own writing and via other Scottish writers, to get thoroughly good Scottish work published under your imprint.

Yours,
C.M.G.

P.S. By the way I am not quite sure what happens finally – do you

538

automatically publish the books in this series once you receive the MSS from the various authors contracted with – or does Gibbon have to O.K. them first – or do they come on to me for my reader's opinion?

UR   Whalsay,
                                                                          12/4/35

My dear Pat,

Sorry about the tooth trouble; trust O.K. again. Am having also to get my eyes seen to and if funds permit new dentures when South in beginning of next month. All these consequences of our biological limitations are a damned nuisance.

Note what you say re question of advance to T. D. MacD[onald][1]. Of course I was not thinking of this book as confined to an academic public but as susceptible of a considerably wider sale. The trouble is, I imagine, that MacD. will hesitate to take on the job unless he gets enough to keep him going till he gets the book done. He'd be afraid of being completely stumped in the middle of writing it by destitution.

I have a note today from George Scott-Moncrieff (who, incidentally, is reviewing Walkinshaw for *The Criterion*).[2] He tells me John Lorne Campbell[3] has finished his Barra book and is looking for a publisher. Mackenzie may have mentioned this to you when suggesting Campbell for the Meanings Series. I have no idea what sort of a book it is, but I have written Scott-Moncrieff suggesting that Campbell should give Routledge's a look at it.

Yes, I'll get in touch with Cleghorn Thomson[4] again at once.

[1] When Gibbon died, in February 1935, MacDiarmid took over his editorial duties and Meanings In Scotland became Meanings For Scotland. MacDiarmid suggested that Fionn Mac Colla (T. D. MacDonald) should contribute a title on 'What Gaelic Has Meant to Scotland' though Paterson felt it was too specialised a subject.
[2] In *The Criterion*, Vol XIV, No LVII, July 1935, George Scott Moncrieff reviewed *The Scots Tragedy* (1933) by Colin Walkinshaw (J. M. Reid).
[3] John Lorne Campbell, Gaelic scholar and folklorist, author of *Highland Songs of the Forty-Five* (1935); Routledge published his *The Book of Barra* in 1936.
[4] David Cleghorn Thomson edited *Scotland in Quest of Her Youth* (1932) and was, in 1935, running a Scottish literary agency; MacDiarmid was interested in this as a possible source of books for Routledge.

I am returning as requested in today's note one copy of the typescript – uncorrected. I hope the American firm 'bites'. But of course I feel that this portion of typescript doesn't do the book justice. I would rather they had seen some of the more interesting chapters. But no doubt they will be given an idea of the considerably more popular character of the bulk of the contents.

Re the completion of the typing, this is, of course, all right as far as I am concerned, so long as it suits your firm – tho' it would have been a Godsend from my point of view if the typescript had been duly delivered sooner as then £40 would be payable to me as per contract. Alas! What sharks we authors have to be under this blasted system!

Valda tells me that one day she met you and a friend of yours and said something about a novel she was contemplating – and you then suggested she should offer it, through you, to this friend's firm. I mention this because Routledge's don't touch fiction and I think you said don't mean to on Scottish side either. Now I am putting together a book to be called *Thirty Scottish Stories* by Hugh Mac-Diarmid – all but two entirely new (the two exceptions have already appeared in periodicals) – and I want to find a publisher to bring this out this autumn. I haven't approached any firm yet. The stories are (if I says it as shouldn't) very varied and represent some of my best work and something new in Scottish fiction but yet not highbrow or limited in appeal. I have twenty of them all ready now – the other ten I am still revising and polishing a little. But I could send the lot in a week or so. Some of them I think will be found very amusing. The total runs to 50,000 to 60,000 words. Let me know what you suggest I should do with them – i.e. whether after all Routledge's might consider them, or, if not, whether (along the lines of your suggestion to Valda mentioned above) you would act as my agent (on commission basis) and sell the first book rights for me to some firm with whom you are in touch. I know the prejudice against short stories – and also the prejudice many firms have against a volume of short stories by a writer who has not done a novel or two first. I think these prejudices are wrong, because most of the best short story writers have been very poor novelists; the short story and the novel are different forms altogether and very few writers excel in both. But my reputation in other fields would, I fancy, stand me in good stead and ensure a sale for this collection that a new book of poems or a non-fictional prose work of mine could not command. I know of course that I could get a publisher easily for these stories, but I want a good publisher as I contemplate if all goes well doing a good deal in this line in the next few years and so much depends on having such a new departure properly launched. So I'll be very glad to have your advice and if you wish post on the dope for your inspection.

Valda joins me in wishing you all the best.

Yours,
Chris.

P.S. It has just occurred to me – in view of the size of the *Eccentrics* book – that you might care for an illustration or two. I couldn't furnish portraits of all those dealt with, but I could furnish good illustrations of several of them – Urquhart, Christopher North, Hogg, McGonagall. Of course I haven't any idea what this means from a costing standpoint; I only throw out the suggestion in case it's of any use to you.

UR

Whalsay.
17/6/35

Dear Mr Warburg,

Many thanks for your letter. There is, of course, no need for you to send me the *Eccentrics* in its revised form[1] before you send it to the printer. I have complete confidence in your revision.

I do not know whether Mr Paterson is back, so I am enclosing to you herewith the MSS of the Lenin book[2]. As Mr Paterson knows I have no facilities here for having my work typed (hence my arrangement with him re the typing of the *Eccentrics*). Can you please arrange to have the Lenin book typed for me too – typed copy, and duplicate – and the typing account sent to me.

I like the title *Red Scotland* you suggest, and, as you see, have adopted it.

The book (which incidentally includes some of my best recent poems) is likely to create a sensation in Scotland; and the fact that I am standing as Nationalist candidate for the Lord Rectorship of

---

[1] Frederick Warburg asked MacDiarmid to cut the introductory chapter, 'The Caledonian Antisyzygy', place it at the end of the book rather than the beginning, and shorten the sentences in the book. Although he had reservations about abbreviating his introductory chapter MacDiarmid accepted these suggestions and was content to leave the shortening of sentences to a Routledge copy-editor.

[2] *What Lenin Has Meant to Scotland* was now called (at Warburg's suggestion) *Red Scotland*.

541

Edinburgh University in October[3], and will thus be prominently in the news, will be good publicity for it if it is out before, or by, that time. With best wishes.

> Yours sincerely,
> C. M. Grieve.

UR

Whalsay.
21/6/35

My dear Pat:-

I will write you again by next post. This is just a brief note enclosing a rough draft of the sort of thing I'd suggest for leaflet letterpress re Meanings series – if need be you could also have photos of the authors on the leaflet. Also I enclose list of Scottish papers for review copies. Let me know if you also think of a few of the principal ones – the only ones I think it is worth bothering about. So far as my own book is concerned I think review copies should be sent to *The Daily Worker*, *The Left Review*, and *The Labour Monthly*.

Hope these suggestions may help.

All the best.

> Yours,
> Chris.

How stands Scotland in the world today? A kind of national stock-taking has been going on since the War ended. Revaluations and new departures of all kinds have been the order of the day; and along with these has developed a many-sided new national political and literary movement. Most of these tendencies, though they have roused widespread interest, alike in Scotland itself and in other countries, have not yet crystallised out into any definitive form. There is a general desire to get them into clearer perspective. Messrs Routledge's new series of 'Meanings For Scotland' is designed to

---

[3] In the Edinburgh University Rectorial Election of 1935 the votes were cast as follows: Viscount Allenby (825), Dr Douglas Chalmers Watson (792), Lord Clydesdale (292), C. M. Grieve (88).

perform this service in regard to many of the most important aspects of Scottish arts and affairs. These concise, trenchantly written, and attractively produced little volumes are each by one of the well-known writers of the younger Scottish group, who has won recognition as an authority on the subject he has taken; and, collectively, the Series will prove a valuable and highly stimulating Intelligent Man's Guide To The New Scotland. The initial issues in this very timely and useful series are as follows:-

[*Scott and Scotland*]

by Edwin Muir, the well-known poet, translator, and literary critic.

[*Whisky and Scotland*]

by Neil Gunn, the distinguished Highland novelist, whose *Morning-Tide* was one of the outstanding successes of 1930.

[*Is Scotland Educated?*]

by A. S. Neill, an experimental educationist of European reputation and author of *The Problem Child* and other challenging books.

[*Literature and Oatmeal*]

by William Power, Scotland's leading literary journalist and descriptive essayist.

[*Red Scotland*]

by Hugh MacDiarmid, the poet and stormy petrel of Scottish arts and affairs.

[*The Lion and the Unicorn*]

by Eric Linklater, the world-famous author of *Juan In America* and other highly diverting novels.

etc.

In this series each of these noted writers chose his own subject as one in which he is specially interested and about which he feels that he has something of consequence to say. The result is a particularly brilliant and lively collection of thoroughly well informed and in many respects highly provocative and controversial pronouncements on a wide range of important Scottish subjects. They are volumes of, at once, great topical interest and permanent value, and, as such, are sure to command an unusual measure of public attention and excite discussion to an exceptional extent.

543

Whalsay.
21/7/35

Dear Mr Warburg:-

I was very sorry to receive your letter of 15th inst., and enclosures. I had thought that my acquiescence (against my own judgement) in cutting what was originally intended as the preface[1] and transferring it to the end, and in agreeing to your editor cutting down some of my long sentences had met your requirements. Indeed you yourself suggested in your last letter on this subject that the typescript, after it had been treated by your editor (which, you assured me, would involve very slight changes) could go direct to the printers, without further reference to me, and I agreed.

I think you will agree that I have shown myself willing to meet your suggestions in every possible way. But what is suggested now is a radical reordering and virtual rewriting of the book. Also postponement of publication till next spring.

Even if on other grounds I could agree I am alas debarred for reasons of health. I was ill off and on all winter and I have had a very serious collapse during the last few weeks. I am now advised, and have no option but to follow the advice, that I must absolutely avoid all work and worry for at least a year. In these circumstances I could not begin the altering of the book until next June or July – if then, or, indeed, at all. That is to say, the postponement of publication would have to be till autumn next year at earliest or perhaps spring 1937.

Postponement of a book after announcement like this is in my opinion very damaging to an author; and even then I would have no guarantee that the new text could please you any better than the present, while that it would sell any better than the present only the event could show.

In reply to your editor's main points I would like to say:-
1) That I have published some thirty books (all characterised by long sentences, numerous quotations, etc) and have had no previous trouble of this kind with any publisher. What your editor calls my 'own set of ideas about Scottish culture, etc' is the substance of almost all these books. And it is precisely these ideas which have gained me an international reputation, which never fail to attract attention and create discussion when I re-present them in new connections, and which have had the practical effect of calling into being the present new literary and political nationalist movements in Scotland. I am not a mere 'maker of books' nor (except to a very

[1] Of *Scottish Eccentrics*.

secondary extent) a writer for money – I am a serious writer and write to express and re-express my own views and develop them in various directions. I would not consider it worth while to write except with this intention. In other words, what your editor regards as my Scottish obsession is the very raison d'être of my work. I agree that this, and the lack of certain superficial graces, does not endear me to the reviewers, but most publishers find that reviewers' opinions whether favourable or unfavourable do not affect the sales of a book one way or another, save in an occasional very exceptional case. I have so little regard for reviewers' opinions that I have never troubled to subscribe to a press-cutting agency; but I know that my work is of permanent value and that is what I am concerned about.

2) With regard to the extensive reference to, and quotation from, a very wide and unusual range of reading, the important thing to realise here is that almost all these quotations are drawn from old out-of-print little-known and generally inaccessible sources, and will be completely new to the vast majority of Scottish, let alone non-Scottish, readers. The book involved a great deal of reading and research in out-of-the-way directions; and the virtues of the bulk of the quotations, in addition to their relevance, is that their quaint phraseology conveys the temper of bye-gone ages and helps to illuminate the characters of my Eccentrics in a way modern phraseology could not do. With regard to the scantiness of bio-graphical material in some of the essays this is due to the fact that further biographical material about the characters in question does not exist.

3) With regard to your editor's constructive suggestions – i.e. the following order of eccentrics:-

Lord George Gordon
Sir Thomas Urquhart
MacGonagall
James Hogg
Christopher North
William Berry
Thomas Davidson
Elspeth Buchan
Lord Monbaddo
Ossian

and also that (as, indeed, I suggested to you myself) the word 'epilogue' should be omitted and that it should simply be printed as the last essay in the book under the heading 'The Strange Process-ion', with the 'introductory' 'Caledonian Antisyzygy' following it – I am, of course, entirely agreeable to these changes.

Even if I could alter the book along the lines you now desire in time for publication early next spring that would be a serious matter for me. Although I write for money only to a very secondary extent, I sign contracts for just the small sums I require but I am dependent upon the payment of these at the expected times. Postponement till spring would mean that I could not receive £40 I expected this autumn, which would be bad enough, especially when I am not in a condition to earn in other ways, but postponement for a full year or longer is, of course, far worse; besides I would be devoting a considerable amount of time unremuneratively and in the curious task of writing a book in a way my readers would recognise as entirely different from any of my previous work and (if I modified my 'Scottish ideas') in accordance with an outlook entirely other than my own – in short, to an elimination of my own characteristic methods of, and reasons for, writing.

The state of my health, however, entirely precludes any such effort.

Over and above all that, I am also seriously concerned now as to what your attitude will be to my other book, *Red Scotland*.

With best wishes,

Yours sincerely,
C. M. Grieve.

UR   Whalsay,
                                                                        3/8/35

Frederic J. Warburg, Esq.

Dear Sir:-

Many thanks for your kind letters re *Scots Eccentrics*, the new arrangement[1] re my services in trying to introduce Scottish authors and Scottish books, and the publication next spring of *Red Scotland*, which would give me time to cut it down to the necessary size for the series. My delay in replying to you is wholly due to the fact that I am still very ill.

[1] Instead of a retainer of £52 per year, paid quarterly in advance, MacDiarmid would, under the 'new arrangement', be entitled to 'a lump sum somewhere in the neighbourhood of £10 for each book introduced and for which we sign a contract' (letter from Routledge, 19 July 1935).

I am extremely pleased about your decision in regard to the publication of the *Eccentrics* and will look forward to proofs.

With regard to *Red Scotland* I am wondering if you have retained the duplicate typescript. I wrote so much beyond the number of words desired[2] quite inadvertently and was very much surprised to find that I had so greatly overshot the mark. But I am not anxious to cut the MSS down (indeed I have certain additions I would like to make to the book which would, I think, improve it greatly – additions amounting to about 2,000 words). It will certainly be a month or two before my condition of ill-health will permit me to begin to work on the task of cutting down the MSS to the necessary size for the series, and in these circumstances I am wondering if you would not consider publishing the book as it stands independently of the series.

Apart from the cutting down of the MSS I am anxious about whether, even if I do this, the material then remaining will be acceptable to you for publication – or whether you may not possibly take exceptions to portions of it as too violently expressed, too revolutionary in tone, or perhaps dangerous under the Incitement to Disaffection Act. It would be a pity to do all the cutting down and then be confronted with such objections as these. I certainly think it would be better for you to read the MSS. before I tackle the cutting-down.

With best wishes.

Yours sincerely,
C. M. Grieve.

UR

Whalsay,
Shetland Islands.
Sunday, 13th Oct. 1935

My dear Pat,

Salutations!
Here I am, back home again, and beginning to try to get the

2 The books in The Voice of Scotland series (as Meanings For Scotland was now called at the suggestion of Frederic Warburg) were not to exceed 50,000 words. In a letter of 22 July 1935 Paterson had written to MacDiarmid: 'Alas for your fervid

thread of things into my hands again. I expect Valda told you that I was suffering from no ordinary illness[1] but a touch-and-go one – a horrible imminence of death from which I was only rescued by a miracle of specialist treatment.

I haven't had time yet since I got back (after the worst sea-jostling I've ever had – a terrible experience for a fellow straight from a hospital bed) to see all the correspondence that passed in my absence or consider how Valda in my name dealt therewith but I gather from one of Mr Warburg's kind letters to her (GR/FJW 21/8/35) that the preparation of *Red Scotland* for the press is left to me.

I will tackle this right away and send it in to you immediately I have it of the right size for the series. I have been thinking this over very carefully and with due regard to a letter of yours in which you indicated that your directors had some definite views as to how this should be done, viz. by the excision of irrelevancies. That is the method I will adopt, baring the central theme of the book as clearly as possible and cutting out irrelevancies, redundancies, and passages in which I tease out the main theme into too highly specialised issues the connection of which with the former is not too obvious to the layman and the mention of which for that reason weakens rather than supports the essential argument. I have also some strong stuff – well within the general understanding and strongly consolidatory of the central theme – which I will add to the MSS, without, however, swelling the total beyond the precise prescribed limit of the series. I trust this result, and the methods by which I achieve it, will be entirely satisfactory to your directors, but, of course, I shall be only too glad to have their comment and to follow any suggestions they may make with regard to special points affecting the excisions and the impression created by the book as submitted with these effected.

I wired you on the eve of leaving hospital, lest there should be any point on which you were specially anxious to get into touch with me. I understood that under the agreement I had with the firm re reading and advising etc. on Scottish books, that I was to get a copy of each of the latter you published. But so far I have not seen copies

enthusiasm, it has produced a book of more than twice the length contracted for, with the result that it is rendered hopeless in its present form for inclusion in the series.'

[1] MacDiarmid had been increasingly under a strain and in August his health broke down completely. F. G. Scott arranged to have the poet admitted to Murray Royal Hospital in Perth, at his expense, and, on 20 August, Valda wrote to Routledge from Scott's house in St Andrews: 'Mr Grieve had a serious relapse & for some days it was a matter of life and death. With the help of the island Dr [David Orr] I brought him South & I am now glad to say – we have every hope that he will be on his feet again in about six weeks.'

of Gunn's or Linklater's[2]. I was anxious to do so. I trust they are going well and have already done sufficiently well as to amply justify the venture.

I enclose the marked copy of the first few pages of proof of *Scottish Eccentrics* received the other day from Messrs Clark, the printers. I like the page-size and type adopted, and the proof is very free from error.

I trust everything is going well with you personally. Alas, there is no likelihood of my being in London soon. The expenses of my illness were utterly ruinous, and I am by no means out of the wood yet – still under the doctor and likely to be for long enough, obliged to be exceedingly careful, and sadly diminished in working power. Still – alive! Which is always something. In fact quite a lot!

With love, Valda joining.

Yours,
Chris.

Kindest regards to Richardson.

UR

Whalsay.
Monday.
[Nov 1935?]

My dear Pat,

So glad to hear from you again. Hope weather on your Scandinavian tour was better than the absolutely hellish conditions prevailing here since my return. Am having a somewhat precarious convalescence, complicated by a painful and disabling accident to my right arm.

I enclose revised proofs; and also beg to submit to the consideration of your firm enclosed study of *The Wolf of Badenoch*[1].

---

[2] The Voice of Scotland series had got under way in 1935 with Neil Gunn's *Whisky and Scotland* and Eric Linklater's *The Lion and the Unicorn*; in the Linklater book there was 'a list of volumes in the series' with MacDiarmid's *Red Scotland* third on the list.

[1] Routledge rejected MacDiarmid's *The Wolf of Badenoch* and though another firm, Rich and Cowan, accepted it the book never appeared. However it is alluded to

I expect to get the *Red Scotland* – reduced to series size – off to you by next post.

I was delighted to get Power's and MacClure's books[2] – both tip-top; format most attractive. The excellence of Power's book rather astonished me; and I have written heartily congratulating him. Gunn's and Linklater's I haven't seen. Hope all go well!

I was surprised to find that, not only *Red Scotland* but also the *Eccentrics* is postponed publication till January. As I explained to Mr Warburg in a previous letter I do not write for more than a minimum of money but am absolutely dependent on receiving such small sums as I contract for at time originally anticipated; otherwise I am badly in the soup. What the postponement of both books means is that I have to live out of both sums – £40 and £20 – months longer than I reckoned on, and the result is disastrous. While Mr Warburg, in one of his most kind and considerate letters to my wife while I was ill, indicated that the firm could not at that juncture consider paying the £40 for *Eccentrics* before the actual publication of the book, I hope that now since matters are so much further advanced they may be able to do so. You will appreciate that being three months unable to do work and the need to pay doctors' bills, typists' bills, etc. prompts this hope, so will you please add to your many past kindnesses by transmitting it to the proper quarter.

Excuse haste – must rush to catch mail boat – will write again on other matters next post.

Love and best wishes.

Yours,
Chris.

and quoted from in *Lucky Poet* where MacDiarmid presents Alexander Stewart (1342–1406), The Wolf of Badenoch, as a fourteenth-century freedom fighter: 'It was a little country that the Wolf fought for, "about the size of Palestine", but it is permissible for a Scot, under present circumstances, to speculate as to just what was lost by its liquidation. The Wolf was destined to go under, but the fight he fought is not finished.' (LP, pp. 215–16).

[2] The Voice of Scotland series continued, in 1935, with William Power's *Literature and Oatmeal* and Victor McClure's *Scotland's Inner Man*.

UR   Whalsay,
                                                      28/11/35

My Dear Pat,

I enclose copy for *Red Scotland* revised and reduced, and trust this
may be found all in order now. If any further reduction is required all
the poems may be cut out except the long one in the Chapter entitled
'Looking At Glasgow'.

I am sorry to have been so long with this, but you know the reason.
I am now keeping better however as are Valda and the boy.

I trust you are. It seems a long time since I heard from you – the
last letter was a short one saying you'd be sending a longer one next
mail, but that has not materialised. My last note to you was merely
agreeing, gratefully, to accept the £10 the firm were willing to pay me
as an additional advance, but that has not come to hand either.

I know of course how busy you all are, and trust things are going
well.

I'll be sending you the balance of the corrected proofs of *Scottish
Eccentrics* by next mail.

Valda joins me in all affectionate regards.

                        Yours,
                        Chris.

UR   Whalsay.
                                                      6/1/36

My dear Pat,

Hope you safely got my new book of poems[1] (in lieu of a Christmas
card) and that you and your wife and family have had a good time
over the Festive Season and that 1936 will prove a bright and
prosperous year for you all. Valda joins me in every good wish.

I have excised all the poems from *Red Scotland* (to my great regret!)
and cut out 8,000 words of prose. I have gone over it carefully and
make it just under 50,000 words in the shape in which I now return it

[1] *Second Hymn to Lenin and Other Poems* (London 1935).

551

to you. I trust you will find this all in order. I am sorry if I have taken a little time to do this; I am keeping fairly well but have still to go very canny. Besides cutting down to this extent is very difficult.

All the best,

Yours,
Chris.

UR

Dear Mr Patterson,

Your Reference. GR-AJBP. 15/1/36

I have to acknowledge your letter of above date and note that your Directors do not wish to publish *Red Scotland*, but are willing to pay me the balance of advance due in respect thereof, any money I receive from another publisher by way of advance on *Red Scotland* to refund your firm to the amount they have paid me.

I appreciate this offer and have no option but to accept same and will be glad to receive the cheque in question at their earliest convenience. And I hereby undertake to repay them the total sum advanced me when and as I succeed in placing the book with another publisher on terms which allow me a sufficient advance to do so.

I shall be glad to have back at the earliest possible opportunity not only the last (cut down) manuscript but also the duplicate copy of the original typescript in its entirety (i.e. before my first – inadequate – excisions were made on it) which I believe (and earnestly hope, since it alone is of any use to me) is in your possession.

But while, without prejudice, I am thus willing to accept their offer and acquiesce in their rejection of the book, I need not say that – as joint instigator with the late Lewis Grassic Gibbon and yourself of the 'Voice of Scotland' Series – I am extremely disappointed, and anxious that your Directors should consider the inclusion in that series of one or both of two other volumes; viz. *The Tragedy of Robert Burns* and *Scottish Gaelic Literature* which I would guarantee to submit to them within three months from the present date, typescripts not to exceed 50,000 words.

With regard to the first of these, some years ago I created a world-wide sensation by an attack on the Burns Cult.[1] This has since been stupidly misconceived by many people as an attack on Burns himself, which is nonsense as I have been a lifelong student of Burns and am his legitimate successor in Scots Poetry. I want to correct that misunderstanding – and to show that the real tragedy of Burns is the failure of the world-wide Burns Clubs to embrace and exemplify the true Burns spirit and to continue his work.

With regard to the second of these, please see Power's *Literature and Oatmeal* p 29 (beginning 'What is most needed' down to the end of the first paragraph on p. 30).[2] Mr Power is not the first to express the need for this. Mr Angus Robertson[3] and other leaders of the Gaelic Movement have also done so repeatedly during the past ten years. For another purpose I have had occasion to make, for the first time, complete English verse-translations of all the leading Scottish Gaelic poems. Two of these[4] have been published, and widely acknow-

---

[1] MacDiarmid's most devastating dismissal of the Burns Cult is contained in the opening section of *A Drunk Man Looks at the Thistle* (1926). He renewed the attack in a speech of 21 January 1928 when he addressed the Glasgow branch of the Scottish National Movement.

[2] The full quotation reads as follows: 'What is most needed, as a central inspiration of all kinds of progress, is a thoroughly good, thoroughly readable history of Scots Gaelic literature, written by a Scots Gael who should be as nearly as possible an opposite number of Dr Douglas Hyde. Such a man would not go out of his way to pay court to Imperialism or any other ism, to lords or chiefs alive or dead, or to any particular sect or creed; he would not think a man a better writer because he had uttered religious or moral sentiments, or a worse writer because he had written erotic or Rabelaisian passages: his main concern would be with artistic and human values; he would assign authors their places according to purely literary standards, and he would be able to show clearly what Scotland had gained and then lost by departure from the central Gaelic tradition, exactly why and in what respects Scots Gaelic literature had declined after 1800, and how, granting the occurrence of genius, a virile revival might be achieved. His book might not be well received by the average Anglified or Sundayfied Gael, but it would be eagerly welcomed by literary scholars all over the world, and its ultimate reactions in Scotland would be irresistible. It would give substance and foundation and background to the Gaelic mind in Scotland. It would be the right preliminary to the fulfilment of Mr Angus Robertson's plan for a Gaelic University in the Highlands.'

[3] Angus Robertson was involved in the twentieth-century Gaelic literary revival; in *A Companion to Scottish Culture* (London 1981, p. 138), edited by David Daiches, D. S. Thomson refers to 'the upsurge of Gaelic publication at the beginning of the twentieth century, including the relatively ambitious if unsatisfying attempt to write Gaelic novels (by John MacCormick and Angus Robertson).'

[4] 'The Birlinn of Clanranald' (515–32), translated from the Scots Gaelic of Alasdair MacMhaighstir Alasdair, appeared in *The Modern Scot*, January 1935, and was reprinted in a limited edition of one hundred copies by the Abbey Book Shop the same year. 'The Praise of Ben Dorain' (587–600), translated from the Gaelic of

ledged by competent authorities to be the best things of their kind yet executed. Doing this work has necessitated a complete new survey and rereading of Scottish Gaelic literature on my part and I am now thoroughly equipped to write this book, which is a 'felt want' in Scottish Gaelic circles, in literary Scotland generally, and in Scottish communities abroad, especially in the Scottish Gaelic communities in Canada. The Gaelic Movement is developing greatly and such a book is a sine-qua-non of its further advance. There is undoubtedly a great opportunity here and I think I can meet it with a concise, thoroughly competent, and attractively written book.

I would propose to send in these books for the favour of your directors' consideration without previous contract or advance in respect of them. I shall be glad to know at the earliest whether they will be willing to think of these, and, if possible, include them in the 'Voice of Scotland' Series.

To revert to the general position between us in regard to *Red Scotland* I must say that, while not myself much enamoured of it in its cut-down condition I am amazed that the attitude to it your Directors now express was not conveyed to me months ago, if at all. This is the first time that the question of its quality has been raised at all. From previous letters I had gathered that – while it was too long – they thought well of it and were only anxious that the necessary cutting should be carefully carried out to preserve its essential structure. This – in loyalty to the series – I have, while not myself pleased with the results, done my best to do. I am now faced not only with the need to revert to the original un-cut-down type-script but owing to political developments during this long delay to considerable alterations to bring the book up to date in several essential respects. This – *Red Scotland* – is a book which is being eagerly awaited all over Scotland and elsewhere and the imminence of its publication has already had repercussions in Communist Headquarters. Friends of mine whose judgement I trust, who have seen portions of the typescript, are – in contradistinction to your reader[5] – of the opinion that it strikes the nail on the head and is sure

Duncan Bàn MacIntyre, was included in MacDiarmid's anthology *The Golden Treasury of Scottish Poetry* (London 1940).

[5] The reader's report on *Red Scotland* included the following comments: 'Well over fifty per cent of the book consists of quotations, not all of them apt, and none of them, I think, written with the fervour and power which the author himself could have instilled into the argument, had he chosen to state it in his own words. [Also] there are passages here and there which are definitely libellous, and would inevitably lead to prosecution and/or the suppression of the book were they published – notably references to the King and Queen and the Royal Family, the Duke of Kent/Princess Marina wedding, and the Queen and the new giant

to create a furore and to have important consequences. You can appreciate from this the grave difficulties in which this eleventh-hour rejection places me, apart from its unheard-of character in relation to a book by any author of established reputation. This is bound to react very detrimentally on my influence, and the fact that you have advertised the book may very well increase my difficulties in now placing it elsewhere.

I am particularly aggrieved at your reader's reference to libellous matters re the King, etc. as – so long ago as 7th August 1935 – yours, (GR-CAF) of that date – says: 'As to *Red Scotland* we have no objection to the work on account of its revolutionary nature, nor do we think there would be any trouble with the Incitement to Disaffection Act.'

Prior to that time, a publisher friend of mine hearing I was writing such a book was anxious to secure it for his firm and although, since the necessity for very considerable cutting-down had then arisen, I was tempted, loyalty to your firm and to the Voice of Scotland series, made me refuse.

Your reader opines that these allegedly libellous or treacherous elements could be excised. I do not agree. I restricted them to a minimum to start with and now, if I can induce this other firm to publish for me now, I shall, of course, increase them very considerably.

As to the other questions of the amount of quotations in my text, raised by your reader, I do not know whether he is the same reader who adversely criticised *Scottish Eccentrics* but certainly the same point was raised in connection with that book – and I promptly disposed of it, to Mr Warburg's satisfaction. I think it is even easier to do so in this case. My book required that I should show that the line I advocated was in keeping with the pronouncements of the acknowledged leaders of Marxian thought and the practice of Communist Parties in other countries. I had to make the necessary quotations to do so. My own declarations or attractive development of the theme would have been of no consequence whatever unless I could show that it was reconcilable at every point with the doctrines of Marx, Lenin, Stalin and others. I have therefore precisely the same reply to make to this reader as to the reader of *Scottish Eccentrics* and hope your directors may consider it as conclusive in disposing of his contentions as Mr Warburg assured me he did in the other instance.

I recognise, of course, that owing to my illness the book was by no

Cunarder. The latter criticism could be dealt with simply by excision, but the former is a much more serious criticism. Quite frankly, I can see no sale for this book at all.'

means what it might have been, and that the subsequent troubles re cutting-down, etc. were due to my original mistake in sending in a typescript double the required size; and that this has involved time and trouble, not only at my end but at yours; and I must conclude by once again expressing my regret for this and my hope that my subsequent relations with your firm may be of a happier character, alike from my point of view and theirs.

Yours sincerely,
C. M. Grieve.

To Leslie and Rhea Mitchell

James Leslie Mitchell (1901–35) was a prolific writer who produced several fine books in English, including the novels *The Thirteenth Disciple* (1931) and *Spartacus* (1933). His finest achievement, written under the pseudonym Lewis Grassic Gibbon, is the trilogy *A Scots Quair* comprising *Sunset Song* (1932), *Cloud Howe* (1933) and *Grey Granite* (1934). This work uses a Scots prose whose elemental oral rhythms root the main character, Chris Guthrie, in the 'coarse, coarse, land' of the author's native Mearns (Kincardineshire). MacDiarmid was enormously impressed by Mitchell's intellectual energy and the two men collaborated on *Scottish Scene or the Intelligent Man's Guide to Albyn* (1934). After Mitchell's early death Mac-Diarmid corresponded with his widow, Rhea (Ray), with a view to increasing the accessibility of the work of a man he regarded as a 'great passionate soul [whose] rich talents happily combined a soaring lyricism with a passionate love of Nature as embodied in his native landscapes, a robust vernacular idiom and humour, profound and clear-etched characterisation, scrupulous fidelity to life, monumental qualities of epic appropriate to his wide-ranging theme, and a forward-lookingness natural to his wholesome love of life' (Company. p. 222).

NLS

Whalsay,
Shetland Islands.
27/1/35

My dear Leslie,

I feel very guilty – a feeling I like to have in other connections but not in matters of personal friendship! But, as I was saying, I feel very guilty at leaving your *Earth Conquerors*[1] so long unacknowledged (just

---

[1] *Nine Against the Unknown* (1934) by James Leslie Mitchell and Lewis Grassic Gibbon; issued as *Earth Conquerors: The Lives and Achievements of the Great Explorers* (1934) in New York.

557

as Valda – with, however, a much less sensitive conscience – feels guilty for not yet writing to Rhea; an epistolary feat she has been vowing to accomplish for months now).

I was delighted to have it. The publishers have made a good job of it; I liked the get-up greatly, and the illustrations came out splendidly. I had read fair swatches of the letterpress in proof at Welwyn, but I was glad to have the whole thing on my knees and to go right through out – vivid and most interesting studies. Many thanks. I hope it has gone well in America – and its counterpart here. I see few literary or other papers and have consequently missed any reviews that may have appeared (not that I overestimate the value of reviews or do not know that, save in a most exceptional case, they have practically no bearing on the all-important matter of sales). I was glad however to come across excellent notices of *Grey Granite* in several quarters and trust all the others were up to these samples.

What are you doing now? The Burns book, I expect – and – a new novel?

I have been in the horrible position of taking on too much – contracting to have far too much done by a given date. Apart from the various lets and hindrances connected with getting re-installed here and having various essential repairs carried out on the house, such a plight instead of spurring me to greater efforts semi-paralyses me and I keep on saying 'I'll never get it done' and not even trying to until the fateful date draws so near that I have to make a really heroic effort. However this – and not any undue Christmas and New Year dissipation – accounts for my delay in writing you; and I have really been working hard, though my total of words per day falls far short of the requirements if my various MSS are to be delivered up to contracted dates.

I'm in good form physically tho' conditions here are Arctic and my peat-stack is like a mass of cast-iron, while to draw the daily supplies of water means breaking ice every time. Valda isn't so well; she has a racking cough that is making us very anxious since (as I think we told you) the specialist at the Clinic in London warned us that any settled cold would be dangerous and that in such an event she would have to leave the Shetlands pronto. and get to Cornwall or somewhere.

I trust Rhea and Rhea Sylvia and Daryll and yourself are all O.K. Please remember me to John Paton.[2] And write sometime and let me know what's doing. There's no need to add – if anything – in your

[2] In a letter of 12 June 1983 to the present editor Rhea Martin, Mitchell's daughter, writes; 'John and Florence Paton were friends of my father who lived in Welwyn Garden City ... both husband and wife were Labour MPs in the 1945–50 Parliament.'

case; you're sure to have enough on your plate to make the diet of work I'm jibbing at so violently seem a mere trifle.

All the best to all of you.

> Yours,
> C. M. G.

NLS

Whalsay,
Shetland Islands.
Saturday (for Monday's mail)
[10 February 1935]

Dear Rhea:-

As you will know the practically simultaneous wires I got yesterday from you and from Helen Cruickshank in Edinburgh announcing Leslie's death came as a great shock to Valda and I.[1] We are extremely sorry and have been able to think of little else since. I am very glad that after delaying too long I had written to thank him for the copy of *Earth Conquerors* and so got in reply his welcome and cheery letter just the other day. Nothing could have been further from my mind than that it was to prove the last I should have from him. It told me, of course, that he had been ill with acute gastritis but seemed to indicate that he was well on the mend. I expect he had a relapse and peritonitis developed very suddenly. Your wire says there was an operation; we hope from this that he may have been spared a great deal of agony at the end, though if he died under the anaesthetic, without recovering consciousness, the shock must have been all the more terrible for you. Our heart-felt sympathy is with you and we trust that you are well yourself and so the better able to bear up under your tragic bereavement. Will you please write us later on and tell us what plans you have decided on? We hope you will keep in touch with us. It is a great consolation to us that we had that delightful week-end with you last summer.

Leslie's untimely death is a serious blow to Scottish literature. I think his best work was all to come – he was just getting into his stride. All the same he had achieved a very remarkable tale of work

---

[1] Mitchell died on 7 February 1935.

in various directions for his age and won a definite place in the history of Scottish literature. His *Scots Quair* has a permanent value which will preserve his memory. I see few papers away up here and these always very belatedly, but I hope that here and there notices have appeared doing justice to his great gifts and very substantial achievement.

I do not know what dispositions he may have made or what order he may have left his work in – I mean, how far he had succeeded in writing books for which he had contracted. He had many friends and if you need assistance of any kind in dealing with any MSS he may have left or in protecting your interests in his published books I am sure you will have no difficulty in securing it. I only mention the matter in order to say that if I can assist or advise you in any way I shall be only too happy to do so.

At a time like this it is very difficult to say anything at all of a comforting or helpful nature. We shall be very anxious to hear later on how you are fixed. Our warmest sympathies are with you and the children, and we sincerely trust that you may be enabled to bear up under this fearful blow and that you may not be involved in any hardship in material matters. Leslie hadn't long to secure the position he had so quickly made for himself and make provision for you against such an unlooked-for eventuality, so if you should be in difficult circumstances do please let us know and give us and other friends an opportunity to rally round and do what we can.

All love to Rhea Sylvia, Daryll, and yourself.

From,
Valda and Chris.

NLS

Whalsay,
Shetland Islands.
12/4/35

My dear Rhea,

Valda (who will be writing you herself) and I were very glad to get your letter on Wednesday. We were worrying about you and wearying to hear what was happening. Do not take this as any reproach for not writing us sooner. We did not expect that knowing the shattering grief and subsequent burdens you have had. I know of the Scottish PEN's effort to help and I knew about the Royal Literary Society hope. I am more than relieved to hear of the latter's grant: I know of course that alas! it won't go far – but it is a great help at the moment – and the Scottish PEN will do their best too. I haven't heard from Helen for a week or two but she had told me you thought of getting back into the Civil Service – it is terrible to think that even if you do the pay is so inadequate. It is impossible in circumstances like yours to say or do anything that does not seem horribly helpless and irrelevant. I agree with all you say about the wanton cruelty and utter senselessness of such a bereavement – and personally I can accept that; it squares with my irrationalist philosophy of life – but what I do find absolutely appalling and unendureable is not that ultimate meaninglessness from any human standpoint, but the fact that within our human scheme of things it should be added to by readily preventible ills which are in many ways still more immediately torturing and terrible. However brutally and unintelligibly the blind forces of nature cut across all that seems decent and reasonable, there is no earthly reason why to such unspeakable outrages on human sensibility should be added horrible economic jeopardies and humiliation, and obligations of drudgery and anxiety superimposed on an irreparable loss. The latter – the thrust-back of the hapless victims into toil and need, and the intolerable savaging and neutralising of the best human hopes and efforts – is perfectly avoidable. In other words, I can face up to the inhuman cosmic course of things and have no religious belief of any sort or any consolation derived from a philosophy that relies on ultimate good in any human sense of the term; but every fibre of my being protests to the uttermost against the needless degradations and difficulties that arise from a remediable economic system. I am terribly touched by all you say of the children and the sudden reversal and circumscription of their happy and promising lot. It is sheerly damnable and I have, I am afraid, no point of contact with those who find any means of comfort in religious or other fugues from reality; and yet I know how supremely difficult it is while refusing to relapse on such false consolations to tackle the day-to-day burden bravely. But it is useless, at least in a letter, to try to pass on such an attitude. I am glad, anyhow, that Muir, Linklater, Ivor Brown and others have rallied to your support and I feel sure that they, and others of the Scottish PEN and outside it, will continue to stand by you and the children in any and every way they possibly can. To turn then to the few practical points that arise out of your letter:-

1/ Mirsky[1] was greatly taken with *Spartacus* and thought something might be done about a film. I haven't heard from him again, *but will write him at once.*

2/ I'll sound John Grierson, the film producer, about *Sunset Song*. I do not think he could do anything himself – he runs the GPO Film Unit but that's mainly a question of publicity and propaganda films for Government departments – but he's a first-class man and in touch with the whole film world and we'll see what he suggests.

3/ I'll write you again on receipt of replies from Mirsky and Grierson.

4/ Surely Hale is very pessimistic – I cannot believe that the Scottish *Quair* will not remain for years in some demand. It may be small – I do not know enough about that side of the book business – but a complete black-out, such as Hale suggests will happen, seems to me impossible.

I am afraid I am not very helpful but if any other point arises in which I can be of any conceivable service to you please do not hesitate to let me know and I will do my best immediately.

I've been off colour and all my work is sadly in arrears: but I'm picking up again. We've had a dreadful winter here – bitterly cold, gale winds, and lashing rain every day except seven in the six months since we got back. Neither Valda nor Michael are too fit. We'll all be very glad when a spell of sunshine and dry weather comes round. I hope you and Rhea Sylvia and Daryll, and Catherine,[2] are at least physically fit and keeping clear of illness.

My dear Rhea this is a very unsatisfactory letter. I will write you again soon and give you any general news that is going, and you'll hear from Valda herself next week. I do not know what our plans this summer may be – I won't be in London unless something urgent calls me there but Valda most likely will – she'll probably be in Cornwall or at least depositing Michael there if she and I are going elsewhere – but if either of us are within hail at all you may be sure we will look you up.

Kisses to the children from all of us and every warm good wish to yourself.

Yours,
Chris.

P.S. I have said nothing of Leslie, or about the details you give of the

[1] Ex-Prince D. S. Mirsky, to whom MacDiarmid's 'First Hymn to Lenin' (297–9) is dedicated. Mirsky wrote various books on Russian literature including *A History of Russian Literature, from the Earliest Times to the Death of Dostoevsky* (1927).

[2] Catherine, Rhea's step-sister.

illness which a better doctor or prompter treatment might have kept from being fatal. I agree with all you say yourself and find myself instinctively trying not to think about it all – it has hit me very badly too. I cannot trust myself to say more.

NLS

Whalsay,
Shetland Islands.
22/10/35

My dear Ray,

Valda and I were very glad to get your letter and to know that you have got a fairly decent sort of post. Also that all of you are fine and fit. During my first week or so in hospital when I was in a very dazed and hallucinated condition and not altogether responsible, I conceived the idea that I had had a long and urgent letter from you. I could not remember what was in it. Which worried me greatly. As soon as I was allowed out of bed I hunted through all my stuff for it, but to my consternation could not find it. The matter continued to worry me all the time I was in hospital and it was one of the first things I asked Valda about after I got home.

I am particularly sorry that Lindsay has failed to find a publisher for the symposium.[1] That is another matter I have not ceased to worry about – the fact that I hadn't managed to get off my promised essay to him prior to my complete collapse. I hope he is still trying and may yet succeed. I cannot understand the complete cessation of interest in Leslie's books to which you refer – interest will certainly revive – but it is a great pity that that inevitable revival has had to be preceded by such a complete drop.

But of all the devilish incalculable careers the author's is the worst.

I sweated blood during the earlier stages of my developing illness to get various books completed for publication this autumn; but, having got them all done and sent in, I emerge from hospital to find two of them delayed till January, another in an altogether uncertain position, and only one actually out up to now.

---

[1] In a letter of 17 June 1983 to the present editor Rhea Martin writes: 'The symposium was, I think, intended as an appreciation of my father after his death ... I can't be very helpful about the man (Lindsay).'

I hope you are having better weather at least than we are. I had the worst sea-tossing I have ever experienced on the voyage home – but the weather since has made our islands indistinguishable from the floor of the ocean. And James Michael, considerably grown since you saw him, is running wild in this chaos and looks exactly like some wild gnome indigenous to the wasty deep.

Apart from colds, however, he is hardy enough. Valda is keeping remarkably fit considering the anxiety she has had and the fact that, in my deplorable state, she has to do all the outside chores – fetch water, peat, etc. I am doing nicely since my return and nibbling hungrily but as yet somewhat ineffectively at my work.

Love and best wishes from us all to you all. Do write again ere long. You are often in our thoughts and we are always glad to hear from you.

Yours,
Chris and Valda.

NLS

Whalsay,
Via Lerwick,
Shetland Islands.
23.5.38

Dear Ray,

I am quite ashamed to have been such an unholy time in writing about. No, I hadn't – and haven't – forgotten about you by any means; but for the past six months or so I've been having a deuce of a time – I took on far too much, for one thing – too many books, I mean – and they proved unexpectedly difficult to do. In fact they aren't done yet, though I am seeing the end of the tunnel at last, thanks to the fact that I have now a resident secretary-typist.[1] So in the autumn I should have quite a spate of books coming out, or, if, as is probable, I have even now delayed too long for autumn publication, by the spring at latest. I'll be glad to finish them all and get on to something else; but confusion and delay has been partly at least my own blame – due to the fact that poetry comes first with me and where I ought to have been concentrating on these commissioned

---
[1] Henry Grant Taylor, who typed *Mature Art*.

books I have instead completed an enormous poem[2] of upwards of 10,000 lines (in words, double the length of an average novel). Besides I've been extremely taken up with political matters, and in that connection am just on the point of launching a new quarterly magazine of Scottish arts and affairs – the first issue of which will appear next month.[3]

I do hope you have not been having things too difficult and that you, and Cathie, and Rhea Sylvia and Daryll are all fine and fit. We are all in good form here. Valda also feels very compunctious about not writing you, but sends you her love and says she really will write you soon, it having been with her a clear case of the spirit having been willing but the flesh weak.

The delay in getting these tomes off my chest has also meant a devilish shortage of bullion, and, as a consequence, I've never got down to London again. Afraid I won't this year yet, alas, but Valda may late summer or autumn, and if so, will of course look forward to seeing you.

I've a fine half-tone block of myself in full Highland Rig. I'll try to get some prints made off it soon and send you one.

Do forgive me and write soon and give us your news. I'll not be long in writing you again.

Love to you all from all here.

Yours,
Chris.

---

[2] *Mature Art.*
[3] The first number of *The Voice of Scotland* is dated June–August 1938.

To Fiona Mac Colla

Fiona Mac Colla was the pseudonym adopted by Thomas Douglas MacDonald (1906–75), the Scottish novelist. He was born and brought up in Montrose as a Plymouth Brother and grew to detest the religion of Knox and to believe that the glory of Scotland lay in the Gaelic past which, he asserted, had been obliterated by genocidal atrocities inflicted by the English after Culloden. In the late 1920s he was living a few doors from MacDiarmid in Links Avenue, Montrose. As he puts it in his autobiography *Too Long In This Condition* (Thurso 1975, p. 80):

> To be precise we were in No 12 Links Avenue, Aunt Annie in 14, and C. M. Grieve in 16. I used to step across the fence, walk across Aunt Annie's lawn, and step across another fence into C. M G.'s. When I made the return journey there was seldom anyone around to observe what course I took, MacDiarmid and I having been setting the world to rights till morning.

MacDiarmid was enormously impressed by Mac Colla's first novel *The Albannach* (London 1932) and believed that the Scottish Highlands had at last found an eloquent voice and appropriately angry fictional form.

NLS

Whalsay,
Friday.
[1935]

My dear Tom,

Yes. There has been some discussion back and forward between Routledge's and me re your book on the Gaelic position.[1] Incident-

---

[1] MacDiarmid wanted Mac Colla to write a book on Gaelic for the Voice of Scotland series; nothing came of the notion.

ally Compton Mackenzie was trying to secure this commission for J. Lorne Campbell but I strongly opposed that, while admitting Campbell's qualifications, on the ground that his book while no doubt academically all right would have a narrower appeal than yours, be less well written, and fail to set the subject effectively against the whole background, cultural and political. I suggested an advance of £50. Paterson[2] wrote that my arguments had convinced them you were the man to do the book but said that he did not see how they could give an advance of £50 – the practice in connection with academic books of which they publish a lot is to base any advance on the number of advance subscriptions, the latter being obtained via prospectus or via academic channels or guaranteed by various University and other endowment funds. I replied that I quite understood this but that the whole point was that your book would not be restricted to an academic appeal but would be general interest and that it ought therefore not to be treated on the former basis. Nothing more has been said about it in subsequent letters to me. So my advice to you is to write acknowledging the receipt of the form of contract but asking that it be amended to provide a certain payment in advance of royalties instead of the provision added to Clause 6 for payment of royalties earned after one month. Say you had thought that for a book of this nature and size an advance on signature of contract of £50 would be a reasonable sum but that you do not know much about this side of the business and perhaps they would suggest a figure. Add, however, that your circumstances are such as to make it difficult for you to apply yourself to the task of writing this book unless a reasonable advance is forthcoming. – You'll gather the sort of line I think you should take. I have no doubt that you'll get the advance all right and hope it'll be adequate to enable you to go ahead. If not we'll have to scrounge round and see if there aren't some other pickings going.

I am keeping much better but have still an unconquerable aversion to applying myself to the tasks most urgently demanding my attention. All is not lost, however, for in lieu of said tasks I have contrived during the past week or ten days to write a book of thirty short stories and I am now engaged in endeavouring to secure a publisher for that, as still another autumn production of mine. They are of course Scottish short stories – and of a different order to anything of that sort we have yet produced – nothing Kailyairdic about them, very varied, simply and straightforwardly written, anecdotal like Maupassant's in kind and without any involved psychologising. They make in fact a very lively collection; I've

[2] A. J. B. Paterson, Routledge's sales manager.

enjoyed writing them and be confident I've communicated that pleasure.

I'm going down to lecture in Manchester University on 10th May and will, going or coming, have a few days in Glasgow with F. G. Scott, and a day or thereby in Edinburgh. I'll be glad of the break. I'm hoping to have my Wolf of Badenoch book[3] off to the publishers before I go South; I finished my big book on *Scottish Eccentrics* a week or so ago; and I'm getting ahead not so badly at last with my Lenin book.[4] Another week's work if all goes well should put me well abreast of my commitments, and leave me free to complete my *Golden Treasury*[5] in the latter half of May and early June. – Then I'll have to snoop round for other jobs to do. What a life!

I agree entirely with your comments on the political situation. It wouldn't be so bad if there were even media enough in which to write in the absence of scope for anything else. As it is I'm without any journalistic outlet at all now. I hear this week that strenuous efforts are being made to restart *The Free Man*[6] – by forming a limited liability company – but tho' I'd be glad enough to have it going again, as a place in which now and again I could say things I felt needed saying, even that doesn't enthuse me and any hopes I have of it are more than offset by a sense of the poor fish most of the other contributors will inevitably be. I wish something would happen to electrify us; the terrible lassitude you describe hasn't affected me much for many years but I have had an unwelcome spell of it too now and am eager to be shaken right out of the hangover of such a feeling.

I'll be hearing how this contract business pans out, and trust it comes off satisfactorily.

Valda joins me in all good wishes.

Yours,
Chris.

P.S. Probably better write to Patterson, I think. He knows I've stressed need of advance – and you're writing to him will give him *locus standi* in further discussion from that angle.

[3] MacDiarmid's book on *The Wolfe of Badenoch* was rejected by Routledge and though subsequently accepted by another firm, Rich and Cowan, the book never appeared. MacDiarmid quotes from the *Wolfe of Badenoch* manuscript in *Lucky Poet* (pp. 210-17, 365-6).

[4] *Red Scotland*, see pp. 536-5.

[5] MacDiarmid's anthology *The Golden Treasury of Scottish Poetry* (London 1940).

[6] The Social Credit weekly *The Free Man* was published in Edinburgh from 1932 to 1934, continued as *New Scotland* (Glasgow, weekly) from 1935 to 1936, then again as *The Free Man* (Glasgow, weekly) until 1947. .

Whalsay,
Shetland Islands.
11/3/35

My dear Tom,

I wrote my last note to you in a hurry – Pat[1] having besought me for speedy suggestions. But he has had since to delay matters in one way and another, one of his partners being in America and the other having been injured in a motor collision in which his eighteen-year-old daughter was killed. Pat has consequently not been in a position to clinch things; he could not commit himself without the authority of one or other of the heads of the firm. On receiving your letter I was writing to him anyhow and added to that letter my sincere hope that he would follow up his suggestion that you should do a separate – i.e. not for the series I wrote you about – volume on the Gaelic question, stressing the increased interest now attaching to this, the reorientation of opinion going on, and your exceptional ability to deal with the matter comprehensively and constructively. I urged him to write you again and to fix up a contract as quickly as possible. If before receiving this letter of mine you have not already heard from Pat again I would suggest that you wait until you do. When a contract comes to be arranged, you will either be asked what terms you wish or it will be necessary for you to ask for an advance. The practice of the firm is to include in the contract the payment of an agreed-upon advance – half of which is payable on signature of contract, the other half on delivery of completed MSS. The firm is wealthy and you should ask for an adequate advance. A good deal depends on what size of book is projected. For a small book to be published in a series for selling at, say 5/- a big advance is out of the question. For my own in this series I got £20 on signature of contract and will get another £20 on delivery of MSS. But if you arrange to do a separate, larger book sellable at 7/6 or 10/6 you could ask safely for more. I would not if I were you raise any question about whether they will be willing to publish what you write. That is their look out. Your MSS would be submitted to a reader for his opinion. In this case – as in regard to all the firm's Scottish books – I will be the reader in question. You will know that I will not raise any difficulties as to the nature and direction of the views you express; any quibbles I may conceivably make will only be on any points which may possibly affect the firm's interests in relation to the Libel Law or the Disaffection Act. Any such points

[1] A. J. B. Paterson, Routledge's sales manager.

would be matter for amicable adjustment. But you need have no fear of any difficulties arising on matters of principle.

If, on the other hand, you are asked to outline the book you propose to write – indicate the subject matter and line of treatment – I would suggest that you do this in very broad terms, stressing the increasing interest in these questions in Scotland and elsewhere and the number of organisations (An Comunn, the Gaelic Texts Society, etc.) concerned with them. Do not condescend to much detail: but simply describe the book you contemplate in very general terms to which none can deny that what you actually do write does in fact conform. If they form false ideas as to what sort of book it will be that is their look-out. In my advisory capacity I have strongly urged the timeliness of such a book, the extent to which the issues involved are in the melting pot, the growing attention aspects of the matter are receiving in all sorts of quarters, the certainty of a good public for a thorough and controversial handling of the subject etc. I'll be hearing from Pat, of course, how things go: but I greatly hope that you may come to satisfactory terms and have the matter speedily settled.

I am exceedingly distressed that you should be having such a horribly trying and difficult time and that your new novel[2] is still so far from completion. I quite understand of course the impossibility of doing good work under such circumstances and can only hope that some fortunate 'break' may soon open up matters and enable you to go ahead with some confidence and good heart. The desperate straits in which you find yourself are, alas, common to a great measure amongst the bulk of my literary friends today: and I myself am just able to carry on very quietly. I have a good few contracts and so enough money in the offing to enable me to maintain this mode of life for a year or more ahead, but at the moment I am worried because my work is in arrears (apart from the fact that I would not be writing the things I have in hand if I could help it – but devoting myself to other subjects and other literary forms). This lag in my working time-table is due to the fact that I took on too much, left myself too little time relying upon an intense burst of activity, and then – about a fortnight ago – suddenly collapsed as the consequence of a chill. I have been suffering since from almost complete nervous and mental prostration. If I had been able to go full steam ahead these last two weeks I would have been well abreast of my programme: but I have been able to do scarcely anything. I am a bit better now; but still unfit for the sheer grind the situation calls for. I have, inter alia, a big book on *Scottish Eccentrics* for Routledge's delivery of which is due now; my Lenin and Scotland book for the

---

[2] Mac Colla's second novel, *And The Cock Crew*, was not published until 1945 (by William Maclellan); it was reprinted in 1977.

series; a biographical study of *The Wolf of Badenoch* for Messrs Rich and Cowan – which should have been delivered last week and won't be for at least a fortnight yet; and a Golden Treasury of Scottish Poetry for Macmillan's.

It was for this last I made the Birlinn translation,[3] which I am glad you like. It seems to have proved a very lucky stroke: I have had a surprising number of congratulations on it. My idea is that a Scottish Anthology which does not include all the best Scottish Gaelic poems – or good verse-translations of them – is absurd. And so I have set myself to provide such translations for this volume. That will sharply differentiate it from all previous Scottish Anthologies, and will, I feel sure, exert no little influence in various directions – including the one you indicate; of serving as a corrective to the stupidities of the Official Nationalist people. I need not tell you how extreme the difficulties are of making even passable translations; nor will you think I am complacently disposed to underestimate them or make any false over-claims for the translations I furnish. I have done Duncan Ban's Moladh Beinn Dorain and am busy still with poems by Iain Lom, William Ross, William Livingston, Donald Sinclair, and others. I am determined not to let the Anthology go to press until I have translations of which I need not be ashamed of 20 to 30 of the best of our Gaelic poems. I would like to have gone further and given a fair proportionate representation of all the Gaelic poets equal in merit to the poets in English or Scots I include; but that is a task beyond me. I can only in this Anthology by giving a score or so of such translations initiate this process of insisting on giving Scottish poetry in Gaelic its rightful place alongside Scottish poetry written in other tongues. Alas! the Birlinn, thanks to its objective character, was somewhat easier to get a decent English version of than most of the others.

I am rambling on; but must close. I too should have written you long ago but am, as you say, a wretched correspondent wherever letter-writing is avoidable at all. But I am delighted to hear from you again, do hope that circumstances will soon improve, will eagerly await further news re this projected volume either from Pat or yourself, and will be glad to have further word from you whenever you care and can.

Every good wish.

Yours,
Chris.

[3] MacDiarmid's translation of 'The Birlinn of Clanranald', from the Scots Gaelic of Alasdair MacMhaighstir Alasdair, was first published in *The Modern Scot*, Vol V, No 4, January 1935, reissued as a limited edition of 100 copies (St Andrews 1935) and included in *The Golden Treasury of Scottish Poetry* (London 1940).

To W. R. Aitken

W. R. Aitken, co-editor with Michael Grieve of MacDiarmid's *Complete Poems 1920–1976* (London 1978), is a leading Scottish bibliographer. His Check List of MacDiarmid's work appeared in *MacDiarmid: A Festschrift* (Edinburgh 1962), edited by Kulgin Duval and Sydney Goodsir Smith, and he updated this material in his bibliographical guide to *Scottish Literature in English and Scots* (1982). He was educated at Edinburgh University and later taught bibliographical studies at the University of Strathclyde. He acted as manager of MacDiarmid's periodical *The Voice of Scotland* (Dunfermline 1938–9).

Whalsay,
31st July '37

Dear Bill,

Very many thanks for all the books, your several letters, and the photos. Orr[1] says to thank you for those you sent him too – he'll write you in a day or two.

Davie's[2] letter is very distressing. He seems to have broken down – or been broken down – completely. I am very fond of him and hoped great things of him, and so hesitate yet to take an objective view of the whole matter. He may come through all right; but he is just as liable, I am afraid, to go the other way now as the way I had hoped and confidently anticipated. I am still very much worried about his going to Germany in particular.

So I do not propose to make any complete reply just now to

---

[1] Dr David Orr of Whalsay; he was instrumental in persuading the poet to settle on the island.
[2] George Davie, author of *The Democratic Intellect* (1961), was a fellow-student of Aitken's at Edinburgh University.

Davie's letter. But there are two outstanding points. He speaks of 'rational justification, co-ordination', etc. (as wanting behind my artistic and political standards). Certainly, I am an Anarchist. Such things are ruled out by definition from my standpoint; I do not need them – indeed I have been at great pains to avoid them. And then: 'the one thing to be said is something you do not need to be told – method in reading and circumscription of aims until you find one central aim are alone fruitful to us younger Scots.' Nonsense. Method implies (forestalls) the aim; circumscription of aims has the inevitable result of precluding certain things from your purview and limiting the choice out of which a central aim will emerge – and the very idea of a central aim, of course, begs the issue.

George hopes to have freedom of thinking later on, and to do fundamental brain work then. What – after the pass has been sold? The whole thing is tragic. I have been through the mill and I know. He is surrendering the key position (the only thing that has enabled me to resist all the pressures, influences, etc.) at the very outset.

I'll be very interested to hear shortly what he has to say about the CP manoeuvre.

Excuse a short letter this time. I have had a sort of flop since you left; seemed drained of about 99 per cent of my necessary (and much needed) energy. Still, I'm making progress – but have still a devil of a lot of work to do.

Some of these books are extremely helpful. I'm returning the Maitland pamphlet to Aberdeen University Library today; I hope I've a big week's productivity next week, and then I'll return all the others.

Glad you enjoyed your unconventional holiday.[1] You didn't enjoy it more than we enjoyed having you here. We'll always be delighted to see you again any time it's possible. I'll write you more fully shortly on divers matters.

Valda and Mike join me in every kind regard.

Yours,
C. M. G.

P.S. Valda'll be writing you and sending you some of the snaps from her film shortly.

[1] A reference to Aitken's first visit to Whalsay.

Dear Bill,

If you do see Davie, please thank him on my behalf for the comments on the CP question in his letter to you of which you sent me a copy, and also for his amplifications thereof in a subsequent letter he has sent direct to me. I will not write him again myself until he invites me to do so and signifies that the coast is clear for such a resumption of direct intercourse between us. But please assure him of my deep concern for his successful emergence from this very trying phase, and of the anxiety with which I will await news of his progress in Germany. His reservations in these two above-mentioned letters have been very helpful to me; I have joined issue with the CP in a series of extensive letters on the whole subject. If the CP cannot be brought round to the clear Scottish Workers' Republican line, I will at least have copies of these letters of mine, and their replies, as evidence in the case; and will, if need be, publish these with suitable comments and send copies to the Comintern in Moscow, etc.

If you see Davie you may also have an opportunity to show him the enclosed verses.[1]

I am snowed under with all sorts of work. So please excuse this brief note.

Oh, that reminds me. I wonder if amongst the Chapbooks you have, you have one in which I have a short poem, called 'Science and Poetry' (or 'Poetry and Science') dedicated to Sir Ronald Ross.[2] If so, I'd be greatly obliged if you'd copy it out and send on to me.

Love from us all. We'd a distressing spell of very cold weather for a

[1] Professor Norman Kemp Smith, author of *The Philosophy of David Hume* (1941), was Professor of Philosophy at Edinburgh University. In a letter, of 7 October 1983 to the present editor, George Davie explained the background to the poem as follows: 'In a personal way so far as it affected me the question at issue was of very little importance. Briefly, Kemp Smith had been reported to me as saying that he would not give backing to my career as a student unless I ceased my association (writing etc) with Chris, who was in Shetland at that time. I told Chris about this before I spoke to Kemp Smith who emphatically and unembarrassedly denied that what he had said bore any such construction and there for me that matter ended. I do not know if Chris had any communication with Kemp Smith after that but he evidently read the introduction to Kemp Smith's edition of David Hume's *Dialogues Concerning Natural Religion* (1935) and this was the beginning of his interest in an attempt to identify with Hume . . . Previously he had spoken of Hume as a pygmy but the connection with Kemp Smith, for whom he had developed a high regard, altered his perception.'

[2] 'Science and Poetry' (1220). A longer poem, 'Poetry and Science' (630–1) begins with a quotation from Sir Ronald Ross.

while after you left. But these past few days have been very hot, and we've been whelmed in dense sea fogs.

Love from all here.

P.S. Can the Dunfermline Press people supply 500 letter-headings as per enclosed sample, and 500 unheaded second sheets of same paper, and send, together with account?

To Professor Norman Kemp Smith

You have separated me and my friend
With treachery bent to a wretched end,
And separated yourself in doing so
(Though none but he and I – and perhaps you – may know)
   From all that is worth while.

You have separated me and my friend
But since he and I are both fully aware
And equally contemptuous of your means and your end
Only for a little can you prevail 'twixt us there
   Ere we reconcile.

Ere we reconcile in a final reckoning
And repudiation of all you are and stand for and serve
When he with his science and I with my song
Sweep you and your world off the single nerve
   Of our one purpose, joined in lightning's style.

You have separated me and my friend,
The lightning is hidden awhile in the cloud.
Gape at the sky and say there's no fear.
Exchange assurances with the myopic crowd.
   Lightning bides its time and is full of guile.

And no trace of Kemp Smith
Will be left to foul the air with
When at last it launches its humbug-shrivelling smile.

Dear Bill,

My ill-luck continues. My new secretary[1] was just getting on nicely with the typing and I was having visions ere long of getting some of the books-in-hand completed and away, when he went ill with swollen neck-glands. This put him out of action for a week; then, just when he'd fairly recovered and was buckling to again, news came of his mother's death. So he had to go South on Monday and I'll be minus his services for at least a week and probably nearer two. Damn!

I had a long and most important letter from Davie – re Prof. Brie's book on Scottish Literature[2] and Muir's *Scotsman* review thereof. And have written him in reply.

As to the Edinburgh Lit. Socy's. idea,[3] I think it is first-rate and am anxious to do all I possibly can to help it. I'm afraid my Montrose experience with the *Chapbook*, etc. does not afford any good guide to the probable demand for such a series – I am certain the interested public is now many times larger than it was then.

I suggest that letters be sent to the editors of as many Scottish papers as possible, saying what is being done, and naming the first issues decided upon for the series, and inviting subscriptions. This will be at least a free advt. in many quarters and will bring in, I feel sure, a lot of enquiries. In particular, in addition to all the dailies and evenings and the leading local papers, periodicals like *The Scots Independent, Scotland, The Scottish Educational Journal* should not be overlooked. At the same time – or as soon as the response evoked by these letters is seen – leaflets should be sent out to all possible quarters, e.g. branches of the National Party of Scotland, all the members of the Scottish PEN, all the members of the Saltire Society – and bookshops like Grant's, Thin's, etc. should be canvassed for an initial order, and also given a supply of the leaflets to hand to customers, put in windows, on counters, etc.

Perhaps before either of these are done, estimates should be taken to find the cost of putting out booklets similar in size, get-up, quality of paper, etc. to the Augustan Series. These should be taken

---

[1] Henry Grant Taylor.

[2] Friedrich Brie, *Die Nationale Literatur Schottlands Von Den Anfängen Bis Zur Renaissance* (1937).

[3] The idea was to issue a series of studies of Scottish literature.

simultaneously from several different printers and the replies compared – also in asking for quotations, they should ask for cost per thousand – up to say 5,000. They can then work it out but I fancy the price should be about 6d (to sell at – less of course trade commissions for supplies to booksellers, etc.). As soon as they do this if in the absence of any definite assurance as to an adequate sale, they feel that they might be committing themselves to too big a thing, I suggest a guarantee fund. I would myself guarantee £5 – I can get Orr to do likewise – and I am prepared to write personally to a lot of others I am certain will also do so. There would, I know, be no difficulty in securing guarantors for £200; and that would certainly suffice to enable the enterprise to be launched with every security against loss to the Scottish Literature Society.

If there are any points I have not covered in these remarks, if either yourself or Ian Ross[1] – to whom please my best regards – writes me thereanent I'll reply immediately. I am most anxious to see this admirable scheme launched as speedily as possible and will do all I possibly can to help it in any way.

Many thanks for the *Daily Worker* cutting – it contains a few stupid misprints but is not so badly mutilated as I had feared – Valda had to 'phone it through to Lerwick to be telegraphed thence to London, so the possibility of error was large, especially as my script was in telegraphese and required to be expanded into journalistic English by the receiving office.

Orr was saying last night that he ought to have written you long ago, but will now. He's a bad correspondent.

I'll not trust myself to comment in any way on the question of your lady or ladies – I don't know enough of the circumstances anyhow – all I can say is that I am anxious for your happiness, pleased to hear of anything calculated to promote it and sorry to hear of anything that has any other effect.

As to your kind comments on last July and the future, I need hardly tell you we'll be more than delighted to see you again any time you can possibly manage.

And now for another matter – could you please ask Mackie's[2] – and at the same time any other printer in your area capable of doing such a job – to give an estimate for printing a quarterly devoted to Scottish arts and affairs – about the size (32 pp – this size of page – and cover, wired) and similar quality paper to enclosed copy of *Wales* (which please return later to me). Ask them to quote for 1,000 copies, 2,000 copies, and 3,000 copies, to begin with – and on the under-

[1] Ian Ross is Father (Ian) Anthony Ross, see p. 871.
[2] J. B. Mackie, the Dunfermline printer of *The Voice of Scotland*. Aitken became manager of MacDiarmid's periodical.

standing that if an order is placed (necessary bank references given, if desired) it will run for at least 4 issues (i.e. a year). I am anxious to have estimates as soon as possible. You need not however at the moment mention on whose behalf you are inquiring.

I will write fully about the intentions of this later. The only other point I can think of the printers might need to know to enable them to quote is that – in contradistinction to what obtains in the enclosed copy of *Wales* – about 75 per cent of each issue will be in prose, and only 25 per cent at most in verse.

And Orr and I venture to hope if we find that we can launch this that you may (tho' I know you are busy yourself) be able to help us in the way of accepting bulk delivery (to save cost of sending the copies up here) and sending out the issues to subscribers, etc. Please let me know if you can see your way to this – and to reading the proofs at times and generally keeping an eye on the matter? Whoever prints it may let you use a room in their place, from which you could send out the copies, store the extra supplies etc.

We are all O.K., except Mike who has been at home a couple of weeks with a particularly nasty bronchial cold.

And we all join in kindest regards.

Yours,
Chris.

Whalsay,
Via Lerwick,
Shetland Islands.
23-3-38

My dear Bill,

Very many thanks for your letter with Mackie's and Lindsay's quotations for the proposed quarterly. We're on! – Mackie's quotation. And extremely glad you can see your way to act as editorial assistant and help us generally at the printing end. The thing to do now is to tell Mackie's we are accepting their quotation – that we guarantee to go for a year (4 issues) at least – and ask them to put their terms in black and white on receipt of which we will formally accept. But neither Orr nor I wish Mackie's – or anybody else – to know that we are the people who are running the magazine. So one of two things can be done – either you get Mackie's to send you the quotation (refusing to disclose who's behind you in the matter) – or if, as is likely, that course is not desirable, ask them to send the quotation to Mr H. G. Taylor, Bridgend, Southwick, Dumfriesshire, and have the envelope marked 'Please Forward' (as Mr Taylor may be away from home). In either case – i.e. whether the quotation goes to you (and is accepted through you) or comes to Taylor (and is accepted by him), Mackie's would probably want a bank reference, and that would be forthcoming.

We would aim at putting out the first issue very early in May.

Prior to that I'll draw up copy for a one-page prospectus and send that to you to have printed and then we'll have it sent out to all the people I can think of – or whose names and addresses I can get through the PEN, Saltire Society, etc. to see what initial subscribers we can get. The subscription will be 3/- per annum (i.e. 9d per issue).

We haven't quite decided on the name yet – perhaps *Hammer and Thistle*. But I'll let you know definitely about that in a day or two. I'm writing George about it – but if you are writing him you can mention it too. And I'll be glad if you can enlist the interest of the E.U. Scottish Literature Society, and others with whom you are in touch.

It'll be quite a devil of a business putting across a militant anti-English anti-Imperialist communistically-inclined Scottish Separatist Republican organ at this juncture – but we'll try to do it in a way that those who are intelligent enough will 'savvy' all right and that yet will be sufficiently guarded to be printable all right without trouble by Mackie's. And along with the political side I fancy we'll print some good literary criticism, short stories, and poems.

Hope you're in good form.

Mike's been off school again with a nasty persistent kind of cold. But the rest of us are O.K. – Orr and Valda taking part in Chekhov's *The Bear* for a concert which comes off on Friday night.

I'm devilishly busy.

Excuse this scrappy letter. I'll have the details – name of quarterly, etc. – finally decided on, and at least a rough idea of the contents of No 1, in a day or so; and will then write you again. But please have Mackie's send on that formal quotation for acceptance as quickly as possible in whichever of the two ways I've suggested seems best to you.

All the best from all here.

Yours,
Chris.

My dear Bill,

You must be thinking I have basely deserted you. Not so. I have been as seriously concerned with the debt to the printers as yourself and more especially with the debt to yourself. I have of course been having an excruciatingly difficult time myself, but the issue is in sight now. Orr is back here – as locum for MacCrimmon – and while still short of cash for various reasons anxious to meet his obligations and likely to be able to do so very speedily now. I expect my own position to improve very soon now and if by then Orr hasn't wiped out the debt I'll probably be able to – or most of it – and certainly that to yourself – myself. My Autobio[1] is in my agent's hands. Gollancz is considering it, and several American firms are keen about it. It is a very big work – over 200,000 words – (it'll probably need some cutting down) and apart from the general difficulty of the subject matter and the legal dangers involved on many scores, it is exceedingly controversial and politically intensely radical and most vigorously – and indeed violently – expressed. So it is not just anybody's pigeon. In fact there are only two or three publishers in Great Britain who could possibly publish it. Nevertheless I hope to get a good break with it.

The Golden Treasury of Scottish Poetry is now all fixed up and at the printers and will be out in the spring.

Finally, there is the big poem.[2] I enclose a prospectus. It is not the sort of thing of course to send a young married man in times like these, and in fact it is almost an impossible proposition in war-time. At no time at all is there any overabundance of people able and willing to spend 2 guineas on a poem even if it is as long as 3 novels at one whack. So it'll need every subscriber I can possibly muster. Do you know of any other possible subscribers? If so I will be only too glad of course to send you – or them – copies of the prospectus. Perhaps the Library would order a copy? It'll certainly be a Collector's Piece par excellence. I don't know how the Obelisk Press will manage at all, since, apart from the sheer amount of setting, the thing will be of the utmost typographical difficulty and complexity. However, here's hoping.

I trust you are O.K. yourself. It is a long time now since I heard from you. I heard that your father had been ill – and had a Whalsay nurse (Ina Spence). I hope it was not serious and that he is all right

[1] *Lucky Poet* (London 1943).
[2] *Mature Art.*

again now. Is there no word of your brother's book yet?[1] And have you heard anything more of the Urquhart project? And are you settled into your own home yet? I trust your wife[2] is in good form. I have no other news. I wrote George Davie some time ago but have not heard from him. (You'll understand that if all goes well with my Autobio etc. I'll be in a position to resume, and intend resuming, the publication of the *Voice* at the earliest possible moment.)

Love from us all to your wife and yourself, and the rest of your family, with best wishes for a happy Christmas and every good wish for a bright and prosperous 1940.

                              Yours,
                              Chris.

                                                    Whalsay,
                                                    Shetland.
                                                    21/4/41

My dear Bill,

I was extremely glad – we all were – to have your letter and to know you are fine and fit and taking not too badly at all to the vie militaire.[1] I have been a little longer than I had hoped in replying but you will understand that in Grant's[2] absence and in the increasing economic and other stringencies of war-time I have plenty to do one way and other. The collection of gulls' eggs for pickling (last year's collection lasted us nicely all winter) and the necessity of cutting, drying, and getting home and stacking as ample a supply as possible of peats are the two major operations looming up on my horizon at the moment. And unlike Grant I am not an expert cragsman (as he proved to be last year) while I hate to think what a hash I'll make of peat-cutting. I'm now being subjected also to the first premonitory blasts of spring cleaning and understand sadly that this must soon develop into an all-involving whirlwind to the utter disruption of my peaceful labours.

[1] James M. Aitken, *The Trial of George Buchanan Before the Lisbon Inquisition* (1939).
[2] Betsy, Aitken's wife.
[1] Aitken served in the Royal Air Force from 1941 to 1946.
[2] Henry Grant Taylor, MacDiarmid's honorary private secretary.

These at the moment are heavy. The *Golden Treasury*'s appearance involved me in a lot of correspondence. It was extremely well reviewed in all the important quarters – and by a lot of well-known writers (Edmund Blunden, Louis MacNeice, Edward Shanks, Herbert Palmer, etc. etc.). Only *The Glasgow Herald*, *The Scotsman*, and the *Aberdeen Free Press* gave it extremely poor and grudging notices; I expected this of course – but not quite the shabby misrepresentation and feeling against myself they showed. However in all the important quarters the reviewers held my case for Scots against Muir fully made out. I haven't seen anything by Muir himself on the subject. In case you haven't seen it I enclose cutting of the full-page special article on it which appeared in *The Times Litt Supp*.[3] This was a surprise in its enthusiasm. The book has sold well, I understand, and is now to be produced in an American edition.

Methuen's were to have published my Autobio this spring but the blitzing in London made it impossible for them to get it out so quickly and September was then fixed. I hope recent events have not thrown out this time schedule next.

Almost simultaneously I got out of the blue two requests from American publishers to let them issue in USA selections of my poems. The firms were the Colt Press, San Francisco, and New Directions, Norfolk, Connecticut. Instead of selections of previous work however the former is issuing – provisionally in August – a volume of my new poems. I'm not sure yet whether the 2nd firm is to go ahead with a volume of selections or not; but at any rate in the 1941 issue of their big annual book magazine, *New Directions*, which appears in the autumn they are to have 1,000 lines of new poems by me.[4]

An American Professor – James G. Southworth of Toledo University (Ohio) has an excellent Chapter on my work (if written from a too-English angle and not concerned with its purely Scots significance and place in the separate Scots tradition) in his book *Sowing the Spring: Studies in British Poets from Hopkins to MacNeice*.

I am busy of course with my book on *The Faroes*,[5] and have a lot of other things in hand.

If I do not refer to the War at all in this letter you will understand why not.

F. G. Scott had the windows of his house broken and some of the

---

[3] *The Times Literary Supplement*, 14 February 1941.
[4] *New Directions in Prose and Poetry* (1941), edited by James Laughlin, contained MacDiarmid's poem 'The Divided Bird' (712–20). The American editions of MacDiarmid's poems never materialised; the first American edition, *Speaking for Scotland: Selected Poems of Hugh MacDiarmid*, was published in Baltimore in 1946.
[5] This book never appeared.

doors knocked squint in the Glasgow blitz: and has since been living with his family at Taynuilt.

Letters these days are scarce: but I had cheery – and cheering – letters lately from Sam Maclean and Paul Potts (both in the Army): Orr is very busy with his big new practice at Leith; Arthur Donaldson is still publishing his *Scottish News and Comment*, Harry Miller's *Scots Socialist* (formerly roneo'd and now printed) is the best thing by far the growth of Scots Nationalism has yet produced and is growing in strength – it advocates the V of S programme of Scots Republicanism à la John Maclean. The Scottish National Convention has forced the London body now to agree to the principle of Scots autonomy. In one way and another things are moving pretty rapidly at last.

Here of course I am hopelessly marooned and feel, in Lawrence's phrase, like a 'paralytic convulsed with rage'. We seldom see anyone even to exchange so much as the time of day with. I told you perhaps in a previous letter that after War broke out we were consigned to Coventry – not because we had thrown our weight about in an unpopular way but simply because it was generally 'understood' that we did not see eye to eye with the consensus of opinion, which latter however was uninformed with any real sense of wherein the difference lay. So since then we have been completely ostracised – the Bruces, Dr MacCrimmon, everyone.

Grant was turned down by the Tribunal but refused medical exam. and went to gaol and intended going the whole way. However on the expiry of his gaol sentence he was reclaimed by the Forestry Commission for whom he'd been working. Since then he has been promoted head sawyer and it seems that the Forestry Commission are going to claim his complete exemption.

I have no news, of course. We have all kept very well except for minor ailments, and at the moment Valda and I are both O.K. while Michael is confined to bed with a heavy cold of a type that is epidemic here just now.

Please give our kindest regards to Betty. It is fine she was able to get a job; also that she managed down to Morecambe.

I've just found your letter again and see you ask about Frank Miller – Yes, I know him to the extent of being in correspondence with him and having read his *Poets of Dumfriesshire* and some other writings of his.

Please excuse this scrappy epistle. Write me again ere long and let us keep in touch. I wish to God you were coming up here this summer. But I'm afraid we can look for no visitors this year yet – and Heaven only knows for how long ahead.

I'll write you again soon too and may be in a better writing mood then than I appear to be now – tho' when I started this letter I thought I was in the right form: but since then my lamp has gone wonky, carbonising and flaring up, and that has put me off my stroke.

Forgive my shortcomings; see and look after yourself; and accept warmest love and good wishes from us all.

Yours,
Chris.

Brownsbank,
by Biggar,
Lanarkshire.
22/2/53

Dear Bill,

It was a great pleasure to get your most interesting and warm-hearted letter of 5th inst. I have been away from home in the interval or I would have replied to it sooner. Why we have failed to get in touch with each other all these years is, as you say, quite inexplicable: but I do agree it's high time to put an end to the mystery. If I am ever over Perth way I'll certainly get in touch with you. I may be, I have just recently managed to establish relations again (after over 20 years!) with my daughter Christine. She is married to a Dundee doctor[1] and mother of a boy and a girl. So I will lose no opportunity of getting to Dundee, and Dundee and Perth are near enough to enable any visit to the former inclusive of the latter too.

I am delighted by all you say about the bibliography of the Scottish Renaissance Movement and of my own work. The devilish muddle the latter is in has been forcibly impressed upon me during the past year or so, when I have had to try to answer questions concerning it by American and French students doing theses – only to find to my disgust I couldn't lay hands on things, and couldn't even remember all sorts of details they wanted. Professor Barker Fairley (now of Toronto) and others have been urging me for a long time to put my affairs in order in this and other respects, and (not

[1] Alastair McIntosh.

584

that I am getting cold feet, but with a view to easing the labours of a possible literary executor) I have of late begun to redd up a little. In these circumstances apart from everything else I regard you as a tower of strength, and you can be sure that if and when you are ready to go ahead with anything about recent Scottish literature I will be only too glad to help in any way I can. You are certainly the man for the job in every way. I think I told you that a friend of mine, and of Geoffrey Wagner's and David Daiches's, Kenneth Buthlay (over from America and at present busy on a thesis under Aberdeen University direction) might be writing you as I'd suggested he should. He is having a very stiff row to hoe and I haven't been able to help him as much as I should have done. But I hear from him now that he has been in touch with you and that you have been very helpful. At the same time he feels he should not trouble you too much, as the sort of information, etc. he wants is really poaching on a territory you have made you own and naturally want to reserve for your own use later. I am afraid there are likely to be quite a lot of applicants for such information in the next year or two. You'd see *The Scotsman* letter the other day from Herr Guder, German lecturer at Glasgow University, regarding a young German scholar who has been commissioned to do an article on modern Scots poetry by a leading German review. I know that in Italy and France as well work is now being done on the subject. So I hope all the heavy work that must be involved in your PhD thesis on the history of the public library movement in Scotland will soon, and triumphantly, be discharged now and leave you free to undertake these other things which are nearer to your heart and in regard to which you are indeed the only competent person so far as I know.

Looking at your letter again I see I may have misled Wagner when I told him I knew nothing of the cancel in *Lucky Poet*.[2] I certainly never saw a copy myself in which the change had been made, but I did know of course that Edgell Rickword had kicked up a row and that to satisfy him and avoid an action Messrs Methuen had cut out the offensive reference. I have the correspondence somewhere, also letters from Nancy Cunard and others offering to give evidence if I decided to fight Rickword's action on the grounds of veritas and absence of malice – since they were in a position to

[2] Originally the reference in *Lucky Poet* (London 1943, p. 172) read 'Edgell Rickword is about the only person with some idea of Nationalism, but even he was in the Black-and-Tans. . . .' After Rickword had complained to the publisher pp. 171–2 were removed and a replacement page was tipped in which deleted the reference to Rickword and substituted the following sentence: 'Hardly one of the London *literati* has any idea of Nationalism or does not aid and abet Imperialism in one way or another.'

prove that as I said, tho' he now denies it, that Rickword was in the Black and Tans.

I enclose a pamphlet you may not have seen (unless I sent you one with my last letter). I mustn't ramble on any more just now as I have a whole file of other letters to get written. But I wholeheartedly agree with your suggestion that we should try to meet somewhere. Apart from the possibility of my being in Perth, it occurs to me that you may occasionally be in Edinburgh. Any time you should be, drop me a postcard, and I could almost any time meet you there. I get into Edinburgh in 40 minutes by bus – an hourly service – and I can always stay in Edinburgh overnight. I needn't tell you we'd be glad to see you here any time, but this is a small cottage and we cannot put anybody up overnight.

Mike[3] is in Glasgow doing a part-time typing job while studying for his University matric. He is going to be a journalist, but the call-up question has delayed his start. It was not sure until recently that the authorities would not 'cat and mouse him'. But it seems clear now that having done his spell in gaol they are not going to trouble him any further.

Valda joins me in every good wish to you all.

My compliments to your wife and to Christine[4] whom I look forward keenly to meeting.

And all the best to yourself.

Yours,
Chris.

Brownsbank.
20/8/57

Dear Bill,

Sorry to have been long in acknowledging receipt of Wagner's book on *Wyndham Lewis*,[1] which I have been reading with great interest (I also saw, of course, the *TLS*. article on it), and your other two enclosures. But I am desperately busy and likely to be so for the

[3] Michael Grieve, the poet's son.
[4] Christine, Aitken's daughter.
[1] Geoffrey Wagner, *Wyndham Lewis* (1957).

remainder of this year. Inter alia I am again giving lectures in Edinburgh for the WEA on Scottish Literature, and also a series (for the WEA too) in South Wales: and I'm addressing Glasgow University Literary Society on the relations of English & Scottish literature. Over and above that I expect to be going to Poland in October or November. Nevertheless my own work goes on. I've now passed the final proofs of *The Battle Continues* (a long poem on the Spanish War in reply to late Roy Campbell's *Flowering Rifle*), and also of *Three Hymns to Lenin* in the series of my books being put out by the Castlewynd Printers, Edinburgh.

With regard to the Scottish Fiction scheme[2] I certainly think Sydney Goodsir Smith's *Carotid Cornucopius*, put out by the Caledonian Press, Glasgow, 1947, should be included, and also *Heid or Hert* by R. L. Cassie (Aberdeen: Aberdeen Press & Journal Office, 1923), the only novel I know completely in Scots since *Johnny Gibb o' Gushetneuk*.[3] But other items will come to my mind, and I'll list them and send on to you, for what it may be worth.

I've also begun making lists (a) of the books dealing with my work (i.e. not mere passing references but chapters or at least extended passages of some critical value), and (b) articles of some permanent value about my work and/or modern Scottish literature generally (the latest which you'll have seen being that in the supplement to the TLS last week).

David Lindsay was a teacher – not at Fettes – but at Loretto. I do not see (unless I missed – I haven't it by me at the moment) in your catalogue of Scottish Fiction mention of his militant Scottish Nationalist novel, *David Go Back*.[4] Many thanks for the copy of Gollancz note about him. I'll look further into him when I get a chance, and also into 'Benjamin Swift'.[5]

It was a great pleasure to Valda and I to have you and your wife and daughter here and we certainly share your hope that henceforward we may continue to keep in regular touch.

Like your own (on your own admission) this isn't a real letter, of course – I simply haven't time to emit more than the most matter-of-fact communications just now. But I'll write you later on when some of the things I mention above get done.

[2] W. R. Aitken, *Scottish Fiction Reserve: A List of the Authors Included in the Scheme* (1955). The Scottish Fiction scheme is an alphabetical list of Scottish novelists showing the collecting libraries responsible for the authors associated with their area.
[3] William Alexander, *Johnny Gibb of Gushetneuk* (1871).
[4] MacDiarmid is confusing David Lindsay, author of *A Voyage to Arcturus* (1920), with John Connell (1909–65), author of *Lyndesay* (1930) and *David Go Back* (1935).
[5] 'Benjamin Swift' was the pseudonym used by W. Romaine Paterson.

Every kind regard to you all.

Yours,
Chris.

P.S. I note you're in no particular hurry for the return of the Wagner book. So I'll keep it for a while yet. But if you should need it please just send me a p.c. and I'll post it back to you straight away.

Brownsbank,
Biggar.
12/3/63

Dear Bill,

Many thanks for your letter and enclosure. I've had you on my conscience for some time but then I've a dreadful back-log of correspondence I just can't get tackling at all. Valda and I are going off to London tomorrow. Tonight we're attending a lecture on my poetry by a Roman Catholic priest in Edinburgh.[1] On evening of 14th I'll be on BBC TV Tonight programme. Then on 19th I'm doing a Border TV interview in Carlisle. I hope I get a chance in the train to put my thoughts in order, so as to give some sort of coherent address in Hamilton[2] – I'll go straight there from Edinburgh. Will be delighted to see Betty, Christine, and you – and the students. There have been some very stupid reviews of *Aniara*[3] – the writers seem to have misconceived the thing all together, misled into regarding it as simply a Science Fiction essay, and paying no attention to what the distinguished Swedish physicist says in his Introduction, but preferring their own quite inadequate ideas on what is scientifically accurate. *The Times Lit. Supp.* review[4] was extraordinarily contra-

[1] Father Anthony Ross.
[2] MacDiarmid addressed the West of Scotland branch of the Scottish Library Association in Hamilton; Aitken chaired the meeting.
[3] *Aniara* (1962) by Harry Martinson. Adapted from the Swedish by Hugh Mac-Diarmid and Elspeth Harley Schubert.
[4] The review in *The Times Literary Supplement*, 15 February 1963, ended: 'The present volume is unlikely to add many to the large numbers of Mr MacDiarmid's admirers who consider him to be among the finest of modern translators from a number of languages which include German, Russian, and Gaelic, yet it was a

dictory – how on earth could the reviewer reconcile the two statements in his final paragraph 1/ that the translation would not add to my reputation 2/ that nevertheless the translation might well prove a seminal work for English literature. Of course every kid knows Jupiter is not a star but a planet – but what is poetic licence for, if it is not permissible to call a planet a star. And the stuff about the use of Hades and its relation to the myth of the underworld was quite irrelevant – the word Hades had no such associations as used simply to mean the abomination of desolation of outer space and the absence of any Heaven or Hell.

My *Collected Poems* sold out very quickly both in America and in the Oliver & Boyd edition here, and there's no word yet when reprinting will put supplies on the market again tho' there is a steady demand.

We've had a terrible winter here – roads blocked – no 'buses or even private cars on main road for days at a time – water frozen up since 12th Jan. and no sign of coming on yet – we've been boiling snow for washing water for nearly 2 months.

Still we're both in good form. Michael was very lucky but his right arm is still in plaster of paris, owing to fractured wrist. Hope you are all fine and flourishing.

Love from Valda and I.

Yours,
Chris.

Brownsbank,
Candymill,
by Biggar,
Lanarks.
30/3/75

Dr W. R. Aitken.

Dear Bill,

Many thanks for your letter of 25th and report on progress of the complete *Collected Poems*. I think I have told you before – and need

bold move to translate this work and it may well prove a seminal volume in the history of English letters.'

not repeat – how remorseful I am at all the work I've involved you in.

Replying to certain points you raise

1/ re glossary I agree with you – there should only be a glossary (conflated as you suggest from those I supplied for the separate books drawn upon) and no additional explanatory annotations and/or elucidations at all. For various reasons I am against having bottom of page glosses rather than a general glossary at the end. And I certainly do not want any scholarly notes, etc. anywhere.

2/ There is no proper sequence in which poems I attributed to *Impavidi* can be presented. I simply abandoned the whole project – and the *Haud Forrit* idea which I later substituted for the Latin title. I haven't alas a copy of Bridson's script[1] nor can I recall what poems it included. Some of these I have probably published since as separate poems, and/or had even published separately before I thought of including them in the abortive *Impavidi* scheme. Unfortunately I've lost touch with Bridson. He retired from the BBC several years ago. I wrote him at Christmas time but have had no reply and think he and his wife may be abroad. I know they were going to Australia.

3/ Re the separate bits in *Lucky Poet* I'll see what I can suggest when I get the photostats. One longish bit, which I entitled 'The Song of the Seraphim' I have had published separately. If you haven't a copy of this let me know and I'll send you one.

4/ Valda and I will of course be very pleased to see you at Stirling if you can be there. The reading on 4th April is in the Studio Theatre, MacRobert Centre of the University at 7.30. We are staying overnight as the Annual General Meeting of the 1320 Club is in Stirling on the 5th April.

With gratitude, and warmest regards from Valda and I to Betty, Christine, Robin and yourself

Yours,
Chris.

---

[1] MacDiarmid's conversation with D. G. Bridson was broadcast, under the title 'Aims and Opinions', on the BBC third Programme on 4 and 9 March 1960. A selection of MacDiarmid's comments is included in *The Thistle Rises: A MacDiarmid Miscellany* (London 1984) edited by Alan Bold.

W. R. Aitken, Esq.

Dear Bill,

Many thanks for your letter with details of proofing, etc. I have had no word at all from Timothy O'Keeffe but Mike told me the other day that instead of being out early in May the book won't be published now till early in June.[1] This is disappointing since I'll be almighty glad once I have the volume in my hands. I can hardly plead guilty to impatience!

The one really satisfactory thing about the whole business is my incredible good luck in having you seeing to the collection and ordering and proofing of the contents. I could not have been better served, and there does not seem any way in which I can repay you.

Whether I'll be able to go to Dublin in July for the capping is still very doubtful.[2] I have been having a very bad time, with a great deal of pain. I would have to be a great deal better before I could make any sort of public appearance. For one thing I am very tottery and to stand for even a few minutes is out of the question.

Finally in aesthetic matters judgment becomes just a question of personal taste. I too think the *Dìreadh* sequence good but I am quite sure 'On a Raised Beach' is one of the very best things I've written and recently for the first time in several years I re-read the *In Memoriam James Joyce* and am more than ever convinced that it is a poem running right through from start to finish. There was one of these Men of Ideas interviews on BBC TV with Professor Gellner[3] the other night, and I was delighted to find it covered precisely the same ground as the JJ poem and came to a similar conclusion.

I hope you keep well – ditto Betty and Christine and her husband and children.

I am of course house-bound and haven't been out of doors since New Year's Day, so there is little or no chance of our meeting since as I'd like a long talk with you on various matters.

But that'll have to await the pleasure of whatever Gods there be.

[1] MacDiarmid died on 13 September 1978. *Complete Poems* (London 1978), edited by W. R. Aitken and Michael Grieve, appeared posthumously.
[2] MacDiarmid was awarded an Honorary Litt.D. by Dublin University.
[3] Ernest Gellner.

With gratitude and appreciation.

Yours,
Chris.

Brownsbank,
by Biggar.
18/6/78

Dr W. R. Aitken.

Dear Bill,

There is no limit to your generosity. You promised me a copy of the Douglas Young book, but the Murison pamphlet on Scots and John Carswell's splendid book on *The New Age* group, all of whom I knew, are unexpected extras for which I am very grateful.[1] Especially the Carswell book. I gave him some information but I would probably never have seen the book but for your kindness. It is by far the best of the books on that group – all of which I have read – but even so it has omissions. For example, he says nothing of the important contributions by Sorabji – makes only one passing reference to the greatly underestimated Denis Saurat – and likewise only refers to Charles Lahr who deserved a whole chapter to himself. These three – Sorabji, Saurat, and Lahr – I have always intended writing full essays on. But don't suppose I will be able to now. Anyhow my warmest thanks.

I've been a week out of hospital now and as I think I told you had two major operations there – one of which confirmed the fact that the basic cause of my troubles is a cancer of the rectum. It is temporarily quiescent. Cancers do that – go into latencies. The doctors had told Valda and Mike I'd probably 6 months to live, but I'm a tough old guy and may live far longer. I'm not anxious to and feel I've done my best work and am unlikely to be able now to add to that, so there's no point living on.

I still expect to go to Dublin for the July 6th affair. But I am very weak and apt to have a lot of pain.

Love to Betty and you – and to Christine and her husband and family.

Yours,
Chris.

[1] The books mentioned by MacDiarmid are *A Clear Voice: Douglas Young, Poet and Polymath* (1977) edited by Clara Young and David Murison; David Murison's *The Guid Scots Tongue* (1977); and John Carswell's *Life and Letters* (1977).

To John Lehmann

John Lehmann (born 1907) was an influential advocate of socially conscious poetry; from 1936 to 1950 he edited *New Writing* and from 1938 to 1946 he was a partner and general manager of the Hogarth Press. He was sympathetic to MacDiarmid's poetry and printed his story 'The Case of Alice Carruthers' in *New Writing* in 1939 (see *The Thistle Rises: a MacDiarmid Miscellany* edited by Alan Bold).

HRC

Whalsay,
via Lerwick,
Shetland Islands.
6-6-38

Dear Mr Lehmann,

I enclose a 'Third Hymn to Lenin' which has not yet been published anywhere, in the hope that you may find it acceptable for *New Writing*.

I have just been reading your article on recent tendencies in English poetry in one of the 1936 issues of *International Literature*[1] in which you make kind references to my own work which I missed at the time. But suggest, 1/ that I might have been included in *New Country* but for my use of Scots, so difficult for Southern Englishmen to understand, and 2/ that my influence – and that of 'First Hymn to Lenin' – must have been very small.

---

[1] In *International Literature*, No 4, 1936, John Lehmann wrote, in 'Some Revolutionary Trends in English Poetry: 1930–1935': 'It is probable that if his best work had not been written in Scots dialect, "Hugh MacDiarmid" would have been included in [Michael Roberts's anthology] *New Country* [1933], though he stands alone, completely outside the Auden-Spender-Day Lewis group and its particular pattern of ideas.'

The facts are, of course, that the 'First Hymn to Lenin' was written for, and appeared initially in *New English Poems*[2] edited by Lascelles Abercrombie and published by Victor Gollancz, while with regard to the second point, my work was well known to most of the younger Left Wing poets from 1926 (when my *Drunk Man Looks At The Thistle* appeared) and I have letters thereanent from many of them, showing incidentally that my Scots medium did not trouble them much if at all, while later Auden was of course a school-teacher in Scotland and a contributor to *The Modern Scot* and my work was well known to him.

I would not in any case have contributed to anthologies run by Mr Michael Roberts (though I knew him personally in London in 1930-31) because I have no respect whatever for his judgment and anticipated long ago that he would take up the positions (with which of course I have no sympathy whatever) he, in fact, does take up in *The Modern Mind* and his new book on T. E. Hulme[3] – i.e. pro-Christian, and holding that civilisation can only be saved by submission to the authority of a Church.

If I have stood very much alone, as you say, it has been because I have been very careful not to be found in questionable company; and beyond that is the fact that while, following my expulsion from the CP and subsequent reinstatement on appeal to the Annual Conference, the Scottish Secretariat of the Party had to admit that its line in regard to Scottish Home Rule had been wrong and altered it to go some little way to meet my demands, the English C. Pers for the most part have not done anything of the sort, and still retain an English Ascendancy attitude and a lack of interest in or patronising attitude towards Scottish affairs which is quite un-Communist and makes it impossible for me to work along with them. Because of this (apart from the fact that I do not think much of Auden, Spender, and Day Lewis as poets and believe them to be grossly overrated) I view with deep suspicion the whole nature and tendency of the left wing literary movement in England – knowing that you have only to scratch it to find English Chauvinism and a 'superior' inability to believe that any good can come out of anywhere but Oxford and Cambridge. Besides if the unfamiliarity of my Scots dialect were the main cause of my isolation from these writers, it would be very difficult to explain how the Left-Wing writers in America, with most of whom I am on very good terms, do not find any difficulty on this score, and welcome me in their magazines and anthologies. I fancy

2 (Ed) Lascelles Abercrombie, *New English Poems* (London 1930).
3 Michael Roberts (1902–48) was an influential anthologist of the English leftist poetry of the 1930s; *The Modern Mind* appeared in 1937, *T. E. Hulme* the following year.

that the real root of the trouble lies in the fact that I am not only a Scotsman, not an Englishman, but also that unlike almost all the English Left-Wing poets and other writers, I have the advantage of belonging to the working class, have always remained in it and never earned enough to lift me into any 'higher' category.

You will appreciate, of course, that these comments on your extremely interesting essay are made in a perfectly comradely way, and simply to set down certain facts and suggest that the almost automatic or instinctive evasion of any consideration of the British international question in the light of dialectical materialism which has all along been a very curious and outstanding feature of the British Social Democratic and now equally of the British Communist movement is what really explains the attitude of my English literary comrades to me.

With every good wish.

Yours fraternally,
C. M. Grieve.

P.S. The traditional English dislike of, and incapacity for, theory is much in evidence in all the work I have seen (and I've seen most of what has appeared) of English Marxists; and in particular the Scottish issue of the *Left Review*[4] (from which – although the only Scottish writer of any international reputation who is a member of the CP – I was deliberately excluded) was scandalously bad in this way and scarcely a statement in it was capable of bearing analysis by any competent dialectician.

HRC

c/o Donnelly,
35 Havelock St.,
Glasgow, W.
10/1/43

John Lehmann, Esq.
My dear Lehmann,

This is a note to introduce my young friend, Ian Finlay,[1] who is

---

[4] The Scottish issue of the *Left Review*, Vol II, 1936–7, contained nothing by MacDiarmid but printed a poem by William Soutar and articles by Neil Gunn, James Barke, J. H. Whyte, Edwin Muir, Catherine Carswell and Willa Muir.

[1] Ian Hamilton Finlay (born 1925), later to gain an international reputation for his visual and sculptural poetry and to provoke some of MacDiarmid's liveliest polemics against experimental art.

travelling down to London tomorrow in the hope of finding some employment of a more congenial kind than offers in this barbarous country. I am sure you will find him a very delightful and most personable young fellow, extremely well read and with excellently developed interests in literature and the arts. I hope you may be able to help him. Not that I imagine that even in these days of labour shortage either the Hogarth Press or *New Writing* have jobs a-going, but that you may be able to give him helpful introductions. What he has in mind is employment with some publishing firm or in journalism or in a bookshop. It will be very kind of you if you can help my friend in this way and both he and I will be very grateful.

I hope things are going well with yourself and with *New Writing* and the Hogarth Press. For myself, war conditions have made me take up engineering and I have been employed in big Clydeside munitions works for close on a year now, doing very heavy work, long hours, etc., but really liking it very much. Writing is practically out of the question, but I am not worrying as when War broke out I had several books ready for publication both in this country and in America, but paper shortage and other difficulties has held these up so far. One of them, however, – a huge Autobiography – is appearing shortly now, *via* Messrs Methuen.

With every kind regard.

Yours,
C. M. Grieve
('Hugh MacDiarmid')

To Douglas Young

Born in Tayport, Douglas Young (1913–73) was one of the most colourful and combative figures in the history of modern Scottish literature. As a poet he wrote the lively Scots verse collected in *Auntran Blads* (Glasgow 1943) and *A Braird O Thistles* (Glasgow 1947); his love of polemics is seen to advantage in *'Plastic Scots' and the Scottish Literary Tradition: An Authoritative Introduction to a Controversy* (Glasgow 1947) and *Scots Burds and Edinburgh Reviewers* (Edinburgh 1966). Young was a gifted linguist who produced a fine Scots translation of Valéry's 'Le Cimetière Marin' and two vigorous versions of Aristophanes: *The Puddocks* (Tayport 1957) and *(The Burdies* (Tayport 1959). He earned his living by lecturing in classics at St Andrews University and his home, Makarsbield in Tayport, was well known to Scottish poets and politicians.

In 1937 the Scottish National Party was persuaded, by its radical wing, to oppose conscription unless advocated by an independent Scottish government. When the Second World War came Douglas Young, then a lecturer in Greek at Aberdeen University, refused to accept his call-up papers from what he regarded as an alien government. Thus he became the centre of a legal struggle in which, largely as a result of his being imprisoned twice, he featured prominently as a martyr to the cause of Scottish independence. Young's election as chairman of the SNP, on 30 May 1942, was welcomed by MacDiarmid who rejoined the party, served on the National Council, and stood as a candidate for Kelvingrove in the 1945 general election. With MacDiarmid, Young was one of the founders of the left-wing nationalist 1320 Club in 1967.

NLS
Whalsay,
Shetland Islands.
20-1-39

Douglas Young Esq.

Dear Mr Young,

I have been away from home, hence my delay in thanking you for your very interesting letter. The 3rd issue of *The Voice of Scotland* which should have been out last month has been delayed by a variety of causes, but is on the point of being issued now. In the 4th issue I am going to publish your letter (not giving your name and address however) and append a note in reply. I sympathise very largely with your point of view, but, since theoretic inadequacy and anti-intellectualism have been the great weakness in turn of the Scottish Radical, Liberal, Social Democratic, and now Communist elements cannot agree that there is not need for an organ which disregards personal feelings and all considerations of compromise. Still less can an organ one of the primary purposes of which is to publish original literature adapt itself to the tender susceptibilities of non-specialist readers. In any case to be stronger in doctrine than in propaganda is not only the express function of this quarterly, but with a small periodical with only a very small and very special circulation, it is impossible to try to compete with the great mechanisms of mass propaganda and appeal to a big public. But even such an organ can exercise a potent influence on those who are mainly responsible for propaganda, and that is, I think, our function, and I have reason to know that we are in fact having that effect in important directions.

Again thanking you for your expressions of support and good wishes.

Yours fraternally,
C. M. Grieve.
('Hugh MacDiarmid')

NLS
c/o Donnelly,
35 Havelock Street,
Glasgow W.
17/1/43

My dear Douglas,

It was a great treat to have your letter and your own assurance that you are, all things considered, in such excellent health and spirits. As requested, I have written to your mother and to David Murison.[1] I hear from MacLellan that the latter has at last returned the proofs of *Auntran Blads*[2] and hope this book will be forthcoming speedily now. Sorley was wounded in both feet at the Battle of El Alemein and is in hospital in Egypt. I hope that while entailing no permanent crippling these wounds may secure his return to this country and discharge from the Army soon. I am writing him tonight. MacLellan tells me Sorley's poems[3] are now in book form and expresses his satisfaction with Wm. Crosbie's illustrations thereto. I am looking forward keenly to this volume also. I have not heard of or from Hay for a long time now, but Scott's settings of some of his lyrics were included in the recent Edinburgh concert programme of Scott's songs and scored a great hit.[4] They are really magnificent. I'll be glad to add my urgings to yours that he should put a volume together and if he agrees and so wishes I'll be very pleased of course to supply a preface. I've mentioned this to MacLellan too as a volume he ought to publish if he is really going to do what he has a great opportunity of doing, i.e. establish himself as the progressive Scottish publisher we've been praying for ever since the end of the last War. Of Davie[5] I can glean no news whatever. Black[6] I haven't seen for many weeks, since (1) I have been working extremely long hours and seven days a week i.e. Sundays too (2) in addition to that, practically all my free time has had to be devoted to the proofs of my enormous Autobiography which Methuen's are

---

[1] David Murison is the Scottish scholar responsible, with William Grant, for *The Scottish National Dictionary* (10 vols, 1929–76).

[2] Young's *Auntran Blads: An Outwale o Verses* was published by William Maclellan, in Glasgow, in 1943.

[3] Sorley Maclean, *Dàin Do Eimhir Agus Daine Eile* (1943).

[4] George Campbell Hay's poems were, like MacDiarmid's, sympathetically set to music by Francis George Scott. After being conscripted for military service, in 1940, Hay evaded the authorities for eight months before being caught, incarcerated in Edinburgh's Saughton prison for a few days, then registered as a soldier.

[5] George Davie, author of *The Democratic Intellect* (1961).

[6] Robin McKelvie Black, editor of *The Free Man*.

publishing almost immediately now, and (3) my wife and boy arrived some weeks ago and she and I are now installed in a flat at above address while the boy is at Aitkenhead's school at Kilquhanity House, near Castle Douglas. For various reasons Robertson's publication of pamphlets of my new poems has not materialised, and now seems unlikely too, but a pamphlet of my *Cornish Heroic Song for Valda Trevlyn*[7] is in type and copies should be available any day now. The only other literary news I have is that the London Scots Self-Government Committee have at last succeeded in issuing their *New Scotland* symposium.[8] I contribute the literature article to this. My contribution was written in the Shetlands i.e. about 18 months ago (the publication as you probably know has been hung up – questions were asked about it in Parliament months ago) and if I remember rightly I had something to say in it about you and Sorley and Hay and others. But I don't really recall just what line I took in it, and a copy hasn't reached me yet.

As you perhaps heard some months ago I had a very serious accident at work – pulled a pile of copper plate down on myself and disabled both legs and one of my arms. I was extremely lucky not to be killed. My injuries responded excellently to treatment and while I was off work for weeks and even after I returned was a pathetic sight hobbling about with the aid of walking sticks, I was speedily O.K. again except for a slight limp of the left leg, which since it is due to a severe rupture of the muscles, will probably continue to affect me for years – but happily does not prevent my working, entail any pain, nor much impede my movements.

It is splendid to think that if all goes well you'll be amongst us again in a matter of eight weeks now.[9] We must have a real celebration. It will be a great occasion.

Congratulations on your great spirit, and every cordial greeting and good wish.

Au revoir.

Yours,
Christopher.

[7] Hugh MacDiarmid, *Cornish Heroic Song for Valda Trevlyn* (Glasgow 1943).
[8] MacDiarmid's essay 'Scottish Arts and Letters: the present position and post-war prospects' appeared in *The New Scotland* (London 1942), a symposium published by the London Scots Self-Government Committee.
[9] This letter was addressed to Young in HM Prison, Saughton.

NLS

c/o Donnelly,
25 Havelock Street,
Glasgow. W.
Wednesday.
[1943]

My dear Douglas,

Many thanks for your letter. I am, of course, willing to accept
office as a member of the SNP Council, regard it as a great honour,
and look forward keenly to doing all I can as a colleague of yourself
and the others.[1]

Yes I could speak at Stirling on the evening of 26th June under the
auspices of the Russia Today Society.

I will hope to get time to write something suitable in Lallans prose
for the proposed broadsheet this week-end. I send you in the
meantime a poem[2] which may be appropriate to the purpose. I'll
hunt out one or two other shorter and more specifically Communist
poems and send them with the prose on Monday so that whoever is
dealing with the matter may have a choice of material.

In the meantime I send you this poem, as you do not say to whom
I should send the material.

I'll be hoping to see you on Saturday at the Council meeting – and
to hearing them all about the Conference, 'nary a' word concerning
which have I seen in any paper.

With compliments and every good wish.

From,
Valda and Chris.

[1] Douglas Young was elected chairman of the Scottish National Party on 30 May
1942; as a result of this victory for radical nationalism William Power (Young's
rival for the chairmanship) and John McCormick resigned from the SNP while
MacDiarmid rejoined.
[2] 'Lamh Dearg Aboo' (1323-5) which eventually appeared in *Poetry in Scotland*, No
2, 1945.

32 Victoria Crescent Road,
Glasgow W.2.
25/11/48

Dear Douglas,

Many thanks for your letters of 22nd Nov.

I am, of course, willing to act as Hon. Pres. of the Renaissance Society if so desired and regard it as an honour. But in view of developments, and likely developments, it will be quite all right with me if the Society decides to cancel my election to that post.

Blythman and Kincaid told me on Saturday about Montgomerie raising the Soutar Poems issue at the meeting.[1] I cannot understand how this was permitted. So far as I know Montgomerie was not a member of the Makars Club and is not a member of the Renaissance Society. Surely he should have been ruled out of order. In any case the matter should not have been discussed – or even broached – in my absence.

What Blythman and Kincaid told me was the first I had heard about it. Yesterday however F. G. Scott brought me Monday's *Scotsman* and showed me Bridie's and Montgomerie's letters. I am vouchsafing no explanations. If I had been asked by any of my friends – or any other bona fide inquirer – about the matter I would of course have given my explanation. But the matter was raised in public first, without any consultation with or warning to me. And of course I take the strongest possible exception to Bridie's claim that a clear case has been made out for the appointment of a Committee of Inquiry by the Saltire Society or PEN. I am not a member of either of these bodies; nor have they any official standing. Bridie might as

---

[1] MacDiarmid's edition of Soutar's *Collected Poems* (1948) was incomplete and omitted important works such as 'The Auld Tree'. 'As a result of its unfortunate omissions,' writes Alexander Scott in *Still Life* (Edinburgh 1958, p. 160), 'this book was poorly received both by press and public, and eventually remaindered.' After the book was reviewed in *The Scotsman* of 11 November 1948 James A. Finlayson wrote to *The Scotsman* (16 November 1948) pointing out that Soutar could not be adequately appreciated unless major poems (such as 'The Auld Tree') were considered. William Montgomerie (*The Scotsman*, 18 November 1948) claimed 'it would be wrong to call [MacDiarmid's edition] even a selection . . . Too much of his best work, including all his long poems, is just not there.' On 22 November 1948 *The Scotsman* printed two more letters on the subject. Montgomerie itemised the omissions he already commented on; James Bridie stated that 'there is a clear case for the setting up of a committee of inquiry by either the Saltire Society or Scottish PEN while Soutar's friends are still alive and the truth is still available.' Maurice Blythman ('Thurso Berwick') and John Kincaid were leftwing Scottish poets sympathetic to MacDiarmid.

well have suggested that I should be hauled at once before a Court Martial in Edinburgh Castle. Scottish Command has certainly as much right to intervene in the matter as either the Saltire or PEN – or for the matter of that the Renaissance Society: and I would on the whole expect fairer treatment from Scottish Command.

Bridie affects to be very concerned about Soutar. But he did not manifest any such concern during Soutar's lifetime nor has he shown any like concern in any direction with regard to other living Scottish writers. The fact is that this is just another example of his methods – i.e. to overpraise the third rate in order to occlude the first rate and so lower the standards generally. He can do nothing else being utterly mediocre – and grossly overpaid – himself. It is precisely the same technique that has always been employed against F. G. Scott – i.e. not to mention him without also dragging in the names of others like Ian Whyte, Thorpe Davie, Chisholm, etc.[2] to suggest that they are all 'much of a muchness': all 'contemporary Scottish composers'.

My position is therefore that the editing by me of S's poems was a private arrangement with his parents and that I am answerable to no one else. I have a letter from Mr Soutar himself expressing his complete satisfaction that I 'had made a fine job of it'. That being so, I regard the matter as closed. If I care for any other reason later to afford certain explanations I shall do so in my own way and at my own time and for my own reasons. I am not disturbed by anybody else's ideas of Soutar's 'importance'. I have my own and I am not prepared to admit that anybody else's can weigh against mine. Nor am I disturbed at any suggestions that I have withheld a lot of the best of S's poems from the Collected book in order to make him out less than he really is vis-a-vis myself. The withheld poems have all been published and are available, so I cannot be accused of having suppressed the evidence! In any case all such questions will 'come out in the wash'. I can afford to bide my time: and am certainly not going to allow myself to be forced to fight on ground not of my own choosing.

This means you will understand that I am amazed that the Renaissance Society should have instructed you to ask me for explanations – which does not seem to me to be their business at all – and that I will not, as I had intended, be at the meeting in Glasgow on 17th Dec. if the Society is to persist in raising the matter in any way at that meeting.

I'll look forward to your *Record* article and think your plan is an excellent one at this juncture. I will be glad to help in any way I can.

---

[2] Ian Whyte, conductor of the BBC Scottish Orchestra, Cedric Thorpe Davie and Erik Chisholm are Scottish composers.

All the best.
Yours
Chris.

P.S. I do hope something is being done for Chiari.[3]

NLS   32 Victoria Crescent Road,
                                                   Glasgow W.2.
                                                   28/2/49

Douglas Young, Esq.
My Dear Douglas,

   This is just a brief formal note to say that if I am offered a Civil List
Pension I will accept it very gratefully. I have just this moment got
back home from Oxford and Manchester, so I must defer a little in
expressing my gratitude to yourself for moving in this matter and to
all the signatories you have secured.
   With every kind regard.

                                        Yours,
                                        Christopher Grieve.

NLS   32 Victoria Crescent Road,
                                                   Glasgow W.2.
                                                   24/3/49

Dear Douglas,

   Just a line to let you know (as I think I ought to do – in case you
have not heard direct – altho' the Prime Minister's letter pointed out
that such awards have, as one of their conditions, that they must be
'kept strictly confidential') that, instead of a Civil list pension Mr

---

[3] Joseph Chiari, a man of letters friendly with MacDiarmid.

Attlee has recommended on the basis of the representations regarding my services to literature made by yourself and other friends that I should receive a sum from the Royal Bounty Fund and tells me I'll receive this next month.

My reason for this breach of the condition of confidentiality is that I feel you ought to know that your effort has been successful, that this award will be very helpful to me, and that I am very grateful to you and all the others who so kindly helped.

With my warmest thanks, therefore, and kindest regards to all of you from Valda and myself.

Yours,
Chris.

NLS

Dungavel.
6/12/49

Dear Douglas,

The young poet you are thinking of was my friend John Bogue Nisbet, who died in the 1st Battle of Loos – a captain in the Royal Scots. Alas, I have no MSS of his. He was writing a lot just prior to the 1914 War, but I don't know if any of that – even if available – would be worth using. It was all very apprentice work. I feel he might have done a great deal if he had lived. As it was he was only trying his wings, and published nothing except a few poems in the school magazine. His parents died, his only sister married and went to live in Canada, and I lost touch.

While on this subject of the Nelson Anthology[1] – which I presume is the same one as Linklater is connected with, and for which I have just sent back proofs of my own poems for it – there are one or two other names I might mention.

A poet in whom I have long been interested – who also died young but with a considerable body of work accomplished – was Lewis Morrison Grant, an Aberdonian, of whom a biography by Jessie Annie Anderson was published. (I've lost my own copy but you should be able to get it in the library. I believe it was published by

---

[1] (Ed) Douglas Young, *Scottish Verse, 1851–1951* (1952).

Leng's of Dundee[2] – in any case I got my own copy as a prize in some competition of the *People's Journal*, I think.) Something of his might well be included.

Then there is 'J. B. Selkirk' (James Brown, Selkirk). You can probably get hold of his *Collected Poems* – and therein I think your choice might well be his Flodden poem, the one with the verse ending 'In Branksome's deidly barrow'. It is, I think, perhaps the most hauntingly powerful of all Flodden poems. Brown was a very interesting man – a very suggestive critic of literature and the other arts, as well as a poet.

Amongst those who were at school with Albert Mackie and myself (at Broughton Junior Student Centre) was Edward Albert, the novelist, author of *Herrin' Jenny* etc. I believe his widow is still alive in Edinburgh; Mackie will know, I expect. Albert wrote some excellent poems. I do not know that he published any of them except a few in the school magazine, but I think it would be well worth finding out what poems were left among his papers.

Then there was F. V. Branford (to whose work Middleton Murry devoted an essay in his latest volume a few months ago). While Francis Thompsonesque in its Latinity of language, I think his poem in memoriam Francis Thompson a very splendid poem indeed. And there are others, especially a very fine one on Loch Goil. I would have included both of these in my Golden Treasury – did indeed include them, as also J. B. Selkirk's Flodden poem – but they had, alas, to be eliminated when I had to cut down the contents to keep that Anthology within the prescribed series size.

I can come to Edinburgh – Thin's[3] – all right for book-signing purposes on Thursday forenoon, 22nd inst., and am getting in touch today with MacLellan to see if he has stocks of my *Selected Poems* available.

In haste, with every kind regard to all at Makarsbield.

Yours,
Chris.

P.S. I hope some of the Shetland poets are represented in the Anthology – particularly (among the contemporary writers) W. J. Tait, who has done some really first-rate work both in Shetland-Scots and in English.

---

[2] It was published by the Caxton Press, Aberdeen.
[3] James Thin, an Edinburgh bookshop.

Dungavel,
by Strathaven,
Lanarkshire.
13/9/50

Dear Douglas,

   As I think I mentioned to you my son Michael, who has now
registered as a Conscientious Objecter provisionally, is basing his
claim on 1/ Scottish Nationalist grounds – the illegality of cons-
cribing Scots for overseas service, etc. and 2/ on his conviction that
all war is wrong. I understand that it will help if he has letters
(addressed to the Clerk of the Tribunal or to whom it may concern)
from people who know him and can testify to the fact that he has held
these views for a considerable period. Can you find it in your heart to
furnish him with such a document, testifying, from your own
knowledge of him over a period of years, that he has long and
consistently held these views? I will be very grateful if you can. He
needs to have such letters as soon as possible now. Address:-
Michael Grieve, The School, Kilquhanity House, near Castle
Douglas, Kirkcudbrightshire.
   Hope you are all O.K. after the hectic PEN time.
   All the best.

                    Yours,
                    Chris.

Brownsbank,
By Biggar,
Lanarkshire.
24/8/51

Dear Douglas,

   I have just got back from Germany and Poland. I hope you
received a postcard I sent you from Berlin, passing on greetings from
Stephan Hermlin whom I had the pleasure of meeting at the
Writers' Club and with whom I had a good talk – as also with Pablo
Neruda, Nazin Hikmet, Anna Seghers, and others.

I hope the delay in replying to the points re 'The Seamless Garment'[1] have not inconvenienced you.

Stanza 6, Line 6, – 'But you're owre thrang wi puirer to tak' tent o't' means you're too occupied with inferior matters to give due attention to that. Puirer, in this context, means inferior, or of less consequence.

Stanza 9, Line 4, – 'Your poo'ers a' delivery taught' means your powers all sufficiently instructed or developed as to become expert.

Coopers o' Stobo, re Lenin and Rilke, means prodigies or exceptional cases.

In haste. Looking forward to your anthology ere long now. Trust all O.K. with you – and with Mrs Young and the children. Valda joins me in kindest regards.

Yours,
Chris.

P.S. Michael[2] will, I expect be picked up by the police any time now and intends then to let matters take their course and serve whatever sentence he gets. There is no prospect of our being able to take a case to the Sheriff and the High Court on constitutional grounds, alas!

---

[1] 'The Seamless Garment' (311–4).
[2] Michael Grieve, the poet's son, who was imprisoned in June 1952 when the Edinburgh Appellate Tribunal rejected his application to be registered as a conscientious objector.

To Sorley MacLean

Sorley MacLean – who was born in Osgaig, Raasay, in 1911 – is widely recognised as the most gifted Gaelic poet of the twentieth century. After attending school at Portree he graduated from Edinburgh University in 1933 then returned to Skye to teach English. At university MacLean had read MacDiarmid's poetry in Scots and felt that '*A Drunk Man* probably influenced me more than the lyrics.' He met MacDiarmid in 1934 and the two poets became close friends and colleagues. MacLean helped MacDiarmid with his Gaelic translations of the poetry of Alexander MacDonald and Duncan Ban MacIntyre and in 1935 visited his friend on Whalsay shortly before MacDiarmid's breakdown that year.

Appalled by the tragic events in Spain, MacLean began work on his sequence *Dàin do Eimhir* (1943) in which an intense love affair is played out against the background of the Spanish Civil War. In 1940 MacLean joined the Signals Corps and was posted to Egypt; he was seriously injured in the Battle of El Alamein. After recovering MacLean taught in Edinburgh before taking up the headmastership of Plockton Secondary School, Wester Ross. When he retired in 1972 he settled in Peinnachorrain, Braes, Isle of Skye. MacDiarmid wrote (Company, p. 237) that 'There is no doubt that [Sorley MacLean] is one of the greatest poets Scottish Gaeldom has had, but his experiences during the Second World War in North Africa silenced him.' This was not in fact the case as was demonstrated by the appearance, in 1977, of *Spring Tide and Neap Tide: Selected Poems 1932–72*.

Whalsay.
5/6/40

My dear Sam,

I am sorry to have been so long in writing to you anent the typescript of your great poem.[1] You will understand that I am not in a letter-writing mood these days – too trapped under the Ossa-on-Pelion of current events and forebodings (not to mention immediate personal difficulties of all kinds). But equally you must understand that the arrival of your poem is a tremendous event in my life – and its dedication to me an honour equivalent to (and because of poetry and in respect of a contribution to *Scottish* Literature even greater and more brain-seizing) than Sorabji's dedication to me of his stupendous *Opus Clavicembalisticum*. Nevertheless you must let me write to you of it again – and not just now. You will see a little of what it means to me however in the enclosed essay, which will you please, after perusal, send to, along with the accompanying note to him, Johnston-Stewart[2] of the *New Alliance*. (Incidentally if you happen to be seeing him you might also before transmitting it to Johnston-Stewart give a read of it to Sydney Smith.) I don't expect Johnston-Stewart to use it: but I'll be able to place it elsewhere. And I have in mind one or two other shorter essays on your work and Hay's I intend to write and send to other quarters.

The poem I quote from in the essay I enclose also a typescript of to you which – since it is my only copy – you might please return to me later. It will also serve to give you some indications of how your work has excited and pleased me.

I do wish we could foregather. I realise in large measure the difficulties of Englishing your shorter poems: but I fancy that if we were together we might between us succeed in writing English lyrics

---

[1] The reference is to MacLean's long poem 'An Cuilithionn' (The Cuillin). It was conceived as 'a very long poem, 10,000 words or so, on the human condition, radiating from the history of Skye to the West Highlands to Europe and what I knew of the rest of the world.' In a letter of 18 October 1982 to the present editor MacLean explained why the poem was unfinished: 'I was on the point of getting it published in 1944 [when] the Polish business of that year shocked me terribly, and some of my perceptive friends condemned it. I do myself because, apart from my pre-1944 uncritical support of the Russian government, the symbolism of it is inadequate to the theme. Besides it was never really finished, but stopped abruptly by a personal tragedy I suffered in Dec. 1939.'

[2] In a letter of 18 October 1982 to the present editor Sorley MacLean writes: 'Johnstone-Stewart [was] a Galloway laird associated with [George] Scott Moncrieff in the *New Alliance*, and, as I remember, associated with the *Free Man*, a Scottish Nationalist then [and] a very likeable man.'

which would do a far greater measure of justice to them than these prose renderings. And it would be enormously worth it. Some of them are very great lyrics indeed.

I haven't heard further from the Hogarth Press people, but I will write you at once if the project goes ahead and arrange with you what of yours I'll include. We must get really good renderings of some of these lyrics; and I'd also use the Highland Woman I had in the *V of S*, and, I think, the Clio part from the big poem.[3] But we'll see shortly. You will understand how difficult it is to get things published just now – and with what infernal delays.

I am extremely sorry to hear of the death of your brother's wife[4] whom I have a happy recollection of meeting at Edinbane. Please give John my deepest sympathy in his terrible trial.

I hope you are in good form yourself, and liking your sojourn in the Borders. I haven't had a cheep from Davie[5] for ages.

I note what you say about the War but do not agree although the Germans are appalling enough and in a short-time view more murderously destructive, they cannot win – but the French and British bourgeoisie can, and is a far greater enemy. If the Germans win they could not hold their gain long – but if the French and British bourgeoisie win it will be infinitely more difficult to get rid of them later. That is my point of view.

I am sorry the raising of the reservation age ropes you in. Please keep in touch with me. I earnestly hope that you may yet be spared this terrible waste of your time (to say the least of it) but if not I will be glad to know your whereabouts as continuously as possible. Being marooned up here is bad enough for me as things are, but to have people like you and Hay[6] and others just vanish into the all-consuming maw and drag on indefinitely not knowing how and where you are would add terribly to the torment. I hope Calum[7] is still safe in Dublin.

[3] The first published version of 'Ban-Ghaidheal' (A Highland Woman), by MacLean, was published in 1938 in MacDiarmid's *The Voice of Scotland*. The poem was written on Mull. MacLean clarifies the reference to 'Clio' thus: 'The "Clio" part is from "The Cullin". There is a series of verse paragraphs, each beginning "I am the Clio of Scotland or Ireland or England or France or Italy, etc. etc."'

[4] MacLean writes: 'My eldest brother John, who died in 1970, was first married to Morag MacDonald [who] was an outstandingly beautiful woman. She died in late January or early February 1940. I took Chris and W. D. MacColl to Edinbane during their visit to Raasay and Skye in Sept. 1937, but I don't think Morag was at home them.'

[5] George Davie, author of *The Democratic Intellect* (1961); a philosopher and friend to both MacDiarmid and MacLean.

[6] The poet George Campbell Hay.

[7] MacLean's brother Calum, a Scottish Nationalist and opponent of the War, got a post-graduate scholarship to Ireland in 1939.

Valda, Mike, Dr Orr, and Grant Taylor join me in every kind regard. Please convey my best respects to your father and mother. I'll write you soon again.

Yours,
Chris.

P.S. I have Oliviera's book about Rilke's poetry; also a collection of R. F. C. Hull's translations (better than Leishman's, Sackville West's, etc.) and Rilke's own books in German. I'll send you any of these if you care.

Brownsbank,
Candymill,
by Biggar,
Lanarkshire.
23/1/77

Dear Sorley,

Many thanks for your letter. You have always been over-indulgent about my poetry and too modest about your own. There is, I think, no doubt about you and I being the two best poets in Scotland today, but it is all nonsense of course to go further than that. Poets cannot be put in a list with a betting figure attached to each. By definition every good poet does something that is sui generis – something that is his alone and couldn't be done by anyone else. Like can only be compared with like. Your work and mine is utterly different, so it is rubbish to say – or try to say – which of us is greater.

[. . .]

There is no question, I think, but that you'd have had much greater international recognition if you'd written in a language accessible to a greater readership. I have had certain advantages, i.e. in being more controversial, but all that amounts to is that a vast deal of claptrap has been and is being written about me. But only a tiny part of it is of real critical account at all. Already things seem to be piling up fearsomely for my 85th birthday next August. I know of 3 books about me due out before then. Eddie Morgan has done a comprehensive essay on all my poetry for the Writers and Their Work series published by Longman's for The British Council. Then there is Gordon Wright's illustrated biography, and Norman Wilson tells me he is including a book about me in the series about great Scots which already includes Knox, Hume, etc. But he does not tell me who has written it.[1]

And I understand that a full-dress Omnibus programme about me has been filmed by Granada TV for production on the great occasion.[2] I also know that my daughter Christine and all my Canadian grandchildren are proposing to come over for the event, and no doubt I'll be beset with hordes of other visitors. I really can't cope with it and wish I could go into hiding on some remote island.

I should have gone into hospital again on 15th inst, but we've been snowed up with all roads blocked. The lane from our cottage to the main road has just been cleared, so I hope to go in tomorrow. I also hope I won't need to be there long but it is impossible to tell. I think they'll decide I need to have another operation for rectal ulcer. Though I am very easily tired I am on the whole not too bad. Valda has been having the worst of it having to do all sorts of chores I'd normally be doing or helping with.

Hope you are in good fettle yourself, also Renee[3] and your family. Love to you all.

Yours,
Christopher Grieve.

Brownsbank,
by Biggar.
12/7/78

Dear Sorley,

I am sorry I've been unable to write you sooner to ask about your daughter. I don't hear well by 'phone, but I do hope your daughter's

---

[1] MacDiarmid is referring to Edwin Morgan's *Hugh MacDiarmid* (1976), Gordon Wright's *MacDiarmid: An Illustrated Biography* (1977) and *John Knox* (1976) – a book published by Norman Wilson's Ramsay Head Press and containing essays by a Roman Catholic (Anthony Ross), a Church of Scotland Minister (Campbell MacLean) and MacDiarmid.
[2] *The Hammer and Thistle* (1977), a film by Murray Grigor and Gus MacDonald.
[3] MacLean married Renee in 1946.

injury was not serious and has healed quickly.[1] It was a dreadful thing to happen.

The Dublin ceremony went off splendidly.[2] I was shaking in my shoes and afraid I might collapse at any moment. But the authorities were most understanding and had posted a stalwart 6-foot graduate at my elbow, alert to see I didn't stumble and giving me a helping hand whenever I had occasion to move.

Despite the flatteries of the Public Orator, I am afraid my fearful reputation is too well known. At any rate the Irish poets had taken flight. John Montague was away in Galway. Seamus Heaney had had to go off to Belfast early that morning, but sent me a nice letter explaining.

I kept a very low profile but tho' tired out enjoyed the occasion, as did Valda. Needless to say the kindness, courtesy, and helpfulness of the Irish left nothing to be desired. I've had to rest since I got home and have had a fearful lot of pain, but I do not think my going to Dublin tho' a great risk did me any real harm.

Yes, I got the card with the many signatures but most of them were unknown to me and I'd have been glad to have your comments on just who and what they are.

I hope you and Renee are none the worse of your Dutch and German travels and the terrible worry your daughter's accident must have been causing you.

Hope we may meet again somewhere ere too long. In the meantime thanks again for your kindness. Valda joins me in love and best wishes to you all.

Yours,
Christopher.

[1] MacLean's daughter Ishbel had fallen through a window but there were no permanent injuries.
[2] On 6 July 1978 MacDiarmid received his Honorary Litt.D. at Trinity College Dublin.

To Nancy Cunard

Nancy Cunard (1896–1965) was known as a minor poet and notorious for her major break with her mother Lady Emerald Cunard. One of the radical causes she pursued with devotion was the plight of the French People and in 1944 she edited, and published under the imprint La France Libre, the anthology *Poems for France*. MacDiarmid's contribution, 'The Fall of France' (1320–1) appears on pp. 75–6 where it is described as 'A portion of a long, unpublished poem'.

<table>
<tr><td>HRC</td><td>27 Arundel Drive,</td></tr>
<tr><td></td><td>Battlefield,</td></tr>
<tr><td></td><td>Glasgow, S.</td></tr>
<tr><td></td><td>5/12/43</td></tr>
</table>

Dear Miss Cunard,

Many thanks for your most kind note inviting me to submit a poem to you for the projected collection of poems on France. I am so sorry your initial letter to me miscarried – probably because I have had so many changes of address during the past couple of years. I am working as an engineer in a big munitions factory and the long hours, etc. do not leave much time to write, but I enclose an unpublished poem about France which I hope may suit your purpose. I will certainly look forward keenly to the book when it appears, and wish you the best of luck with it. May I add that I remember very well our meeting in London some years ago, and that I have continued to watch for and follow your own writings ever since. Please accept my comradely greetings and every cordial good wish for the success of this present project and for all your work.

Yours fraternally,
Hugh MacDiarmid.

P.S. I'm so sorry – I haven't a typewriter just now.

27 Arundel Drive,
Battlefield,
Glasgow, S.
21-3-44

Dear Miss Cunard,

Please excuse just the briefest note in reply to yours to hand tonight. You ask for a quick reply re the translation; and I haven't time for more than just that, tho' I fear I owed you a letter (before yours came today) since I haven't yet acknowledged your own poem, which I liked very much, or – what is more to the point – returned that typescript to you. I don't know if you expected me to do so; but I should have done so – and would now, but I've just had a hunt round and can't lay my hands on it at the moment. Which is an infernal nuisance. But I have literally no time to myself at all these days – working seven days a week from 7 a.m. to 6.30 p.m., and two nights to 9.30 and when I say working I mean it – real hard physical toil. So I have no time for anything at all save work, eat, and sleep. I'm not complaining – only explaining, why I can't keep track of things properly, reply in reasonable time to letters, etc. And of course one of these things I simply can't do is to keep abreast in reading. So I miss all sorts of things; and missed alas! Miss Warner's[1] review of *Lucky Poet* in *Our Time*. Many thanks for telling me about it. I'll try to get hold of a copy. Reviews I have seen have nearly all been terribly bad (I do not mean unfavourable – but incompetent, lying, and vindictive). However I have had heaps of letters, like your own, from all over the world expressing great appreciation of it. So much so, that I'd be all the better myself if I could have a good read of it again too on some such place as the top of Maiden Castle (which, incidentally, I do know – I've a great liking for Dorset and Somerset, Devon, and, of course, Cornwall). It is at any rate good news that the book has attracted Miss Warner's attention; I know her work – and Miss Ackland's[2] – and have a high regard for both of them. The book was selling well, but has been withheld from sale for a month or two, until my reference, on page 172, to Edgell Rickword[3] was altered to suit the representations of

---

[1] Sylvia Townsend Warner (1893–1978) reviewed *Lucky Poet* favourably in *Our Time*, Vol 3, No 7, February 1944.

[2] Valentine Ackland was Sylvia Townsend Warner's companion; the two women joined the Communist Party in 1935 and MacDiarmid was familiar with their political work as well as with Warner's writing.

[3] As printed in *Lucky Poet* (London 1943, p. 172) MacDiarmid's reference to the left-wing poet Edgell Rickword ends elliptically: 'Edgell Rickword is about the only person with some idea of Nationalism, but even he was in the Black-and-Tans ...'

his lawyers, who, however, don't seem to be satisfied yet, but are holding out for a sum of money by way of damages, plus substantial costs. However, the publishers think they'll be able to have it on sale again very soon now.

As to the translation, I am of course delighted that my poem should be one of those chosen – proud you're going to do the translating of it yourself – and quite agreeable in this matter to receiving no payment, of course.

I haven't a copy of my poem about the place either, it seems, and can't remember just how it ran – either in the form in which I sent it to you or in the abridged form you decided to use. But I have come across in one of my notebooks the following lines which I evidently thought ought to be inserted somewhere and which I now send you since you may think they will strengthen the poem – repeating as they do, with a closer application, the binnacle image with which the poem opens – this, however, is just a suggestion; I leave the matter to you entirely. Here they are, then.

> So I hold my faith in France today
> As a binnacle holds a ship's compass,
> Rocking under and around it, but holding it
> In miraculously isolated suspension.

Hope all goes well with you and your own. Please give my comradely greetings to Miss Warner and Miss Ackland too when you see them again. I'll be looking forward eagerly to the appearance of 'Poems for France'.

Yours fraternally,
Hugh MacDiarmid.

To Maurice Lindsay

Born in Glasgow in 1918, Maurice Lindsay has combined his prolific literary activities with a public career as a broadcaster, television personality and (from 1967 to 1983) Director of the Scottish Civic Trust. As editor of *Poetry Scotland* (1943–6) and author of *Hurlygush: Poems in Scots* (1948) he became one of the most prominent figures in the second wave of the Scottish Literary Renaissance. His admiration for MacDiarmid was expressed in the poem 'To Hugh Mac-Diarmid' from *The Enemies of Love* (1946):

> For you are not contained by the edge of an age,
> easing the sharp, contemporary itch
> with a trumped-up tag or a newly polished adage
> for the anxious eyes that stare at their own last ditch;
> but one who, on Time's only mountainside,
> searches the clouds for where the heavens divide.

Lindsay's forceful character insisted on a strongly independent point of view and in later years he and MacDiarmid were often at odds on crucial cultural issues. In the *Glasgow Bulletin* of 7 June 1952 Lindsay attacked a provocative speech MacDiarmid had made at a concert of works by F. G. Scott and Erik Chisholm at the Institute of Contemporary Arts in London; in *The Lowlands of Scotland: Glasgow and the North* (1953) Lindsay denounced MacDiarmid as 'a ranting politician'; in his collection *Snow Warning* (1962) Lindsay dismissed Lallans as an idiom entirely irrelevent to contemporary life; and in his anthology *Modern Scottish Poetry* (1976) Lindsay infuriated Mac-Diarmid by attributing the lyric 'The Little White Rose' (461) to Compton Mackenzie. Despite these basic differences there were interludes of friendship and co-operation; Lindsay clearly regarded MacDiarmid as a lost leader whose Communism had obliterated his lyric impulses while MacDiarmid recognised Lindsay as a formidable foe.

32 Victoria Crescent Road,
Glasgow W.2.
Thursday. [March 1949]

Dear Maurice,

Many thanks for your letter. There is nothing in this matter, of course, that should affect our personal friendship, which I too value highly. Nor did I think your remarks were directed against me. What I did think, wrongly it seems, was that they were directed against Blythman and Kincaid, and the linking of the Scottish Literary Revival with Communist propaganda as in the Maclean meeting, the Robeson reception, etc.[1] I did not remember about Hamish Henderson, though I agree he has been asking for retaliation on your part. What I really objected to was certain phrases – e.g. dishonest pseudo-criticism in the Russian manner. The fusion of political propaganda and literary criticism is by no means peculiar to the Soviet Union, and is not necessarily dishonest in any case. If we Communists make our political bias more obtrusive, that is more honest – the fact is that reactionaries are none the less pushing their propaganda just as persistently, if more insidiously, all the time. It is, for example, generally taken for granted that good poetry must be 'on the side of the angels' – to be anti-Christian is to be subversively propagandist, to be Christian is in the nature of things, and so on. My own view has not changed, save in detail in accordance with developing history, for many years; see *Albyn*, the General Strike passages in *A Drunk Man Looks at The Thistle*, the Hymns to Lenin, etc. I do not agree with you that there is less freedom of the artist in the Soviet Union than in Britain or the United States; only the incidence of lets and hindrances is different. Even in regard to music, I cannot agree that music has not political implications – even in this country (and rightly, I think, up to a point) there have been objections to the prevalence of jazz on the grounds of public health and morals; and I cannot for the life of me see that conscription for military and industrial purposes is acceptable and not intellectual and artistic conscription. We accept the principle ourselves in the compulsory educational system. That is directed to ends acceptable

---

[1] On 4 December 1948, the 25th anniversary of the death of the Scottish Republican leader John Maclean, a rally was held in St Andrew's Hall, Glasgow. Under the chairmanship of Hamish Henderson, MacDiarmid spoke on 'The Cultural Heritage of John Maclean' and poems were read by, among others, Maurice Blythman ('Thurso Berwick') and John Kincaid. Paul Robeson, the bass whose Communist sympathies curtailed his career in the USA, was well received when he visited Scotland.

619

to our own economic system – the Russians are equally entitled to mould their people to the requirements of their very different system. But there is no question of the reproduction here of the Russian state of affairs; we have a very different background and are at a very different stage of historical development; our application of Communism will differ accordingly from the Russian. I cannot, however, see that it is possible, let alone desirable, to keep our arts and our politics in water-tight compartments; and certainly the major danger to our arts now is not from the Communists, who are a small and largely a cultural minority, but from the forces of reaction which are, as in America, engaged in an incessant witch-hunt and eager, and able, to keep us under a statute of Mortmain. It is this equating of artistic values with the extent to which they are 'safe' to the existing order and to which they stuff themselves with religious, moral, social and other anachronisms of the most infantilist and vicious character than I am up against.

Above all, it must be insisted that a man who uses his literary gifts as a weapon in the social struggle and makes his means of artistic expression a vehicle for Communist propaganda, cannot be said to have no real concern for literature (Scottish or any other). These two things are not necessarily exclusive, and to suggest that they are implies the assumption that Communism in this respect is in a different case from Conservatism or any other brand of politics. And, of course, the pretence of being 'non-political' or 'above-politics' is the worst form of political partizanship.

I set out all these considerations simply because it is inevitable that this issue will become more and more important, and I want you to realise that I have chosen my side and am utterly and irrevocably opposed to Christianity, capitalism, and all the social *and artistic* forms these have produced or that are compatible with them. This must lead to a state of civil war – indeed, people of my point of view are already all but outlawed in this country and in the United States. I must exercise all the influence I possibly can, in my own writing and through all the organisations with which I am connected and all my personal contacts to press home my point of view and that is why I took the initiative in forming the Writers' Section of the Scottish-USSR Society and in helping with the Maclean and Robeson meetings. That is also why I have had to continue to dissociate myself from the Scottish PEN, the National Party of Scotland and other organisations. I am sure you will understand all this and forgive me for thinking it expedient to set it out here – very boringly, I am afraid. The matter will probably emerge in an acute way next year in connection with the International PEN Conference in Scotland – even to the extent of those of

620

us who are out-and-out pro-Russian and anti-Western-Union organising a separate demonstration in Edinburgh (or Glasgow); while internationally I am finding myself involved in a host of arrangements in which I will have no hesitation whatever in speaking for Scottish Literature in a Communist sense.

Well, well, I'll be seeing you again ere long, I hope. Kindest regards to Joyce[2] and yourself, in which Valda joins me.

Yours,
Chris.

EUL

Dungavel,
by Strathaven,
Lanarkshire.
14/5/50

Dear Maurice,

Many thanks for your letter. As editor[1] you are of course perfectly entitled to accept and reject as you think fit and I have no quarrel with you on that score. I have no use for other people's opinions on my work. Nearly all my books have been very adversely criticised — at first! My most successful book has been my *Lucky Poet* — successful, I mean, not only in sales but in the influence it has exercised on people's lives. I still get letters about it from all over the world, and have ample evidence of the effect it has had, is having, and is likely to continue to have. And I have no doubt whatever that in this and other respects the second volume will be even more successful. My article about 'Travels In The North' was an excerpt from this book. I have no doubt it reads better in its proper context than as a separate article. It may not be on my best level but all writers of any consequence are very unequal and the real question is not whether it is on my best level but whether it is on a level comparable with much that appears in the *Scots Review*. However that is a matter of opinion and you have every right to your own.

I quite agree that I am very conceited. We all are. By that I mean

[2] Joyce, Maurice Lindsay's wife.
[1] Maurice Lindsay took over the editorship of *The Scots Review* in May 1950; it ran for a further seventeen issues, the last one being dated September-October 1951.

every human being, and the more conceited the less one has to be conceited about. As to my suggestion that everyone in the Scottish Literary Movement is a place-seeking creature, except myself, I do not quite go so far as that: but I do know that I could always have made a lot of money if I had chosen to write the sort of thing all sorts of periodicals want – I have always refused to do anything of the sort. I have never written for a ready-made public or to evoke the most easily-evoked responses. I have always been utterly opposed to the fetishism of the capitalist system, which turns art, ideas, and everything into things to sell. But my suggestion springs from a deeper source – I believe that everyone who in any way acquiesces, fits into, 'succeeds' under the Capitalist system is a knave or fool or both.

I am very sorry indeed to hear that the *Scots Review* (like all other Scottish newspapers and periodicals) is to maintain an 'iron curtain' between its readers and the USSR and International Communism. Communists are to be attacked – but not allowed to defend themselves. It is a base and cowardly procedure, the only consolation being that the dialectic of history is such that in the long run this sort of attitude fosters instead of inhibits the development of Communism.

However I need not go any more fully into the matter here. My own attitude is precisely the opposite of yours. I certainly cannot contribute to – and must oppose by every means in my power – a Scottish periodical that takes up such a position. I regard the 'democratic system' in non-Communist countries as a monstrous fraud. Communism in my view is the only guarantee of individuality in the modern world and the USSR the only real democracy the world has yet seen,

I agree that it is not quite fair to you to complain that I am excluded from the *S.R.* because of poems I have never sent in. But what I really mean is that the poems I am now writing or likely to write in the future are – even where they are not explicitly on what you call Communist propaganda themes – so essentially and unmistakably Communist that if you saw most of them you could not (in your present attitude and policy) dream of publishing them, while if you didn't 'get' their implications it would certainly be unfair on my part to take advantage of that to smuggle into the *S.R.* pages matter so utterly incompatible with its policy.

I hope the BBC symposium on Friday[2] may allow certain things to

---

[2]'Scottish Poetry: A Symposium of Views by poets and critics', BBC Scottish Home Service, 2 June 1950. Both MacDiarmid and Lindsay took part.

be said which in my view at any rate will redeem the thing from the –
as I agree – usual feebleness and futility of such occasions.

Love to you all,

Yours,
Chris.

You complained some time ago of Hamish Henderson's criticisms of
your own work as judging it from a Communist point of view: but the
S.R. policy now is just the same sort of thing – no matter how well
written, how penetrating and timely, no article is to be admitted if it
favours the Communist side!

EUL

Dungavel,
by Strathaven.
5/8/50

Dear Maurice,

Many thanks for your letter and copy of July *Scots Review*. I think
you must be right about the poem – i.e. Rilke, not George – but have
no means of checking here.[1] I have only the Duineser Elegies of Rilke
by me – none of Leishman's translations – and none of Stefan
George's stuff. I made translations of quite a lot of the latter in the
Shetlands but have not been able to lay my hands on these again.
The copy I found of this one was clearly marked 'From Stefan
George' but that may have been an error too, as I was dealing with a
lot of Rilke's stuff at the same time. Nor does my recollection of the
originals help; I never had anything of a verbal memory.

I've been meaning to write you for a good while about your
Wood's Edge book.[2] Yes, I think quite a few of the Scots poems show
a definite advance and I feel that you have opened up a line for
yourself in this along which you may go a long way. I may be wrong
but I think you are more likely to achieve really distinctive work in

---

[1] Lindsay pointed out that MacDiarmid's 'You Know Not Who I Am' (22) was
not 'After the German of Stefan George' but after Rilke. In fact the original is by
George.
[2] Maurice Lindsay, *At the Wood's Edge* (1950).

Scots than in English. If I had to make any criticism of your book, indeed, it would be that you should be warier in regard to what you publish in volume form, since several of the English pieces are markedly very much inferior whereas several of the Scots pieces raise the level of the collection quite a lot.

Excuse this brief note. We're still unsuccessfully house-hunting and haven't long to do it in – since we're to be in Edinburgh by the 18th and, in addition to securing a house by then and if possible effecting our actual removal, I am up to the eyebrows in accumulations of papers and books which I must pack so as to have them readily accessible again.

Love to you all.

Yours,
Chris.

P.S. Can you tell me what the position is now re my Saltire *Dunbar*[3] selection of which I have never heard another word?

EUL

Brownsbank,
Candymill,
Biggar.
21/10/64

Dear Maurice,

Many thanks for *One Later Day*.[1] I have read the poems again and that confirms my belief that this is one of your best books and opens up a distinctive line along which you will reap further rich harvests. In short, the remarks quoted on the over-turn of the jacket from Daiches and Alvarez hit the mark. I'll watch for reviews and wish the book the good luck it deserves. And thanks again for the dedication which I appreciate greatly.

If I have been a little long in writing you, you'll understand I've been away in Kinross and West Perthshire. We had a very strenuous

[3]Lindsay, as general editor of the Saltire Society series of Saltire Classics, made some cuts in MacDiarmid's introduction to his edition of *Selections from the Poems of William Dunbar* (Edinburgh 1952).
[1]Maurice Lindsay, *One Later Day* (1964).

campaign.[2] If this was not reflected in the vote, we didn't expect it to be. In fact we polled a good deal better than we anticipated in such a feudal (and enormous – 8,000 square miles) constituency at the first time a Communist candidate had stood. But votes were not the real object of the exercise. That was to achieve the maximum of world-wide publicity and we achieved that all right. No other candidate of any party had anything like it, and that of course accrues to the prestige and influence of the party. We can now set up a good branch in the constituency too and build on that for next time. It was all great fun but terribly exhausting. Incidentally – if we were denied our own TV and Radio appearances – we had French National Television and Belgian Television interviewing me and televising several of our meetings.

As I've just said I'm extremely tired, but there's no rest for the wicked and I'm just entering now on an exceptionally busy spell with debates and/or lectures and/or poetry readings at Oxford, Aberystwyth, Edinburgh, Glasgow, St Andrews etc. The Oxford thing is a Union debate in which I'm seconded by Professor Isaiah Berlin, and my opponent is Humphrey Berkeley MP whose seconder I don't know yet. Heaven help me!

I expect you've flitted from Annan now and hope you're liking your new abode (tho' not I imagine without some regret for that splendid house you had at Annan).

Kindest regards to Joyce and your daughters and yourself from Valda and I.

Yours,
Chris.

[2]In the General Election of 15 October 1964 MacDiarmid contested the Kinross and West Perthshire constituency for the Communist Party: the result was Sir Alec Douglas-Home (Con), 16,659; A. Forrester (Lab), 4,687; A. Donaldson (Scot. Nat.), 3,522; C. M. Grieve (Comm.) 127.

NLS   Brownsbank,
                                                             Biggar.
                                                            11/12/64

Dear Maurice,

   Our cottage is between 3 and 4 miles from Biggar on the Edinburgh road.[1] After leaving Biggar there is (on your right, going
towards Edinburgh) only one little collection of county council
houses, and an old ruined mill. That is Candymill. As you pass the
last house the Edinburgh road swings round – a blind corner – but in
a straight line with the road you've come is a farm road going uphill
to our cottage – a very short distance. Ours is the first, and only,
cottage you come to. I trust this is clear enough, but, if not, anyone in
the Candymill houses will direct you.
   Looking forward to seeing you.
   All the best,

                              Yours,
                              Chris.

NLS   Brownsbank,
                                                             Biggar.
                                                            12/4/65

Dear Maurice,

   Glad to have your letter. I'd been wondering about the film. I note
you say October for putting it on. I'd been afraid I might miss it if it
were earlier, as I am going to East Germany next month and then to
Cuba. As to your coming up with still camera man I don't know
what you want to do, i.e. whether you need me here. If so, it may be
difficult to fix a date when I'm not away. Valda will of course be here
and delighted to give any facility needed – unless later on she is away
in Cornwall.

[1] Lindsay came out to see MacDiarmid to discuss the Border TV film *Rebel With a
Cause* (1964). At the time Lindsay was Programme Controller of Border Television.

I'd heard about the expanded Faber anthology.[1] Good. The trouble with Macmillan so far as I am concerned (apart from the fact that they take an unconscionable time to answer correspondence and agree to anything) is that I get little or nothing out of it. They get the fees, and in due course my share will figure in their statements to me. For this reason I have asked other recent anthologists not to select anything that appears in my *Collected Poems*, but to use instead poems which don't or, if they have the necessary space, longer poems represented in the *Collected Poems* only by short extracts. One such Anthology[2] has just agreed to use in full 'On A Raised Beach' which I regard as one of my best poems. The Anthologist in question had not seen that poem but on doing so not only hailed the chance of using it but came to the conclusion that it would prove to be the best poem in the book.

Macmillan's have now agreed terms with Tom Scott for his Oxford University Press anthology. But it is a big selection and has cost plenty – of which I'll only ultimately get a small proportion. So I am feeling disgruntled about that.

As to the titles you list my feeling is that they do not represent my work – they only represent my poetry as it was 30 to 40 years ago. Apart from 'A Glass of Pure Water' and 'The Eemis Stane' I really feel they do not do me justice. I would have suggested instead – if longer poems are ruled out – 'Prayer For a Second Flood' from *1st Hymn to Lenin and Other Poems*, and two of the three poems quoted in a recent centre page article on me in the *Times Literary Supplement* (leaving out of course the poem 'Perfect' about which as you will know there has been controversy on copyright grounds). Poems not in *Collected Poems* are my copyright and for them I would of course receive the fees.

There has been a change recently in the person to write to on such matters at Macmillan's: but if you write to Trade Editor, c/o Messrs Macmillan's, New York, that will be O.K.

I had heard with delight about the EUP *Poetry Scotland*[3] and will of course be glad to send stuff when I know the date by which you should receive it. There is one thing however about which I must be absolutely frank. I deplore Edwin Morgan's association with you and George Bruce in the editorship. Morgan's prominence in connection with 'Concrete Poetry' and with Ian Hamilton Finlay

[1] The second edition of Lindsay's anthology *Modern Scottish Poetry: An Anthology of the Scottish Renaissance* (1966).
[2] 'On a Raised Beach' (422-33) was included in David Wright's anthology *Longer Contemporary Poems* (1965).
[3] *Scottish Poetry*, (1966–76) an Edinburgh University Press poetry annual edited by Maurice Lindsay, George Bruce, Edwin Morgan and others at various times.

rules him out completely as far as I am concerned. I will not agree to work of mine appearing in any anthology or periodical that uses rubbish of that sort, which I regard as an utter debasement of standards but also as a very serious matter involving the very identity of poetry. These spatial arrangements of isolated letters and geometrically placed phrases, etc. has nothing whatever to do with poetry – any more than mud pies can be called a form of architecture. And I feel so strongly about the need to fight this sort of thing *a l'outrance* that I, and I am happy to say several other poets, have refused to allow any poems of ours to appear in the Oxford anthology if stuff of that sort by Morgan or Finlay or anybody else is to be included.

I had thought I might have heard from you by now too about your projected comprehensive *Selected Poems*[4] you wrote me about months ago.

Hope you are in good form and everything going well. Kindest regards to Joyce and your daughters.

All the best.

Yours,
Chris.

---

[4]Lindsay's *Selected Poems* appeared in 1973, his *Collected Poems* in 1979.

To John Laidlaw

John Laidlaw (1873–1964) was the poet's cousin. He worked as a printer in Langholm.

32 Victoria Crescent Rd.,
Glasgow W.2.
11/6/49

Dear John,

I've just had a note from John Ritchie of *The Glasgow Herald* telling me he's seen in this week's *E & L* that Bob died suddenly on 3rd inst.[1] I am very sorry to hear this. He looked so well when I saw him at the Common-Riding last year. I was sorry he felt that what I had said about T. S. Cairncross in *Lucky Poet* precluded our being friends.[2] I had seen nothing of him for many years as you know, but he and I had been so friendly in my early teens and I owed so much to him then – teaching me shorthand and lending me literary papers and books and talking with me on all sorts of subjects I was interested in.

---

[1] John Ritchie was, like MacDiarmid, a Langholmite; Bob Laidlaw (1882–1949) was John Laidlaw's brother. As a young man Bob Laidlaw had an office job, hence MacDiarmid's reference to shorthand. He later became a shoe repairer and retailer. The E & L is the *Eskdale and Liddesdale Advertiser*, the local paper.

[2] After acknowledging that the Rev. T. S. Cairncross encouraged him as a youth in Langholm, MacDiarmid says '[Cairncross] subsequently ceased to be friendly with me because he was of fastidious upper-class temper, while my work from the beginning was Socialistic and anti-Christian, so that any association with it was likely to compromise his chances of ministerial promotion and the degree of DD, while the fact that from the very outset my work attracted far more attention, and in important quarters at that, than his had ever done, chagrined him sorely and, on the part of a working-man's son, affected him as a piece of intolerable presumption' (LP, p. 222).

Please accept for yourselves – and convey to Janet, Maggie and the others when you see them – my sympathy in this bereavement. Also Alice to whom I feel in the circumstances I cannot write direct, and Nan, whom of course I have never met. I hope you are all well.[3]

I think Ritchie is going to write a short appreciation of Bob for the *E & L* and I'll see that in due course.

I hope I may be in Langholm for the Common Riding, and Valda and Michael will probably be with me. But it is a little early to know definitely yet. Besides we are flitting – that is to say, when we get a new house, which is no easy matter. As matters stand we're half packed up to move which is a nuisance as it means half my books and papers are not available to me, which makes things difficult as I am desperately busy.

We are, however, all in good form and trust this finds Maggie and yourself in like case.

> Love to you all,
> Yours,
> Chris.

> Brownsbank,
> Candymill,
> by Biggar,
> Lanarkshire.
> 10/7/57

Dear Cousin John,

I've been inundated with congratulatory letters of all sorts, of course, but none I was more pleased to get than yours. The statement in the Hickey paragraph[1] was apocryphal – I did not make it, but I might well have done. Honoured and humble was exactly how I felt, 'humble' in this context meaning conscious of how

---

[3] Janet and Maggie, Bob Laidlaw's sisters; Alice, Bob Laidlaw's wife and sister-in-law of Rev T. S. Cairncross.

[1] The William Hickey column, in *The Scottish Daily Express*, 6 July 1957, noted 'Christopher Murray Grieve (Hugh MacDiarmid, the poet) was capped as Hon. Doctor of Laws of Edinburgh University yesterday ... Said Grieve later: "I feel honoured and humble..."'

much more I want to do and of the fact that it does not become easier as one gets older. However we'll see. I have a lot more books on the stocks.

But I have a host of claims on my time in addition to my own writing. As you probably know I only got back from China two or three weeks ago. I was over a month in China, flying there by way of Belgium, Czechoslovakia, and Russia. It was a wonderful experience. China is an enormous country but I managed to cover a great part of it, by 'plane, train, and boat. I lectured in Peking and Nanking Universities and gave poetry readings and/or had conferences with writers' groups in half-a-dozen other cities. Nanking University wants me to go back for six months next year to lecture on literature. Application for me has been made to the Higher Education Authority in China and if it is approved, and the invitation comes through officially, I will accept and take Valda with me. Nanking is a very lovely city in the subtropical South-West of China.

In the meantime I have my usual writers' course of lectures to give in Edinburgh for the Workers' Educational Association, and in October I've also to give a set of lectures in South Wales.

So I am kept busy enough. Happily like you I keep in good health. I was glad to hear you were keeping so nicely and wouldn't mind if I could stand just far enough behind you not to cast my shadow on the water, and watch you having that cast you speak of. I knew you were over 80, but had not remembered Janet[2] was older than you. Fancy her being 89 this year. If you remember please send me a note of the date and of her address and I'll send her a greetings telegram when the time comes. Accept now for yourself my congratulations and best wishes, and may the occasion still have many happy returns.

My life has been in many ways a chequered and difficult one, and I am well aware that many features in it are apt to be misunderstood and disapproved. But, as you say, while I don't think they'd ever have understood the course I have taken, I think this Edinburgh degree business would have pleased my father and mother if they'd been alive. And I'd have been particularly pleased if your Maggie[3] had lived to see it. I know she always hoped great things from me.

Valda enjoyed the Edinburgh doings greatly, and so did Michael, who has been doing very well as a journalist and is now deputy chief-sub, on the Glasgow *Daily Record*.

Please give my kindest remembrances to all the clan as and when you see them. It is a long time since I had any Langholm news before

---

[2] Janet was John Laidlaw's sister.
[3] Maggie was John Laidlaw's wife.

your letter, tho' I had a short note from Joan Wilson,[4] the teacher, a few days ago. But there was little news in it. Michael saw J. M. Ritchie[5] of *The Glasgow Herald* the other week and Ritchie was asking if I wouldn't be down for the Common-riding. I wish I could, but I have far too many engagements looming ahead and many of them I have to prepare speeches for. So I decided I couldn't manage this year yet.

Talking of the broadcast about me, we're having another one on 17th inst. for F. G. Scott, in which I am taking part.[6] Whatever Langholm may think of me, at least Langholm folks should be proud of the fact that three out of the five in this new series 'Men of Mark' on the Scottish Home Service have a Langholm connection – Scott, Thomas Telford, and myself. Not bad for one wee Border burgh.

Valda and Michael join me in every kindest regard to you, and all the other members of the clan.

Yours,
Chris.

---

[4] Joan Wilson, MacDiarmid's contemporary, became a primary teacher at Langholm Academy.

[5] J. M. Ritchie, a journalist from Langholm.

[6] 'The Indivisible Man', a radio portrait of MacDiarmid introduced by Norman MacCaig, was the first of five programmes on 'Scottish men of stature'. The series was broadcast as follows: C. M. Grieve (3 July 1957), Francis George Scott (17 July 1957), Thomas Telford (6 August 1957), Very Rev R. F. V. Scott (25 August 1957), Lord Cooper (25 September 1957).

To Sean O'Casey

MacDiarmid's admiration for the great Irish dramatist Sean O'Casey (1880–1964) was reciprocated warmly. *Sunset and Evening Star* (1954), the sixth and final volume of O'Casey's autobiography, is dedicated 'To My dear Friend Hugh MacDiarmid/Alba's Poet and one of Alba's first men' and in the narrative O'Casey writes (Pan edtn 1980, pp. 528–9):

> His mind was vexed and wonderful with the thoughts of a poet, Hugh MacDiarmid, set down in *To Circumjack Cencrastus* and his *A Drunk Man Looks at the Thistle*, books of new thought, daring, and lyrical with fine songs. Lord God, this fellow is a poet, singing a song even when pain seizes him, or the woe of the world murmurs in his heart. Evidently a scholar, too, knowing Latin and languages, with philosophies from Christ's to that of Nietzsche housed comfortably in his head. He wrote in the Scottish manner, adding riches to the rich music of the Lallans. His verse tore along like a flood through a gorge, bubble, foam and spray flying from the deep rushing stream.

There was, however, a personal issue that kept the two men apart for some years. MacDiarmid's first wife Peggy Skinner left the poet in 1930 to go and live with Billy McElroy, a London coal-merchant and friend of various artists including O'Casey. He was, moreover, O'Casey's best men at his marriage to Eileen Casey in 1927; the financial backer of the first London production of *Juno and the Paycock*; and the original of Poges in *Purple Dust*. In a letter, of 3 June 1983 to the present editor, Eileen O'Casey wrote:

> [Shortly] before I was married, Billy McElroy, Augustus John, and Sean used to be about together. I saw a great deal of Billy after we were married. I also met MacDiarmid and his wife Peggy who came to see us once or twice when we lived in St John's Wood; and I met Peggy after she had left MacDiarmid and was with McElroy only about once as I was working on the stage. Billy McElroy was a coal merchant, a Scotsman, and great company; the friendship between him and Sean petered out in Sean's later years.

In a letter published in David Krause's *The Letters of Sean O'Casey* (New York 1980, Vol 2, p. 161) O'Casey writes to Leslie Daiken on 10 February 1944:

> I'm not conscious of ever having done anything to hurt Hugh MacDiarmid. He went through a hell of a time when I knew him – I saw him but once – we went with some friends to a Revue in Chelsea Palace. I thought him a grand fellow. He was in great poverty at the time – I was a little better myself. His wife (Peggy Skinner) left him & went away with another. A long time after he wrote to me from the Shetlands saying he had another woman [Valda Trevlyn] whom he loved, & who loved him; but his mind was on the bairns, & asked me if I thought he should leave the woman he was with, & go back to the first wife. I didn't answer the letter, for I knew this was not for me to say. That he, & he alone, must decide such a question. And that is the one and only injustice I did to Hugh.

When MacDiarmid wrote to O'Casey on 6 October 1949 – see p. 635 – O'Casey (9 October 1949) replied clarifying the situation with reference to McElroy:

> When I came first to England, I was just a gaum, having practically no experience; possessed only of an honesty I thought all had as well as myself. McElroy was, I knew, something of a business rascal, but he was a character, and, in my mind then, a friend to artists. I thought he was standing me by you through Peggy, & he gave me his word of honour that this was all he had in mind. It was long after, through conversations with his son that I discovered what an untrustworthy man he was. I for a long time was sure he'd never do anything mean or underhand to an artist. I was just a gaum.
>
> I honestly don't remember receiving a letter from you asking me to try to get you in touch with your children. What I do recollect is that you asked my advice about a young lass of Shetland; whether you would or would not hold her fast, seeing you were anxious about your children, & still had a gradh for Peggy ... As far as I know, McElroy is still alive & kicking ...McElroy was the most egoistic & selfish mortal that ever crossed my path.

Dear Sean O'Casey,

I have been meaning to write you ever since Hamish Henderson showed me letters of yours with regard to the next issue of my quarterly, *The Voice of Scotland* which is to be an Irish number with poems, etc. by a round dozen of younger Irish writers. I was greatly moved by your kind references to myself, and above all by what you said about understanding that I had some grievance about you.

That is not the case at all. I have always regarded my meeting with you as one of the red letter days of my life, and only been sorry not to have had further opportunities of meeting you. I have followed with joy all you have written and been glad to find you and I were on the same side – e.g. on the British Peace Committee. I have been doing a great deal in Scotland in that connection, speaking alongside the Dean of Canterbury, Paul Robeson, John Platts Mills, and others all over the country, and now I am wondering if you are going to be at the Conference in London on 22nd and 23rd inst, as I am coming down for it.

Amongst other things, as you probably know, I am a Director of Theatre Workshop Ltd, which I regard as one of the best experimental theatres in the English speaking world and which as you probably know has had a great success in Czecho-Slovakia, Poland, etc. I was through in Edinburgh at the Festival time and saw Theatre Workshop's wonderful production of Ewan MacColl's great play, *The Other Animals*. While I was there both MacColl and the producer, Joan Littlewood, told me of their great wish to produce your *Cock-a-Doodle-Dandy* and their disappointment that you had been unable to allow them to do this. They asked me if I would write you and see if this could not possibly be arranged yet. I agreed to do so, while pointing out that I had no special influence with you and that in any case I did not know the grounds of your refusal – e.g. you might be already committed to others by contract precluding any arrangement with Theatre Workshop, and besides there were financial and other considerations, so all I could do would be to urge you to give any further consideration to the matter you possibly could, and that is what I am venturing to do now on the grounds that Theatre Workshop deserves any support you can possibly give it and that if permitted to put on your play would certainly make a superb job of it – a better production, in deeper sympathy with your own genius, than any other company I know of either in this country or in America. However, all I can do is simply to say that and leave the matter there.[1]

As to the alleged and non-existent grievance against you, the only thing to which this can possibly refer is the fact that fifteen years ago or thereabouts I wrote you, pointing out that since before my divorce I had never been allowed to see or hear from or (hardly at all – and not for years now) hear about my children, Christine and Walter, and I had asked in that letter if you could not possibly, if still in touch with them, have a word with McElroy or Peggy and see if they would not let me see them occasionally – as, of course, the Court would have allowed me to do if I had had the money to take legal action to that effect. I had no reply to that letter. You may not have received it; or you may have thought, it was not a matter with regard to which you could do anything or I had any right at all to approach you. I wondered if you had had my letter and I was very disappointed not to receive any reply: but there was never any question of my having a grievance against you or feeling that I had had the slightest right to expect you to intervene on my behalf in such a matter in any way.

As things stand, I know nothing whatever about the children; have heard nothing about Peggy for 14 or 15 years; and do not know whether McElroy is still alive or not.

I hope you are in good form and better health and that your family are all well and happy. I read your *Inishfallen Fare Thee Well* with intense appreciation – a joy in your creative genius and, simultaneously a sharing of the agony which underlay so much of the narrative, that together made the reading for me one of the few major experiences any contemporary writing has given me.

Please accept my best wishes, and every fraternal greeting.

Yours,
C. M. Grieve.

[1] O'Casey replied on 23 October 1949 explaining that he'd already secured an American production of the play and that the producer had an option on a British production.

Dungavel,
by Strathaven,
Lanarkshire.
20-12-49

Dear Sean,

Many thanks for your two kind letters. I am extremely sorry to hear you are so unwell. I ought to have written you in reply ere this, but as you will see by the change of address I have flitted; also I have been desperately busy, addressing meetings all over the country – first of all with Alexei Surkov and Pavlo Tychina, the Russian poets, and then with Professor J. D. Bernal. You will have noticed too that the Scottish Movement has taken a great leap forward. The National Covenant calling for a Scottish Parliament has already over $\frac{1}{2}$ million signatures and there is no doubt it will secure the target of 2 million by February. This development – tho' only a beginning, since the Covenant itself is only the thin end of the wedge – is involving an infinite amount of work. However I like such work and am in splendid form.

I don't know if you'll have seen enclosed book; it's the latest volume of verse I've put out. But the CP are now going to publish my *Hymns to Lenin* and other Communist poems.[1]

Excuse this brief note, just to wish all of you the season's greetings. I'll write you soon.

Yours,
Chris

Brownbank,
by Biggar,
Lanarkshire.
12/9/52

My dear Sean O'Casey,

I cannot tell you how proud I was to receive your letter. As always, of course, it praises my poems far beyond their due, but I am at least

[1] This project never materialised.

glad that you should feel that way about them. I am enclosing a small pamphlet,[1] recently published, which at any rate, I think, accurately describes the spirit that animates me.

I would have replied immediately to your most welcome letter, but as you no doubt saw from the *Daily Worker* I have been up to my eyebrows in the work of the People's Festival in Edinburgh. I only got back home a couple of days ago, after a spell of lectures, poetry readings, and other functions, held in honour of my 60th birthday, which, nevertheless, proved just a little bit too strenuous for a man of my years.

It is good to be back for an interlude of quiet again to this little hill-farm cottage of mine and to my garden, now sadly dishevelled by the autumn winds, but still amazingly attractive with its profusion of giant marguerites, hollyhocks, and red and yellow nasturtiums.

Not that I'll get long here. I'm off again on 22nd inst. to Falkirk and Grangemouth to talk to the Labour League of Youth about 'Poetry as a Political Force' and then for the three days beginning 27th inst. I have to take part in a Youth Festival at Clydebank.

But I keep fine and fit and in excellent voice, and as I go about in my red kilt I find it difficult to realise that I am really 60.

Amongst the men of whom I have seen a great deal recently was the Africaans poet and dramatist, Uys Krige a tremendous admirer of yours and anxious if he can manage it to meet you. I gave him your address and promised I would write you by way of introducing him; and he said he would run down from London to see you if he possibly could. I hope he can. You will find him a most delightful fellow – a splendid poet and folk-singer and constitutionally incapable of being on the wrong side in anything. Although he is acknowledged to be the leading Africaans poet and can attract a popular audience anywhere in South Africa, he is *non persona grata* with the Malan people, of course.

My constant absences from home entail, amongst other things, difficulty in keeping abreast of my reading and I haven't yet got hold of your latest volume of reminiscences but I have read many excellent reviews of it and have it on order. So I am looking forward to another of the great treats you have given me four times before with this series. I hope it is selling well.

This brief note carries with it my love and every good wish to your wife and family and yourself. I do hope we can meet again some day ere too long and have a real crack together.

Ever yours,
C. M. Grieve.

[1] Hugh MacDiarmid, *Cunninghame Graham: A Centenary Study* (Glasgow 1952).

P.S. There are one or two small misprints in this pamphlet but you will spot these for yourself.

Brownsbank,
By Biggar,
Lanarkshire.
17/11/54

Dear Sean,

How can I thank you for the dedication of *Sunset and Evening Star* – and for all you said in it about me, and for the copy of the book itself with your holograph on the flyleaf? I am immensely proud of it – and a little ashamed, becasue I do not really deserve it.

Save in one respect. My regard for you. I know no other man I feel so close to. There is scarcely anything you say in the book that is not just my own opinion and in my own spirit too – if only I'd had anything like your genius of expression. I've seen the *Times Literary Supplement* review – and Worsley's[1] in the *New Statesman* – and your brief letter in reply to the latter. These homunculi are multiplying and practically monopolise the literary field now in all the so-called 'free nations of the West'. I think we are bound to go right down. You are the only survivor now in English Literature of a breed that produced many great figures in the past – but yields hardly the veriest midget of a throw-back now.

Congratulations anyhow on this magnificent completion of a series of books against which the gutlessness of all else that is being produced in England today can be measured. I have read and re-read it with immense appreciation, much laughter, and pride, and I will often turn to it again when I feel in need of reassurance that our portion of the human race once produced a real man or two, and the English language can still even in these diminished and dubious days furnish a medium for passionate and worth-while expression.

I am not endowed with your energy and staying power. A great deal of my time and strength is taken up with public speaking all over Scotland – I have about thirty addresses in my diary now to give before the end of January – to Workers Educational Association, CP

---

[1] T. C. Worsley, the literary journalist.

Branches, Scottish USSR Society, and other organisations. The Connolly Association too! Yet I do manage to keep on writing too. My huge poem, *In Memoriam James Joyce*, which runs to over 6,000 lines, should be out before the end of the year, and I will send you a copy. It is in English (and other languages), but I am getting back to Scots – I feel that this long detour has been necessary to me – and with a little luck in the course of the next few months I hope to have another volume to form a companion to *A Drunk Man Looks At The Thistle*.

I hope you, and Eileen, and your family are all well and liking your new home. (I have mislaid the address so I am sending this c/o your publishers.) I heard some time ago that you had had a poisoned hand and trust you have completely recovered from anything of the kind.

We are all well here. My son Michael is a journalist in Alloa and doing very well. Valda joins me in all love to Eileen and yourself and your family.

Ever yours,
Chris.

To Jean White

Jean White is the daughter of MacDiarmid's cousin Maggie Laidlaw although the poet always referred to Jean as his cousin. She joined her father's watchmaking and jewellery business, in Langholm, in 1946. From 1950 to 1960 and 1963 to 1975 she served as a non-political member of Langholm Town Council.

Dungavel,
by Strathaven,
Lanarkshire.
27/7/50

Dear Jean,

Glad to hear from you. I had never learned what had happened at the Municipal Election time at Langholm but am delighted to hear that you got in without a contest. A good deal of Council business is 'gey dreich', no doubt, but you never know when a burning issue may emerge. The reporting of speeches certainly leaves a great deal to be desired often enough and with the increasing shortage and curtailment of space this is not likely to improve in the near future.

I had no hesitation in accepting the Civil List Pension since it was given for literary – and not political – reasons only, carries no strings with it, and was given despite the knowledge that I am an out-and-out Republican and entirely opposed to the present Government. I knew nothing about it until I had a letter from the Prime Minister saying that he had had a letter signed by many leading writers urging him to recommend it to the King and that he was prepared to do so. While it is nominally a Royal Pension, it is actually nothing of the kind. It comes out of a Government Fund and recipients are recommended by the Prime Ministers on the basis of representations received. The King has no option save to endorse what the Prime Minister recommends.

Yes. It is a nuisance having to flit — and houses are appallingly difficult to get. So far we have not been able to secure one, but we must be out of here by the end of August. This place suited us extremely well and I have been very busy. I have several big books in hand and to have to pack up all my stuff and get installed somewhere else means an indefinite delay before I can get down to the work again. However we've had a splendid year here and knew when we came that we could have no security of tenure. In fact, we've been here nearly twice as long as we originally expected. Valda, who loves the country, has been happier here than anywhere else we have lived during the past twenty years, and in splendid form as a consequence.

I wrote to the Buck and Eskdale Temperance,[1] but could not get rooms. Even so, we would have come down for the Common-Riding and stayed in Carlisle overnight, but as matters stand, since we are already beginning to pack up, we have decided not to do so. All of us — Valda, Michael, and myself — will be in Edinburgh for a fortnight at the end of August for the International PEN Congress.

I am very sorry to hear that 'Maggie John',[2] as we called her when boys, has been ill. I'll drop John a line.

Every kind regard to all of you from all here.

Yours,
Chris.

P.S. If Jim[3] turns up, please remember me with kindest regards to him and his wife and family (as also, of course, to Willie[4] and his wife). I was down lecturing some time ago in the University of Wales at Aberystwyth and also in Manchester University, and spent some time in Manchester and Birmingham. I had thought of popping over to Sheffield and looking Jim up — also reviving old Sheffield acquaintances of my own, since I spent a year in barracks there at the

[1] A hotel in Langholm. In 'Water of Life' (314–19) MacDiarmid writes:
    The Buck and Croon Hotels — guid judges baith
    O' credibility I've cause to ken;
    A wee hauf wi' the emphasis on the wee,
    And day and daily d'they no' see again
    A miracle clean-flypit, in the maitter
        O' wine turn't back to water?
[2] Maggie John was the wife of MacDiarmid's cousin John Laidlaw.
[3] Jim White, Jean's brother, was Professor of Ceramic Technology at Sheffield University and retired in 1978.
[4] Willie White, Jean's brother, was a bank manager who died in 1972.

beginning of World War I. But I had to change my plans and come back here sooner than I had intended.

Brownsbank,
Biggar,
18/12/61

Dear Jean,

It seems a very long time since the Common-Riding. I had meant to write you long before this, but we've had an immense upheaval here. This has been the modernisation of this cottage with the introduction of electric light, etc., piped water supply, the building of a kitchenette, bathroom, flush lavatory, etc. I was assured the whole thing would be done in three weeks – actually it has taken about four months. With all my books, papers, etc. having to be moved, I still don't know where anything is – at least I haven't got them into working order yet. All this happened too when I was having an extremely busy time – addressing meetings all over the place, and correcting the proofs of my forthcoming books – all of which are now overdue for one reason or another, but will be out soon.

I hope all's been well in interval with your mother and yourself. I'm writing this mail also to John Laidlaw.

I expect Valda and I will be in Langholm about 23rd February for a wedding. The bridegroom is the son of neighbours of ours here;[1] the bride's name is Warbeck and she belongs to Chapelknowe, near Langholm. Our party is coming by 'bus. I don't suppose we'll be long in Langholm but we may, I hope, get a glimpse of you.

All the best to you and your mother, and all friends, for a happy Christmas and a good New Year.

Yours,
Chris.

[1] The bridegroom was related to Valda Grieve's neighbour and domestic help, Mrs Jackson.

Brownsbank,
Biggar,
Lanarkshire.
15/12/65

Dear Jean,

It seems a very long time since we had any news of you. Hope you
are O.K.; also Jim and Willie and their households.

Valda and I are in good fettle, tho' I have had a very busy time
and am now in training, among other things, for a series of Burns
Suppers.

I saw from *The Scotsman* the other day of the death of the fair-
haired friend of my boyhood – Jeannie Wilson – and wrote to her
sister Joan.[1]

All kindest regards and season's greetings.

From,
Valda and Christopher.

Brownsbank,
Biggar,
7/5/68

Dear Jean,

Major Boothby was over yesterday and showed me your letter to
him, and his reply. As he said I wouldn't trust Wendy Wood[1] as far
as I could throw her if both my arms were broken – and I've known
her for forty years. If I'd been present when she was proposed for
1320 Club membership I'd have opposed it. I am sure she is just
using the Club to try to deflect people into her Patriots, and in
particular to try to take over the Symposia, now Dr Philp has left the
Club. I was told yesterday by Ted White that the next symposium
has been arranged for Edinburgh yourself with Professor

[1] Jean and Joan Wilson were contemporaries of MacDiarmid's; both became
primary teachers at Langholm Academy.
[1] Wendy Wood, founder of the Scottish Patriots, was one of the most flamboyant
figures in Scottish nationalist politics. A South African by birth and a sculptor by
inclination she believed in the politics of publicity.

T. B. Smith (the greatest authority on Scots Law), another legal luminary, and Wendy as speakers. She's no blate!

As to getting down to Langholm this month I'm afraid that's out of the question now. I've had no further word from George Bruce and Douglas Gray about our filming journey to Crowdieknowe, etc. And shortly I must really get down to hard work. My new Garden Studio is now in situ – and a splendid erection it is. Valda is busy painting the floor, etc., and a joiner is coming out this week to put in shelves. Then I'll have to tackle the sorting out of my books and papers and their proper disposition on the said shelves. After that I'll have months of steady writing and do not intend to go anywhere except for brief visits to Cheltenham Arts Festival and – in October, with Valda to East Germany.

Valda is going off for a few days in Ireland next week and I'll spend them in Glasgow at Michael's.

This week we've been inundated with visitors – authors, publishers, etc. And on Friday I'm going to the 1320 Club Executive Meeting in Edinburgh.

Just now I'm expecting Kulgin Duval and Colin Hamilton, and once they've been and gone, we'll settle down to hear and see the Radio and TV programmes on the municipal election results. Expect you'll be having a late night of it too for the same reason. Hope the SNP do well, tho' I'm afraid they are too optimistic in some of their press statements.

Hope you're in good form and behaving yourself.

With love from Valda and I.

> Yours affectionately,
> Chris.

> Brownsbank,
> Candymill,
> by Biggar.
> 12/6/78

Miss Jean White.
Dear Jean,

Or, as privately I call you, Miss Persil! I was disappointed when I got home on Saturday, after two more major operations, not to find you here and learn you were not coming up but had something else on. Your visits have given me great pleasure. Alas, the first of two operations mentioned above confirmed that my main trouble is a rectal cancer. So I am near the end of my tether. I still hope to go to Dublin for July 6th but it is very uncertain whether I'll be able to, and I'm afraid now Langholm Common-Riding is out of the question.

I've asked Michael to give you 30 or 40 of my books (not paperbacks but substantial books) either for the Library or for yourself if you so wish.[1]

Love and best wishes to you and all Langholm friends.

Yours,
Chris.

[1] Jean White writes: 'These books were not by MacDiarmid but taken from his book-shelves. He actually selected them himself, not long before he died. At present they are stored in my house as the Library premises have never been fit for re-opening to the public. The building has been badly attacked by dry rot and is standing empty at the moment. The owners, the Annandale and Eskdale District Council, have plans to repair it and alter the internal lay-out.' (Letter of November 1982 to Alan Bold.)

To Alex McCrindle

The distinguished actor Alex McCrindle was one of MacDiarmid's closest friends. The two men had political views in common and were both committed to the radicalisation of culture through such ventures as the People's Festival, launched in Edinburgh in 1952, and Theatre Workshop. McCrindle's wife – who wrote, under the name Honor Arundel, Marxist criticism and also children's books – became a prominent figure in Scottish literary circles and a champion of MacDiarmid's poetry.

EUL

Brownsbank,
By Biggar,
Lanarkshire.
5/10/51

Dear Alec,

I will of course be very glad to do anything I possibly can in connection with the projected show on April 12th next year.[1] That includes coming to London and reading poems or anything else the Committee wants me to do. I hope Sean O'Casey can do something but I question if he'd be able to come to London. He is an old friend of mine and I'd love to see him again but he has had, and is still having, a terribly hard time of it. I do not know off hand whether it will be possible to find a piper and one or two good dancers to represent Scotland, but I should think so. The ideal would be if we could get the piper Burgess[2] who took part in the People's Week Festival. He is one of the best in Scotland. However I'll set about finding what can be done in this connection right away – consult

---

[1] The projected show was a garden party to raise funds for the Edinburgh People's Festival which was launched in 1952.
[2] Jimmy Burgess.

Hamish Henderson and others – and let you know as soon as possible.

I haven't seen Norman McCaig since he came back from London tho' his wife and children were out here the other week. I'll be on the qui vive to hear the broadcast,[3] of course. The last one sounded good enough to me tho' other folk (less aware of the difficulties) hardly shared my good opinion of it and were inclined to make too much of the mistakes in pronunciation, interpretation, etc. I am sure I won't need to make so many allowances this time anyhow and feel sure it will be a great deal better. I haven't heard again from Ewan McColl either and do not know exactly what poems are included: but I do know that he intended to include that very shy-making masterpiece of mine, 'Harry Semen'. I just can't imagine that coming over the air, but I'd give a great deal to hear it, if McColl really has managed to smuggle it in past the BBC's moral censorship. Its inclusion is almost certain to evoke a storm of horrified protests. I've only one complaint to make – the BBC ought to have invited me down in an advisory capacity. An interlude in London with Norman, Ewan, Honor and yourself would have suited me extremely well.

I haven't heard just what has been done about putting the People's Festival on a permanent footing and extending the organisation to include Committees in Glasgow, Aberdeen, and Dundee. But I understand all that is going ahead and plans being made to have artistes next year from the Eastern Democracies, etc.

Re the play for the Scottish mining villages there just isn't one, you know. The only things – and they are popular enough – are plays by Joe Corrie. But they are on the kitchen level and just not nearly good enough. Ewan and I talked about this and I suggested that he should write one for you based on the Knockshinnoch disaster.[4] It lends itself to something that would fit in too with our Peace propaganda. The miners are of various nationalities – Scots, Irish, Poles,

---

[3] The broadcast was 'The Lallans Makars', BBC Third Programme, 23 June 1952, compiled by Ewan McColl, featuring as readers of MacDiarmid's poetry John Laurie, Alex McCrindle, Norman MacCaig (who read 'Harry Semen').

[4] On 7 September 1950, 129 miners were entombed in Knockshinnoch Castle Colliery, New Cumnock, Ayrshire; thirteen men died as a result of the disaster. In his final statement, on 16 November 1950, Abe Moffat – President of the National Union of Mineworkers (Scottish Area) – told the Knockshinnoch Colliery Inquiry: 'The main point I want to make here, contrary to all previous disasters from an inflow of moss, is that never had we so many warnings of an impending disaster and so little attention given by those responsible at the colliery. As a matter of fact, I would go further and say that there was a complete disregard of those previous warnings by those responsible at the colliery.' The full details of the disaster are given in William Pearson's *The Tragedy of Knockshinnoch* (Edinburgh 1951).

Ukrainians, etc., and have all sorts of feuds running amongst them. Then the disaster takes place and the human element comes to the fore, triumphing over all the racial religious and political differences. I think Ewan could make a very useful play along these lines. The Knockshinnoch disaster has created a very profound and widespread impression everywhere in Scotland, and as you will know the NCB officials are now being tried, so anything effectively pegged on this issue will have not only the advantage of topicality but be in alignment with matters which are of vital consequence to the National Union of Mineworkers and to the whole body of Scottish miners and their wives and families. In other words if he can use this theme Ewan's work is more than half done for him in the minds of an immense public already and the thing could have tremendous repercussions. I think Ewan is coming up here shortly so that he and I can work together on a Macbeth play and other things, and if so I am hopeful that he will do this Knockshinnoch thing too.

I'll look forward keenly to hearing how the Kilmarnock negotiations[5] pan out. Kilmarnock is quite reasonably handy for us by 'bus.

I missed the *D.W.*[6] with Honor's thing about the People's Week and its references to myself. Thank her all the same. It was a great pleasure to meet you both. Here's to our better acquaintance in the near future. Valda joins me in love to you both.

Yours,
Chris.

P.S. I'd have written you ere this, only I had mislaid my note of your address – I won't be guilty of that again.

---

[5] There was a plan to reopen the Kilmarnock theatre.
[6] *Daily Worker.*

EUL

Peking Hotel,
Peking,
China.
5/5/57

Dear Honor & Alec,

I got to China all right but two days later than expected owing to some slip-up in the arrangements so that after flying from Prague to Moscow by jet plane we did not get going on by jet, but had to take the ordinary plane service through Siberia and the Gobi Desert, with two overnight halts at guest houses. However we arrived in good time for the May Day celebrations which were magnificent beyond words, and along with our contingent included parties from 46 nations. ½ a million took part in the parade before Mao Tse Tung, Chou en Lai, and Voroshilov. Since then we have been having in splendid sunny weather, a tremendous round of receptions, garden parties, outings to places of historic and/or scenic beauty, art shows, exhibitions, concerts, and operas. Tomorrow I am going off early by plane on a fortnight's tour – Sian, Chungking, down the Yangtse Gorge to Hankow by boat, then on by plane again to Shanghai and back to Peking. I hope (if I can get a seat on the jet plane) to be back in London on 3rd or 5th June. I can't begin to say anything about my impressions yet – they'll take a long time to digest – but I have given a poetry reading along with Alberti the Spanish poet and several of the best Chinese poets, have addressed the Writers' Club, and have still to initiate discussions at Peking University and at the Foreign Language Institutes. Have seen a lot of Nan Green, Ted Brake, Alan Winnington, Wilf Burchett, and Andrew Condron, etc.[1]

Love to you all. Hope good news of your play, Honor.[2]

Yours,
Chris.

Sorry my ink ran out.

[1] Nan Green was married to Ted Brake who succeeded Alan Winnington as *The Daily Worker* correspondent in Peking; Wilfred Burchett reported on China and Korea for *The Daily Worker*; Andrew Condron, a former Royal Marine, was taken prisoner in Korea and subsequently decided to stay on in China for several years before returning to Britain.

[2] Honor Arundel's play *The Three Brothers*.

Brownsbank,
Biggar,
14/10/60

Dear Alex,

Writing to you because I don't expect to be in Edinburgh for a while now and am desperately busy here. But Mike was down last night and told me you had got 4 or 5 people to put up £50 each.[1] That is marvellous. Perhaps later on you can tell me who they are so that I can thank them privately. But I am very anxious that there should be no leakage of any kind with regard to this matter and indeed can only accept if that is agreed. That does not mean I won't be very grateful to you and to the contributors, but just that there must be no publicity whatever about the thing.

You will probably know that I've agreed to repeat the Lewis Grassic Gibbon lecture for the Party in Aberdeen next month; also I've just agreed to stand for the Rectorship there.[2]   Hope you are all well.

With our love.
Yours,
Chris.

[1] Concerned about the poet's predicament, Alex McCrindle wrote to some Scottish writers (such as Compton Mackenzie and Naomi Mitchison) asking them to contribute £50 to a fund that would enable some improvements to be made to MacDiarmid's home at Brownsbank. MacDiarmid himself wrote of his cottage: 'We had no "mod cons", and were getting too old to put up with really primitive conditions. In a year or two, however, some of the Edinburgh University students, members of the Young Communist League, and other friends came to the rescue and did all the necessary digging, draining, etc., and we soon found ourselves equipped with a kitchenette, bathroom, hot and cold water, flush lavatory, and electric light and other gadgets.' (Company, p. 189).

[2] At the Aberdeen University Rectorial Election, 1960, the voting was: Peter Scott (277), C. M. Grieve (248), Cliff Michelmore (188), Sir Colin Anderson (187), Donald Campbell (85).

EUL   Brownsbank,
                                                Biggar.
                                                24/4/68

Alex McCrindle Esq.
Dear Alex,

                        Re 1320 Club
    You've probably heard that Dr Geo. Philp[1] has resigned from the
Club. It seems likely he has decided to throw in his lot with Wendy
Wood and her Patriots. I've know Wendy for 40 years and I
wouldn't trust her an inch. I think she has been trying to use the
Club for the purposes of her own organisation – endeavouring to
detach members from the Club and enlist them in the 'Patriots'. Geo
Philp's resignation may mean that the Symposia (of which Philp was
Convener) may be transferred to the Patriots. This will be most
unfortunate. The initial symposium[2] at Glasgow University was a
great success. Our intention was to have similar symposia soon in all
the other Scottish Universities. I hope no divisiveness in the Club
will frustrate this intention.
    I was glad to hear from Valda that Honor on the 'phone was
keeping her courage high and do hope that the treatment she is
presumably having will be speedily effective. Please give her our love
and best wishes.
    And that of course goes to all of you.

                        Yours,
                        Chris.

EUL   Brownsbank,
                                                Biggar,
                                                Lanarkshire.
                                                1/8/72

Dear Alec,

    Valda and I were very sorry indeed to hear what you said on the
'phone about Honor. It is terrible. I cannot write her alas! but please

---

[1] A doctor active in Scottish National politics.
[2] There were plans for a series of symposia on Scottish culture.

give her our love. Death is so horribly arbitrary and indiscriminate. I feel ashamed of being nearly 80 when others who are younger and have more still to give are taken away. It is especially sad that Honor should be just when she had been enjoying successes. We love her, of course, and are desperately sorry – and our hearts go out too to you and the girls. If the end is inevitable we can only hope that she will have all the alleviation and easement possible in the circumstances and that she may pass peacefully and painlessly. We will not forget her great gifts and wonderful courage.

Yours,
Chris.

EUL

Brownsbank,
Biggar.
11/6/73

Alec McCrindle, Esq.
Dear Alec,

I do not need to tell you how sorry Valda and I were to hear that Honor had died.[1] It was obvious to us when we came down to Hume that the end could not be long delayed. And we can only hope that she passed away peacefully and without pain.

We send you – and Sussanah, Catherine, and Jessie[2] – our love and deepest sympathy. We are so glad that we managed to see her so recently and were able to appreciate her wonderful courage.

I do not know if I can get to Mortonhall[3] on Wednesday. I will if I can, but the bus service does not fit in. I do not know if I can get a lift in someone's car. And of course I am hard pressed for time as we go to Holland on Friday, and I have still a lecture on Celtic Literature to write for delivery in Amsterdam.

[1] Honor Arundel died, of cancer, on 8 June 1973.
[2] Sussanah is Honor Arundel's daughter by her first husband; Catherine and Jessica are the twin daughters of Honor and Alex McCrindle.
[3] Mortonhall is a crematorium in Edinburgh.

Michael will be at Mortonhall representing Valda and I. With kindest regards,

Yours fraternally,
Christopher Grieve.

To D. G. Bridson

As Assistant Head of Features with the BBC in the 1950s, D. G. Bridson was one of the most influential admirers of MacDiarmid. He arranged for broadcasts from MacDiarmid's later poetry at a time when it was not widely known. In 1959 he recorded a long conversation with MacDiarmid which was broadcast on the BBC Third Programme on 4 and 9 March 1960; the substance of MacDiarmid's contribution to the programme is included in *The Thistle Rises: A MacDiarmid Miscellany* (1984) edited by Alan Bold.

LLI

Brownsbank,
Candymill,
by Biggar,
Lanarkshire, Scotland.
11/6/56

Geoffrey Bridson, Esq.,
Assistant Head of Features, B.B.C.
Dear Geoffrey,

Many thanks for your most encouraging letter of 8th inst. I was indeed very pleased with the Joyce poem broadcast[1] and have had many most appreciative letters from all over Scotland.

I will of course be delighted to furnish some of the unpublished sections of the whole poem from which another 1/2 hour reading may be selected.[2] But I cannot do so immediately. I do not know

---

[1] A reading of MacDiarmid's *In Memoriam James Joyce* (Glasgow 1955) was broadcast on the BBC Third Programme on 31 May 1956.

[2] A reading from *Impavidi Progrediamur*, the uncompleted section of MacDiarmid's *Mature Art* sequence, was broadcast on the BBC Third Programme on 19 December 1956.

whether you wish it at once and trust some delay will not affect your arrangements.

The position is this. I wrote the whole immense thing in the Shetland Islands just before the War. Then I had to come to Scotland and go into engineering for a year or so, and subsequently, for another year or so, into the Merchant Service. Towards the end of that period my wife packed up all my books and papers and brought them down. We were in digs at first and had no room for a huge mass of trunks, boxes, etc. and had to store them. Later we succeeded in renting a house and later again moved here. In both of these moves we were obliged to leave a large amount of our stuff still in storage – and have not yet recovered a large proportion of it.

When I prepared the Joyce poem for the printer I had great difficulty in recovering my MSS – and did not recover it all. So I had to write fresh stuff to fill these gaps. Also in the interval some of my ideas had changed – and there had been many developments in linguistic thought; so I had to do a considerable amount of amending, adding, etc.

The same thing will happen with the unpublished sections of the whole poem when I lay hands on my original drafts. I will go ahead at once but I will require say six weeks before I can send you a typescript of roughly as much again as the Joyce poem from which you may choose. I hope this will do. I will give it priority but unfortunately I have other commitments just now which I cannot switch off the main line to let this express pass unless the BBC could commission the work – stipulating a definite delivery date. If they did so, however, I would be able to concentrate entirely on this, and I am sure you would not be disappointed in the quality of the material sent you by the appointed date.

I will, by the same token, be very glad to have the kind of informal discussion you suggest, in which I could explain my aims and theories, with Ewan and James McKechnie.[3] I understand you would wish to record this to follow the reading of the second lot of selected pieces. But if you cared to have it done rather in the interval between now and the delivery of the new material I'd be very willing to come down & do it.

A third edition of my *Drunk Man* has just been published, and I enclose a copy for you, with my thanks & best wishes.

Yours sincerely,
Christopher Grieve.

[3] James McKechnie and Ewan McColl were, with Seamus Ennis, the readers in the broadcast of *Impavidi Progrediamur*.

LLI
Brownsbank,
Biggar.
14/9/56

D. G. Bridson, Esq.
Assistant Head of Features, B.B.C.
Dear Geoffrey,

Many thanks for your letter today. I am delighted to know you have been able to record 1/2-hour of selections from *Impavidi Progrediamur* with McKechnie and McColl. The copy of the script you said you were sending so that I might know the portions selected hasn't reached me yet but I look forward to it in due course.

I agree of course that Waddell's position re the Edda[1] does not find favour with the consensus of scholars and is no doubt in some respects quite heretical. But there is a quality of imagination of a rude and grotesque kind which is more in keeping with the Scottish than with the English poetic tradition, no doubt, and it seems to me that, waiving the question of scholarly accuracy altogether, elements could be drawn from him which could be worked up in verse-drama form very effectively (e.g. his treatment of Loki): but of course the proof of the pudding is in the preeing of it and I know it is useless merely to suggest that that can be done – the thing is to do it. I have certain definite ideas on the subject and I will hope a little later to draft something and send it to you in the hope that its poetic quality may justify it no matter what the objections to it might be from the standpoint of exact scholarship. I agree also of course that tho' I like some features of his work Waddell's own translations *qua* poetry are for the most part extremely bad and need thorough re-writing.

As to the talk I note what you say and if it is possible for you as you hope to arrange this for the same week as the *Impavidi* selections I will, of course, be available whenever you need me.

I hope you have a most enjoyable holiday. You do not say where you are spending it, but at worst the weather can hardly be worse than it has been most of the summer and indeed, here at any rate, it seems to be steadily improving and the latter half of this month and

[1] 'I have mentioned Charles Doughty, but all that Charles Doughty did in regard to the ancient British requires to be supplemented by a thorough assimilation of Dr L. A. Waddell's *The British Edda* (1930) . . . Dr Waddell's book was of course virtually stillborn; English historians and *litterateurs* are not open to fundamental revaluations or any displacement of the upstart English tradition in favour of the far more important elements that tradition has so far wholly occluded and is all intent to keep in occlusion.' (LP, pp. 291–2).

657

October promise, as is often the case, to be much better than the popular holiday months.

    With kindest regards.

                Yours,
                Christopher Grieve.

To Ian Milner

Ian Milner (who was born in Oamaru, New Zealand) is Associate Professor of English at Charles University, Prague. He has published *The Structure of Values in George Eliot* (1968) and many poetic translations from the Czech including, with George Theiner, Miroslav Holub's *Selected Poems* (1967).

Brownsbank,
Biggar.
24/3/60

Dear Mr Milner,

Many thanks to Jarmila[1] and yourself for your kind messages re our motor smash, and also to Linda for her card. We had a very close call indeed. We are out of hospital now but suffering from shock reaction and will be obliged to take things very quietly for some time. Our various cuts and bruises have healed nicely but Valda has internal injuries to her right side and the back trouble for which she got ultrasonic treatment and radioactive mud-baths in Sofia – and which seemed cured as a consequence – has been reactivated by this accident and is giving her a great deal of pain and trouble. I had a lot of facial and other injuries but the most troublesome is the fact that my dentures were smashed in my mouth and the splinters of the vulcanite plates gashed my gums and pierced the roof of my mouth, with the consequence that I cannot get new dentures until my mouth heals. So I have been obliged to cancel various lecturing engagements, etc. The only outing I've had since the accident was to Edinburgh the other day to a reception given by the Italian Circle to

---

[1] Jarmila, Ian Milner's wife.

meet the Nobel prize-winning poet, Salvatore Quasimodo. I hope to go to Sweden about the end of April and/or beginning of May, but whether I will have teeth by then I don't know and certainly I'll not get rid of various scars on my brow and round my eyes so soon. I had a letter from Alana and have just written her.

The BBC have been very good to me recently. They sent a TV team up here to do a film interview with me. That has not been telecast yet, but while the team was here I did various recordings – reading poems and giving my views on the present position and prospects of poetry, what I thought of various contemporaries, etc. – and that material was broadcast in three separate Third Programme 45-minute talks recently.[2] Also on the Scottish Home Service I gave a long talk on Lewis Grassic Gibbon, the novelist who died 25 years ago.[3] Otherwise, alas, my work is sadly in arrears, and my correspondence is in a hopeless condition from which I despair of ever being able to retrieve it. Certainly I can't do much about it meantime, as my doctor insists that I must do only a minimum of reading, let alone writing.

I hope you three are all in good form. Valda is eager to visit Czechoslovakia but I am afraid it is unlikely we can do that this year now.

Kindest regards and every good wish to you all, and to any other of my Czech friends you may be seeing.

Yours,
Christopher.

Brownsbank,
Biggar,
Lanarkshire.
5/12/60

Dear Mr Milner,

I'm afraid all my correspondence is still dreadfully in arrears. I had thought I'd have made up long ere this for the loss of time, etc.

---

[2] The three talks were broadcast on the BBC Third Programme on 4, 9 and 14 March 1960.

[3] The programme on Lewis Grassic Gibbon, 'A Vision of Scotland', was broadcast on the BBC Scottish Home Service on 29 February 1960.

my car-accident entailed; but no! – and other things have kept on adding to the difficulties. Just recently I was one of five candidates for the Lord Rectorship of Aberdeen University. I didn't think I had any chance in view of my politics, but I came in second – and only missed the office by 4 votes.[1] Just after the result was announced I had several meetings to address in Aberdeen, for the CP and for the Scottish Nationalist, and got back here grudging the time I had so lost and anxious to get on with my writing again. Alas! It was only to find an outbreak of Foot and Mouth Disease. So all the cattle and sheep on this farm had to be slaughtered and my movements, and Valda's, were under police control and confined to the actual farm land. So that was another infernal nuisance. And now I'm working hell for leather on the huge Swedish translation.[2] The publishers – Hutchinson in London and Knopf in America, are clamouring for its completion. But that's not a thing that can be hurried since it's a verse translation and the author insisted that the original verse structure should be retained. I had hoped to have got over to Sweden to discuss various points with him but haven't been able to do so.

At long last the – still unexplained – long delay with my *Collected Poems* which Macmillan's, New York, are publishing is over and they say they are pushing ahead with it as rapidly as possible now. So I'm hoping it'll be out very early in the New Year.[3]

My own health is O.K., but Valda is still having a lot of trouble with her nose which was broken, and with her back as a consequence of the car smash reactivating a trouble which we had thought the treatment she got in Bulgaria had disposed of.

I can't recall just how long ago it was since I had your last letter – nor can I put my hand on it at the moment but I do remember you hadn't had very favourable conditions on your holiday and were coveting the Black Sea and Bulgarian sunshine again. I hope all three of you are in good form nevertheless.

A dreadful illustration of the condition my affairs have been in is the fact that I haven't managed to write to Jessie[4] at all since she was here.

I noted what you said about the translations and am grateful to

---

[1] The result of the 1960 Aberdeen University Rectorial Election was Peter Scott (277 votes), C. M. Grieve (248), Cliff Michelmore (188), Sir Colin Anderson (187), Donald Campbell (85).

[2] *Aniara* by Harry Martinson – adapted from the Swedish by Hugh MacDiarmid and Elspeth Harley Schubert – was published by Hutchinson of London and Knopf of New York in 1962.

[3] MacDiarmid's *Collected Poems* was published by Macmillan of New York in 1962.

[4] Mrs Jessie Kocmanová (née Scott) has been resident in Czechoslovakia since the Second World War; she teaches at the English Department of Purkyne University, Brno.

you but of course I know these things are difficult to arrange and can take a very long time.

Since we are into December Christmas and New Year are not far away, so please accept Valda's and my best wishes.

Yours,
Christopher.

Brownsbank,
Biggar
10/4/65

Dear Ian Milner,

I am very sorry to have been so long in writing you. Many thanks for postcard from the mountains, and your letter. The copyright controversy has, it seems, died now. It certainly raised interesting points. The 'Perfect'[1] matter was most unfortunate. As to other cases – e.g. Hugh Gordon Porteus's instance – as an American poet wrote me: 'Copyright is a legal – not a literary – matter.' I certainly haven't been worried. We don't invent the information – we get it somewhere – and retail it without acknowledging sources. It's the use we put things to that counts. If part of a loaf is torn out, beaten up into dough, and baked anew as a biscuit, that is not any plagiarism of the loaf. Anyhow as Dr Johnson said when somebody complained about the employment of too many quotations in a piece of writing, 'It is one thing to use quotations – Those who don't seem to are in fact as a rule doing nothing but quote all the time.' Quotations show a proper social spirit.

Yes, you are quite right. I must ease off. I've just had a desperately busy time – Newcastle, Durham, Manchester, Leeds, and Cambridge Universities – and I'd have had Bangor and Coleg Harlech too; but couldn't because Welsh communications were all bedevilled by snow. Still they are only postponed. Also I've Nottingham, Sheffield, and Lancaster still to do – and poetry reading at Edinburgh Festival. Fortunately that's August. Because before that I'm going to East Berlin (14th to 22nd May) for International Writers'

---

[1] For details of the 'Perfect' controversy in the *TLS* see pp. 828–31.

meeting to mark 20 years since liberation from Nazi tyranny. Also I'm going to Cuba, but date not yet fixed. If it clashes with East Berlin date then I'll have to cancel the latter. What a life!

I'm interested to hear of new periodical and your translations – also looking for the one you mention in *Times Literary Supp.*[2]

Also I've signed a contract for a new autobiographical book (*A Scottish Poet and his Friends*) of 80,000 to 100,000 words which I must deliver by 1st October.

The real reason for my delay in writing you has been annoyance with Valda. She is a hopelessly bad letter-writer. She's been meaning to write Jarmila ever since just after we saw you. I told you she'd a brooch for Linda.[3] I kept urging to send it. But she delayed – and then couldn't find it. She's just found it now, so I expect she'll send it any day now.

Hope you are all well. We are, and send our love and best wishes to all three of you, and the poodle, and all friends.

Yours,
Chris

[2] The *TLS* of 29 July 1965 published Milner's translation of Miroslav Holub's poem 'Fall of Troy'.
[3] Linda, Milner's stepdaughter.

To Jonathan Knight

The scientific precision and political passion of MacDiarmid's work attracted the attention of Professor Jonathan Knight and his wife Frida. B. C. J. G. Knight (1904–81) was a microbiologist who pioneered the study of the nutritional requirements of microbes; from 1951 to 1969 he held the founding chair of microbiology at Reading University. Frida Knight worked for the Free French in London after escaping from a German camp in 1942. She has translated and written various books including one on *The French Resistance* (1975).

Brownsbank,
By Biggar,
Lanarkshire.
27/7/60

Dear Professor Knight,

'It wasn't only that he had no enemies; but he hadn't even any friends', I read this sentence in a who-done-it the other day. Neither of these assertions is true in my case. I have plenty of enemies, of course. Friends, as distinct from acquaintances, are scarce on the ground however. So I am very happy to have found Mrs Knight and yourself. Letters such as you and she have sent me are very encouraging to a stormy 'petrel' accustomed to more kicks than ha'pence. You'd be surprised if I could tell you of the way I have been – and still am – treated by, for instance, the Scottish Press. The leading papers have not reviewed any of my books for over 30 years. Controversies are always raging in their correspondence columns about my work – if 'raging' is the proper term for what is so one-sided, since my detractors are given a monopoly of the field, letters from my supporters are seldom printed, and when they are, they, like my own, always have the guts taken out of them, and the effect given is therefore one of character and reputation assassination and the other elements of a sustained 'smear' campaign. I'm not complaining but simply stating the fact, so you will understand what a tonic it is to get letters like Mrs Knight's and yours occasionally.

If health and harness hold I think I'll do a lot yet. I have quite a number of books both prose and verse on the stocks. Most of them are whales of poems, of course, and I question very much if I will ever pour myself out in a novel as you suggest. But sequelae to *Lucky Poet* there almost certainly will be. The trouble is that the people I write, or want to write, about won't stay put till I get them into print. They die on me, and then I have to amend or amplify what I've written. And as for ideas they too keep changing in the most baffling way. I no sooner get a nice array of them lined up than the whole atmosphere of thought changes and I find either that I've wasted a lot of words on issues that have gone out of fashion or failed to keep sufficiently abreast of emergent subjects or because of my incorrigible cussedness want to change the emphasis in this way or that, promote certain notions and demote others. It's a devil of a life, but again I'm not complaining – I like the infernal process far too much.

With every kind regard to you all.

Yours,
Hugh MacDiarmid.

Brownsbank,
Biggar,
Lanarkshire.
17/9/60

Dear Professor Knight,

There are a couple of passages (in the typescript of *The Kind of Poetry I Want* which I gave you) of which I do not seem to have any copy. I am putting the whole thing together now for early publication and I am anxious not to have to omit the passages in question, so I will be grateful if you will kindly send me the typescript by registered post. I will return it to you safely in a day or two. I am sorry if this is a nuisance to you but this poem became badly fragmented – parts of it appeared in *Lucky Poet*, another long piece of it in *A Kist of Whistles* and other portions elsewhere; and, of course, I want to put the whole thing together and probably add to it or re-order parts of it and the passages I have in mind in your typescript are vital to what I have in mind.

I had the pleasure a week or two ago of seeing McCance[1] again when he was in Ayrshire.

I wonder if Mrs Knight sent her Thomas Muir play to Theatre Workshop and if so if she has heard from them about it.[2]

I also saw Ian Fletcher[3] in Edinburgh a few days ago. I promised one of your boys some Bulgarian match-box labels. I haven't been able to hunt them out yet. But will.

With kindest regards to you all.

Yours,
Hugh MacDiarmid.

Brownsbank,
Candymill,
Biggar,
Lanarkshire.
9/12/60

Dear Professor Knight,

I am sorry to have retained this typescript[1] so long (not that there has not been a certain advantage – I noted that there were a few blanks where there should have been Greek words, and these I have now inserted). I have been very busy. As you may have seen from the papers I was one of the five candidates for Aberdeen University Lord Rectorship, and came in second. While in Aberdeen I had several meetings to address on the Peace Movement and especially the

---

[1] MacDiarmid's friend William McCance was lecturer in typography and book production at Reading University where Knight was professor of microbiology.
[2] The Thomas Muir play was never produced.
[3] Ian Fletcher, lecturer in English at Reading University.
[1] *The Kind of Poetry I Want.*

anti-Polaris-base campaign. Then when I got home I found that there was a Foot and Mouth disease outbreak here and all the cattle and sheep on this farm had to be destroyed and our own movements were under strict police control and we were confined to the actual land of the farm. This was a great nuisance and held me up in various ways.

I enclose also the Bulgarian match-box labels and hope they may please the young collector.[2]

Will you please tell Mrs Knight that I am afraid there will be nothing doing so far as Theatre Workshop is concerned in the meantime. Despite the succession of plays that have done well – e.g. Brendan Behan's, Frank Norman's, and Shellagh Delaney's – Theatre Workshop is £20,000 in the red and must work very cautiously for some time ahead. There was a Directors' Meeting in London recently which I had hoped to attend – but I didn't manage; I was too busy with the campaign throughout Scotland against the Polaris base.

McCance tells me he thinks I'll be asked back to Reading to give a talk to the University Literary Society. I'll certainly come if I can.

Christmas and New Year are drawing very near, so I take this opportunity of wishing Mrs Knight and the children and yourself all the compliments of the season and best wishes for 1961.

Yours sincerely,
Hugh MacDiarmid.

Brownsbank,
Biggar,
Lanarkshire,
Scotland.
17/12/62

Dear Professor Knight,

I do not know how long I've been owing you replies to your very kind and encouraging letters. The birthday business in August

2 Robert Knight, the professor's son.

overwhelmed me altogether, and I've had no let-up since. I hope all's well with Freda and yourself and the children.

You'll be interested to know both the Macmillan and Oliver & Boyd issues of my *Collected Poems* are sold out. They'll reprint of course but that may take a little time. The *Festschrift* sold extremely well too. And now I am waiting for my translation of *Aniara*, due out (Hutchinson) on 4th February. I've been expecting it since September, but they postponed publication without advising me. Perhaps you heard some of the Third Programme readings from it.

I'm feeling very bucked today since Professor Carstairs in his final Reith lecture[1] last night paid a tribute to the Lallans poets and quoted a poem of mine – as a little oasis of sanity and hope in a mentally increasingly unhealthy world.

Love to you all and best wishes.

Yours,
Christopher Grieve.

Brownsbank,
Candymill,
Biggar,
Lanarkshire,
Scotland.
3/9/63

Dear Professor Knight,

I am sorry to have been so long in replying to your far too kind, but most welcome, letter. This is due 1/ to my having been away in Newcastle-on-Tyne and elsewhere; 2/ to involvement in the Edinburgh Festival; and above all 3/ to the fact that I have been conducting a sort of rival British Association here. I've had a spate of Professors and Lecturers visiting me. Professor Barker Fairley,

---

[1] In his sixth and final Reith Lecture G. M. Carstairs said: 'I must confess that much of Lallans is Greek to me, and yet sometimes I catch the excitement of feelings which can only be expressed in one's mother tongue; for example, when Hugh MacDiarmid likens the moonlit earth to the tear-streaked face of a sleeping child in his line: "Earth, thou bonnie broukit bairn" [17].' G. M. Carstairs, *This Island Now* (London 1963, p. 101).

Chair of German, Toronto and his friend Dr Brill, St Andrews University German Dept; Professor Kenneth Buthlay, Chair of English Sao Paulo, Brazil; Professor G. Ross Roy, Texas (who has just launched a new quarterly *Studies in Scottish Literature*); Louis Simpson, poet and lecturer at Harvard – and I'm now expecting Professor M. L. Rosenthal, Chair of English, New York University. How's that for a roll-call?

Certainly with regard to what you say of my scientific interests as revealed in my poems, it would seem that what Sir Charles Snow says about the gulf between the two Cultures does not apply to me. Another scientist wrote me recently listing over a dozen statements made by me which anticipated scientific findings not established till some twenty years later. I wish I could lay my hands on that letter. I'd like to refer that list to you for checking.

Which reminds me that another of my recent visitors was the Professor of Metallurgy at Sheffield University who is a cousin of mine.[1]

Yes, I'm hoping to perpetrate a lot more poetry. But I won't get down to concentrated work on it till after mid-November. I've too many meetings before then. What is likely to happen quickest is an outburst of books about me. Two of these[2] are at the printers but won't I think be published until March, while the third is being written by Louis Simpson who thinks it'll take him about two years!

I was delighted to hear Mrs Knight's translation of the Rumanian play on the Third Programme.[3] I wonder if you are still on your own? I've seen or heard nothing of McCance and don't know his new Girvan address or I'd probably have gone over there for a week-end ere this.

As you probably saw in *The Observer* John Wain had another stab at me![4]

Kindest regards to you all. When all the other Professors in the world are beating the path to my door I just can't understand why you fail to come too. Still here's to the next time we do meet.

Yours,
Christopher Grieve.

[1] Jim White, Professor of Ceramic Technology at Sheffield University; retired in 1978.
[2] Duncan Glen, *Hugh MacDiarmid and the Scottish Renaissance* (Edinburgh 1964); Kenneth Buthlay, *Hugh MacDiarmid* (Edinburgh 1964).
[3] The play was *The Lost Letter* by Ion Luca Caragiale.
[4] See pp. 817–8.

57 Miller Street,
Glasgow, C.1.
14th October 1964.

Professor B.C. Knight,
Chair of Microbiology,
University of Reading,
Berkshire.

Dear Jonathan,

Many thanks for your telegram and for your generous contribution towards the Election fund. We have firmly inserted the thin edge of the Marxist wedge into this feudal 8,000 square miles constituency[1] and must, after Friday, do all we can to hammer it home.

Yours,
Christopher.

---

[1] Kinross and West Perthshire, the constituency of the then Prime Minister, Sir Alec Douglas-Home. MacDiarmid fought the seat for the Communist Party but lost his deposit.

To Bertrand Russell

In 1960 Bertrand Russell (1872–1970) announced the formation of 'The Committee of 100 for Civil Disobedience against Nuclear Warfare'. MacDiarmid was asked to join the committee and accepted, in a letter of 29 September 1960 to the Rev Michael Scott. On 18 February 1961 MacDiarmid and Russell shared a platform at a massive peace rally in Trafalgar Square, London.

McM

The Cottage,
Brownsbank,
Biggar,
Lanarkshire.
4/8/62

The Earl Russell, D.M., F.R.S.
43 Hasker Street,
London, S.W.3.

Dear Lord Russell,

I'll be very pleased to join you in signing advertisement for funds for Committee of 100.

If I had had any hesitation it would be simply because practice is better than precept, and I am not in a position myself to help financially at the moment. I hope to be so a little later however, and will not forget. Also I have been so incredibly busy lately that I have not been able to serve the Committee as I should have done, but I expect to be freer shortly and I'll try to get contributions from my friends.

Please give my kindest regards to Lady Russell, and accept same yourself.

Yours sincerely,
Hugh MacDiarmid.

671

McM

The Earl Russell, D.M., F.R.S.

Dear Lord Russell,

I might have replied to your letter of 15th inst. a day or two days more quickly, but I understood you would be attending the Writers' Conference in connection with Edinburgh International Festival and thought to see you there.

However I appreciate all you say and will certainly arrange to be with you, as you desire, in the demonstration on 9th September. Alas, I have been so busy lately that I do not remember – or, if I had them, have mislaid letters thereanent – just where this demonstration is to be held. Can you please give me the necessary particulars?

I join with you with regard to its vital importance at this juncture and share your hope for a very large and determined turn-out.

With warmest regards to Lady Russell and yourself.

Yours sincerely,
Hugh MacDiarmid.

To Edwin Morgan

Edwin Morgan, author of a perceptive monograph *Hugh Mac-Diarmid* (1976) is an accomplished essayist and poet whose style ranges from work in Scots to experimental concrete poetry. He was born in 1920 in Glasgow and lectured in English at Glasgow University from 1947 to 1980 when he retired as Titular Professor. His poem 'To Hugh MacDiarmid' – included in his *Poems of Thirty Years* (1982) – pays tribute to the man who 'out of scraps of art and life and knowledge ... assembled that crackling auroral panorama/ that sits on Scotland like a curly comb/or a grinning watergaw thrown to meteorology.'

Brownsbank,
Biggar,
Lanarkshire.
5/1/62

Dear Edwin Morgan,

Many thanks for your letter. The line you ask about in my poem on Charles Doughty[1] is difficult and probably grammatically indefensible, but what 'where you lie needs tells' means just as you suggest 'where you lie (no other sign is needed to tell)' or 'necessarily' for 'needs'. Petavius, Langrenus, and Arzachel are all place-names in the landscape of the moon. Hope this makes things clear.

Here's wishing you a good creative New Year. My own has begun

---

[1] As Morgan had included MacDiarmid's 'Stony Limits. In Memoriam: Charles Doughty, 1843–1926' (419–22) in his *Collins Albatross Book of Longer Poems* (1963) he sought clarification for his explanatory notes.

in style, with the appearance of my *Collected Poems* (Macmillans, New York), and *The Kind of Poetry I Want* (K. Duval, Edinburgh).

Yours sincerely,
Christopher Grieve.

Brownsbank,
Biggar.
5/2/62

Dear Edwin Morgan,

Many thanks for your letter again. 'Lunation' in my poem[1] refers to the first of the two possible meanings of the term, viz. the period of the full moon. The reference, of course, assumes the (non-existent) lunar influence, but I understand it is a fact that at the time of the full moon there is an apparent growth on that part of the moon's surface which the poem calls 'the north-easterly garden'. I hope this clears up the point for you.

With every kind regard.

Yours,
Christopher Grieve.

Brownsbank,
Candymill,
Biggar,
Lanarks.
15/1/75

Dear Edwin Morgan,

My wife wanted to give me a book of my choice for Christmas and I asked for the Carcanet volume of your essays.[1] I chose rightly and

[1] 'Stony Limits' (419–22).
[1] Edwin Morgan, *Essays* (1974).

have been absorbed in them ever since. And I do not mean the essays dealing with my work, some of which of course I had seen and appreciated before. They are indeed among the best things so far written about my poetry – welcome oases on the desert of contemporary literary journalism. That's not as you know, to say I agree with them – only I am glad to encounter high intelligence anywhere.

There are one or two points which may interest you. I am especially struck by the passage at end of p 220 and top of p 221 in which you deal with the 'enormous gap of ordinary human experience which my poetry hardly represents at all'. That is of course true: but why should I concern myself with that sort of thing at all. Poetry has never had more than a very small percentage of the reading public – readers, I mean, who really understood and appreciated it. I believe it is true that ever since the start of recorded history, in all countries and all centuries, all the arts and sciences, all the constituents of civilisation have been created (often in the teeth of public opposition and certainly always of mass indifference): and that if this infinitesimal element in the population were eliminated all the rest of mankind could do nothing at all to rebuild the arts and sciences. So it is only with that infinitesimal element that I have any need to be concerned.

I do not like people – I'd be ashamed to profess any regard for the mass of mankind – I may love or have friendship for an individual here and there, but that is all. I am essentially a loner and practise what I preach. For years I have gone without a word with anyone else apart from my wife for weeks or months at a time: and I have always eschewed intimacy – I have an enormous number of acquaintances but that relationship is mostly maintained by correspondence and not by personal contact. And I cannot see how it can be held that I have missed anything worth having.

You probably know George Steiner's *In Bluebeard's Castle*[2] with almost every word of which I agree. 'At seminal levels of metaphor, of myth, of laughter, where the arts and the worn scaffolding of philosophic systems fail us, science is active. Touch on even its more abstruse regions and a deep elegance, a quickness and merriment of the spirit come through. ... The "poetry of facts" and realisation of the miraculous delicacies of perception in contemporary sciences already inform literature at those nerve-points where it is both disciplined and under the stress of the future. ... The absence of the history of science and technology from the school syllabus is a scandal. It is an absurdity to speak of the renaissance without knowledge of its cosmology, of the mathematical dreams which

[2] George Steiner, *In Bluebeard's Castle* (London 1971, pp 100–2).

underwrote its theories of art and music. To read 17th and 18th century literature of philosophy without an accompanying awareness of the unfolding genius of physics, astronomy, and algebraic analysis during the period is to read only at the surface.... It is not only that the humanities have been arrogant in their assertions of centrality. It is that they have often been silly. We need no poet more urgently than Lucretius.'

In addition to your essays – and some of Prof. David Daiches – one of the greatest compliments I have been paid is by Professor D. M. MacKinnon, Professor of Divinity, Cambridge who in his *The Problem of Metaphysics*[3] – a summing up of his arguments in his Gifford Lectures – devotes a whole chapter to my poem 'On a Raised Beach' in the course of which he says: 'At first sight we seem in this poem a very long way from the sort of issues that have concerned us in the discussion of Aristotle's ontology. Again, both in the lines quoted and in the poem as a whole, the mood is very different from that of the tentative essays on theism with which a considerable part of this work has been concerned. Yet the grave atheism expressed in the lines quoted effectively latches on to the discontentment expressed in what has immediately preceded it. The poet is concerned with what is; he is not inviting the reader to an exercise in "seeing as". In some measure this is conveyed by the actual use in the poem of technical terms from geology, of setting in the organisation of the whole the effective language of the northern isles. It may sound paradoxical to say that the philosopher who reads this poem may suddenly find himself reminded of Kant's treatment of substance in the first *Analogy* ...'

And he goes on: 'The poet's language has a bite of which over-indulgent use across the centuries has deprived the idiom in which religious poets have spoken of divine eternity. Certainly, if God exists, then "a thousand years in his sight are but as yesterday". But Aristotle's first mover, whose activity is defined as *noēsisis noēsēos* is too lightly dismissed by Christian theists as too coldly indifferent an ultimate to be bearable; this because to recall Aristotle's theology in the light of this poem is to be reminded that at least it honestly faced the question of what ultimately is, without prejudging the answer that it must be an ultimate concerned with the human scene. MacDiarmid writes as an atheist, and his poem is eloquent testimony that out of an atheist ontology a great poem may spring. To say this is not intended as the insult so often offered by the religious of claiming that no man is a serious atheist. But it is to remember that atheism and theism have this in common; that both alike are

[3] D. M. MacKinnon *The Problem of Metaphysics* (Cambridge 1974, p. 166–8).

ontologies and that in the relatively loose sense of the term in which it may be applied to a conspectus of Aristotle's metaphysics that includes his theology as well as his anatomy of being. If it is insulting to the atheist to speak of him as unknown to himself a religious man, it is permissible to remember that unlike the positivist he allows himself to be concerned with what is, in the very special sense of demanding an unconditional validity for what he says. Hence indeed the violence of Lenin's polemics against Bogdanov, for the latter's readiness to substitute Ernst Mach's sensationalism for materialism. No one would call Lenin's *Materialism and Empirio-Criticism* philosophy. It is polemic of the kind of which its formidable author is master. Yet it is the sort of work that the philosopher who is concerned with the problem of metaphysics would do well to remember, and that not least in the present context as we recall the poetry that MacDiarmid has written in Lenin's honour.'

While then I have no use whatever for 'the brotherhood of man' or 'my fellow-men' or anything of that kind – derivates all from the notion of the fatherhood of God – I must tell you that 'The Watergaw'[4] was not written about my dying father – or the dying of any other person – and suffers I think because it can be read in that way, whereas my actual 'inhuman' attitude is much more truly expressed in 'At my Father's Grave':-

> The sunlicht still on me, you row'd in clood
> We look upon each ither noo like hills
> Across a valley. I'm nae mair your son.
> It is my mind, nae son o' yours, that looks
> And the great darkness o' your death comes up
> And equals it across the way.
> A livin' man upon a deid man thinks
> And ony sma'er thocht's impossible.

I've been ill with 'flu since Christmas and can scarcely write. Hence this ill-written scrawl. But I thank you again for writing about my work in a way helpful to me – something one seldom

---

[4] Though MacDiarmid denied that 'The Watergaw' was about his father's death there is poetic evidence to suggest that it was. In 'The Watergaw' (17) he cites 'the last wild look ye gied/Afore ye deed!'. In 'Kinsfolk' (1147–50) he refers specifically to his father and says:
> Afore he dee'd he turned and gied a lang
> Last look at pictures o' my brither and me
> Hung on the wa' aside the bed, I've heard
> My mither say.

receives from any commentator – and I send you my best wishes for your happiness and prosperity in this New Year.

Yours,
Christopher Grieve.

P.S. Owing to my illness I have had to cancel the Poetry Afternoon at Ayr on 1st Feb.

To Sydney Goodsir Smith

Born in New Zealand, the son of a Professor of Forensic Medicine, Sydney Goodsir Smith (1915–75) came to Scotland at the age of twelve. As a poet he embraced a Scots muse and developed as one of MacDiarmid's most gifted disciples. He was a convivial character well known in the bars of Edinburgh where he self-consciously assumed the role of the boozy bard of Auld Reekie.

NLS   Brownsbank.
                                                                    20/3/62

Dear Sydney,

The Third Hymn[1] was written while I was in the Shetlands – but bits of it at different times. The only bit published before *The Voice of Scotland* in 1955 was what appeared in *Lucky Poet*. I should think 1935 would be the main date of composition.

Hope all goes well with you. I'll not likely be much in Edinburgh now till Festival time. But I'll be about at the Writer's Conference.[2] I see I'm to orate on the second day on Scottish Writing Today. 'God' help me!

I'm off to London on Saturday to do a ½ hour interview with Malcolm Muggeridge on Granada TV.

[1] In *Hugh MacDiarmid: A Festschrift* (Edinburgh 1962), which he edited with the publisher Kulgin Duval, Smith wrote an essay on 'The Three Hymns to Lenin'.
[2] The Writers' Conference was organised by the publisher John Calder and held as part of the official Edinburgh International Festival. It was not repeated after a 'happening', featuring a naked girl in a wheelchair, was devised by avant garde writers participating in the proceedings at the McEwan Hall.

All the best.

Yours,
Chris.

My 'author's copies' of *Collected Poems* haven't reached me yet!
Damn!!

NLS   Brownsbank.
                                                         26/4/65

Dear Sydney,

Congratulations – and many thanks on your demolition of David
Craig[1] and effective exposure of the Anti-Scottish lobby in the
current *Studies In Scottish Literature*.

I've felt for a long time I must get back to writing poetry in Scots –
but I got so tangled up in all sorts of things I couldn't manage. But
your article has finally tipped the scale. I must do it – and will –
without further delay.

You'll have seen Sparrow's statement in *Times Lit* – that I simply
lifted the poem 'Perfect' from Keidrych Rhys.[2] I've written denying
this absolutely. If I had the money (since even winning the action
would cost several hundred quid) I wouldn't have bothered to reply
at all but simply instituted legal proceedings. But we'll see.

All the best.

Yours,
Chris.

---

[1] David Craig's *Scottish Literature and the Scottish People 1680–1830* (1961) applied
Marxist criteria to Scottish literature and was particularly severe on Mac-
Diarmid's Scots-writing disciples.
[2] See p. 830–3.

To Duncan Glen

Duncan Glen, Head of the Department of Visual Communications at Trent Polytechnic, is one of the most energetic and accomplished advocates of the work and worth of MacDiarmid. Born in Cambuslang, Lanarkshire, in 1933 he founded the periodical *Akros* in 1965 and has edited it as a platform for poetry in Scots and English. Under the Akros imprint he has also published many books and pamphlets including several by MacDiarmid and various collections of his own poems. His *Hugh MacDiarmid and the Scottish Renaissance* (1964) is an impeccably researched and greatly informative account of the literary movement initiated by MacDiarmid.

NLS

Brownsbank,
Candymill,
Biggar.
19/9/62

Dear Mr Glen,

Many thanks for your letter and the two proof copies of *The Hawthorn*.[1] It is an elegant job, beautifully printed and produced.

And I am delighted to hear what you say re your biography and Messrs Chambers's reaction thereto. I hope they decide to publish. On the basis of what's been happening re my *Collected Poems* and the *Festschrift*, I believe such a book would sell all right just now, and of

---

[1] Hugh MacDiarmid, *Poetry Like the Hawthorn. From In Memoriam James Joyce* (Hemel Hempstead 1962). 'These pamphlets of poems by MacDiarmid which I published in the sixties are now rare and booksellers are asking high prices for them. The first one I published was *Poetry Like the Hawthorn*, 1962, and recently I saw a bookseller advertising one of the twenty-five signed copies, which I sold at 10/6d (less 33⅓ discount to booksellers), for £50!' Duncan Glen, *Forward from Hugh MacDiarmid* (Preston 1977, p. 11).

course the tremendous wave of publicity I've been having should ensure that.

I'll be very pleased to sign the 25 copies as you suggest, and I think Kulgin Duval would sell them for us. But I can't, of course, accept your too generous offer to give them to me. You must be recouped for the cost and expenses you've incurred at any rate, and there is no question of a fee to me. If the poem had been in an anthology I'd have got anything between two and ten guineas and if it had been broadcast I'd have got 1½ guineas per 8 lines. But these figures have nothing to do with this matter. I am delighted with the booklet, and regard your publishing it in this way as a fine compliment.

I couldn't myself see or hear the ABC Bookman TV programme. I simply flew down to Teddington Studios, did the job, stayed at the Skyway Hotel overnight, and caught the earliest plane back to Edinburgh the following morning, arriving 9.30 a.m. and getting out here about 11 a.m. That's the way I like things, but I've had just too much lately – with sound radio, TV, miscellaneous speaking engagements, not to mention birthday parties and presentations. All too much of a good thing for a septuagenarian of retiring disposition. All my correspondence is still hopelessly in arrears – and, you know, I got literally hundreds of cards, letters, telegrams from all over the world! I must see it doesn't happen again.

I am glad you saw so many of the articles about my work; they'll have helped to fill in details about my career perhaps. As to your queries, I do not know just what Ewan MacColl had in mind about the American lecture tour offer. It is true that such a thing has been suggested quite a number of times – generally by friends (American authors, University lecturers, etc.) who did not weigh sufficiently the fact that I'm a member of the CP and wouldn't have been allowed beyond Ellis Island. But these were all just suggestions – not definite offers – and I can't think what specific instance MacColl had in mind (tho' I have a notion that he is probably right, and that I've just forgotten).

Yes, I contributed to *The New Age* as Pteleon (among other names) and that must have been between 1926 and 1929. Also to *The Scottish Educational Journal* as James MacLaren and that must have been in the same years. The *Vox* articles signed AKL and Stentor were mine all right. As you say, my output in the early to middle 'twenties was incredible – how the devil I did it I can't now imagine; I only wish I had the same energy now – and yet you know, perhaps I have; only instead of pouring out articles, it goes now into correspondence – my range of letter-writing nowadays is really phenomenal.

I mustn't write any more just now. If you have other queries cropping up you'd like to put to me, please don't hesitate – or anything else I can do to help in any way. I hope you are fine and fit after your holiday – tho' the weather was scarcely holiday weather! It hasn't improved since.

My wife joins me in best wishes.

Yours,
C. M. Grieve.

Brownsbank,
Candymill,
Biggar,
Lanarkshire.
24/4/63

Dear Mr Glen,

Many thanks for your letter. I am glad to know you have effected the translation from England to Scotland and hope Mrs Glen and you are beginning to feel yourselves at home. I am very sorry, however, to hear of your son's illness and trust he is making a good recovery. My son is O.K. again – he had a very narrow squeak indeed, but is fine and fit again and back to work. His address is 2 Park Terrace, Glasgow, C3 and he is in the 'phone book. I mention this in case you should want quick news at any time of my whereabouts, etc.

It is splendid to know that *Poetry Like the Hawthorn* did so well. Scottish booksellers are not really booksellers at all – they are mostly deep in a rut and have no initiative or knowledge of, or interest in, literary matters.

I continue to be excessively busy but after doing a TV piece for Grampian TV in Aberdeen on 6th May, my wife and I hope to have a week's badly needed holiday – in Langholm, just to show that the Philistine stupidity of a small group on the local Town Council has not daunted me and that I have no intention of allowing it to come between me and my love of my native place.

My wife joins me in every kind regard to Mrs Glen, Ian, and yourself.

Yours,
Christopher Grieve.

683

Brownsbank,
Biggar.
13/7/69

Dear Duncan Glen,

I got home from Canada a few days ago – in very bad shape, alas. In Canada, I suffered a virus infection, which in turn upset most of my internal organs and culminated in a bout of pneumonia. Fortunately I was in good hands, my son-in-law being a doctor.[1] But the whole thing left me terribly weak, and under the necessity of continuing a heavy course of anti-biotic drugs. I was very glad to get home, but am still quite exhausted and spend most of my time in bed. Tomorrow I'm to go into Edinburgh for another X-ray examination, and will probably stay in Chalmers' Hospital there for about a week. The main reason for that is that my trouble may flare up again at any time and if I were here neither Valda nor I would know how to deal with such a relapse, whereas in the hospital I'd have the necessary immediate attention.

Many thanks for the paste-up of the photo-book.[2] The photos have come out splendidly – especially the early ones. I do not know if you want this paste-up back. If so, just let me know and I'll have it sent to you at once.

Of course I entirely approve your effort to get a publisher to take it up, and I hope in particular that Messrs MacGibbon & Kee may do so.

Naturally all my other work is at a complete standstill for the time being. I have five books to write which should have been in the hands of the publishers by now. Heaven knows when I'll be able to do them. Also, of course, I've had to cancel all sorts of other things – e.g. poetry reading in Dublin, etc.

Hope all goes well with you. I'm still looking for your poems from the Caithness publishers.[3] Kindest regards from Valda and I to Mrs Glen and your family and yourself.

Yours,
Chris.

---

[1] Christine's husband Alastair MacIntosh.
[2] Hugh MacDiarmid and Duncan Glen, *The MacDiarmids: A Conversation* (Preston 1970).
[3] Ronald Eadie Munro (pseudonym of Duncan Glen), *Kythings* (1969).

Brownsbank,
Biggar.
8/8/69

Dear Duncan,

Many thanks for the copies of *Akros* – an excellent issue again.

Willie Neill and Major Boothby have passed on to me the suggestion for an article for *Akros* reviewing the issues of *Catalyst*, and I am willing to do this. Please let me know when it should reach you.

In return Neill wants me to do an article for *Catalyst* on you and your activities. This too I have agreed to do. It does not need to reach him until the end of September or beginning of October.[1]   I am keeping better but still suffering from seriously reduced energies, and still failing to make anything like the headway I need to with my host of commitments.

As to publishing 'Ode to All Rebels', I think I'd greatly prefer to have you publish a pamphlet of new lyrics – in Lallans. As you know I've intended for a long time to get back to writing in Lallans and carry my work in that medium a stage further. I am sure I can do this now and have been mulling over a lot of themes in my mind. I'd hoped to have had the poems written ere this, but my illness has thrown my work schedule completely out of kilter. Still I think (d.v. and W.P.) I'll have a batch ready in a month or two and I'll only send them to you if I am satisfied that they are as good as my early lyrics.

Hope your own recovery is continuing. All the best to you and to Mrs Glen and your family.

Yours,
Christopher Grieve.

If you don't want the *Catalyst* review article please let me know. I'm hoping to write it and send it to you within the next few days.

---

[1] Neither of the projected articles (for *Akros* and *Catalyst*) materialised.

Brownsbank,
Biggar.
10/8/70

Dear Duncan Glen,

Valda and I only got back from Kilquhanity School – which has
been celebrating its 25th year of existence – late last night, to find
amongst the mail awaiting me your letter of 6th inst. and the
provisional Contents list of the Critical Survey.[1] I am very pleased
Tom Maschler[2] has encouraged you to go on with this. The selection you have chosen includes most of the best essays on my work –
by Scottish writers! But that fact implies grave limitations. I have
had occasion to say in a recent preface that 'critics are as rare in
Scotland as snakes in Ireland' and that John Holloway was correct
in saying that most of what purports to be literary criticism is 'mere
personalia'. This is especially true of Helen Cruickshank's essay –
which I wish you would leave out. I have little or no use for the
'mainly domestic' – i.e. gossip column rubbish. Helen as you say is
a very old friend of mine – on certain levels which, alas, are
irrelevant to literary appreciation. She has never really understood
my work at all and has remained a virtually unredeemable Kail-
yairder.

It follows from the above that I prefer commentators of a certain
high sophistication – and these are almost all non-Scots. It is,
however, impossible for you to include in such a collection essays in
German, Magyar, Swedish, etc. But I think an exception could –
and should – be made of French in virtue of the Auld Alliance. So I
am enclosing a copy of *Critique* which contains an essay on my
Joyce poem by Michel Habart.[3] I don't think you will have any
difficulty in securing permission to republish it in your book, and
think it well worth it, as a corrective to those insular reviewers who
condemn my later work. It is my only copy, so please return it to
me in due course.

Valda and I had a good time in Langholm – and subsequently at
Kilquhanity – and now I must get down to a monstrous amount of
work I've delayed doing too long.

[1] (Ed) Duncan Glen, *Hugh MacDiarmid: A Critical Survey* (1972).
[2] Tom Maschler is Chairman of Jonathan Cape; the book was published eventually
by Scottish Academic Press.
[3] Helen Cruickshank's essay 'Mainly Domestic' appeared in *MacDiarmid: A Festschrift* (1962), edited by Kulgin Duval and Sydney Goodsir Smith. Glen did not
reprint it in his symposium. Michel Habart's essay 'Hugh MacDiarmid: Vision-
naire du Langage' was included in Glen's symposium.

Love to you all,

Yours,
Chris.

Please excuse this inadequate note – written in haste.

NLS   Brownsbank.
                                                        7/10/70

Dear Duncan Glen,

Many thanks for the *Akros Anthology*, an excellent production.[1]
While I agree with you about the number of young poets now writing
in Scots you have gathered round you, I wish they were setting their
sights higher and using a lot more Scots vocabulary. Their work for
the most part is simply in the kind of Scots still in conversational use
– and that is not the kind of Scots in which high poetry can be
written, and what can be done in it, and is being done by these poets,
is qualitatively little, if at all, above Kailyaird level, viz. emotion
without intellect, and fancy without imagination. Still in sum it is
perhaps the thin end of a wedge that will yet force through the
barrier to a full use of Scots as a language.

I finally decided not to bother about Scobie's ridiculous article.[2] I
haven't been at all well recently and can still make little or no
headway in making up the mountain of work I am still in arrears
with.

I was extremely sorry to hear about your accident[3] and hope you
have made a complete recovery and have no troublesome after-
effects, as I have even yet from my accident several years ago.

With kindest regards from Valda and I to Mrs Glen and yourself
and other friends at Preston.

Yours,
Chris.

[1] (Ed) Duncan Glen, *The Akros Anthology of Scottish Poetry, 1965–70* (1970).
[2] Stephen Scobie's article on MacDiarmid and Ian Hamilton Finlay appeared in
Akros, No 15, August 1970.
[3] Glen had been knocked off his bicycle by a van but was not badly injured.

Brownsbank,
Biggar.
16/12/70

Duncan Glen, Esq.
Dear Duncan,

It seems a long time since I heard from you (except for your Christmas card which came yesterday). You have so accustomed me in the last year or two to frequent communications that a cessation of these gives me an uncanny feeling of being cut off. I can only hope you – and Mrs Glen and your family – are all O.K. As to business that is another matter. I note that you are to bring out a new periodical and understand that *Akros* may not appear so frequently. The double McDiarmid number[1] must have presented a formidable obstacle to further developments. As no business man myself I can only observe with astonishment all you have done.

As you probably know Valda and I had a very happy holiday in France and Italy. At Aix in Provence the widow and one of the daughters (who teaches, as does her husband, in the local University) of my old friend Professor Denis Saurat received us and threw a big party of their colleagues for us. Then we crossed the French Alps into Italy and in Venice I had a long and most happy session with Ezra Pound. We had lunch with the Pounds and then Ezra and I crossed the Grand Canal in a vaporetta and walked together in St Mark's Square and had coffee in the famous Café Florian there.

I keep saying I must cut down my public commitments. I am too old to carry on. So I say – but I can't. On getting back from Milan I was once again caught up in the whirl of engagements. I gave a poetry reading at Bristol University (and to get there had to go to – and travel up from – London) then went back to London in order to travel to Newcastle-on-Tyne where I did a Colour TV interview for the Tyneside TV. Then back to Glasgow, and then to London again to read poems and speak on behalf of the Irish political detainees. What a life!

However I must not exacerbate things by writing a long letter – I have a mountain of Xmas and other mail to attend to – to say nothing about arrears of work! So this is just a passing note to wish you all a happy Xmas and a prosperous New Year from Valda and I. As above details of my recent movements will show

[1] *Akros*, Nos 13–14, April 1970.

you, I actually passed Preston twice but could not of course break my journeys there and see you, as I'd fain have done!!

Yours,
Chris.

NLS   Brownsbank,
                                                              Biggar.
                                                             14/3/71

Dear Duncan Glen,

Since the Postal Strike was ended I have felt like someone standing in the way of the almighty onrush when the retaining wall of a reservoir gives way. It will certainly take me a good while to discharge my epistolary obligations.

Many thanks for *Knowe* and *In Appearances*.[1] The latter is I think by far the best thing you have done. It is as you know a kind of poetry at a great remove from my own. It is very personal and intimate, and expressed at a conversational level – staccato often. But I agree with the excellent statements in the excerpt from Paul Duncan quoted on the jacket. It is good to know you have a stock still to publish which will furnish another couple of books. By that time it should be possible to see your work in the round, and I'll have to put my thinking cap on. I owe you that in any case, but just at the moment I can't attempt to do justice to *In Appearances*. I hope I may have time to try to shortly.

Re Alex Scott-David Craig. I'm a bit tired of that sort of thing, but regarding Craig in *Akros* you have my permission (I'll write him too) to let him quote in his article any of the poems of mine he and Manson have been exhuming from the early days of Lallans.[2] I think nothing of them myself and will not permit Manson and Craig to publish their collection of them except with a note by myself explaining just why I think them worthless as poetry unless they are clearly stated to be mere juvenilia and discarded trial shots.

[1] *Knowe*, a monthly supplement to *Akros*, ran from January to April 1971. *In Appearances* (1971) is a book of Glen's poetry.
[2] Alexander Scott and David Craig had been at odds in the pages of *Knowe*. Craig's essay was never published in *Akros*.

Good news that Critical Survey of McD is likely to be published in November by Edinburgh Academic Press.

I'll try to send you the Pound photos in a day or so. I am very grateful to you in this connection of trying to get enlargements.

You do not mention *Whither Scotland*.[3] I hope all goes well with it too. The Bodoni Press, Verona, are going to publish in expensive de luxe editions both the three Direadh poems (as one book) and the *In Memoriam James Joyce*.

I've had a desperate downpour of TV and Radio engagements – an hour-long programme for BBC TV, an interview with James Cameron for BBC2, an interview in James Mossman's 'Review' magazine, and a 25 minute poetry reading for London Weekend Television for which I've to go down to Wembley about the end of the month. Also I've just agreed to do a programme for STV early in April. I hope too to go to America for International Poetry Forum at Pittsburg, and also to Canada to speak and read poems at Carleton College, Ottawa, and at the Laurentian University at Sudbury.

And if in the interstices of these engagements I can manage to do some writing I hope to send you some new poems.

In the meantime all the best to Mrs Glen, yourself, and family, and the others at Preston who've been here.

Yours,
Chris.

NLS

Brownsbank,
Biggar.
27/9/71

Duncan Glen, Esq.

Dear Duncan,

It was good of you to call on me in the hospital. I was very pleased to see you but thought you were bearing traces of overwork and obviously needed a good holiday, which I hope you had.

I made a good recovery from my operation but got out of hospital too quickly perhaps – anyhow I've had a good deal of trouble since.

[3] (Ed) Duncan Glen, *Whither Scotland? A Prejudiced Look at the Future of a Nation* (1971).

It takes time for one's organs to regain their normal functions after the shock and displacements of a surgical invasion.

Both the surgeon and my son-in-law, who is a consultant physician, told me there was no need to cancel my projected American and Canadian engagements – that, indeed, I'd be more fit to fulfil these than if I'd gone before having the operation.

Alas, I am now advised that it is too soon after the operation – it will be all right in a few months' time, but not now – so I've been obliged to cancel the whole thing which was to have been from 25th October to mid-November. I think I had a hidden feeling that in proposing to go on with the tour I was taking a big risk, since the fact is that I just haven't been more than a yard or so from the toilet any time.

Otherwise apart from congenital laziness I am not succeeding yet in reducing my appalling backlog of work. I hope I acquire more energy soon. I am really in dreadful arrears.

I was glad to see in the last issue of *Stand*[1] an appreciative notice of your poems, and I certainly think highly of the one that was reproduced.

I hope *Whither Scotland?* has gone well. I don't know how *Akros* is shaping, but there is a new American anthology called *Twenty-Three British Poets*, which is an important attack on official British Poetry which is stigmatised as largely museum stuff – out of touch with or opposed to the most important trends and needs of poetry today. I'd like to write you a short article about this if you want it.

Valda joins me in kindest regards to you, Mrs Glen and your family.

       Yours,
       Chris.

---

[1] Reviews of work by Glen appeared in *Stand* Vol 12, No 1, and Vol 12, No 2.

Brownsbank,
Biggar.
21/11/71

Duncan Glen, Esq.

Dear Duncan,

Many thanks for the copies of *Feres* and *The Individual and the Twentieth Century Scottish Literary Tradition*.[1] These have just arrived. I have not had a chance to read *Feres* yet, and have only riffled through, and not yet carefully read, *The Individual*, etc. but even on that inadequate basis of study I am sure it is one of the best things you have done. That does not mean that I agree with a lot of it, but merely that I welcome it as an extension of the field for debate. My main objection of course is that while welcoming all the diverse usages of Scots it does not indicate how good poetry is to be distinguished from negligible rhyming. The critic's job is to 'distinguish and divide' and that cannot be done if all comers are to be equally welcomed and any insistence on particular standards dismissed as cliqueish. However, your essays fortify the basic demands for the revival and extended application of the Scots language and bring to the task quotations and considerations from a wide range of literary and philosophical phenomena, many of which are new and as such were not available to me when I was busy indicating possible or desirable lines of development 40–50 years ago.

These two additions to the bibliography of your works are excellently produced and I hope (not knowing anything about costs of production) that this also means economical as well as excellent.

I think you are wise to ease off a bit, you have certainly had a very heavy time of it, and that must have depleted your physical resources.

While I am O.K. again, I do not yet find it possible to work as hard as I'd wish to do – and indeed need to do if I am to make up the arrears I incurred during my illness. All I can do so far is just tinker at the circumference of my problem. I mean write short pieces – new introduction to *Lucky Poet*, essay on Robert Henryson to preface my Penguin selection of his poems, a note for the sleeve of the Claddagh record of Sorley Maclean's poems, and I have a round dozen of such small things to do yet. But the major jobs I haven't the strength to venture upon yet, tho' I hope to do so soon.

One little point re one of your essays is that McLuhan is a Scot, or

---

[1] Duncan Glen's *Feres: Poems* (1971) and his essay *The Individual and the 20th Century Scottish Literary Tradition* (1971).

thinks of himself as such.[2] I met him in Toronto at the big Roman Catholic Seminary which incidentally houses one of the finest libraries of mediaeval literature in the world. And McLuhan told me he belonged to a Scottish family transplanted to Ulster at the time of the Plantation of Ulster. Incidentally he is a most entertaining conversationalist and has an enormous repertoire of anecdotes. When he'd fired off a whole series of stories at me I felt it was up to me to tell him a few he probably hadn't heard, and he brought out his notebook and jotted down the stories I told him!!

I haven't been out of this cottage since I left hospital but this week I'm going in to Edinburgh to attend a dinner of the Edinburgh branch of the English Association of which Charles King is the secretary.

I'd meant to send you an article based on a recent American anthology, but do not know when this should reach you to be considered for the next *Akros*.

Also as you probably know Alex Scott is getting together a volume of essays on Neil Gunn as an 80th birthday tribute to him.[3] I've promised to write one but haven't done it yet. Gunn was in hospital too with trigeminal facial neuralgia which is one of the most hellishly painful things man suffers. He's home again now the doctors having decided not to operate in the meantime.

Dr George Davie is also in hospital, with suspected TB I'm told, tho' that seems unlikely. I wrote his wife Elspeth, but haven't heard yet how he's doing or what exactly is the matter.

Vada joins me in best wishes to your wife and yourself.

With renewed thanks,

Yours,
Christopher Grieve.

P.S. I wonder if your friends have been able to do anything with the Ezra Pound snaps yet.[4]

[2] Marshall McLuhan, the culturologist and author of *Understanding Media* (1964) and *The Medium is the Message* (1967).

[3] (Eds) Douglas Gifford and Alexander Scott, *Neil M. Gunn: The Man and the Writer* (1973).

[4] Valda Grieve took photographs of MacDiarmid's meeting with Pound in Venice in 1971; two of them were reproduced in Gordon Wright's *MacDiarmid: An Illustrated Biography* (Edinburgh 1977).

Brownsbank,
Biggar,
Lanarkshire.
16/7/75

Duncan Glen, Esq.

Dear Duncan,

Many thanks for your letter and for the copies of *Akros* and of your *Mr and Mrs J. L. Stoddart at home*,[1] which last I have just received and not had any chance to read yet, so I must write you later regarding it.

As to *Akros*[2] the various surveys by decades of the position of Scottish Poetry are full of information and will be useful to many people interested in but not too well informed on the matter. So the issue should serve a very useful purpose since the number of such people is steadily and substantially increasing and will be further extended by students and school pupils who have the advantage of courses in Scottish Literature not available to earlier generations of their kind.

But as to the value of these essays as criticism I have my doubts. I notice the view expressed that Robert Garioch and Ian Hamilton Finlay are poets of some importance, which I don't believe at all – and certainly they and most of the others commented on have not managed to secure any international recognition or establish a reputation for themselves for technical and other initiatives such as characterise leading poets of most so called civilised countries today – except England. Wales and Ireland are far ahead of the last named in this respect, and Scotland is slowly I think coming abreast of them.

I note no mention of Tom Law, who I consider one of the best in Scotland today, or of Robin Munro whose new volume (published by Dent) I have just received – and find in every way confirmatory of the high promise I discerned in his first Shetland poems.

I'll send Robert Duxbury a poem as you suggest. You ask about my *Complete Poems*. These have now been assembled and ready for the publisher – but this as you will appreciate has been a big job and I don't know yet just when the book (or books – for I think it will take two volumes) will appear, but not this year now but in the spring '76 perhaps.

Kindest regards to Margaret and yourself and congratulations on

---

[1] Duncan Glen's poem *Mr and Mrs J. L. Stoddart At Home* (1976).
[2] *Akros*, Vol 10, No 28, April 1975. In this issue David Black praised the work of Robert Garioch and Ian Hamilton Finlay.

having carried *Akros* on so long and with every confidence in its contrivance albeit with full understanding of the labours it entails for you.

Yours,
Chris.

NLS   Brownsbank,
                                                                by Biggar.
                                                                 15/2/78

Duncan Glen, Esq.

Dear Duncan,

A horrible thing has happened to me. Some weeks ago Philip Pacey wrote and told me in strict confidence that he and some others were planning to issue a sort of festschrift[1] testifying to their high opinion of you on the occasion of your leaving Preston for Trent. He wanted a poem or two from me for this purpose, and stressed that all concerned were specially anxious that the matter should not be divulged to you. So if it hasn't already leaked out to you I am sure I can trust you not to tell I've given the game away.

But I have to do it because I'd have been very pleased indeed to acquiesce in Mr Pacey's request – but I just can't. I'm having a very bad time indeed and can't write, or read, or even watch TV. And this is likely to last for an indefinite period ahead.

The trouble is that I underwent half-a-dozen operations and then it was found that instead of helping me my condition had 'gravely deteriorated'. So some other treatment was needed and it was agreed I shall have a course of radio therapy – not the old X-ray business but the new Neutron treatment. Alas, the specialists just don't know what dosage (strength of treatment) any individual needs, and that varies greatly. So they told me they had modified the strength of my exposures. But evidently not nearly enough. I did sustain one radio burn, externally, in my left groin. This healed very quickly. But I was still having extreme pain and difficulty in the performance of my natural functions and it now seems I am badly burned internally and

---

[1] *Our Duncan, who art in Trent* (1978).

that condition will take time to overcome. I have so much pain that I am simply drained of all energy for anything else.

I am sure you will understand and appreciate how very sorry I am to be missing from the forthcoming festschrift.

I hope your move to Trent is a good one and that you are all well. With every kind regard and gratitude for all you've done.

Yours,
Christopher Grieve.

NLS

Brownsbank,
Candymill,
by Biggar.
20/2/78

Dear Duncan,

My laggard condition is emphasised by your most kind and understanding letter just received – before I have managed to thank you for the copy of Alex Scott's Anthology of *Modern Scots Verse*.[1]

This is not only a great compliment to me on my recent 85th birthday but as your 100th publication there could scarcely have been any book better fitted to mark the century of *Akros*.

I am particularly pleased at the inclusion at last in such a selection of worthy representations of yourself, of Tom Law, and of Tom Scott.

I wholly agree with you that your best tribute to my example is just to follow your own star and do your own thing.

Certainly the anthology puts paid to Maurice Lindsay's idea that the Scots Renaissance has petered out – all he really means by that is that he has not been accorded the prominent place in it he thinks he deserves. I think on the contrary and the two poems by which he is represented are quite enough, and indeed that they might well have been left out.

I wonder if, in the throes of flitting from Preston, you have copies left of the *Akros*[2] with the articles by Mulrine and others on my work

[1] (Ed) Alexander Scott, *Modern Scots Verse 1922–1977* (1978). The anthology was published in honour of MacDiarmid's eighty-fifth birthday.
[2] *Akros*, Vol 12, Nos 34–5, August 1977. Special Hugh MacDiarmid Double Issue.

– the issue with the Coia drawings. If so, please send me a couple, and I will of course pay for them.

With every kind regard to Margaret and yourself, and of course I'll be delighted to see you if you can come – tho' the visit must be a brief one; I hate having friends undertake the long journey to come here when I can only see them for a very short while.

As always.

Yours,
Christopher.

To George Bruce

George Bruce was born in Fraserburgh where his father ran the oldest curing firm in the north of Scotland. His first book, *Sea Talk* (1944) made his reputation as the poet of Buchan and one of the most fastidious exponents of English verse to emerge in Scotland since Edwin Muir. After working for some time as a teacher of English he was, from 1946 to 1970, a BBC producer in Aberdeen and Edinburgh. As such he was responsible for many broadcasts in which MacDiarmid's cultural impact was analysed and his poetry promoted. George Bruce's interview with 'MacDiarmid at Eighty-five' is included in *The Thistle Rises: A MacDiarmid Miscellany* edited by Alan Bold. For the letters MacDiarmid wrote to Bruce at the BBC see pp. 525–31.

NLS

Brownsbank,
Biggar.
4/8/65

Dear George,

I am writing you just because you are the quickest to get in touch with. I have just learned with horror that the book to be issued by Edinburgh University Press edited by Maurice Lindsay, Edwin Morgan, and yourself is to be called *Scotch* Poetry.[1] Well, I certainly won't allow any poem of mine to be scotched. Unless the title of the collection is altered to something more acceptable, I have to give you notice now that no poem of mine must appear in it. I'm not blaming you – I don't know who is responsible. But it just won't do, and I must dissociate myself from any such monstrosity.

[1] The annual anthology (Edinburgh 1966–7) was eventually entitled *Scottish Poetry*.

Long time no' see. Hope you and Mrs Bruce and your family are O.K.

All the best.

Yours,
Chris.

NLS

Brownsbank,
Biggar.
9/5/71

George Bruce, Esq.
Dear George,

Just a line to congratulate you on the Glasgow University Fellowship and wish you the best of luck with it. I've just been listening to the Bookmark discussion on Arts Council grants to authors. I think University fellowships much better – tho' I would never have liked one myself. In most cases, like John Davidson, I think the only useful advice that can be given to young literary aspirants is just the advice Punch gave to those thinking of marrying, namely Don't!

I also hope that the Glasgow Fellowship would be only a one-year appointment or just from year to year, but like Norman's[1] at Stirling (in contradistinction to the Edinburgh University one) a permanent job.

Anyhow so far as encouragement of Literature is concerned I think one criterion should be that nothing popular or likely or designed and intended by the author to give the public what it wants should be encouraged at all but on the contrary discouraged by every possible means. Literary value is not a matter of opinion – there are objective standards independent altogether of whether many people or indeed any like or dislike a particular work or not.

All the best to Mrs Bruce and yourself.

Yours,
Chris.

[1] Norman MacCaig.

699

NLS

Brownsbank,
Candymill,
Biggar,
Lanarkshire.
7/12/72

George Bruce, Esq.

Dear George,

Many thanks for *Lines* and the inscription of your poem 'The Desert' to me.[1] I am delighted by this evidence that (a) you are having a good creative period, and (b) that you have about you in Glasgow University such a promising group.

I think 'The Desert' *is* successful, but whether it is political in the sense I advocate is another matter. Any strengthening of the intellectual content of poems I welcome, and, of course, the inclusion of political and social material and scientific material and indeed all sorts of material hitherto regarded as not poetic. But of course the test of political poetry is not only that it should be poetry but that it should have political effect, as I think some of mine has had (witness the telegrams of appreciation I had on my 80th birthday from *all* the European Communist Parties and also some from further afield – also the fact that my Hymns to Lenin were broadcast in Moscow on the occasion of Lenin's anniversary).

Valda and I have just had a very good time down South where I had a Poetry Reading in the Mermaid Theatre in London, and in Cambridge University under the auspices of the English Faculty.

These 80th birthday affairs are nearly over. People have been extremely kind but I have found the whole business a bit too much. I've still to go down to Langholm for a few days starting on 14th inst. when friends in Langholm are going to present me with an armchair.

I am in very good form apart recently from a cold in the head. Valda has also had that, but we are both in good shape really. Hope this finds Mrs Bruce and yourself in like case. And now, as the time draws near, we wish you a happy Christmas and a good New Year.

Yours sincerely,
Christopher Grieve.

---

[1] *Lines Review*, Nos 42 and 43, September 1972–February 1973, contained George Bruce's poem 'The Desert'.

To Tom Scott

Tom Scott, born in Glasgow in 1918, is a poet who found his Scots voice in 1950 and has written powerfully in both Scots and English as witness the work in *The Ship and Ither Poems* (1963) and *The Tree* (1977). With Professor John MacQueen of Edinburgh University, Scott edited *The Oxford Book of Scottish Verse* (1966), an entertaining and educational anthology. MacDiarmid, as the letters show, took a great interest in the project. Scott's *Dunbar: A Critical Exposition of the Poems* (1966) did much to draw attention to Dunbar's living presence in Scots verse.

Brownsbank,
Biggar.
13/3/65

Dear Tom,

I appreciate fully all you say in letter received today.

I think probably the best thing to do is just (if M's delay or refuse permission or ask too big a fee) to go ahead and print the 'Wheel' from the *Drunk Man*. I think Moray MacLaren did just that when he included it in his *Wisdom of the Scots*[1] – with impunity. But in any case you have my permission and if there is any trouble I am willing that a deduction should be made from the fees payable to me to compensate M's for the unfortunate oversight!

I note what you say re Norman McCaig, David Craig, etc. gunning against Lallans. They can gun all they like – the ricochetting will blow them off their little perches in the long run.

As to Alan Bold he is a problem. I was for a little while in two minds about acceding to his request that I should introduce his

[1] (Ed) Moray McLaren, *The Wisdom of the Scots* (1961).

pamphlet of poems.[2] But I took my courage in both hands and am now glad I did so. I think he has the root of the matter in him and will come through all right. So I'm glad you're hoping to include one of his poems.[3] The one read over the Scottish Home Service in Alex Scott's and Walter Keir's report on the Scottish University Verse Competition[4] came over very well; and Bold's use of the science of colour (red light, etc.) to establish his political point was very effective.

All the best to you and yours. Anthologising is a heart breaking job.

Yours,
Chris.

Brownsbank,
Biggar.
24/3/65

Dear Tom,

I am returning herewith the copies of correspondence re Ian Finlay.[1] This kind of pressure is certainly not to be tolerated and I will be very shocked if the OUP people are influenced by it. In any case, I feel strongly on the subject that if Finlay – or any 'Concrete' stuff – is included then I must refuse to be. There have been all sorts of changes in poetry in different countries and throughout the ages; nevertheless all that is worth while constitutes a unity. No one wants to exclude the possibility of new developments, but there is no justification for using the term 'poetry' to cover something utterly different – and whatever else may be said about Finlay's work, and

[2] MacDiarmid wrote an introduction to Alan Bold's first collection of poems, *Society Inebrious*(1965).
[3] Tom Scott originally wanted to include Alan Bold's poem 'Recitative' in *The Oxford Book of Scottish Verse* but it was eventually decided to exclude younger writers.
[4] 'Red Sunset' was included in 'University Notebook', BBC Scottish Home Service, 11 March 1965.
[1] Several of Ian Hamilton Finlay's admirers wrote to Oxford University Press insisting that his concrete poetry should be represented in *The Oxford Book of Scottish Verse*. It was not.

that of his many associates, it certainly has nothing in common with what down the centuries, despite all changes, has been termed 'poetry'.

However, there you are – I am sorry if this in any way adds to your troubles and further complicates your tasks – but I am utterly unwilling to have any poems of mine included in an anthology in which any of Finlay's productions are also included. I leave it to you to advise the OUP to that effect, if insistence on Finlay's inclusion necessitates it.

All the best.

Yours,
Chris.

Brownsbank,
Biggar.
5/11/65

Dear Tom Scott,

Many thanks for your letter. I am sorry but not surprised OUP have turned down Garioch's collected poems, tho' I agree that the long delay is inexcusable. I do not know why OUP should have delayed because it must have been clear right away that the publication could not be commercially successful. I am of course sorry that Garioch should have had to endure this long suspense and then find his hopes disappointed. But in so far as I know his work there is very little of it of value. His strength lies in his knowledge of Scots, and particularly of demotic Edinburgh dialect but he has no elevation and is in general I think not only dull but vulgar in the worst sense. Edinburgh University Press is a possibility, perhaps, but I cannot think of any other likely publisher. A grant from Carnegie would, of course, be a great help.

The Noel Stock book re Pound should be out.[1] It's called *Perspectives* and was to be published by a New York firm. But I've heard

---

[1] MacDiarmid contributed an essay, 'The Return of the Long Poem', to Noel Stock's symposium *Ezra Pound: Perspectives* (1965).

nothing yet. Pound's birthday has gone with practically no notice in this country so far as I've seen.

Glad your *Dunbar* has reached proof-correcting stage – even if some of the corrections necessary shouldn't have been required especially the irritating punctuation business.

Also, of course, glad the OBSV proofs are beginning to come in. I can't suggest another book you might like to tackle, but I'll think about it, and let you know if I come up with anything.

Anyhow all the best to you and yours.

Yours,
Chris.

Lanarkshire.
23/4/66

Tom Scott, Esq. M.A. Ph.D.

Dear Tom,

Every conceivable congratulation you on your magnificent *Dunbar*. I do not expect that I will often – if at all – again thrill so greatly on receipt of a book. O & B have printed and produced it splendidly. I have of course, as you will understand, only had time yet for a first run-through, but nothing that comes within the compass of my own interests and knowledge in it can I think be faulted. I look forward to long spells of absorbed reading and reflection in its company. Who knows but what it may trigger off my aged and lazy muse again – to say nothing of its effect on younger writers, and the authors who, I feel sure, will in the next decade or so bestir themselves to supply the other studies you list as so greatly to be desired alongside your own.

I hope some editor asks me to review it. Anyhow I'll certainly be on the qui vive for the notices it gets in all the important quarters.

We should really meet to celebrate the occasion. But I am not likely, alas, to be in Edinburgh in the near future. I am suffering from a serious diminution of energy, and must eschew any activities I possibly can in the near future anyhow.

Hope you are feeling fit and fine now your long darg has reached this happy consummation.

With best wishes to your wife and children and yourself.

Yours,
Chris.

To Timothy O'Keeffe

Timothy O'Keeffe, the publisher, was with MacGibbon and Kee when that firm published three collections of MacDiarmid poems – *A Lap of Honour* (1967), *A Clyack-Sheaf* (1969), *More Collected Poems* (1970) – and *The Uncanny Scot* (1968), a selection of MacDiarmid's prose edited by Kenneth Buthlay. O'Keeffe left MacGibbon and Kee to found his own publishing house of Martin Brian and O'Keeffe who published MacDiarmid's *Complete Poems*, post-humously, in 1978.

> Brownsbank,
> Biggar,
> Lanarkshire.
> Scotland.
> 14/11/66

Timothy O'Keeffe, Esq,
Messrs MacGibbon & Kee Ltd,
Publishers.

Dear Mr O'Keeffe,

Many thanks for your very kind letter. The position with regard to my *Collected Poems* is that Messrs Macmillan, New York, have now in hand a new edition of this. The more egregious errors in the first edition have been corrected and the glossary greatly expanded. This is to be published early in May.

Messrs Oliver and Boyd have nothing to do with the matter. I have no arrangement with them. They simply bought a number of sets of sheets of the original New York edition and had these bound up and given their own imprint. They grossly underestimated the demand and sold out their supply immediately. Messrs Macmillan refused to give them any more. The New York edition also sold out very quickly.

As you probably know, I was ill-advised enough to consent to Messrs Macmillan using only brief passages from some of my longer poems. These passages were practically meaningless taken out of their context in this way. I would like now to publish these poems in full. This would entail Messrs Macmillan's permission to use the passages which did appear in *Collected Poems*.

Also I found that I had forgotten to include a number of poems. These are among my best poems.

So I wonder if you would like to consider publishing a volume containing 1/ these longer poems in full and 2/ a number of poems not included in *Collected Poems*.

I need not tell you how gratified I am at your continuing interest in my work, and how pleased I would be to have such a volume over your imprint.

With best wishes.

Yours sincerely,
C. M. Grieve.

Brownsbank,
Biggar,
Lanarkshire.
9/5/68

Timothy O'Keefe, Esq,
c/o Messrs MacGibbon & Kee,
Publishers.

Dear Timothy O'Keeffe,

Many thanks for your note. My wife and I greatly enjoyed your all-too-brief visit here. It was a pity we couldn't put you up overnight. I was glad to have you confirm my high opinion of *Glen Fiddich*. As it happened the following day I fell heir to a couple of bottles of Moranjie, another malt whisky, but blander than Glen Fiddich and not quite so authoritative.

I had meant to tell you about the books. As I said in a previous letter you'll have the typescripts of two them by the end of the summer – one a prose book, the other poetry. I have done all the research for the former now and have the material under my hand, so it is only a case of straightforward writing. Poetry is not so amenable to a strict timetable. But I've kept the next three months clear of other engagements, and that will suffice. I hope this is O.K. with you. The other prose book I've done some preliminary work on also, but I don't think I'll be able make any headway on it now till I get the foregoing two off my hands.

In the meantime I'm looking forward to proofs of the Buthlay book[1] of stories.

With best wishes to you and your colleagues.

Yours,
Christopher Grieve.

Brownsbank,
Biggar,
Lanarkshire,
Scotland.
20/2/70

Dear Timothy O'Keeffe,

Many thanks for your letter of 17th. I had a very happy time in Dublin from which I got back on Wednesday. But what a pity we missed seeing you. I note with much regret that you have now left MacGibbon & Kee, and can only hope you have the best of luck in quickly securing another post.

I have been wondering what the position is re *More Collected Poems* having heard nothing since I returned the book proofs.

Also I had hoped to have sent in by now two other books – the prose book surveying the whole field of Scottish national character, and the long poem, *Haud Forrit*[1]. But I have been held back by illness and it will be a month or two before I can complete and send them in now. I hope this delay is not an infraction of the terms of my contract. I will send them in as soon as I possibly can, but I am still unable to do any sustained work.

[1] Hugh MacDiarmid, *The Uncanny Scot* (London 1968), a selection of prose edited by Kenneth Buthlay.
[1] *Impavidi Progrediamur*, or *Haud Forrit* as he referred to it in his last years, was projected as the final part of MacDiarmid's huge *Mature Art* project.

With every kind regard from my wife and myself.

Yours,
Christopher Grieve.

Brownsbank,
Candymill,
by Biggar,
Lanarkshire.
21/1/78

Timothy O'Keeffe, Esq.

Dear Timothy,

I suppose something unexpected came in the way and prevented your projected visit to Scotland. Anyhow I hope I did not miss you for any other reason. True, I was in hospital over most of the relevant time. I have in fact been having one hell of a time – and as if the main trouble were not enough, the course of Neutron ray therapy I underwent left me with a nasty radiation burn which is infernally painful and requires constant dressing by a nurse.

In the absence of all news I keep worrying about the *Complete Poems*. I had really thought I'd have had Vol I by this time. I do hope there are no serious causes of delay but will be glad to have any reassurance you can give me, and in particular, any hard and fast date of publication. I do not want the book to be 'posthumously published', but am anxious to see the completed article while I am still able to see.

I hope things are going well with you. They won't with me for some time ahead anyway. I had to cancel my intended visit to Canada after all, which was a great disappointment since it was an event which I regarded as extremely important. I have also within the past couple of weeks had to refuse invitations to Paris, London, Dublin, and Cardiff.

With kind remembrances to your wife, and to Martin Green,[1] and of course your good self.

Yours,
Christopher Grieve.

[1] Martin Green was, with O'Keeffe, one of the founders of Martin Brian and O'Keeffe.

Timothy O'Keeffe, Esq.

Dear Timothy,

Many thanks for jacket of *Complete Poems*, I am very pleased with it. It should stand out in any bookshop display.

I note what you say re publications, but I am of course waiting as patiently as I can.

I go into hospital again on 7th inst. and expect operation the following day. But if all goes well I hope to be only two or three days in hospital and think I should manage to get to Dublin for the ceremony[1] on 6th July all right. Hope to see you there.

Every kind regard to your wife and yourself.

Yours,
Christopher Grieve.

[1] The Honorary Litt. D. conferred on MacDiarmid by Dublin University.

To David Wright

Born in Johannesburg in 1920, David Wright was educated at Oxford and made his literary reputation as a poet and editor – of the magazines *Nimbus* and *X* and the Penguin anthologies *The Mid-Century: English Poetry 1940–60* (1965) and *Longer Contemporary Poems* (1966). Wright included MacDiarmid in both his Penguin anthologies and urged Penguin Books to publish MacDiarmid's *Selected Poems* (which they did in 1970). He regularly came to Langholm in the 1970s for the annual Common-Riding and enjoyed meeting MacDiarmid there. Wright's wife Pippa – Phillipa Reid – was born in New Zealand, trained at the Old Vic Drama school and was for many years a leading actress with the Century Theatre.

Brownsbank,
Biggar,
Lanarkshire,
Scotland.
18/4/67

Dear David Wright,

Many thanks for your letter and pamphlet of poems. I was pleased to see your tribute to Robert MacBryde, a counterpart to George Barker's on Robert Colquhoun.[1] I owed – if I am a poet! – elegies to these two also, but I am no good at occasional verse, and will I am afraid fail to render the tribute I should.

I am extremely interested to hear of your proximity to the Scottish Border. All being well, I hope to be at Langholm as usual for the

[1] David Wright's pamphlet *Poems* (1966) contains the poem 'For Robert Mac-Bryde' (including the line 'I owe one to you if I am a poet' alluded to by Mac-Diarmid). MacDiarmid knew the Scottish painters Colquhoun and MacBryde well.

711

Common-Riding, but may not manage this year, as I have a truly terrific programme ahead. I go to USA on Thursday 20th, and in May to Canada. I'll be back here in the beginning of June and will be in Edinburgh for the opening of the MacDiarmid Exhibition in the National Library of Scotland on 3rd July. From 6th to 12th July Valda and I will be in London for the International Poetry Festival, and on 6th August in Edinburgh for a big gathering the CP are organising for my birthday. Then I am going to the German Democratic Republic and to Hungary. But do get in touch if Pip and you are to be in Edinburgh!

It is good of you to suggest a MacDiarmid paperback to Penguin. I hope it comes off. But I have so many books in the offing, by me or about me, that I mustn't be greedy.

I think the best thing to do about your grandfather's uniform, etc.[2] is to offer this to the Scottish Museum of Antiquities, Chambers St, Edinburgh. I am sure they'll be keen to have it. You might write in the first place to

Dr Ian Inglis,
Curator,
at above address.

Every kind regard to Pip and you.

Yours,
Christopher Grieve.

Brownbank,
Candymill,
Biggar,
Lanarkshire.
4/7/73

Dear David and Pippa Wright,

Good to hear from you again and to know you expect to be at Langholm Common-Riding – which is not on 28th June (as your

---

[2] Wright's grandfather John Murray was a member of the Ayrshire Volunteers. The uniform, dating from c. 1860, was presented to the Scottish United Services Museum on 3 July 1967.

712

letter says) but on Friday 27th July. Unless something unexpected intervenes we'll be there.

We are both at the moment very jaded and just recovering from an exhausting time in Rotterdam and Amsterdam, and afterwards in London. We went to Holland to take part in an International Poetry Festival and had a very enjoyable, if extremely busy, time. It was just over 50 years since I'd been in Holland last and I had expected the climate would not differ much from that of Scotland. Instead it was terrifically hot – as blindingly sunlit as Salonika. I do not like too much sun or heat. Valda revels in them and benefits accordingly. Such conditions energise her, but enervate me. I had one consolation, however, if ere long, as I expect, I go to Hell, it won't be to an eternity of weeping and wailing and gnashing of teeth. I am satisfied I could never stand the climate, so my sojourn there would be brief and surcease of my sufferings speedy.

London wasn't much better. I took part in the Poetry Book Society's Poetry International '73 and finally did a TV appearance, but this was really grilling and I still feel half-incinerated.

Hope all goes well with both of you. As you say, all news when we meet.

Love from Valda and I.

Yours,
Christopher Grieve.

Brownsbank,
Biggar,
Lanarkshire.
9/8/73

Dear Pippa and David,

I need not tell you how sorry I was to miss seeing you at the Common-Riding. Valda and I were in Langholm nearly a week, but after the Common-Riding day I wasn't up town at all but just had to lie low and rest. I felt quite O.K. on the Common-Riding morning, went up to the Market Place, heard the first Crying of the Fair, then went up the Kirk Brae to watch the cavalcade of horses galloping up. It was a splendid morning and I was looking forward to a very happy

713

day. I went down to the Market Place – looked into the Eskdale Bar to see if you'd arrived, and then stood outside awaiting the second Crying of the Fair. And then suddenly collapsed. A doctor was sent for and sounded me, took my blood pressure, etc. – and found nothing whatever the matter with me. He simply thought I'd be standing in the sunshine too long and that my collapse was due to some inadequacy of the blood supply to the brain – but he could discover no cause for that.

A few years ago I used to take these collapses fairly frequently, but had not had any for a long time. On all the previous occasions the various doctors who examined me all found my heart, lungs, etc. perfectly O.K. – the only clue to the cause being perhaps the fact that I have a very low blood pressure. That of course can be worse than high blood pressure and in certain circumstances prove fatal.

Heaven only knows, it deprived me of your company to which I had been looking forward. These collapses of course leave me very shaky, so I could do nothing for the remainder of my stay in Langholm but just lie about on a sofa or in bed. It was all most unfortunate. I can only hope it did not entirely spoil the day for you. Incidentally drink was *not* the cause. I'd only had two small whiskies.

Better luck next time!

Valda joins me in every kind regard.

Yours,
Christopher Grieve.

To Alexander Scott

Alexander Scott was born in 1920 in Aberdeen and educated at Aberdeen University. During World War Two he was awarded the Military Cross and after the war he became a combative force in the cause of Scottish literature; he was appointed head of the Department of Scottish Literature at Glasgow University in 1971 and has made his presence felt on various academic boards, editorial committees and anthologies. His own poetry, in *Cantrips* (1968) for example, is characterised by a linguistic flair evident in incisive and satirical poems in both English and the aggrandised Scots he has employed since 1945. His book on William Soutar, *Still Life* (1958), is an outstanding piece of biographical-critical work and his interest in MacDiarmid is expressed in *The Hugh MacDiarmid Anthology* (London 1972) which he edited with the poet's son Michael Grieve.

Brownsbank,
Biggar.
26/6/67

Alex Scott Esq.

Dear Alex,

Many thanks for sending me the copy of *Void*,[1] per Mike, to Stirling – and for your excellent (if too flattering) article therein. Congratulate Ewan[2] on the issue. *Void* compares favourably with several other such productions I see.

As to your article I am not convinced that my effort to write

---

[1] *Void*, edited by Ewan Scott, and fellow students at Sussex University, appeared on only one occasion: this issue (of April 1967) contained an article by Alexander Scott on 'The Scottish Renaissance in Poetry'.

[2] Ewan, Alexander Scott's younger son.

philosophical poetry in Scots has failed. In my new book[3] I include 'Depth and Chthonian Image', a poem that has been largely overlooked by my commentators. There is quite a lot of very archaic Scots in it, but that doesn't bog down the poetry – on the contrary I think the movement of the verse carries with ease even the most difficult elements of vocabulary. I remember a very shrewd critic, who himself was a well-posted philosopher saying when it first appeared that if I contrived to write philosophical poetry of that quality I need have no fear. Apart from that two other poems I recently republished (both are in my new collection) – 'Whuchulls' and 'Wauchopeside' – both seem to me successful in this way. However, yours is the third article within the past fortnight on my work – and the best of the three and I've no doubt will hold its own all right against all the others that will be appearing shortly now.

Glad STV suggestion is likely to prove fruitful.

All the best to Cathy[4] and yourself.

Yours,
Chris.

Biggar.
13/12/67

Dear Alex,

The suggestions you propose making to the Scottish Books Council are excellent, and I would of course be willing to serve as Chairman of such a Scottish Poetry Book Society as you propose. The composition of the Committee you indicate – viz. Norman, Sydney,[1] yourself (as Managing Editor) and Stewart Conn seems to me O.K.

I had an excellent – and extremely busy time in Dublin. I don't like Guinness and didn't drink any, but made up for that with plenty of John Jamieson. The Poetry Reading (for the Anti-Apartheid Movement funds) was an enormous success – an audience of between 600–700, and a sum of over £80 clear for the Cause.

[3] Hugh MacDiarmid, *A Lap of Honour* (London 1967).
[4] Cathy, Alexander Scott's wife.
[1] Norman MacCaig, Sydney Goodsir Smith.

On the plane back I was very thirsty and with the best intentions in the world eschewed Whisky and took a couple of cartons of iced orangeade. This completely upset my stomach and I have been very much under the weather since. Also, unfortunately, Valda put her back out again and is suffering a lot of pain and will have to do as little as possible for some time.

With every kind regard to Kathy and yourself.

Yours,
Chris.

Brownsbank,
Biggar.
10/7/68

Alex Scott, Esq.,

Dear Alex,

Congratulations on your *Cantrips*, a copy of which I've just got from Glen. Beautifully produced – and worthy of it. I think it is your best book – and certainly almost the only substantial verse contributions to the Lallans Movement outside mine. Sydney is a different category. All the others, including Soutar, are very minor. Here you have displayed a full range – Douglas Young's over-anthologised 'The Minister' is hopelessly poor, compared with such things as 'Doun Wi Dirt', 'Screened on Sunday' (an excellent jeu d'esprit, splendidly clinched with the X certificate) and 'Lit. Crit', with its magnificent last two lines. Of a very different kind is 'The Gallus Makar', one of the two or three best poems inscribed to me – and the only one in Lallans that is a first-rate poem in itself. I hope the book has the success it deserves – both in respect of purchasers and reviewers. I shouldn't end my remarks about it without saying that 'Supermakar Story' dispatches Young in quite devastating and conclusive manner. No wonder he's hyne awa' in America.

I'm enclosing a copy of an American educational service, issued to all American Universities and senior educational establishments. As you will see it is in two parts – one addressed to the teacher, the other to the student. This seems an excellent idea to me, and one which might well be copied for classes (University and other) in Scottish

Literature. Leaflets such as this are relatively very cheap to produce, and a dozen or so issues could cover pretty well the whole field and be very useful indeed in the absence (or too great cost) of more substantial text books.

All the best to Cathy and yourself and the boys.

Yours,
Chris.

Brownsbank,
Biggar.
10/10/69

Alex Scott, Esq.

Dear Alex,

Many thanks for your letter. I'm sorry the University of Massachusetts Press budget has been cut, with the consequence that Jack Weston's edition of *The Drunk Man* can't now appear until Sept. '70.[1]

Re the two points you ask about.

1/ Certainly 'saxpenny planet' refers to Hogg's statement, and obliquely to the general depreciation of all things Scottish and at the same time to the usual imputation of meanness on our part, viz. 'Bang goes saxpence'.

2/ Stertle-a-stobie. On certain roads when they were deep in dust a puff of wind could set balls of dust rolling along, and as children we used to chase these. Stertle-a-stobie was the name given to this sport. It is certainly so given in the large-paper edition of Jamieson's Dictionary.

I can't imagine where Weston got the gloss 'weak beer' for No 1. This is almost as bad as George Bruce's gloss to the line in 'Crowdieknowe' where the angels are stigmatised as a trashy bleezin' French-like gang, and he glossed bleezin' as drunk![2] Of course we have the term 'Bleezin' drunk' but in the context it should

---

[1] Weston's edition of *A Drunk Man Looks at the Thistle* (Amherst 1971) was vetted by Scott before publication.

[2] George Bruce's erroneous gloss of 'bleezin' occurs in his anthology *The Scots Literary Revival* (1968).

718

have been clear that it was the meretricious gaudiness of the angels that was referred to.

Yes, I was very sorry indeed to miss the Taliesen Congress, and hope you enjoyed it.[3]

Today I've received an advance copy of the *Selected Essays* of Hugh MacDiarmid dedicated to Cathy and you. It is very handsomely printed and produced and I hope you'll like it. Publication date is Nov. 6th. I'm afraid – like *The Uncanny Scot* and *The Company I've Kept* – it is not the sort of book likely to be considered for, let alone get, one of the Arts Council's publication awards! I'm afraid I'll survive all the same.

Kindest regards to you all.

Yours,
Chris.

Brownsbank,
Biggar.
3/12/69

Alex Scott, Esq.

Dear Alex,

I hear from Alec McCrindle that the Scottish Actors Coy would like to include in their next year's plans the play I asked you to collaborate with me in writing – viz., a sort of conflation of Brecht's *Threepenny Opera*, Gay's *Beggar's Opera*, Burns's *Jolly Beggars*, Graham's *Skellat Bellman*, and Chambers on the Lord of Misrule. So we'll have to begin planning it in some detail.[1]

As you know I've been in hospital again and while all the tests I underwent there were highly satisfactory and showed that there is nothing whatever organically wrong with me it is clear that I'll have

---

[3] *Taliesen* is the literary periodical of the Welsh Academy; in September 1969 the Taliesen Congress in Cardiff covered 'Literature in Celtic Countries'. Scott represented Scotland, substituting for MacDiarmid who was unable to go.

[1] As Alexander Scott explained, in a letter of 21 September 1982 to the present editor, 'Owing to Chris's ill-health, the play he suggested we should collaborate upon never got further than the rather nebulous definition made here.'

to ca' canny and abate many of my usual activities. Inter alia I've had to cancel many engagements in Ireland and elsewhere.

But I'll try to set out and send you in considerable detail a sort of synopsis of what I have in mind – as soon as possible. In the meantime I understand Mike is coming out here tomorrow, and if so I'll send you per him my Brecht translation.[2] It's my only copy, so I'll want it back.

You'll be interested to know that the University of California Press are to put out an edition of my *Selected Essays*. G. S. Fraser's review in *The Times Literary Supplement* was, I thought, excellent.

Hope all's well with Cathy and you and the boys.

Yours,
Chris.

---

[2] MacDiarmid's adaption of Brecht's *The Threepenny Opera* was first performed at the Prince of Wales Theatre, London, on 10 April 1972.

To John C. Weston

John C. Weston, Professor of English at the University of Massachusetts at Amherst, has done fine editorial work on MacDiarmid's poetry. He prepared the revised edition of MacDiarmid's *Collected Poems* (New York 1967) and an annotated edition of *A Drunk Man Looks at the Thistle* (Amherst 1971) with the spelling standardized. As he explained, in a letter of 2 February 1983 to the present editor, he wanted Macmillan of New York to bring out a Selected Poems of MacDiarmid:

> I approached Macmillan with a proposal to publish a selected poems because the *Collected Poems* [of 1962] was unreadable. They said yes at first and then insisted on a new edition of the CP instead. After the new edition I again proposed a selected poems and they seemed interested, pursued this for a while, then dropped it for reasons I could never fathom.

In the two letters to Weston, MacDiarmid discusses the notion of a Selected Poems, as edited by Weston, and responds to queries about *A Drunk Man*.

Brownsbank,
Biggar,
Lanarkshire,
Scotland.
21/8/68

Dr J. C. Weston.

Dear Jack,

Many thanks for your air-mail letter. I know both David Craig and John Manson.[1] I wouldn't have chosen either to do a selection

[1] David Craig and John Manson edited the Penguin edition of MacDiarmid's *Selected Poems* (Harmondsworth 1970).

of my poems. [. . .] All I can do is wait until I hear from Macmillan's and/or the Penguin people. I think I'll have to approve or disapprove of the actual selection (and almost certainly I'll take absolute objection to any prefatory or other remarks they make). Then I'll have my say about the actual selection.

In these circumstances I am all the more delighted that the Mass. U. Press still wants you to go on with your selection, and that will include the whole of the *Drunk Man* with marginal glossing. I do hope you will be able to do this; it will be an effective counterweight to the Penguin one.

I have just received a note from Norman,[2] enclosing your airmail letter to him and asking me to reply to you direct about the 'I'm fu' o' a stickit God'.[3]

We have a popular phrase 'the stickit minister', meaning a student who hasn't been able to qualify as a minister or alternatively has qualified but is so unfortunate that no church will call him to a ministry. 'A stickit God' simply means the feeling that one has a conception of the Divine that one cannot effectively formulate but is always grappling with. 'A fork in the wa'' is an old Scottish idiom for the practice in many countries by divers means of transferring a woman's labour pains to her husband or at least ensuring that he shares the agony when her time comes. Mary, the mother of Christ, did not invoke any such showing of her travail by Joseph. She was a gentle woman ('canny' has several meanings, including not only quiet or gentle, but also cunning). She hadn't a hold on Joseph at all i.e. she didn't pierce him with the prongs of the fork or force him to share her pangs. My outcry about the Second Coming means that Jean's travail is being shared by me and that the difficult birth with which I am coping is 'the second coming' in the sense that Christ's birth was the first and that a successful deliverance of a new conception of the Divine comes chronologically second to that, i.e. is not a Second Coming of Christ but of my own unknown personal God. I agree of course that it is utterly unfair to blame Jean, since,

---

[2] Norman MacCaig, the Scottish poet (born in Edinburgh in 1910) was one of MacDiarmid's closest friends.

[3] MacDiarmid is referring to two quatrains from *A Drunk Man* (134):

> *I'm fu' o' a stickit God.*
> *THAT's what's the maitter wi' me,*
> *Jean has stuck sic a fork in the wa'*
> *That I row in agonie.*
>
> *Mary never let dab.*
> *SHE was a canny wumman.*
> *She hedna a gaw in Joseph at a'*
> *But, wow, this seecund comin'! . . .*

unlike Joseph, I am the father of this infant. But as you say there is a tremendous overhang of religious ideas in the poem and by definition in giving voice to them a drunk-man may not be very logical in his attributions of blame, and may even be confused or contradictory. The point is not to be logical, but to deal with a diversity of ideas shooting from all directions on an intoxicated mind and be concerned only in dealing with them that poetry is made of them. I trust this is clear enough. The poem is in point of fact a favourite of my own – just from the qualities in it you discern – 'deliciously outrageous, bawdy, screechingly irreverent'.

This letter is not as full and coherent as I'd have liked it to be. I am having a devil of a time of it. I've been plagued all day with phone calls, etc. from journalists, the BBC, TV, etc. ever since the news broke about the invasion of Czechoslovakia, and now I've to go off to London to do a radio talk about the contingency of a civil war breaking out yet between England and Wales, or between England and Scotland. I am assured I'll be given scope to say all on the matter I wish to say – and heaven knows I've plenty to say. But I wanted to get this explanation of the poem off to you as quickly as possible, to avert the possibility of your having to cut this poem out of your essay.

With every kind regard to Joan, the children, yourself and other friends.

Yours in haste.
Chris.

Brownsbank,
Biggar,
Lanarkshire,
Scotland.
20/7/70

Professor J. C. Weston.

Dear Jack,

You would understand, I think, that I did not realise that your working trip over here was to be so very short, and that I wasn't to see you again. I had thought to come into Edinburgh on the Tuesday or Wednesday following your visit, but when I 'phoned Norman[1] I learned you were already away. I was very disappointed but hope your various engagements panned out successfully.

Many thanks for sending me the inscribed copy of your essay on the *Drunk Man*. Also the galley proofs of the Mass. Univ. edition. The critical note is excellent (I'd seen the introductory essay before, of course, and expressed my appreciation of it.) But the critical note really grapples with the poem and is a first-class exposition. What you say about the 'translations' being from English sources is only partly true.[2] I read not Russian but French, Spanish, and Italian – and I had read most of Blok in French. I've said elsewhere that a knowledge of the language of the originals can be a disadvantge to a translator. It is better not to know the language but to use a crib – or preferably cribs. What a translator does need is command of his own language. However, I agree my 'scholarship' is spotty and promiscuous. So was Yeats's. But I really do know much more than may be readily imagined. I remember for example an English Professor, who had been in South America challenging me on what I said of the different usages of certain words in Brazil, Chile, and Argentina. But he had to admit later that he was wrong and I was right. I am a very industrious Autolycus.

In the galleys themselves the only point I note is that the sentences about the Langholm Common-Riding (to which Valda and I are going this week-end) is that the event is not in June but on the last Friday of July; and that barley bannocks and salt herring are not had as refreshments. A barley bannock fixed to a circle of wood, and with a twelve-penny nail driven through its centre, is carried in the procession. It has some ancient historical significance, but I forget the precise explanation. When I was a boy there was still a great deal of home baking – indeed bread, cakes, etc. were all baked at home and not bought from shops. And barley bannocks were common fare then. My mother used to bake them every now and again. I question if any are to be had in Langholm now – except the one carried in the procession and specially baked for that purpose. Salt-herring too are

[1] Norman MacCaig.
[2] 'I believe that MacDiarmid began writing [*A Drunk Man Looks at the Thistle*] sometime in 1925 (line 290 was written then, anyway) and up through the early part of the next year thought of it primarily as a demonstration piece of Scottish literary expansionism, a star witness in his case for Scots intellectual poetry, but that as he progressed he came to realize that he had a great poem in itself. The original purpose still shows through in its shrill intellectuality and flashy learning, for example the ostentatious assertion in footnotes of translation directly from Russian (11.169,241,353) when in reality the source is English, a language to be eschewed according to the original purpose of the poem.' (Weston's edition, p. 116).

seldom or never seen. They are still common fare in the Orkney, Shetland, and Hebridean Islands of course.

I sent the letter right away to Miss Deas at the Scottish National Library regarding *The Voice of Scotland*.[3]

The trip to Israel has been postponed till later in the year – October or even November, which will be better anyhow weather-wise than August. But I hope that arrangements when finally made won't clash with my intended visit in October to various Canadian Universities.

With kindest regards to Leonard Baskin, Professor Kaplan[4] and other friends, and to Joan[5] who will, I hope, come with you next time – it was disappointing she couldn't this time. And of course all the best to the children, and yourself.

Yours,
Chris.

[3] Margaret Deas of the National Library of Scotland arranged for photocopies to be taken of MacDiarmid's magazine *The Scottish Chapbook*, not *The Voice of Scotland*.

[4] Professor Sidney Kaplan, of the Department of English, University of Massachusetts at Amherst, wished to include a book by MacDiarmid in a series he was editing. The book was to be illustrated by the artist Leonard Baskin; the plan, however, never materialised in print.

[5] Joan, Jack Weston's wife.

To David Craig

David Craig, author of *Scottish Literature and the Scottish People, 1680–1830* (1961) and co-editor (with John Manson) of MacDiarmid's *Selected Poems* (1970), is a prominent Marxist critic who has consistently claimed that MacDiarmid's late poetry in English – the *Mature Art* project – represents the collapse of a great creative talent. In his essay 'MacDiarmid the Marxist Poet' (*Festschrift*, pp. 94–5) he argues that 'MacDiarmid's work runs out into a vast graveyard of ideas' and laments 'the running-out of a wonderful creative flow'.

Langholm,
Dumfriesshire.
29/7/70
Until 3rd August. Then
Brownsbank.

Dr David Craig

Dear David Craig,

Kulgin Duval sent on your letter today and by the same delivery I had a letter from John Manson telling me the publication of the Penguin *Selected Poems* has been postponed till September. I'd been expecting it any day and am disappointed – as I am sure Manson and you are – by the delay. However I'd been afraid that rumours of a take-over or at least merger – with the American McGraw-Hill firm might have entailed a change of publishing policy.

I had not thought you were the author of the *TLS* article.[1] The acerbity of my reply was of course due to the dismissal, as spoil-

---

[1] The *TLS*, 14 May 1970, carried an anonymous full-page review of MacDiarmid's *A Clyack-Sheaf* (London 1969) and *More Collected Poems* (London 1970). MacDiarmid replied in the *TLS* of 4 July 1970.

heaps, of my later poetry to which I continue to attach far more importance than I do to my early lyrics. I know of course you have an opposite view.

What I could not – and still cannot – understand was the reference to my uncollected pre-*Sangschaw* Scots lyrics. I recognised the one you printed in your article in *TLS*[2] – it is not too bad. But I just cannot for the life of me recall any others. And while I am perfectly agreeable that you and Manson should edit these (and indeed pleased you should wish to do so), my only stipulation is that I must see and approve what you intend to include in the book. If they are good, it seems strange to me you did not include them in the Penguin. If they are not good enough to bear comparison with the contents of the Penguin then I should be very chary of allowing them to be reprinted – tho', so long as they are dated, I probably don't need to be.

On another matter you'll be interested to know I am (temporarily at least and without abandoning the long discursive stuff you dislike) reverting to Scots poems and have contracted to deliver MSS of 30 or so new Scots lyrics for a book by the end of September. I hope to keep that deadline, but I am meanwhile smothered with other work and besides have plans to go to Israel and then to Canada in October.

Kindest regards to Jill and your children, and to yourself from Valda and I.

Yours,
Christopher Grieve.

Brownsbank,
Biggar,
Lanarkshire, Scotland.
3/6/74

Dear David Craig,

I am very sorry indeed to have had to cancel my Swansea engagement and to have caused Mr Thomas[1] so much trouble. I

[2] Craig cited the poem 'On an Ill-Faur'd Star' (1233).
[1] Tom Thomas, who ran the annual Dylan Thomas Summer School for the extramural department of Swansea University.

delayed advising him of the likelihood of my being unable to travel to Swansea, since I kept hoping to fulfil the engagement. But a couple of very bad 'turns' forced my doctors to insist on my cancelling the arrangement. My health on the whole is surprisingly good, though my energy, and powers of concentration and sustained application are greatly diminished. But the real trouble is that it is not safe for me to undertake such engagements now. I am apt to have sudden collapses without warning. The doctors cannot account for these but say they think there are spasmodic occlusions of some of the small blood-vessels supplying the brain. The 'turns' do not last long but leave me severely shaken and the sudden collapses, of course, alarm the people I happen to be with. I can be seemingly all right and then suddenly crash as if I'd been poleaxed.

I haven't actually written my Dylan Thomas piece yet, but will try to do so in the course of the next fortnight and have it typed and sent on. I'll be very glad to have you read it.

I will of course be glad to see John Manson and you here when you are in Scotland. So far as I know I'll be at home until the end of August, when I have to go – if I can – to a granddaughter's wedding in Rochdale.

I hope this finds you and Jill and your family all O.K.

Yours,
Christopher Grieve.

To Ronald Macdonald Douglas

Ronald MacDonald Douglas (1896–1984) was one of the most energetic editors of *Catalyst*, a magazine which ran from December 1967 to Winter 1974 as the organ of the 1320 Club. When the 1320 Club was founded, in June 1967, it claimed to be a centre of research rather than a political party; MacDiarmid accepted the position of the Club's first president and spoke and wrote in praise of the radical outlook of the organisation.

As editor of *Catalyst*, author and journalist, Douglas kept in close contact with MacDiarmid of whom he wrote (in a letter of 12 August 1982 to the present editor):

> He was an extremely kindly man. He went out of his way to do anything he possibly could for anybody and for any cause with which he agreed.

In the same letter Douglas clarified the references to Roísín and Marjorie and, in a different tone, to Major F.A.C. Boothby who founded the 1320 Club and was imprisoned in 1975 on a charge of conspiracy to import explosives for the purpose of damaging property in connection with the Army of the Provisional Government of Scotland:

> Roísín Napier and Marjorie Brock and I have lived together for over forty years – and, believe it or not, without ever in all that time having had anything that could be called a serious row. We worked together. Roísín is a linguist [and Marjorie] is the best sub-editor in Scotland . . . The Boothby story is a long, involved, and very dirty one. Boothby was a police agent. That was eventually proved . . . I suppose you know that he died three or four years ago.

Ronald MacDonald Douglas, Esq.

Dear Ronald,

I have been away talking to the students at Stirling University. Hence the delay in replying to your letter of 9th inst. but also because I could not gather just what the position is re *Catalyst*. I was glad to think you might be taking it over, but something Major Boothby[1] said over the 'phone to Valda seemed at variance with that. So for two days I tried to get in touch with him to ascertain precisely what was happening, but he was away somewhere and I couldn't contact him. Now it seems the question of editorship is still unsettled, and indeed the question of the periodical's contrivance. The latter is not surprising. The figures you gave (£370 for each issue – over £800 debt) horrified me. I'd never been told anything about this.

I'll certainly send you an article or articles as soon as I know definitely that *Catalyst* is continuing and that you are editor. But I won't be able to write them until mid-November. Valda and I are going to Verona in Italy on 5th Nov. We'll fly over to France and then motor. I have people I want to see en route – at Avignon, at Aix, and at Lyons, and then we'll motor right through to Verona. I'll only be away about a week and will fly back.

The poetry is a problem. Most of what *Catalyst* has printed is very poor. The trends in fashion – particularly amongst the young – are in my view deplorable. Your experience of living in a different world altogether from these people is of course mine too. They know nothing, and care less, for the great poetry of the past. They simply want to 'express themselves' – and have nothing worth a curse to express. The sonnet is poor and as you say not correct technically. But then there have been all sorts of experiments with the sonnet

[1] Major F. A. C. Boothby was one of the founders (in June 1967) of the 1320 Club. On 29 March 1975 Major Boothby was arrested and charged with conspiracy to import explosives for the purposes of damaging property in connection with the Army of the Provisional Government of Scotland. MacDiarmid appeared at the trial as a character witness on Major Boothby's behalf. Major Boothby was sentenced to three years' imprisonment of which he served thirteen months before being released on parole. Discussing the SNP's refusal to recognise the 1320 Club as an authentic expression of Scottish Nationalism, Christopher Harvie, in *Scotland and Nationalism* (London 1977 pp. 249–50) writes: 'The ban turned out to be justified: the Club's conspiratorial and authoritarian tendencies came to the surface and in 1975 landed its secretary, Major F. A. C. Boothby, in prison on a conviction for terrorist conspiracy.'

form (or two forms – Petrarchan and Shakespearian) – Gerard Manley Hopkins for example opened it out to all manner of lengths of line and abandonment of any particular prescribed number of lines. But then he was a genuine poet, and the liberties he took seldom lacked justification. 'The Girl From the IRA' is slightly better. But I do not think either of them merit publication – even as fillers for odd bits of space. I re-enclose both of them to you. Also the Rayne MacKinnon piece. He has written much better things, but is very unequal. He is a patient (voluntary) in Carstairs Mental Hospital (Home Office) and I hear from him every other day.

I hope this finds all of you – Roísín, Marjorie, and yourself – in good form and look forward to meeting at the Symposium. Valda and I are both well enough but unaccountably tired and lacking in energy. I'm still badly in arrears with various books I should have delivered to publishers before this.

Every kind regard from Valda and I.

Yours,
Christopher Grieve.

Brownsbank,
Biggar,
Lanarkshire.
27/11/70

Ronald MacDonald Douglas, Esq.

Dear Ronald,

I have just got your letter of 22nd inst. We had a strenuous but vastly enjoyable time in France and Italy, particularly at Aix in Provence where friends at the University threw a big party for us – and at Venice where I had a long session with Ezra Pound. I flew back from Milan on 15th inst. Valda went on into Austria and only got back here a week ago. Then I had to go off again to read poetry to the students at Bristol University, and then do a colour TV programme at Newcastle-on-Tyne. Now I'm exhausted but must rally, as I've a lecture and poetry reading to give at the Arts Theatre at Solsgirth, Kirkintilloch on Monday and then I'm going to London to address a rally on behalf of the Frank Roche and Irish Political Detainees Fund in Islington Town Hall.

However I'll certainly get an article done for you (about 1500 words) and post it to you early this incoming week. Probably on the necessity of extremism and a complete break with England. I have read with great interest and sympathy all you say in your letter re John Herdman[1], etc. – how young fellows like him get so infernally conceited on the basis of having produced a tom-tit's clutch of eggs I just don't understand.

What you propose to try to do with *Catalyst* – make it a real revolutionary magazine and seek to regain the lost dynamic in the Scottish Movement – is of course precisely what is so urgently needed and I'll certainly do anything I can to help. But I fear that so far as a very large part of our population is concerned the process of Anglicisation has gone so far that they are just utterly hopeless. However, as long as there are a hundred of us there is still hope.

Every kind regard from Valda and I to Roísín, Marjorie, and you, – hoping you are all well and that we may meet again ere long.

Yours for Scotland,
Christopher Grieve.

Brownsbank,
Candymill,
Biggar.
24/4/72

Ronald MacDonald Douglas, Esq.

Dear Ronald,

I had hoped to have had a good talk with you when we met at the 1320 Club Symposium in Edinburgh. But, alas, things did not work out that way.

[1] In a letter of 22 November 1970 Ronald MacDonald Douglas told MacDiarmid of an altercation with John Herdman, then editor of *Catalyst*: 'It all seems to have begun with my being deputed to offer young Herdman a bit of help professionally. This he refused in a most high-handed manner, telling me that he had a double first in English from Cambridge.' John Herdman subsequently made a name for himself as a witty novelist who played ingenious variations on perennially Scottish themes in books such as *Pagan's Pilgrimage* (1978).

You (and Roísín and Marjorie) have done a wonderful job with *Catalyst* (vide the excellent current issue), and I am very sorry indeed – but not surprised – to hear via Valda that you feel you must give up the editorship after the issue of the coming of summer and autumn issues.

Apart from the inherent difficulties of the job – let alone people like Boothby, and the general divisiveness of our folk and their chronic lack of any unity of purpose (apart from the unity of not having any!) – the task must have laid a great burden on you. What is so regrettable is that just as you have pulled the thing up, literally by its boot-straps, and have it even minimally solvent and however inadequately increasing its circulation, you feel you must resign the editorship. I do not know anyone who can take it over with any hope of success. Valda mentioned it to Michael the other day but I doubt if he could take it on – he has already far too much work on his hands, and must concentrate on things that are financially rewarding.

I do not know what you think of doing now. So far as I am concerned I am ashamed to have been able to do so little to help. My own affairs are in chaos. I am in hopeless arrears with several books, and other writings; and while I am not bad physically, it is a different matter mentally and psychologically. I am quite incapable still of the necessary concentration of power of sustained application. And I am afraid this state of things is not likely to improve soon, if at all.

However, I hope we can meet and have a thorough talk on the whole Scottish Question ere long. In any case I will certainly let you have an article for the autumn issue (and perhaps for the summer one too).

I hope your own health is improving, and that Roísín and Marjorie are not too much 'under the weather' as a consequence of their labours.

With every good wish to all three of you from Valda and I.

Yours,
Christopher Grieve.

P.S. I don't know if you are still in process of taking action against Boothby, but I agree with you that he must be made to behave himself, and if indeed he is playing a double game, exposed and got rid of. If the action does go on I'm certainly with you all the way and will be glad to give you my fullest support in any way.

Dear Ronald, Roísín and Marjorie,

Sorry for the delay in thanking you for your all-too-kind gifts on my recent 80th Birthday.

Yes. I have survived it – but only just! The response from friends all over the world was terrific – and terrifying. I had hundreds of cards, letters, presents – and I am afraid it will take me well into nonagenarian status before I can acknowledge them all.

If only all those who on this occasion have praised my work had really followed my lead and worked as wholeheartedly for our great Cause that would no longer be dubiously successful. However 'Rome was not built in a day' and I have no doubt whatever of our ultimate victory.

I have a sweet tooth and Terry's chocolates are among my topmost favourites, and Borderer tho' I am this is the first time I have possessed a garment of Border knit-wear.

With my grateful thanks and every good wish to all three of you – in which Valda joins.

Yours for Scotland,
Christopher Grieve.

Brownsbank,
Candymill,
Biggar,
Lanarkshire.
17/8/75

Dear Roísín, Marjorie, and Ronald,

Many thanks for your greetings on my 83rd birthday and the splendid box of chocolates. I am sure you did not send me the latter to imply that I needed any sweetening, but your discovery that I have a sweet tooth suggests to me that you may well have had access to my dossier at New Scotland Yard. I am sure the fact is mentioned there.

If I have been a week in writing to thank you that is simply because my birthdays in recent years have overwhelmed me in a mass of cards, letters, telegrams and visitors. And it takes me some time to recover.

Otherwise I am well enough, and trust you are all so too. I wish we lived nearer and could meet more often. I seem to get more and more isolated from all other Scottish Nationalists and seldom hear what (if anything) is going on at all. Though I am sure it will yet – despite all the fools and knaves who usurp the arena.

With renewed thanks and every high regard to you all.

Yours,
Christopher Grieve.

To Morven Cameron

Morven Cameron, an English teacher resident in Glasgow, wrote an expressive poem in praise of MacDiarmid. It is reproduced in Gordon Wright's *MacDiarmid: An Illustrated Biography* (Edinburgh 1977, p. 145) and the second stanza runs:

> When I put my ear to the great conch of your words
> they bawl and hiss
> of a universe in labour;
> and hush to a woman's sigh
> and quiet
> when her waters break for the birth.

MacDiarmid liked the poem and became friendly with Miss Cameron who corresponded with him fairly frequently in the 1970s.

Brownsbank,
Biggar,
17/4/73

Dear Morven,

I do not need to tell you how much I enjoyed my time at your school.[1] You were all very kind to me, and I especially appreciated the letter I had from one of the girls. I will not forget the delicious sole, and the unusual whisky, the name of which I failed to get, with which you regaled me.

It was all the greater pity that I should have astonished or shocked you on the way back with what you call my 'condemnations'. But I should have thought you would have known how little time I have for almost all other people. I get on well with most people when I

---

[1] Glasgow High School for Girls where Morven Cameron was Head of English.

736

want to – but that is just a social superficiality. I do not really like people – save for an individual here and there. I have an enormous acquaintanceship but it is only very seldom I allow that to become more than acquaintanceship with an individual or two. I have no wish to increase the number of my real friends, and real friendship in my sense of the term implies community of insight, if not necessarily community of interest.

I have never failed to make my attitude plain. In *The Company I've Kept* for example. Or in many poems, as, say, 'Lament for the great music', where I say:-

> I am as lonely and unfrequented as your music is.
> I have had to get rid of my friends . . .
> If one's capital consists in a calling
> And a mission in life one cannot afford to keep friends.
> I could not stand undivided and true amongst them.

My concern with politics and poetry is not the shallow thing most people mean when they aver that they have their own opinions and likes or dislikes: but a veritable matter of life and death. There is ample evidence that I have helped a great many Scottish writers and that my influence has made it much easier for them than I ever had it myself. But I am disappointed in them. They call themselves friends of mine, but they do not share – nor understand – either my politics or my poetry, and are actually exemplifying or condoning the very things I have all along fought most strenuously against. What then does the alleged friendship consist of?

The essence of the matter lies in what I have always stressed as one of my basic principles, viz. that the good is the enemy of the best.

I am sorry if I distressed or angered you, but I thought you knew, and would allow for the fact that I am an Ishmaelite.

Valda and I are going up to Loch Tummel to Kulgin Duval's and Colin Hamilton's house on Monday for a day or two. On 25th we are going to London for a Foyle lunch at the Dorchester and will stay a couple of days. Then on 15th June we are going to Rotterdam for a Poetry Festival at which the second half of the week's programme will be devoted to the language and literatures of the Celtic countries. We'll be there for several days.

Every kind regard to your father and yourself from Valda and I.

Yours,
Christopher.

737

Dear Morven,

We were of course very sorry you couldn't come down, and sorrier still that that was due to your father's deteriorated condition, which we hope has now taken a turn – or several turns – for the better. And that we'll see both of you ere long.

Old men are unaccountable creatures. Valda and I were at the RSA reception in Edinburgh. A big turn out. Hundreds of people. Valda will confirm that I was very careful indeed. Had only one small whisky at Norman MacCaig's before the event: and two glasses of very light white wine at the affair.

Enjoyed it and talked to all sorts of people. But I was on my feet too long. Towards the end, while waiting transport home, I suddenly collapsed – crashed as if I'd been pole-axed, and gave my forehead a lovely bruise where I contacted with the tiled floor. What a carfuffle! Sir John Bruce attended to me, and Mrs Chalmers Davidson and Selby Tulloch (all friends of mine) were in the offing. I recovered consciousness to find about half-a-dozen policemen trying to lift me (when, if they'd had any first-aid sense they have just stretched me out flat, instead of which, crushed up in their arms, I was deprived of oxygen); and an ambulance had been summoned.

Of course most of those present would attribute my downfall to drink. But that was not the case – on this particular occasion. Indeed, I'd have fallen much less heavily and awkwardly if I had had a good intake of the pure spirit of Scotland.

The taxi arrived, and I was quite O.K. again (except for a very painful head) by the time we got as far as the outskirt of Edinburgh.

Despite this deplorable lapse Valda will assure you (if assurance is necessary) that I behaved in an exemplary way in Wales. We had a very good time at Lampeter College, and subsequently in Aberystwyth and Cardiff, and I met many very interesting people – some of whom I hadn't seen for 30 years. The weather throughout was splendid.

Now I have engagements looming up at Oxford University, The University of Sussex, University College at Swansea, and at Ochtertyre House, Crieff.

Valda joins me in warmest regards to you and your father.

Love,
Yours,
Christopher.

Brownsbank,
Candymill,
by Biggar.
15/10/76

Dear Morven,

I hope your injury is healing satisfactorily. But what's this I hear about you having such difficulty in getting your clothes on, that you didn't manage it in time for a caller to whom you had to present yourself 'starkers'? There is no need for any such conretemps, as you must know that if you need a valet (or feminine equivalent thereof) or lady's maid or whatever I'd be very pleased to serve you in any such capacity.

What's happened to Maurice Lindsay?[1] He sent me a long letter of an indescribably waffling sort which only made matters worse. He alleged that the little White Rose poem carried my name – and then he excised that and substituted Compton Mackenzie's name as author – on the advice of Alex Scott. Can you imagine anything more irresponsible? If I were to take action against him and the publisher, the ludicrous weakness of their explanation would land them in a very heavy penalty. I cannot think any sane person – let alone an experienced author and journalist, could have expected to get away with such a high-handed action.

You'll be glad to know that, thanks to your representations, the Schools Poetry Scheme have paid me not £15 but £20!! for the reading I gave at Laurel Bank School.

I've been having – and am still having – a bad time with a heavy bout of gastric 'flu – just at the time when I've shoals of work which I cannot begin to tackle at all.

Hope your father is O.K., also Marguerite and Gillie. I am in touch with Deirdre, of course.[2]

With love from Valda and I.

Yours,
Christopher.

[1] In his anthology *Modern Scottish Poetry* (1976) Maurice Lindsay attributed 'The Little White Rose', MacDiarmid's celebrated lyric, to Compton Mackenzie.
[2] Marguerite Macdonald is Morven Cameron's sister; Gillian ('Gillie'), whose bust of MacDiarmid was purchased by Glasgow University, and Deirdre Macdonald, are Marguerite's children.

739

To David Daiches

Born in Edinburgh in 1912, David Daiches is a distinguished academic and author. He taught in universities in England and the USA and was Professor of English at the University of Sussex from its foundation in 1961 until his retirement in 1977. His introduction to the second edition of *A Drunk Man Looks at the Thistle* (Glasgow 1953) is an admirable account of MacDiarmid's masterpiece.

Brownsbank,
Biggar,
Lanarkshire.
23/9/69

Dear David Daiches,

It is a long time since we met or corresponded. So it was extremely good of you to have a copy of your book on whisky[1] sent to me. Many thanks to you and your publishers. I have, or know and have read, all the books listed in your bibliography. And have no doubt yours is the best of the lot, tho' I enjoyed both Neil Gunn's and Dr McCulloch's.[2] I thought the latter, comprehensive as he was and drawing all the time on personal experience, had missed one malt whisky, Clynelish. But I had read too hastily, and found I was wrong. He had not missed it. As an old whisky man myself I nearly missed it, but my son-in-law, from Brora, produced some of it one day and I remedied this omission.

Talking about whisky I'll never forget how you saved my life when after an orgy of sherry at Downing,[3] I streaked over to Jesus and you regaled me with a bottle of Morangie.

---

[1] David Daiches, *Scotch Whisky: Its Past and Present* (1969).
[2] Neil Gunn's *Whisky and Scotland* (1935) was included in the Voice of Scotland series; R. J. S. McDowall's *the Whiskies of Scotland* (1967).
[3] In the late 1950s when Daiches was a Fellow of Jesus College, Cambridge; MacDiarmid had been invited to Downing College to give a talk to The Doughty Society.

I thought I knew Irish Whiskey well too, but last time I was over in Ireland I found one equal to the best Scottish single whisky – namely Middleton's. It is not well known and only available in two of Dublin's pubs even. But I was staying at Rathfarnham and nearby there was a hostelry called 'The Tuning Fork'. That instrument never struck a wrong note! Middleton's is distilled in Cork by a firm called Beamish, which reminded me of Lewis Carroll's Jabberwocky.

Until a few days ago I had an enforced abstention for several months, owing to the amount of penicillin and terra-mycin in my system. I'd gone to Canada and caught a virus infection which upset all my organs in turn and ended by giving me a bad dose of pneumonia. I was taken aboard the aeroplane in Toronto in a wheel-chair. On getting home I went into Chalmers Hospital in Edinburgh and X-rays showed I'd still pneumonia on my lungs. That happily cleared away in a week or so but left me extremely weak. Convalescence in Langholm rehabilitated me, but I have had to reduce my activities very considerably. Not to be wondered at since I am 77, and I am afraid this curtailment of energy must now be permanent. Still I am not so bad. Alas, all this meant a piling up of arrears of work and I am quite unable yet to tackle the writing of several books contracted for and due to be delivered to the publishers months ago.

I hope you are not likely to incur any such abatement for many years to come. I haven't encountered your son Alan since we had a Border foray together for BBC TV[4] But I have been very seldom in Edinburgh this past year or two.

Since your essays on it did so much for the *Drunk Man*, you will be interested to know that this is that book's big year. Massachusetts University Press are producing a really scholarly edition of it; the Bodoni Press, Verona, a de luxe edition illustrated by the veteran Belgian artist Franz Mascreel, and Claddagh Records, Dublin, 2 LP covers of the whole of it read by myself.

With renewed thanks and every kind regard to Mrs Daiches and yourself.

Yours,
Christopher Grieve.

[4] Alan Daiches did photographs for a series of programmes of poems on different Scottish regions by different Scottish poets. MacDiarmid's contribution to the series was his poem 'The Borders' (1423–1430); it was transmitted on BBC TV on 17 March 1966.

Brownsbank,
Biggar,
Lanarkshire.
Scotland.
17/6/74

Professor David Daiches,
Sussex University.
Dear David,

How can I thank Mrs Daiches and you for all your kindness. I thoroughly enjoyed my visit and am grateful to all concerned.[1] On the Wednesday instead of taking one direct to Gatwick, Angus MacIntyre[2] gave me a splendid run to Steyning, where my son Michael was born 42 years ago, and then to Thakeham where we lived at that time. I had not been back in that area in the interval, and this return visit enchanted me.

I have been having a great time reading the anthology[3] you gave me – contriving so many things I liked immensely years ago and had not reread since. The article on myself is probably too kind but I was very pleased by the comment on *In Memoriam James Joyce*, which almost everywhere else has been condemned as worthless and a deplorable waste of my powers. I was also very pleased by the section on David Jones – whose exclusion from Larkin's Oxford Anthology I protested strongly about at the Foyle celebration of its publication in the Dorchester.

The book as a whole puts me in possession of a whole library of books I love – but of which I do not possess copies.

Please thank Isobel for me and accept my most grateful regards.

Yours,
Christopher Grieve.

---

[1] MacDiarmid had visited the University of Sussex to give a talk after which he stayed at the Daiches home in Burgess Hill, Sussex.
[2] Angus MacIntyre, Public Relations Officer of the University of Sussex.
[3] *The Norton Anthology of English Literature* (4th edtn 1962); Daiches edited the modern section (from 1880 onwards).

Professor David Daiches,
University of Sussex.
Dear David Daiches,

How good of you to send me a copy of your delightful *Was*.[1] I have been reading it with great interest and appreciation. If I have been a few days in acknowledging it that is because (though books are so dear now) I have just had an unexampled influx of gifts of books from the most diverse quarters – a volume of poems by Nathaniel Tarn from America; an anthology of relevant Communist poems in translation (including one of mine) from a poet in Hanoi I met in Sofia a few years ago; Lady Antonia Fraser's beautifully produced anthology of *Scottish Love Poems*; an advance copy of a new biography of Keir Hardie (price £8 – which would have kept Hardie and his family for a month at least), and so on.[2]

You applied the description trans-human to some of my poetry. I am afraid I was launched across that 'trans' long ago. Edwin Morgan complains in one of his essays that there is a lack of concern for the normal preoccupations of ordinary folk in my work; and I have had to confess that on the whole I do not like people – and have no love of mankind en masse, but regard them as a failure and can only find interests in common with an individual or two. So I could never write a book like *Was* (apart of course from the quality of the writing and the organisation of the content) or *Two Worlds*[3] for the simple reason that although I have known a great number of people I have always avoided intimacy with them and never really knew them at all. So to essay anything of a like kind to these two books of yours would be trying to make bricks without straw. The men and women who have interested me most I only have my idea of what their interests and affiliations were – that is, my idea of them, and never any ordinary human understanding.

However, I have written far too much anyway, and it is far

---

[1] David Daiches, *Was* (1975).
[2] The books mentioned by MacDiarmid include Nathaniel Tarn's *Lyrics for the Bride of God* (1975), (ed) Antonia Fraser's *Scottish Love Poems* (1975), K.O. Morgan's *Keir Hardie* (1975).
[3] David Daiches, *Two Worlds* (1956).

better to have such books from you than that I should attempt anything of that sort.

Please give my regards to Professor Nuttall[4]. Angus McIntyre, I believe, has come back to Scotland, but I haven't run across him yet.

And of course give my warmest regards to your wife and accept same yourself.

With renewed thanks.

Yours,
Christopher Grieve.

---

[4] Tony Nuttall, Professor of English at Sussex.

To Mary Macdonald

When Fionn Mac Colla died in 1975 he left three novels that had been rejected by publishers during his lifetime. His widow Mrs Mary Macdonald – with the help of John Herdman, Ruth McQuillan, James B. Caird – secured posthumous publication for *The Ministers*. Since the publication of Mac Colla's *The Albannach* in 1932, MacDiarmid had applauded his achievement and was evidently anxious to introduce *The Ministers* (which eventually appeared, under the imprint of Souvenir Press in 1979, without an introduction).

Brownsbank,
Candymill,
by Biggar,
11/7/78

Mrs Mary Macdonald.

Dear Marie,

I will of course do as you ask – if I can. That last phrase simply expresses my doubt as to whether I can do the job well enough. And it must be well done – or not at all.

You do not tell me by what date you must have it. But I notice from the publishers' letter that they must have 'copy' early in September. That suits me all right. I couldn't write it just now. Indeed I haven't been able to write anything of any consequence for 18 months.

I am still very ill and in constant severe pain. As you may know cancer is a very tricky thing. It can go into recess and stay latent for long periods. Mine is quiescent at the moment. I do not anticipate having to go into hospital again but both Valda and I greatly appreciate your kind offer to do anything you can to help us.

We were in Dublin last weekend when the University there gave me an honorary D.Litt (Doctorate in Literature). That was a real ordeal, with a 6 ft. student at my elbow I was afraid I'd collapse at any moment. But I didn't and the affair went off splendidly. Valda and Michael, of course, enjoyed themselves.

I'll write you again as soon as I can write anything. If you don't like what I write – or anything in it – please don't hesitate to say so and refuse it. I'll do my best, you may be assured.

Hope you and all your family are well. I am of course, as you know, delighted that *The Ministers* is to be published. I'll be still happier when all Tom's unpublished books are published. I think I'll probably keep living till that happens. John Herdman's article of which you enclosed a script is excellent.

All the best from Valda and I.

Yours,
Chris.

Brownsbank,
by Biggar.
8/8/78

Dear Marie,

I hope you are not worrying about my delay in sending you the introduction to *The Ministers* – and still more that the publishers aren't worrying. I've been having a bad time – far too much pain to leave me any energy to attend to anything else.

However I've sorted out my ideas now and will write the thing tonight and send it to Deirdre in Glasgow (Michael's wife) who'll type it and send it to you. Please consider yourself free to reject it or cut it down or otherwise alter it in any way. The more I think about it – and about Tom – the more I wish now I had 20,000 or 30,000 words to do. But I think I've solved that problem now, and what you get in the next day or two will certainly be short and to the point.

Give my regards to John Herdman whose excellent essay on Tom's unpublished books has of course been most helpful. And to

Ruth McQuillan. I hope all goes well. And that the other books will speedily follow *The Ministers.*

Yours,
Christopher Grieve.

Brownsbank,
by Biggar.
10/8/78

Dear Marie,

I am terribly sorry, but I stupidly overestimated my strength when I wrote you last. All I wanted to say was in my mind – it was only a matter of writing it out and sending it to Deirdre to type and send it to you. So I began to write it. I had only written a few sentences when I had a very bad turn, and it was physically impossible for me to continue. I thought I might manage the following day. Alas, I was incredibly weak and couldn't do anything. I have decided now to abandon the whole thing – and several other things I had intended to do. You can hardly believe how sorry I am.

I've told you before one of my main troubles is that it is infinitely easier for me to write 20,000 or 30,000 words than just a hundred to two. All I have thought about Tom and his work since I agreed to your request will not be lost. If I recover any strength I'll write a long essay which will be one of the best things I've ever done. But that lies in the future. Even to write a short letter takes more out of me just now than I have to give. The other night's experience was a terrible one. Valda can tell you how hard I struggled to do the job, but it was no good. I ceased to be able to write at all. My hand and arm just seized up – very painfully, and the ideas I had meant to express and had so nicely sorted out in my mind collapsed into a chaos it was quite hopeless to try to get into any order again.

I hope you understand and that John Herdman or someone will come to the rescue. Later if I'm still alive and in better condition I'll do the long essay and have it published in pamphlet form, but I'll have to read the unpublished poems first – and as matters stand I can't read let alone write – the pain that attacks me absorbs all my attention and I have no energy left to do anything – even watch TV.

And that state of affairs may end suddenly or drag on for months or even years.

    With all my love and regret.

                    Yours,
                    Christopher.

Open Letters

All his life MacDiarmid used the correspondence columns of news-papers and periodicals as a series of platforms on which to promote the various causes he was committed to. This was an extension of his belief that literature was a calling rather than a remunerative career and he gladly contributed feature-length letters to the press in the hope that a polemical presentation of his views would attract attention and lead to debate on political and poetic issues.

Diminutives in the Doric

A few months before he adopted (in the August 1922 issue of *The Scottish Chapbook*) the pseudonym 'Hugh MacDiarmid' and began publishing the Scots poems that would establish him as a major poet, C. M. Grieve unleashed an attack on contemporary vernacular literature in Scots. It was always MacDiarmid's intention to use Scots in an experimental manner in order to break from the post-Burnsian tradition and give Scotland an intellectually demanding modernist literature. Hence the term Synthetic Scots and Mac-Diarmid's opposition to dialect verse on the grounds that it was contaminated by the kailyard school of Scots writing. Grieve's opportunity for an attack on Scots vernacular verse came when the *Aberdeen Free Press* of 18 December 1921 featured on the front page a story headlined 'Diminutives in the Doric':

> Dr J. M. Bulloch read a paper on 'The Delight of the Doric in the Diminutive' to the Vernacular Circle of the London Robert Burns Club on Monday night. . .Dr Bulloch remarked upon the persist-ence in the use of the diminutive, more particularly in the north-east of Scotland, where by far the most vigorous and idiosyncratic form of the vernacular was retained. He retorted

upon the 'Doubting Thomases,' found particularly in Scotland, who questioned the usefulness of study of the vernacular, and he went on to deprecate the use of what he had nicknamed more than once 'Albyn Place English.' The speakers of Albyn Place English were essentially grotesque because they invariably had Scots mentalities, and therefore the very minimum of the art of successful mimicry . . . The diminutive remains dominant to this day in the Scots mind, distinguishing it very distinctly from the mind of the pukka English, who use hardly any genuine diminutives of their own.

John Malcolm Bulloch (1867–1983) was editor of the *Graphic* from 1909 to 1924 and had a reputation as an astute book reviewer and an accomplished genealogist.

ABERDEEN FREE PRESS
15 December 1921

12 White's Place,
Montrose,
December 13, 1921

Sir,

The space you have given to Dr J. M. Bulloch's lecture on 'The Diminutive in Doric' encourages the hope that you will in fairness spare a corner for one who strongly differs from him.

Those who use what Dr Bulloch terms 'Albyn Place English' (whatever they may be) will probably – if they exist – have no difficulty in replying to the 'little Eccelfechanities of Peckham and Tooting' (whom we all know). But Dr Bulloch's plea for Doric infantilism is only worthy of the critical consideration of nursery-governesses. A critic capable of referring to 'Mr John Mitchell's delightful crack with his grandson' is capable of anything – and nothing. Most contemporary grandchildren would take steps to have us examined in lunacy if we afflicted them with such talks in Doric.

Miss Symon's[1] opinions I respect: but her views of Scottish

[1] In his lecture Bulloch had praised 'Miss Mary Symon, of Dufftown, the author of the moving poems on "Neuve Chapelle," and "The Soldier's Cairn." Miss Symon is not only a constructive artist of a very high quality, but she is an extraordinarily incisive critic of our psychology, and a past-master of our most distinctive Doric.'

psychology have been determined geographically. If she lived in Lanarkshire or West Fife she would know that the processes of evolution have carried the most important sections of the Scottish nation far beyond the hill-plaid and 'sleevid weskit' stage.

The main objection to the Vernacular Circle's propaganda lies in the fact that it emphasises the part at the expense of the whole, and puts the cart before the horse. Had the aim been to encourage all that is finest and best in Scottish literature, whether written in Doric or English, the movement might have merited support – although, after all, prizes do not produce literature.

Is the expression of Scottish mentality in English – even Albyn Place English – essentially grotesque? Synge, Yeats, and other great Irish writers found no difficulty in expressing themselves in an English which they yet made distinctively Irish. Is the psychological difference between, say, Oscar Wilde and Joseph Conrad not as profound as the difference between an Englishman and a Scot?

Some of the 'perfervids' attached to the London Vernacular Circle (not themselves particularly distinguished as creative artists) are making claims for the Doric which even writers such as Mrs Violet Jacob, John Buchan, and Professor Alexander Gray – who have added to its glories – repudiate. The latter recognise its insuperable spiritual limitations, as Burns did, and as future writers must increasingly do.

Dr Bulloch in London retorts upon the '"doubting Thomases", found particularly in Scotland, who question the usefulness of the study of the vernacular.' As one of them, I may be permitted to counter-retort that, living in Scotland as I do, I question the usefulness mainly because I entirely disagree with Dr Bulloch's opinion that the mentality of our countrymen has not varied very much.

The variation between an R. L. Stevenson, a John Davidson, a Robert Buchanan, a William Sharp, a John Barlas, shows that Dr Bulloch is generalising about an insignificant minority.

It is curious that Thomas Campbell charged Burns with being un-Scottish – because he was so unself-conscious. How does this agree with what Dr Bulloch says about one of our 'cruxes'? He makes the same mistake as Campbell. No Scottish writers of our times are further out of the Burns tradition than the Doric-writing group: and the continuity in all but language of those contemporary writers of what Dr Bulloch calls 'Albyn Place English' with all the great Scottish makers is easily demonstrable – as Professor Gregory Smith[2] has shown.

I am, etc.
C. M. Grieve.
(Editor of *Northern Numbers)*

ABERDEEN FREE PRESS
23 December 1921

12 White's Place,
Montrose.
December 21, 1921

Sir,

Permit me to thank Dr J. M. Bulloch for his most courteous and candid reply to my remarks regarding his paper on 'Diminutives in the Doric.'[1] I did not venture to crave from you sufficient space in which to essay any comprehensive criticism, and since Dr Bulloch's reply takes thrice the lineage of my letter it is obvious that even at the outset the conditions of adequate controversy are haplessly imbued with a diathesis of giantism which destroys all hope of accommodation in the columns of a daily newspaper such as yours.

I quite and unregretfully agree that the gulf between Dr Bulloch enjoying, if not deliberately stimulating, the responsiveness of a large audience (including those astute business men who replace with such ineffable appropriateness in these changed circumstances – since 'the poor we have always with us' – those readers whom Shelley in his day justly feared would associate the sentiments of his 'Epipsychidion' with the philanderings of the nursemaid and the butcher boy) to Doric infantilism, and myself, rejoicing in the belief that progress in sexual ethics is at last removing the 'specific aboulia' which has so long been responsible for the prevalence of the diminutive in Scotland, cannot be bridged.

Dr Bulloch's letter is largely a cerebration of the unconscious –

[2] In *Scottish Literature* (London 1919, pp. 138-9) G. Gregory Smith scoffed at the spectacle of the Scots-writing 'poeticule [who] waddles in good duck fashion through his Jamieson, snapping up fat expressive words with nice little bits of green idiom for flavouring.'
[1] Bulloch's lengthy reply appeared in the *Aberdeen Free Press* of 21 December 1921.

which is a sort of treachery to his caste. True to the principle he indicates of descending to the level of his audience, how fortunate for him that the vernacular interested them! Circumstances are conceivable when on precisely the same grounds he might have found himself constrained to encourage cannibalistic proclivities. Surely the Burns cult is a phenomenon of which only a literary pathologist can be proud – an unique abnormality of mob-consciousness pickled in whisky. Burns only occupies the role of an eponym giving a name to a cult in spirit and essence entirely different from anything traceable to him. How did Burns Clubs originate? The active 'non-literary' vernacularists of today are the competent successors of the perverters of the original idea of the Burns Club, who began that syncretism which has resulted in creating an atmosphere in which even such a Scotsman as Dr Bulloch can complacently observe that 'Burns is loved by thousands of people all over the world who never read a book, and least of all a book of poetry,' and speak of a strength which can only be concentrated in the remarkable sinews of class – a Bolshevic argument!

I am sufficiently destitute of humour actually to dislike witnessing Dr Bulloch 'Syncretising' Burns by speaking deprecatingly (by implication at any rate) of 'mere culture,' and emphasising some occult unphraseable accessibility to the moderately literate and illiterate alike (but not to the 'literary' whom, of course, 'much reading hath made mad') as the vital quality of his genius, and the essential virtue of the vernacular.

The fact that the Vernacular Circle issued a world-wide appeal for funds to subsidise vernacular conservation and, if possible, restoration is surely propaganda – the constituent paragraphs of that appeal did not float together from the ends of the earth like the pieces of a jig-saw puzzle – and I am glad to see Dr Bulloch disassociate himself from the extravagant claims made by others more or less closely associated with the Vernacular Circle.

A final point! If the English Dr Bulloch adjectivally belittles is mainly the mark not of aesthetic or literary equipment, but of mere caste mimicry is the use of the vernacular (or any language) other than that – and is there anything to choose between them so far as mob-psychology goes, other than the peculiar virtue die-hards may attach to minority manifestations?

Is not, in fact, the only criterion literary merit – and are not spiritual values of infinitely more consequence than values which are merely psychological?

I am, etc.
C. M. Grieve.

753

12 White's Place,
Montrose.
January 27, 1922

Sir,

Since I was responsible in the first instance for this controversy in
these columns, I must point out that Miss Symon's via media is
unfortunately, so far as I am concerned, a cul-de-sac which does not
penetrate into the debatable land at all.

I was brought up in a braid Scots atmosphere. No one relishes the
peculiar virtues of the Doric more heartily than I do. No one can be
more anxious than I am that these should not be lost or Scottish
vernacular literature cease to be read – dangers which I believe to be
greatly exaggerated. But I am very much more anxious that the
habit of reading should be controlled by literary factors alone. Mere
patriotism is a Caliban's Guide to letters. What shall it profit a man
if he remains a Scot but lose his own soul? The great need of every
civilised country is for a thinking public. In Scotland there is ample
reason to know that no intensive insistence on the Doric will conduce
to that. The people do not think in the Doric or in any other language
– and the problems that it is most urgently desirable that they
should, if possible, be made to think about are those problems
created by our industrial civilisation which there is no terminology
in the Doric to deal with. For the most part the Doric tradition serves
to condone mental inertia – cloaking mental paucity with a trivial
and ridiculously over-valued pawkiness! – and bolsters up that
instinctive suspicion of cleverness and culture – so strongly in all
peasants – which keeps the majority of the Scottish public wallowing
in obsolete and really anti-national tastes – anti-national, for the
latent spirit of Scotland showed its potential stature when a determined effort was made (in the last half of the 18th century) to cast off
the swaddling clothes of the Doric. Alas! reaction fastened them still
more tightly about the unfortunate spirit (kept a Peter Pan of
national consciousness against its will) and its struggles ceased – and
are only now being resumed in a new and almost incredible access of
hope! Compared with other countries comparable in size – Belgium,
for instance – Scotland stagnates in an apparently permanent
literary infancy owing to the operation of certain forces of which the
Doric sentiment is the principal.

The Doric is as much mine as anybody's. I love it as jealously. My
accent could be cut with a knife. Not only so! I have had the temerity

to address myself to the solution of the two great problems of the Doric – the facts that no serious Doric prose and no Doric drama ever evolved, in which respects Doric is singular amongst all European dialects and languages. I believe that both were capable of being evolved from the Doric. I believe I know exactly why neither ever did develop out of the Doric. And I believe that I can show that if certain factors had not operated, and if certain other factors had operated – and if history had followed a different course and Doric had today been exclusively used for all purposes in Scotland – how the difficulties which prevented the development of both would have been overcome. That thesis – illustrated with original examples of the Doric prose which might have so evolved (examples purposely on sufficiently abstruse subjects) and with excerpts from the possible drama of that conceivable Doric age full of precisely the sort of feeling the ordinary vernacularist would call 'the Scottish' or 'anti-Scottish' – I am now preparing for issue in book form – for private circulation only, for the simple reason that though (or perhaps because) I am interested very deeply in these matters myself, I consider that any attempt to create a Doric 'boom' just now – or even to maintain the existing vernacular cult in anything like its present tendencies – would be a gross disservice to Scottish life and letters.

My main points here are that the Vernacular Circle have not really addressed themselves at all to the root problems of the Doric as a literary medium, and that the Vernacular Cult in its present form – like its wider aspect, the Burns Cult, which Dr Bulloch has significantly admitted is mainly maintained by people who read little or nothing and poetry least of all, and must accordingly be regarded as a great inhibiting agency, preventing the development of an atmosphere in Scotland congenial to modern ideas and ideals – cannot be dissociated from its reactionary elements and from the consequences of an inherent contempt for culture and the tendency to regard people of progressive culture and ideas as 'superior' and snobbish.

I wish I had space here to quote from the enormous mass of newspaper and other cuttings I have collected during the past year. The plea of coincidence could scarcely rebut the charge of propaganda. The collection certainly shows that the friends of the Vernacular Circle have taken advantage of the natural anti-cultural sentiments of the mass of their readers to decry all progressive and creative tendencies in Scottish literature. For instance, it is iterated and reiterated incessantly that 'the true tendency of Scottish literature lies along the line of the vernacular' – a statement that will not bear a moment's examination, yet so persistently and recklessly repeated that a widespread prejudice against the work of Scotsmen writing in English has been created, and reviews of Scottish books as a direct consequence demand that shibboleth and totally disregard those inherent psychological elements which betray the true Scot – elements hideously murdered in the average vernacularist's conception of Scottish psychology.

Dr Bulloch may disclaim having ever said that this or that bit of Doric infantilism, affectionately quoted, was literature. What I am concerned about is that any amount of people have been so influenced by the attitude that Dr Bulloch and others like him have adopted towards the vernacular that they have been confirmed in their anti-cultural prejudices, become practically idea-proof, and afflicted with a mental and spiritual agoraphobia which has driven them – and to all intents and purposes the rest of Scotland with them! – into a cul de sac, where they bury their minds (as ostriches bury their heads) in the shadow of the blind wall which blocks them out from literature and from life.

I am, etc.
C. M. Grieve.

THE GLASGOW HERALD
15 May 1922

16 Links Avenue,
Montrose.
May 11 [1922]

Sir,

It is pretty generally recognised (by those who recognise such things) that something in the nature of a revival of Scottish poetry is at last manifesting itself, or would be but for adverse commercial conditions. In connection with *Northern Numbers*, the *Scottish Poetry Annual* (so generously reviewed by *The Glasgow Herald*), I and others associated with me in that venture have had in view for some time the possibility of issuing a monthly chapbook of current Scottish poetry. The fall in printing costs which we have been awaiting now renders that practicable, provided a certain measure of support is forthcoming.

I am in close touch at the present moment with the constantly developing work of over thirty young Scottish poets (not to take into account others who have already secured a certain – inadequate – amount of recognition), and these in course of intercourse discover,

756

I find, a common difficulty. There is no Scottish literary paper: and newspaper editors, while according more or less space to verse, have seldom any use for really significant work, particularly if in technique and for ideation it presents, as it generally must, unfamiliar features. The majority of newspaper readers are thus sedulously guarded from those aesthetic surprises which they would probably find unintelligible and intolerable however welcome and exhilarating they might prove to an elusive minority. I would be the last to seek to deny them this protection, but I believe that that minority in Scotland, sufficiently interested or capable of becoming interested in experimental poetics, is now quite large enough to justify the publication of such a monthly periodical as is indicated.

To these I would briefly declare that there is being produced in Scotland today, under circumstances which amount to a conspiracy of silence, an increasing body of really significant poetry, and that a monthly selection of it, containing no item that is not considerably above what may be called 'magazine level' is feasible if they so desire.

Sufficient evidence of that desire is all that is needful. *Northern Numbers* has been extensively praised, and the standard of *Northern Numbers* at least will be maintained in this monthly auxiliary. It must be emphasised that the great majority of the poems included will be poems which cannot otherwise secure publication at all. The excellence of many of these (rejected by what might naturally be accounted the likeliest existing papers) will, I am confident, quickly prove how great the need for such a periodical has been, and to what an extent the absence of it has inhibited Scottish poetical potentialities.

The venture is not to be a commercial one. It is intended to cover expenses and no more. The size of the monthly (which will consist only of new poems and short essays in criticism) will depend entirely upon the response to this appeal. Yorkshire supports a magazine of this kind devoted to Yorkshire poetry. Liverpool has a 'left-wing' chapbook. Surely Scotland is not incapable of maintaining a similar periodical. This is certainly one of the prerequisites of a Scottish literary revival. Only a very limited number of subscribers at 10s. annually (for which they will receive the twelve monthly issues post free) are needed. Will those interested please communicate with me at the above address, at their earliest convenience. In the event of an adequate response the first number will be issued in August.[1] I am, etc.

C. M. Grieve.
(Editor of *Northern Numbers*)

[1] The first issue of *The Scottish Chapbook* appeared in August 1922.

THE SCOTSMAN
13 November 1924

16 Miles Avenue,
Montrose.
November 11, 1924

Sirs,

My attention has just been directed to Dr Kitchin's article[1] under above title in your issue of November 8, and since that involves gross misrepresentation of a matter with which I am perhaps primarily concerned – apart from incorporating without permission the poem entitled 'The Eemis Stane,' of which I hold the copyright – I shall be obliged if you will spare me space to reply.

Dr Kitchin would have been fairer to himself – and perhaps even to our group – if, like my friend Saurat, he had first familiarised himself with our work. The name 'Scottish Renaissance Group' was merely the title Saurat gave one of his articles about us – not one we have ourselves adopted.[2] Dr Kitchin's article, however, shows throughout that his knowledge of our movement is practically restricted to what is said about it, or reproduced from it in an abridgement in the October *Marsyas* of a much longer article of Saurat's, which appeared in *La Revue Anglo-Américaine*. Surely a movement which has had several periodical organs and, apart from the association with it of such writers as John Buchan, Neil Munro, Sir Ronald Ross, Sir George Buchanan, Lady Margaret Sackville, and Mrs Violet Jacob, has enlisted the active support of between sixty and seventy younger Scottish writers, deserves better, on the basis of these facts alone, than to be thus cavalierly treated.

As to what Dr Kitchin says of 'the manners of the newcomers', I plead impenitently guilty, as one of them, to an inability to suffer fools gladly or, in fact, at all. That is 'my own funeral', however, but I challenge Dr Kitchin to name any other of my associates in this group who have in any way similarly transgressed. Apparently Dr Kitchin is of the opinion that any writer who refuses to 'bow the knee to Baal' should be forced to go through the mill; but he over-estimates the power, even in Scotland, of what Mencken terms the

---

[1] 'The "Scottish Renaissance" Group' by George Kitchin, *The Scotsman*, 8 November 1924.

[2] The reference is to Denis Saurat's article 'Le groupe de "la Renaissance Ecossaise", *Revue Anglo Américaine*, Première Année, No 4, April 1924. Still it was MacDiarmid, or rather Grieve, who coined the phrase 'Scottish Literary Renaissance' in his 'Causerie: a Theory of Scots Letters' in *The Scottish Chapbook*, Vol 1, No 7 February 1923. The article is reprinted in Hugh MacDiarmid, *The Thistle Rises* (London 1984), a MacDiarmid miscellany edited by Alan Bold.

'Boobocracy', and it is absurd to stigmatise as unthought-of writers, a group whose work appears more or less regularly in most of the world's leading literary reviews, and has excited interest in two continents.

In other respects, Dr Kitchin's article is a tissue of misrepresentations. Who, for example, other than Saurat, has referred to M'Diarmid as 'the new Burns'? And why does Dr Kitchin choose to reproduce one of the least successful of Mr M'Diarmid's early experimental poems,[3] when, from the same source, and with French translation, he could have taken what, in Saurat's opinion, was up to then M'Diarmid's chef-d'œuvre, 'The Watergaw'? Almost any poet can be so misrepresented by taking a bit of juvenilia as a representative selection. As one who has had access to all that M'Diarmid has written, I agree with some competent critics in like case that M'Diarmid's finest work to date is in a lengthy poem, such as 'Ballad of the Five Senses', or such short poems as 'Overinzievar' or 'Ex Vermibus' (both conceived in a very other vein than 'The Eemis Stane').

Again, it is assuredly a gaffe of the first magnitude to pretend that there is anything 'intensely local' about the work, for example, of Edwin Muir or George Reston Malloch, two prominent members of the group, both of whom have been commended by critics of high international standing.

And who are the 'painters, sculptors, and musicians', Dr Kitchin avers are connected with our movement?

I am, etc,

C. M. Grieve.

[3] Kitchin quoted 'The Eemis Stane', then Saurat's translation, then commented: 'It is impossible to judge here of the claims made for Mr M'Diarmid. No doubt some of them are extravagant, but there are certain pieces of his which raise him above the common level of writers in dialect – above (in the writer's opinion) Mr Charles Murray. He has – it is strange to say it of a dialect poet – a certain high seriousness which Mr Murray never attempts. For Mr Murray's craft, delightful as it can be, definitely accepts the local limitation, whereas it is the ardent aim of the new group to be something more. And the spirit they represent is not confined to verse. Painters, sculptors, and musicians are enlisted in this movement, which is at once intensely local and European at the same time.'

THE SCOTSMAN
17 November 1924

16 Links Avenue,
Montrose.
November 13, 1924

Sirs,

Your correspondent signing himself 'A Northern Numbers Contributor' in your issue of today makes a serious and quite unfounded suggestion.

The idea that the original contributors to *Northern Numbers* formed a group was created not by me as editor, but by various reviewers, and I took occasion in *The Glasgow Evening News* and elsewhere to deny that we were a group in the sense of subscribing to any particular programme or theory of letters, or in any other sense than as co-contributors to the volume in question. But only one contributor – Dr Neil Munro – protested against the suggestion, and declined on that ground to contribute to subsequent collections.

If your correspondent will give his name and the names of the two friends he indicates I think I will be able to satisfy your readers that the reason the trio in question were not included later was not because of any protest or refusal on their part, but for very other reasons.

Incidentally it may be pointed out that Mr Hugh M'Diarmid's work was never included in *Northern Numbers*.

I am, etc.

C. M. Grieve.

ABERDEEN PRESS AND JOURNAL
15 September 1925

c/o 'The New Age',
70 High Holborn,
London, W.C.

Sir,

Reference 'A.K.'s' article on my book of poems, *Sangschaw* in your issue of 12th September, I know better than to ask you for space in which to justify the theories under-lying my work against your contributor's criticism, and I am, or course, unconcerned as to his opinion of its value or lack of value as poetry, but I must respectfully solicit space to controvert what he says, or insinuates, in regard to matters of fact.

I do not understand the obscure allusion that underlies his statement that I am 'generally accepted as the Maconochie[1] of Mr C. M. Grieve'. What does 'generally accepted' and 'Maconochie' mean in this connection? I shall be glad if 'A.K.' can refer me to any issue of *The Scottish Chapbook* or any other periodical in which, as he avers, my name 'used to be bestooned with inverted commas'. I know that there is curiosity in certain quarters – which I do not intend to gratify – as to the relations between Mr Grieve and myself: but that does not justify 'A.K.' or anyone else jumping to conclusions. I may suddenly tire of their antics – with unpleasant and expensive consequences to them.

To deliberately misrepresent the nature of a writer's work in a public place may not be actionable: but I defy 'A.K.' to substantiate his statement that I have acquired the 'habit of giving to words meanings which they either don't possess or which no one can say they did possess'. He cites my use of 'antrin' in 'The Watergaw'. I speak the Doric as well, I fancy, as anyone does, and I do not 'realise the mistake'. But even if he were right in regard to that one example, it does not justify his generalisation.

As to the 'toning down to melody' and 'acquiring the music which is the soul of lyricism' almost all my poems have been set to music. 'A.K.' presumably has not heard any of them sung, but I can safely promise him that when he does, he will find that there are more things in music as well as in poetry than his philosophy wots of.

He omitted to mention that my book contains a preface by John Buchan, and quotes critiques by Professor Denis Saurat, Dr Kitchin, and others. I am content to leave it to the public to decide whether 'A.K.'s' opinions or theirs carry most weight.

Yours faithfully,
Hugh McDiarmid.

---

[1] M'Connachie is the fanciful alter ego J. M. Barrie acknowledged in his speech 'Courage' delivered as a Rectorial Address at St Andrews University on 3 May 1922.

TLS
14 January 1926

16 Links Avenue,
Montrose.
[January 1926]

Sir,

May I be permitted to break a lance with your reviewer[1] on matters of fact? He says that 'Jamieson knows the noun "knedeuch," but no such adjective as "knedneuch." ' As a matter of fact Jamieson gives the word as follows:-

'Knedneuch (ch. gutt.). A peculiar taste or smell: chiefly applies to old meat or musty bread, Fife: synon, knaggim. S.'

I have no apology to make for using it adjectivally. Yowdendrift is the opposite of erddrift, and, despite Morrison, I am quite entitled to use it in its primary sense of direction irrespective of the question of content, but, as a matter of fact, my use of the word in 'The Eemis Stane' is consistent in both respects. There is nothing absurd about the phrase 'yon antrin thing'. 'Antrin' is still used in certain parts of Scotland – as in the commonest phrase 'an antrin word' – to mean unusual, rare, seldom seen. A rainbow, especially an indistinct rainbow like a watergaw, is seen 'beyond' a downpour. The spectator is not immersed in the rainbow but in the rain; the rainbow is 'ayont' the 'onding'.

There is no reason why Scots writers should be precluded any more than English writers from using slang terms, foreign words, localisms, &c., or from seizing upon subordinate or obsolescent aspects of the significance of the words and endeavouring to give them a new force – i.e., to 'make' the language.

Where literary and linguistic considerations cannot be happily reconciled I have no hesitation in giving precedence to the former; this accounts for the other differences between your reviewer and myself. The contrary practice has been largely responsible for the provincialization of Scots poetry; we have been far too much under the thumb of the dictionary makers.

Hugh McDiarmid.

[1] *Sangschaw* (Edinburgh 1925) was reviewed in the *TLS* of 7 January 1926 under the heading 'A Scottish Renaissance'. After making the remarks to which MacDiarmid takes exception in his letter the reviewer concluded 'Still, there is a true vein of poetry in Mr M'Diarmid – how rich, or how thin, his future work will show.'

16 Links Avenue,
Montrose.

Sir,

An author can scarcely foresee perhaps all the anticipations with which readers may turn to a book entitled *Contemporary Scottish Studies*. Your reviewer[1] (in your issue of January 6) evidently feels that it ought not to deal mainly with literature. Perhaps not; it ought perhaps to deal mainly with vaudeville artistes; but, while my book is mainly concerned with literary issues, three of its thirty-odd chapters are devoted to music; three to drama; two, and parts of others, to politics; one to education: and, inter alia, I deal with linguistics, economics, and many other subjects. Moreover, my volume is marked 'First Series' and I indicate omissions which may be overtaken in a second. In the light of these facts surely your reviewer's complaint is singularly absurd. An author's style may be a matter of some importance, but in a book such as mine surely the fundamental contentions can be considered apart from the perhaps unfortunate way in which they may be expressed. And, since most of my book is devoted to a plea (not without interest, surely, even from an English point of view) for a cultural decentralization, and its expression, in Scotland, in Braid Scots or Gaelic rather than in English (which, I contend, is, for a variety of reasons stated, an inferior and undesirable medium for Scottish expression), I cannot help feeling that your reviewer would have dealt more fairly with my book, and better exemplified these virtues he deems desirable in a critic and declares to be lacking in me, if he had mentioned that fact rather than concentrated on the faults of my English, to which, I myself, quite unapologetically, draw attention in my book.

But my main purpose in writing is with reference to your reviewer's statement that I base my consideration of one novelist on a book which he (or she) has not, in fact, published. Will he please enlighten me further as to this? Since he makes such a point of it I assume that he is not referring to some mere mistake or misprint in regard to a title but to something that is really the touch-stone as to my competence or otherwise he declares it to be.

It is suggested to me that the novelist your reviewer referred to

---

[1] The *TLS* of 6 January 1927 began its brief notice of *Contemporary Scottish Studies* (London 1926) by saying 'Mr Grieve's title arouses expectations, even though one finds that his imposing-looking volume confines itself almost wholly to Scottish literature.'

was Miss Agnes Mure Mackenzie. I only make the most casual reference to her work in three short consecutive sentences in a volume of well over 300 pages, and do not name her novels at all. I mention, however, that she is also the authoress of a volume of criticism and a volume of verse, and it may be that either or both of these have not yet been published but only announced. I do not know. But, if it was this that your reviewer referred to, it is certainly altogether insufficient to bear out the general charge against my book he based on it. My brief reference to Miss Mackenzie's work has no bearing one way or another on the central contentions of my book to which he makes no reference. Can he find no more material mistake in a volume of close on 100,000 words to justify his summary dismissal of its claims to attention?

As to the charges of lack of breeding, lack of knowledge, &c., it would surely have been fairer to have substantiated these with some examples. I can quite understand that, as another writer has said, 'to the ordinary Anglicised Scot' my studies 'may appear unintelligible and in some cases biting and bitter'; but one does not expect a reviewer in *The Times Literary Supplement* to dismiss a book on the basis of such prejudices. The Scottish Renaissance Movement, of which the book is part and parcel, may not commend itself to English or Anglo-Scottish critics, but that scarcely disposes of the matter.

Yours sincerely,
C. M. Grieve.

TLS
6 October 1927

[Montrose, September 1927]

Sir,

Apropos the review of my first volume of poems – *Sangschaw* – in 'synthetic Scots' (as a matter of fact few of them are: most of my poems there, and subsequently, are in simple, unmixed dialect) in *The Times Literary Supplement*, I replied to your reviewer's challenges as to my usages of certain words and showed conclusively that I was right in every instance. He did not return to his charges. When he reviewed my second volume, *Penny Wheep*, however, he again made a series of similar strictures. I refrained from a second rebuttal. But in your issue of September 22, reviewing my third volume, *A Drunk Man Looks at the Thistle*,[1] he comes away with another 'bill of exceptions' of the same type. It is bad enough in such columns as these that (apart from a hint or two of moral prejudice) a volume of poetry should be denied criticism qua poetry and reviewed entirely from a quasi-philological angle; but this surely becomes intolerable when the reviewer persists in repeating errors already rebutted and making new ones of the same order. Even so, all he can find fault with amounts to about 1 per cent, of the terms in the glossary. The futility of such 'criticism' is obvious when it is recognized that in certain cases, for all that he knows, or all the bearing it has on my work properly considered, I might be indulging in 'creative linguistics' like the Russian Klebnikov or in forms of *skaz* or *zaumny*. Several of the words he says 'should have been glossed' actually are glossed; three of the others 'poulp,' 'keel,' and 'seam' – are not glossed because they are English words and by no means out-of-the-way ones at that. I do not know what dictionaries your reviewer uses, but I cannot be held bound by their limitations. 'Grieshuckle,' 'foudre,' &c., are all given in well-known Scots dictionaries. I have also ample oral sanction for them – as for the use of 'cude' for 'barrel' as well as 'tub'.

In other cases your reviewer depends upon the 'meaning' a certain lexicographer attaches to a word – but the way it is used by certain Scottish writers, and defined by other lexicographers, is not so limited, and, of course, it is very seldom that a dictionary entry presents all the shades of 'meaning' attaching to a word, let alone foresees all the legitimate extensions and figurative usages thereof, while dictionary-makers in general are not perhaps the best people to interpret the precise sense in which a given term is employed or intended, in texts either old or new. With regard to the word 'comb', I do give the Scots as 'kaim' (which is the same as your reviewer's 'kame'); I know 'coom' as coal-dust – not as a variant of comb; but the way in which I use 'coom' shows that I am dealing with an altogether different word than either comb (kaim or kame) or coom in these senses. I am concerned with it in this instance as a 'collection of cells', e.g. honeycomb. Your reviewer has apparently paid more attention to my glossary than to my text or he would not have made so irrelevant a comment. As to the four lines quoted at the end of his review, I have no notion of the ideas your reviewer may harbour as to

[1] A brief notice of *A Drunk Man Looks at the Thistle* (Edinburgh 1926), in the *TLS* of 22 September 1927, suggested that 'it is idle to attempt a coherent account of a poem so deliberately and provocatively incoherent.'

the convenances inebriety of the kind postulated should – or would –
observe. There is no need for ideas on the subject; the 'drunk man' 's
conduct is – the 'drunk man's' conduct. There are no 'pretensions' –
only the actualities. Your reviewer has committed the very fault
against which my preface was designed as a warning.

Yours sincerely,
Hugh McDiarmid.

JOHN O'GROAT JOURNAL
27 April 1928

16 Links Avenue,
Montrose.
April 17, 1928

Sir,

My attention has been drawn to the extraordinary paragraph
regarding the above in the 'Glasgow Caithness Notes' in your issue
of 13th April.[1]
Even if Scotland were admittedly the most cultured and artistic
country in the world, there would surely be nothing essentially
contemptible or absurd in an endeavour to still further increase the

---

[1] The *John O'Groat Journal*, 13 April 1928, contained the following paragraph: 'The
"highbrows" who are conducting the Scottish Renaissance campaign are getting
to be hysterical as well as lyrical. Take this, for example, from the current issue of
The Scots Magazine: – "Artistically in the modern world Scotland doesn't exist. No
music, no drama, no letters, of any international significance. Why is this
all-round sterility so complete, so without parallel in the life of any modern
nation?" The answer supplied is that Scotland has not got Home Rule! The
accusation is grotesquely untrue. It is not many months ago since the Prince of
Wales was at Edinburgh to open the finest war memorial in the world of which a
Scotsman was the architect. In art Sir D.Y. Cameron and Muirhead Bone are the
two greatest living etchers. The most successful play running in London just now
is *Thunder in the Air,* by Robin Millar, assistant editor of the *Glasgow Evening News*.
It is said to be a better play than *Mary Rose* by Barrie – another Scotsman. Our
Scottish newspapers – daily and weekly – are better written than those of
England. We have our Scottish school of fiction boasting such names as Neil
Munro, John Buchan, George Blake, and Neil Gunn. Artistically we don't exist?
Blethers!' *The Scots Magazine* article referred to 'Defensio Scotorum' published in
Vol IX, No 1, as the work of 'Dane M'Neil', a pseudonym used by Neil Gunn.

excellence of its art products and deepen and intensify the aesthetic consciousness of its people. Scotland, however, is nothing of the sort. All the more need then for a movement with these objects which are, in fact, the objects of the Scottish Renaissance movement. It is admittedly a 'highbrow' movement. Does your contributor hold any brief for a lower level of effort and appeal than it is within anyone's power to take and make? If his objection to our 'highbrowism' is that it is not genuinely or sufficiently 'highbrow,' can he point to any 'highbrowism' more genuine or adequate in Scotland today – or to any achievements on his own part which entitle him to adopt a superior or hostile attitude? I venture to suggest that if he discards his anonymity his comments would promptly appear in their proper perspective.

As to the sentence he quotes from *The Scots Magazine*, surely the best way of ascertaining the relative literary and artistic standing of any country is to see how it is regarded in other countries. There is no work of reference, literary history or criticism, etc., dealing with European Arts of Letters today which so much as mentions Scotland or any Scottish artist, author, or composer. Every other country in Europe may be separately dealt with – may even require lengthy special sections to themselves, with long lists of authors, artists, and musicians of not only national but international calibre. Scotland alone always passes unmentioned. Why? Because it is the unanimous opinion of the leading European authorities on contemporary literature, art, music, drama, etc., that modern Scotland has produced nothing of the slightest consequence. Neil Munro, John Buchan, George Blake may seem big figures to your contributor, but they are never mentioned in serious literary discussion, and their relative stature is so small that in books dealing with modern letters and canvassing hundreds of names drawn from every other country in Europe they are not deemed worthy of so much as a passing mention. Let your correspondent write to Buchan and ask him for his honest opinion on this, and he will find that Buchan agrees with the writer in The *Scots Magazine*.

Your correspondent is sadly at odds with himself in citing the name of Neil Gunn – for Neil Gunn is one of the Renaissance group and thoroughly at one with our propaganda. His first novel, *The Grey Coast*, was an excellent bit of work and foreshadowed a higher development of the Scottish novel than anything since *The House with the Green Shutters*, but neither Gunn nor his friends are so fatuous as to think it is on a European level.

Then to drama, Barrie's popularity and wealth proves no more in regard to his merit as a dramatist than the fact that Annie S. Swan is regarded as a great novelist by thousands of readers makes her anything of the sort. Both are quite negligible in their respective fields; and if your contributor cares to invite the opinion of any litterateur of European standing he will get an immediate endorsation of this statement.

The less said of the Scottish War Memorial and the work of Sir D.Y. Cameron and Muirhead Bone the better. All three are to modern art what Mid-Victorian fashions in female attire are to the current modes.

I am, etc.,

C. M. Grieve.

P.S. Oh, and does your contributor honestly think the *Aberdeen Press and Journal*, the Dundee *Courier and Advertiser* and *The Scotsman* anything like on a level with *The Manchester Guardian*, *The Daily Telegraph* and *The Times*? He will be telling us next that in *The Scots Magazine* itself we have more than enough to compensate us for having no Scottish *Spectator*, *Nation and Athenaeum*, *New Statesman* or *Punch*.
C. M. G.

SCOTS OBSERVER
7 January 1933

[December 1932]

Dear Sir,

I am a violent person; I fight when I am attacked! It may be time my work and personality were brought under serious review; but the anonymous writer of the long article on the subject[1] in your issue of 22nd December certainly does not initiate the process. Surely

[1] The *Scots Observer* of 22 December 1932 carried an anonymous article, prompted by the appearance of *Scots Unbound and Other Poems* (Stirling 1932), accusing MacDiarmid of 'intellectual bullying', 'continuous assertion of his brain power' and being 'purely imitative of certain artists he respects'. MacDiarmid's reply, in the issue of 7 January 1933, was augmented by a letter in his defence by Valda Trevlyn (the poet's second wife) who strongly objected to 'the extraordinary attack on Hugh MacDiarmid in your last issue.'

something of value might have been said in three of your short columns even. The general suggestion that I ought to return to my earlier type of work and eschew my later proclivities implies that the writer is much wiser than I am, and in a position to advise me. I cannot be expected to take him at his own valuation in this way. His article is studded with unwarrantably derogatory remarks and vicious innuendoes, e.g., 'versification of my latest reading', 'straining of credulity in the learning implied', etc. What foot-notes I give refer to books which are far from recently published, and which it should have seemed I had probably had little occasion to read only recently, while the reflection on my scholarship is one which the writer cannot justify. The legitimate functions of a critic is to deal with my work – not to imagine I would be better employed doing something else, or to discuss issues concerning my personality and equipment for which in the nature of things he cannot possibly have the requisite data. No one is under any obligation to purchase my books, and your contributor's hypothetical new reader who would resent the price and linguistic difficulties of my work is a highly improbable person. He can always buy a leather-bound Tennyson or an Edgar Wallace instead. If I care to fix the price at a guinea a line (and send gratis copies to reviewers) that is entirely my own affair, and it is a piece of mere impertinence to suggest that I should sell my stuff cheaper. As to those earlier lyrics of mine – and the *Drunk Man* (which is as full of out-of-the-way references, foreign translations, etc., as my recent publications) – which according to your reviewer so many people admired, not only did that admiration fall short of spending the relatively low price in purchasing the same (thus complicating my subsequent publishing problems), but these same earlier books evoked precisely the same criticisms (of high-browism, obscurity, out-of-the-way allusions, etc.) to which your reviewer now subjects my latest production. Those who have really befriended my work from the beginning have a very different point of view, and I find in them an audience which, though small, is one of which I have every reason to be proud, because it consists of men and women who have themselves done distinguished work. From the style of his article I cannot imagine that your reviewer falls into that category; and significantly (in addition to his grudging references even to those brief lyrics in which he admits I still show myself a 'poet in my own right') he fails to mention one of the poems in *Scots Unbound* which is free of most of the 'faults' of which he accuses me, but which is generally regarded by those whose opinions I respect as one of the very best things I have yet done. I refer to 'Tarras'. It is high time that Scottish reviewers tried to understand what a writer is trying to do instead of presuming to advise him to do something

769

which falls more easily within their ken; and the suggestion that I owe anything to the Scottish reading public or ought to consider them in any way or confine my personal hobbies to commoner lines is one which I entirely repel. The whole article is moreover vitiated by its insincerity. If my later manifestations are a deplorable departure from my earlier quality, and it would be any service to Scots letters that I should revert to the latter, no article could be less calculated to induce me to try to do so. Instead of speculating on my motives and methods your contributor ought to have had recourse to the various essays in which I have explained and defended my practices, and joined issue with these. Scotland has always taken away far more with her left hand than she gave with her right from any poet of the slightest consequence she ever had. Your contributor credits me with quick wit, vision, intricate responses to life, intellectualism, and a lyrical faculty of a high order. In view of the way in which, on top of all that, he proceeds to treat me one wonders whose is the stupendous intellect that can presume to lecture the possessor of such gifts, and how he would have treated some unfortunate poet who was destitute of these attributes – which, after all, have not been possessed singly, let alone jointly, by more poets than can be numbered on the fingers of two hands, in the whole course of Scottish literary history. To exemplify these and yet expose oneself to such treatment is almost enough to inhibit any further effort, and certainly can hardly fail to imbue the victim with an invincible prejudice against anything which such a 'critic' approves.

Yours sincerely,
C. M. Grieve.

THE FREE MAN
9 December 1933
Sir,

In reply to Dr Mary Ramsay's interesting letter,[1] may I say that I draw a distinction between the synthetic use of a language and all

[1] In *The Free Man*, of 25 November 1933, Mary P. Ramsay's letter on 'Nationalism and Vernacular', asked 'Can a distinction be drawn, when we speak of literature, between vernacular and *synthetic* Scots? . . .Poetry has no partnership with philology.'

other uses of it, either of what is called 'a full canon' or of such restricted forms as any dialect, any particular 'poetic diction', or any so-called 'standard' (e.g. King's English). All of these use parts of the common stock of what may be called 'the accepted vocabulary.' It in a phenomenon observable in all languages that, despite minor differences, all these usages employ only a very small fraction – and for the most part all the same fraction – of the expressive resources of the language in question, and that the differences in vocabulary of a Shakespeare, a dialect writer like Barnes, a linguistic experimenter like Charles Doughty or Gerard Manley Hopkins, any other writer, and 'the man in the street' are so slight in relation to the vast mass of available words they all exclude as to be practically negligible. The reason why nineteen-twentieths of any language are never used is shrewdly related to the problem of the freedom of the consciousness. As Dostoevski said, all human organisations tend to stabilise and perpetuate themselves – to become 'a church' and to short-circuit human consciousness. This is most marked in our language-habit, our helpless submission to a fraction of our expressive possibilities – and in this connection it is vitally necessary to remember that language is just as much a determinant of what is expressed in it as a medium of expression. By the synthetic use of a language, then, I mean 'the destruction of toothless ratio' – 'freedom of speech' in the real meaning of the term – something completely opposed to all our language habits and freely utilising not only all the vast vocabulary these automatically exclude, but illimitable powers of word formation in keeping with the free genius of any language. Theoretically – and to some extent practically – I go further and agree with Joyce in regard to the utilisation of a multi-linguistic medium – a synthetic use, not of any particular language, but of all languages. Personally, I write in English, or in dialect Scots, or in synthetic Scots – or in synthetic English – with bits of other languages. I recognise the values of any language or any dialect for certain purposes, but where I am concerned with the free consciousness I cannot employ these – I must then find an adequate synthetic medium. The 'Free Man', ultimately, can make do with none other than le mot libre. I hope this is clear enough for Miss Ramsay to appreciate from it the distinction I draw between a synthetic use of a language and any other; I could only hope to express myself completely on the subject by such a synthetic use of words as would inevitably be completely unintelligible to anyone except myself. I do not agree then, that either the passage she quotes from Shakespeare or from myself represent what I mean by a synthetic use of language at all, but if she would care to set against what I regard as one of my more successful experiments in synthetic Scots an equivalent passage in synthetic English, I would proffer the following which I wrote this summer:-

In The Caledonian Forest[2]

The geo-selenic gimbal that moving makes
A gerbe now of this tree now of that
Or glomerates the whole earth in a galanty-show
    Against the full moon caught
Suddenly threw a fuscous halation round a druxy dryad
    Lying among the fumet in this dwale wood
As brooding on Scotland's indecrassifiable race
    I wandered again in a hemicranic mood.
She did not change her epirhizous posture
But looked at me steadily with Hammochrysos eyes
While I wondered what dulia might be her due
And from what her curious enanthesis might arise,
And then I knew against that frampold background
This freaked and forlorn creature was indeed
With her great shadowed gastrocnemius and disipient face
The symbol of the flawed genius of our exheredated breed.

As in Antichthon there among the apoproegmena
A quatr' occhi for a long time we stood
While like a kind of springhalt or chorea
The moonshine flickered in the silent wood,
Or like my own aporia externalised,
For her too slight kenosis made it impossible for me to woo
This outcast Muse, or urge the long-lost cause we might
    advance even yet
Conjunctis viribus, or seek to serve her, save thus, ek
    parergou.

I am, &c.
C. M. Grieve

[2] The poem (391-2) was collected in *Stony Limits and Other Poems* (London 1934).

NEW SCOTLAND
26 October 1935

[Whalsay,
October 1935]

Let the English do what they will
We Scots to France must be steadfast still!

Dear Mr Editor,

Congratulations on the first issue of *New Scotland*[1] which has just reached me in my hyperborean home.

While agreeing with the tenor of most of the articles in it, may I express the hope that, it will, in subsequent issues, get into closer and closer grips with actual affairs and possibilities in Scotland itself and in particular concentrate the attention of its readers on the fact that any professedly Scottish Nationalism that is not radically proletarian and Republican is not worth a damn. In a recent article Professor Saunders Lewis, President of the Welsh Nationalist Party, wrote: 'The Welsh working people see now that the English Labour Party and Trade Union Congress are imperialists, pro-Capitalist organisations, prepared to go to war in defence of the English Empire. Welsh Nationalism is the Welsh working people's only defence against English militarism.' It is high time the Scottish working people came to a similar realisation with regard to Scottish Nationalism and *New Scotland* will be a sorry disappointment unless it drives that home.

The 'Auld Alliance' can still rouse the hearts and claim the allegiance of thousands of Scots and it is vitally necessary at this moment in the interests of Scotland and of France and of Europe as a whole that this old allegiance should be greatly intensified and effectively related to current issues and practical affairs. England is playing the opposite game and despite denial after denial our Foreign Office, and National Government generally, is working hand in hand with Hitlerite Germany.

The Auld Alliance of Scotland and France may seem at first glance to have little enough to do with proletarian interests today; but those who think this, need to think again.

It is not only vitally related to proletarian interests, alike in France

---

[1] *New Scotland* – a combination of *Alba Nuadh* with the Social Credit weekly *The Free Man* – was launched in October 1935. MacDiarmid's letter was featured as the main lead on the front page of Vol I, No 3, 26 October 1935. An editorial note pointed out that 'Part of the above letter is an extract from MacDiarmid's forthcoming book *Red Scotland*.'

and Scotland and everywhere else, but to the issues of the Douglasite propaganda to which *New Scotland* is specifically devoted. Let me illustrate this: but let me first quote a passage, which every true Scot should have off by heart, from a poem by a great Scottish poet (though he wrote in Latin) – to wit, George Buchanan. That poets frequently have a remarkable prophetic faculty is a fact amply attested in literary history; and the following passage might well enough have been revised as an apt reminder to us at the present time and a piece of the shrewdest practical counsel, viz. (I quote from a prose translation by Mr Geo. E. Davie):-

'Charlemagne, too, who to the French gave the Latin fasces and Quirinus' robe (i.e. the symbols of European hegemony), and the French by treaty joined the Scots; a treaty which neither the War-God with iron nor unruly sedition, can undo, nor mad lust for power, nor the succession of years, nor any other force. Tell over the list of France's triumphs since that age and of the conspiracies of the world in all its airts for the destruction of the French name – without the help of Scottish soldiers never victory shone upon the French camp; never really cruel disaster crushed the French without the shedding of Scottish blood, too; Scotland – this one nation – has shared the brunt of all the vicissitudes of French fortune; and the swords that threatened the French it has often diverted against itself. The bellicose English know this, the wild Netherlanders know this, to this the Po's waters are witness, and Naples attacked again and again by unsuccessful invasion. This is the dowry your wife offers you (i.e., Mary, Queen of Scots, in marrying Francis of France, to whom the poem was addressed), a nation for so many centuries, faithful to your subjects and conjoined with them by a treaty of alliance – a people unsubjugated by arms through so many dangerous crises.'

This is the real meaning for Scotland of 'Soutra's' warning (in *New Scotland* No 1) that 'the alignments in the coming war will thus probably be England, Germany, Italy, and Japan against France and America.' There is no question about that – and Scotland must stand by France then through thick and thin. The whole aim and object of Scottish National Policy now should be to hamper England in effecting that new alignment – and when the crisis comes Scotland's part must be to divert and destroy England's power in this connection, by secession from her and the transformation of the impending war into a civil war in Great Britain itself.

In considering the full bearings of these contentions it would be well if readers remembered that Buckle justly said of Buchanan that he was the first to define popular rights, and in his *De Jure Regni Apud Scotos* 'justified by anticipation all subsequent revolutions'.

774

If any reader should ask, 'But what about proletarian interests, and about Douglasism, in particular' it would be well that he or she should remember what has been happening in France and realise the true inwardness of the following passage from a recent issue of *The Week* (which clearly reveals the relationship which makes the present author believe, not only that Communism and Nationalism can go hand in hand, but that Communism is the only safe-guard of nationalism, and ultimately of human personality, in the world today), viz:-

'Hard facts behind the more or less disingenuous interpretation placed upon the now famous Moscow-Paris communiqué issued after the Stalin-Laval talks in Moscow indicate a movement in the position of the Third International which is none the less sensational for the fact that it is a change very different from that suggested by the "wishful thinking" of the big press. Subscribers – particularly those who read the *Daily Telegraph* and the *Daily Herald* – will recall that in the course of that communiqué Stalin "approved the considerations" which have led the French to adopt defensive measures against the Hitler menace. "Wishful thinkers" – not least those in the Second International who have developed politically disastrous self-deception into a habit – happily concluded that this, in fact, foreshadowed the co-operation of the French Communist Party – now the strongest single party in Paris – with the "defence" armament schemes of the Comité des Forges and Marshal Pétain. According to one of our Paris correspondents, this ludicrous suggestion was not only broadcast but actually believed by certain elements in France, who gleefully hailed the alignment of the Third International with the armaments policy. The real situation – which is of basic international importance – is as follows. The victories of the Communists in the French municipal elections have consolidated a position already extraordinarily powerful. The Moscow communiqué, without of itself altering the position of the Third International, in fact signalised a movement of major importance. The movement is in the direction of the consolidation around the Third International of those who in each country are genuinely "patriotic" – are genuinely in favour of the defence of "la patrie" – as opposed, for example, to the Comité des Forges, the Bank of England, and the other "patriotic" leaders who have "patriotically" armed Hitler Germany in a manner comparable to the now notorious supply by the notably patriotic firm of Vickers of the guns which killed the Anzacs, etc., at Gallipoli. The immediately interesting and important fact is that the Third International is now stressing the fact that national defence is of course a necessity – in the sense of the defence of the people and their country against Fascist attack from at

775

home or abroad. But (and here are alike disappointed the hopes of the big press and of the Second International, which demands "co-operation with the capitalist governments for national defence"), the Third International and especially the French Communist Party are making clear that in their view the first step towards effective defence of the workers of any country against Fascist aggression – internal and external – is the control of the Army by and for the workers. The French Communist Party is putting forward the demand for the "elimination of Fascist elements from the Army". On this demand are implicit (a) the demand for workers' control and organisations of a genuinely anti-fascist workers' defence corps – and it is now evident that the French Communists will be content to support nothing less; (b) the fact that the Third International in France is now advanced to the position where it can begin to put forward this demand effectively as a step on the road to its ultimate objective, namely, the upset of the whole Capitalist set-up and all that that implies, and the establishment of a revolutionary regime for the protection of French civilisation from its enemies, external and domestic.'

The Communist Party is right in regarding the official National Party of Scotland as a Fascist organisation. That was the whole aim and object of the *Daily Record's* manoeuvre – its precious Plan For Scotland and the formation of the Scottish National Development Council – to which the old National Party succumbed, and, as a result, fused with the Duke of Montrose's Scottish Party and fell under the leadership of people like the Duke of Montrose, Sir Alexander McEwan, Professor Dewar Gibb, and 'Annie S. Swan'. The real nationalists left it en bloc, and have since occupied themselves in other directions.

I accurately described the *Daily Record's* and Duke of Montrose's fascistic manoeuvre at the time.

All these people – these pseudo-nationalists – are Anglo-Scots, with no real knowledge of Scottish language or literature – insulated from it by English, and by the fact that they are cut off from the Scottish proletariat, all their concrete connections being with the denationalised Anglicised bourgeoisie. From this point of view, what is wrong with them – as with our Scottish Socialist Movement – is a complete failure to appreciate the truth of Count Keyserling's realisation that 'until a vital nucleus of individuals stands for a programme which shall be only the external expression of a vitally existing inner state, it will remain powerless'. It cannot be fairly said that any reformers have as yet adopted this attitude. I know of no Socialist who really wills what he advocates; if he comes into power he very soon lives and acts in the spirit of the very life-philosophy he

formerly opposed and for that matter may go on opposing out-
wardly. That is where the importance of realising that you cannot be
a Socialist, let alone a Communist, without breaking not only with
Capitalist politics and economies, but Capitalist culture as a whole –
that you cannot be a Scottish Nationalist without breaking with
English culture, lock, stock and barrel – comes in. The French
Communists are not concerned with the preservation of French
civilisation as it has been – but with getting down to French
Ur-motives, under Communism.

The workers in Scotland must do likewise. It is the only way out.
Continued association with England, either in the present relationship or any other, or even continued allegiance to the dangerously
and anti-democratically conspiring clique of cosmopolitan care-
erists in Windsor Castle, cannot but commit us to Fascism, the
antithesis of the Scottish genius and the negation of its natural
destiny and world-function. We can only rightly direct our affairs at
the present time and in the future by rigid adherence to the policy
that inspired us in the past – unbreakable alliance with France and
continual war with England.

Yours for Scotland,
Hugh MacDiarmid.

TLS
22 February 1936

[Whalsay
January 1936]

Sir,

In your issue of January 4 appears a review of my translation of
The Birlinn of Clanranald[1] in which, after admitting that my translation is the most successful yet made, your reviewer goes on to

[1] The review in the *TLS* of 4 January 1936 claimed, 'The translator's remarks on
the metres used in the original are confused and misleading . . .The space that is
given to the metres would have been much better used to describe the rigging and
appearance of the galley that is the subject of the poem, since this type of vessel is
not likely to be familiar to the modern reader any more than the classical Gaelic
metres are to Mr MacDiarmid.'

777

suggest that my acquaintance with classical Gaelic metres is less than most people's knowledge of this particular type of ship, i.e. nil. As an author who has written a great deal on this very subject, and who has made English verse translations of the majority of the most important Scottish Gaelic poems, I must ask you to grant me space to protest against this singularly uncalled for and completely unjustified suggestion. I am in a position to prove that I have a specialist's knowledge of the field in question.

Hugh MacDiarmid

TLS
4 September 1937

Whalsay,
Via Lerwick,
The Shetland Islands.
[August 1937]

Sir,

I am gathering material for a biographical study of Arthur O'Connor (1763–1852), the Irish rebel and later appointed a general of a division by Napoleon, and of his brother, Roger O'Connor (1762–1834), who in 1882 published the *Chronicles of Eri*, which I entirely disagree with the *Dictionary of National Biography* in regarding as being 'mainly imaginative' or indeed as at all imaginative or otherwise than completely authentic.

I am very eager to secure letters, written by them and to have access to family papers, &c. Any letters lent to me for this purpose will be guarded carefully and returned with gratitude. I would be thankful, too, for any information pertaining to letters written by them, or indicating other sources of material regarding them. I may add that I am in correspondence with Mr L. Albert, the editor of the latest edition of *The Chronicles of Eri* (Berlin and London, 1936).

Hugh MacDiarmid.

Whalsay,
Via Lerwick,
Shetland Islands.
[May 1938]

Sir,

In the recent Scottish section[1] of *The Times Literary Supplement* your contributor Doris N. Dalglish opines that Mr Lewis Spence's 'auld Scots' poems are more appealing to the average reader than my 'synthetic Scots'. It would be interesting to know how she arrives at this conclusion, which I have very good reason for believing to be exactly the opposite of the truth. Certain sorts of data are available with regard to matters of this kind. Miss Dalglish does not appear to have troubled to resort to any of these data, but in the absence of that her comment is surely simply an impertinence in both senses of the word – a kind of presumption deplorably common among contemporary criticasters and constituting almost their whole stock-in-trade.

What are the data to which I refer? To begin with there is the evidence of anthologies, whose compilers must be assumed to cater for the 'average reader' and to have as good a knowledge of the average reader's likes as Miss Dalglish. In the last twenty anthologies that have come my way – including Mr W.B. Yeats's *Oxford Book of Modern Verse* and Mr Maurice Wolman's *Poems of Twenty Years* – my work is represented. Mr Spence's is not. The evidence from volumes of critical essays and surveys of contemporary poetry – such as Miss Babette Deutsch's *This Modern Poetry* and Mr Cecil Day Lewis's *A Hope for Poetry* – is to the same effect. So is the evidence to be drawn from the extent to which my poems have been translated into other languages, and been the subject of critical studies in other countries, whether through essays in periodicals, pamphlets, academic theses, or lectures. I quite understand how at first blush my work seems (to those who have a certain patronizing attitude to the general public) insusceptible, because of its linguistic difficulty and for other reasons, of much popular appeal: but those who have lectured on it to popular audiences in connexion with the Adult Education Movement and to societies at Aberdeen, Manchester, and other universities, assure me that they had no difficulty

---

[1] The 'Scottish Literature Today' feature in the *TLS* of 30 April 1938 included Doris N. Dalglish's article 'Towards a Nationalist Literature – The Scottish Renaissance'.

whatever in 'putting it across' – a result which accords with my own far more varied experience in connexion with popular audiences in all parts of Scotland. The anticipated difficulties in this matter are simply a figment of what Lord Tweedsmuir has called 'the interpreting class' and do not present themselves in actual practice. It would occupy far too much space to detail this evidence here, but what it amounts to is that Miss Dalglish had nothing whatever to go upon in making the remark in question and that she is demonstrably quite wrong.

Mr Peter MacCallum Smith is, of course, right in what he says in his able letter in your issue of May 7 on the question of the Back to Dunbar slogan. I invented this slogan some fifteen years ago to signify an opposition to the post-Burnsian 'Kailyaird' usage of Scots, and also a break with 'popular' anti-intellectualism and an intention of returning not only to a full canon of Scots and a repudiation of mere dialect circumscription, but a claim to deal with the full range of subject matter of a truly national poetry as opposed to mere 'local' material. But Mr Neil M. Gunn, the novelist, rightly stated in an article about that time that what I really meant was not 'Back to Dunbar' but 'Forward to MacDiarmid', and all my later work – none of it pastiche of the Auld Makars and most of it concerned with dialectical materialist and contemporary scientific subject-matter – has amply vindicated Mr Gunn's discernment. Unlike Miss Dalglish and other commentators who attach far too much importance to that early slogan, Mr Gunn has not held to the letter in disregard of the spirit.

C. M. Grieve ('Hugh MacDiarmid').

THE SHETLAND TIMES
8 July 1939

Whalsay.
June 1939.

Dear Sir,

Will you please allow me to thank 'R. W.' for his appreciative review of my new book, *The Islands of Scotland*, in your current issue, and to reply very briefly on two points he raises.

The first is with regard to the practice of 'bundling' in the

Shetlands. I am glad 'R. W.' pointed out that I did not deal with this 'critically', i.e., I did not condemn it. The Author of a recent history of the same practice in New England shows the geographical circumstances responsible for it – the lack of outside shelter and privacy for courting couples, etc. – but, after a full survey of all the health and other factors involved, comes to the conclusion that the practice is eminently justifiable and compares favourably with the conventional practices elsewhere. This is my own opinion, and if I criticise the Shetlanders it is not because of the practice in question (the prevalence of which nowadays is in any case an arguable matter), but because of their tendency to deny that it exists and their failure to take an honest stand and defend it. If what I say on this score may inadvertently mislead people outside the islands, 'R. W.'s' phrase about my conclusion as to the 'lax morality' of the young Islespeople may also mislead those who have not read my book, and I may therefore be allowed to make it clear that I regard the practice of bundling as much better on all counts than the practices of the majority of young folks in Scotland and England. There is more immorality there than in the Shetlands; the relations of the lovers are conducted there in a far more surreptitious and furtive fashion, and the consequences in disease, illegitimacy, irregular relationships of all sorts, and divorce are evil out of all proportion to anything that happens in the Shetlands.

The other point is with regard to what 'R. W.' says of the extreme unlikeliness of a renaissance along Norn-autonomous lines. I quite agree that ninety-nine people out of a hundred would share this 'commonsense view', but in precisely the same way the vast majority of Russians in 1916 would have regarded the overthrow of the Czarist regime and the establishment of the USSR as a dream outside the bounds of all probability, while the hundreds of thousands of German Socialists a few years ago would have found the possibility of Hitler's Nazis coming to power just as fantastically incredible. 'Common-sense', in other words, is no guide in these matters. I do not say that Shetland Autonomy based on Scandinavia rather than Britain is likely – I only say that far less likely, and less desirable things are continually happening in the field of politics, and that, whether the Shetlanders want this or not, it is the only way in which they can conserve what remains of their ancient traditions and their characteristic way of living, and that there are extremely good reasons why, as this juncture, their minds should consider the chance of such developments just as increasing numbers are being forced by circumstances to consider similar chances in regard to Scotland, Wales and Ireland. Circumstances are undoubtedly forcing our people on to lines most of them still regard as utterly

781

impracticable. A well-known Scottish poet writes me in this connection: 'I was particularly interested to your remarks upon the premonitory significance of island life as anticipating a condition, at least in essence, to which Western man must approximate. The rediscovery of earth, with its concomitant of increased sensuous awareness, is obviously our major need: and in the knowledge of this necessity (for I assume you will agree that if men refuse to act in a creative fashion they foredoom themselves to disasters which drive them to the choice which they would deny) one can accept even the bomber as a necessary agent for the rehabilitation of the land.'

If ideas of Norn-autonomist renaissances are incredibly farfetched, it must at any rate be remembered that the system under which we are living is far more fantastic and incredible – the world our shrewd commonsense people have brought about in which, as Neil Gunn, says, in his Foreword to Peter Anson's admirable pamphlet, *The Sea-Fisheries of Scotland: Are They Doomed?* 'What, then, has gone wrong with Scotland? It cannot be the quality of her fish because it is the best in the world. Her fishing banks are famous. Our herring catches are deliberately restricted by a Government Board. Often vast quantities of our fish are dumped. Yet one-quarter of our home-consumed herring is imported from Norway. More astonishing than that: we used to export an enormous quantity of our cure to Russia: now, as Mr Anson shows, we are not only not exporting to Russia, but, in 1937, Russia exported to Great Britain fish to the value of over £1,800,000. And Japan sent us fish to the value of nearly £2,000,000.'

For people who live in a world which is full of such appalling absurdities to complain of the farfetchedness and fantastic improbability of anybody's alternative ideas is for them to busy themselves with the mote in somebody else's eye and ignore the beam in their own with a vengeance. The great mass of 'commonsense people' have no ground whatever to gibe at the impracticable visions of any poet; they are simply straining at a gnat of fantasy while they swallow a whale of far more stupendous – and harmful – irrationality.

David's victory over Goliath must have seemed unlikely enough. But such victories are as possible today as ever they were.

Yours,
C. M. Grieve.
('Hugh MacDiarmid')

Footnote:- There are only these two ways of it, and the Shetlanders, like all other peoples, are free to choose either the creative way or the way of disaster and death.

FREE MAN
8 August 1942
The Editor
Sir,

Opinions differ. My view of Sydney Smith's poems in *Skail Wind*[1] differs very sharply from that of your reviewer, 'W.S.', and from that of Mr Douglas Young, expressed in *New Alliance*, where he passed similar strictures on Smith's use of Scots, and alleged unScottish-ness, to those of 'W.S.' in these columns. Even if Sydney Smith were not half Scottish by birth, and domiciled in Scotland, and deeply involved in the Scottish Literary Movement, his devotion to the Scots language would be very welcome, as a rare kind of compliment indeed for any non-Scot to pay to the Scots tongue. Save us from any 'little Scotlandism' in this connection. 'W.S.' and Douglas Young seem to me 'dog-in-the-mangerish' in their attitude. Nor do I attach any value whatever to the petty pedantic points they make about Smith's use of Scots. On the contrary I welcome and approve his experimentism and the rich synthetic vocabulary he employs, and so far as poetic quality goes I regard him as by far the best young poet writing in Scots who has emerged in our midst for over twenty years. He deserves every encouragement.

To devote oneself to poetry – and to succeed in these times in getting a volume of it published – is no light matter, and it is deplorable that the first venture of an enthusiastic young writer like Sydney Smith should have cold water dribbled on it in this way by two fellow-poets who should have been among the first to give him the hand of fellowship, and the freedom of the little clan of Scots authors to which they belong, and to which I feel sure Sydney Smith will soon prove himself a very distinguished acquisition indeed.

In the meantime, it is good to see him in this first book 'feeding his oats' no matter how indigestible his 'fine, confused feeding' may seem to some of his dyspeptic seniors.

Yours, etc.
Hugh MacDiarmid.

---

[1] Sydney Goodsir Smith, *Skail Wind* (1942).

Plastic Scots

In a broadcast lecture, delivered in November 1946, James Fergusson used the term 'plastic Scots' to ridicule the Scottish Renaissance Movement which had by then attracted a whole school of poets anxious to emulate MacDiarmid. Fergusson complained that the users of plastic Scots wrote bad poetry in a bastard language. MacDiarmid's letter of 13 November 1946 launched a lively correspondence that was eventually closed by the editor on 29 November 1946; in the course of this controversy MacDiarmid was supported by Maurice Lindsay (12, 21 and 26 November), Edwin Morgan (15 and 26 November), Douglas Young (16 and 22 November) and R. Crombie Saunders (19 November).

THE GLASGOW HERALD
11 November 1946

> 32 Victoria Crescent Road,
> Glasgow, W.2.

Sir,

Mr James Fergusson's strictures in his broadcast last week on synthetic (or, as he prefers to call it, plastic) Scots sound very Rip Van Winkleish at this time of day. It is not only that the experiments towards a synthetic Scots and what has been produced in that medium in poetry, prose, and drama – by the late Lewis Grassic Gibbon, Robert MacLellan, myself, and others – have won the praises of many famous critics and creative artists, and been no barrier to appreciation in other countries.

Even if Mr Fergusson's opinion weighed anything against the recorded praises of the late W. B. Yeats, the late A. E. (George W. Russell), ex-Prince D. S. Mirsky, the late Professor George

Gordon, the late Lord Tweedsmuir, Mr Sean O'Casey, Mr T. S. Eliot, and a host of others, the fact remains that – so far as poetry at least is concerned – English anthologists and writers like Messrs Stephen Spender, Louis MacNeice, and Cecil Day Lewis have found cause to pay attention to it and to eschew almost all contemporary Scottish poetry not written in it, while all recent English critics and literary historians have testified to the fact that wherever modern Scottish poets have written both in English and in Scots their best work has been done in the latter. All modern languages are synthetic – none more so than English. Norway and other countries provide examples of the successful creation – by purely arbitrary methods – of modern linguistic media on the basis of old and obsolete or obsolescent stocks. Language experimentation of various kinds has been a feature of every modern literature. Why should Scottish literature be an exception? Did it not need revival by such methods more than that of any other European country?

Burns's Scots, too, was highly synthetic – disregardful of dialect demarcations and drawn from a variety of historical periods. The arguments Mr Fergusson uses were all used, against Burns. One had thought one had heard the last of them long ago.

That synthetic Scots, as used by myself, Mr Sydney Smith, Mr Maurice Lindsay, Mr Douglas Young, or others, is not intelligible to the man in the street is no argument against it. Great Poetry and other literature have been and are being written in very many languages that not five in a million Britons know. If they do not know synthetic Scots that is their loss – their ignorance in no way invalidates the medium.

The fact of the matter is, of course, that one never hears such arguments against synthetic Scots except from an Englishman or an Anglo-Scot. My own poems have had no difficulty in finding French, German, Icelandic, and other translators. No matter what Mr Fergusson or anyone else similarly minded to him in this connection may think, the synthetic Scots movement will go on. It is attracting more and more of the younger Scottish writers of ability – and as it belongs to a class of literary phenomena well understood in most modern European literatures – and in American literature – it will have no difficulty in securing consideration throughout the civilised world, however little honour it may have in Anglo-Scotland and in insular England, with their notorious incapacity for foreign languages.

A distinguished French scholar and critic – Professor Denis Saurat – was responsible for inventing the term 'Synthetic Scots'. I have no objection whatever to Mr Fergusson's suggested alteration to 'Plastic Scots'. The requirements of modern expression are so complex and countless that the greater the degree of plasticity in any linguistic medium the better! –

I am, etc.
C. M. Grieve. ('Hugh MacDiarmid')

THE GLASGOW HERALD
13 November 1946

32 Victoria Crescent Road,
Glasgow, W.

Sir,

Permit me to protest against the way in which the writer of the paragraphs in Saturday's Editorial Diary on 'Short Course in Plastic Scots'[1] misrepresents contemporary Scots poetry. His references to concealment of meaning in such poetry are particularly absurd. A great deal has been written about obscurity or unintelligibility in modern poetry. Scots poetry, even in synthetic Scots, is singularly free from it, its main characteristic indeed being clarity and directness of statement. That the philosophical implications of such poetry are not less profound than those of any other contemporary poetry is another matter susceptible of easy demonstration; but it is not a matter of opinion but simply of fact that contemporary Scots poetry is far more direct and easily intelligible (given a knowledge of the language, of course – but that is requisite for the understanding not only of poetry in Scots, but in French, Russian, or any other language, not excluding English) than that in any other European language.

English poetry, on the other hand, is, in the case of many contemporary practitioners, exceedingly obscure and ill to under-

[1] *The Glasgow Herald* of 9 November 1946 ridiculed the notion of plastic Scots: 'It is, of course, much easier to write plastic Scots than to read it, and the art can easily be mastered with the help of a few simple rules.

'Manner is your concern rather than matter. Your subjects need be few – Hugh MacDiarmid, Glasgow, the Highlands, the English, love, drink, and Hugh MacDiarmid. You should write at least one ode to Hugh MacDiarmid: this is *de rigueur*. After all, he invented synthetic Scots, from which the plastic form is derived.

'It is not necessary for what you write to have no meaning, but it is vital to conceal your meaning, if any, as much as possible.'

stand, and even, in many cases, devoid of meaning. Contemporary Scots poets may, like Burns, use an occasional phrase even many Scots do not understand without recourse to a dictionary – e.g., 'a daimen icker in a thrave'. But the works of almost all modern English writers of high literary standing are full of words and phrases of which this is also true – words and phrases also no less far removed from the ready comprehension of the average English speaker or reader – e.g. Meredith, Hardy, etc.

Critics of linguistic experimentation like your paragraphist may seem to the ordinary common-sense reader to be obviously right in such strictures: but they ought to reflect that far more distinguished critics than themselves who have taken a similar line have been woefully mistaken – e.g. the late Dr Robert Bridges in those ludicrously 'Blimpish' comments on the poetry of Gerard Manley Hopkins which delayed the publication of the latter but failed eventually to prevent its becoming one of the greatest influences in modern English poetry. 'What is sauce for the goose is sauce for the gander' – and if Hopkins can sweep the board in English poetry in this way, it is only reasonable to suppose that a similar phenomenon may operate in Scots poetry.

Incidentally, 'cwa' is not an ejaculation but simply means 'come away' and is still in regular use in that sense in various parts of Scotland. Why should an occasional stanza not commence with it?

Even if all the efforts that have been, or are being made to refurbish Scots as a literary medium are as ludicrous as your paragraphist seems to find them, the fact remains that the work of Scottish poets in plain, straightforward English cuts no ice whatever. English anthologists almost wholly exclude it – and rightly! It is obviously – and demonstrably – utterly inferior. What, then, is the Scottish poet to do but try to extend and strengthen his own native language in precisely the way that all languages, including English, have extended and strengthened themselves – and that is all synthetic Scots has attempted!

It is not the case that modern Scots poets have invented new words to eke out their vocabulary. Nor is it the case that they have had undue recourse to Jamieson's Dictionary. Most of them write on the solid basis of the speech they first spoke as children and were familiar with in their homes – the speech, incidentally, of the vast majority of the Scottish working class still, and, judging by the scant headway made against it by English during the past two centuries, likely to remain so! – I am etc.

C. M. Grieve.
('Hugh MacDiarmid')

32 Victoria Crescent Road,
Glasgow, W.

Sir,

There is no question of my trying to enforce (as Mr John R. Fethney[1] phrases it) Lallans on our Southern neighbours. What I object to is their enforcing their English on us. But with regard to the question of English as a medium for Scottish poets, it is the English critics, anthologists, etc., who have unanimously insisted upon the inferiority of the Scottish poets in question. The entire Scottish contribution to English poetry could be excised without noticeable detriment to the latter. In these circumstances it has simply been my contention that it would be better for Scottish poets to cease using a medium in which time has shown they have an irremediable inferiority and see if they cannot do better in the very different Scottish tradition, first of all in the 'halfway house' of Scots, and ultimately in a resumption of Gaelic.

I am little interested at this time of day in the opinion regarding my own work of people who have not themselves built up a sufficient reputation as creative artists or as critics to command, if not my agreement, at least my interest and respect. Enough of my contemporaries so qualified have approved my work to satisfy me.

With regard to Mr Fethney's query about contemporary Scottish prose-writers, here again no Scottish prose-writer has contributed anything essential and indispensable to the English prose tradition. The work of Mr Neil Gunn and other Scottish prose-writers in (or mainly in) English today has certain qualities, but English critics do not regard them as front-rank figures nor agree that their work is contributing anything material to the maintenance or further development of the English prose tradition.

In reply to Mr Matthew Forsyth,[2] it was certainly my impression

---

[1] John R. Fethney's letter, in *The Glasgow Herald* of 18 November 1946, suggested that Scotland would fare better if 'she – her poets, rather – pursued the old Hielan' custom of beating the Sassenach on his own ground, at his own game? After all, to try enforcing even 'standard' Braid Scots on the Southroners is rather like an 11–80ths tail wagging a dog.'

[2] Matthew Forsyth, of the Citizens' Theatre, Glasgow, wrote (in a letter in *The Glasgow Herald* of 18 November 1946): 'Mr C.M. Grieve (Hugh MacDiarmid) is reported to have stated in a lecture at Clydebank on November 12 that James Bridie was in favour of foreign plays, including, "English" plays, being translated into Scots before being played in Scotland, and that this would be the policy of the Citizens' Theatre in future . . . It will not be the policy of the Citizens' Theatre to

that Mr Bridie stated at the conference in question that it was to be the policy of the Citizens' Theatre in future to translate foreign plays into Scots, beginning with Shakespeare's *Midsummer Night's Dream.* Others shared my impression, and the matter was one which occasioned a good deal of discussion among us later. I am sorry if we were mistaken. Mr Bridie may indeed have been joking. But the English language lends itself to all kinds of misunderstandings, and as a foreigner I am no doubt apt to be deceived by it. –

                    I am, etc.
                    C. M. Grieve.
                    ('Hugh MacDiarmid')

THE GLASGOW HERALD
27 November 1946

                    32 Victoria Crescent Road,
                    Glasgow, W.2.

Sir,

I thought the plastic Scots controversy had perhaps gone a little too far when I saw in a Glasgow evening paper recently the caption – 'Judge Sees Film of Operation for Burns'.

So far as the majority of the letter-writers opposed to synthetic Scots are concerned, I feel myself very much in the same position as John McCallum, the Australian star now filming in Britain, who is holding out against a suggestion that he should change his name. 'It's too hard to spell' he was told.

Most of these letter-writers are practically re-echoing Mr Somerset Maugham's statement:- 'I have never had much patience with the writers who claim from the reader an effort to understand their meaning.'

But it must be retorted to them in no uncertain fashion, as Mr Cyril Connolly retorted to Mr Maugham in this connection:- 'This is an abject surrender, for it is part of the tragedy of modern literature that the author, anxious to avoid mystifying the reader, is afraid to

translate foreign or English plays into Scots. Further, as director of this theatre, I am in fairly close touch with James Bridie, and I feel quite safe in saying that at no time, publicly or privately, has he advocated such a policy.'

789

demand of him any exertions. "Don't be afraid of me," he exclaims. "I write exactly as I talk – no, better than that – exactly as you talk. Imagine painters painting or Beethoven composing exactly as he talked"! The only way to write is to consider the reader to be the author's equal: to treat him otherwise is to set a value on illiteracy, and all that results from Mr Maugham's condescension to a reader from whom he expects no effort is a latent hostility to him, as of some great chef waiting on a hungry Australian. As Richards says of the poet:- "It is hard, and, in fact, impossible, to deny him his natural and necessary resources on the ground that a majority of his readers will not understand. This is not his fault, but the fault of the social structure. For a book to be written at the present time with any hope of lasting half a generation, of outliving a dog or a car, of surviving the lease of a house or the life of a bottle of champagne, it must be written against the current, in a medium which makes demands on both the resources of our language and the intelligence of the reader."'

Mr Laurie[1] is wrong when he says that Scots is not my native language. It is. And his notion that because poems can be translated fairly satisfactorily into other languages they could just as well have been written in one or other of these languages in the first instance is so manifestly absurd that there is no need for me to say anything further in reply to his letter.

I do not agree at all with Mr Maxwell[2] that I 'must allow that the final judgment on my works rests with the ordinary people'.

Homer, Plato, Plotinus, Catullus, Horace, and scores of others of whom 'the ordinary people' know nothing are nevertheless immortal.

'The ordinary people' do learn a little about some of the great figures in literature during their school years, but they do not read them afterwards. What they do read is for the most part beneath contempt. Their final judgment is shown by the kind of books that achieve best-sellerdom. Such books are almost invariably of no

---

[1] John Laurie's letter, printed in *The Glasgow Herald* of 20 November 1946, asserted that 'The real test of great poetical work is not in the language used to produce it, but in the quality of the thought which the language makes known. It is certain that a poem which translates satisfactorily into French, German, and Icelandic, as Mr C.M. Grieve assures us his poems do, could clearly have been written in any of them to begin with, suggesting that the choice of an obscure language, especially when it is not his natural one, is made out of perversity.'

[2] R. Maxwell's letter, in *The Glasgow Herald* of 22 November 1946, suggested that 'Mr C.M. Grieve . . . must allow that the final judgment on his works rests with the ordinary people, the modern counterparts of the old-time ploughman and dairymaid . . . [The Scots vernacular] is useless for profound thought, but unequalled for humour and pathos, and as a weapon in controversy it is no match for the fine, vigorous English which Mr Grieve wields with such power.'

literary value whatever, and the overwhelming verdict of 'the ordinary people' fails to establish these books in any permanent repute or to secure for them even the barest mention in books of literary criticism or literary history.

All the great things in the arts and in the sciences have been the creation, very often 'against the current' (i.e. in the teeth not only of unutterable ignorance and indifference, but even of active hostility on the part of the hoi polloi), of a very small minority of people – a minority that is practically constant throughout the whole of history. It is that minority with which I am concerned. The opinions of the others do not matter a rap to me.

Mr Maxwell, says that this means that I must be considered merely a member of a mutual admiration circle or a cult. I agree. The whole of literary history has been the product of a succession of such cults; and human society consists in every connection of a number of mutual admiration circles. But he is wrong when he says that the efforts of myself and my associates are 'futile'. If they had been they would not have occasioned this controversy, which has created a degree of interest and discussion all over Scotland – and farther afield – which even I find far beyond anything I expected. And the publishers of my synthetic Scots poems – and those of some of the other poets in this movement – can show that there is a demand for these books comparable to (and in Scotland itself far in excess of) the demand for even the best-selling volume of contemporary English poetry. We have in fact quite an adequate buying public to ensure the continuance, and indeed in the near future the intensification, of our efforts. – I am, etc.

C. M. Grieve.
('Hugh MacDiarmid')

NATIONAL WEEKLY
29 October 1949

Sir,

I regret that owing to absence from town I have been unable to reply sooner to Mr Sneddon's admirable letter in which he asks me to give chapter and verse for my statements that the crisis, is only

English, that Scotland if free from England would have a favourable trade balance, and that Scottish interests are being sacrificed all along the line to help England in its well-deserved and really immedicable economic mess, or, in other words, that Scotland is being compelled to subsidise England heavily at the cost of perpetuating (and, indeed, worsening) grave Scottish social problems, of thwarting Scottish initiative in all directions, and imposing on the Scottish population lower wages, more unemployment, greater dereliction of the potentialities of our vastly superior natural resources, and, in sum, all manner of unnecessary and unjustifiable hardships, restrictions, and frustrations.

The article to which Mr Sneddon referred is not, however, to be taken singly but should be read in conjunction with all I have written on this matter in the past twenty years. In these writings such facts and figures as can be secured from behind the iron curtain the Westminster Government so vigorously maintains between Scottish affairs and the Scottish people have been set out from time to time. Admittedly they are not enough. But as I have always emphasised that is precisely the trouble. The Westminster Government has persistently refused to make the necessary facts and figures available. They have good reason for doing so. That refusal is in itself a sufficient pointer to the truth. But it is supported by all manner of indirect evidence susceptible of no other explanation. Such facts and figures as are available are to be found in Mr Arthur Donaldson's admirable pamphlet, *Exports: Opportunity or Menace*, to which I devoted a long article in the *National Weekly* on 18th June 1949; and also in the newly published pamphlet *Scotland and the Crisis* by Harry Gardiner.

The nature of these facts and figures – stemming directly as they do from the state of affairs disclosed in the last return, over a quarter of a century ago, in which the relative contributions of Scotland and England to the National Exchequer were separately given – is in itself sufficient to warrant my statements queried by Mr Sneddon, and such supporting declarations as that embodied in one of the resolutions submitted to the policy-making conference of the Scottish National Party in Edinburgh last week-end, namely that 'Scottish has a favourable trade balance with other countries and that the austerity and restrictions now imposed upon the people of Scotland are a direct consequence of England's bankrupt economy.'

I would be glad to follow up the valuable suggestions made by Mr Sneddon and endeavour to bring together all the available information in the most concrete fashion. Unfortunately personal considerations make it impossible for me to undertake this task at the present time. But even without such detailed information it is perfectly clear that my statements were correct, as are such supporting statements as Dr MacIntyre's declaration that 'Scotland is perhaps the last milch cow of the Empire. Scotland is an exporting country to a very much greater extent than England. The consequence of devaluation is that the people of Scotland are going to work a great deal harder for a great deal less. They, particularly those in the West, will be the first to suffer.'

Along the same line, and equally incontrovertible, is Mr Austin Walker's statement in Edinburgh on Friday, that Scottish Nationalism provides a policy 'which would draw Scotland out of the economic crisis and even help the English at the same time. Scotland, with her own Government, could maintain adequate social services and provide jobs with decent wages because she has a surplus of exports over imports.'

Alongside all other considerations involved should be placed the indisputable truth voiced the other day by Sir Steven Bilsland when he was asked what special advantages Scotland had to offer to Americans to induce American companies to set up precision engineering and chemical factories employing male labour in Glasgow, Lanarkshire and Renfrewshire.

Sir Steven said: 'I think we provide better labour than the English.'

There is no doubt about it, and that is the crux of the whole matter.

Yours etc.
C. M. Grieve.

THE SCOTSMAN
9 December 1950

Dungavel,
by Strathaven,
Lanarkshire.
December 5, 1950.

Sir,

In 'A Scotsman's Log' in your issue of 30th ult. Mr William Montgomerie, editor of *Scots Chronicle* is quoted as stating that in his opinion the balance in our literature is 'now weighted unduly in favour of the writers in Lallans' and that 'it is writers of poetry in English who now feel frustrated in Scotland by the growing monopoly of a Scottish Renaissance too narrowly defined'.[1] Without going into the question of Mr Montgomerie's motives in making (not for the first time) these statements, I would crave a little of your space to examine the actual facts.

The principal Scottish poets writing in English today are Messrs Edwin Muir, Andrew Young and W. S. Graham. All of these have published a number of volumes of poems (i.e. they have not been so frustrated as to be unable to find publishers); two of them are frequent contributors of poems to leading literary periodicals, and all three have been extensively reviewed and enjoy widespread recognition at home and abroad.

As to other Scottish poets writing in English today there are none of any consequence save Mr Norman MacCaig. I regard Mr MacCaig as one of the finest Scottish poets writing in English we have ever had, and I do not think he has had anything like his proper need of recognition yet, but assuredly that is not due to the extent to which attention has been focused on the Lallans movement, and I know Mr MacCaig well enough to know that he would be the last to think anything of the kind.

Most of the leading Lallans poets also write poems in English themselves and do so better than any of those who confine themselves to English, with the exception of the four poets I have named. It is also a fact that the various periodicals which have been run in connection with the Lallans movement have always given a fair amount of their space to poems in English by contemporary Scottish writers.

That English and American anthologists have frequently passed over Scottish poems in English and preferred in recent years to select Lallans poems instead cannot be represented as a log-rolling manoeuvre on the part of the Lallans poets. Several of these anthologists have expressed the highest opinion of the relatively far superior quality of the Lallans poems to any in Scots-English. Not only so, but the consensus of English and American literary critics holds that wherever modern Scottish poets have written in the two media of Scots and English, by far their best work has invariably been done in Scots, their English poems being comparatively negligible.

To turn to the opinions of leading English poets, it is significant

[1] 'A Scotsman's Log', in *The Scotsman* of 30 November 1950, also quoted Montgomerie as saying 'Scots has not yet been recreated as a language.'

that Messrs Day Lewis, Stephen Spender, and others have praised Lallans poems in the highest terms and envied the vitality of Lallans expression as compared with the great bulk of contemporary verse in English. Mr T.S. Eliot has even gone so far as to say to certain leading Lallans poets that they are serving literature better than they could have done by confining themselves to English.[2]

The late Mr W. B. Yeats was an enthusiastic supporter of the Lallans movement and used to go about reciting certain Lallans lyrics which he greatly admired and had memorised. Dr Oliver St. John Gogarty, Mr Frank O'Connor, and other Irish writers who, like myself knew Mr Yeats, can corroborate this. At their request I once sent Mr Yeats and 'A.E.' (the late Mr G. W. Russell) representative collections of contemporary poems in English by Scottish poets like Mr Edwin Muir, the late Messrs William Jeffrey, William Soutar, Frederick Branford and others. They found the entire collection quite devoid of merit and said that this confirmed them in their support of the Lallans movement.

It would seem, then, that Mr Montgomerie has simply made himself the mouthpiece of some negligible Scottish versifiers in English, who are jealous of the success of the Lallans movement. The full absurdity of his contentions must be realised when the facts, that it is infinitely easier to get work in English published and that, while Lallans-using periodicals are very few and far between, hosts of media exist for English verses, are taken into consideration.

On the broad issue of English versus Lallans I wish to say nothing in this letter except to point out that the guardians of the English tradition, from John Dryden onwards, have frequently warned Scottish writers to 'keep off the grass' and protested that any attempt on the part of Scottish writers to use English, especially in verse, could have no good results.

Perhaps the latest to do this is Mr Herbert Read, who has said, 'I have always been chary of committing myself when any but the poetry of my native language is concerned. For poetry is such a function of language – almost an impersonal fount of its slow growth – that it seems contrary to nature that anyone not born to a language should be capable of extracting its essence. I would even go farther and suggest that no one whose blood is not coeval and congenital with the language he uses ever attains the last perfection of poetic expression. There is no great English poetry written by a Scotsman.'

[2] Eliot's observation was confined to MacDiarmid. In a letter of 15 August 1948 to Albert Mackie, Eliot expressed his regret that he could not attend a lunch in honour of MacDiarmid and concluded: 'It will eventually be admitted that he has done more also for English poetry, by committing some of his finest verse to Scots, than if he had elected to write exclusively in the Southern dialect.'

And later, in the same essay, Mr Read says: 'I would never trust a Scotsman with our poetry.'

I entirely agree with Mr Read, and for that reason think it better that we Scots poets should attend to our native tradition rather than attempt to use English when it is clear that we can only do so in a very inferior way and, as all our literary history shows must fail to attain first, second, or even third rank in that alien medium.

Finally, I would ask Mr Montgomerie to name the English poets in Scotland who 'feel frustrated' so that a collection of their work can be examined by a panel of well-known English poets. I am confident that the opinion of the latter would be that the occlusion of such work, whether by Lallans or anything else, is no loss to literature, however it may rouse the envy and spite of its perpetrators.

I am, &c.
Hugh MacDiarmid.

NATIONAL WEEKLY
5 July 1952

Brownsbank,
By Biggar.
28/6/52

Sir,

Circumstances prevented my associating myself with John MacLean when I came out of the army after the First World War. My friend, Archie Lamont, is wrong in thinking I was demobilised in 1918. I was not demobilised until 1920. It was not until two decades later that I lived in, or had much to do with, the West of Scotland (apart from a period in Clydebank in 1911). During the time between 1920 and 1923, when MacLean died, I was for some time in Montrose and then in an isolated part of Ross-shire, 12 miles from the nearest village. As soon as my health was re-established and I returned to Montrose, I threw myself into Socialist and Scottish Nationalist activities of all kinds. I had been enormously influenced by John MacLean and James Connolly and have consistently advocated their line, of combined Socialism and Nationalism right throughout the subsequent thirty years. But in the light of what

I have just said, and the circumstances in which MacLean was placed during these last two to three years of his life, Archie will understand why closer relations between MacLean and myself were impossible – a fact nobody regrets more than I do.

Yours, etc.
Hugh MacDiarmid.

Honour'd Shade

Honour'd Shade: An Anthology of New Scottish Poetry To Mark the Bi-centenary of the Birth of Robert Burns was edited by Norman MacCaig, sponsored by the Arts Council and published by Chambers of Edinburgh in 1959. An anonymous review in The Scotsman of 19 November 1959 criticised the collection as unrepresentative:

> There are certainly many fine pieces in the anthology, but the editor does not seem to have ranged very far in making his selection. Edwin Morgan is represented by four pages, while poets such as Hamish Henderson, Alan Riddell, Tom Law and David McEwan do not appear at all. This is surely a surprisingly disproportionate balance, and, in the opinion of this reviewer at least, deprives the collection of much of its claim to be considered truly representative of modern poetry in Scotland . . . As perhaps might be expected, Hugh MacDiarmid is given most space . . . The anthology itself, which of course neither mainly nor chiefly consists of poems in Lallans, might perhaps almost have been called, like one of the poems it contains, 'The Muse in Rose Street'.

Rose Street, known as the amber mile of Edinburgh on account of the proximity of so many pubs, contains two bars especially loved by the literati. Milne's Bar, downstairs off Hanover Street, was Mac-Diarmid's 'favourite howff'; the Abbotsford, just along the road, is a more elegant establishment. MacDiarmid was regularly to be seen, at this period, in Milne's and the Abbotsford with his close friends Norman MacCaig and Sydney Goodsir Smith.

THE SCOTSMAN
21 November 1959

Edinburgh.
November 20, 1959

Sir,

The reviewer of the anthology of Scottish poetry sponsored by the Scottish Committee of the Arts Council thinks the book might well have been entitled *The Muse in Rose Street*. Well, why not? The Rose Street group of contributors are certainly head and shoulders above all the contemporary Scottish versifiers and several of them, in the opinion of leading critics in England and other countries, are of very high rank indeed.

Probably what lies behind your reviewer's suggestion, however, is the common and utterly stupid objection to 'a clique'. Why, however, should poets be excluded from the rule that 'birds of a feather flock together'? Most of the best work in literature and the other arts has generally been done by such groups – and has always been bitterly resented by the inferiors excluded from such groups.

Your reviewer does not think this anthology fully representative of the best recent Scottish poetry. Strength might have accrued to his contention if he had named other and better poems not included in it which meet the express condition of not having already been included in any of their author's books. I know none such.

So far as I am concerned I would like to say that I am satisfied that no contemporary Scottish poet deserving inclusion has been excluded. I have the highest opinion of some of Mr T.S. Law's work but I doubt very much if he had any poems available which met the condition on which the anthology rested as stated above – I am, etc.

Hugh MacDiarmid.

Brownsbank,
Biggar.
November 27, 1959

Sir,

I was very careful in what I said and broadcast about 'T. T. Kilbucho',[1] namely, that his verse was in my opinion the best of its kind being written in Scotland now, i.e. folk-poetry of the traditional post-Burnsian sort, and that he was one of the few – and certainly the best – practitioners of 'crambo-clink' belonging to the same class of farmers or farmworkers still extant. The operative phrases are 'of its kind' and 'to the same class'.

There is no inconsistency such as Mr W. Little alleges between what I said then, and what I have since said about the *Honour'd Shade* anthology. One may fully appreciate the beauty of a daisy or even of a dandelion, and yet either for some special occasion or in general prefer roses or even orchids, and deem it inappropriate to add daisies or dandelions to bouquets of these.

Even if I were inconsistent some of Mr Little's expressions are quite unjustified. He is another of these ''umble, all too 'umble' people who are nevertheless so overwhelmingly conceited that they seem to think they are divinely commissioned to keep other people on the straight and narrow path of their own severely and incorrigibly limited comprehension. Witness his attribution of unintelligibility to some of the poems Mr MacCaig chose. Why should what is intelligible to him be taken as a standard?

In the same way my use of the term 'Inferiors' was not offensive. It was merely exact. It cannot be denied that there are greater and lesser poets; the latter are inferior as poets to the former, and a Gresham's Law operates that to put even a little of the latter among the former is apt to reduce the value of the whole. – I am, etc.

Hugh MacDiarmid

[1] T. T. Kilbucho was the pseudonym used by Tom Todd, a farmer-poet who became friendly with MacDiarmid. On 13 August 1952 the BBC Scottish Home Service broadcast 'On the Shoulder of Cardon', an interview between MacDiarmid and Kilbucho. MacDiarmid's introduction to Kilbucho's *Clachan and Countryside* (Glasgow 1956) asserted that 'the poems of Tom Todd (T. T. Kilbucho) are the best that have been produced in this kind in Scotland since Burns and Hogg.' In a letter in *The Scotsman* of 27 November 1959, W. Little recalled this championship of Kilbucho and accused MacDiarmid of inconsistency on the grounds that a poet he had praised so highly was omitted from an anthology he claimed as representative of the best contemporary Scottish poetry.

Brownsbank,
Biggar.
November 24, 1959

Sir,

A great American scholar said 'A preference for the inferior is one of the commonest disguises of envy', and the truth of this is well exemplified in your reviewer's strictures on *Honour'd Shade*.[1]

Underlying several of his phrases there is a suggestion that I had something to do with choosing the contents of this anthology. I had not, I have been abroad most of the year, and had no idea at all what poems were included or by what poets.

Earlier this year I was one of the adjudicators in a poetry competition. Of the hundreds of entries I did not think any one of them deserved any prize. This is a common experience in such matters: 99 per cent of the entries are worthless rubbish. If an anthology is to be 'fully representative' all these writers should presumably be included.

This seems to be what your reviewer contends: but 'representative' and 'all-inclusive' are not synonymous, and even if *Honour'd Shade* had been confined to half-a-dozen poets it might still be thoroughly (or even more) representative of the 'best' in contemporary Scottish poetry. There are thousands of versifiers in most countries at any time, but time is a great winnower, and it is a fortunate country that produces even one or two of any real worth in any generation.

I do not agree with Mr Douglas Young[2] about the bevy of Scottish songstresses today, and think that perhaps his regard for them is due to his objection to modernistic trends in poetry and determination to uphold superannuated kinds of verse. He may find certain poems in Mr MacCaig's anthology 'dullish prose masquerading as verse', but literary reactionaries have condemned much modern poetry on the same ground.

This point of view is endorsed by the overwhelming majority of readers. Hence the fact that versifiers like Miss Wheeler Wilcox,

[1] 'Your Reviewer' wrote to *The Scotsman* (24 November 1959) defending himself against MacDiarmid: 'He is a fine poet; he should not attempt to pontificate on the work of those whose aims are perhaps different from his own.'

[2] Douglas Young's letter (*The Scotsman*, 24 November 1959) complained of the unrepresentative nature of the anthology since there was 'not a single woman poet' among the contributors.

Miss Wilhelmina Stitch, and Mr John Oxenford appeal to a far greater public than the poems of Mr W. B. Yeats or Mr T. S. Eliot. In other words Mr Young and your reviewer on the one side, and I on the other, are arguing about different things altogether, and it is their kind of contention and conception of poetry that has bogged Scottish verse in ruts of worthlessness so long. But the interest of the qualified literary world, and the judgments of all critics of any international repute, lie in the opposite direction.

If I 'should not attempt to pontificate on the work of those whose aims are perhaps different from my own', what qualifications has your reviewer to pontificate about poets whose aims are different from his – or Mr Young's – and no 'perhaps' about it? – I am, etc.

Hugh MacDiarmid

THE SCOTSMAN
7 December 1959

Brownsbank,
Biggar.
November 28, 1959

Sir,

I thank you for your assurance that your reviewer did not suggest that I had anything to do with the *Honour'd Shade* selection.[1] I was not unjustified however in thinking he had. What else did he mean when he wrote 'Whether Mr MacDiarmid likes their (Alan Riddell's and Hamish Henderson's) work or not, they deserved inclusion in such a collection'? That certainly seems to imply that I had some say in the matter. My likes or dislikes were otherwise quite irrelevant and there was no justification for speculating about them in this connection.

Again, he thinks that for various reasons I 'may not be the best person to decide on the composition of the anthology'. Since I did not decide and had nothing whatever to do with it, what is the point of this typically 'wormy' remark?

---

[1] An editorial note, appended to MacDiarmid's letter of 24 November 1959, denied that *The Scotsman* reviewer had suggested that MacDiarmid had undue influence over the contents of *Honour'd Shade*. 'Your Reviewer' returned to the epistolary battle in the issue of 28 November 1959.

I can only conclude that your reviewer is clumsy and insensitive in his use of English, and indeed that is seen elsewhere in his letters. I said that I thought Mr Douglas Young's attitude was perhaps due to his dislike of modernistic poetry, but your reviewer objects to my bracketing him with Mr Young as an opponent of 'modern poetry', which is a different thing altogether and shows that he missed my point by a million miles.

Then he finds little to say about another letter of mine because I do not reply to points he raised but content myself with 'a barrage of insults and inaccuracies'. I have carefully reread my letter and consulted friends about it, and utterly fail to find 'insults and inaccuracies'. Perhaps your reviewer will explain. I was arguing about literary matters, not personalities, and certainly did not intend to be impolite, nor do I think I was so, having regard to the fact that your reviewer can hardly expect to be taken at his own valuation. It is true I think him a Quisling, a snake in the grass, and a journalistic opportunist truckling to the accepted views of the English literary ascendancy, and admirably exemplifying the tactics of 'the bourgeois, panicking at the thought of his nakedness and making a fussed and pompous escape into the commonplace the lieu commum and ideé reçue'.

How else can I possibly construe his remarks about Lallans?[2] He simply repeats what the late Mr Edwin Muir said about it. But Mr Muir subsequently recanted in public. I hope your reviewer will have a similar integrity in due course. In the world today many languages that previously had no literature have recently acquired one, and several lapsed languages have been successfully revived and applied to modern literary purpose.

Arguments similar to your reviewer's were levelled against Burns's use of Scots by the Edinburgh literati. He was solemnly warned that if he persisted in using Scots he would limit his reading public to a fraction of the population of Scotland whereas by using English he would command a vast world-wide body of readers. Where are these Edinburgh literati now? Burns by adhering to Scots became perhaps the most international poet the world has ever seen. Why then, it may be objected have I recently written mostly in English? I can only say to such questioners 'Aufgeschoben ist nicht aufgehoben'.

It must be remembered that prior to his unfortunate and sub-

---

[2] In his letter (28 November 1959) 'Your Reviewer' argued that Lallans was artificial 'because only a small minority of Scots speak a language anything like it, and, with the continuing influence of television, radio and films, that number, for good or ill, will dwindle to nothing. Poetry must be based on the natural speech of the particular country.'

sequently recanted lapse, Mr Muir (in these very columns) had hailed my Lallans poems as 'having rendered an incomparable service to Scotland in making Scots once again a medium like any other language for the whole range of literary purpose, and bringing Scots poetry again into the mainstream of European literature'. Mr T. S. Eliot has said the same thing: so has Dr Kurt Wittig: and *The Times Literary Supplement* like Mr Eliot, has welcomed the renaissance of Scots both for its own sake and as advantageous to English poetry itself.

It must always be remembered, too, that if your reviewer is right about the inevitable disappearance of Lallans we will also lose not only Burns but a great body of the best Scots songs (which certainly shows no signs of loss of popularity) and balladry. I do not believe the world, let alone Scotland, will willingly let these go. In Burns's case we might well reflect 'eventus stultorum magister'. The success of my own work in many countries – and that of Mr Sydney Goodsir Smith as expressed by the superlative praises of Dame Edith Sitwell[3] – may well mean that the same schoolmaster is busy now giving a much-needed second lesson.

To turn to another matter, why is your reviewer so insistent on the merits of Alan Riddell and Hamish Henderson? Although he does not hesitate to accuse me of 'inaccuracies', you reviewer says I have persistently implied that Mr Hamish Henderson is an 'inferior' poet. I challenge him to cite any comments I have ever published on Mr Henderson's poems. 'Silence gives consent,' perhaps, and I will not deny that Mr Henderson's work is hardly 'my cup of tea'. But the matter is beside the point so far as *Honour'd Shade* is concerned. Mr Henderson was invited to contribute but ignored the invitation until months later, by which time the anthology was already at the printer's. If Mr Henderson was one of the 'notable poets' omitted, the editor was certainly not to blame in this case. (Parenthetically, since questions have been asked about it, I think and hope the phrase in question about 'notable poets' was used ironically, meaning poets omitted who might think themselves notable!)

I am unaware – and do not believe – that any critic of international repute has praised Mr Henderson's poetry (unless Mr G. S. Fraser is to be so accounted, as I certainly do not account him!). Anyhow, whatever may be said about Messrs Riddell and Henderson, I do not think they are poets of such consequence that it matters one way or the other whether they appear or do not appear in any selection.

[3] Sydney Goodsir Smith's *So Late into the Night* (London 1952) was introduced by Edith Sitwell who praised some of the poems in the collection as 'amongst the few poems by a poet now under forty to which the word "great" can be applied'.

With regard to cliques, even in that portion of English literature to which your reviewer seems so absurdly devoted, the charge 'Squirearchy' comes readily to mind. Then there was the Pre-Raphaelite Brotherhood and then Mr Harold Monro and his Poetry Bookshop and Georgian Poets. But unlike your reviewer, I do not see Scottish literary matters against an exclusively or predominantly English background, and I think at once of Stefan George and the 'Blätter fur die Kunst' circle, for example or of the Mallairoi ('the hairy ones') in Greece (Kostes Palamas, Alexandros Pallis, Jeran Psicharis, and the rest), or of Guillaume Apollinaire in France and his 'close friendship' with Matisse, Picasso, Dérain, Braque, Henri Rousseau, André Salmon, Max Jacob and Pierre Reverdy or of the Dadaistes (Philippe Soupault, Tristan Tzara, Louis Aragon, etc); or in Russia of Vladimir Mayakovsky drafting in collaboration with David Burliuk and others, the first historic manifesto of the Futurist Movement, 'A Blow in the Face of Public Opinion' in 1912; or in Vienna of Hermann Bahr and the Jung Wien movement; or in Spain Azorin and the other leaders of the so-called 'Generation of 1898'; or, again in France, Charles Maurras and 'L'Action Française' group.

Your reviewer accused me of 'sweeping generalisations', but surely the prize goes to his declaration that 'artists have usually made poor critics'. The opposite is much nearer the truth. Hardly anything worth writing has been written about poetry save by poets. Think, for example, of the critical work of Coleridge, Keats, Goethe, Paul Valéry, T. S. Eliot.

When your reviewer claims 'a mind less blinkered' than mine, this is presumably another example of his mis-handling of English. If by 'blinkered' he means 'more parti pris', more extreme in my advocacies and antipathies, I grant it, but 'blinkered' comes strangely from a nonentity who cannot deny for a moment that my purview of literature is immensely greater than his, and not like his myopically confined to English literature, but at home in many literatures, friendly with contemporary authors in over twenty countries, and with his own work translated into many languages.

It is not the case that modern Scottish writers are abnormally addicted to denigrating each other. I can easily prove that almost all the denigration has come from anti-national reviewers like your reviewer or from other Anglo-Scots. But whatever may be said of 'dictionary dredging' and all the rest of it, the truth about the use of Lallans remains simply a case of 'abusus non tollit usum.' – I am, etc.

Hugh MacDiarmid.

805

THE SCOTSMAN
16 December 1959

Brownsbank,
Biggar.
December 12, 1959

Sir,

I had not forgotten – nor have I altered in my opinion – what I wrote about Hamish Henderson's *Elegies for the Dead in Cyrenaica*[1] ten years ago in the *National Weekly* and, later, about his 'John Maclean March' in the same paper and elsewhere. But *Honour'd Shade* could not use anything from the former in accordance with the express condition of the anthology, and the merits of the latter as a song, and the question of its quality as poetry are two very different matters. Like Mr Henderson, the other poets in *Fowrsom Reel* seem to have petered out, unfortunately.

At the time I hailed their work because it seemed to me to herald a long-overdue development in Scottish poetry. That has not materialised, however. I am glad to hear that Mr Henderson is engaged on another long poem and hope it will justify my anticipations poetically and politically. All this, however, is irrelevant to *Honour'd Shade*, Mr Henderson's exclusion from which was, as he told us, his own fault.

Miss Cruickshank's letter[2] expresses a point of view which I have been fighting against as strenuously as I could for the past 40 years. The foreign writers and artists I listed may be 'caviare to the general' but they have had a great deal to do with modern achievements and tendencies in literature and the other arts in Europe, and to cite them in substantiation of my claim regarding cliques was certainly relevant. Scottish literature has suffered sufficiently from restriction

[1] Hamish Henderson, in a letter in *The Scotsman* of 12 December 1959, reminded MacDiarmid of the high praise he had given to *Elegies for the Dead in Cyrenaica* (London 1948) in an article in *The National Weekly* of 9 April 1949: 'In form and substance it compares with most of the war poetry of Rupert Brooke, Sassoon and even Wilfred Owen.' Henderson closed his letter by pointing out that *Honour'd Shade* contained nothing by the four writers – John Kincaid, George Todd, F.J. Anderson and 'Thurso Berwick' (Maurice Blythman) – represented in *Fowrsom Reel* (Glasgow 1949), a Clyde Group anthology introduced by MacDiarmid.

[2] Helen B. Cruickshank's contribution to the *Honour'd Shade* controversy was an epistle in *The Scotsman* of 11 December 1959. The second stanza opened:
Noo, what dis Hughoc think he can impress
Wi's fremit learnin' ? Fegs, wha is't unless
It's Chambers' Brithers, whase braw Dictionar'
Supplied the borrowed words he writes wi' vir.

to the kailyard and I need make no apology for my internationalism. In any case, all my work has been activated by the principle enunciated by J. R. Lowell when he wrote: 'Not failure but low aim is crime.'

As to Chambers *Dictionary*, all our words are borrowed from somewhere or other – we do not invent them – and all that matters is how and to what end we use them. It is a pity more people do not have recourse to dictionaries for the extension and subtilisation of their vocabularies. Miss Cruickshank asks for whom I write and the answer is; Certainly not for those who, in discussing literary matters, are proud of their ignorance and fain to use it as a Procrustean bed, or for those (and Scotland is full of them) who reduce discussions on artistic matters to a question of 'scoring cheap laughs' or think they can dispose of great issues by remarks on the level of a gamin's cry: 'Get your hair cut', and ignore all the real problems raised in a lengthy correspondence in favour of an inane giggle which lets loose more than a whiff of sour grapes. – I am, etc.

Hugh MacDiarmid.

SCOTTISH FIELD
February 1962

Brownsbank,
Biggar.
[January 1962]

Sir,

May I point out in reply to Mr Tom Wright's article on 'Burns and the Poets of To-day'[1]
(1) That non-Lallans writing poets were never excluded from the periodicals, anthologies, etc., run by myself and others. On the contrary, they always predominated in numbers if not in quality. It was the stated aim of the Scottish Renaissance Movement to encourage better work by Scottish poets not only in Lallans but also

---

[1] In the February 1962 issue of *Scottish Field* Tom Wright criticised the 'attitudes and dogmas of the older poets', claimed that the 'Lallans boys' monopolised editorial control of outlets for Scottish writing, and complained of the 'massive road block' inhibiting the progress of the younger Scottish writers.

in English and Gaelic and there is ample testimony that this was successfully achieved.

(2) Since these publications included poems by over 60 writers, it is absurd to assert that they were operated by an exclusive clique. Writers who failed to secure entry may well reflect that they were kept out not because they did not belong to a clique but simply because they were just not good enough.

(3) After all, Messrs Tom Wright and Hugh Rae,[2] failing admission to the Scottish Renaissance publications, were not debarred from appearing in the hundreds of English, American, and British Colonial organs. Yet the fact remains that Lallans Poets like myself appeared in far more of these than Scotland's self-pitying jeunes refusés.

(4) Mr Wright may assert that Scottish Nationalism in poetry and elsewhere is out of date, but his mere assertion proves nothing. I am of the opposite opinion entirely, but in reply to what he says about foreign editors recognising the worth of a poem *per se* how does he explain the fact that the work and worth of the Lallans poets has been recognised and highly praised by leading critics and fellow poets of many nations who do not appear to have been at all similarly impressed by the poems of Messrs Wright, Rae, and the other young poets mentioned in their articles.

Hugh MacDiarmid

THE GUARDIAN
5 March 1962

Brownsbank,
Candymill,
Biggar,
Lanarkshire.
[March 1962]

Sir,

Knowing that I live in an isolated country place, a correspondent

---

[2] Hugh Rae's article, in the same issue of *Scottish Field*, supported Tom Wright's position.

has just sent me a cutting of Mr John Wain's letter[1] from your issue of February 28. I think I need say little more in reply to it than quote what this correspondent says, and with which I entirely agree –

'It's a letter from our pseudo-angry young man John Wain attacking your politics in an inaccurate and irrelevant way. He seems to feel you should get involved in a muck-raking session with him – presumably to boost his fading fortunes. If nothing else, it confirms English insularity.'

Like many of my friends in Moscow, Prague, Sofia, and Budapest, I have always had and retain many American friends and by no means regard the United States and the John Birch Society, or the late Senator McCarthy, as synonymous. I know the strength of the Peace Movement and of the Communist Party in America too well for rubbish of that sort, and the point of my reference to exiled Scots in America is simply that University lecturers there have told me that they have had less difficulty in putting across to their students the Scots poetry of the fifteenth-and sixteenth-century Makars than that of the English Chaucerians.

Interest in my work in America is nothing new, as Mr Wain can find if he consults a bibliography of essays about me, and the extraordinary width of the haggis belt, coterminous with the circumference of the globe, may be plain to even his jaundiced eyes later on, if he adds to consultation of such a bibliography, a perusal of the names and locations of my correspondents during the past half-century when that correspondence becomes available to students in the National Library of Scotland.

The despicable character of Mr Wain's letter must be clear to your readers if they reflect for the moment on his reference to 'some hogwash written by a Government hack in Budapest'. This is an ignorant jeer at a long and scholarly discussion of my work published in a famous learned journal, and in Magyar. Unscrupulousness can hardly go further. Mr Wain should be thoroughly ashamed of himself, but then he would not have written as he has done if the sentiment of shame was not alien to his nature.

Yours etc.
Hugh MacDiarmid.

[1] *The Guardian* of 22 February 1962 printed 'MacDiarmid on MacDiarmid', a feature to which John Wain took exception in his letter (printed 28 February 1962): 'The reason Grieve cuts no ice in England or (outside the haggis belt) in Scotland, is there plainly enough. He can't make up his mind. He is simultaneously truculent (to Whitehall) and fawning (to Moscow). He simultaneously praises some hog-wash written by a Government hack in Budapest and thumbs his nose at the Americans who print his work. Simultaneously the bold border-reiver and the flunkey of international communism.'

NEW SALTIRE
Summer 1962

Brownsbank,
Candymill,
Biggar
Spring 1962

Sir,

Is there even ane o' thae Beatnik poets[1]
Wi' which the place is sae raji rife
Da'en mair than juist feelin' a lassie's bloomers
And thinkin' he's seein' Life?

Yours, etc.,
Hugh MacDiarmid

---

[1] This epistolary quatrain appeared, under the heading 'Question to Edwin Morgan' in *New Saltire 4*, Summer 1962 as a riposte to Edwin Morgan's article 'The Beatnik in the Kailyaird', *New Saltire 3*, Spring 1962. Morgan lamented the lack of interest in Scotland in the Beat movement: 'Almost no interest has been taken by established writers in Scotland in the important postwar literary developments in American and on the Continent. Ignorance is not apologized for. The Beat writers are dismissed as a throwback to the 1920s.'

Teddyboy Poetasters

Edwin Morgan's article 'Poet and Public', in *The Scotsman* of 12 May 1962, referred to MacDiarmid's letter in *Scottish Field* (see p. 807) which was written in response to articles by Tom Wright and Hugh Rae castigating the Scottish Renaissance movement as an institution that had become reactionary. In defending the 'younger Scottish poets' Morgan drew attention to the experimentalism of Ian Hamilton Finlay whose Wild Hawthorn Press publications had been attacked in *The Glasgow Herald* by Douglas Young:

> The Wild Hawthorn Press has started, in addition to its volumes of poetry, an attractive monthly broadsheet of new poems, international in scope and cheap in price, with the title (or anti-title) *Poor. Old. Tired. Horse.*

THE SCOTSMAN
18 May 1962

Brownsbank,
Biggar.
May 12, 1962

Sir,

I am 'a wicked animal. I defend myself when I am attacked'. But in his article in your Week-end Magazine today, Mr Edwin Morgan uses forms of words which suggest that in this case I was the aggressor. That is not the case. Messrs Tom Wright and Hugh Rae did more than 'question the present usefulness of some Scottish Renaissance assumptions'. Their arguments were ad hominem: not only so, but involved demonstrably false statements and unjustifiable personalities.

My adjective 'self-pitying' was correct. During the past forty years my motto has been 'contra nando incrementum' and young writers who have not yet proved their worth at all, but who instead of similarly fighting their way against the current complain that old contemporaries (whom they simultaneously vilify) are not helping them, are obviously actuated by self-pity and envy.

In any case, it is absolutely untrue that the Scottish Renaissance Movement has held down these younger writers. The Scottish Renaissance writers have never been in a position to do anything of the sort. They have not themselves had access to most of the outlets Mr Morgan enumerates (and his list is not complete). It was precisely for this reason that ad hoc periodicals of their own were launched. As these were produced specifically to publicise 'a propaganda of ideas' and to publish creative writing on that basis, today's younger writers were not even born by the brief period during which most of these periodicals ran. They might therefore just as well accuse Burns or Dunbar of being an 'establishment' which has not helped them but actually blocks their way.

It is indeed like blaming *Punch* or *Encounter* for not publishing articles on poultry keeping, and especially on keeping chickens not yet hatched.

The truth, as ample evidence can be set out to show, is that I personally have gone out of my way over the years to help scores of other poets, most of whom, however, 'came to nothing', and many of whom were writing kinds of poetry very different to any in which I was personally interested. The 'sturdy beggar' is not a new phenomenon in Scottish life, but hitherto very infrequently encountered in Scottish literature. How otherwise can we describe young writers whose truculent attitude to their elders is 'You help me, or else . . . '? Such mendicancy under threats of vilification is what Mr Morgan is defending.

It is all very well to say that I will 'have to come to terms with the criticism that my own kind of aggressive, exclusive, dogmatic, proprietorial Scottishness may not be the best for Scotland', but Mr Morgan does not show that these adjectives correctly describe my work (and in particular my poetry, which is what the argument is really about), and I think he knows that the great majority of critics who have written about my poems have come to very different conclusions about them.

Anyhow, I have, not only in prose statements, but in verse, again and again explained in detail just exactly what I have done or tried to do. I will be quite ready to do so again whenever I am challenged in rational argument. As I have said in some of my poems, the kind of poetry I want is

A learned poetry wholly free
Of the brutal love of ignorance;
And the poetry of a poet with no use
For any of the simpler forms of personal success.[1]

To want that 'may in fact be the very thing that is holding Scotland back at the present time'. But holding it back from what? Time will tell, but I cannot for a moment believe that accelerated progress to any desirable end will be achieved under the impetus of a group of teddyboy poetasters who have in any case written little enough in justification of their own attitude. In short, while I agree that older writers should (and generally do) help their juniors when the latter seem to show promise, I cannot see any obligation to assist in the promotion of work diametrically opposed to my own and especially when claims to such assistance are advanced under menaces of abuse eked out by false statements and callow incompetence generally. – I am, &c.

Hugh MacDiarmid.

P.S. – I should add that so far from evading 'coming to terms' with this opposition I have discussed the literary issues involved at considerable length in a pamphlet, now at the printers and to be published shortly, entitled *Ugly Birds without Wings*.[2] In the meantime I may say to the younger writers in question and to Mr Morgan, that my general attitude is that expressed by Mr Graham Hough, in a recent Third Programme talk, when he said:

'It is necessary to encourage the struggling shoots of what the critic sees as most desired: and it is necessary, in Ezra Pound's phrase, to keep down vermin. By vermin I mean not people but ideas. Let me say that there are two kinds of vermin that need keeping down at present. The first is the anti-culture that our culture has recently produced: the hatred of arts and letters: the grudging enmity to the high culture of the past. I do not mean mere popular indifference or hostility but the intellectual abetting of these things, the malevolent corrosion of values from within: the pop version of the trahison des clercs.'

That is precisely what I object to in the work of these younger writers and the reason why the broadsheet Mr Morgan finds

[1] *The Kind of Poetry I Want* (1030).
[2] Hugh MacDiarmid, *The Ugly Birds Without Wings* (Edinburgh 1962) in which extreme exception was taken to Ian Hamilton Finlay's poetry broadsheet *Poor. Old. Tired. Horse.*

'attractive' strikes me on the contrary as utterly vicious and deplorable.

THE SCOTSMAN
22 May 1962

Brownsbank,
Biggar.
May 19, 1962

Sir,

Your readers would have no difficulty in appreciating that Mr Ian Hamilton Finlay and Miss Jessie McGuffie in their letter in today's *Scotsman*[1] made no reply to the points raised in my letter, and, in particular, completely failed to substantiate the charge that I had in any way prevented younger Scottish poets securing publication.

The gibe 'Stalinist' is, of course, an easy one, since I am a member of the Communist Party, but to equate the 'Thaw' in the USSR with that vast undergrowth of mediocre verse which has always flourished in all literatures, and never more so than today, is simply nonsensical. If to believe that poetry of any value is an extremely rare thing, and that an infinitesimally small proportion of published or even unpublished verse ever emerges into that category – and that there are ways of spotting what is likely to do so, and what not – means that a man belongs to an 'Establishment', then, of course, I do, and am proud of it.

I note what your correspondents say of the current issue of their broadsheet, but to provide a smoke-screen of exotic translations (and the quality of the originals and of the translations is not condescended upon) only serves to show the lack of substantive creative work. Poetry does not live by poets taking in each other's washing in this way.

[1] Writing as editors of *Poor. Old. Tired. Horse.* in their letter to *The Scotsman* (19 May 1962), Ian Hamilton Finlay and Jessie McGuffie said: 'We have read Hugh MacDiarmid's letter [and] think it hilarious that the Russian literary "scene" is being duplicated, in miniature, in Scotland. That is, Hugh MacDiarmid is a "Stalinist". He therefore defends the "pravilnye" poetry. The poets of the Scottish "Thaw" have to be abused as "stilyagi" – teddyboys. For a poet who denies being part of an "establishment" this is a rash line to take.' They then itemised the contents of the current issue of their broadsheet drawing attention to the international range of contributions.

To write of 'those notorious "teddyboy" poets, Leopardi and Apollinaire' is a characteristic wriggle as your readers know. I made no reference to these poets as 'teddyboys', but I am glad that they appeal (if they do) to readers under 40 and do not fall into that category of 'the anachronistic' to which I have been consigned.

The fact remains that for many years I have received countless 'poetry' magazines not dissimilar to this broadsheet, their contributors running into many hundreds of names I had never seen before and happily have never seen again: and all these productions were also purportedly 'international' (not really international, however, but simply cosmopolitan), while hardly anything, if anything at all, in their contents was of the slightest worth.

As the Dutch epigrammatist, Multatuli, pointed out long ago, the opinion of 10,000 fools is worth no more than the opinion of one fool, and the banding together of no matter how many bad versifiers even if from all the ends of the earth, is not a healthy literary phenomenon, while, though I may not unfairly be called a Stalinist, to denounce Mr Douglas Young, who is far from sharing my odious position in this respect, simply because he made it clear in a review that he did not regard Mr Ian Hamilton Finlay's 'poems' as products of a heaven-sent genius, shows clearly enough what is really biting these writers. – I am, &c.

Hugh MacDiarmid.

ESKDALE AND LIDDESDALE ADVERTISER
30 January 1963

Brownsbank,
Biggar,
Lanarkshire.

Sir,

I have read Mr J. M. Ritchie's letter suggesting I should be made Langholm's first freeman, and also an article in *The Sunday Express* dealing with the bitterness said to be entertained against me in Langholm because of two scandalous stories I published in one of my books over twenty years ago, and quoting remarks by Provost Grieve, the Town Clerk, and some garage proprietor expressing the view that any decision to confer the Freedom on me would be highly unpopular in the burgh, and is, for that reason, very unlikely.[1]

I am a little tired now of public honours and in no way anxious for more. My 70th birthday last August brought me many hundreds of congratulatory letters and telegrams from all over the world and I was the recipient of many presents and fêted at many parties. My work was also the theme of scores of articles in leading papers and periodicals in this and many other countries and gatherings in my honour were held in places as far apart as Prague and Toronto. In addition to these manifestations of widespread appreciation, I had earlier, as Mr Ritchie pointed out, been honoured by Edinburgh University, Her Majesty the Queen in her Honours List, and many literary and political societies.

In these circumstances I can readily dispense in what remains of my lifetime with any further public eulogising – especially on the part of people whom I have no reason to suppose know my work and are in any way qualified to judge it. The assumption seems to be that I would be flattered if the Freedom were offered to me. No doubt I would be for various reasons, but I would certainly have cause to regret that those who had it in their power to decide the matter were men of stuffy 'respectability', ignorant of literary values, small-minded, and full of petty prejudices. One should not look a gift horse in the mouth perhaps, but neither should one forget another saying which advises us to beware of 'the Greeks bringing gifts.' What Langholm (at least in its present official representatives) thinks of my character and career is not in the least likely to be of the slightest consequence in the long run.

There is only one other point I would like to clear up, and that is the suggestion that there is a certain feeling against me because I have so seldom visited Langholm in the past 50 years. I love Langholm and am always glad to return to it. During the half-century in question, however, it ought to be remembered that I was in Macedonia and France for over five years in the First World War, at sea in the Merchant Service in the Second World War, ten years on a small island in the North East of the Shetland Archipelago, a

[1] In the *Eskdale and Liddesdale Advertiser* of 2 January 1963 there appeared a letter from John Murray Ritchie, a Langholmite and journalist with *The Glasgow Herald* who suggested that the first Freeman of Langholm should be MacDiarmid: 'Langholm has shown a strange indifference to the achievements of this distinguished native.' *The Sunday Express* of 29 January published a feature by James Wightman who described the bitterness in Langholm resulting from two stories about the burgh published in *Lucky Poet* (London 1943, pp. 227–8). Wightman then quoted remarks by Town Clerk Edward Armstrong, garage proprietor Andrew Jeffrey and Provost James Grieve who said, 'I do not think there is much chance of his being made a freeman.'

couple of years in London and Liverpool, and that in recent years I have travelled in Russia, China, Czechoslovakia, Bulgaria, Rumania, Hungary, and East Germany. That has not left me time or opportunity to revisit Langholm. But I have thought of buying a house there and settling down in the evening of my days, and may yet do so. Whether I do so or not will in no way depend either upon the praise or dispraise I may encounter in the Muckle Toon.

Yours, etc,
Christopher Grieve
(Hugh MacDiarmid)

THE OBSERVER
18 August 1963

Biggar.
[11 August 1963]

Sir,

In his review of Sean O'Casey's books,[1] Mr John Wain is hard up to find people to attack on the ground of inhumanity, but lies when he asserts that he does not single out O'Casey and myself on political grounds. My attitude to the Hungarian affair in 1956 seems to have become an obsession with him, but if he had been actuated solely by humanitarian feelings he could surely find more cause to pillory the active or passive supporters of the Governments responsible for Hiroshima, Nagasaki, Dresden, Algiers, Angola.

Terrible as many of these events were, I do not remember Mr Wain dissociating himself from or protesting against any of them – nor should I expect that of a man whose kindly spirit is so well

[1] In his review, in *The Observer* Weekend Review of 11 August 1963, John Wain (commenting on O'Casey's *Under a Colored Cap, Feathers From the Green Crow*, reprinted *Autobiographies*) criticised O'Casey for being 'loud in his praises of a Scottish poet, Hugh MacDiarmid, who showed his love of humanity by rejoining the Communist Party in 1956, when more squeamish souls were leaving it, to show his delight in the repression of Hungary'.

revealed by his attack on my octogenarian friend Sean O'Casey, the latchets of whose shoes Mr Wain is unfit to tie.

Hugh MacDiarmid.

THE SCOTSMAN
4 November 1963

Brownsbank,
Biggar.
October 29, 1963

Sir,

I have read with interest but far more disagreement than agreement the four articles on 'The Arts in Scotland', by your literary editor, Mr W. H. C. Watson,[1] in which, inter alia, he opines that the movement towards a Scottish Rennaissance has been fought – and lost. This judgment in so far as there may seem to be an element of truth in it is surely premature. Forty years is hardly long enough to arrest and reverse the overwhelming tendency of the preceding two centuries and more. I know of course that many people, like Mr Watson, think that a revival of Scottish Nationalism today is a hopeless anachronism, and in particular that several of our younger writers have protested against the conscious and deliberate Scottishness of the work of myself and some other writers and advanced the contention that all they wanted to do was to write as well as they could without any such commitment to 'Scotland the Nation' and an independent Scottish literary tradition.

Literature is not written in a vacuum, however, and they would do well to perpend again what W. B. Yeats wrote in *Letters to the New Island*, viz:-

'To our greater poets everything they see has its relation to the national life, and through them to the universal and divine life: nothing is an isolated artistic moment; there is a unity everywhere; everything fulfils a purpose that is not its own. . . . But to this universalism, this seeing of unity everyhere, you can only attain

---

[1] In his fourth, and final article, W. H. C. Watson, wrote (*The Scotsman*, 30 October 1963): 'The Renaissance has achieved what it is going to achieve, and must now accept its pension.'

through what is near you, your nation, or if you be no traveller, your village and the cobwebs on your walls.'

As Professor Peter Ure says in his excellent brochure on Yeats in Messrs Oliver & Boyd's paperback 'Writers and Critics' series: '. . . Yeats's decision, which was taken quite deliberately when he was about twenty, to make himself an Irish poet', resulted in his going in *The Wanderings of Oisin*, *The Countess Cathleen*, and *The Land of Heart's Desire* to ancient mythology and supposedly Irish folk-tales since 'these were the two principal sources at which the Irish imagination might strengthen itself by drinking at the fountains of its youth and the traditions kept alive amongst the people. In the reviews which he wrote for American journals between 1887 and 1892 he insisted that Irish writers must stick to Irish subject-matter – "We peer over the wall at our neighbour's instead of making our own garden fresh and beautiful" – and that they must get to know the literature of the imaginative periods of Irish history.'

Again, 'the tortured history of Ireland in rebellion and civil war filled Yeats's poetry. . . . The use of the "inherited subject-matter", the mythology, was not to be an educational device nor an aesthetic one, but something more deeply political – a deepening of the political passion of the nation by strengthening its imagination, by going back to the place where it is most itself and not any other country', or, as Yeats himself put it in his Autobiographies: 'I could not endure . . . an international art, picking stories and symbols where it pleased. . . . Have not all races had their first unity from a mythology that marries them to rock and hill?'

I do not think the Scottish Renaissance Movement has failed. The leaven is working, and a Movement that has thrown up in a couple of years, books like Dr George Davie's *The Democratic Intellect*, Dr David Craig's *Literature and the Scottish People*, and Mr Moray McLaren's *The Wisdom of the Scots*, with only a little earlier, Dr Kurt Wittig's *The Scottish Tradition in Literature* cannot be written off as a failure. Dr Wittig shows that 'about the middle of the sixteenth century, Scottish literature was among the richest, the most accomplished, and the most distinctive in Europe. The concept, therefore, that it is a tributary to the larger English stream cannot be defended for a moment'. It is our duty therefore to resume and carry forward our own tradition, not to seek to contribute to an alien and utterly different one, even if we could without (as has been the case up to now) – serious creative inferiority. – I am, &c.

Hugh MacDiarmid.

Scottish Folksong

On 19 February 1964 the BBC Third Programme broadcast 'Scotland Today', a survey of Scottish culture introduced by David Daiches. Among the contributors to the programme were MacDiarmid and Norman MacCaig who criticised the low intellectual content of folksongs. David Craig, the Marxist critic and author of *Scottish Literature and the Scottish People, 1680–1830* (London 1961) took up the defence of folksong in a letter to *The Scotsman* of 7 March 1964:

> Scotland should be proud to have, living in Aberdeen, Jeannie Robertson, a noble singer whose huge repertoire of songs gives us in living form that great body of tales, worksongs, and irrepressible sallies of comedy with which our people have kept themselves going and nourished their imaginations from time immemorial. . . Scotland's lays are the ballads, and it is thus no exaggeration but the sober truth to say that in Jeannie Robertson Scotland has her Homeric-type singer, whose work is the equal in quality, in beauty and truth if not in scale, to the great European epics.

The correspondence that followed involved, principally, MacDiarmid, Craig and Hamish Henderson whose work with the School of Scottish Studies, Edinburgh University, included researching the oral tradition and recording singers such as Jeannie Robertson.

THE SCOTSMAN
13 March 1964

Brownsbank,
Biggar.
March 7, 1964

Sir,

Mr David Craig's letter on depreciation of folk-song is altogether beside the point. In all literatures there is a vast undergrowth of doggerel and mediocre versifying, but it is a remarkable instance of 'trahison de clercs' if Dr Craig would have us believe that this is to be valued as equal to or better than acceptedly great poetry simply because, thanks to their minimal literacy and because is corresponds to their ignorant tastes and reflects the sorry condition of their lives, it is more popular among the broad masses of the people than the poems of, say, Shakespeare, Dante, Goethe, Rimbaud, Rilke, Pasternak, Montale, &c. &c.

Judged on this basis, MacGonagall must be accounted a great poet, since he keeps going into edition after edition and comes only second to Burns in this respect. So must Robert Service be accounted as a great poet, because he, too, achieved great popularity and made a fortune out of the millionfold sales of his books. No doubt he reflected the lives and dispositions of the Yukon pioneers, but that does not mean he ever wrote a line of poetry. He didn't.

Dr Craig does not hesitate to suggest that some of us who took part in the discussion on the Scottish Home Service underrated folk-song because of ignorance. The suggestion is unworthy of him. I for one have been bored to death listening to more of it, including the renderings of Jeannie Robertson, Jimmy MacBeth, and others, than I venture to suggest Dr Craig has ever suffered, and I certainly never want to hear any more of it.

Unlike Dr Craig I think the BBC has already given much more programme prominence to 'corn-kisters' than they deserve, and certainly of our great treasury of Scottish song only a small fraction has yet been broadcast. We hear the same hackneyed songs, Gaelic, Scots, or Anglo-Scottish, again and again and again, and the BBC would do well if it could induce some of its artistes to extend their repertoires. It has been estimated that of the over 200 songs of Burns the great majority are never sung at all and only about 20 are frequently (and in my view far too frequently) heard.

The demand everywhere today is for higher and higher intellectual levels. Why should we be concerned then with songs which reflect the educational limitations, the narrow lives, the poor literary abilities, of a peasantry we have happily outgrown? The study of such productions may be of some historical value, but is certainly of no literary value, in regard to which, as in every other connection in life, surely our regard and, if possible, emulation, should be given to the best and not to the lowest in past literary productivity. And above all we should not allow ourselves to be bogged in nostalgia for an irrecoverable way of life, and one, I think, in every respect fortunately irrecoverable. – I am, &c.

Hugh MacDiarmid.

THE SCOTSMAN
24 March 1964

Brownsbank,
Biggar.
March 19, 1964

Sir,

Mr Hamish Henderson[1] points out that on radio I quoted three lesser-known poems of Burns which I regard as much better than those for which Burns is usually praised. I was quite aware of their debt to folk sources, but Mr Henderson is quite wrong in thinking that my praise of these poems contradicts what I wrote in reply to Dr Craig. One point is that in thinking these poems better than the others I do not thereby think them great poetry.

I cannot deny that in Scottish literary history there have been fruitful interactions between folk-song and art poetry, and that this happened in some of my own early lyrics. But that was nearly 40 years ago, and my meeting with Montale was 17 years ago. The folk-song movement I was attacking in my letter had not then assumed its present menacing form, and in my own development as a poet I have had to abandon many of my early ideas and during the past 30 years I have been writing kinds of poetry quite unindebted to any folk-song source and for the most part utterly opposed to anything of the kind.

Mr Henderson seems to have a curious idea of what constitutes a *mot juste*. The fact that I attach a certain value to some poems of Burns, based on folk-song originals, does not invalidate my general condemnation of the folk-song cult today, and it is quite a different thing to single out what has been achieved on such a basis by a poet of standing as opposed to approving generally of the unimproved

---

[1] Hamish Henderson, in his letter to *The Scotsman* (19 March 1964) wrote:
'Since [Jeannie Robertson] was discovered in 1953 she has repeatedly received invitations to visit both the United States and the Soviet Union. Her records have sold thousands of copies. And yet, as Dr David Craig has pointed out, she has never been given one single 15-minute programme to herself on the Scottish Home Service.

'Among the "accepted, great" poets, Mr MacDiarmid lists Montale . . . Having introduced Mr MacDiarmid to Montale in 1947, and acted as interpreter during their conversations, I well remember how keen Mr MacDiarmid was to stress the fruitful interaction from which folk-song and art-poetry have always benefited in the Scots literary tradition. . . There can be no doubt that by denigrating Scots popular poetry now, Mr MacDiarmid is trying to kick away from under his feet one of the ladders on which he rose to greatness. . . Mr MacDiarmid has taken exception to the term "ignorant" applied to his comments on folk-song by Dr Craig, but ignorant – in this case, at least – is unfortunately the *mot juste*.'

mass of such 'songs'. In any case, a tremendous change has taken place since Burns' day, and since I wrote my own early lyrics, and apart from the fact that I think poets today have far other and much more important things to do, I do not believe that folk-song sources can now supply spring-boards for significant work. – I am, &c.

Hugh MacDiarmid.

THE SCOTSMAN
31 March 1964

Brownsbank,
Biggar.
March 28, 1964

Sir,

I am very tired of the unscrupulous way in which correspondents like Dr David Craig use the few lines from my 'Second Hymn to Lenin' beginning:

Are my poems spoken in the factories and fields,[1]

to support their anti-literary demagoguery.

In honesty, they should go on to show that my subsequent verses point out that no poet of any consequence has achieved that – not Shakespeare, Dante, Milton, Goethe, Burns – or, in fact, anyone at all worth a docken.

We all know of the great vogue and inter-traffic of European balladry. Most of it is rubbish, but in a few of our Scottish ballads it soars for a verse or two into the realm of great poetry. But all that arose out of an entirely different state of society from ours today or any ever likely to recur in 'advanced' countries.

---

[1] David Craig's letter to *The Scotsman* (28 March 1964) praised such traditional ballads as 'Edom o' Gordon' and 'Waly, Waly' to demonstrate the emotional depth of folksongs and quoted from MacDiarmid's 'Second Hymn to Lenin' (323):
> *Are my poems spoken in the factories and fields,*
> *In the streets o' the toon?*
> *Gin they're no, then I'm failin' to dae*
> *What I ocht to ha' dune.*

Dr Craig knows perfectly well that I was not referring to that very small number of pieces of high literary excellence, of which, 'Waly, Waly' is one: but to the bulk of the songs sung in connection with the current folk-song movement, and in particular the 'corn-kisters'.

I have been a Socialist and active in various ways in the working-class movement for over half a century. One of the main factors by which I have been actuated has always been the realisation of the very inadequate and seriously defective character of popular education, and I have never been – and am quite incapable of being – impressed by the preferences of the great mass of people adequately characterised by Professor Kenneth Buthlay in his recently published study of my work[2] when he says, apropose the Burns cult, that it has been, and still is, largely a matter of 'fulsome lip-service paid to his genius by people who had little but contempt for poetry in every other respect, and not even in rudiments of standards by which to judge it'.

Dr Craig attempts to dissociate himself from the promulgation of 'the unimproved mass of such songs', but his original letter was largely devoted to praise of Jeannie Robertson – and what else is she doing? And what proportion of the great collection of recordings of the School of Scottish Studies is more than rubbish? Dr Craig's tribute to the two songs[3] he mentions by Hamish Henderson shows that he falls holus-bolus into the class defined in the final clause of my quotation from Professor Buthlay.

In any event, I have always made my position clear enough, and Dr Craig would have been fairer, if, alongside the lines he quoted, he had also quoted these (written over 30 years ago, as were those he quoted):-

> I'm oot for shorter oors and higher pay
> And better conditions for a' workin' folk,
> But ken the hellish state in which they live's
> Due maistly to their ain mob ignorance.
> Yet tho' a' men were millionaires the morn,
>   As they could easily be,
> They'd be nae better than maist rich folk noo
> And nocht that matters much 'ud be improved
>   And micht be waur![4]

I am, &c.

Hugh MacDiarmid.

[2] Kenneth Buthlay, *Hugh MacDiarmid* (1964).
[3] 'Fareweel to Sicily' and 'The Freedom Come-all-ye'.
[4] The stanza occurs in *To Circumjack Cencrastus* (228–9).

Brownsbank,
Biggar.
April 7, 1964

Sir,

Despite the efforts of Messrs David Craig, Hamish Henderson, and others to demonstrate that I have resiled from my previous attitude to poetry and the people, the fact is that they are basing their 'case' on fragments of my work torn out of context, whereas if they had considered my work as a whole they would have realised that I was taking up the same position over 30 years ago and have maintained it consistently since.

For example, in an essay on 'Problems of Poetry Today' in 1934, I say, 'It is impossible to believe that the vast majority of contemporary poets, believe that poetry is vitally important, let alone the rarest and most important faculty of the human mind, or are prepared, for example, to consider the relatively enormous publicity given to some murder or divorce or stupid political "stunt" as against the lack of "news value" considered to attach to any good new poem. They acquiesce in the socio-economic-politico-journalistic debauching of educational interests – the organised subversion and stultification of even those beginnings of popular education in which so much public money is spent: but poetry ought to be the mainstay of these educational interests.

'And it is precisely here that I reinforce my line of argument – it is the parasitical "interpreting class", those who "talk down to them" and insist that the level of utterance should be that of popular understanding, and jeer at what is not expressed in the jargon of the man-in-the-street, who are the enemies of the people, because what their attitude amounts to is "keeping the people in their place", stereotyping their stupidity. The interests of the masses and the real highbrow, the creative artist, are identical, for the function of the latter is the extension of human consciousness. The interests of poetry are diametrically opposed to whatever may be making for any robotisation or standardisation of humanity or any short-circuiting of human consciousness.'

It is significant that Dr Craig[1] accuses me of 'cultural defeatism' and sneers at the extremely long poems with which, in lieu of my

[1] David Craig's letter (*The Scotsman*, 7 April 1964) cited some examples of the popular appreciation of highly accomplished works of art and claimed that 'all this makes cultural defeatism inexcusable'.

early lyrics, I have been preoccupied in the last thirty years. The trouble is that he, and other professedly Communist or Left-wing advocates of regression to the simple outpourings of illiterates and backward peasants, do not know what, in fact, poets are doing in the Communist countries. Our century, our society, promotes the synthesis of the arts, synthetic thinking. The art of Communism will present us with ever more edifying artistic alloys, superior forms of Lenin's 'monumental propaganda'. Indeed, the term monumental has struck root in the theory of cinematography, the theatre, and music as well. Eisenstein's films *Battleship Potemkin*, *Alexander Nevski*, *Ivan the Terrible* are monumental, epos-like in the highest degree.

The 'epic drama' of Bertolt Brecht, an innovator through acquiring the monumental traditions of Sophocles, Shakespeare, and others, possesses the same basic character. A sonata by Enescu can also be sublime: in *Oedipus*, however, 'the work of my life', as the composer called it, the fruit of a quarter of a century's creative preoccupations and ten years' labours, the sublime is specifically monumental.

In music especially those great compositions such as operas, concertos, symphonies, symphonic poems, oratorios and cantatas can be monumental. The monumental was expressed by Bach, Beethoven, Brahms, Berlioz, Wagner, Bruckner, Mahler, Dvorak, Mussorgski, Borodin, Balakirev, Bartok, or Prokofiev. Symphonism implies vast generalisations, broad planes, comprehensive dimensions. By its very nature it quite favourably suits sharp conflicts, powerful dramatism, the combination of the epic and the dramatic genres (at times even the lyrical one).

Symphonism promotes the monumental. A recent conclusive proof is the creation of Dimitri Shostakovich. Shostakovich's symphonies form a grandiose 'musical chronicle' of the revolutionary decades. The 1905 revolution (Symphony No 9), the Socialist revolution (Symphony No 12), the Great Patriotic War (Symphonies No 7 and No 8) – these are its main stages, each of them monumental.

The grandeur of the time requires grand syntheses – not only in fine arts or music, but also in literature, not only in prose but also in poetry. Mayakovsky's poems 'Vladimir Ilyitch Lenin' and 'Harasho' ('The Poem of October') render in an impressive epic and lyrical synthesis the history of the preparation and carrying out of the first Socialist revolution in the world. The Chilean Pablo Neruda celebrates the fight for national liberation in monumental cycles of poems, such as the well-known *Canto General* or in the more recent *Canicion de gesta*, devoted to revolutionary Cuba – not unlike the huge mural frescoes painted by the Mexican painters.

Nazim Hikmet worked out a colossal poetical edifice, planned in nine volumes, with more than 3000 heroes, suggestively entitled *Human Panorama*, or *History of the Twentieth Century*. Vladimir Lugovski wrote, in 14 years, the great work of his life, *The Middle of the Century*, a book of poems which he called *His Century's Autobiography*, the result of profound lyrical and philosophic meditations on man, mankind, Communism.

The passage from my 'Second Hymn to Lenin' is, I think deliberately, misunderstood by Messrs Craig and Henderson. The aim of all great poetry is universalisation, but in so far from attaining it, great poetry is known only to a tiny fraction of the population. The isolated cases Messrs Craig and Henderson mention prove nothing to the contrary. We even used to have an occasional shepherd in this country taking a volume of Greek poetry with him to the hills. But one swallow does not make a summer – or even a good drink! Voicing the vain desire to get through to the people, realising that I, and all literature, were failing to do so, it is noticeable that I refer to Dante, Goethe, &c – in other words, to the great world poets, and not to the folk-poetry broad masses of the people already know.

There is no solution to the problem via the latter: the multiplication of mediocre writers is no contribution to literature.

I do not propose to do it here, but it would be useful to consider just why Messrs Craig, Henderson, and others are so concerned with inferior stuff and so indifferent to the peaks of human achievement in the arts.

As to Mr William Smith,[2] I am quite aware that I must not confuse song with poetry, but this correspondence so far as I was concerned was one regarding literary values. On the musical side of the matter I said all I needed to say in my essays on Francis George Scott and Sir Hugh Robertson in my *Contemporary Scottish Studies* in 1926. As to my own poetry, Mr Smith ought to know that a great deal of it has been set to music – and that, if his musical tastes, like mine, appreciate Schoenberg, Webern, Berg, and the like, all of it could be, albeit backward-looking people may regard it as 'not really poetry at all', and would certainly regard such possible settings as 'not music', since indeed they would be as remote from folk-song as the atmosphere of any intelligent house-hold is from 'the home-life of our dear Queen'. – I am, &c.

Hugh MacDiarmid.

---

[2] William Smith's letter (*The Scotsman*, 7 April 1964) accused MacDiarmid of 'failing to apply the proper standards in confusing song with poetry'.

Perfect

On 31 December 1964 the *TLS* published an anonymous review of Duncan Glen's *Hugh MacDiarmid and the Scottish Renaissance* (1964) and Kenneth Buthlay's *Hugh MacDiarmid* (1964). After commenting on MacDiarmid's use of Scots the reviewer added 'An English reader can at least appreciate this small imagist masterpiece ["Perfect"] . . . "The above", comments Mr Buthlay, who quotes it, "is the poem that Ezra Pound and the Imagists talked about but did not write".' For the record 'Perfect' (573), as included without any reference to authorship in *The Islands of Scotland* (London 1939), reads as follows:

Perfect

On the Western Seaboard of South Uist
(*Los Muertos abren los ojos a los que viven*)

I found a pigeon's skull on the machair
All the bones pure white and dry, and chalky,
But perfect,
Without a crack or a flaw anywhere.

At the back, rising out of the beak,
Were twin domes like bubbles of thin bone,
Almost transparent, where the brain had been
That fixed the tilt of the wings.

The Welsh writer Glyn Jones responded to the *TLS* review in a letter (*TLS*, 21 January 1965) in which he quoted 'Perfect' then stated:

These words, attributed by Professor Buthlay to Hugh Mac-Diarmid, and appearing in Hugh MacDiarmid's *Collected Poems* were written by me – except the first line – as prose in a volume of short stories entitled *The Blue Bed* and published by Cape in 1937. This is not a question of similarity or echoes; the words are identical – apart, I repeat, from the first line – and describe in my story the skull of a seagull found on the shore. What Hugh MacDiarmid has done, no doubt through some inadvertence or forgetfulness, is to arrange my prose in the form of the poem quoted above. The earliest date on which the lines appear over the name of Hugh MacDiarmid is, as far as I can discover, 1944.

I ought to add that I have no personal quarrel with Hugh MacDiarmid at all and that I have long been an admirer of his poetry.

TLS
28 January 1965

Brownsbank,
Biggar,
Lanarkshire.
[January 1965]

Sir,

I exchanged letters with Mr Glyn Jones about the poem, 'Perfect', prior to the appearance of his letter in your columns. I have used quotations from many books in some of my poems but have always been careful to attribute such quotations to their sources when I knew these. In this case it is impossible for me after thirty years to recall the circumstances. I certainly never saw Mr Glyn Jones's book, *The Blue Bed and Other Stories*, published in 1937 by Messrs Cape. I was living on a small island in the Shetlands at that time (1932–39) and had no access to new novels or volumes of short stories. I seldom read fiction in any case. But like many poets I kept notebooks in which I jotted down passages from my reading, some of which I subsequently used. I have asked Mr Jones whether his story had not appeared prior to book publication in one or other of the periodicals I used to see – e.g. *Wales* and *The Welsh Review*. I learn from him that Mr John Brophy reviewed it in *The Listener* and quoted the relevant passage in his review. I either automatically memorized it and subsequently thought it my own, or wrote it into one of my notebooks with the same result. Any plagiarism was certainly unconscious. The poem has been published many times and this is the first time the identity with Mr Glyn Jones's words has been noted and brought to my attention. Mr Glyn Jones says he has not been able to trace any publication of it by me before 1944, but I included it in my *Islands of Scotland* (Batsford), published in 1939 and written in 1938, and I am pretty sure printed it earlier in *The Voice of Scotland* or some other periodical, and an artist friend of mine liked it so much that she did a painting of a pigeon's skull on the seashore at that time.

Such things occur. Many poets wittingly or otherwise have used passages from other author's prose word for word in their poems and I remember a writer I knew who published a poem over his own name in *The New Age* and was incredulous when it was pointed out to him it was one of Blake's most famous lyrics. Mr A. R. Orage, the editor, had also failed to recognize its provenance when he passed it for publication.

I have made the necessary explanations and apologies to Mr Glyn Jones and he has generously accepted these. The poem will of course not appear again over my name.[1]

Hugh MacDiarmid
(Christopher Grieve)

TLS
6 May 1965

Brownsbank,
Biggar,
Lanarkshire.
[May 1965]

Sir,

I have previously explained in your columns how I inadvertently came to use Mr Glyn Jones's words in a rearranged form and claimed the result as a poem of my own. Mr John Sparrow[1] (while very kindly saying he accepts my bona fides, which I find impossible to reconcile with what he now purports to disclose) carried the

---

[1] 'Perfect' was included, without Glyn Jones's concurrence, in *Complete Poems* (London 1978).

[1] John Sparrow's letter (*TLS*, 22 April 1965) asserted that no credit should go to MacDiarmid for rearranging a passage from Glyn Jones's story 'Porth-y-rhyd' as verse since 'The transformation had already been made – quote innocently, as a literary experiment or *jeu d'ésprit* – by Mr Keidrych Rhys, who sent the resulting "poem" to Dr Grieve.'

matter a stage farther and says that Mr Keidrych Rhys was the original misappropriator of the words in question and made a poem out of them which he sent to me and which I then appropriated and published as a poem of my own. I will be glad to know how Mr Sparrow comes to this conclusion. There is no basis for it whatever. Mr Keidrych Rhys never sent me any such poem – if he published such a poem anywhere I have never seen it – if he published the poem in the form in which it has been published and claimed in various quarters as a poem of mine, then he took it from me and not I from him. I have all my correspondence in the early 1930s with Mr Rhys intact somewhere and will be able to check the matter conclusively, I think. But I have not access to a lot of my papers in the meantime nor time at the moment to make the search of the great quantities of correspondence, etc., presently available to me, since I am on the point of going to east Germany and thereafter to Cuba. All I can affirm at the moment is that the rearrangement of Mr Jones's words as published in 'Perfect' was unquestionably mine.

Hugh MacDiarmid

TLS
13 May 1965

Brownsbank,
Biggar,
Lanarkshire.
[May 1965]

Sir,

I am glad Mr Keidrych Rhys[1] does not think the charge of conscious plagiarism against me can stick, and I enjoyed the

---

[1] Keidrych Rhys's letter (*TLS*, 6 May 1965) endorsed John Sparrow's claim that he (Rhys), not MacDiarmid, had rearranged the Glyn Jones passage as verse: 'What Mr John Sparrow wrote is true. Except for the one added line of his own, and the omission of inverted commas, and the title "Perfect", Mr Hugh MacDiarmid's line arrangement happens to coincide with mine. His previous hunch about *Wales*, etc., in these columns is right; but the date was 1937. . . . It is with some reluctance that I intervene between the Scottish and Welsh high-priests and their supporting troops, for like Mr Sparrow I do not think the charge of conscious plagiarism sticks.'

effective reply to the classic question, 'quis custodiet ipsos custodes?' given to some other contributors to this correspondence in the concluding sentences of his letter. For reasons I have already given (i.e., inability at the moment to search my correspondence files and the papers for the relevant years, and my impending absence abroad) I cannot carry the matter further just now and effectively dispose yet of Mr Sparrow's very positive, and, I am sure, quite unjustified accusation.

On the general issue involved my sympathy is entirely with an American poet who writes me reassuringly to remind me that copyright is a legal matter and not a literary one. As Mr T. S. Eliot said: 'Minor poets borrow, major poets steal' and my own practice is much of my later work has been like that of Mr Ezra Pound who, in one of his essays, says he takes his material from wherever he can find it and endeavours to transform the assemblage into an artistic unity, the test being that in the upshot the whole (i.e., what in sum he makes of these discrete materials) is more than the sum of the parts.

In any case I acknowledged in my book the source of the passage on Karl Kraus[2] and there may well be differences of opinion about the extent to which, in the 'current drawn from many sources' of an immense poem, I effected aesthetically effective transformation of the material. Mr Herdan thinks I did not do so. Professor Kenneth Buthlay thinks I did, going in detail into the changes I made in his book about my work.

Incidentally in the long preface to *In Memoriam James Joyce*, I explain and seek to justify, my method – to judge what requires

[2] A letter (*TLS*, 6 May 1965) by G. Herdan observed: 'In [MacDiarmid's] poem *In Memoriam James Joyce* in the Section headed "And above all Karl Kraus" (published in Penguin Poets: *English Poetry 1940–60*) I find an almost word for word copy (except for the last 15 lines) of the review in *The Times Literary Supplement*, May 8, 1953, of Karl Kraus's book, *Die Dritte Walpurgisnacht*.' In the preface to the fourth edition of his *The Disinherited Mind* (London 1975) Erich Heller clarifies the Karl Kraus passage: 'Part of my essay on Karl Kraus was originally written for *The Times Literary Supplement*. It appeared anonymously . . . I was surprised as well as flattered to discover much later that with this article I had contributed not only to the *TLS* but also to the poetry of Hugh MacDiarmid (Dr C. M. Grieve), the renowned Scots poet. His poem "And above all, Karl Kraus", from his cycle *In Memoriam James Joyce*, consists of 157 lines of which 149 are taken from my essay – with their essential identity preserved – even though they suffered a little breakage in the process of being lifted into the poetic mode. My slight anxiety that this transference might be detected by some readers and ascribed to me as plagiarism is caused by the (may I say deserved) notoriety of Hugh MacDiarmid's poem. It was selected, without acknowledgement of my *TLS* essay for the Penguin Book *The Mid-Century English Poetry 1940–1960*, which enjoys wide circulation.' The 'Karl Kraus' section of *In Memoriam James Joyce* is printed on pp. 767–771 of *Complete Poems*.

consideration of the whole poem and not just the Karl Kraus section – but perhaps the quickest verdict on the matter is that I have always in such work used 'a strong solution of books' and acted in accordance with what Dr Johnson (wasn't it?) said in defending an alleged overuse of quotations from other writers, viz., that that showed a better sense of social obligation, since those who did not so use quotations (acknowledged or unacknowledged) never in fact did anything but quote all the time.

Hugh MacDiarmid.

THE SCOTSMAN
13 April 1965

Brownsbank,
Biggar.
April 10, 1965

Sir,

Mr Ian Finlay (his letter today)[1] should have passed his comparison of certain writers to footballers like Jim Baxter and Denis Law a little further, and he might have realised that such careers are short and have no enduring value, and that is certainly true also of the 'avant-gardists' he espouses. It is also true that that so-called avant-gardism has produced no comparable stars, and certainly no Scot is in the running.

But the comparison with the aces of commercialised sport has a certain justification perhaps. The alleged avant-garde work in question has no more to do with literature than it has to with football. What is in question here is the very identity of literature. It is no use using terms like literature, drama, or poetry to cover

[1] In a letter, in *The Scotsman* of 10 April 1965, Ian Hamilton Finlay pronounced ironically on Scottish culture: 'What we need is hamely, Scottish Second Division fare. Away with your Jim Baxters and Denis Laws. The international avant-gardism – not to speak of the panache and art – of such players, is a disgrace to the native tradition.' Jim Baxter and Denis Law were the leading Scottish international players of the period and were celebrated for the virtuosity of their footballing skills.

activities which are utterly outside all that has been recognised under these names throughout the history of the arts.

Judging by the way these 'avant-garde' activities are being promoted to create an illusion of internationalism, the whole thing has more resemblance to the organisation of Murder Incorporated than to any programme not dependent on blackmail, wanton obscenity, and incredible scurrility, and it would have been more consonant with the facts if Mr Finlay had cited not Baxter and Law but Al Capone and Lucky Luciano, types who could also claim a certain, and not dissimilar, internationalism.

As to mediocrity, I will be ready to agree that Mr Finlay and his friends may well have 'inside information' which ranks them as authorities on that. – I am, &c.

Hugh MacDiarmid.

LINES REVIEW
Summer 1968

Brownsbank,
Biggar.

Dear Sir,

I wonder what Dr Douglas Young seeks to imply when he writes: 'How I wish somebody would get the facts straight about F. G. Scott's share in the arrangement of the bits of that masterpiece'?[1] In several of my publications I have given all the information that is to be had on this matter. Does Dr Young not accept what I have said, and, if so, why? There is no mystery about the matter at all. When I was writing the *Drunk Man* I had poured out a great mass of verse. Scott came to Montrose and in an all-night session he helped me to discard a great deal that was inferior,

---

[1] Reviewing the revised edition of MacDiarmid's *Collected Poems*, in *Lines Review* No 25, Winter 1967–68, Douglas Young wrote, 'How I wish somebody would get the facts straight about F. G. Scott's share in the arrangement of that masterpiece [*A Drunk Man*]. I remember his telling me that he went off to Montrose one weekend with a bottle of whisky, and spent a night sorting the work out from the odd bits and pieces that Christopher had accumulated; but just how much Scott did to organise it all I did not gather.'

repetitive, or not essential. I had ceased to be able to see 'the wood for the trees'. Scott was in a happier position and helped me to discard the inessential material in my manuscripts and bring out what he regarded (and I agreed) was the most effective arrangement of what was left. That was all. It is not a new phenomenon in literature and the other arts.

Scott had nothing to do with the actual writing any more than Edwin Muir (who was also privy to what I was doing, and saw various portions of my manuscript as I wrote them). There is, despite Dr Young's insinuation, nothing further to be learned. Scott, Muir, my first wife, and others who were in touch with me when *A Drunk Man* was being written are all dead now, but I think it is likely that correspondence from them when my letters are finally published, will fully bear out what I say. If not, there will remain only the explanation I myself have given, and if that is not accepted, I would like to know why.

Yours, etc.,
Hugh MacDiarmid.

THE SCOTSMAN
28 September 1968

Brownsbank,
Biggar,
September 1968

Sir,

Kindly accord me a little space in which to make a statement that will be of interest to all concerned with the use of Scots as a literary medium now and in the future.

A distinguished American scholar[1] who has published several important books on Scottish literary subjects writes me as follows: 'I've decided to risk your displeasure by making a bold suggestion. I find your Scots orthography perfectly dreadful and have never been

---

[1] Professor John C. Weston, see pp. 721. In a letter, of 30 August 1983 to the present editor, Weston says, 'with his usual aggrandizing when he speaks of his admirers he confuses my articles and editions with books! I wrote the letter but I never have published an important book.'

able to understand the apparent contradiction between your nationalism and your use of vile truckling apostrophes. I also don't know why you weren't invited to the Makars' Club meeting in 1947. Perhaps they felt it was too late for you to change your Scots poetry. But if you were to want to change, the procedure is very easy; merely make a public announcement (in *The Scotsman* say) that in future reprintings of your Scots poems you want them respelled by a competent Scots editor to conform with the Scots Style Sheet as it appeared in *Lines Review*, No 9, August 1955. This act could have a tremendous effect on the history of Scottish literature and if it were a public one would be particularly appropriate now with the rise in nationalism. Besides, it would be a way of twisting the English lion's tail.'

The editor of another volume of mine just on the point of being published says in his introduction: 'The spray of philologically gratuitous apostrophes has its uses in providing many readers with clues to the meaning; and it is of more importance to show what the author did with his resources at the time of writing than to super-impose at this point an editorial apparatus of standardisation. If MacDiarmid's Scots is linguistically erratic, that is true of prac-tically all modern Scotsmen. Also, there is rather a fine line between standardising the medium as such and a tendency to diminish the individuality of those of the author's characters who use it.'[2]

Without in any way resiling from my belief that the spelling of 'tyger' in William Blake's famous poem has a value lost if the word is modernised and made 'tiger', I have after careful consideration decided at last to accept my American friend's advice and will see that those ultimately likely to be involved in a definitive complete edition of my poems or whoever I name as my literary executors are instructed to that effect. – I am, &c.

Hugh MacDiarmid

[2] Kenneth Buthlay in his Introduction to MacDiarmid's *The Uncanny Scot* (London 1968, pp. 7–8).

THE SCOTSMAN
7 November 1972

Brownsbank,
Biggar,
November 3, 1972

Sir,

Your report today on the death of Mr Ezra Pound says of Mrs Olga Rudge that she was 'the only person he had talked to for years'. This is not the case. In November 1970 I and my wife and two friends (Messrs Kulgin Duval and Colin Hamilton) were with Mr Pound and Mrs Rudge in his house in Venice and I had a long talk with him about mutual friends, especially Messrs T. S. Eliot, C. H. Douglas, A. R. Orage and Peter Russell.

We subsequently went out and had lunch together, and then we crossed the Grand Canal in a vaporetta and walked in St Mark's Square and had coffee in Florian's Cafe. Mr Pound was in good trim and walked very briskly. He had some affection of the throat and his speech was not very clear, but he was very animated and discussed economics and other matters very connectedly and incisively.

I am, etc.
Hugh MacDairmid.

THE SCOTSMAN
8 May 1978

Brownsbank,
Candymill,
by Biggar.
May 3, 1978

Sir,

In all countries today there is a conflict between what has generally been regarded as poetry in the past and certain modernist tendencies. Admirers of the former have usually little or no regard for the latter. Their attitude is well shown in Christine Creech's letter on Alan Bold's football poems.[1]

---

[1] By way of celebrating Scotland's participation in the World Cup finals in Argentina in 1978 *The Scotsman* featured a front page spread of prepublication extracts from Alan Bold's *Scotland, Yes!* (1978), a book of football poems. Several hostile letters appeared in the paper before MacDiarmid rose for the defence.

I belong to the opposite camp and think that in these poems Bold has scored a real triumph. High intelligence and football fanaticism seldom go together. It would have been easy enough to write 'pop' poems on the subject – to write on the level of most discussions of football matters. Bold instead invests his subject-matter with an unwonted dignity. His poems are all intelligent commentaries, stated with a fine directness and economy. Those of us who have followed Bold's career have been wondering what line of development he would take.

Years ago I said that Scotland had had in Burns a grand popular poet, and I thought it was time it had a great unpopular one, a role I thought might be mine. Unlike Bold, I have no use whatever for anything that commands a great public following, but with his qualifications it now seems that Bold will assume the role I had thought might be mine.

I would like to congratulate him on the splendid achievement and *The Weekend Scotsman* on him giving him such a splendid spread. I do not say this in any patronising way. Bold and I are in many respects polar opposites but while these football poems in subject matter and treatment are altogether beyond my scope, I think I can recognise good poetry when I see it, no matter how different it may be from anything I have written or could attempt, and it is in this spirit that I venture to applaud Alan Bold's achievement.

C. M. Grieve,
('Hugh MacDiarmid')

Miscellaneous Letters

MacDiarmid took as his motto Rilke's statement that 'the poet must know everything' (v. LP, p. 67). He certainly gave the impression that he knew everyone and corresponded with a wide range of people, invariably responding to every letter that came his way.

TO KAIKHOSRU SHAPURJI SORABJI[1]

321 High Holborn,
London, W.C.1.
5/1/32

My dear Sorabji,

How can I possibly thank you for so magnificent a dedication and presentation copy?[2] I am extremely sorry I was not in when you called with it (if – as my office[3] people think – it was you); I hate to think in a matter of this kind that you did not have – and gave me – the added pleasure of handing it over directly. It is a stupendous volume – marvellously printed; any odd loose page one could lay one's hands on would be admirable to frame and hang on a wall. Be sure that I will treasure the volume as one of my dearest possessions

---

[1] The composer Kaikhosru Shapurji Sorabji (born 1892) is one of the most prominent figures in MacDiarmid's pantheon. Introducing the chapter on Sorabji in *The Company I've Kept* London 1966, p. 38) MacDiarmid says: 'No matter how many friends I wish to write about in this book I feel I must give pride of place to Sorabji . . . merely to think of him, let alone see him, still gives me the same thrill I experienced when we first met [in the early 1920s].'

[2] Sorabji's colossal piano work, *Opus clavicembalisticum*, which lasts for more than two hours, was published in June 1930. It is dedicated 'To My Two Friends (E Duobus Unum): Hugh M'Diarmid and C. M. Grieve Likewise To The Everlasting Glory Of Those Few Men Blessed And Sanctified In The Curses and Execrations Of Those Many Whose Praise Is Eternal Damnation.'

[3] The office of the Unicorn Press.

and that no one will ever pay me a greater compliment than you have done. Of the stupendous power of the composition, and the certainty of its eventual recognition – as of your work and place as a whole – I am equally satisfied, albeit keen to see the latter expedited. You have had to stay far too long in the wilderness overshadowed by placemen and morons. But your day will come and surely cannot be long delayed now. Would that one were sure that due recognition once secured would in any way make up for the period of stupid neglect! But I am as contemptuous, I am afraid, of most people's opinions when they reach the stage of accepting any man of calibre as I am of their infernal stupid slowness in reaching that point. Sursum corda. All the best to you. I hope you have other big projects in hand and that these are shaping themselves securely to your mind. To go on with the great work – that is all that matters. For the moment let me just accept your wonderful gift, which I can never repay, with a simple I Thank You, but adding – and do let us meet soon. I trust you have been keeping well. I myself have had a very up-and-down time with a recurrent 'flu and am besides bogged in a mass of private troubles of all kinds (including a divorce suit against me which culminates this month) – not a good atmosphere for work, tho' I too have lots of things in hand.

I am still retaining your essays – anxious to do something about them yet and hoping to be able to undertake their publication yet after I see how some other ventures go. At least let me keep them until we have met and had a talk.

Ever Yours,
C. M. Grieve.

TO PEGGY GRIEVE[1]
NLS

Cootes, Thakeham,
Sussex.
1/6/32

Dear P.,

I am extremely sorry to hear about Christine, poor little soul, and also about yourself. I do hope you will both be much fitter soon. I am writing Christine by this post and sending her a small postal order to buy some little thing. I am also sending you herewith the Pageant of Scottish History for her, and Walter; and the descriptive booklet. I am having a tremendous spate of article writing this week and have sent out articles or suggestions for articles to all sorts of papers, and do hope I may have some luck. But I wish I could get a regular job of any kind, tho' it seems hopeless. There is so little offering. I try every likely advertisement I see but nothing ever comes of it. I do hope things will ease soon for yourself and above all that you will soon be in better form. Kindest regards to Ina and all friends.

Yours,
Chris.

---

[1] MacDiarmid met Margaret ('Peggy') Skinner in 1918; he was working in Cupar as a journalist with *The Fife Herald* group, she was a copyholder in the same office. The couple were married on 13 June 1918 in Edinburgh then moved to Montrose after the war. MacDiarmid and Peggy had two children, Christine (born 1924) and Walter (born 1928). When the poet went to London in 1929 he and Peggy both became friendly with Billy McElroy, a coal-merchant who was friendly with various writers including Sean O'Casey. Peggy lived with McElroy after separating from MacDiarmid in 1930. She divorced MacDiarmid in 1932, emigrated to Canada in 1955 and later returned to England to settle with a Canadian husband. She died at Deal in Kent, in 1962, at the age of sixty-five.

TO JOHN MACNAIR REID[1]
NLS

Cootes, Thakeham,
Sussex.
23/7/32

My dear Reid,

Delighted to have your letter. I quite understand your point of view in regard to *The Albannach*[2] and agree with some of the things you say, and certainly respect the others, but all these are issues not for a letter but for a long talk.

I did not mean in what I said about being careful not to dedicate a political or otherwise not perhaps generally acceptable poem to you to impute any funk or undue concern for your job or anything of that sort to you. On the other hand, even where there is nothing of that sort, one does not want to associate a friend with an expression of ideas or sentiments he might not approve – since – apart from anything else, that would impair any satisfaction he had in the dedication perhaps.

I had not seen you frequently enough or had long and intimate talks enough with you to relate you intimately to my work in the way that might have been possible if (as I hope we may yet have) we had had such a basis of profound spiritual intercourse and accord – which may well be (and I think is) there latently but not yet clearly established as more prolonged personal relationships would make it. So, in that way, any poem I can dedicate to you is a shot in the dark – it may or may not establish a profound spiritual bond between us, no matter how, more superficially considered, its content may be something we have much in common, as, e.g. almost any Scottish nationalist subject would be.

But I have given the matter very deep consideration and come to the conclusion that what I should wish to dedicate to you should be something that would at least rely upon what we have most essentially in common – the fact that we are both poets; and that therefore would have to be 1/ a good poem, and 2/ as complete and effective an expression as possible of my basic belief qua poet.

[1] John Macnair Reid (1895–1954), to whom MacDiarmid dedicated the long philosophical poem 'Depth and the Chthonian Image' (346–53) was a journalist with *The Glasgow Herald*, Inverness *Courier*, *Glasgow Evening Times*, *Glasgow Evening News*. He wrote novels such as *Homeward Journey* (1934) and the posthumously published *Judy from Crown Street* (1970) as well as the poems in *Symbols* (1933).

[2] Fion Mac Colla, *The Albannach* (1932). MacDiarmid saw in Mac Colla the representative novelist of the Scottish Highlands and encouraged him as such. Reid had reservations about the novel.

I accordingly propose to inscribe to you a long poem 'Depth And the Chthonian Image' a copy of which I enclose. Let me know what you think of it. To my own mind it is an important poem and likely to take a key place in my work.

I also enclose a copy of *Second Hymn to Lenin* and will be glad if the *Evening Times* can review it (and, if so, if you'll send me a copy – the price, by the way, is 5/-, in case mention might be made of that). Which reminds me, to revert for a moment to the disgraceful Unicorn Press matter, that I hope your editor, knowing I was associated with that firm, hasn't any idea that I was in any way whatever connected with that affair. MacDonald is devilishly touchy; he just mentioned your adverse review in a letter I had the other day – I don't think he'll have any feeling that you were moved by malice or anything of that sort, but I'll be writing him in a day or so, and will take the opportunity of giving him a right angle.

Every kind regard to your wife and yourself.

Yours,
C. M. G.

TO HERBERT READ[1]
UV

1 India Buildings,
Victoria St,
Edinburgh.
2/1/33

Dear Professor Read,

Just a note to thank Mrs Read and you for yesterday's lunch. A man like myself, though leading a very active life and concerned in politics and all sorts of things, is essentially lonely to an extraordinary degree in Scotland, to the detriment of his work too. There are so very few people with whom one can discuss the things that matter most to one. But for practically the one exception of

[1] Herbert (later Sir Herbert) Read was, in 1933, Professor of Fine Art at Edinburgh University and editor of the *Burlington Magazine*. Read (1893–1968) gained a reputation as a poet and a prolific writer on art who championed avant garde developments.

F. G. Scott Scotland is in this sense simply a howling void to me. You can imagine from this how glad I am to find you in Edinburgh and have occasional meetings with you – though, alas, we are too shy to talk frankly and freely on real issues and tend rather to confine ourselves to small talk. The language and other aspects, of course, constitute very difficult problems in this matter of work like Scott's and mine and the possibilities of a Scottish Movement. I wonder if Mrs Read and you would let me, as a memento of yesterday, inscribe these two short poems to you.[2] I have written them out in English but though actually they are written in a very slightly Scoticised medium, the slight changes in the sound make a good deal of difference and I prefer them greatly in the Scots form.

With compliments and best wishes.

Yours sincerely,
C. M. Grieve.

TO EZRA POUND

Ezra Pound (1885–1972) was one of the most prominent figures in MacDiarmid's personal pantheon. The two poets shared a faith in the heroic qualities of epic poetry, a belief in Social Credit economics and a determination to embody a whole cultural philosophy. The tautness of MacDiarmid's early lyrics has qualities in common with Pound's cycle *Hugh Selwyn Mauberley* (1920) but the main impact of Pound on MacDiarmid is to be seen in the *Mature Art* plan to write a Celtic epic in the multilingual mode used in the Cantos. Mac-Diarmid contributed to a commemorative symposium on Pound, held at Queen's University, Belfast on 21 February 1973, and said:

Of all the men I have known (and I know them all over the world, I know most poets from many countries), I loved Ezra Pound. I think he was the most lovable man I met and I was happy to know

[2] The two poems were 'Durchseelte' (1288) and 'Riding in a Fog' (1289). MacDiarmid's English versions comprise a slight orthographic alteration except for the first quatrain of 'Durchseelte' which involves a change of rhyme: 'I thought when I saw it first/There was little call/For one bird to appear in a world/Where nothing else lived at all.'

that my affection for him was reciprocated. (*Paideuma*, Vol 3, No 2, Fall 1974, pp. 151–2).

BRB

Whalsay,
Shetland Islands.
19/12/33

My dear Ezra Pound,

I am glad to have your letter. How amazing that we have never corresponded before. I have been on the point of writing you scores of times these last fifteen years, but. . . .

I am, of course, a fraud as you will see from my address. I still contrive by a species of magic to maintain an appearance of being au fait with all that is happening in welt-literatur. The review in *New English Weekly* of *Dictionary of Foreign Literature* (7th inst.[1]) was by me – quite a feat to evolve it in this hyperborean preserve where I am reduced to the possession of a mere handful of books. But it must become increasingly difficult for me to produce these occasional effects of omniscience. Gone are the old *New Age* days when I could – and did – really keep abreast, and might jabber in fifteen languages in a single article. I get no foreign papers and can scarcely ever afford to buy a book, nor can I get any reviewing whereby to keep in touch in a hit-or-miss sort of way. So I haven't seen Active Anthology; nor your Cantos XXXI/XLI (my reference[2] to the passages in XIX and XXII was only a safeguard – what I really meant was that I knew

---

[1] In *New English Weekly*, Vol IV, No 8, 7 December 1933, there was an anonymous review of R. Farquharson Sharp's *A Biographical Dictionary of Foreign Literature* (1933).

[2] The same issue of *NEW* as above featured MacDiarmid's article 'Poets, Consider!', an argument for 'a congress of representative poets' who would spread the Social Credit gospel. MacDiarmid noted 'I have seen nothing so far germane to my present concern. Ezra Pound's passages in defence of Douglasism (Cantos XIX, XXII) are another matter, a solitary exception.' Pound, on reading this, wrote to MacDiarmid from Rapallo on 7 December 1933. 'My Dear MacDiarmid, I don't know quite how complete an exception you are trying to make me. I don't think the passages in XIX and XXII are in any way isolated from the mass of the Cantos. Though the more specific locus of economics is in Cantos XXXI/XLI, I can't write everything all at once on the same page. Also I am probably a more boycotted, trimmed, excluded author than you apparently think. AND the question how far an economic concern (by a writer of verse) can be or shd/ be confined to lyric or matric expression . . . seems to me variant.'

that in respect of what you had written on economics, and, as a poet, how you had dealt with them made you an exception I found it necessary to point out – pending a more thorough research of your recent poems than I was able to make. Besides my article was a very incomplete one. I see Eliot in his *Use of Poetry*[3] refers to Wordsworth's Distributivism!) – I take your points, and agree so far as these go, but mine was, of course, that no poet today is standing to the powers that be as even Wagner once stood. 'In his person there was nothing of the militant, but through his music he was not far from displacing from his pedestal that man of blood and iron, Bismarck himself. And Bismarck was well aware that it was not wholly by means of soldiery that the German States had been liberated from the dominance of Napoleon, but by minstrels and ballad-singers. The man who feared neither bullet nor bayonet took heed of this outlaw.'

The Schablone[4] a man needs to produce such an, and greater, effects as a poet today on public opinion and on the financial and political system is indeed a Schablone – the very question resembles that word which means so many entirely different things – I am afraid I find the antics of most of the poets who attempt such a task no better than those split slippers of comparses which last barely a week owing to their *wooden* pointes!

But of course the show has to pay its way and it is sometimes very difficult, I admit, to do as Holtei did towards that end and 'bring along ladies of a loveliness which is contrary to police regulations (polizeiwidrig hubsch)'!

With compliments and every high regard.

Yours,
Hugh MacDiarmid.

[3] T. S. Eliot, *The Use of Poetry and the Use of Criticism* (1933).
[4] MacDiarmid liked the word; when he issued a prospectus in 1939 it was headed *Mature Art: An Exercise in Schlabone, Bordatini, and Scordattura*. The spelling was corrected in the second impression of *In Memoriam James Joyce* (Glasgow 1956, p. 35) in the line 'In schablone, bordatini, and prolonged scordatura'.

TO VICTOR GOLLANCZ LTD

c/o Mrs Wells
6 Acacia Place
SW8
18/3/34

Miss Dorothy Horsman,[1]
Messrs Victor Gollancz Ltd

Dear Miss Horsman,

I got the proofs of my book[2] just as I was leaving the Shetlands and hope to return corrected copy in a day or two. I will call with it personally and we may be able to discuss the matters arising in your letter of 16th inst. which I received late last night.

Apart from the fact that I knew you have proofs 'vetted' by a lawyer prior to publication, I was myself particularly careful with this book. I recognise that the legal adviser in such a case must be extremely careful but I find that very frequently this leads them to exaggerate the possibilities of action. It seems to me that anything of the kind, whether on the score of libel, sedition, obscenity or blasphemy is unlikely in this case, because 1/ In each of the cases to which their letter refers I have expressed similar types of opinion more moderately than in previous volumes of mine where, although the grounds for possible action might have been more legitimately apprehended, actually nothing happened – despite in certain cases newspaper outcries against my work on these grounds.
2/Each of the poems to which their letter refers has already been published, word for word as it now appears in my book, and no action was taken or attempted.

So far as the actual facts go I am of course guilty of frank expressions of Communist and anti-religious opinion and of outspoken sentiments on sexual matters; but in all those cases these do not transcend the common practice of those who hold similar views, and can only be constructed as open to proscecution on grounds of sedition, obscenity, or blasphemy if the tenets of the Communist Party, the Rationalist Association, and advanced sexologists are denied promulgation on such grounds – as they are not.

The poem on pp. 99[3] where your lawyers advise that it might

---

[1] Miss Dorothy Horsman, Production Manager of Victor Gollancz.
[2] *Stony Limits and Other Poems* which Gollancz published, with various deletions, in 1934.
[3] 'On the Oxford Book of Victorian Verse' (449–50). Originally the poem ended with the dismissive quatrain:
    So when this book is revised for reissue

provoke doubtful claims for libel on the part of certain living poets is an instance of over-caution – no ingenuity could construe what is said of these poets into more or other than a disbelief that they are more than 'very small beer' and of no greater rank than certain extremely poor poetasters of the past. This is a piece of perfectly legitimate literary criticism – with no libellous insinuation of any kind.

The poem on p. 78[4] cannot be libellous. It does not go beyond the simple statement of the Chief-Constable's extraordinary resemblance to the late King Edward – a fact well-known and frequently commented on in Scotland, and absolutely undeniable. To state a resemblance of this sort, which is patent and indisputable, cannot be held to imply or suggest any reflections which verge upon libel. It is a simple statement of fact.

I am glad your advisers think prosecutions on the score of blasphemy unlikely as I could not make the very numerous alterations which would be required to render the book innocuous in that respect except with a great amount of re-writing.

I had all these matters very carefully in mind when I sent you my MSS, and particularly the question of libel against individuals. I am certain nothing in the book falls into that category, and that any grounds for possible prosecution are political or religious and that these, judging by all my past experience and the fact that all these poems have already been published with impunity, are as remote as it is possible to make them without wholly emasculating the volume.

But I shall be very glad to discuss these matters further with you when I return the proof, either in person or by correspondence.

With best wishes,

Yours sincerely,
C. M. Grieve

Let us have you included lest somebody should miss you.
Here with your peers – Squire, Church, and Strong,
Masefield, Noyes, de la Mare. *Oh Lord! how long?*
As these real names were, despite MacDiarmid's letter, found objectionable the closing couplet of the poem was changed to read:
Here with your peers – Spoof, Dubb, and Blong,
Smiffkings, Pimple, and Jingle. *Oh Lord! how long?*
[4] 'Edinburgh Toun' (483). This describes the police setting down steel boxes
To shoot the workin'-classes doun
Under a Chief Constable – Whoa, horsie, steady! –
Juist the spit-image o' 'Peacemaker' Neddy.
The poem was deleted from the first edition and restored, with other excluded poems, in *Stony Limits and Scots Unbound* (Edinburgh 1957).

TO STANLEY NOTT[1]
SUNYB   [1934]

My dear Stanley,

I had hoped to see you today but am too worried over personal matters.[2] I owe you 10/- but it is not this that has kept me away, but simply the desperate circumstances in which I am involved. I expected to receive my share in my mother's estate last week, but, though I have wired and written to my brother who is settling it, it has not come to hand yet. Nor have I yet got my promised advance from Victor Gollancz, while a new contract with Jarrolds for an autobiography, with an advance of £50, cannot be definitely concluded and the advance paid for a few days yet. In the meantime I am in desperate straits – detached from all my belongings which are held in a hotel I had to leave because I had no more money and to which I owe 5/9; (and incidentally for this reason without my papers and unable to keep working on *Forty Songs* with which I was making excellent progress before these troubles beset me). You will understand the situation when I tell you that I spent two nights in the open – one of them on a bench in Trafalgar Square.

If you possible can will you let Gawsworth[3] have a pound or two to keep me going until some of these other things come through, and make a definite date with him to see me on Monday or Tuesday?

I am anxious to talk about pushing the essays, since they are a little late for PEN Congress publicity, and need all the more energetic publicity work now.

                             Yours,
                             Chris.

---

[1] Stanley Nott was the publisher of MacDiarmid's *At the Sign of the Thistle* (London 1934) and *Second Hymn to Lenin and Other Poems* (London 1935).
[2] The poet's mother had died on 11 April 1934. The same year MacDiarmid travelled to London to participate in a plan to remove the Stone of Destiny from Westminster Abbey. This letter was probably written during that visit.
[3] John Gawsworth (1912–70) was the pseudonym of Terrence Ian Fytton Armstrong, poet, critic, and editor. MacDiarmid dedicated 'The Little White Rose' (461) to Gawsworth.

TO J. H. WHYTE

J. H. Whyte, who ran the Abbey Bookshop in St Andrews, founded *The Modern Scot* to provide an attractive outlet for the outstanding Scottish writers active in the 1930s. Understandably Whyte was enthusiastic about the work of both Edwin Muir and MacDiarmid – who frequently contributed poetry and prose to the magazine. MacDiarmid's translation of Alasdair MacMhaighstir Alasdair's 'The Birlinn of Claranald', for example first appeared in *The Modern Scot*, Vol 5, No 4, January 1935 and was then issued as a limited edition by Whyte's Abbey Bookshop. *The Modern Scot* ran from Spring 1930 to January 1936; in April 1936 it was incorporated into *Outlook*, edited by Whyte and David MacEwan. By then Mac-Diarmid advocated an extremist Scottish Republican position and disliked the 'St Andrews school of polite literature'. He felt particularly aggrieved, and vulnerable, at this time since his book *Red Scotland* had been announced by Routledge and was not now to be published by that firm (see pp. 536–56). However, as general editor of The Voice of Scotland series, for which *Red Scotland* was written, he had to live with the fact that all the other titles had appeared or were about to appear. Edwin Muir's *Scott and Scotland* (1936) was to be the most provocative title in the series for it argued that Scots was inadequate to the expression of a truly modern cultural programme. In *Outlook*, Vol 1, No. 3, June 1936, there was a substantial extract from Muir's forthcoming book containing the contention that Scots was an anachronism:

> Scots has survived to our time as a language for simple poetry and the simpler kind of short story, such as [Stevenson's] 'Thrawn Janet'; all its other uses have lapsed, and it expresses therefore only a fragment of the Scottish mind. One can go further than this, however, and assert that its very use is a proof that the Scottish consciousness is divided. For, reduced to its simplest terms, this linguistic division means that Scotsmen feel in one language, and think in another; that their emotions turn to the Scottish tongue, with all its associations of local sentiment, and their mind to a standard of English which for them is almost bare of associations other than those of the classroom.

MacDiarmid was horrified since the argument apparently dismissed as anachronistic his achievement in creating Synthetic Scots in general and *A Drunk Man Looks at the Thistle* in particular; indeed Muir went on to say that MacDiarmid's attempts to revive Scots were irrelevant for 'he has left Scottish verse very much where it was before.' By way of reply MacDiarmid sent a letter to *Outlook* but its

850

belligerent tone offended Whyte who rejected it. MacDiarmid's next step was to circulate an open letter to Whyte. It was prepared like a press handout with the headline PROLETARIAN-SEPARATIST LITERARY LINE IN SCOTLAND and launched an attack on *Outlook* as 'the Scottish literary and fascist-nationalist quarterly' and Whyte as 'the wealthy literary editor of *Outlook*'.

NLS
TS

Whalsay,
Shetland Islands.
Wednesday 1/7/36

My dear Whyte:-

Many thanks for your letter.[1] Though I use ridicule and invective (which are after all dialectical weapons of a perfectly valid kind, tho' their use is deprecated for reasons I do not approve – a là Marx's own practice – by the very mealy-mouthed English-polite people I must needs oppose in all directions) you know perfectly well that my line against Muir and others is not dictated by any meanly personal considerations, but by the facts (1) (the minor one) that I am entitled to fight them with their own weapons – or sharper weapons than their slick suavities and sniggerings, and (2) (the vitally important one) that all the decent work done in connection with the Scottish Movement has been, and can only continue to be, done along the Communist proletarian separatist-Republican line, whereas what has happened to the *Outlook* is that just as the Nationalist Party was captured at the time of the fusion by the MacEwans[2], so now our cultural organs have been captured and no interest whatever is shown in the developing War and Fascism situation or in the day-to-day struggles of the Scottish Workers.

If Muir's article was, as you allege, only an incidental bit of a *Scott* book[3], and illustrated a general thesis, so does my letter (which is

---

[1] Whyte took strong exception to MacDiarmid's description of Muir as 'one of the leaders of the white mouse faction of the Anglo-Scottish literati and a noted connoisseur of buttered bread.'

[2] MacDiarmid believed that the Duke of Montrose, Sir Alexander MacEwan and others had sidetracked and subverted the revolutionary Scottish Nationalist Movement, as originally conceived by Cunninghame Graham and MacDiarmid himself.

[3] Edwin Muir, *Scott and Scotland* (1936).

851

part of *Red Scotland* in its 'white mouse faction' and other phrases).
Muir's fatuous concern with Scott is an unmistakable pointer at this
juncture. In any case, as can be gathered from Brandes[4], Scott's
only value is his objective treatment of parts of Scottish history and
the partial revivication by his influence of Catalan and Flemish and
other minority literatures. The whole direction of Scott's line was
his regret for the quite needless passing of Scottish institutions,
mannerisms, etc. into English, as exemplified in many of his famous
sayings, i.e. about an un-Scotched Scotsman becoming a damned
bad Englishman, etc. This leads on naturally to the separatist
position and Muir cannot do justice to those – the only important –
elements in Scott save in contradiction to his own (Muir's) anti-
Scottish-separatist line. Properly used, Scott can only be used as a
battering-ram to drive home the failure of 19th century and subsequent Scottish writers to crystallise phases of Scotland's developing history in the way Scott, though only poorly, did for certain
previous periods. The significance of this grave national-historical-
literary leeway is clear enough from a Marxist standpoint. Muir
himself has also in the past pointed out that Scott's best artistic
work was done in the Scots Vernacular, i.e. in 'Wandering Willie's
Tale'. That Muir now denies this, or turns a blind eye to its
contemporary implications and applications, is typical of the
irremediable confusion and constant self-contradiction of his own
pretendedly-objective but wholly subjective pseudo-critical position
– what the late Lewis Grassic Gibbon well called his 'anaemic
Blah'.

Besides, why was my *At the Sign Of The Thistle* (1934) never
reviewed in the *Modern Scot*? For the same reason that Muir refused
to review it in his *European Quarterly*? You signed the testimonial[5] to
me, but either you do or do not believe in what you signed, and I am
driven to the latter conclusion since you prefer Mary Ramsay's[6] and
Scott-Moncrieff's[7] and Muir's views of what is in the interests of
Scotland to mine, prefer silly articles by Henderson Stewart, MP,

[4] Georg Brandes (1842 –1927), the Danish literary critic.
[5] In the spring of 1936 MacDiarmid was presented with a public testimonial
signed by Sir James Barrie, Sean O'Casey, Compton Mackenzie and all the
leading Scottish writers – which expressed 'our profound sense of great services
you have rendered to Scots letters and to literature in general'. After quoting the
testimonial in *Lucky Poet*, MacDiarmid comments 'this Testimonial largely
represented a disposal of me – the signatories (or some of them) felt that they
had done the gallant and generous thing and so for the future I could be safely
ignored.' (LP p. 44).
[6] Mary Ramsay, author of *Calvin and Art* (1938)
[7] George Scott-Moncrieff, editor of *Scottish Country* (1935) and a contributor to
Outlook.

Tom Johnston, MP[8] and the like to substantiate works – poems etc – by myself, and amongst all the things *Outlook* promised to do there was conspicuously no mention of poetry – which presumably only comes within your new purview in homeopathic doses for fill-up purposes.

I must obviously completely dissociate myself from this line and do so now with the direct warning that you are betraying the Scottish Movement – that the people who took no previous interest in that Movement with whom you are now getting into touch are not worth getting into touch with, but are a worthless set of people – a historically doomed class of petit-bourgeois due for speedy liquidation.

Yours sincerely,
C. M. Grieve.

P.S. Your suggestion that I should reply to Muir in an 'objective dispassionate article' is only an invitation to me to do some of the piffling ('interesting, however misguided')[9] playing with ideas Muir is doing; and I must of course decline to waste time writing anything of the kind.

P.P.S. Your Fascistic line is clear in any case, I must remind you, since your first issue of *Outlook* recommended an Economic Advisory Committee – the very thing set up under Sir James Lithgow's chairmanship – playing the game of the Anglo-Scottish authorities in forms of alleged decentralisation giving a specious pseudo-satisfaction to Scottish 'interests' in lieu of genuine Nationalism (i.e. the nemesis of Socialism and Social Democracy's neglect or mis-prizal of the Scottish Nationalist issue, and Scottish Nationalism's blindness to, or Fascistic line towards, the Class War) – a rec-ommendation with which you said all your readers must agree, though it is obviously a line out which separatism cannot emerge at all, at any rate in any proletarian Republican sense of the word. In any case, this consensus of opinion and alleged open forum business of yours are purely Fascist notions.

Another important point is your provision of a platform for Dr

---

[8] The first issue of *Outlook*, Vol 1, No 1, April 1936, contained 'My Plan for Scotland' by J. Henderson Stewart, MP; the second issue, Vol 1, No 2, May 1936, contained 'Fascist Boards for Scotland?' by Tom Johnston, MP.

[9] The quotation in parenthesis is from Whyte's letter to MacDiarmid refusing to publish his response to Muir's article.

Bowie[10] with his idea that the Second Industrial Revolution in Scotland must lie along the capture and development in Scotland of luxury trades of all kinds, a line that has nothing whatever to do with the real bases of our national economy or the masses of the workers, but is in significant and sinister alignment with the establishment in Italy today of branch factories by big English motor firms, etc. In other words, Whyte, I might have written 'the Whyte mouse faction' – your game is up – we see through it at every point – and you will no longer be able to dodge and gloss over the political situation with the reptilian dexterity that has hitherto characterised your (and Muir's) manoeuvres, nor will you any longer be able to get away with giving space to Fascist articles and then making a pretence of editorial impartiality by putting up straw men of your own choosing, and Socialists like Tom Johnston and Lennox Kerr, to give what purports to be the Socialist reply (as the BBC did in putting up Joseph Duncan against Scottish Nationalism recently). I am now in close and constant touch with thoroughly competent dialectical materialists in all our Scottish Universities, and the Red Scotland line we are now developing (e.g. in the coming Edinburgh University Rectorial Election and at an Inter-University United Front – Socialists, Communists, and Scottish Nationalists – Conference) will completely expose and speedily put an end to all such manoeuvres of yours and Muir's.

You have raised this question of personalities. You need not therefore try to burke the purely impersonal line I have taken in the foregoing pages by entertaining any feeling now that I have been basely ungrateful and that this is any case of my biting the hand that has fed me.

C. M. G.

10 *Outlook*, Vol 1, No 1, April 1936, contained 'The Next Ten Years' by Dr J. A. Bowie whose 'Literature: Class or National?' appeared in *Outlook*, Vol 1, no. 3, June 1936.

TO WILLIAM BURT[1]
EUL

Whalsay,
Shetland Islands.
Saturday 16/7/39

My dear Burt,

Many thanks for your letter, and the two periodicals. I am glad that, tho' still obliged to lie pretty low, you are in fair tide again. The 40 minutes bus to school sounds pretty strenuous – all right perhaps in decent weather, but apt to be very trying, I should think, in the winter-time. It's nice however that you are so acceptably settled forenenst the Pentlands, and with trees, squirrels etc. close at hand. I hope Billy likes his job in the Town Clerk's Office. Gosh, how the years have gone by. It is perfectly amazing to think that the boy I wrote that lyric to is 18 already – and John 14! I read with keen interest what you say about the Depth and Chthonian Image poem. You – and F. G. at the time it was written – are the only two who seem to have spotted it at all. I personally think it is one of my best things. Lord only knows what's going to happen to all my stuff – I have MSS of poems by me amounting to at least five or six times all I have yet published. It is not becoming easier to get things – especially longish things – published anywhere, either in volume form or in periodicals. *The Criterion*[2] was the only periodical in Great Britain in which the *Cornish Heroic Song* could have appeared – and that was the last issue of it, and put an end also to the only outlet I've had recently for critical writing – except this little quarterly of my own,[3] copies of which I send you herewith. I'll also send you a copy of the new issue which will be out in a few day's time – since, inter alia, it contains a slashing reply to Muir's *Scott and Scotland*. The Clann Albain got shunted aside by my marital and economic disasters, and I have not reverted to it. But some day I hope to. It would not be a very difficult job to put all the parts of it I've already done into their proper sequence, and complete the structure in which they were to

---

[1] William Burt (1883–1949) was born in Tarbert, Argyll; educated at St Andrews University; and taught English at Langholm Academy, where C. M. Grieve was one of his pupils, then at Linlithgow Academy. It was Burt who drew F. G. Scott's attention to the MacDiarmid poems in *The Scottish Chapbook* and arranged a reunion in 1923. MacDiarmid duly celebrated the occasion by writing the poem 'Hungry Waters' (52) for Burt's son Billy and the poem is dedicated to 'a little boy at Linlithgow'. Billy Burt (1920–42) was killed when serving as a Pilot Officer in the RAF.

[2] *The Criterion*, Vol XVIII, No LXXI, January 1939, contained MacDiarmid's 'Cornish Heroic Song for Valda Trevlyn'.

[3] *The Voice of Scotland*.

take their place, and add the other unwritten parts as originally planned. But I can't do that until I get my present load of projects off – and that includes an Autobiography, a huge novel (of a rare kind – a philosophical novel) on which I am working pretty hard just now, and various other things. But the way would probably be cleared if my big *Mature Art* poem is published by that Paris-American firm,[4] as I think it will be. In any case I'm getting back to Scots again now after my long detour, and although I have so much else in hand I have no doubt that if I can organise my time so as to make proper progress with these, then as at Montrose – when also most of my time was taken up with other things I'll be able to write a good deal of poetry too in the interstices of these other tasks.

I mustn't write more at the moment. But as I told you in my last letter I'm to be lecturing in Edinburgh about the end of November and I'm hoping to see you then and have a good crack.

All the best to Carrie and the boys. Valda and Mike are O.K. He's growing too – 7 now – and a perfect little Berserker type.

Yours,
Chris.

[4] Jack Kahane's Obelisk Press.

TO ARTHUR GEDDES[1]
NLS

32 Victoria Crescent Road,
Glasgow, W.2.
20/1/48

Arthur Geddes, Esq, D. ès L., PhD
President, The Outlook Tower,
70 Cluny Gardens,
Edinburgh.

Dear Dr Geddes,

I have to thank Miss Finlayson for sending me on your behalf a copy of the particulars regarding the General and Research Editorship for your father's MSS; and also the Rev J. A. C. Murray BD, for his note received today telling me that the Secretary has been on holiday but that my application will be considered very soon now by the Publications Committee.

I applied, not because I was short of other work or particularly interested in the money aspect, but because 1/ of the fact that I knew your father and have been progressively interested in his life and work with which I have thoroughly familiarised myself in so far as it has been available to me; and 2/ because I regard a more complete knowledge of it as essential to certain aspects of my own life-work. In this latter connection I may mention that in the second volume of my Autobiography (the first volume of which, *Lucky Poet* was published two or three years ago) a chapter of some 12-15,000 words is devoted to your father, and other chapters to friends of mine like W. B. Yeats, A. R. Orage, 'A. E.' (George Russell), Major C. H. Douglas, and others – some of whom were also friends and associates of your father.

I noted the word 'academic' in the advertisement to which I replied: but on reading the particulars relating to the proposed Research Fellowship you have now sent me (and particularly Clause 3 thereof which stresses the necessity of University qualifications if an application is to be made to the Carnegie University Trust for

[1] Dr Arthur Geddes, son of Sir Patrick Geddes (1854–1932) who was, in MacDiarmid's opinion 'one of the outstanding thinkers of his generation, not merely in Britain but in the world, and not only one of the greatest Scotsmen of the past century but in our entire history . . . His published works do nothing like justice to his genius. He had a profound distrust of what he used to call the modern habit of "verbalistic empaperment" and in consequence it has to be said of him that like Thomas Carlyle's hero in *Sartor Resartus* he left behind bags and boxes of notes, mountains of diagrams; and a huge bundle of correspondence all of which has still to be gathered, deciphered, and appraised by the generation which will one day, I trust, hail him as its prophet.' (Company, 82).

Scotland) I realise that I am probably ineligible, as, of course, I have no academic qualifications – and that while I might be considered to have some countervailing qualifications of my own these are not of a nature which would enable me to receive such financial assistance.

I regret this greatly, as the work would have been very much after my heart, and I fully realise the immense importance of the work to be done and regard its proper discharge as in line with all my major interests.

I note your postscript, however, with regard to 'qualified editors for particular books'. Of those listed earlier in the typescript I am particularly interested in Number 8 and 9 (i.e. Selection of Letters etc., and Contemporary Civilisation) and would regard it as a very great honour, indeed, to be entrusted with the editorship of either or both of these.

With compliments and best wishes.

Yours sincerely,
C. M. Grieve.
('Hugh MacDiarmid')

TO BERNARD FERGUSSON[1]

32 Victoria Crescent Road,
Glasgow W2
5/3/48

Brigadier Bernard Fergusson,

Dear Sir:-

Reference your verses in today's *Daily Record* may I point out that you are a liar, and that it is a cowardly thing to write in that way in

---

[1] As the late Bernard Fergusson (Lord Ballantrae) explained, in his collection *Hubble-Bubble* (London 1978, p. 46), 'In 1948 the literary editor of the Scottish *Daily Record* induced a few Scottish writers to flyte against each other, and invited me to participate. This was when the writers of the so-called Scottish Renaissance were in full spate, pouring out verse in what they called "Lallans" or Lowland Scots, which my brother James Fergusson happily dubbed "Plastic Scots".' The first stanza of Fergusson's poem 'A Flyting', in the *Daily Record* of 5 March 1948, ran as follows: 'Frae midden-tap tae midden-tap,/These Scottish Chauntecleers/Craw loud and lang, and vaunty flap,/Forbye their wings, their ears./Shoogling their kaims like cap and bells/They cry at me and you:/'Ye're

the press about professional authors about whose work you are either ignorant or grossly-misinformed? Most modern poets' work – at least during the life-time of these poets – is hardly known outside their own countries and to that extent in your elegant phrase they may be said to 'craw on their ain midden-taps'; but that confinement of their reputation to their own countries does not apply only – or more – to the Scots poets you slander than to the vast majority of their contemporaries in every country. In any event it does not apply to me. My work has been translated into many languages; critical works concerning it have been published in Germany, France, America, Iceland and elsewhere, and many of the most distinguished poets and critics in the world today in France, Russia, India and elsewhere have praised it very highly. If you know anything of it, it does not follow that your opinion of it, good or bad, is worth a rap – you have not manifested any special competence in this connection, and even if you had your opinion would weigh nothing against the opinions of the late W. B. Yeats, AE (George Russell), T. S. Eliot and many other writers of international repute who have come to very different conclusions than those implied in your verse regarding its merits – and regarding the Scottish Literary Movement in general of which my work is one of the products.

I do not expect any apology from a person of your disposition, nor would a retraction overtake the harm you have done to a movement many of whose proponents are as able, honest, and selfless as the leading writers of any other Western European country, or even as you are yourself – in your own estimation.

Yours sincerely,
Hugh MacDiarmid

a' kailyairders bar oorsels;/Sing Cock-a-doodle-doo!'/ But cocks that only craw at hame/Are aye kailyairders just the same.'

TO CLEMENT ATTLEE
PMO

Dungavel,
By Strathaven,
Lanarkshire.
Scotland.
10/3/50

To
The Right Hon Mr Clement Attlee, PC
The Prime Minister.

Sir:-

I beg to thank you for your letter of 2nd inst, telling me that His Majesty the King has been graciously pleased on your recommendation to grant me a Civil List Pension of £150 per annum, and to say, with great gratitude, that this most helpful and generous proposal is entirely acceptable to me.

I have duly completed the form you enclosed and return it to you herewith as requested.

With deep appreciation and sincere thanks.

I remain, Sir,

Your obedient servant,
Christopher Murray Grieve.

TO ROBERT MACLELLAN[1]
NLS

Dungavel,
By Strathaven,
Lanarkshire.
14/4/50

Dear Robert,

How kind of Kathleen and you! The matter[2] was not supposed to be divulged until the Honours list comes out sometime next month – but the Prime Minister's letter arrived when I was away in Wales,

---

[1] Robert McLellan (born 1907) is an outstanding Scots dramatist whose *Jamie the Saxt* (1937, printed 1970) has established itself as one of the classics of the modern Scottish theatre.

[2] MacDiarmid was granted a Civil List pension of £150 a year.

Valda opened the letter, and divulged the contents to a chap who was staying here. Immediately I got back I emphasized to the fellow that the matter must be held strictly confidential until officially released and he promised to do so – but the chance of getting a guinea or two for a *Daily Mail* exclusive was too much for him and he spilt the beans. One or two papers lifted it from *The Daily Mail* – but papers like *The Glasgow Herald*, *Scotsman*, etc. know, of course, to wait for the official announcement.

The pension will of course make a big difference to us, and together with the fact that we are now ensconced in this fine big house[3] with all modern conveniences in the middle of a pine wood on the estate of Scotland's premier duke there can really be little excuse if I fail to do a good few of the many things I ought still to do but have not had suitable circumstances to attempt up to now.

Valda and I were delighted to see that you had carried off first place in the Drama Festival and that the McKemmie Trophy had gone to the company playing *The Changeling*.[4] We hope the new play[5] is coming along. The Festival Committee are still fighting a desperate rearguard action, but can't continue much longer. You'll come into your own all right too.

Excuse this hasty scrawl. Love to you all from all here.

Yours,
Chris.

[3] In 1950 the Duke of Hamilton offered MacDiarmid a five-apartment outhouse at his home, Dungavel House, near Strathaven, Lanarkshire. After a few months the National Coal Board purchased the entire property and MacDiarmid moved to Brownsbank Cottage, Candymill, by Biggar, his home for the remainder of his life.
[4] McLellan's play *The Changeling* (1938, printed 1950) was produced by the Paisley Old Grammarians in the Community Drama Association Festival and won the McKemmie Trophy in the Scottish finals.
[5] Robert McLellan, *Mary Stewart* (1951).

TO WILLIAM MONTGOMERIE
NLS

Dungavel,
By Strathaven,
Lanarkshire.
26/9/50

Dear Wm. Montgomerie,

Many thanks for your letter of 23rd inst. I have pleasure in giving you permission to print 'Crowdieknowe'.[1] The copyright is my own and you do not require to write any publisher for permission.

Yes. I was just getting down to writing a lot more Scots Lyrics, when the sale of this estate and the necessity of packing up and getting ready to move to another house if and when I can get one forced me to suspend my work. I do not know when it will be possible for me to resume it yet. In any case I have to be very careful and very sure now. These new lyrics must carry forward my work from the point reached in the best of my early lyrics. I feel that unless really substantive work of this kind can be done soon either by myself or some other the whole Movement is going to peter out. I will be glad to send you a few of these new poems to read as soon as I am ready to release them.

I am looking forward eagerly to the *Scots Chronicle* and hope it will have great success.

With kindest regards and best wishes to Mrs Montgomerie and yourself.

Yours sincerely,
C. M. Grieve.

---

[1] In 1950 the poet William Montgomerie decided to retitle the *Burns Chronicle*, which he then edited, the *Scots Chronicle* and devote it to Scottish poetry in general rather than Burns in particular. 'Crowdieknowe' was included in the *Scots Chronicle* of 1951 after which the title *Burns Chronicle* was restored.

TO KENNETH BUTHLAY[1]

Brownsbank,
by Biggar.
4/3/53

Dear Kenneth,

I am sorry to have been so long in acknowledging your last letter. This is only a brief note even yet, but I'll write you fully in a day or two now. Only part of the 'Ode to All Rebels' appeared in *Stony Limits*; the whole thing (or at least one complete version of it) was published in two instalments in successive issues of *The Voice of Scotland*. But that version is not what I'd now have taken as the final one. I am rooting out my MSS of it and will make a copy and let you have it very soon.

I hope by the time this reaches you you'll have received a galley proof of Daiches's preface for the new edition of the *Drunk Man*. The printer promised it for yesterday and I asked my son, who is in Glasgow, to send you a copy as soon as it is available.

To go into the matter fully is more than I can manage in this letter, but the reason why Doughty influenced me so greatly[2] is 1/ that I think English poetry has been on the wrong lines for centuries and that Doughty's attitude to language indicated the proper corrective. 2/ that I have always wanted to resume our great Gaelic heritage and have always had it in mind that the need to penetrate the crust that has formed during these centuries and get down to our real foundation has teased in vain the minds of a whole succession of great poets, all of whom have thought of essaying epics on the subject but for one reason or another found the thing too difficult. Milton, Blake, Matthew Arnold. And our Scottish-Latin poet George Buchanan. Doughty was made of sterner stuff and penetrated deeper, and achieved more towards that common objective, than all of them. The Irish literary Renaissance people only tinkered with the fringes; the whole Celtic Twilight business was a dodging of the issue.

3/ I have always felt that the resumption and redevelopment of Scots as a literary medium was only a stage in that return to our Gaelic background which alone would enable us to conceive and achieve major work.

[1] Kenneth Buthlay is author of *Hugh MacDiarmid* (Edinburgh 1964) and editor of *The Uncanny Scot* (London 1968), a selection of MacDiarmid's prose.
[2] MacDiarmid's admiration for Doughty is expresssed in his *Charles Doughty and the Need for Heroic Poetry* (St Andrews 1936), a reprint of an article published in *The Modern Scot*, Vol 6, No 4, January 1936.

4/Doughty had to travel to Arabia and elsewhere to recover the genius of the English language; Yeats and other Irish poets went to Scandinavia (the Eddas) and then to India with a view towards recovering the master-key – I have accompanied all of them in all these travels and possessed myself of all they found and even that is far too little for the purpose – but via Scots rather than English I am sure I have had an instrument that has enabled me to get far nearer to the goal – and although time is going on I believe I will still be able to do a very great deal towards consummating all these efforts.

5/ I do not suggest that when I read all Doughty's poems in the early years of the century I was immediately seized with their full significance in this sense, but I certainly realized at once that I found in them a clue to the most essential if as yet quite unformulated purpose of my spirit.

6/ As you know I have been silent and comparatively unproductive for a good few years now, but I have not been idle and I have been pursuing the purpose of which these statements give you only the faintest adumbration unceasingly all the time, and I have now a tremendous programme of poetry in hand which I hope will carry the whole complex process into the sunlight of achieved poetry ere long.

7/ With all due modesty I must admit that I agree entirely with the summary you give of the position in regard to Scots poetry since Burns and you sum the whole thing up when you say: 'But yours is a highly individual achievement, and it will need big talents to digest it, let alone develop it, in Scots.' What I have had to do for several years past is to ask – not if there was any sign of anybody else who had a clue at all and might develop these big talents: there isn't, and, on the law of averages, isn't, I think, likely to be; but whether I myself could not do it and carry the whole business a good many stages further (however destitute I might be, like Melchizidec, of either progenitors or progeny in such a matter!). And now at last I think I can – and that if I can't it is extremely unlikely that anyone else will. We'll see – within the next year at most. I think I have all the strings in my hand now. And believe me I am not boasting – it is far too big and difficult a task to contemplate except with humility and devotion.

You will understand that the big programme of poetry I speak of will be in Scots – and not like the great bulk of what I have written in recent years, in English or a multi-linguistic medium.

I wish you were within reach to talk to on all this business and hope that'll come ere long yet: but I must stop now. The only other thing I mustn't forget is that I am sorry I must have misled you re the *Rural Reform*[3] book – the Fabian Society suggestion on the back of the form I return herewith is correct.

All the best to Sheila and yourself.

Yours,
Chris.

TO EDWARD ARMSTRONG[1]
AEDC

Brownsbank,
Candymill,
Biggar,
Lanarkshire.
28/3/63

Edward Armstrong, Esq.,
Town Clerk,
Langholm,
Dumfriesshire.

Dear Sir:-

I see from one of the Sunday papers[2] that the suggestion having been made that I should receive the Freedom of the Burgh of Langholm, the Town Council went into Committee to discuss the matter and decided not to do anything about it in the meantime. Baillie Murray is reported as saying that that did not preclude the matter being raised later.

I write because it would be a pity if the time of these gentlemen were wasted in further fruitless discussion. Please inform your Council that if at any future time they should offer me the Freedom I

[3] MacDiarmid contributed to the Fabian Research Committee's publication *The Rural Problem* (1913).
[1] Edward Armstrong, the Town Clerk of Langholm, read this letter to Langholm Town Council on 11 April 1963 as the minutes record: 'The Town Clerk was instructed to confirm the opinion he had expressed when acknowledging the letter that Dr Grieve's wishes would be respected.'
[2] *The Sunday Express*, of 20 January 1963, carried an article by James Wightman headed 'Honour Hugh MacDiarmid – The Old Bitterness Flares Up'.

will refuse it, and will also refuse any other public recognition offered
to me by Langholm.

> Yours sincerely,
> Christopher Murray Grieve.

TO FORBES MACGREGOR[1]
NLS

> Brownsbank
> Candymill
> Biggar
> Lanarkshire
> 12/2/64

Forbes Macgregor,
Author of *The Gowks of Mowdieknowes*.[2]

Dear Sir (or Sirs – as I am told the pseudonym 'Forbes Macgregor'
covers two authors):-

My attention has just been called to your booklet *The Gowks of
Mowdieknowes*. I do not know any reason why you should get away
with your stupid vituperation and lying about a writer – or number
of writers – whose latchets you are unfit to tie, and I certainly do not
intend to let you off. I will make it my business forthwith to find out

[1] Forbes Macgregor. Born in Edinburgh in 1904 he was educated at Broughton
Higher Grade and taught in Edinburgh for forty-one years, ending his teaching
career as headmaster of South Morningside School. He has published many
collections of humorous poems in the vernacular.
[2] *The Gowks of Mowdieknowes: A Study of Literary Lunacy* (Edinburgh 1963) is
Macgregor's satire on the Scottish Literary Renaissance whose leader is
identified as Kirsty MacGrumphy (an allusion to Grieve's celebrated
pseudonym and the fact that as a boy in Langholm he was known as Kirsty). As
presented in MacGregor's book MacGrumphy is a megalomaniacal opportunist:
'With that naive cunning, *simplicitas munditiis*, or what you will, which is so often
the greater part of the Scotch village idiot's stock-in-trade, young MacGrumphy
early realised with what facility he could obtain that adulation his soul thirsted
for. But he was rather at a loss to find the Pierian springs at which he first must
needs fill his cracked jug. However, by perusing one or two obsolete volumes of
Geography, or Cosmography, History and Astronomy, which the scientific
world had finished referring to for the best part of four generations, the stripling
MacGrumphy, like that other stripling of destiny before him, readily had to his
hand the equivalent of the five smooth stones from the brook, wherewith to
conquer the Goliath of popular incredulence.' (*The Gowks of Mowdieknowes*, p. 14)

precisely who you are, and then if as I am told you are a school teacher I will call a meeting of the parents of the pupils of any school in which you may be still teaching (a job for which you are obviously monstrously unfit), and at the same time I will issue a pamphlet dealing faithfully with your booklet and distribute that to these parents and to the press and others. These steps will ensure publicity in the national press.[3]

Yours sincerely,
Hugh MacDiarmid

TO P. H. BUTTER[1]

Brownsbank,
Biggar,
Lanarkshire.
22/12/66

Professor Butter,
Department of English,
The University,
Glasgow.

Dear Professor Butter,

It is very good of you to send me the copy of your book on Edwin Muir. It may seem a poor return that I can only say, in the Pauline words, 'Almost thou persuadest me'. I have read the whole book several times. I do not think the case for Muir could have been better put but one speaks of a man as one finds him. I was pleased with the way you dealt with his opposition in *Scott and Scotland* to the revival of Scots for literary purposes. He himself of course recanted in part at least but that did not get the same publicity as his attack. I do not

---

[3] MacDiarmid decided to forget the matter though he did not forgive, as Forbes Macgregor explained in a letter of 17 September 1982: 'MacDiarmid never forgave me and even when I wrote and had published by *Akros* a long essay on Scottish education agreeing with all MacDiarmid's principles, he would not read it because I was the author; so said Duncan Glen to me.'

[1] P. H. Butter, Professor of English at Glasgow University, has published a short monograph *Edwin Muir* (Edinburgh 1962) and – the book MacDiarmid discusses – *Edwin Muir: Man and Poet* (1966).

however think it is the case that my ceasing to write in Scots did more harm to the movement than Muir's attack. Some of the young poets who were trying to write in Scots may have been discouraged – but they did not matter in any case. The few who could use the medium have not been discouraged – T. S. Law, Robert Garioch, Alastair Mackie. I know of no others of whom it is of any consequence whether they have or have not continued their efforts. I myself have not discontinued writing in Scots. Like Heine, at a given stage, I found it necessary to abjure lyrics – try to 'break up the tonality of the lyric' and import all manner of new material. That took Heine years of effort but his later poetry, in which he finally succeeded, never of course achieved anything like the tremendous acclaim of his early lyrics. I think the parallel is exact. But I think I too have now succeeded and that the detour represented by my long poems in English has now paid off. Certainly several of my poems in Scots not yet published in volume form seem to me among the best things I have done. They are not short lyrics like my early work, but poems of 50 to 100 lines or so. I hope to publish a volume of them next year (1967).

Apart from the merits of the argument, the trouble was that Muir had been privy to what F. G. Scott and I were doing and had never voiced any disagreement with our aims. So his sudden attack in *Scott and Scotland* was a stab-in-the-back. I have said so, and argued against Muir, in various quarters but I have not, as you suggest, pursued him vindictively ever since.[2] On the contrary. I have not dealt with the matter – and with Muir – fully anywhere. But I felt I must do so now. I cannot agree that he is a good, let alone an important, poet. I do not believe at all from my knowledge of him in his professed Christianity or his near saint-hood of character. On the contrary I do not believe he had any intellectual integrity at all. I cannot exemplify my reasons here, but if I write a long essay as I now intend to do, that will be easy enough. The trouble with Muir in my acquaintance with him is that one simply couldn't get through to him at all – Willa always answered for him. It was her stated intention to develop him into a successful little literary gentleman – and she succeeded, and he acquiesced in the process. It was a process that involved many very dubious proceedings. I remember how I introduced the Muirs to Professor Sir Herbert Grierson – and my disgust at the way they immediately leeched on to him. And that was by no means a solitary case within my knowledge of a very adroit trimming of sails to meet a favourable breeze. Also, it is just not true

2 In fact MacDiarmid 'dealt with' Muir in the introduction to *The Golden Treasury of Scottish Poetry* (London 1940) and in *Lucky Poet* (London 1943). See also his open letter to J. H. Whyte on pp. 851–4.

that they were desperately hard up. Poverty is a relative thing. They never knew the kind of hardship I underwent at all. And it was at a time of particular difficulty for me (as they knew) that *Scott and Scotland* appeared, incidentally rubbing salt into the wound by the fact that the book in question was published in a series initiated and jointly edited by 'Lewis Grassic Gibbon' and myself.

There is a great deal in your book of great interest to me – and of new information – and despite all I say about my own attitude to Muir and to his poetry I have read it with great interest and will think very carefully over the whole matter before I write on him (and if I do it won't be on the subject of the use of Scots – but on his poetry which I think is thoroughly bad and reactionary).

You will understand I have felt it necessary to be quite frank in this letter. Yet I am truly grateful to you for sending to me (and inscribing) the book and I will be very pleased to see you again at the OUP cocktail party.

With renewed thanks and best wishes for health and happiness in 1967.

Yours sincerely,
Christopher Grieve.

TO IAIN CRICHTON SMITH[1]
NLS   Brownsbank,
TS   Biggar,
                                Lanarkshire.
                             2nd July 1967

Dear Iain Crichton Smith,

Duncan Glen has sent me a copy of your *Golden Lyric* essay on my work, admirably printed and produced (but not alas free of misprints!), and I feel I must write and thank you very sincerely although I do not agree at all with most of your statements. What I think I must do now (in appreciation of the concern you have devoted to my work) is to write an essay in which I deal with all your

---

[1] Iain Crichton Smith's *The Golden Lyric: An Essay on the Poetry of Hugh MacDiarmid* (1967) contends that MacDiarmid's early lyrics are the most achieved expressions of his poetic vision.

points seriatim, and I am confident that in such an essay I can prove that there is a higher synthesis in which all the apparent (and on a certain level, real) contradictions and inconsistencies in my work can be resolved – showing indeed as I said in *Lucky Poet* that they are all essential elements in a *summa* I have not yet furnished.

However, that can't of course be done off the cuff, and I am desperately busy and will remain so for the next three months, till all the fuss about my 75th birthday is past – if I survive it!

There is only one point, however. You use the terms 'appalling apartness' and 'conscious loneliness' and say that in certain poems a 'certain inhumanity emerges'. That is, of course, perfectly true. But I think David Daiches in the current *Literary Review* puts the matter better when he says: 'The more I read and reread him the more convinced I am that basically he is a rather terrifying kind of mystic (I know he dislikes the word, but I can only express the matter as I see it) who seeks after a truth too uncomfortable for ordinary vision, a truth to which the normal categories of argument may well be irrelevant. I think that this is a clue to his splendid early lyrics, too.'

Calling me 'A Hero For Our Time', Denis McWilliams in the University of Kent magazine, justifies the shy-making title, by saying 'True to his first motto, he must be one of the few poets to have faced not formal but architectonic problems' and argues as follows: 'MacDiarmid's "Diamond Body" is partly an expression of his understanding of the intuitive process present in his earlier poetry. So differentiation and then resolution is a means to an understanding of what was initially intuitively "clear". The later poetry needs this understanding, for MacDiarmid uses it. He differentiates between the ways of understanding experience as a method of writing. He uses on the one hand the "mechanistic" factual precision of the experience of the intellect; on the other he uses intuition and a feeling for the vitality of life. . . . The later poetry reaches an overt synthesis of the two responses to experience.'

There will be a great deal of writing about my poetry from all sorts of angles in the next few weeks and my attitude is simply 'Let the debate continue'. I am not really concerned that many people do not think me 'a Communist in any ordinary sense of the word'! They are hopelessly mistaken. So are all those who think Communism is concerned with 'ordinary humanity'. . . . least of all with humanitarianism. They forget that our objective is 'to change human nature'. You are perfectly correct when you say I have no more use for the masses than they have for me. There is scarcely anything that appeals to any considerable body of people that I have anything other than contempt for.

Finally I say in the prefatory note to my new volume of poems (due out almost immediately): 'It is believed in some quarters that in recent years I have ceased to write in the aggrandised Scots in which I wrote my early lyrics in the 'Twenties. The fact is that after the success of these, I, like Heine after the success of his lyrics, found (as the late Professor Laura Hofrichter brings out so convincingly in her book on the subject) I could no longer go on with that sort of thing but required to break up the unity of the lyric and introduce new material of various kinds on different levels of significance. It took Heine years of agonised effort to find the new form he needed, and his later work, in which he did find it, never won a measure of esteem like that secured in his early work. So it is in my case.'

With renewed thanks and best wishes, and the hope that we may meet one of these days and talk matters out.

> Yours,
> Christopher Grieve.

TO ANTHONY ROSS[1]

> Brownsbank,
> Biggar,
> Lanarkshire.
> 'Phone – Skirling –
> Biggar 55.
> 22/9/67

Rev Anthony Ross OP.

Dear Father Ross,

Many thanks for your letter of 20th inst. re *Scottish International*, and inviting me to become one of the five trustees. I note that Alex Gibson of the SNO[2] is also being invited to be one of the trustees.

You say: '*When you have more information about what is aimed* at we hope you will honour us by becoming one of the five trustees.' I will

---

[1] Father Anthony Ross (who entered the Dominican Order in 1939 and was ordained a priest in 1945) was RC chaplain to Edinburgh University. He was one of the leading figures associated with the magazine *Scottish International* (1968–74).

[2] Sir Alexander Gibson, Principal Conductor of the Scottish National Orchestra.

certainly need a great deal more information. Pending that, please regard this reply as merely provisional. My suspicions may not be well founded but I think it necessary to be quite frank and to say that I regard the whole matter with the gravest suspicion.

I have devoted many years to seek to overcome the inability of the academic authorities and literary circles in many countries to recognise that Scotland is a separate and very different country from England, that Scotland has an independent literary tradition at odds in many vital respects with the English tradition – and that it has always been, and remains, the aim of the latter to eliminate the former and assimilate Scottish Standards completely to English. Government agencies like the Arts Council, the British Council, British consulates, etc. have pursued this policy and been largely responsible for the general identification abroad of what is merely English as British, and these agencies have actively endeavoured to frustrate my efforts to give foreign countries a true sense of Scotland's difference, of the need for Scotland to build on its own separate traditions without regard to England, and in particular to revive our native languages, Scots and Gaelic.

This propaganda of mine has been increasingly successful. I have now established innumerable contacts in many countries. This has accelerated greatly in the last year or two – to such an extent that I have no doubt the English are now determined to counter or at least abate my influence, and that is at least one of the reasons for the present manoeuvre to establish *Scottish International*.

Organs committed to the aims and objects of the 'Scottish Renaissance' never had any hope of financial support from the Arts Council or other bodies. Why is the Establishment ready now to help *Scottish International* if not just because it is designed to betray the aims of the Scottish Renaissance? It is significant that two of the editors – Robert Tait and Edwin Morgan – have not only never taken any active part in Scottish Nationalist developments either literary or political, and are associated with very questionable international developments like 'concrete poetry' and other pro-Beatnik and 'with it' tendencies. Nor are either of these gentlemen of sufficient weight as writers themselves to justify their appointment as editors unless the object is to serve undeclared ends at complete variance with the proclaimed purpose.

I think you will agree that I cannot lend my name and influence to a project which does not accept as of prime importance the encouragement of Scots and Gaelic, the necessity of Scottish Independence, and the recognition that in contradistinction to the situation in England a deep-seated Radicalism is the chief, and an

872

irreversible, element of the Scottish political tradition and a prime requirement of Scottish conditions today and henceforth.

Unless therefore I can be assured that these matters are all safeguarded in a way in keeping with the programme I have pursued for the past half-century I am not only unable to be associated with the project in any way but will be obliged to expose its real aims and to oppose its development in every way I can.

Also, I note you stress that the new organ is designed to be essentially encouraging to the under thirties. Personally I have always sought to encourage and help new Scottish writers no matter of what age. But I view with deep suspicion the stress laid on the young. There are always thousands of literary aspirants, not one per cent of them ever come to anything of consequence, and the effect of encouraging young writers generally is simply to ham-string the development with an ever-heavier weight of mediocrity. I am quite opposed to the way in which the Arts Council's bursaries for writers operates. I am sure no good can come of it, and certainly the objectives for Scotland with which I am mainly concerned cannot be served in this way.

Ever since you gave the memorable lecture on my poetry I have hoped we might meet again and get to know each other better. I am therefore all the more sorry to have to give a reply to your letter which may seem churlish and unhelpful. But on reflection I am sure you will agree that I have no option, and that the tenor of my letter in no way runs counter to my high regard and good wishes for yourself.

> Yours sincerely,
> Christopher Grieve.

TO CHARLES LAHR[1]
ULL

> Brownsbank,
> Biggar,
> Lanarkshire, Scotland.
> 2/3/68

Charles Lahr, Esq.

Dear Charles,

Glad to hear from you, and many thanks for sending me the

---

[1] Charles Lahr was a bookseller and friend MacDiarmid occasionally met in London.

Newsletter with the article on Scottish Nationalism and Fascism. It is of course nonsense. The 1320 Club is a group of people to conduct research into various aspects of Scottish economy, culture, etc. with a view to having these thoroughly studied and the results available when, and if, Scottish Independence is secured. The people concerned are competent and willing to carry out such researches and make them available to the public at large. Like all clubs the membership is limited and not open to everybody. So it is attacked as anti-democratic, elitist, and so on. As with other struggles against Imperialism, I do not believe that the Westminster Parliament will grant Scotland any useful measure of Self-Government no matter how strong the popular demand may be. Consequently contingency planning must include measures in case armed struggle is forced upon us. The popular demand is certainly very great. The Scottish National Party has over 100,000 paid-up members and is now the strongest political party in Scotland, able financially and determined to contest every seat at the next General Election. But in the opinion of myself and the 1320 Club it lacks leadership. The officials are reactionaries, poudjadists, and complete Philistines. Their appeal is wholly on the emotional plane. What we want to do is to give them effective intellectual backing. Of course this implies that we of the 1320 are better equipped intellectually (as we are) and the National Party resents being regarded as mainly morons (which they are).

Ian MacCalman whoever he is is ill-informed. He says, for example, that I am no longer a member of the Communist Party. I am, of course.

However the issue is hotting up and the next year or two will see big developments.

We are very sorry indeed to hear that Esther is in such a bad way. Please give her our kindest regards. Her condition must make things very difficult for you and Donagh. It is distressing that P. should be so crippled by rheumatism – especially as she has no one to help her. Give her our love and best wishes.

I don't know when I'll be in London again. I had a spell in hospital recently with a bad dose of Asian flu, but thorough examination showed that my general condition (heart, lungs, etc.) was O.K. However my doctors insisted that I should reduce my public speaking and other activities, particularly if they involve travelling, to a minimum, and so I have had to refuse all sorts of requests (including one from Cambridge, which would have meant a night or so in London).

Valda is in good form tho' she racked her back some time ago and that – and a bad knee – still troubles her.

874

However if I do get to London be sure I will let you know and make a point of seeing you.

Yours as always.
Chris.

TO GEOFFREY ELBORN
EUL
Brownsbank,
Biggar,
Lanarkshire.
7/7/68

Geoffrey Elborn, Esq.

Dear Mr Elborn,

Many thanks for your very kind letter. I have had pleasure in inscribing your copy of Buthlay's book[1] with 'The Little White Rose of Scotland'.

I am afraid I cannot at the moment give you my assessment of Yeats and Eliot. I was friendly with both of them but not with many of their ideas which were of a pro-Fascist character. I believe that owing to this their reputations will decline – particularly Eliot's (as a poet – not as a critic where his work has been, and will continue to be, enormously influential). Yeats on the contrary will, I feel sure, continue to hold his place as the greatest poet of his period in the English language, but mainly by virtue of his later work. His early 'Celtic Twilight' poetry has already been almost wholly discounted.

I am very sorry I can't go into this matter more fully, I am really desperately busy and have four or five books coming out shortly and am consequently overwhelmed with proofs, correspondence, etc. But you can read what I say of Yeats and Eliot in my last autobiographical book *The Company I've Kept*.

With renewed thanks and best wishes.

Yours sincerely,
Christopher Grieve
('Hugh MacDiarmid')

[1] Kenneth Buthlay, *Hugh MacDiarmid* (1964).

TO RORY WATSON[1]

Brownsbank,
Biggar,
Lanarkshire
20/12/71

Dear Dr Rory Watson,

I should have written you ere this to thank your wife and you for your kindness when I was in Stirling. But in addition to a post-operation lack of energy (and no small sub-structure of natural laziness) I have been reading an enormous volume – your thesis on the Cencrastus element in my work, which Norman MacCaig has lent me. It is a splendid piece of work and I am torn between admiration for it and remorse at having entailed so great a labour of exegesis on a friend.

Norman, I think, indicated that there was some likelihood of it, or part of it, being published in the ordinary way; and in the absence in all the vast amount of writing that has been devoted to me of any worth-while criticism at all I certainly hope so.

I do not know how many copies you had done or what libraries copies have to be lodged in. But if there is a copy still available I'd love to have it or, better still, to buy one.

I am not going to make any detailed comment, but when you point out the paucity of references to Shestov[2] in my work despite the fact that I acclaim him as my master, I would point out in return that poems like 'The Impossible Song' and parts of 'Ode to All Rebels' are pure Shestov. Also note might be taken of the fact that subsequent to my concern with Dostoevski and Shestov and Jaspers, Heidegger, and Kierkegaard, I state that I found a subtler dialectic in some of the Indian materialist philosophers and particularly in Sankara and the *Adviata* – and not at all of course in any of the gurus Aldous Huxley and many American cultists draw upon.[3]

---

[1] Roderick ('Rory') Watson, born in Aberdeen in 1943, did his postgraduate thesis, at Cambridge, on 'A Critical Study of the Cencrastus Theme in the Poetry of Hugh MacDiarmid'. Since 1971 Watson has taught at the University of Stirling.

[2] MacDiarmid referred to Leo Chestov as 'my favourite philosopher' (LP, p. 28) and acclaimed 'my great master, Shestov' (745).

[3] In 'The Meeting of the East and West', a section of *In Memoriam James Joyce* – which is part of the *Mature Art* project – MacDiarmid writes:
Fichte in his essay 'Anweisung zu einem seligen Leben'
Comes near to the Adviata doctrine most amazingly
– So much so that Otto has even attempted to give
Whole passages of Fichte in the language of Shankara. (854)

With every kind regard and renewed thanks, to your wife, and Christopher, and you.

Yours,
Christopher Grieve.

TO CHARLES NICOLL[1]
EUL
Brownsbank,
Biggar,
Lanarkshire.
8/1/73

Charles Nicoll, Esq.

Dear Mr Nicoll,

Many thanks for your letter, and the poem attached.[2] The latter certainly hits off quite accurately the position in which I found myself in Mechan's, and I don't know what would have happened if you had not saved my bacon by taking me on in the Copper Shell Band section.

It is true that I had – or could have – little in common with most of

[1] Charles Nicoll was an engineer who worked in Mechan's Engineering Company in Scotstoun, Glasgow, when MacDiarmid was employed as a precision fitter during the Second World War after being conscripted in 1941. In a letter to Kulgin Duval (in the Grieve Archive of Edinburgh University Library) Nicoll wrote: 'Christopher was drafted into the department where gun shields were being made. Work in this department meant a lot of heavy filing. A type of work for which Christopher was physically unsuited. Also he was unfortunate enough to have a most inconsiderate foreman and he had little or no help from his fellow workers. His life in this department was a misery. However, relief, to some extent, was at hand when he was transferred to the copper shell department, which was under my charge. I made it as easy as possible for him by making his main job that of checking and keeping count of all incoming and outgoing material to and from the department.'
[2] In an undated letter Nicoll sent MacDiarmid a poem called 'McDiarmid' which began
>   They treated ye wi scant respect,
>   The workers o' the Clyde.
>   Their tools ye didna understaund,
>   An' few wad, willin', guide
>   The haund that, skillfu', moved the pen
>   In richtfu' place, denied.

877

the workers, and they in turn had no understanding of or interest in the things that really concern me. Nevertheless it was a valuable experience and on the whole, thanks largely to you, I enjoyed it.

I am still incredibly busy. Now that I have passed the 80 mark I am trying to ease off, but circumstances won't let me.

We had a quiet Christmas with our son, daughter-in-law, and grandsons in Glasgow, and they were all here over New Year. A family party is about as much now as we want. But of course we still get a lot of visitors.

We hope you had a happy Christmas too, and that 1973 may be a good and prosperous New Year for you.

> Yours,
> Christopher Grieve.

TO RUTH McQUILLAN[1]
NLS

Brownsbank,
Biggar.
30/4/73

Dear Miss MacQuillan,

Many thanks for your long and most interesting letter. I had no idea that your Oral would be such (it seems to me) a gruelling experience. I can only hope that the examiners give you (or recommend) the best degree in their power. I am not sure whether PhD or M Litt. ranks best. I note what you say about Holloway's treatment of Rory Watson, but I don't know what that was – i.e. how cruel or disgraceful, etc. it was.[2]

With regard to your own experience Erskine-Hill while here – and in Cambridge – was very genial. I did not discuss my Communism

[1] Ruth McQuillan submitted a thesis on Hugh MacDiarmid to Cambridge University at the end of 1972; it was accepted in April following an 'Oral' (or viva).

[2] Rory Watson, the Scottish poet and critic, was at Cambridge doing a PhD on the *Cencrastus* theme in MacDiarmid's poetry. His recollection is that John Holloway, of Queen's College, had many demands on his time but there was nothing 'cruel or disgraceful' in his approach. Holloway, in fact, is an admirer of MacDiarmid's work.

with him, or, indeed, there was no concentration of enquiry or response about my Langholm beginnings or how these had influenced my subsequent development either in politics or as a politician.[3] I can't understand his insistence with you that Langholm must have determined me along the Communist Line, and that insistence (or what seems to me largely irrelevant so far as your thesis is concerned) savours to me of a bit of witch-hunting or on Erskine-Hill's part of a rabid anti-Communism.

I might, I realise, have gone into the matter rather more fully with you. I had completely forgotten, and have now no recollection whatever, of the Prize-Giving with the young Buccleuch ladies.[4] But I was not wrong in saying that the officiating of such people in public matters would have been resented. That this solitary instance appears to show that it was occasionally accepted in no way invalidates my statement. Langholm people then were intensely radical, republican, and anti-English. My father was a trade-unionist, a co-operator, and a radical.

But it must be remembered I was even then an omnivorous reader. My instincts always propelled me to the Left extreme. When I was 16 in Edinburgh I joined the ILP and the University Fabian Society. These bodies were at that time much more revolutionary than they became later. We all read a great deal. I was familiarised then with Anarchism and Marxism, and read not only the *Labour Leader* and the *Clarion* and the Glasgow *Forward* but other more extreme organs like *Justice*.

Then I went to Wales to run a paper (the *Monmouthshire Labour News*) for the South Wales Miners Federation, and while there I associated not only with Right-Wingers like Stanton of Aberdare and other Welsh Labour MPs but with the Communist Tom Mann, and more important still with many young Welsh students at Ruskin College and these were of course au fait with Marxist doctrines.

Even in Edinburgh prior to that there were not only the ILP but branches of the SDF and SLP and the memory of James Connolly

---

[3] In a letter, of 8 July 1983 to the present editor, Ruth McQuillan writes; 'Dr Howard Erskine-Hill, then of Jesus College, was my Internal Examiner [and] thought there must have been something in the social and cultural environment of Langholm which had predisposed the poet to Communism. I disagreed. Dr. Erskine-Hill had entertained the Grieves in Cambridge and visited them in Scotland. There was a mutual respect and liking between them. Not only is Dr Erskine-Hill certainly not a "rabid anti-Communist": I don't for one moment believe Dr Grieve thought he was!'

[4] 'The young Buccleuch ladies must have been daughters of the Duke of Buccleuch who were among those invited to distribute prizes at Langholm Academy.' Ruth McQuillan, letter of 8 July 1983.

was still potent.[5]

I do not know if you saw the tribute paid to me on my 80th birthday by the Communist Party of Great Britain. It was signed by John Gollan, General Secretary of the Party, and unanimously endorsed by the whole Executive. I had letters in similar terms from Russia, East Germany, Czecho-Slovakia, and Poland. So my position as a Communist is very widely understood and it is only British commentators who are amateurs in the matter who hold that if I am a Communist I am a very unorthodox one.

So there was a long history of moving towards actual membership of the Party before I actually joined it.

I spoke at Foyle's Lunch in the Dorchester on Philip Larkin's *Oxford Book of 20th Century English Verse*. But I spoke sarcastically and a stupid (or unscrupulous) *Daily Express* reporter took what I said au pied de la lettre, and published me as having berated Larkin for leaving out Mary Wilson[6] whom (he said) I regarded as the very cream of contemporary verse in the English language! Imagine it! I haven't bothered to protest at the way he interpreted my remarks as the very opposite of what I said and think.

Valda and I are going to Holland on 15th June and we'll be in London again towards the end of June when I'm giving a poetry reading in the Festival Hall.

I hope all's well with you and that your labours will be well rewarded soon – not only in the sort of job you secure, but also in your emergence with the sacred Circle of Doctors.

Valda joins me in every kind regard.

Yours,
Christopher Grieve.

[5] The SDF is the Social Democratic Federation; the SLP is the Scottish Labour Party.
[6] Mary Wilson, wife of the former Prime Minister Harold Wilson, had considerable popularity with her collections of her own poems.

TO WILLIAM OXLEY[1]

Brownsbank,
Biggar,
Lanarkshire.
Scotland.
6/9/73

Wm. Oxley, Esq.

Dear Mr Oxley,

Many thanks for your letter of 4th inst. I am glad you are so appreciative of my poem, 'The Divided Bird' in *Stand*.[2] I think it is one of the most nearly successful attempts to write the kind of poetry I want in English I have so far succeeded in writing, but I observed to my wife when I showed it to her that I doubted if any one of my contemporaries in Scotland – Edwin Morgan, Norman McCaig, Iain Crichton Smith etc. – could make head or tail of it or even make any intelligent comment on it.

The Yellow Rose of Space and Time (which are aspects of the same thing, of course) is designated as Yellow because 1/ their life depends on the Sun, 2/ Yellow is forsaken – and I am positing the condition of dispensing with such conventional things. What you say about Pound and the whole Modernist movement is, of course, what is as always in my mind, when I write 'Craftsman-ship not for its own sake now, etc'.

My abandonment of so much of the furniture of poetry – strict metres, stanza forms, etc. – and introduction of all sorts of scient-ific and other material commonly regarded as non-poetical – is due to my assumption of the same position, and carried further in the portion about Erika Storm, Webern, H. E. Apostel, etc., since my position in regard to poetry is paralleled by my preference in music for atonalism, the mathematical music of Berg and others. And I have the same attitude to such music on that in the Italien-isher Liederbuch as I have to most Victorian or Georgian verse.

And now business matters. The Toftcombs Hotel, in reply to Valda's phone just now, assures us that while they have not written you your booking there for 12th–13th October is O.K. I am worried, however, about the Newcastle Festival – I have as you know a reading there on 14th but I am afraid I'll have to go down to Newcastle on the 13th. The last bus from Edinburgh on

[1] William Oxley, the poet, was born in Manchester in 1939 and has edited several literary magazines including *Littack*.
[2] MacDiarmid's poem 'The Divided Bird' (712–20) was included in *A Kist of Whistles* (Glasgow 1947) and reprinted in *Stand* Vol 14, No 4, 1973.

Friday is at 9.35 from St Andrew's Square bus station, Edinburgh.
I enjoyed Anthony Johnson's[3] visit very much.
Every kind regard to your wife and yourself.

                              Yours,
                              Christopher Grieve.

P.S. I have engagements Mermaid Theatre, London on 25th Nov.,
Ewell (Surrey) on 26th, with Greater London Arts Association to
record for Dial-a-Poem service on 27th and to talk to the Union
Society at Oxford that (27th)night.

TO GORDON WRIGHT[1]
EUL   Brownsbank,
                                            by Biggar.
                                            7/1/77

Dear Gordon Wright,

   Many thanks for photostat of Compton Mackenzie's address in
Scots Independent,[2] and your suggested passage for inclusion in the
biography. I have no objection to what you propose, but the matter
of the alleged plagiarism of the 'Little White Rose of Scotland'
ascribed in Maurice Lindsay's anthology[3] to Compton is *sub judice*
and any reference to it must be made with great caution. Personally I

---

[3] Anthony Johnson, Professor of English at the University of Pisa. *Littack* Vol 2,
No 2, contains an interview with MacDiarmid based on conversations
conducted by Oxley and Johnson.

[1] Gordon Wright is a photographer, publisher and author of *MacDiarmid: An
Illustrated Biography* (Edinburgh 1977).

[2] In his MacDiarmid biography, Gordon Wright quotes – from the December
1929 issue of *The Scots Independent* – Compton Mackenzie's broadcast of 5
November 1929 in which he used the following words: 'You know our wild Scots
rose? it is white, and small, and prickly, and possesses a sharp sweet scent which
makes the heart ache.' When MacDiarmid included 'The Little White Rose'
(461) in his anthology of *Living Scottish Poets* (London 1931) he footnoted the title
'With acknowledgements to Compton Mackenzie' and attributed the poem to
Anon. In *Stony Limits* (London 1934) the poem appeared under his own name.

[3] Maurice Lindsay's *Modern Scottish Poetry: An Anthology of the Scottish Renaissance
1925–1975* (1976) begins by citing 'The Little White Rose' as the work of Sir
Compton Mackenzie.

prefer no reference to be made at all, since I do not think the general public has any right to be informed at all. If any of them suspect plagiarism they are welcome – but if they voice or publish any suspicion they render themselves liable to prosecution. Maurice Lindsay has now agreed that the poem is mine, and not Compton's and his publishers, The Carcanet Press, have agreed to insert an erratum in all the copies of the book and to alter the attribution of the poem from Compton to my name. I am not satisfied with this. I am insisting that the poem be removed from the book, and also that all my other poems in the book be removed too. As to the erratum I have forbidden that that should include any explanation whatsoever, and am insisting on an explicit apology from Maurice Lindsay and the publishers for the wrongful attribution. The whole thing is in the hands of the lawyers.

In what you propose to publish you end: 'From these last lines, C.M.G. was inspired to write the following poem.' This should be altered to read: 'From these last lines, CMG was, it has been suggested, inspired to write the following poem (i.e. "The Little White Rose") but it may also be pointed out that other phrases in Sir Compton's address (viz. "We have grafted ourselves upon the rich rose of England. It has flourished on our stock", etc.) express precisely the same thing as is expressed in that section of "A Drunk Man looks at the Thistle", which begins:

> 'I might hae been contentit with the Rose
> Gin I'd had ony reason to suppose – etc.

down to the verse

> 'I might ha' been contentit – ere I saw
> That there were fields on which it couldna draw
> (While strang-er roots ran under't . . . etc.'

The Drunk Man was published in 1926 and enthusiastically reviewed by Compton then, so he was familiar with the passage in question, and his address only appeared in 1929.

I am sorry you've been ill or quarantined with suspicion of chicken pox and trust you are O.K. again now. I've not been well myself and am going into Chalmers Hospital again on 15th inst. for, I expect, another abdominal operation.

We'd a quiet Christmas (in Glasgow) and New Year here, and hope you had a good time too and will have a bright and prosperous 1977.

With all the best from Valda and I.

Yours,
Christopher Grieve.

TO RONALD STEVENSON[1]

Brownsbank,
by Biggar.
5/3/77

Ronald Stevenson, Esq.

Dear Ronald,

Herewith the Cardenal book.[2] I hope my retention of it has not been a trouble to you. There can be no question of refunding the postage. I am only too glad to have had a loan of it. As I think I told you in a previous letter, Cardenal is an absolute find so far as I am concerned. He is like Pound but better than Pound in several quintessential ways.

Thank you also for the script of your talk on F.G.[3] It is excellent. I wish a really big event could be organised to mark the centenary of FG's birth – a concert at which all the best of his songs could be sung by competent singers.

As you know I have been in hospital again and had a third operation. I have to have another on 11th May – which is expected to be the last of the series to finally dispose of the cause of the trouble.

Valda and I were sorry indeed to miss Mr King and you.[4] Hope you – and Marjorie and the children – are all O.K.

With every high regard and good wish.

Yours,
Christopher Grieve.

---

[1] Ronald Stevenson, the Scottish composer and musicologist, was born in 1928. He shared some of MacDiarmid's musical interests – in Sorabji and F. G. Scott for example – and contributed an essay to *MacDiarmid: A Festschrift* (Edinburgh 1962), edited by Kulgin Duval and Sydney Goodsir Smith. Stevenson's best-known work is *Passacaglia on D.S.C.H.* which is published by Oxford University Press and recorded by John Ogdon on the EMI label. He has set many of MacDiarmid's lyrics.

[2] Ernesto Cardenal, *Homage to the American Indians* (1973). Seventeen poems translated by Monique and Carlos Altschul.

[3] 'The Songs of Francis George Scott' by Ronald Stevenson, broadcast on BBC Radio 3, 20 February 1977.

[4] Charles King who taught, as did Stevenson, at Broughton School in the 1950s.

TO WALTER PERRIE[1]

Brownsbank,
Candymill,
by Biggar.
21/7/77

Dear Walter Perrie,

If I do not reply now to your letter of 19th inst. Heaven only knows when I'll manage to do so. Alas I can only reply very inadequately. The reason is that I am still far from well, and must go into hospital again and undergo another operation shortly (probably about 15th August). In the meantime several things prevent my writing much. Firstly my looming 85th birthday means I'm going to be inundated with all sorts of visitors here and there are all sorts of public and private functions arranged to mark the occasion – at hardly any of which I'll be able to be personally present. Secondly I am going away to Langholm for a week on Sunday (24th inst).

Your outlined scheme is certainly on the right lines. But it is so long ago now that I was immersed in the writers you name (Soloviev, Rosanov & others) that I just can't recollect in detail how I came to know their work. One source certainly in Soloviev's case was the *Hibbert Journal*. And of course I had several of his books in English translations. But I was also told about him by ex-Prince D. S. Mirsky, who wrote very appreciatively of him in his two volumes on Russian literature. So far as Shestov and Buber are concerned, I derived most of my knowledge of their work from articles, reviews, etc. in a French Philosophical periodical, of which I had access at the time to a complete file. Rosanov was available in translation by Koteliansky and articles about him appeared in Middleton Murry's *Adelphi*. Buber's books are available in English translations, and I read much of him too in the French periodical mentioned above.

In the Double Number of *Akros* just published Ruth McQuillan has interesting things to say about the source in Soloviev's works on which I was drawing. In this she follows Dr Rory Watson's Cambridge PhD thesis in which he goes into the matter in great detail.

I was of course as you suggest familiar at the time with French, Tarot symbolism, and the Apocalypse of St John – also with Gabriel Marcel and with Berdyaev and of course Kierkegaard.

[1] Walter Perrie, the Scottish poet and critic whose conversation with MacDiarmid on *Metaphysics and Poetry* was published in 1975, wrote to the poet as part of his preparation for a philosophical study of *A Drunk Man Looks at the Thistle*; part of this study has appeared in Perrie's book *Out of Conflict* (1982).

Many thanks for your good wishes for my birthday. I note that you expect to be at the Edinburgh Conference[2] and may see you there – but not at any of the lectures; the only event I expect to be able to attend is the Concert on the Saturday night.

Hope you are in good health and that your various work goes ahead successfully.

With best wishes,

Yours sincerely,
Christopher Grieve.

TO PATRICK CROTTY[1]

Brownsbank
Candymill
by Biggar
Lanarkshire
Scotland
21/11/77

Dear Patrick Crotty,

I am sorry to have been so long in writing you, but I have been having a bad time and have been literally quite unable to write.

The papers given at the Conference[2] will, I understand, be published and I am looking forward to reading yours and others – if the publication is quick enough. For there has been a drastic deterioration of my condition. I had a sixth operation in Chalmers Hospital in Edinburgh a week ago today. Alas! these operations have not been successful. A few weeks ago the chief surgeon told Valda I had *perhaps* six months to live.

[2] The conference in honour of MacDiarmid's 85th birthday was held on 12 and 13 August 1977 in the Assembly Rooms, Edinburgh.

[1] Patrick Crotty, born in Fermoy in 1952, is a primary teacher in Cork, Eire. While at University College, Cork, he worked on an MA thesis on MacDiarmid.

[2] To mark the 85th birthday of MacDiarmid, on 11 August 1977, a two day conference was held in the Assembly Rooms, George Street, Edinburgh on 12 and 13 August. The papers given at the conference (organised by Akros Publications and the Scottish International Institute) were not, in fact, published as a collection.

It has now been agreed that more drastic steps must be taken and I am to have a course of radio therapy in the Western General Hospital in Edinburgh, beginning in the first week of January. The ominous implications of this will not escape you and I am now making my final dispositions accordingly. It is not the old X-ray therapy I'll be having – but the new neutron therapy sponsored by Dr Arnott[3] of Glasgow which is regarded as a great breakthrough in this treatment and avoids the grave disadvantages of the X-ray treatment.

As to your question, there is no ruined mill at Langholm.[4] There is, ironically, a ruined distillery which has not been producing the stuff in my lifetime. The use of the word 'epopteia' covers both the possible references you mention – with main emphasis of course on the sense of 'general illumination' than on the recondite transmission of the secrets of the dead.

All the best to you. I had hoped my *Complete Poems* (two volumes – about 1,000 pages each) would have been out by now. Whether it will be published in time to be other than posthumous is now very questionable.

Excuse more at the moment – and in particular my atrocious handwriting. It has been good knowing you and I am very sorry our meetings have been so few and so brief. Valda joins me in every kind regard.

Yours,
Christopher Grieve.

---

[3] Sidney John Arnott (born 1939) is Senior Lecturer in Radiation Oncology at the University of Edinburgh. In a letter of 15 October 1982 to the present editor Dr Arnott explained: 'My particular research interest was the giving of Neutron therapy for patients with various forms of cancer – particularly rectal cancer. I think that all [MacDiarmid] could have meant when he mentions "sponsored" is that it was my recommendation that we gave this treatment. Unfortunately he has the name of the town wrong – it is really Edinburgh.'

[4] As part of his plan to submit a PhD thesis to Stirling University on MacDiarmid's *Clann Albann* project (comprising a huge autobiographical poem) Patrick Crotty examined 'Depth and the Chthonian Image' (346–53) which is subtitled 'On looking at a ruined mill and thinking of the greatest'. In the ninth stanza of the poem MacDiarmid refers to 'your final epopteia' and Crotty asked the poet whether 'epopteia' as used in the poem had anything to do with the 'epopteia' achieved by initiates to the Eleusian Mysteries.

TO TOM NAIRN[1]

Brownsbank,
Candymill,
by Biggar,
Lanarks.
1/3/78

Dear Tom,

Many thanks indeed for the copy of *The Break-up of the U.K.* and for your inscription of it to Valda and I. I am still in a sorry condition, with a great deal of pain, and I find it difficult to read (or even watch TV). I just cannot concentrate on anything else as long as this pain continues – as it will do for an indefinite time ahead. And in the meantime I can do nothing to bring my correspondence up to date or write anything else, and I am refusing all invitations to speak, read poems, etc etc, or indeed do anything at all I can avoid doing. I haven't been out of the house since I left hospital. I go back to Chalmers Hospital on 13th inst, but do not expect to be kept in there.

I do not know what Neal Ascherson will make of our interview.[2] He seemed to have made up his mind without really interviewing me at all. But we'll see when the thing appears in *The Sunday Times Magazine*.

I have so far only read a fraction of your book – but with great interest and general agreement 'tho I don't really feel competent to discuss many of the points that concern me most. So much of the essential reading you have done has not come my way – nor as matters stand could I have done justice to a reading of it. I must reconcile myself to be away out on the side-lines – so far out that I can't really see the action at all.

Part of the trouble – in addition to my infernal abdominal trouble – is that I never see anyone who can discuss these matters. I think it is a pity I don't see you – and the others I don't know at all; Chiene, Lynda Myles, etc.[3]

As you have probably heard Dublin University are giving me a Litt. D. in July (if I am well enough to be able to be there!). It must

---

[1] Tom Nairn, author of *The Break-up of Britain: Crisis and Neo-Nationalism* (1977), was born in Freuchie, Fife, in 1932. In 1977 he was Director of the Scottish International Institute who – with Akros Publications – organised a conference in celebration of MacDiarmid's 85th birthday.

[2] Neal Ascherson, 'The Last of the Giants', *Sunday Times Magazine*, 14 May 1978.

[3] Peter Chiene was a member of the Scottish National party and editor of *Q Magazine*; Linda Myles, Director of the Edinburgh Film Festival, arranged for films about MacDiarmid to be shown at the 85th birthday conference.

be the first time an Irish institution has honoured a declared 'Communist'.

Do you know Robert Mulholland whose book just published, *Scotland's Struggle for Freedom*, represents my own position better than any previous position? But I have my grave doubts. The last time I heard from Mulholland he was pleading with me to leave the CPGB and join Sillars and the Scottish Labour Party.[4] The fact that he could make such a plea to me threw a strange light on all he says on my side of things, and could not have been made unless he misunderstands my whole position fundamentally.

One of the things that keeps recurring is the charge that I am hopelessly contradictory in the positions I take up. But then all my positions are just a spin-off from my poetry. Like the Russian Rozanov I am vitally interested in ideas – like to savour them one after the other – appreciate the taste of each of them – but do not commit myself to any of them. A stance of moral anarchy, of course.

I hope your book goes well. It is about the only serious work on Scottish nationalism. Hanham[5] wasn't bad – but did not go nearly so thoroughly into the matter.

With renewed thanks & best wishes,

Yours,
Christopher Grieve

---

[4] Jim Sillars, the Labour MP, was briefly involved in promoting his own breakaway Scottish Labour Party.
[5] H.J. Hanham, *Scottish Nationalism* (1969).

INDEX

The arrangement of *The Letters of Hugh MacDiarmid* is by correspondent; those listed in the Contents as 'miscellaneous' are indicated in the index by '(correspondence)'. Readers interested in a particular chronological period should refer to the 'home and career' section of the Grieve reference. Names and publications in the letters have frequently only cursory mention; however, these have been consistently noted, together with the explanatory footnotes (n), as they pinpoint recurring patterns and descriptions of events in MacDiarmid's life. Published works are italicised, poems, broadcasts, articles and speeches are enclosed in speech marks; unpublished works have no distinguishing marks.

894

Flowering Rifle (Campbell), 413, 587

Forsyth, Matthew, 788, 788n

Forward, 97, 274, 285, 287–9, 287n, 390

Forward from Hugh MacDiarmid (Glen), 681

Foulis, T.N. (publishers), 37–8, 44, 65, 65n, 69, 75, 107, 139n

Fowrsom Reel (Clyde Group), 806, 806n

'Francis George Scott: a Centenary Song Recital' (disc), 476

Francis George Scott and the Scottish Renaissance (Lindsay), 475

Free Man, The, 105, 149, 151, 243, 245, 420, 420n, 477, 478, 534n, 568, 568n, 610n; (correspondence), 770, 783

From Daer Water (MacArthur), 457

Frost, Robert, 94

Fury of the Living, The (Singer), 192, 192n

Gaelic Movement, 553–4, 553n

Gallery (Bason), 403

Gallipoli Memories (Mackenzie), 395

Galsworthy, John, 218

Garioch, Robert, 514n, 694, 694n, 703, 868

Garnett, Edward, 210, 210n

Garten, Millig, 443

Gawsworth, John, 503, 849n

Geddes, Arthur, (correspondence), 857

Geddes, Professor Patrick, 85, 85n, 112, 201, 271, 524–5, 857–8, 857n

'Gentlemen' (Gunn), 200

George, Stefan, 310, 623, 623n

Georgian Poetry (ed. Marsh), 3

Gibbon, Lewis Grassic *see* Mitchell, James Leslie

Gifford, Douglas, 693

Glasgow Herald (correspondence), 756, 784, 786, 789

Glasgow University: Literary Society, 587; Poetry Society, 133

Glen, Duncan (Ronald Eadie Munro), 471, 471n, 681, 681n, 684, 684n[2], 686, 686n[2], 687, 687n[2], 689, 689n, 690–1, 690n, 692[2], 692n, 694, 694n, 719, 828; Festschrift, 695, 695n

Glenconner, Lady, 45

Goethe, Johann Wolfgang von, xii, 103, 805

Gogarty, Senator Oliver St. John, 101, 214, 225, 349–50, 349n, 373, 374–5, 374–5n, 795; *Contemporary Scottish Studies*, 385, 385n, 485

Golden Lyric, The, (Smith), 869–70, 869n

Gollancz (publishers), 233, 248, 250, 359; (correspondence), 847

Gordon, Professor George, 784

Gould, John, (ed. *Broughton Magazine*) 2, 79n

'Gowk, The' (Soutar), 167n

Gowks of Mowdieknowes, The (Macgregor), 866–7, 866n

Graham, R.B. Cunninghame, 44, 198, 217, 485, 638, 638n, 851n

Graham, Rt. Hon. William, 84

Graham, W.S., 794

Grant, Lewis Morrison, 605

Graves, Charles, 332, 332n

'Greenside' (Munro), 160, 160n

Grey Coast, The (Gunn), 194[2], 204–5, 205n, 206, 210, 211, 212, 391, 767

Grey Granite (Gibbon), 558

Grierson, Professor Herbert J.C., 84, 84n, 110, 110n, 148, 148n, 217, 306, 868; 'Braid Scots Poems', 307–8, 335, 336; *Sangschaw*, 85, 86; Scott biography, 450–1

Grierson, John, 562

Grieve, Andrew Graham (MacDiarmid's brother), 12, 20, 196, 367, 367n

Grieve, Christine (MacDiarmid's daughter), xxxi, 223n, 228, 320, 636, 841; as baby, 85, 89, 92, 315, 316; doctor husband, 584, 684; school, 400; tonsils operation, 223

Grieve, Christopher Murray (Hugh MacDiarmid): Aberdeen University Rectorial election, 1960, 651, 651n, 661, 661n, 666; American recognition of work, 167, 405; appreciation: Mackenzie, 374, 374n, O'Casey, 633, Thomson, 83n; attacks 97, 517–22; basic essentials, need for, 117, 118, 121, 164–7, 183, 406, loan from Mackenzie, 406, from Muirhead, 295–6, 296n; beard, 267–8; childhood and youth, xxvii–iii, Civil List Pension, xxxiv, 604–5, 641, 860–1, 860n; Committee of 100, member, xvi, 671; correspondence, vii–iii, x, xxi–iii, 111, 860[2]–1, 860n; *curriculum vitae*, 11–13, 340, 366, 366n, 367–8, 367n; description of MacDiarmid, at 16, 2; Dinnieduff, 'Prophet's Chamber', 105; Dublin University:

Grieve, C.M. *continued*

'Crowdieknowe', 862, 862n; 'Crown of Rock, The', 478; Cultural Heritage of John Maclean, The, 619n; *Cunninghame Graham*, 638, 638n; 'Dante on the Edinburgh People', 484n; Dimidium Animae Meae, 96; 'Depth and the Chthonian Image', 116, 116n, 225n, 359n, 477, 716, 842–3, 842n, 855, 887n; 'The Divided Bird', 184, 184n, 487n, 582n, 881, 881n; 'Dìreadh', 116n, 126, 126n, 268, 268n, 522n, 591, 690; 'Dr. Kitchin, Moscow and the Scottish Renaissance', 84n, 85; 'Donald Sinclair', 259, 259n, 346–9, 356n; *Drunk Man Looks at the Thistle, A*, viii–ix, xi–xii, xxxi, 88–9, 90, 91, 94, 206, 207, 209, 211, 273, 273n, 318–33, 334, 343, 343n, 346–9, 351–3, 364–5, 364n, 365n, 369, 373, 377, 415, 423n, 433, 457, 475–7, 496, 594, 609, 619, 769, 834–5, 834n, 850, 883, 885, MacDiarmid's translations, 724, 724n, new edition, 517, 863, recording, 471, 741, reviews, 214, 215, 348n, 349n, 350n, 409, 765–6, 765n, revised edition (Weston), 718, 781n, 721, 722–3, 724, 741, sales, 346n, Soutar's rejoinder, 136, 143; 'Durchseelte', 884n; 'Dytiscus', 477; *Early Lyrics*, 1, 369n; 'Eden Regained', 48, 48n; 'Edinburgh', 56, 56n, 57, 484n; 'Edinburgh Toun', 848, 848n; 'Eemis Stane, The', 627, 758–9, 759n; 'English Ascendancy in British Literature', 232, 248, 248n, 356n, 357, 434–8, 434n, 477; 'Essays on Literature' (broadcast), 511n; 'Ex Vermibus', 759; 'Fall of France, The', 615; 'Farmer's Death', 504; Faroes, The, 582; 'Faroese Holiday', 357n; Fier Comme Un Ecossais, 352, 381, 381n, 385, 415; *First Hymn to Lenin*, xxxii, 233n, 237, 240, 250, 357, 359, 360, 360n, 464, 486n, 593–4, 619, 627; 'Following Day, The', 47, 49; Forty songs, 150; French poets translated, 33; 'Future of Scotland, The', 287n; 'Genethliacon for the New World Order', 150; 'Gertrude Stein', 248, 248n, 356n; 'Glasgow, 1960, 154n, 'Glass of Pure Water, The', 163n,

627; 'Glen of Silence, The', 171n; 'Glog-Hole, The', 206, 206n; *Golden Treasury of Scottish Poetry, The*, 119, 119n, 120, 120n, 131, 167, 167n, 171, 172, 176, 177, 178, 312, 430, 481, 486, 500, 554n, 568, 571, 580, 582, 868n, American edition, 186, drastic revision, 174, Mackie selection, 409, 411–12, reviewed, 179, 179n, 187; 'Golden Wine in the Gaidhealtachd, A', 171n, 186; 'Goodbye Twilight', 263–4, 263n; *Handmaid of the Lord, The*, 94, 94n, 295, 295n, 379, 379n; 'Harry Semen', 648, 648n; Haud Forrit (Impavidi), 496, 590, 708; 'Herd of Does, A', 86, 86n; *Hugh MacDiarmid Anthology, The*, 532; 'Hungry Waters', 207n, 490n, 855n; 'I Heard Christ Sing', 307, 309, 338; Impavidi Progrediamur, xv, 496, 496n, 590, 708n, broadcast, 655–6, 655n, 656n, 657; 'Impossible Song, The', 876; *In Memoriam James Joyce*, xv, xxxiv, 453–6, 454–6n, 496, 527, 591, 640, 655[2], 655n, 656, 681, 690, 742, 832, 832n, 876n; 'In the Caledonian Forest', 772; In the Tents of Time, 44; *Islands of Scotland, The*, 120, 120n, 160, 187, 259, 259n, 405, 405n, 479, 481, 502, 780–1, 828, 830; 'John Maclean', 175, 175n; *Kind of Poetry I Want, The*, xv, xxxv, 273, 273n, 530, 530n, 665–6[2], 674, 813, 813n; 'Kist of Whistles, A', 477, 666; Lament for the Children, 412; 'Lamh Dearg Aboo', 601; *Lap of Honour, A*, 706, 716, 716n; 'Larking Dallier', 154n, 'Life in the Shetland Islands', 357n; 'Little White Rose, The', 618, 739, 739n, 849n, 875, 882–3, 882n; *Living Scottish Poets*, 145, 145n, 233, 237, 404, 478, 478n, 537, 882n; 'Lost Pigeons, The', 478; *Lucky Bag*, xxxi, 207, 209, 209n, 215, 215n, 357, 359, 412; *Lucky Poet*, xviii, xxxiii, 1, 120, 120n, 131, 148, 171, 174, 177, 180, 182, 191, 405, 405n, 430, 470, 479–80, 482–5, 488, 491, 550n, 580, 599–600, 621, 665, 679, 856, 868n, 870, Cairncross, 629, 629n, reviewed, 616, 616n; 'Lynch Pin', 477, 477n; 'Macbeth' (script), 524–9, 649; *MacDiarmids, The: a conversation*, 684, 684n; Maidenkirk to John O'Groats,

Grieve, C.M. *continued*
96; Marseilles, Moods and
Memories, 32; Mature Art, xi,
xivv-xv, 122, 130, 168, 169, 171, 175,
263–4, 263n, 265, 266–7, 268, 268n,
408n, 413, 433, 446–8, 447n, 470n,
476, 479, 479n, 565, 580, 844, 856,
876n, *see also* Cornish Heroic Song;
Meanings For Scotland (series), 539,
539n, 542–3; 'Milk-Wort and
Bog-Cotton', 477, 477n, 504, 504n;
'Moment in Eternity, A', 1, 54, 54n,
55, 97, 423n, 478; 'Moonlight Among
the Pines', 338; *More Collected Poems*,
369, 706, 708, 726n; 'Monument,
The', 478, 478n; Muckle Toun, The,
216–7, 244n; National Movement,
book on, 94; 'Neo Gaelic Economies',
97, 219, 219n; *New Directions*, 180,
184, 184n, 186, 487, 582, 582n; 'New
Movement in Vernacular Poetry,
The', 203, 203n; *New Scotsman, see
Scottish Chapbook*; 'Nietzsche and the
Revival of the European Spirit', 215;
'Nisbet', 77, 77n, 80; *Northern Numbers*,
xxx, 3, 37, 38, 39, 51, 51n, 195, 197,
317, 756–7, reviewed, 52, 52n, 53,
53n, 56, 56n, Second Series, xxx, 53,
54, 55, 58, 59, 65, 65n, 69, 70,
reviewed, 69, 69n, 107–8, 195, Third
Series, xxx, 75, 107, 137, 138[2],
139n, 196, reviewed, 80; *Northern
Review, The*, xxx, 198n, 199, 200, 283,
283n; 'O Jesu Parvule', 87; Oddman
Out, 44; 'Ode to All Rebels', 685, 863,
876; 'On a Raised Beach', xiii, 150,
591, 627, 627n, 676; 'On an Ill-Faur'd
Star', 727, 727n; 'On the Oxford Book
of Victorian Verse', 847–8n; 'On Bare
Hill Tops, 478; 'Oon Olympian,
The', 477–8; 'Outstanding Qualities
of the Scots Vernacular' (broadcast),
95, 95n; 'Overinizievar', 759;
Parisian sketch, 32; 'Parley of Beasts',
362n, 478; *Penny Wheep*, xxx, 86n, 88,
206, 207, 324, 334, 337, 343–6, 362,
369, 415, 476, 765, review copies,
344–5, 364, sales, 346n; 'Plan for the
Unemployed, A', 357n; 'Playmates',
57; 'Plea for a Scottish Fascism',
394n; 'Plea for Synthetic Scots', 478;
Poet and His Friends, A, 177, 412,
485, 491, 663; *Poetry Like the Hawthorn*,

681, 681n, 683; Poets of Tomorrow,
172–3, 175; 'Poet's Passing, The',
432n; 'Praise of Ben Dorain, The'
(trans), 553n, 571; 'Prayer for a
Second Flood', 627; *Present Condition of
Scottish Arts and Affairs, The*, 381, 381n;
Present Condition of Scottish Music, The,
xxxi, 209, 209n, 215, 215n; 'Present
Position of the Scottish Nationalist
Movement', 357n; 'Problems of
Poetry Today', 356n, 825; 'Purpose of
the Free Man, The', 356n; *Rebel with a
Cause* (film), 626; Red Scotland, xxii,
153, 157, 257, 426–7, 428, 532, 536,
536n, 541, 541n, 543, 546–55, 547n,
554n, 568, 570, 773, 850, 853; 'Return
of the Long Poem, The', 703n;
'Reviving the Scots Vernacular', 82n,
307n, 309; 'Riding in a Fog', 844n;
Road to Spain, The, 44; *Robert Burns:
Poems*, 269, 269n; 'Robert Burns
1759–1796', 92, 92n, 209, 209n, 537n;
St. Sophia, 96; Salonika Poems, 24,
28, 31, 33, 35; *Sangschaw*, xxx, 85, 87,
135, 143, 201, 202, 314, 334, 337–8,
349–50, 361, 369, 415, 476, 760, 762,
765, review copies, 342, reviews, 86,
86n, 88, 201, 201n, 203n[2], sales,
346n, trans, 86, 86n; Scotland Today
and Tomorrow, 287; Scots Arts
Essays, 8; Scots Church Essays, 8;
Scots Lyric since Burns, The, 324;
Scots Unbound, xxxii, 116, 243n, 248,
253, 359n, 360n, 767–8, 768n;
'Scotsmen Make a God of Robert
Burns', 102, 382, 382n; 'Scott
Centenary, The', 478; 'Scottish Arts
and Letters', 600; *Scottish Chapbook*,
xiv, xxx, 3, 45, 45n, 75, 75n, 76, 77,
77n, 78, 79, 107, 107n[2], 108, 135,
138, 138n, 140, 140n, 195, 196, 196n,
197, 271, 318, 475, 725, 725n, 756–7,
757n, 761, Edinburgh University
Supplement, 139, 139n, financial
quotations, 54, 76, Gunn, 193,
reviews, 77–8, 77n; Scottish Colour –
Thought, 9; *Scottish Eccentrics*, 151,
153, 257, 532–3, 534n, 541, 541n,
544–51, 555, 568, 570; 'Scottish
Home Rule and Revival of Letters',
77; *Scottish Nation, The*, xxx, 79, 79n,
140, 197, 198, 198n, 275–82, 275n,
316, 316n, 394n, Gunn, 193, 196,

Grieve, C.M. *continued*
196n[2], *see also* Northern Review;
'Scottish National Development',
232; 'Scottish National Politics', 284;
Scottish issues articles, 95; Scottish
Poetry (broadcast), 622–3, 622n;
Scottish Review, 207; *Scottish Scene*, 149,
149n, 421, 421n, 465, 533, 557;
Scottish Vortex, The, 9; 'Seamless
Garment, The', 608; 'Second Hymn
to Lenin', xxxiii, 146, 146n, 153,
243n, 246, 247, 360, 360n, 443–5,
443n, 444n, 466, 551, 551n, 823, 823n,
827, 843, 849n; *Selected Essays of Hugh
MacDiarmid* (ed. Glen), 718; *Selected
Poems* (ed. Craig and Manson), 369,
721–2, 721n, 726; Selected Poems (ed.
MacCaig), 530, 530n; *Selected Poems*
(Gollancz), *see Stony Limits; Selected
Poems of William Dunbar*, 269, 269n,
492; *Selections from the Poems of William
Dunbar*, 624, 624n; Shapes and
Shadows, 59; 'Shetlands and the
Faroes, The', (broadcast), 160, 160n;
Six Scottish Poets, 172–3, 172n, 175,
177, 182; 'Skald's Death', 423n;
Socialist Poems of Hugh MacDiarmid,
532; 'Somersault', 362n *Song of the
Seraphim, The*, 590; 'Songs for
Christine', 96; Sonnets, 73, foreign
subjects, 71, 72; 'Sonnets of the
Highland Hills', 40, 40n; Soviet State,
The, 32; 'Spanish Girl, The', 21n, 47,
47n; 'Stony Limits', 673, 673n, 674;
Stony Limits, xxxii, 148, 150, 248,
248n, 359–60, 465, 847n, 863, 882;
'Summit, The', 478; *Tarras*, 243,
244n, 246, 248, 466, 478, 769; Third
Hymn to Lenin, 593, 619, 679; *Thistle
Rises, The*, (ed. Bold), 248, 248n, 351,
351n, 591n, 593, 655, 698, 758n;
Threepenny Opera, The (Brecht), 720,
720n; 'To a French Girl Friend', 29,
29n, 35n, 44n; *To Circumjack
Cencrastus*, xxxi, 91, 94, 96, 100, 101,
103, 203n, 209, 229, 229n, 334, 352–6,
354–5n, 376, 378, 384, 384n, 397, 410,
432n, 457, 457n, 475, 824,
pre-publication articles, 112–2, 113n,
354–5, reviews 103, 113n, 142, 142n,
Watson study, 876, 876n; 'To Lenin',
145n, 233n; 'Towards a Scottish
Renaissance', 201, 201n, 208, 208n;

'Travels in the North', 621;
'Triangular', 33; *Twenty Poems by Hugh
MacDiarmid, with Twenty Lithographs by
William Johnstone*, 467; 'Two
Memories', 486; 'Two O'Clock in the
Morning', 478; *Ugly Birds Without
Wings, The*, 273, 273n, 813, 813n;
Uncanny Scot, The, 434n, 706, 707,
707n, 719, 836, 863n; 'Universal
Man, The', 60, 60n; 'Up to Date',
423n; Vers libre volume, 53;
'Veuchen', 154n; 'Vision of Scotland,
A' (broadcast), 660, 660n; *Voice of
Scotland*: periodical, xxxiii, 171, 171n,
265, 266, 266n, 268, 268n, 407, 407n,
469, 558, 559, 565, 572, 577, 577n,
581, 598, 611, 611n, 679, 855, 863,
Irish number, 635, Muir cartoon,
125–6, series, xvii, 255, 255n, 536,
537–8, 539[2], 539n, 542–3, 547–50,
550n, 552–5, 535–7n, 547n, 549n,
565, 850, 869, MacColla's Gaelic
book, 539, 539n, 566–7, 566n, *see also*
Red Scotland; *Vox, see* main entry;
'Water Music', 243, 244n, 467;
'Water of Life', 73, 74, 74n, 75;
'Watergaw, The', 433, 677, 677n,
759, 761; 'Wauchopeside', 716;
'Welcome to the PEN Delegates',
422, 422n; 'Welt-Literature', 310,
357; What Lenin Has Meant to
Scotland, *see* Red Scotland; 'Wheel',
701; 'Wheesht, Wheesht', 423n;
'Whuchulls', 716; 'Why I Became a
Scots Nationalist', 248; 'Windbags,
The', 48, 48n, 50; 'Wit Turns Poet,
The', 385, 385n; Wolfe of Badenoch,
The, 549, 549n, 568, 568n, 571; 'You
Know Not Who I Am', 623, 623n
Grieve, Deirdre (MacDiarmid's
daughter-in-law), 746, 747
Grieve, Elizabeth, (MacDiarmid's
mother), xxxii, 89, 849, 849n
Grieve, James (MacDiarmid's father),
677, 677n, 879
Grieve, Michael (MacDiarmid's son),
133, 163, 189, 191, 423, 551, 562, 563,
586, 683; Alloa journalist, 640; birth,
247; cold, 578, 583; conscription, 275,
303–5, 303n, 495, 607–8, 608n;
fractured wrist, 589; Glasgow *Daily
Record*, 631; holiday fishing, 490;
illness, 425, 500; MacDiarmid's

Muir, Edwin, xvii–xviii, 94, 125–6, 156, 156n, 157, 187[2], 198 198n, 203, 203n, 209, 209n, 210–1, 213, 225, 271, 300, 339, 348,350, 352, 385, 395, 396, 396n, 424, 426–9, 433, 482, 543, 759, 794–5, 803, 835, 850–4, 851n[2], 855, 867–9
Muir, Willa, 125–6, 537, 537n, 868
Muirhead, Roland Eugene, 274–5, 301n; SNP candidate, 299
Mulholland, Robert, 889
Munro, Margaret T., 160, 160n
Munro, Neil, 44, 212; *Northern Numbers* dedication, 38, 39, 760, 766n, 767
Munro, Robin, 694
Munro, Ronald Eadie, *see* Glen, Duncan
'Murderer, The' (Soutar), 152n
Murison, David, 599, 599n
Murray, Cecilia, 21
Murray, Charles, 307, 307n, 351, 759
Murray, Helen Christine, 14, 14n, 21, 25

Nairn, Tom, 888n; (correspondence), 888
Napier, Roísín, 729
National Movement in Scotland, The (Brand), 274
National Outlook, 44, 44n, 52
National Party of Scotland, *see* Scottish National Movement
National Weekly, 806, 806n; (correspondence), 796
Nationale Literatur Schottlands von den Anfangen bis zur Renaissance, Die (Brie), 576n
Neil M. Gunn (Hart and Pick), 193, 199n
Neil M. Gunn (ed. Gifford and Scott), 693, 693n
Neill, A.S., xxix, 253, 543
New Age, The xxx, 1, 3, 6, 6n, 97, 200, 215, 237, 340, 357, 410, 682; Braid Scots number, 82, 83, 88
New Age Group, The (J. Carswell), 592
New Alliance, 610, 610n
New Education Fellowship, 319
New English Poems (ed. Abercrombie), 145n, 594
New English Weekly, 243, 845, 845n
'New Forms' (Gunn), 202
New Saltire (correspondence), 810

New Scotland, 152–3, 152n, 154, 154n; (correspondence), 773; London Self-Government Committee, 600
New Writing, 593, 596
New Writing in Europe (Lehmann), 486, 486n
Nicholson, William, 364, 364n
Nicoll, Charles, 877n; (correspondence), 877
Nietzsche, Friedrich Wilhelm, 633
Nightwood (Barnes), 263
Nisbet, John Bogue, 10, 10n, 13, 605
Niven, Barbara, 429, 470, 470n
Norman, Frank, 667
Norton Anthology of English Literature, The (sel. D. Daiches), 742, 742n
Nott, Stanley, 849n; (correspondence), 849

'O Sun' (Gunn), 196, 196n
Obelisk Press, 452, 470, 480n, 580, 856n
Observer, The (correspondence), 817
O'Casey, Sean, 183, 234n, 518, 633–4, 635, 636, 639, 647, 785, 817–8
O'Connor, Arthur, 778
O'Connor, Roger, 778
Off in a Boat (Gunn), 264
Ogilvie, George, xxviii, 1–4, 369, 369n; appreciation by MacDiarmid, 3; headmasterships, 2, 81, 89, 93, 93n, 100; MacDiarmid article in *Broughton Magazine*, 51, 51n; MacDiarmid's mentor, 41–43; subject of dedication, 54, 54n, 59;
Ogilvie, William H., 37, 38, 56, 56n, 391n
O'Keeffe, Timothy, 706
One Later Day (Lindsay), 624
Open the Door (C. Carswell), 419
Opus clavicembalisticum (Sorabji), 230, 610, 839n
Orage, Alfred Richard, xxx, 1, 3, 237, 242, 243, 357, 412, 485, 837
O'Rahaille, Aodhagan, 434
Orr, Dr. David, 105, 117, 127, 244, 246, 247, 258, 548, 572, 572n, 577, 578, 579, 580, 583
Other Animals, The (MacColl), 635
Our Duncan, Who Art in Trent (ed. Pacey), 695
Out of Conflict (Perrie), 885n
Outlook, The, 60, 97, 255n, 426–7, 850–1, 853